To Be **Virtuous**

Be what's best! ™

To Be **Virtuous**

SECOND EDITION

M. Gregg Fager

Human Progress™

Library of Congress Control Number: 2012937969

Cataloging Data

Fager, M. Gregg.
 To be virtuous / M. Gregg Fager. —2nd ed.
  p. cm.
  ISBN 978-0-9839215-8-5 (hardcover : alk. paper)
  1. Virtue. 2. Moral education. 3. Ethics. I. Title.

BJ1521.F34 2012
179.9'—dc22

To contact us or to learn more about our books and services, please write to Human Progress L.C., Post Office Box 686, Farmington, Utah 84025 USA, or visit our website at: **www.myhumanprogress.com**.

Know what's best!™ Do what's best!™ Be what's best!™ are trademark slogans of Human Progress L.C. The images found upon and within this book are original works of its author.

*Dedicated to all our posterity of enlightenment, virtue
and integrity who are determined and empowered of
God to perpetuate a priceless legacy of liberty, hope,
peace and joy and to show the world by example,
instruction and virtuous love of Him and of
one another how to preserve that legacy
in virtuous oneness with Him, with
one another and with their
posterity, forever*

*And to all those
who strive choice by choice
in virtuous love of God and man to
perpetuate that legacy in virtuous oneness*

[L]et virtue garnish thy thoughts unceasingly.
—The Lord Jesus Christ

CONTENTS

Virtue is a pattern of thought and behavior based on high moral standards. It encompasses chastity and moral purity. Virtue includes modesty – in thought, language, dress, and demeanor. . . . The paths of virtue lead to happiness in this life and in the life to come. —Elaine S. Dalton

THE AUTHOR'S TRILOGY

Book 1 . . . for those who want to *Be what's best!*™

To Be Virtuous is a reference book, textbook and workbook in one. *The Human Virtues Dictionary,* found only in this book, provides a definitive record of human virtues. This book is well suited to all those capable of learning virtue, beginning with the very young.

This book serves as an overall introduction to the author's trilogy on the languages of human character and human virtue. In its *Foreword,* Dr. Richard G. Wilkins recounts Dr. M. Gregg Fager's twenty-eight-year journey (1984-2012) to identify and definitively record the language of human character and from it the language of human virtue. Dr. Wilkins' "about the author" *Foreword* appears only in this book.

This book has an allegory on human virtue found only in this book. Studying and discussing that allegory can help us better understand and better use some of the essential principles of virtue development.

Chapter Seven is entitled *A Comparison of 19th and 21st Century Definitions.* That chapter provides insights on how language pertaining to human character has changed since 1828, including examples of the corruption and corruptibility of that language. That chapter is found only in this book. Remaining textbook chapters in this book appear in modified form in books 2 and 3.

Book 2 . . . for those who want to *Do what's best!*™

The Language of Human Virtue is the author's second reference book, textbook and workbook in one. *The Building Virtue Dictionary,* found only in book 2, is a compilation of all of the human virtues found in book 1, plus all *relative value* human characteristics we can use to build, preserve and strengthen human virtues (or vices) within ourselves, our families and society. Together, all of these human characteristics form the language of human virtue. That book is for those capable of using enlightened reason to better understand and build virtue, beginning with youth.

Book 2 has three allegories on human virtue found only in that book. Studying and discussing those allegories can help us better understand and better use essential principles of obtaining and maintaining better and stronger virtue within us.

Chapter Seven in book 2 is entitled *Building, Preserving & Strengthening Human Virtue.* There the author describes relative value characteristics and illustrates how we should virtuously use them—along with virtues—to build, preserve and strengthen human virtues within ourselves, our families and society. You may better understand and better use book 2 after you have studied and practiced what you can learn from this book.

Book 3 . . . for those who want to *Know what's best!*™

The Language of Human Character is the author's third reference book, textbook and workbook in one. *The Human Character Dictionary,* found only in book 3, lists and defines essentially all human virtues, all human vices, and all remaining relative value characteristics which can be used to produce, preserve or restore human virtues or vices within us. Together, all of those human characteristics form the language of human character. That book is for those who can use enlightened reason and can safely examine vice to better understand and build virtue.

Book 3 has five allegories on human character found only in that book. Studying and discussing those allegories can help us better understand and better teach one another some essential principles about making better personal, family, organizational and national choices and decisions.

Chapter Seven in book 3 is entitled *Building, Preserving & Strengthening Human Virtue* (as in book 2). Explanatory notes in Chapter Nine are more extensive in book 3 than in the other two books. You may better understand and better use book 3 after you have studied and practiced what you can learn from this book and from book 2.

★★★★★★★

FOREWORD
by Dr. Richard G. Wilkins

For years I have been a personal friend of Dr. M. Gregg Fager. His family name is a German name which, before it was Americanized by his 18th Century Pennsylvania ancestors, was spelled *Feger* (pronounced *fay'gur* in German). Some of Gregg's relatives fought and died in the American Revolution. Subsequent generations migrated from Pennsylvania and Maryland through Kentucky, Illinois, Missouri and Nebraska into Colorado, Wyoming, Utah, Idaho and California. Along the way, they fought in other wars to vigorously defend liberty under the Constitution of the United States, including everyone's inalienable and truly self-evident right to harmlessly worship according to the dictates of personal conscience.

A Yearning for Progress

Throughout his college education, Gregg longed for a class – any class – that would help him get his mind around the topic of *human character*. It did not exist. As an undergraduate student at BYU he settled for *psychology* as a major. When he graduated with honors (B.S. 1974), he had earned teacher certification and was a distinguished military graduate with a commission in the United States Army.

After serving for three years in West Germany during the Cold War, and as a commander for three years in units at home and abroad, Gregg resigned his commission as a captain in 1980. His supervisors repeatedly noted in their evaluations his "moral and character strength" and his "integrity." Gregg went on to receive advanced degrees, licensing and training in *education* (M.Ed. 1978, David O. McKay School of Education, BYU), *business* (M.B.A. 1980, Thunderbird School of Global Management) and *law* (J.D. 1983, J. Reuben Clark Law School, BYU).

As a part-time educator, Gregg taught ancient scripture classes at BYU during twelve semesters from 1979 to 1988. He was highly rated as an instructor by his students, who gave him particularly high marks in "inspires character development." He says part of his job was to teach students how previous generations have identified, recorded and relied upon *words* of truth and virtue in their efforts to build better lives.

A person's life is reflected in their work, just as their work is reflected in their life. Throughout his career, Gregg has endeavored to teach truths and virtues in *word* and in *deed*. He has consistently sought to minister to the needs of those inside and outside of his religion by quietly but regularly participating in or leading groups of volunteers in service projects to benefit the poor and needy worldwide. He says he continues to seek learning about various religious denominations because the truths and virtues they teach have had such a positive influence in his life.

Gregg has also volunteered as counselor and consultant in law and business. For example, some years ago he served for two weeks as a volunteer consultant in Moscow and Volgograd, Russia. In a presentation to members of a Volgograd law firm about how to develop a strategic plan for prospering in a free-market economy, he taught them their long-term prosperity depends upon their good teamwork, which depends upon their good planning, which depends upon their good leadership, which depends upon their good attitudes, which depends upon *goodness* itself. The presentation was well received. He later served in a similar role in Baku, Azerbaijan. In a later note from Baku, Gregg and his wife were told, "I work with foreigners since 1993 and, believe me, I haven't yet met such a kind (in real understanding of this word) people like you are. Thank you very much again, Allah bless you!!!"

An Exceptional Twenty-eight-year Contribution

In the early 1980s, there was much talk in the media of "family values," but no one provided a complete list of family values or a means of identifying them. There is still no complete list. "Character development" was spoken of, but emphasis was placed more on teaching *values* in school systems as *acceptable* ethical and moral standards, rather than on *virtues*.

In the summer of 1984, Gregg began to note the public call for greater social unity in human *values* and for more focused *character development*. At the time, he was working as a vice president of administration at an international economics consulting firm in Menlo Park, California. In his spare time, he began using gathered media articles and reports, as well as other sources, to study and define the relationships among human thoughts, beliefs, values and characteristics. He sought ways to identify *family values*. He began to look for practical ways to help people progress from *talking* about what is better to *doing, being* and *teaching* what is better.

During the next three years Gregg continued his compilation and study of relevant materials. He concluded that human character is spiritual in nature. He recognized that our spiritual comprehension of the Divine is enhanced or limited by our comprehension of *words*. He thus concluded that nothing is more fundamental to the improvement of human character than a clear understanding of language pertaining to human character.

Gregg also concluded that the thoughts, beliefs and values people can embrace are *infinite* in number, but the characteristics resulting from such thoughts, beliefs and values are *finite* in number. At that time, no one had attempted to list the finite number of human characteristics found from A to Z in the English language. And no one had attempted to classify them according to how valuable they are to the progress of humanity.

In 1986, Gregg moved his family to Utah. After a seventeen-month stint at a large Salt Lake City law firm, he entered private law practice. Meanwhile, in the spring of 1987, he began to work nearly 40 hours each week to identify, list and consolidate definitions of human characteristics. He believed that if human *virtues* could be identified from among all human *characteristics*, the resulting list would empower individuals and families to identify *family values* by whether they produce, preserve or restore one or more *virtues* within people, families and society.

In 1988, a year after his written work on human character began, Gregg published a 193-page binder entitled *New Human Character Dictionary and Workbook*. The binder had 140 pages of defined human characteristics and invited readers to provide their own defined numerical values to the definitions using provided criteria. He shared this prototype with a selected audience of educational, government and civic leaders. He sold copies to the general public under the corporate name of Center for Character Development, and gathered feedback from all who would share.

With this test publication, Gregg discovered that academicians were generally preoccupied with the gain or loss of their own academic prestige and, thus, too prone to demand *data* with which to scientifically confirm answers to questions. He also discovered the sad irony of public educators who were determined to teach *values* while excluding spirituality from the public forum. Nevertheless, perhaps the most important thing he discovered was a groundswell of desire within the general public for solid *character building* leadership from someone who could help them and their families make a powerfully positive difference in their own lives with *practical answers* that produce *personally verifiable* positive results.

Among those who applauded Gregg's initial effort was former U.S. Secretary of Education, Terrel H. Bell (1921-1996). Dr. Bell recognized and endorsed the work as "a fundamental, timely and very powerful set of tools." He wrote, "The tools can help anyone develop the clear thinking and correct feelings essential to unobstructed discernment, proper choice and the development of better character." Encouraged by such feedback, Gregg decided to continue his work, but obstacles stood in the way.

In 1988, one simple word search through 140 pages on a good personal computer using WordPerfect 4.2 took several minutes or more. The need to provide for his family and lack of more advanced desktop technology prevented him from pushing his written work forward for a time. Between 1988 and 1997, he built his law practice and continued to regularly observe and study human characteristics. He continued to look for sponsors and to note his conclusions, experiences and observations about human character along the way. Despite his best efforts over the years, he found no one willing to hire or pay him to further his work.

In 1997, Gregg went to work for a large, multinational organization in Salt Lake City. For the next seven years, he was part of that organization's efforts to contribute to global well-being by providing humanitarian and welfare relief in caring for the poor and needy, fostering self-reliance and encouraging service to others. While there, he gained new insights into the practical relationship between human character and humanity's earthly or temporal well-being. He became utterly convinced that the overall progress and well-being of humanity are tied to the development of better thoughts, beliefs, values and characteristics within us, within our families and within society as a whole. He continued to study and write about human character along the way.

In 2004, Gregg and his wife, Trudena, concluded that – together – they would make all necessary sacrifices for him to complete his work on human character and human virtue to benefit humankind. Since then, Gregg has thrown himself into the work full time, and then some. He has shared his work with me and has kept me closely apprised of his progress since 2005.

In 2008, Dr. M. Gregg Fager finally completed his initial manuscript of *The Language of Human Character*. *The Human Character Dictionary* in that book (with its more than 27,000 definitions) lists and defines essentially all human virtues, all human vices and all remaining human characteristics.

In 2009, Gregg completed his initial manuscript of *The Language of Human Virtue*. *The Building Virtue Dictionary* in that book (with its more than 18,000 definitions) is a compilation of all of the human virtues, plus all "relative value" human characteristics found in *The Human Character Dictionary*.

In 2010, Gregg completed his initial manuscript of *To Be Virtuous*. *The Human Virtues Dictionary* in this book (with its 4,900 definitions) is a compilation of all of the human virtues also listed in the other two dictionaries. The first edition of the book was put in print by a New York publisher in the fall of 2010.

In 2011, publication was cancelled when work on the other two books revealed the need for further coordinated editing of all three books. Editing and publication of all three books was then undertaken by Human Progress L.C. Editing the books together was no easy task. Properly accounting for a single change in all affected books sometimes took hours.

In 2012, the second edition of *To Be Virtuous* and *The Language of Human Virtue* were completed. Human vices are excluded from the two books "to protect eyes and minds from premature or excessive exposure to human vices." Gregg says "one can learn more about virtue by studying vice, but one can also more powerfully acquire virtue by taking no more thought of vice than necessary." It is for you to decide which approach is better for you and for those you teach.

The Language of Human Character was also completed in 2012, after twenty-eight years in the making. These three books constitute Gregg's trilogy on human character and human virtue. I have reviewed his manuscripts and have found them not only inspiring and informative, but helpful in improving my own personal and family life. Dr. Fager's contribution is truly exceptional.

A Creative and Innovative Work

Dr. Fager's work is highly creative. Each of the definitions he has written is a creatively assembled organization of *words* designed to provide a realistic and unique portrait of a real human condition. This work is unique in that it uses defined numerical values to classify each definition of each characteristic.

His work is innovative – there is nothing else like it in the world. It is an approach to thinking that refreshes and revitalizes the true meanings of words pertaining to every dimension of human character and human virtue. It stimulates new thinking about how lives can be improved in every truly progressive forum, and especially within the family.

A Rigorous Work

Dr. Fager has been remarkably rigorous in his work. The various chapters of this book reveal provably scrupulous and solid accuracy. For example, the chapter entitled *Words as Representations of Reality* demonstrates how real words represent real life and real things, and how we can understand and use those words to avoid attempts by some to confuse the concepts of *real* and *reality*. The chapters entitled *Definitions as Statements of*

Truth and *Integrated Language as a Treasury of Truth* discuss how words can and should be tested and used to convey truth over time. In the *Glossary* are more than seventy solid definitions of fundamental terms such as *character, reality, truth, virtue* and *vice*. Perhaps the best example of his years and years of rigorous work is found in his definitive research, classification and recording of an exhaustive list of human characteristics.

A Work of Insight

Dr. Fager's work offers profound insight. The foremost tool in each of his three books is its dictionary. For nearly three decades he has worked to clarify, classify and standardize the language of human character, and from it the language of human virtue – much like Noah Webster worked for twenty-seven years to standardize the definitions, spellings and usages of the language spoken by Americans two hundred years ago. Both men relied on the work of predecessors. At the same time, both men had to craft realistic definitions using personal insight to match language to reality.

A Work of Discovery

Dr. Fager's work is a work of remarkable discovery. For example, in his research and writing he discovered that a surprisingly powerful and numerically evident internal consistency of language pertaining to human character has survived through the ages. An explanation of this discovery and its provable findings are described in the chapter entitled *Integrated Language as a Treasury of Truth.*

As part of the evident survival of the internal consistency of that language, Dr. Fager points out that at least vestiges of truth about God and about godliness have survived because they have been treasured and perpetuated in the *treasuries* (or *thesauruses*) of *words* of various languages and in the lives of people who have written and spoken those words through the ages. He says, for example, that those who have received *revelation* from God, past and present, know the true meaning of that word for themselves. So it is, he says, with words such as *faithful, godly, righteous* and *spiritual*. Such words continue to exist because they continue to represent real human conditions within the lives of people.

Meanwhile, Dr. Fager uncovered internal inconsistencies which point to the corruption and corruptibility of the English language pertaining to human character. From his findings, he took painstaking efforts to restore the internal consistency of language, or in other words, to bring the language of human character back into closer harmony with itself and with reality.

His research included a comparison of current definitions of human characteristics with those defined in Noah Webster's 1828 *American Dictionary of the English Language*. The chapter in this book entitled *A Comparison of 19th and 21st Century Definitions* summarizes some of his findings and allows the reader to personally determine whether there has been a corruption of terms pertaining to human character since 1828.

Dr. Fager's work identified not only definitive lists of virtues and vices, but more than 13,400 "relative value" human characteristics which can be used to produce, preserve or restore human virtue (or vice) within us. "Relative value" human characteristics are defined in the *Glossary* and are definitively recorded in his books *The Language of Human Virtue* and *The Language of Human Character*.

Dr. Fager also discovered the need to preserve the true symmetry of opposites within language pertaining to human character, as with true antonyms. This discovery pointed to the need for some corrective realignment of opposites and for some new terminology to account for essential missing opposites. He asks, for example, what is *dirty-minded* without *clean-minded*, *familial* without *antifamilial*, or *atheistic* without *asatanic*? This symmetry is described in some detail in the chapter entitled *An Open Challenge to the World*. It can be thoroughly studied in his book *The Language of Human Character*.

Dr. Fager concluded that a strong affirmation of life's spiritual dimension lies within existing *treasuries* of words in the language of human character. It became obvious to him that, unless humanity builds and preserves an integrated language of human character, plain and precious truths will eventually disappear from the minds and hearts of those who suffer from the effects of disintegrating language, and can learn no better.

A Work of Diversity

Dr. Fager's work recognizes that *human character* is as broad as *human diversity*, and vice versa. This work recognizes that human beings take their spiritual bearings from a range of experiences. This range of experiences is reflected in human characteristics which highlight the reality of true enlightenment, virtue and integrity within good people in every major geographical population on Earth. In this work are human characteristics such as: *aboriginal, African, American, Arabian, Asian, Australian, Australasian,*

Caribbean and so forth. At least one of the definitions of each of these characteristics appears as a *virtue* in all three of his dictionaries.

Notwithstanding the vast diversity which exists in the world, also included are definitions of such human characteristics as: *integrating, intercultural, interdependent, interethnic, intermingling, international, interracial, interrelating* and *interreligious.* These and other definitions reflect the importance of our sharing with one another in *words* the best spiritual bearings we have discovered from our range of personal experiences.

A Work of Impact

Dr. Fager's work has the potential to positively impact the lives of millions of individuals and families all over the world. He has written:

Under the laws of humanity, the truth about an accused person's state of mind cannot be justly assumed. It must be *proven* to a judge or jury by the use of evidence proffered under the rules of evidence. Yet evidence even from the accused person may be corrupted with confusion, error or falsehood. Thus, the truth about that person may not be known, except to that person and to God.

Science is likewise restricted. Scientific conclusions are no better than the data gathered to prove them. Information gathered from or about a person may be corrupted with confusion, error or falsehood. Gathered information is subject to misinterpretation. Thus, the truth about that person may not be known, except to that person and to God.

In the realm of spirituality, however, it can be given to each of us to see clearly the truth about God, who we are in His sight, and who He wants us to become. If we are honest with ourselves and obedient to His promptings, He can give us power to spiritually discern the truth about everything He wants us to know, which may sometimes include the thoughts and intents of other people's hearts. A better understanding of the language of human character can enhance this power of discernment within each of us.

As Dr. Fager's work is honorably tested, verified and improved upon by you and by others, the living of its proven virtues will have a tremendously positive impact upon you, your family and society. He invites each of us to measure the impact of this work for ourselves, and to act accordingly. He says: "As each part of this work is honorably proven to be truly virtuous by you, let it be consistently pondered, performed and taught by you. If you find any part of it to be deficient, you are invited to improve upon it in harmony with steps provided in the chapter entitled *An Open Challenge to the World."*

A Practical Work

This highly practical work begs to be personally tested or proven by you in every honorable, harmless and practical way you can devise. Its potential practical applications are many. Various allegories are found in each of Dr. Fager's books. Each allegory is simple enough to be used by parents to teach their children; yet each one is complex enough to be used by teachers at any level. The definitions in his three dictionaries provide room for meaningful discussion and testing at any level.

People can use this book as a practical reference for progress. The chapter entitled *Some True Statements about Human Character* contains twenty-four true statements placed in logical sequence beginning with the simple statement, "Every person has character." Subsequent statements traverse general principles of human character improvement before directing us to specific statements about how we can personally test and use this book to improve ourselves choice by choice and day by day.

This book invites people to personally explore the finite study of *words* from A to Z pertaining to human virtue, the verified or verifiable truths human virtues do and should convey within their meanings, and how humanity can use informed personal understanding of respective human virtues and their actual social impact value to accurately evaluate the human thoughts, beliefs and values which produce them.

All three of Dr. Fager's books are capable of winning a reputation as outstanding works of solid accuracy and reliability for use in bettering the lives of people across the earth. Proof of this lies in personally living the virtues defined in each of his three books and in virtuously performing the "relative value" characteristics defined in his books *The Language of Human Virtue* and *The Language of Human Character*.

A Work for Virtue-based Leadership Development

One of the best possible applications of Dr. Fager's work is its use in virtue-based leadership training. He has written:

Nearly all respectable authority on leadership points in some way to a leader's ongoing responsibility to acquire more and stronger positive strengths and to fix negative personal flaws. So what are those positive strengths and what are those negative personal flaws? Don't all positive leadership strengths constitute, produce, preserve or restore in leaders such virtues as *humble, selfless, discerning, wise, honest, integrated-at-heart, courteous* and *edifying*? Yes. Aside from innocent errors or mistakes, don't all negative leadership flaws constitute, produce, preserve or restore in leaders such vices as *arrogant, selfish, senseless, dishonorable, disintegrated-at-heart, discourteous* and *maligning*? Yes.

Can bad leaders willingly become good leaders through the acquisition of virtue? Yes. Can good leaders willingly become better leaders through the acquisition of more and stronger virtue? Yes. Can leaders acquire greater virtue without first acquiring a better understanding of virtue? No. Is it possible for willing people to better test and better understand for themselves what is virtuous and what is not by better testing and better understanding the languages of human character and human virtue? Yes. Of what value, then, is the study of those two languages? It is crucial. Is there a pressing need and growing call for these two languages? Yes, especially for the language of human virtue.

Some years ago, Dr. Fager founded Human Progress L.C. as the business arm of his work. His organization's mission is "to help empower the diverse but willing individuals, families, organizations, and nations of the earth to understand, do, be and teach what is truly virtuous well enough to powerfully rise in unison above the world's predatory forces of darkness, vice, corruption, bondage, despair, turmoil and misery." I believe such a mission represents edifying and inspiring leadership at its best.

A Work with Which to Spiritually Comprehend the Divine

Who or what is the Divine? Dr. Fager says *"the Divine* may be defined as God and His virtues, creations, revelations, laws, ordinances, commandments, works and anything else that truly reveals, among other things, who He is, what He knows and what He does."

We cannot impose manifestations of the Divine upon each other, but I believe Dr. Fager's work represents a remarkable quest for progress toward helping every willing person enhance his or her efforts to *personally comprehend* the many and diverse manifestations of the Divine. This book provides tools which can be used for *personal spiritual discovery* by persons of every creed who wish to confirm and affirm life's spiritual dimension through ongoing personal reception and comprehension of manifestations of the Divine.

By living in harmony with the truths found in Dr. Fager's works we can personally come to know that the Creator has manifested and will continue to manifest Himself and His virtues to our hearts and minds, in part, through *words*. By pondering and performing what is *virtuous*, as defined in *The Human Virtues Dictionary*, the truths in this book can be personally proven or verified to each and every sincere seeker of truth. From every resulting increase in *enlightenment*, each recipient of truth will be personally uplifted and inspired toward receiving, comprehending and living in closer harmony with more and greater manifestations of the Divine.

Conclusion

Dr. M. Gregg Fager's pioneering works are a wonderfully positive breakthrough in the field of human virtue research, education and development. His substantial record of achievement exemplifies one of the various ways human beings can express our yearning for spiritual progress. His writings highlight and can help humanity fulfill our needs for powerful reform and improvement in the development of virtue.

I celebrate with Gregg the completion of his twenty-eight-year journey (1984-2012). I celebrate with him his ongoing quest to love and glorify God by sharing with us progressive language tools which can empower each of us to increasingly confirm and affirm life's spiritual dimension through our ongoing personal reception and comprehension of manifestations of the Divine. And I celebrate with him his ongoing quest to love his neighbor as himself by sharing with us progressive language tools which can empower each of us to be better leaders in producing, preserving and restoring virtuously liberating freedom, health, honorable economic prosperity and steady progress among us all.

Dr. Richard G. Wilkins

PREFACE

The true end of life is not mere existence, not pleasure, not fame, not wealth. The true purpose of life is the perfection of humanity through individual effort, under the guidance of God's inspiration.
—David O. McKay

As an honest person, you know it would be dishonest to dismiss the value and power of all or part of this book before you have honorably tested it by its own terms. You understand that one cannot stand at the base of a mountain one has not climbed and, in glancing at it, truthfully tell oneself or others what it is really like to climb to its summit.

To better *understand, do, be* and *teach one another* what is truly virtuous is not an easy downhill slide, but rather a challenging uphill climb out of engulfing clouds of darkness, vice and corruption. With enough focused and honest effort with this book over time, you *will* make that climb and you *will* receive the glorious liberty, hope, peace and joy that come with it.

When it comes to your personal improvement, it is far better to follow your own mind and heart than it is to follow the crowd. While science may offer persuasive evidence and convincing proof of many things, the best laboratories for discovering and improving who you are lie within your own mind and heart, and nowhere else. That will not change. Within those laboratories you are invited to examine whether you agree or disagree with the answers given in the following two conversations.

Conversation on Truth and Error and Virtue and Vice

Do we truly live in a realm of real opposites? Yes, we do. Can those opposites be accurately represented in our minds and hearts by opposing *words*? Yes. Are we granted power as children to learn to identify for ourselves such opposites as *truth* and *error* or *virtue* and *vice*? Normally, yes.

Does choosing truth and virtue in the face of opposition over time increase our powers to see and choose more truth and virtue? Yes. Does choosing error and vice over time diminish our powers to see and choose anything except error and vice? Yes.

Can our knowledge of truth and virtue be distorted or lost? Yes. When our knowledge of them is lost, or when we think they are entirely relative in meaning and value, can we find one choice or standard to be *better* or *worse* than another? Not until experienced natural consequences reveal to us whether its true meaning and its true comparative value are *virtuous* or *vicious.* Can horrible consequences come too quickly for us to change the evil choices or decisions which bring them? Yes. Can such consequences sometimes be delayed, hidden or ignored for a time? Yes. Do vicious people who know this selfishly seek personal gain by seeking the loss or distortion of truth and virtue in themselves and in their victims? Yes.

Can we eliminate the realities of truth and virtue? No. When truth and virtue are found, and are not regarded as relative in meaning or value, can we easily find one choice or standard to be *better* or *worse* than another? Yes—what is *virtuous* or *vicious* become so readily discernible that awaiting experienced natural consequences becomes unnecessary. Do repentant wrongdoers who learn this turn to virtuous unity and the common good for themselves and others by learning and living *words* of truth and virtue? Yes. Do *words* of truth and virtue become valuable to them? Yes, most valuable.

Conversation on Freedom and Virtuous Unity

Can a free people survive under a republican constitution without remaining virtuous and morally strong in *word* and in *deed*? No. Can national freedom endure where vicious equality, diversity, inclusion, individualism or liberality are held above virtuous unity and strength? No.

Can what is made legal or illegal by humankind serve as an adequate substitute for what is right and wrong? Obviously no. Bad laws never produce good results. Neither does the bad enforcement of good laws.

Is it possible to legislate the virtuous love, unity and strength of an unwilling people? No. Is it possible to legally and safely limit the power of those who would impose vicious disunity and weakness? Yes, but only to the extent a willing majority of free people are virtuously united and virtuously strong enough to adequately enact and enforce good laws.

Is it true that a vicious majority allowed to impose unrestrained error and vice will also impose the bondage of anarchy or tyranny? Sadly, yes. Is it true that the freedom to choose virtuous love, unity and strength, the common good and true joy can survive and flourish only where *words* and *deeds* of truth and virtue are valued by a virtuous majority as highly as life, liberty and property? Yes. Then how valuable must *words* and *deeds* of truth and virtue be to a virtuous majority? They must be of greatest worth.

This Book and its Purpose

To Be Virtuous is a reference book, textbook and workbook in one. It has a dictionary plus ten chapters of textbook. The last of the ten chapters explains how the entire book can be used as a workbook. I wrote this book to empower the willing among us to better *understand, do, be* and *teach one another* what is truly virtuous—so that in greater virtuous love we can better progress together toward virtuous oneness.

Virtue is the true foundation of all worthy thoughts, words and actions. It is the true foundation of all worthy laws, rules, standards and values. Human progress depends upon the rate and quality of our improvement in human virtue. Our better development of virtue requires our better understanding of the human virtues found in our language, and of their actual impact values within us.

From human thoughts come beliefs. From beliefs come values. Thoughts, beliefs and values are *infinite* in number. Human virtues from A to Z in the English language (or in any another language) are *finite* in number and are the *fruits* of all virtuous thoughts, beliefs and values. As we acquire a more clear understanding of human virtues, we can more clearly discern virtuous thoughts, beliefs and values, and their true sources.

The Human Virtues Dictionary **in this book** is a definitive record of human virtues from A to Z in the English language. This dictionary has just over 4,900 definitions representing the character fruits of all virtuous thoughts, beliefs, values and characteristics. With its various tools, this book invites and guides our personal validation and verification of each definition of each human virtue, and its defined numerical value (or impact value) as a virtue, clarifies our understanding as we engage in this process, explains and guides our virtue building, and challenges us all to follow provided steps to test and improve upon this work for the betterment of all.

Using the tools in this book can enable us to more clearly understand and better teach the unsurpassed advantages and benefits of building more and stronger virtue. As individuals, families, organizations and nations, we can use this book in our daily efforts to more effectively build greater virtue while forsaking vice, in our efforts to promote virtue-building education and leadership, and in our urgent need to better integrate and safeguard the language of human virtue from corruption and disintegration.

Because this book can help each of us to better discern and reject that which is *evil* in favor of that which is *good*, it can help us work together to decisively win the greatest of victories on the ultimate battleground—the human mind and heart. Understanding, living and teaching well enough the virtues in *The Human Virtues Dictionary* will empower the diverse but willing individuals, families, organizations and nations of the earth to powerfully rise in unison above the world's predatory forces of darkness, vice, corruption, bondage, despair, turmoil and misery.

A Reference Text and Workbook for the Development of Personal Virtue

The rate and quality of our *personal* improvement in human virtue depend upon how well we personally avoid, escape and live without vice. How well we personally avoid, escape and live without vice depends upon how well we personally build, preserve and strengthen virtues within ourselves. Such principles of personal virtue building are explained in Chapter Two, entitled *Some True Statements about Human Character*.

This book is well suited to every person capable of learning personal virtue, beginning with the very young. Each of us can use this book to make better choices and decisions about who we are and will become. Each of us can use this book to evaluate and identify for ourselves those virtuous thoughts, beliefs, values and characteristics which will produce, preserve or restore the greatest true enlightenment, virtue, integrity, liberty, hope, peace and joy within ourselves, our families and society.

A Reference Text and Workbook for the Development of Family Virtue

Every *family's* improvement in human virtue is contingent upon the development of virtue within its individual members. More perfect acquisition of the virtues found in *The Human Virtues Dictionary* will empower the members of any and every family on Earth to use more virtuous love to achieve virtuous oneness with one another and with God, and to experience more true enlightenment, virtue, integrity, liberty, hope, peace and joy in the process.

This book is well suited to every family capable of learning virtue together. Mothers, grandmothers and other women who fill the role of mother are uniquely endowed by our Creator with qualifications suited to reaching out in kindness and love to powerfully build and nourish human virtues within the minds and hearts of children. Society *cannot* progress without this vital nurturing influence from such women. This book provides them with powerful tools with which to raise up better children in an increasingly challenging world. Every child needs a good mother.

This book also provides fathers, grandfathers and other men who fill the role of father with powerful tools with which to better protect and teach their families and to more safely guide teenagers through formative years. A father's irreplaceable influence for good is vital to the progress of the family and, thus, to the progress of society. Every child needs a good father.

A Reference Text and Workbook for the Development of Organizational and National Virtue

There is room for improvement in the collective virtue of the members of every *organization* and *nation*. Prescribed use of this book will empower the members of any and every organization and nation to collectively achieve better virtue and more virtuous love. This, in turn, will help them collectively achieve virtuous oneness with the people of other organizations and nations and with God, and will bring to all of them and to all of us greater true enlightenment, virtue, integrity, liberty, hope, peace and joy.

This book is well suited to every organization and nation capable of learning virtue together. All virtuous citizens, lawmakers, policymakers, professionals and other organizational members, leaders and teachers can use the tools in this book to counter the alarming negative impacts of creeping darkness, vice and corruption. Every business, civic, community, educational, peer, political, professional, religious, social, trade and other organization in every nation of the world can use this book as a reliable resource for sustaining better human progress in organizational or national identity, purpose, policy, behavior, performance and prosperity.

A Reference Text and Workbook for Present and Future Research, Education and Development

Virtue-based research, education and development are becoming more obviously important to our global well-being. This book invites and challenges you to further your own research, teaching and building of more and stronger virtue. Working together to build greater virtue within us will have *a powerfully positive and immediately transformative impact* on our personal and collective ability, accountability, adjudication, administration, character, commerce, conditions, diplomacy, economics, education, ethics, government, health, humanity, jurisprudence, lawmaking, leadership, liberty, management, morality, policymaking, politics, progress, prosperity, purpose, reform, religion, research, responsibility, rights, standards and training, to name some. Without more and stronger virtue, these things *cannot* and *will not* improve.

The needs of humanity are calling for *your* cooperative testing and improvement of this work. The chapter in this book entitled *An Open Challenge to the World* invites the people of all backgrounds, disciplines, languages and nations to follow provided steps to test and improve upon this work for the betterment of humanity. This Open Challenge can and should be undertaken in minds, hearts, classrooms, studies and resulting publications and practices across the world—*especially in your own.*

The Deficient and the Good

As the author of this book, I make no official statement in behalf of any organization or nation. I also make no defamatory, hateful or untrue statement about any human being living or dead. This book emphasizes what is what rather than who is what. In other words, each definition of a human attribute is intended to accurately describe the real human condition represented by that attribute, and is not to be regarded as a statement by the author attributing that condition to the actual character of any particular person. This book is not perfect in its present form. Neither is its author. Full responsibility for the deficiencies of this book is humbly accepted by its author.

I am most grateful for the virtuous influence of my parents and ancestors. With tears of gratitude I acknowledge the loving kindness and the steady encouragement of my wife, Trudena. Through my years of long and difficult workdays, she has been a wonderful helpmate. I am also most grateful to Dr. Terrel H. Bell, to Dr. Richard G. Wilkins, to Boyd J. Tuttle and to all others who have provided valuable assistance and encouragement.

Full credit for anything good in this book belongs to God. Many times when I was at a loss for words, He filled my mind with the right words and confirmed them in my heart by His Holy Spirit. Sometimes He did not wait for me to ask. In the day and in the night He awakened me to things I should write. I could not have written this book without His help. In your study of this book, you may see His hand and feel of His Spirit.

As the Author of Virtue to everyone on Earth, God is bound to teach, perfect, reward and protect every virtuous nation. Without virtue, a nation has no promise. Consequently, to the extent a nation becomes virtuous it becomes liberated, prosperous and defensible, and to the extent it becomes vicious it becomes enslaved, impoverished and indefensible. Hence, by virtuous example and instruction, the wise teach the young to choose what is virtuous for the good of all. For the sake of all, let us continue to *better understand, do, be* and *teach one another* what is truly virtuous.

M. G. FAGER

CHAPTER ONE
An Allegory about Human Virtue

Do men gather grapes of thorns, or figs of thistles? Even so every good tree bringeth forth good fruit; but a corrupt tree bringeth forth evil fruit. A good tree cannot bring forth evil fruit, neither can a corrupt tree bring forth good fruit. Every tree that bringeth not forth good fruit is hewn down, and cast into the fire. Wherefore by their fruits ye shall know them. —The Lord Jesus Christ

The Allegory of the Good Apple Tree

One late winter day a goodly farmer cultivated a spot of ground in his orchard and planted a seed for a new apple tree. Then he watered the soil surrounding the seed. It was a seed from a healthy tree proven capable of flourishing in unusually harsh weather conditions. He was told the seed could grow into a prize fruit tree.

As spring arrived, sunshine warmed the moist ground until the seed sprang into life. From its shell grew a root. As the root's tiny hairs absorbed water and dissolved minerals, a seedling developed and poked its small, leafy head through the surface of the earth into the light of day.

The farmer continued to cultivate, enrich and water the ground around the tree. The root became a strong root system which spread deeper and deeper into the surrounding soil. The roots produced and transported healthy sap into the tree's growing stem and branches. The year the little apple tree became mature enough to produce fruit, it produced just a few apples, but the farmer found them to be unusually tasty.

The tree's roots and leafy branches continued to nourish each other as layer upon layer of heartwood turned seasonal growth rings into a sturdy trunk with more and more leafy branches which reached higher and higher into the sky. The farmer pruned the branches of the apple tree each year so the tree could produce its best and most abundant fruit. In time, the young tree produced an abundance of delicious fruit which sold for the best prices in the market. It was indeed a prize fruit tree.

The farmer had a vicious neighbor who was jealous. By night the vicious neighbor filled part of the farmer's irrigation ditch with dirt to divert its water away from the apple tree. Before the farmer cleared the ditch, the young apple tree drove its roots deeper into the ground where it found water and survived.

The vicious neighbor became angry. By night he poured poison on the ground around the apple tree. The root system somehow detected the difference between the poison and the usual water and nutrients it absorbed from the soil. The root system began to draw good water and nutrients from selected parts of the ground. Elsewhere, threatened roots ejected poisoned water away from the heartwood as soon as it was detected. The tree survived and grew.

The vicious neighbor became furious. By night he brought insects to infest the trunk of the apple tree. The insects bored into the bark and began to threaten the heartwood. The tree changed the color of some of its leaves to signal the farmer of the attack. The farmer noticed the signal and drove the insects away with insecticide. The trunk became even stronger.

The vicious neighbor became enraged. One night he began to cut fruit-laden branches from the tree with his hatchet. The noise awakened the farmer who came running. When the farmer reached the tree the vicious neighbor ran away. The vicious neighbor was livid, but this time he was caught and was banished from the land. The branches and the tree grew back stronger than before.

As the years went by, springtime blossoms covered the tree's wide-spread branches. In the fall, the farmer often picked record harvests of fruit from the apple tree for himself, for his family and for the people who came to the market to buy the best apples in the land. The farmer eventually sold not only apples from his prize tree, but also seeds from its apples. He planted some of the seeds to produce other good trees in his orchard.

The apple tree survived other severe challenges but persevered in producing much good fruit all of the rest of its days. What will become of your fruit the rest of your days? What are you willing to *learn, do, be* and *teach* to make your fruit as truly virtuous as possible? Do you have a more important goal to achieve, a more crucial battle to fight, or a greater personal victory to win in this life? If so, what is it—and what makes it so? What virtues will you learn, live and teach from this allegory?

Youth is the seed time of good habits. —Thomas Paine

CHAPTER TWO
Some True Statements about Human Character

If we work upon marble, it will perish; if we work on brass, time will efface it. If we rear temples, they will crumble to the dust. But if we work on men's immortal minds, if we impress on them high principles, the just fear of God, and love for their fellow-men, we engrave on those tablets something which no time can efface, and which will brighten and brighten to all eternity.
—Daniel Webster

The following statements are written in *first-person form* to help the reader more personally examine and evaluate the truthfulness of each one. Terms in the *Glossary* and definitions in *The Human Virtues Dictionary* may provide additional or missing insights on the following statements:

1. **Every Person Has Character.** Historically, the word *character* is derived from words meaning to *distinctively carve, engrave or inscribe upon or within.* Every person has their own composition or set of human characteristics. For me, that composition or set of human characteristics is the *character* distinctively carved, engraved, inscribed or otherwise recorded upon or within my heart by the choices and decisions I make, over time.

2. **My Character and My Personality Are Not the Same.** Among its various definitions, *personality* means the person I *outwardly* appear or present myself to be in the minds of one or more other people. My personality or image may reflect or represent my true character, or it may not. For example, in the minds of others, I may be esteemed or regarded as highly attractive, colorful and entertaining in *personality*, while I choose to remain *inwardly* hypocritical, masquerading or tawdry in *character*. (This truth is evident in the references of the Lord Jesus Christ to people who are likened unto *wolves* wearing *sheep's clothing* or unto *whited sepulchres* which are *full of dead men's bones.*)

   On the other hand, my *personality* or image may be esteemed or regarded by others as lacking form, comeliness, beauty, desirability or preference, while the inner condition of my *character* is of marvelous true enlightenment, virtue and integrity. My character is who I truly am within me. (This truth is evident in the Old Testament statements: *man looketh on the outward appearance, but the Lord looketh on the heart*—who *triest the heart, and hast pleasure in uprightness*—and who searches *the heart* in order *to give every man according to his ways, and according to the fruit of his doings.*)

3. **There Are Three Dimensions of Human Character.**
   a. One dimension of human character is that certain *composition or set* of definite human characteristics recorded upon or within my heart. To the extent I am aware of them, my certain composition or set of definite human characteristics can be listed.
   b. A second dimension of human character is that certain *impact value* of each of my definite human characteristics and the combined impact value of all of them within me, as recorded upon or within my heart. Virtues have the most positive impact value within me. Vices have the most negative impact value within me.
   c. A third dimension of human character is that certain *degree of strength* of each of my definite human characteristics and that certain combined degree of strength of all of them within me, as recorded upon or within my heart. Increasing the degree of strength of a human characteristic within me can multiply its impact value.

4. **Character Development May Be Likened unto the Growth of a Fruit Tree.** The growth and development of a fruit tree may be used to help me understand the growth and development of my character, as follows (see *italicized* terms in the *Glossary*):
   a. The **roots** of the tree may be likened unto my *mind* or intellect, which is capable of receiving and processing information as thoughts of my *mind*. Many a thought will prove to be either nutritious (with a positive impact value) or poisonous (with a negative impact value) once it is absorbed into my *heart*.
   b. The **sap** made and used by the tree to form its rings of heartwood may be likened unto the thoughts of my *heart*. I can willfully choose to allow certain thoughts of my *mind* to become absorbed into the thoughts of my *heart* by refusing to reject them, or by selecting them to be a part of what I want to do and who I want to be. Either way, each thought of my *heart* continues to form what I do and who I am until I choose, if I still can, to permanently replace it with a different thought within my *heart*.
   c. The **trunk** of the tree may be likened unto my *beliefs*, which grow from, embody and represent the thoughts of my *heart*.

  d. The **branches** of the tree may be likened unto my *values (standards)* — which grow from, embody and represent my *beliefs* — which grow from, embody and represent the thoughts of my *heart*.
  e. The **fruits** of the tree may be likened unto my *characteristics* — which grow from, embody and represent my *values (standards)* — which grow from, embody and represent my *beliefs* — which grow from, embody and represent the thoughts of my *heart*. My entire harvest of fruits in all three of their dimensions is my *character*.

5. **The Number of Possible Thoughts People Can Think Is *Infinite*.**

6. **The Number of Possible Beliefs Which Can Grow from People's Thoughts Is *Infinite*.**

7. **The Number of Possible Values Which Can Grow from People's Thoughts and Beliefs Is *Infinite*.**

8. **The Number of Possible Characteristics Which Can Grow from People's Thoughts, Beliefs and Values Is FINITE.** Human character is defined and circumscribed by the *finite* number of definite human characteristics alphabetically classified from A to Z in the English language (and similarly listed in other languages). Human characteristics represent all of the consequences of human thoughts, beliefs and values known to exist within us. Thus, unlike thoughts, beliefs and values, human characteristics can be circumscribed into one great whole, and can be classified, named and listed as such.

9. **Human Characteristics Can Be Classified According to Their Impact Value.** Each definite human characteristic can be classified with a defined numerical value (or impact value) according to the extent to which it produces, preserves or restores true enlightenment, virtue, integrity, liberty, hope, peace and joy within me, my family and society — or according to the extent to which it produces, preserves or restores darkness, vice, corruption, bondage, despair, turmoil and misery within me, my family and society. [The five defined numerical values (or impact values) used in this book are defined in the *Glossary*. Their use in classification is described in the next chapter.]

10. **Good Characteristics Produce, Preserve or Restore True Enlighten-ment, Virtue, Integrity, Liberty, Hope, Peace and Joy within Me, My Family and Society.** Ultimately, that which is good comes to us from God. Good is revealed and sustained by God's use and by His righteous followers' use of powerfully enlightening intelligence or the pure light of truth. From enlightenment can come virtue, integrity, liberty, hope, peace and joy. Conversely, there can be no lasting joy without peace, no lasting peace without hope, no lasting hope without liberty, no lasting liberty without integrity, no lasting integrity without virtue, and no lasting virtue without enlightenment or the pure light of truth.

11. **Evil Characteristics Produce, Preserve or Restore Darkness, Vice, Corruption, Bondage, Despair, Turmoil and Misery within Me, My Family and Society.** Ultimately, that which is evil comes to us from Satan. Evil is hidden and sustained by Satan's use and by his followers' use of powerfully deceiving darkness. From darkness can come vice, corruption, bondage, despair, turmoil and misery. Conversely, there can be no lasting misery without turmoil, no lasting turmoil without despair, no lasting despair without bondage, no lasting bondage without corruption, no lasting corruption without vice, and no lasting vice without darkness.

12. **Better Discernment Can Result from Understanding the True Merits of Human Characteristics.** Defined numerical values (or impact values) can be accurate reflections of the true merits of definite human characteristics. I must discern *for myself* the true impact value of each of the finite number of definite human characteristics found from A to Z in the English language (or in another language)—no one else can do this for me. Once I have come to know these character fruits for what they truly are, I can use them to discern for myself the *best* thoughts, beliefs and values, and their true sources—and the *worst* thoughts, beliefs and values, and their true sources. (It is for this purpose the Lord Jesus Christ revealed to *each of us* the sure test of discernment: *Ye shall know them by their fruits.*)

13. **Better Character Is Built from the Inside Out, Not from the Outside In.** Better character comes from better choices and decisions, over time. If I am accountable, then my character begins to form in my childhood

as my willfully chosen thoughts, words and actions are formed and performed. While I am still liberated and well enough within my mind and heart to willfully choose for myself, I alone can control what is happening on the stage of my mind and what is being built or changed within my heart, over time.

Over time, improving my environment can help me improve my character, but no one and nothing in my environment can decide my character as long as I choose to do, be and teach only what is truly virtuous—only my willful choices can do that. In this condition I can willfully choose to progress by improving my character with the invited help of God. (God cannot and will not help me progress contrary to my will—He has granted me liberty by granting me freedom of conscience.)

From this condition I can, instead, willfully choose to regress to the point where I empower Satan and his followers to control what is happening on the stage of my mind and within my heart. In doing so, I willfully surrender to them my will, and thus my liberty, to improve my character, regardless of my environment or situation. (Satan and his followers want me to willfully surrender to them my will and my liberty to progress—they seek to impose bondage upon me by taking from me my freedom of conscience.)

14. **Building Better Character Requires a Better Understanding of the Terminology of Human Character.** Each discipline, such as agronomy, horticulture, carpentry, mechanics, law or medicine, has its own unique terminology. As with other disciplines, the extent to which I understand the terminology of human character from A to Z in the English language (or in another language) will determine the extent to which I can understand, do, be and teach within the discipline. For example, if I can better understand and choose what is truly virtuous, then I can make better choices and decisions, do better things and become a better person and a better teacher of virtue.

15. **A Person of Enlightenment, Virtue and Integrity Is Who I Become and Remain at Heart as I Forsake and Withstand Darkness, Vice and Corruption.** I can open my heart to God and to the influence of those who are of true enlightenment, virtue and integrity who want to empower me to define, represent and govern my own self in a manner that is pleasing unto God. If I open my heart to them, they will help me fill it with true enlightenment, virtue and integrity, and with naturally consequent liberty, hope, peace and joy. Choosing true enlightenment,

virtue and integrity leads me *away* from darkness, vice and corruption, and *away* from naturally consequent bondage, despair, turmoil and misery. To the extent I lose a vice I gain one or more opposite virtues. To the extent I gain a virtue I lose one or more opposite vices.

16. **A Person of Darkness, Vice and Corruption Is Who I Become and Remain at Heart as I Forsake and Withstand True Enlightenment, Virtue and Integrity.** I can open my heart to Satan and to the influence of those who are of darkness, vice and corruption who want to empower themselves to define, represent and govern me in a manner that is pleasing unto them. If I open my heart to their influence, they will fill it with darkness, vice and corruption, and with naturally consequent bondage, despair, turmoil and misery. Choosing darkness, vice and corruption leads me *away* from true enlightenment, virtue and integrity, and *away* from naturally consequent liberty, hope, peace and joy. To the extent I lose a virtue I gain one or more opposite vices. To the extent I gain a vice I lose one or more opposite virtues.

17. **Complete Honesty of Heart Is Required of Me to Improve My Character.** Just as filth allows for the spread of biological disease, deception allows for the spread of darkness, vice and corruption. Those already plagued with such evils cleverly use deception to counterfeit, distort or disguise the voices of enlightened certainty, reality and truth, lest they be used by others to forsake or withstand darkness, vice and corruption. Thus, the great moral danger of the day is deception. And the most deadly form of deception is self-deception. With true and unrelenting commitment to my pure and complete honesty with myself I can improve my character. Without it, I cannot.

18. **Positive Change Is and Will Remain an Uphill Battle.** Without real choice and powerfully vicious opposition, human progress would be impossible, and any achievement of human virtue would be rendered meaningless. The ultimate defeat of human virtue would also render its achievement meaningless.

There is abundant evidence for me to ascertain that my negligent or willful loss of true enlightenment, virtue and integrity will ultimately lead to my naturally consequent bondage, despair, turmoil and misery. That same evidence is proof enough that excessive tolerance, attempted neutrality, or willing surrender to darkness, vice and corruption can never lead anyone to lasting liberty, hope, peace and joy. There is no solid evidence to the contrary. None.

Meanwhile, abundant historical and prophetic evidence testifies that in the growing heat of battle, the knowing and the wise will join the camp of those of true enlightenment, virtue and integrity, and shall ultimately prevail with God's help, while the deceived and the foolish will join the growing camp of darkness, vice and corruption, and shall ultimately perish.

19. **Achieving the Best Possible Character Is a Person's Crowning Achievement on Earth**. No other achievement of mine can ultimately compensate for my lack of good character. It has no equivalent and no substitute. I have it or I don't. I can forsake my good character for money or property, but I cannot purchase it with money or property. I can abandon my good character for worldly fame, pleasure, popularity or power, but, unlike image, personality, prestige and reputation, it cannot be bestowed upon me by others. No one else can achieve, acquire or possess it for me.

The best possible character can come to me and can remain with me only through my own consistent, conscientious and sincere efforts, under the guidance of God's inspiration, over time. I will ultimately be judged by Him for who I truly am within my heart, for what I truly desire within my heart, and for what I have thought, said and done as a consequence. Without good character, no other achievement of mine will matter in the long run. Achieving the best possible character will be my crowning achievement on Earth.

20. **I Can Receive Enough Power to Be Rid of All Vices Within Me**. Provided I am not so obsessed or possessed within my mind and heart that I cannot choose for myself, as I choose to use my very best efforts to allow God to help me improve my character choice by choice, I will receive enough power from Him to effectively expel evil or satanic thoughts from my mind — and can thereby prevent them from entering my heart, regardless of my environment or situation. (This truth is evident in the New Testament statement: *God 'is' faithful, who will not suffer you to be tempted above that ye are able; but will with the temptation also make a way to escape, that ye may be able to bear 'it.'*)

By willfully escaping from and preventing such thoughts from entering my heart, I can prevent all evil or satanic powers and personages from gaining any further control over the development or formation of my character. As I do this, I can justly receive from God the power to acquire enough virtue to rid myself of all vices and of all disposition to restore them within me. My retention of virtue and the remission of those vices will thereafter depend upon my daily choices and decisions.

21. **I Can Receive Enough Power to Lead Myself and Others to Achieve Better Character over Time.** With God's help, I can receive that power by prayerfully doing my very best choice by choice to live and teach in harmony with virtues I have selected from *The Human Virtues Dictionary.* By their fruits in me I shall know whether they are virtues worth living and teaching. If they prove to be virtues, then by those fruits I shall know God. (To help us know God, the Lord Jesus Christ taught *each of us* the sure test of knowing His truths and virtues: *If any man will do his will, he shall know of the doctrine, whether it be of God.*)

22. **Choosing Truly Virtuous Thoughts Is an Important Key to Leading Myself and Others to Achieve Better Character.** I can achieve better character by improving the quality of my *characteristics.* I can achieve better characteristics by improving the quality of my *values.* I can achieve better values by improving the quality of my *beliefs.* I can achieve better beliefs by improving the quality of my *thoughts.* Hence, I can consistently achieve better character over time by constantly thinking in harmony with human virtues. (It is for this purpose the Lord Jesus Christ revealed to *each of us* the sure method of personal improvement: *[L]et virtue garnish thy thoughts unceasingly.*)

23. **I Can Honorably Test Whether Use of this Book Helps Me to Better** *Understand* **What Is Truly Virtuous.** Provided I am still liberated and well enough within my mind and heart to choose for myself, I can find out for myself whether this book actually helps me to better understand what is truly virtuous. I can do this by completing at least the first step in Chapter Ten, entitled *An Open Challenge to the World.*

24. **I Can Honorably Test Whether Use of this Book Helps Me to Better** *Do, Be* **and** *Teach* **What Is Truly Virtuous.** Provided I am still liberated and well enough within my mind and heart to choose for myself, I can find out for myself whether this book actually helps me to better do, be and teach what is truly virtuous. I can do this by completing at least the first two steps in Chapter Ten, entitled *An Open Challenge to the World.*

CHAPTER THREE
The Classification of Human Character

What lies behind us and what lies before us are tiny matters
compared to what lies within us. —Ralph Waldo Emerson

Words serve as a classification system for human thoughts. Classification systems provide for the consistent naming and listing of all kinds of beings, concepts, conditions, objects, places and things which, in turn, allow for their common if not universal identification and reference. Historically, classification has proven to be of astonishing benefit to the advancement, discovery, organization and dissemination of human knowledge and experience.

More than 2,300 years ago, the Greek philosopher and naturalist Aristotle classified animals as vertebrates and invertebrates, and plants by size and appearance.[1] His supposed contemporary, the Greek mathematician Euclid, classified mathematical truths called *axioms* and *postulates* into 467 propositions of plane and solid geometry.[2]

Published classification systems began to reemerge in the *16th Century* A.D. The German physician Georgius Agricola (Georg Bauer) developed a classification system for minerals, published *De Re Metallica* in 1556, and became known as the founder of minerology.[3] With the discovery of the microscope by Dutchman Zacharias Janssen in 1590,[4] the science of microbiology and its classifications, names and lists began to emerge.

Early in the *17th Century*, English schoolteacher Robert Crawley, with the assistance of his schoolteacher son, Thomas, published *A Table Alphabeticall*, the first book with a lexical focus entirely devoted to an alphabetical English word list with English definitions. Published in 1604, it was the first English dictionary.[5] With the invention of the telescope by Dutchman Hans Lippershey in 1608 and its improvement for use in astronomy by the Italian Galileo Galilei by 1610,[6] classifications, names and lists pertaining to astronomy were founded.

During the *18th Century*, the Swedish botanist and explorer Carolus Linnaeus framed taxonomic principles for defining genera (groups) and species (kinds) of organisms, and created a uniform system for naming and classifying them.[7] His book *Species Plantarum* (1753) forms the basis for plant classification. The 10th edition of his *Systema Naturae* (1758) forms the basis for animal classification.[8] From 1758 to 1782, the French astronomer Charles Messier compiled *The Messier Catalog*, a list of approximately 100 of the most amazing galaxies, nebulae and star clusters in earth's night sky.[9]

The *19th Century* brought an expansion of classification. American educator and writer Noah Webster published in two volumes *An American Dictionary of the English Language* in 1828. At that time, his twenty-seven-year work surpassed every known dictionary in number of defined words at 70,000.[10]   In 1829, Swiss-American natural scientist Louis Agassiz published *Selecta Genera et Species Piscium,* one of the first works on the classification of fish.[11]   In 1838, French-American woodsman and painter John James Audubon completed publication of his masterpiece, *Birds of America,* consisting of 435 hand-colored, life-size engravings depicting hundreds of bird species.[12]

Creation of the vast *Oxford English Dictionary* was launched in 1857. Its first publication took seventy years to complete, drew from tens of thousands of contributing minds, and organized over 400,000 definitions.[13] Russian chemist Dmitri Ivanovich Mendeleev proposed the classification of the properties of chemical elements in 1869, which led to classifications found in the periodic table.[14]   In 1876, American inventor Melvil Dewey copyrighted his Dewey Decimal Classification system for library books and materials.[15]

In the *20th Century,* German engineers Ernst Ruska and Max Knoll invented the electron microscope.[16] Their 1930s work was improved upon by others who made it possible to view, classify and list molecular structures and viruses for the first time. Gene mapping was launched under the Human Genome Project in 1990.[17] In 1996, American Larry Page and Russian-American Sergei Brin joined as entrepreneurs to develop a computer search engine and two years later founded Google, Inc.[18]   At present, their online services provide the computer users of the world free access to a web index with billions of web pages and other items of classified, named and listed information, with online searches completed as soon as they are entered.

In this *21st Century,* there is a glut of technical information and exploding innovation, yet people are challenged and confused as never before by growing darkness, vice, corruption, bondage, despair, turmoil and misery. *Where* are the classifications, lists and maps of human character-istics, especially the virtues? And *where* is the great young generation of men and women who will understand, live and teach one another what is truly virtuous well enough to powerfully rise in unison above the world's predatory forces of darkness, vice, corruption, bondage, despair, turmoil and misery? What revolutionary things will you do and keep doing to make it *your* generation? What will you do to get as many as possible to join you?

The people of Earth have classified, named and listed animals, birds, fish, galaxies, genes, mathematical axioms and postulates, microorganisms, minerals, molecular structures, nebulae, plants, stars, viruses, words and all manner of other classified, named and listed information. It is likewise possible to classify, name and list the finite number of human characteristics found from A to Z in the English language (or in any other language). Most of those characteristics are found in dictionaries. Each of them has at least one definition which represents or which should represent a *real human condition*. This book explains how some of those definitions can and should be improved upon.

This book also explains how it is possible to use *defined numerical values* to further classify human characteristics, along with their definitions, according to how valuable they are to the progress of humankind. The five defined numerical values (or impact values) used in this book are **positive two** (2), **positive one** (1), **zero** (0), **negative one** (-1) and **negative two** (-2). Together they are a *__classification system__*.

With this classification system one number can be used to truly tell us what any real human condition can do to, for or against us. This book explains how it is possible to use this classification system to create, test and preserve the entire language of human character as an *integrated language* (see related terms and defined numerical values in the *Glossary*).

➤ *To Be Virtuous* contains *The Human Virtues Dictionary*. This dictionary has just over 4,900 definitions. It identifies those human characteristics with a defined numerical value (or impact value) of **positive two** (2). Each one is a human **virtue**.

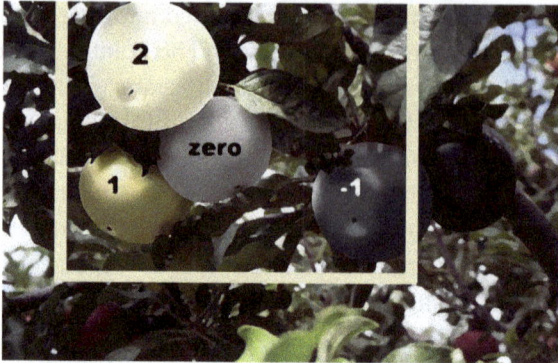

The author's book *The Language of Human Virtue* contains *The Building Virtue Dictionary*. That dictionary has more than 18,400 definitions. It identifies those human characteristics with defined numerical values (or impact values) of **positive two** (2), **positive one** (1), **zero** (0) or **negative one** (-1). All four of them (2, 1, 0 and -1) can be *virtuously* used to build, preserve and strengthen *virtues* within each of us. Each of the last three (1, 0 and -1) can also be *viciously* used to build, preserve and strengthen *vices* within each of us.

The author's book *The Language of Human Character* contains *The Human Character Dictionary*. That dictionary has more than 27,100 definitions. It identifies each human characteristic with its own defined numerical value of **positive two** (2), **positive one** (1), **zero** (0), **negative one** (-1) or **negative two** (-2). Each negative two (-2) human characteristic is a human **vice**.

Human virtue exists as part of human character. A definitive record of human virtues and of the entire language of human virtue can be derived from a definitive record of the language of human character. That is why the dictionaries in *To Be Virtuous* and *The Language of Human Virtue* are drawn from the author's book *The Language of Human Character*.

The Human Virtues Dictionary **in this book** attempts to provide a definitive record of human virtues in English, in harmony with enlightened certainty, reality and truth. This dictionary is a reference book which, along with the textbook chapters that precede it, can prepare you to test the accuracy and truthfulness of any part or all of this book for yourself.

Once you have tested and discovered for yourself the proven nature of the truths within this book, you will then be prepared to use this book to improve yourself and this book. This book can and should be improved upon. A map for doing so is found in Chapter Ten, entitled *An Open Challenge to the World*.

Notes

1. "Development of Classification." *The World Book Encyclopedia*. Chicago: World Book, Inc., 2007. 656. Print.

2. "Euclid." *The World Book Encyclopedia*. Chicago: World Book, Inc., 2007. 376. Print.

3. "Georgius Agricola." *Encyclopædia Britannica*. 2012. Encyclopædia Britannica Online. 5 May 2012. Web. <http://www.britannica.com>.

4. Asimov, Isaac. *Asimov's Chronology of Science and Discovery*. New York: Harper & Row, Publishers, 1989. 124. Print.

5. Crystal, David. *The Stories of English*. Woodstock, New York: Overlook Press, 2004. 280. Print.

6. Mount, Ellis and Barbara A. List. *Milestones in Science and Technology: The Ready Reference Guide to Discoveries, Inventions, and Facts*. Phoenix, Arizona: The ORYX Press, 1987. 83. Print.

7. "Carolus Linnaeus." *Encyclopædia Britannica*. 2012. Encyclopædia Britannica Online. 5 May 2012. Web. <http://www.britannica.com>.

8. "Linnaeus, Carolus." *The World Book Encyclopedia*. Chicago: World Book, Inc., 2007. 337. Print.

9. "The Messier Catalog." 25 Feb 2008. *Students for the Exploration and Development of Space (SEDS)*. 5 May 2012. Web. <http://www.seds.org/messier/Messier.html>.

10. Slater, Rosalie J. "Noah Webster, Founding Father of American Scholarship and Education." Preface to Noah Webster's *An American Dictionary of the English Language.* Sixteenth Printing. St. Louis: A Graphic Resource, Incorporated, 2004. 24. Print.

11. "Louis Agassiz." *Encyclopædia Britannica.* 2012. Encyclopædia Britannica Online. 5 May 2012. Web. <http://www.britannica.com>.

12. "Audubon, John James." *The World Book Encyclopedia.* Chicago: World Book, Inc., 2009. 884. Print.

13. "History of the Dictionary." *Oxford University Press.* 5 May 2012. Web. <http://www.oed.com>.

14. "Mendeleev." *The World Book Encyclopedia.* Chicago: World Book, Inc., 2007. 398. Print.

15. "Dewey Decimal Classification." *The World Book Encyclopedia.* Chicago: World Book, Inc., 2009. 177. Print.

16. "Ernst August Friedrich Ruska." 1 Aug 2003. *Pioneers in Optics. Science, Optics & You.* Molecular Expressions™. 5 May 2012. Web. <http://micro.magnet.fsu.edu/optics/timeline/people/ruska.html>.

17. Pillsbury, Edmund. "A History of Genome Sequencing." 5 May 2012. Web. <http://bioinfo.mbb.yale.edu/course/projects/final-4/>.

18. "Google Milestones." 5 May 2012. Web. <http://www.google.com/corporate/history.html>.

CHAPTER FOUR
Words as Representations of Reality

A word is a package of thought. —The Author

Words may present or represent reality. As words about what is *real* are conveyed and presented to our learning, we can use them to reconvey and represent to each other's minds commonly defined images or descriptive representations of certain designated portions of what is *real*.

For example, we sometimes use real colors, creatures, plants, temperatures and other real things to draw our minds to certain designated portions of what is *real*. Consider the following examples of human characteristics used in English. Some of them are defined in *The Human Virtues Dictionary* in this book.

Words about real *colors* we use as human characteristics:

black	brown	green
black-and-white	color-blind	jaundiced
blackballing	colorful	miscoloring
blackening	coloring	off-color
blacklisting	colorizing	red
blackmailing	colorless	red-blooded
blue	discoloring	white
blue-blooded	gray	yellow

Words about real *creatures* we use as human characteristics:

animalistic	bullying	dogged
animalizing	catlike	dogging
aping	catty	doggish
apish	chicken	dog-tired
asinine	chicken-hearted	eagle-eyed
badgering	clammy	ferreting
bearish	cocky	fishy
beastly	coltish	fleecing
bestial	crabbed	foxy
bugging	crabby	harebrained
bull-dogged	currish	hawkish
bull-headed	debugging	hawklike
bullish	dog-eat-dog	hogging

hoggish	ramming	viperine
hog-wild	serpentine	viperish
hounding	sheepish	viperous
lionhearted	shrewish	vixenish
lionizing	slothful	vulturelike
muleheaded	sluggish	vulturous
mulish	snaky	waspish
parasitic	sponging	waspy
parroting	toadish	weaseling
pigeonholing	toady	woolly
piggish	venomous	wormish
pigheaded	verminous	wormy

Words about real *plants* we use as human characteristics:

blossoming	gingering	starchy
bush-league	nettling	sugary
bushwhacking	oleaginous	syrupy
corny	peachy	thorny
currying	peppering	vegetal
flowery	peppery	vegetating
fructuous	pithy	vegetational
fruitful	robust	weeding
fruitless	sapping	willowy
garden-variety	spicy	withy
ginger	starchlike	wooden

Words about real *temperature* we use as human characteristics:

chilling	hot	tepid
chilly	hot-blooded	warm
cold	hot-headed	warm-blooded
cold-blooded	hot shot	warm-hearted
cool	hot-tempered	warming
coolheaded	lukewarm	warmish

Words about other real *things* we use as human characteristics:

ablaze	afire	aglow
acidic	aflame	airing

anchored	hurdling	stellar
anchoring	inflamed	stoned
anchorless	inflaming	stonewalling
belting	inflammatory	stoning
blitzing	iron fisted	stony
bootlegging	ironhanded	stonyhearted
breadwinning	iron-hearted	storming
bubbly	lofty	stormy
buoyant	loony	straight-arrow
buttery	mercurial	strait-laced
calcifying	mooning	strapping
callous	moonstruck	streamlining
closeted	oily	street-fighting
closeting	rock-ribbed	street-smart
clouded	rocky	streetwise
clouding	rudderless	stringing
cloudless	salty	sunny
cloudy	scumlike	sunshiny
concrete	scumming	tempestuous
crusty	scummy	thunderous
dicey	scurvy	trash-talking
dirty	shadowy	trashy
drained	shady	underground
draining	shoplifting	uniform
dynamite	showboating	volcanic
electrifying	silver-tongued	watery
fair-weather	stargazing	wavering
fiery	starring	waxen
filthy	starry-eyed	waxing
fuming	star-struck	whipping
gravitating	steaming	whistle-blowing
grounded	steamy	windy

Learning to Share Knowledge of Reality through Language

When we are born into the world, most of us soon begin to associate what we are sensing with certain real things, such as *a bright light, a gentle touch* or *a warm meal*. We begin to associate real voices we hear with the real people we continue to see or feel around us. Such thought associations begin long before we learn the names or words associated with the real people and things we are sensing. For example, most of us quickly and correctly associate a certain smiling face, a certain pleasant voice and certain tender nurturing with a certain someone, but it generally takes a year or more before we can learn to call that certain someone by some form of the sound *mother*—a sound which then continues to reconvey and represent to our minds the *truth* of what she has actually done for us.

As little children, our first attempts to say what we have heard might be about *mama*, *daddy* or another family member, or about where someone's real *nose* really is or where their real *eyes* or *ears* really are, and so forth. As we continue to communicate with correctly associated spoken sounds, our common spoken vocabularies grow. With enough common spoken vocabulary comes the capacity to learn to read and write real words.

As most of us begin to use our senses to learn to read, we first learn which sounds are commonly associated with each of the written symbols in the alphabetic letters or pictographs of the language we are taught. With those associations correctly placed in our minds, we can then learn how to correctly sound out and correctly write words like the ones you are now reading (hearing in your mind). Those who learn to do these things in a certain common language can clearly communicate in writing with one another in that language.

From written words can come a vast array of combined sounds we can hear in our minds for the first time, and which introduce us to certain real people or things of which we were not previously aware. As each of us becomes aware of real things and of the words used to describe them, those words can continue to be used to reconvey and represent the *truth* about those things to us and can thereby become descriptive representations of *reality* to us. When we are thinking about words which convey and present to us the *truth* about someone or something *real*, we are then experiencing or observing *reality*.

There are some who are prone—knowing they have not personally ascertained and do not possess an absolute, perfect and verifiable personal knowledge of its truthfulness—to accept, proclaim or sponsor as truth the discernibly unverified or otherwise refutable idea, speculation or theory that: words can never produce a real or true understanding between word sender and word receiver because no one has ever had and no one can ever have conclusive proof or sufficient reason to know that both the words and the distinctive definitions which represent and connect those words to certain designated portions of reality were ever understood in precisely the same way by both word sender and word receiver.

Despite such claims, people constantly and consistently communicate a true understanding of reality with other people by continuing to express commonly used word symbols to reconvey and represent commonly defined images or descriptive representations of certain designated portions of reality. For a very simple example, use spoken words to say to a young child, *"Touch your nose!"* If they touch their nose in response, then there has been pure use of commonly or mutually understood language and a true match of word symbols, their definitions, and those certain designated portions of reality they represent.

For another simple example, have someone sit on a chair. Then, without gesturing use spoken words to say to them, *"Please stand up then sit back down."* If they stand up and then sit in response, then there has again been pure use of commonly or mutually understood language and a true match of word symbols, their definitions, and those certain designated portions of reality they represent.

For another example, say to an older child or to an adult, *"Let's each hold up four fingers when I say 'go.' Ready . . . go!"* A match in numbers you each hold up again equals pure use of commonly or mutually understood language and a true match of word symbols, their definitions, and those certain designated portions of reality they represent.

For further understanding, see *real, reality* and other related terms in the *Glossary*. See also definitions of related characteristics, such as *semantic*, in the author's dictionaries. See also the following chapter, entitled *Definitions as Statements of Truth*. If you remain unsettled about whether the words you are reading, the thoughts you are thinking, the feelings you are feeling or the life you are living are verifiable as reality, then study, ponder and pray about this entire book before deciding whether it is possible for you to discover the reality of these matters for yourself.

CHAPTER FIVE
Definitions as Statements of Truth

To myself I seem to have been only like a boy playing on the sea-shore, and diverting myself in now and then finding a smoother pebble, or a prettier shell than ordinary, whilst the great ocean of truth lay all undiscovered before me. —Sir Isaac Newton

The Evolution of Language

Definitions of words are statements of meaning. People will continue to use defined words to convey meaningful thoughts new and old. The English language never stops evolving. Newly defined words like *yottabyte* are added to explain and represent new phenomena. Defined words like *methinks* become *archaic* in usage. Defined words like *typewriter* become *obsolete* in usage. There is never a need, however, for a language to evolve away from clearly representing unchanging truth about such things as the existence of God and His dealings with humankind on Earth. Note, for example, Shakespeare's use of "God buy you" in *As You Like It* and in *Twelfth Night*. Did he mean *May God redeem you*, or *May God be beside you*, or something else? And how did his words become *God by'e* and then a simple *good-bye* with no thought of God?

Etymologies of Words Pertaining to Truth and Virtue

Etymologies can offer rich accounts of the known or supposed origins, developments, derivations and histories of words and of the definitive meanings they have conveyed in various languages for centuries. If various people centuries ago recorded their own sure knowledge of enlightened certainty, reality or truth about God, it is reasonable to conclude that at least vestiges of that enlightened certainty, reality or truth have survived within the etymologies of their recorded languages. For this reason, many definitions in *The Human Virtues Dictionary* are consistent with many commonly accepted etymologies. However, it is wise for reasons given in the following sections of this chapter to avoid placing too much emphasis on etymologies as sources of the true meanings of words pertaining to truth and virtue.

Discrepant Etymologies

Published explanations of the origins, developments, derivations and histories of words and their definitions are diverse. The etymology provided for each defined word is not the same in all English dictionaries. Foreign languages cited in an etymology, foreign words cited, and translations of the same foreign word may not be the same from one dictionary to another. There can even be disagreement on the language from which a root word originated. When two different etymologies are given in two diverse dictionaries for the same defined word pertaining to truth, then we can mistakenly accept at least one of the etymologies as *authentic* and *authoritative*.

Old Etymologies

We can mistakenly accept an etymology pertaining to truth as *authentic* and *authoritative* merely because it is or seems to be very old. Dates of origin found in etymologies are often neither conclusive nor reliable. For example, the history of the English word *etymology* itself is believed by some to have begun in the 14th Century A.D., and is thought to be derived from the Greek. Does that mean no one who spoke earlier forms of English studied the origins, developments, derivations and histories of words pertaining to truth and virtue before the 14th Century? Does that mean the Greeks were the first to do so? If not, who were the first, and did they understand truth or virtue any better than we can?

Evolving Etymologies

We can mistakenly accept the evolutionary notion that all etymologies and all other definitions of words are and must remain amorphous and vague. As a result of that notion, some evolving etymologies pertaining to light and truth can suffer. For example, when usage of a defined word pertaining to truth is considered *obsolete* because fewer people seem to be using the word, we can mistakenly suppose that the designated portion of truth represented by a true definition of that word has also become *obsolete*. When usage of a defined word pertaining to truth is considered *archaic* because people have not used it for a century or so, we can mistakenly suppose that the designated portion of truth represented by a true definition of that word has also become *archaic*. Once a defined word is classified as *obsolete* or as *archaic,* it can be removed from language and eventually lost to human knowledge. Sometimes light and truth can be lost along with it.

Corrupted or Lost Etymologies

We can mistakenly accept a specific etymology pertaining to truth as *authentic* and *authoritative* merely because evidence of its corruption or loss has been deliberately corrupted or lost by people who likely wanted to hide truth, or to hide from truth, for various reasons. The meanings of words pertaining to truth and virtue can be corrupted or lost over time. For examples see Chapter Seven, entitled *A Comparison of 19th and 21st Century Definitions.*

Cited Quotations

We can also mistakenly accept an etymology pertaining to truth as *authentic* and *authoritative* merely because cited quotations pertaining to it are used to show that the etymology has been or is being regarded by someone or by some as *authentic* and *authoritative.* If a quotation distorts a true meaning of a word pertaining to truth, then that word's meaning is weakened in its descriptive representation of truth and begins to represent a distortion of truth. Such distortions may be sustained through popularized successive approximations, as in twisting the word symbol *wicked* into an accepted misnomer for such realities as an *awesome adventure* or something *wonderfully masterful.* Our failure to consistently preserve or restore the known true meanings of words pertaining to known or knowable truth will result in the consistent disintegration of language.

Verifiable Definitions are Statements of Truth

Definitions of words may be statements of truth. Defined word symbols pertaining to human character from A to Z in the English language (and in every other language) can be used to describe, represent and circumscribe every real human condition of character each of us can understand, do, be and teach. As long as the following combination exists for a named characteristic, then that characteristic, with its definition and its defined numerical value, is an effective representation of reality and a statement of truth to us all, and should be preserved as such (see related terms in the *Glossary*):

- A certain *word symbol* by which a human characteristic is named is preserved in connection with
- A *definition* describing a *real human condition,* which is preserved in connection with
- A *defined numerical value* describing the characteristic's *real impact value,* and
- The *word symbol,* its *definition,* and its *defined numerical value* together form an effective representation of reality and a personally verifiable statement of enlightened certainty, reality or truth.

You are invited to think, feel and act to apply the foregoing criteria as tests to *personally validate* and *personally verify* each human characteristic with its definition and with its defined numerical value as they appear in *The Human Virtues Dictionary* in this book. How to apply the tests is shown in this chapter. Remember, the best laboratories for discovering and improving who you are lie within your own mind and heart, and nowhere else. You are especially encouraged to use the personal testing methods found in this chapter and in Chapter Ten, entitled *An Open Challenge to the World.*

A Word of Caution

Set aside *all* personal, peer and institutional agendas, biases, bigotries, cultures, customs, fads, fashions, favorites, habits, lifestyles, norms, partialities, preferences, prejudices, presumptions, traditions, theories, trends, whims and such—to include any you think the author may have, plus your own—as you honorably test or prove each definition of a characteristic. Make each test a true and honorable test.

Avoid jumping to conclusions during testing. Avoid all disruption and interference. Let go of all doubt and all fear of failure. Release yourself to ponder the words in your mind as you quietly listen well enough in your heart. Be still. Let things settle within you.

Keep in mind a stated definition of a characteristic is *not* a statement of what you must *think.* Instead, it is a description of what you should *personally choose* to prove, and if found to be virtuous, what you should then *personally choose* to ponder as one of your personal thoughts.

Keep in mind a stated definition of a characteristic is *not* a statement of what you must *believe.* Instead, it is a description of what you should *personally choose* to prove, and if found to be truly virtuous, what you should then *personally choose* to adopt as one of your personal beliefs.

Keep in mind a stated definition of a characteristic is *not* a statement of what you must *value*. Instead, it is a description of what you should *personally choose* to prove, and if found to be truly virtuous, what you should then *personally choose* to perform as one of your personal standards.

Withhold final judgment until you have honorably completed the tests in this chapter for personal validation and verification of definitions. When done properly, these tests will help you determine whether or not a stated definition of a characteristic is a *real human condition* that is truly virtuous.

Religion Definitions

The name of a religion may offer various meanings. For example: *Buddha* may be said to mean *awakened one*; *Catholic* may be said to mean *universal*; *Confucian* may be said to mean *benevolence*; *Hindu* may be said to mean of the *religions beyond the river Sindhu*; *Islam* may be said to mean *humble submission and obedience to Allah*; *Jain* may be said to mean *spiritual conqueror of worldly passion*; *Judaic* may be said to mean *of the covenant of Judah with God*; *Methodist* may be said to mean *methodical study and worship*; *Mormon* may be said to mean *more good*; *Shinto* may be said to mean *way of the Gods*; and *Sikh* may be said to mean *able disciple or learner*. These and other such definitions have all been set aside.

Nothing in this book constitutes an official statement of any religious denomination, the meaning of its name, or its teachings. Definitions in this book disclose the *virtuous fruits* of human character which *anyone* can acquire by virtuously pondering and performing *any* form of doctrine, dogma, ideology, philosophy or theology capable of producing, preserving or restoring such fruits within you, your family and society.

What matters most is how *virtuous* or *vicious* you are and can become *as a result* of your pondering and performing a particular religion and its teachings. That is also what matters most with *every* cultural, historical, legal, normative, political, popular, scientific, secular, traditional or other form of doctrine, dogma, ideology, philosophy or theology.

Personal Validation and Verification of Definitions

> *The voice of conscience is so delicate that it is easy to stifle it; but it is also so clear that it is impossible to mistake it.*
> —Madame de Stael

If you have become a person of diligent and prayerful awareness, education, experience, inspiration, observation and study, then you have likely acquired enough familiarity with human character and with the use of this language to be able to personally validate and personally verify whether or not any given definition in a dictionary should be preserved in connection with the word symbol it defines.

Let's take, for example, the second definition(^{2}) of *kind* in *The Human Virtues Dictionary* in this book. It is:

[2*] kind^2 - to be honorably and justly reciprocating

[Note: *This definition of *kind* has been given an impact value of positive two (2) in *The Human Virtues Dictionary*, although a two (2) precedes no definition in that dictionary because all of the definitions are virtues. Underlined sections in the following four tests are fill-in-the-blank sections that can be used to test any human characteristic and each of its definitions.]

Personal Validation Tests

To begin, honorably apply the following two personal validation tests.

❑ 1. Do I think and feel in my heart that the word symbol [kind] should be preserved in connection with the definition [to be honorably and justly reciprocating]? Is the connection valid to me?

❑ 2. Do I think and feel in my heart that the definition [to be honorably and justly reciprocating] represents a *real human condition* as defined in the *Glossary*? Is the condition valid to me?

Keep your answers to these questions in mind. Answer them again, *after* you have applied the following two personal verification tests.

Personal Verification Tests

If you have become a person familiar with real human conditions which produce, preserve or restore true enlightenment, virtue, integrity, liberty, hope, peace and joy within you, your family and society, then you are also familiar with real human conditions which produce, preserve or restore darkness, vice, corruption, bondage, despair, turmoil and misery within you, your family and society. As you ponder and perform this word and its definition, what power does it manifest within you? What impact does it have within you, your family and society as a result?

Using the methods found in Chapter Ten, entitled *An Open Challenge to the World*, honorably apply the following personal verification test without exposing yourself to any temporary or lasting harm:

☐ 3. Have I personally proven and have I thereby come to know in my mind and in my heart that this definition's *defined numerical value* [of positive two (2)] accurately describes this characteristic's *real impact value* within me, my family and society? In other words, do I know this *real human condition* [to be honorably and justly reciprocating] matches the criteria of its defined numerical value [of positive two (2)] as defined in the *Glossary*?

If your answer to this test is in the affirmative, then you have come to know the word *kind*, along with the definition *to be honorably and justly reciprocating* and the defined numerical value of *positive two* (2), is a **virtue** which is truly good because it constantly and powerfully produces, preserves or restores true enlightenment, virtue, integrity, liberty, hope, peace and joy within you, your family and society. You have also come to know that your answers to tests one and two should be in the affirmative.

[**WARNING**: If personal proof is sought by personal experimentation, then this test is *effective* and *safe* in testing positive two (2) characteristics (or virtues). It can also be effective and safe in testing positive one (1), zero (0), and negative one (-1) characteristics, provided the test is of their positive or virtuous use. If personal proof is sought by personal experimentation, then this test is *effective* but *not safe* for testing the negative or vicious use of positive one (1), zero (0), and negative one (-1) characteristics. It is also *effective* but *not safe* for testing negative two (-2) characteristics (or vices).]

You may have learned the hard way that personal experimentation is a poor teacher of vices because personal experience teaches, tests and grades all at once. Unavoidable harmful consequences may follow. To avoid all deception and harm which can come from personal experimentation with vice, remember that to prove a virtue by personal experimentation is to simultaneously prove all opposite vices *without* the use of personal experimentation.

The final personal verification test is highly recommended, even if you have affirmative answers to the first three tests. With some exceptions, every person has acquired or can acquire enough personal revelation from God to ascertain what is enlightened certainty, reality or truth—and what is not—well enough to *personally verify* by that means whether or not any given human characteristic in any dictionary is an effective representation of reality and a statement of enlightened certainty, reality or truth. The final personal verification test is:

❏   4. Have I received a confirming witness within the thoughts of my mind and within the feelings of my heart from God that this characteristic, together with its definition and its defined numerical value, makes a statement of enlightened certainty, reality or truth? In other words, by my sure reception of inspiration or revelation from God do I know within the thoughts of my mind and within the feelings of my heart that the statement made [2 kind - to be honorably and justly reciprocating] is a true statement [of virtue]?

If your answer to this test is in the affirmative, then you certainly know the characteristic, along with its definition and its defined numerical value, is a statement of truth and of God. (Your answer to the third test should also confirm this.) You have also come to know that your answers to tests one and two should be in the affirmative. You have also come to know that every truly defined human characteristic, together with its correct defined numerical value, is an effective representation of reality and a statement of truth to us all, and should be preserved as such.

If you can personally improve upon the definitions or can correct the defined numerical value given to the human virtues defined in *The Human Virtues Dictionary*, then accept the challenge found in Chapter Ten, entitled *An Open Challenge to the World*. Make sure any changes you make meet the criteria prescribed in this entire chapter and in that chapter.

For further understanding, see related terms in the *Glossary* and related characteristics in the author's dictionaries. If you remain unsettled about whether the words you are reading, the thoughts you are thinking, the feelings you are feeling or the life you are living are verifiable as truth, then study, ponder and pray about this entire book before deciding whether it is possible for you to discover the truthfulness of these matters for yourself.

CHAPTER SIX
Integrated Language as a Treasury of Truth

If language be not in accordance with the truth of things, affairs cannot be carried on to success. —Confucius

Disintegrated Language

To disintegrate a language is to take all or part of that language out of context with some portion of *enlightened certainty, reality* or *truth.* Disintegrated language can accurately convey neither *truth* nor its opposites. Disintegrated language can, therefore, accurately convey neither a clear understanding of that which is *good* nor of its opposites. Every person, family and society who causes or allows their language to be viciously disintegrated with semantic darkness and corruption can so distort the truth in their own minds and in the minds of others as to allow or cause themselves and others to stumble and to suffer increasing darkness, vice, corruption, bondage, despair, turmoil and misery. This may result in the tragic downfall or destruction of many of us.

Integrated Language Is a Treasury of Truth

Integrated language is any language with which someone can communicate a true understanding of *enlightened certainty, reality* or *truth* with another person by expressing commonly used word symbols to reconvey and represent commonly defined images or descriptive representations of certain designated portions of enlightened certainty, reality or truth. Hence, definitions of that which is truly good and of God are made and found to be easily recognizable and clearly distinguishable from definitions of that which is evil or satanic.

For example, integrated language will not allow a word symbol like *evil,* and its commonly defined images or descriptive representations of certain designated portions of reality, to represent a designated portion of reality which is commonly known to be *good,* and vice versa. Truth is in harmony with itself. So is integrated language. Integrated language is, therefore, a thesaurus or *treasury* of truth, and should be preserved as such.

Where language pertaining to human character is integrated, someone can also communicate a common understanding of a *real human condition* with another person by expressing commonly used word symbols to reconvey and represent commonly defined images or descriptive representations of certain designated portions of what is real. Where there is integrated language pertaining to human character, all word symbols and definitions representing *imaginary human conditions* are excluded.

An integrated language of human character can be created and tested by the use of defined numerical values, such as those defined in the *Glossary*. In integrated language, as long as each definition for each named characteristic is a verifiable statement of truth, then the entire integrated language becomes an effective representation of reality and an integrated treasury of truth for us all, and should be preserved as such.

Personal Validation and Verification of Integrated Language

> *In matters of conscience, the law of the majority has no place.*
> —Mohandas K. Gandhi

To this day, the language of human character remains amazingly integrated. Commonly used dictionaries provide ample evidence of this. After the entire text of *The Human Character Dictionary* in the author's book **The Language of Human Character** was written, it was discovered that very few changes were needed to meet all of the criteria in each of the following five categories designated in **bold**.

Positive Two (2) Characteristics

☐ Each positive two (2) definition of the characteristic represents a *real human condition,* as defined in the *Glossary*; and

☐ Each positive two (2) definition of the characteristic matches the *defined numerical value* criteria for a positive two (2) found in the *Glossary*; and

☐ None of the characteristics named *within* a positive two (2) definition has a *solely* negative (-1 or -2) defined numerical value that makes the definition negative; and

☐ No *solely* positive two (2) characteristic appears out of character with its definition or with its defined numerical value anywhere within **this book** (or within the author's books *The Language of Human Virtue* and *The Language of Human Character*).

Characteristics named *within* a positive two (2) definition may have definitions with defined numerical values other than zero (0) worth turning to for further study. It is most likely at least one of the characteristics named has a definition with a defined numerical value of positive two (2).

Apply the above positive two (2) criteria as tests within **this book** (or within the author's book *The Language of Human Virtue* or *The Language of Human Character*). Then draw your own conclusions. As used in the testing criteria above and below, the word *solely* means the characteristic has only one defined numerical value, and there is no definition of the characteristic which has any other defined numerical value.

Positive One (1) Characteristics

☐ Each positive one (1) definition of the characteristic represents a *real human condition,* as defined in the *Glossary*; and

☐ Each positive one (1) definition of the characteristic matches the *defined numerical value* criteria for a positive one (1) found in the *Glossary*; and

☐ None of the characteristics named *within* a positive one (1) definition has a *solely* negative (-1 or -2) defined numerical value that makes the definition negative; and

☐ No *solely* positive one (1) characteristic appears out of character with its definition or with its defined numerical value anywhere within the author's books *The Language of Human Virtue* and *The Language of Human Character.*

Characteristics named *within* a positive one (1) definition may have definitions with defined numerical values other than zero (0) worth turning to for further study. It is most likely at least one of the characteristics named has a definition with a defined numerical value of positive one (1).

Apply the above positive one (1) criteria as tests within the author's book *The Language of Human Virtue* or *The Language of Human Character*. Then draw your own conclusions.

Zero (0) Characteristics

☐ Each zero (0) definition of the characteristic represents a *real human condition,* as defined in the *Glossary*; and

☐ Each zero (0) definition of the characteristic matches the *defined numerical value* criteria for a zero (0) found in the *Glossary*; and

☐ Characteristics named *within* a zero (0) definition all have at least one definition with the defined numerical value of zero (0). Otherwise, they have definitions with categories of both positive and negative defined numerical values which indicate the equivalent of a zero (0) definition *space* between the two categories.

Characteristics named *within* a zero (0) definition may have definitions with defined numerical values of zero (0) worth turning to for further study. Definitions of characteristics given a zero (0) can be neither solely positive nor solely negative. Apply the above zero (0) criteria as tests within the author's book *The Language of Human Virtue* or *The Language of Human Character*. Then draw your own conclusions.

Negative One (-1) Characteristics

- ☐ Each negative one (-1) definition of the characteristic represents a *real human condition,* as defined in the *Glossary;* and
- ☐ Each negative one (-1) definition of the characteristic matches the *defined numerical value* criteria for a negative one (-1) found in the *Glossary;* and
- ☐ None of the characteristics named *within* a negative one (-1) definition has a *solely* positive (1 or 2) defined numerical value that makes the definition positive; and
- ☐ No *solely* negative one (-1) characteristic appears out of character with its definition or with its defined numerical value anywhere within the author's books *The Language of Human Virtue* and *The Language of Human Character*.

Characteristics named *within* a negative one (-1) definition may have definitions with defined numerical values other than zero (0) worth turning to for further study. It is most likely at least one of the characteristics named has a definition with a defined numerical value of negative one (-1).

Apply the above negative one (-1) criteria as tests within the author's book *The Language of Human Virtue* or *The Language of Human Character*. Then draw your own conclusions.

Negative Two (-2) Characteristics

- ☐ Each negative two (-2) definition of the characteristic represents a *real human condition,* as defined in the *Glossary;* and
- ☐ Each negative two (-2) definition of the characteristic matches the *defined numerical value* criteria for a negative two (-2) found in the *Glossary;* and

☐   None of the characteristics named *within* a negative two (-2) definition has a *solely* positive (1 or 2) defined numerical value that makes the definition positive; and

☐   No *solely* negative two (-2) characteristic appears out of character with its definition or with its defined numerical value anywhere within the author's book *The Language of Human Character.*

Characteristics named *within* a negative two (-2) definition may have definitions with defined numerical values other than zero (0) worth turning to for further study. It is most likely at least one of the characteristics named has a definition with a defined numerical value of negative two (-2).

Apply the above negative two (-2) criteria as tests within the author's book *The Language of Human Character.* Then draw your own conclusions.

The author invites and encourages comprehensive testing of his book *The Language of Human Character* to prove the numeric integrity and the numeric symmetry of opposites within the language of human character. Some criteria for numeric testing are found above. All virtuously scientific means of numeric testing are welcome.

If you can personally improve upon the integrity of the language of human character, then accept the challenge found in Chapter Ten, entitled *An Open Challenge to the World.* Make sure any changes you make meet the criteria prescribed in that chapter.

For further understanding, see *disintegrated language* and *integrated language* in the *Glossary.* See also the chapters of this book entitled *Words as Representations of Reality, Definitions as Statements of Truth,* and *An Open Challenge to the World.*

CHAPTER SEVEN
A Comparison of 19th and 21st Century Definitions

Truth and virtue are subject to our discovery, but not to our whims. True virtue manifests itself in the wonderfully positive fruits invariably produced within everyone everywhere to the extent we each understand, perform, become and teach each of its respective virtues. —The Author

Noah Webster's 1828 *American Dictionary of the English Language* was the most extensive dictionary of the English language when it was published. The comparative analysis which follows is not exhaustive, but it provides evidence of some *negative* changes in human character since that day. For example, the word *Nazi* did not appear. The analysis also provides some evidence of *positive* changes. For example, the word *ecological* did not appear. Other examples reflect changes in *real human conditions* since 1828. For example, the words *telephonic* and *televising* did not appear.

Webster's 1828 Dictionary was also a widely accepted record of American thoughts, beliefs, values and characteristics pertaining to God's revealed truths and virtues. Since then, no one has proven that God's existence ceases whenever some people believe He does not exist; and no one has proven that God's revealed truths or virtues change whenever some people want to change them. Yet the following analysis provides evidence that, since 1828, some writers and editors of dictionaries have disregarded historically valid etymologies and quotations representing virtuous realities and precious truths in their persistent and sometimes successful attempts to dishonorably alter, distort or remove definitions pertaining to God and to godliness.

A conscientious effort has been made to restore within the author's dictionaries virtuous realities and precious truths represented by the language of early Americans who knew God and trusted in Him. Why restore them? Because God and godliness have never ceased to be virtuous realities or precious truths in the minds and hearts of many of their posterity, and because there is grievous injustice in the fact that descriptive representations of such realities and truths have been removed from our language by said writers and editors of dictionaries *not* because they have ever ceased to be realities and truths in human lives, and *not* because descriptive representations of them have actually become universally *obsolete* or *archaic*, but for no *good* reason at all. Draw your own conclusions from the following comparative analysis.

In the analysis below, wherever the words "did not appear" follow a word in **bold** it means the word in **bold** is _not_ defined in Webster's 1828 Dictionary. Where a word in **bold** _is_ defined in that Dictionary, words from its 1828 definition(s) appear _italicized_.

Cited in parentheses are facsimile page numbers where the _italicized_ excerpts are found in the 2000/2001 _electronic_ version of Webster's 1828 Dictionary published by **Foundation for American Christian Education, Chesapeake, Virginia.** Any notes on definitions found in one or more dictionaries in use in the 21st Century follow (in parentheses). In these notes, words repeated from the 1828 excerpts appear in _italics_.

For further understanding, see related terms in the _Glossary_ and related characteristics in the author's dictionaries. See also the preceding chapters.

A

abortion, in part, meant _miscarrying, or producing young before the natural time, or before the fetus is perfectly formed_ (119). (21st Century: There is also association or reference to voluntary abortion, or the practice of willfully ending the viability or potential viability of a fetus, a practice sometimes used for birth control.)

absurd, in part, meant _opposed to manifest truth_ (123). (21st Century: There is no mention of _truth_, let alone _manifest truth_.)

adultery, in part, meant _violation of the marriage bed; a crime, or a civil injury, which introduces, or may introduce, into a family, a spurious offspring._ A further definition refers to _unchastity_ (143). (21st Century: Association or reference is made to voluntary sexual intercourse between a married person and someone other than their husband or wife. There is no mention of _violation, crime, civil injury, spurious offspring_ or _unchastity_.)

agnostic did not appear.

amoral did not appear.

anticlerical did not appear.

antiracist did not appear.

antireligious did not appear.

apathy, in part, meant _contempt for earthly concerns_ (195). (21st Century: There is no mention of _earthly concerns_.)

B

badmouthing did not appear.

believe, in part, meant _assent of the mind, a yielding of the will and affections, accompanied with a humble reliance on Christ for salvation_ (274). (21st Century: There is no mention of _yielding, humility, Christ_ or _salvation_.)

belittling did not appear.

bellyache did not appear as a verb (275).

benediction, in part, meant _giving praise to God or rendering thanks for his favors_ (277). (21st Century: There is no mention of _praise, God_ or _thanks_.)

Bible is defined as _THE BOOK, by way of eminence; the sacred volume, in which are contained the revelations of God, the principles of Christian faith, and the rules of practice_ (1828 printed version text). (21st Century: Association or reference has been expanded to refer to the sacred writings of any or every religion. There is no mention of *revelations, God* or *faith*.)

blah and **blasé** did not appear.

blasphemy meant *an indignity offered to God by words or writing; reproachful, contemptuous or irreverent words uttered impiously against Jehovah* (295). (21st Century: Association or reference is made to *irreverent* behavior toward what man considers holy, sacred or venerable. There is no mention of *Jehovah*.)

bloodletting meant *the act of letting blood, or bleeding by the opening of a vein* (299).

blue did not appear as a human characteristic (301).

blue-blooded did not appear.

body-piercing did not appear.

bootlicking did not appear.

boycotting did not appear.

brainstorming did not appear.

brainwashing did not appear.

broadcasting meant to *cast or disperse upon the ground with the hand, as seed in sowing; opposed to planting in hills and rows* (327-328).

bureaucratic and **bureaucratizing** did not appear.

C

chaos meant that *confusion, or confused mass, in which matter is supposed to have existed, before it was separated into its different kinds and reduced to order, by the creating power of God* (387). (21st Century: Association or reference is made to the infinity of space and to formless matter supposed to have preceded the existence of the ordered universe. There is no mention of *the creating power of God*.)

charismatic did not appear.

charity, in part, meant *supreme love to God, and universal good will to men* (389). (21st Century: Association or reference is made to Christian *love* and to benevolence or generosity to the poor. There is no mention of *supreme love to God*, and there is no mention of *universal good will to men*.)

chaste, in part, meant *pure from all unlawful commerce of sexes. 'Applied to persons before marriage,'* it signifies *pure from all sexual commerce, undefiled; 'applied to married persons,' true to the marriage bed* (391). (21st Century: Association or reference is made to refraining from sexual intercourse that is regarded as contrary to morality or religion. There is no mention of *true to the marriage bed*.)

chauvinistic did not appear.

clairvoyant did not appear.

class-conscious did not appear.

cloning did not appear.

collectivist did not appear.

communist did not appear.

compunctive meant *causing remorse* (457). (21st Century: The word *compunctive* has been removed.)

conservative meant *Preservative; having the power to preserve in a safe or entire state, or from loss, waste or injury* (477). (21st Century: Association or reference is made to preserving existing conditions and institutions. There is no mention of *safety, loss, waste* or *injury*.)

contrite, in part, meant *worn or bruised. Hence, broken-hearted for sin; deeply affected with grief and sorrow for having offended God; humble; penitent;* (489). (21st Century: There is no mention of *broken-hearted, God* or *humble*.)

cool, in part, meant *to lose the heat of excitement or passion; to become less ardent, angry, zealous, or affectionate; to become more moderate* (494).

creationist and **creationistic** did not appear.

crime, in part, meant *an offense against the laws of right, prescribed by God or man, or against any rule of duty plainly implied in those laws* (522); **criminal**, in part, meant *involving a crime; that violates public law, divine or human* (523). (21st Century: There is no mention of *God* or of *the laws of right prescribed by God. Duty* and *divine law* have been disconnected, and so have *divine law* and *public law*.)

cultural did not appear.

D

decimate, in part, meant *to tithe or take a tenth part* (555). (21st Century: There is no mention of *tithe*.)

decontaminating did not appear.

defeminized and **defeminizing** did not appear.

defusing did not appear.

delicate, in part, meant *effeminate* (568). (21st Century: All association or reference made to the female gender has been removed.)

desegregating did not appear.

desensitizing did not appear.

desolate, in part, meant *deserted of God* (583). (21st Century: There is no mention of *God*.)

deterministic did not appear.

deviate, in part, meant *to wander, in a moral sense; to err; to sin* (587). (21st Century: Association or reference is made to what is considered socially or morally unacceptable. There is no mention of *erring* or *sin*.)

devout, in part, meant *yielding a solemn and reverential attention to God in religious exercises, particularly in prayer* (589). (21st Century: There is no mention of *God* or *prayer*.)

discern, in part, meant *to see or understand the difference; to make distinction; as, to discern between good and evil, truth and falsehood* (603). (21st Century: There is no mention of *good and evil*, and there is no mention of *truth and falsehood*.)

discreet, in part, meant *wise in avoiding errors or evil* (608). (21st Century: There is no mention of *error* or *evil*.)

discriminating carried no racial denotations (608).

disinhibited did not appear.

Divine, in part, meant *pertaining to the true God* (630). (21st Century: There is no mention of *the true God*.)

dog-eat-dog did not appear.

do-it-yourself did not appear.

down-to-earth did not appear.

dysfunctional did not appear.

E

ecological did not appear.

effeminate, in part, meant *having the qualities of the female sex; soft or delicate to an unmanly degree; tender; womanish; voluptuous* (665).

egalitarian did not appear.

egocentric did not appear.

elect, in part, meant *chosen or designated by God to salvation* (669). (21st Century: The word *elect* is placed under *Theol.* to limit it as a strictly theological definition.)

enlighten, in part, meant *to give light to; to give clearer views* and *to enable to see or comprehend truth.* It also meant *to illuminate with divine knowledge, or a knowledge of the truth* (690). (21st

Century: Intellectual and spiritual light are separated. Light and truth are disassociated from one another. There is no mention of *truth*, and there is no mention of *divine knowledge*.)
epistemological did not appear.
ergonomic did not appear.
ethical, in part, meant *relating to manners or morals* (709).
ethnocentric did not appear.
evolutionary did not appear.
existentialist did not appear.

F

fabulous, in part, meant *feigned, as a story; devised; fictitious* (737). (21st Century: Association or reference is made to someone or something exceptionally good.)
facepainting meant *the act or art of painting portraits* (738).
face-saving did not appear.
faithful, in part, meant *firm in adherence to the truth* and *true; worthy of belief* (742). (21st Century: Associations and references made to *belief* and to being full of faith are considered obsolete. There is no mention of *truth*, and there is no mention of *true*.)
faithless, in part, meant *without belief in the revealed truths of religion* (742). (21st Century: Association or reference is made to being without religious faith. There is no mention of *revealed truths*.)
fascist did not appear.
feminine, in part, meant *soft; tender; delicate* and *effeminate; destitute of manly qualities* (760).
feminist did not appear.
first-string and **first-team** did not appear.

foolish, in part, meant *wicked; sinful; acting without regard to the divine law and glory, or to one's own eternal happiness* and *proceeding from depravity; sinful; as 'foolish' lusts* (792). (21st Century: There is no mention of *wickedness, sin, depravity* or *lust*, and there is no mention of *divine law and glory* or *eternal happiness*.)
foresight, in part, meant *foreknowledge accompanied with prudence in guarding against evil* (798). (21st Century: There is no mention of *evil*.)

G

gay meant *Merry; airy; jovial; sportive; frolicksome*. It denoted *more life and animation than 'cheerful.'* It also meant *Fine; showy*. The third definition says *Inflamed or merry with liquor; intoxicated; 'a vulgar use of the word in America'* (832). (21st Century: The word came to mean "homosexual" in the 20th Century, as an adjective and then as a noun. Unlike the noun "gaiety," the word "gay" is rarely used in America to represent enjoyment of healthy and lively merriment during respectable social activities.)
genocidal did not appear.
geopolitical did not appear.
God, in part, meant *The Supreme Being; Jehovah, the eternal and infinite spirit; the creator, and the sovereign of the universe* (851). (21st Century: Association or reference is made to a *Supreme Being*, and to the use of the word *God* as a profane interjection. There is no mention of *Jehovah*.)
grace, in part, meant *the application of Christ's righteousness to the sinner* and *a state of reconciliation to God* (857). (21st Century: There is no mention

of *Christ, righteousness, sin* or *rec-onciliation to God.*)

grief, in part, meant *the pain of mind occasioned by our own misconduct; sorrow or regret that we have done wrong; pain accompanying repentance* (865). (21st Century: There is no mention of *misconduct, wrongdoing* or *repentance*.)

H

happy, in part, meant *being in the enjoyment of agreeable sensations from the possession of good; enjoying pleasure from the gratification of appetites or desires. The pleasurable sensations derived from the gratification of sensual appetites render a person temporarily 'happy;' but he only can be esteemed really and permanently 'happy,' who enjoys peace of mind in the favor of God* (884). (21st Century: There is no mention of *good*, and there is no mention of *real or permanent happiness, peace of mind* or of *God*.)

hard-core did not appear.

hard-line did not appear.

hard-nosed did not appear.

health, in part, meant *salvation or divine favor, or grace which cheers God's people* (894). (21st Century: There is no mention of *salvation, divine favor, grace* or *God*.)

highbrow did not appear.

high-class did not appear.

holocaust meant *a burnt-sacrifice or offering, the whole of which was consumed by fire; a species of sacrifice in use among the Jews and some pagan nations* (919).

holy made reference to the character of God and man. *Applied to the Supreme Being, 'holy' signifies perfectly pure, immaculate and complete in moral character; and man is more or less* *'holy,' as his heart is more or less sanctified, or purified from evil dispositions. We call a man 'holy,' when his heart is conformed in some degree to the image of God, and his life is regulated by the divine precepts. Hence, 'holy' is used as nearly synonymous with good, pious, godly.* Reference is also made to the *'Holy Ghost,'* or *'Holy Spirit'* as *the third person in the Trinity; the sanctifier of souls* (919). (21st Century: Association or reference is made to that which is considered sacred, to that which is venerated in religion as having sanctity, and to the divine — defined as God or a god. There is no mention of *heart*, or *pure*, or *perfectly pure*, or *immaculate*, or *complete in moral character*. There is no mention of *purified* or of *purified from evil dispositions*. There is no mention of life *regulated by the divine precepts. Holy Ghost* is separately defined. There is no mention of *the sanctifier of souls*.)

homosexual did not appear.

honest, in part, meant *chaste; faithful* (921). (21st Century: Associations and references to *chaste* are considered archaic. There is no mention of *faithful*.)

humane, in part, meant *having the feelings and dispositions proper to man; having tenderness, compassion, and a disposition to treat others with kindness; particularly in relieving them when in distress, or in captivity, when they are helpless or defenseless; kind; benevolent* (930). (21st Century: Association or reference is made to *tenderness* and *compassion. Benevolence* and *kindness* are treated as synonyms rather than as elements.)

humble, in part, meant having *a low opinion of one's moral worth, to make meek and submissive to the divine will* (931). (21st Century: There is no mention of *morality*, and there is no mention of *divine will*.)

hypersensitive did not appear.

hypocrite meant *one who feigns to be what he is not; one who has the form of godliness without the power, or who assumes an appearance of piety and virtue, when he is destitute of true religion.* It also meant *a dissembler; one who assumes a false appearance* (938). (21st Century: There is no mention of *godliness, true religion, dissembling* or *false*.)

I

idolatrous, in part, meant *partaking of the nature of idolatry, or of the worship of false gods* (942). (21st Century: The term *idolatry* is qualified as Biblical. There is no mention of *false gods*.)

impatient, in part, meant *uneasy or fretful under suffering; not bearing pain with composure; not enduring evil without fretfulness, uneasiness, and a desire or effort to get rid of the evil.* It is noted: *We are all apt to be 'impatient' under wrongs; but it is a christian duty not to be 'impatient' in sickness, or under any afflictive dispensation of Providence* (952). (21st Century: There is no mention of *evil*, and there is no mention of any *afflictive dispensation of Providence*.)

important, in part, meant *having a bearing on some interest, measure or result by which good or ill may be produced* (956). (21st Century: Association or reference is to that which is of great consequence or

significance. There is no mention of *good* or *ill*.)

incontinent, in part, meant *not restraining the passions or appetites, particularly the sexual appetite; indulging lust without restraint or in violation of law; unchaste; lewd* (969). (21st Century: Association or reference is made to moderation of sexual desire. There is no mention of *lewd, lust* or *unchaste*. Association or reference is also made to failure to control the discharge of human waste.)

inquire, in part, meant *to seek for truth* (992). (21st Century: Association or reference is made to facts or information. There is no mention of *truth*.)

inspired, in part, meant *informed or directed by the Holy Spirit* (996). (21st Century: There is no mention of *the Holy Spirit*.)

integrity, in part, meant *the entire, unimpaired state of any thing, particularly of the mind; moral soundness or purity; incorruptness; uprightness; honesty.* Notes add: *Integrity comprehends the whole moral character, but has a special reference to uprightness in mutual dealings, transfers of property, and agencies for others* (1000). (21st Century: Association or reference is made to ethical principles and moral character, to wholeness, and to honesty. There is no mention of *unimpaired state, purity, incorruptness* or *uprightness*.)

intercultural did not appear.

investigation, in part, meant *the action or process of searching minutely for truth, facts or principles* (1013). (21st Century: Association or reference is made to *facts*. There is no mention of *truth* or of *principles*.)

irreligious, in part, meant *ungodly* and *profane* and *wicked* (1017). (21st Century: There is no mention of *ungodly, profane* or *wicked*.)

irreverent, in part, meant *wanting in reverence and veneration; not entertaining or manifesting due reverence to the Supreme Being* (1018). (21st Century: There is no mention of *the Supreme Being*.)

J

judging, in part, meant *rightly to understand and discern* (1030). (21st Century: Association or reference is made to deciding. There is no mention of *rightly* or *discern*.)

judgment, in part, meant *the spirit of wisdom and prudence, enabling a person to discern right and wrong, good and evil*. Further meanings include: *the spiritual government of the world* and *the doctrines of the gospel, or God's word* and *the decrees and purposes of God concerning nations* and *the final trial of the human race, when God will decide the fate of every individual, and award sentence according to justice* (1030). (21st Century: Association or reference is made to a misfortune regarded as inflicted by divine sentence, and to a *final trial* of all people, both the living and the dead, at the end of the world. There is no mention of *discerning, right, wrong* or *evil*, and there is no mention of *God, God's word*, or *the decrees and purposes of God concerning nations*. There is no mention of God deciding *the fate of every individual*, and there is no mention of His awarding *sentence according to justice*.)

judgmental did not appear.

judicious, in part, meant *adapted to obtain a good end by the best means* (1031). (21st Century: Association or reference is made to judgment. There is no mention of *good end* or *best means*.)

K

knowing, in part, meant *to perceive with certainty; to understand clearly; to have a clear and certain perception of truth, fact, or anything that actually exists* (1041). (21st Century: There is no mention of *certainty, clarity* or *truth*, and there is disconnection of *fact* or *truth* from what *actually exists*.)

know-nothing did not appear.

L

larger-than-life did not appear.

lesbian did not appear.

lewd, in part, meant *given to unlawful indulgence of lust; addicted to fornication or adultery; dissolute; lustful; libidinous* and *wicked; vile; profligate; licentious* (1067). (21st Century: Association or reference is made to *lust* and obscenity. There is no mention of *addiction, fornication, adultery, dissolution, libidinous* or *licentious*. Associations or references made to *vile* and *wicked* have been declared obsolete.)

lust, in part, meant *evil propensity; depraved affections and desires* (1096). (21st Century: Association or reference is made to control and intensity of appetites, *desires* or passions. There is no mention of *depraved* or *evil*.)

M

malfeasance meant *evil doing; wrong; illegal deed* (1106). (21st Century: Association or reference is made to wrongdoing and illegality. There is no mention of *evil*.)

mind-expanding did not appear.

miserable, in part, meant *very unhappy from grief, pain, calamity, poverty, apprehension of evil, or other cause* (1828 printed version text). (21st Century: There is no mention of *calamity* or *evil*.)

mislabeling did not appear.

mismating did not appear.

misperceiving did not appear.

monistic did not appear.

moonshine meant the light of the moon.

moral, in part, meant *relating to the practice, manners or conduct of men as social beings in relation to each other, and with reference to right and wrong. The word 'moral' is applicable to actions that are good or evil, virtuous or vicious, and has reference to the law of God as the standard by which their character is to be determined. The word however may be applied to actions which affect only, or primarily and principally, a person's own happiness* (1161). (21st Century: Association or reference is made to generally accepted customs of conduct in a society. There is no mention of *good, evil, virtuous, vicious* or *happiness,* and there is no mention of *the law of God.*)

movie-making and **movie-watching** did not appear.

mudslinging did not appear.

N

natural, in part, meant *pertaining to nature; produced or effected by nature, or by the laws of growth, formation or motion impressed on bodies or beings by divine power* (1182). (21st Century: There is no mention of *divine power.*)

Nazi and **nazifying** did not appear.

networking did not appear.

newsworthy did not appear.

no-good did not appear.

O

objective, in part, meant *belonging to the object; contained in the object.* Notes add: *'objective certainty'* exists when the proposition is certainly true in itself, and *subjective* [certainty exists] when we are certain of the truth of it (1208). (21st Century: Association or reference is made to what can be known. There is no mention of *certainty* or *truth.*)

obsession meant *the act of besieging; the first attack of Satan antecedent to possession* (1211). (21st Century: There is some association or reference made to occupying. There is no mention of *Satan,* and there is no mention of *possession.*)

off-color did not appear.

offend, in part, meant *to transgress the moral or divine law; to sin; to commit a crime* (1216). (21st Century: There is no mention of *divine law.*)

old-fashioned meant *Formed according to obsolete fashion or custom: as an 'old-fashioned' dress* (1219).

one-upping did not appear.

opportunistic did not appear.

overrate meant *to rate at too much; to estimate at a value or amount beyond the truth* (1241). (21st Century: There is no mention of *truth.*)

oversexed did not appear.

oversimplifying did not appear.

P

pacesetting did not appear.

pagan, in part, meant *a person who worships false gods* (1247). (21st Century: There is no mention of *false gods.*)

panhandling did not appear.

paper-chasing did not appear.

patient, in part, meant *submission to the divine will* (1267). (21st Century: There is no mention of *submission* or *divine will*.)

pejorative did not appear.

perfection, in part, meant *the complete possession of all moral excellence, as in the Supreme Being; or the possession of such moral qualities and virtues as a thing is capable of* (1279). (21st Century: Association or reference is made to the highest degree of *excellence* and to being *complete*. There is no mention of *all moral excellence* or *virtues*, and there is no mention of *the Supreme Being*.)

personable, in part, meant *graceful; of good appearance* (1285). (21st Century: Association or reference is made to agreeable or pleasing. There is no mention of *good* or *graceful*.)

perspicuous meant *clear to the understanding; that may be clearly understood; not obscure or ambiguous.* Notes add: *Language is 'perspicuous' when it readily presents to the reader or hearer the precise ideas which are intended to be expressed* (1286). (21st Century: Association or reference is made to *clear* language as the ready means of presenting *precise ideas* to a reader.)

perversion, in part, meant *the act of perverting; a turning from truth or propriety; a diverting from the true intent or object; change to something worse.* Notes add: *We speak of . . . a 'perversion' of Scripture, when it is willfully misinterpreted or misapplied* (1287). (21st Century: Association or reference is made to what is generally regarded as abnormal. There is no mention of *truth, propriety, misinterpretation* or *misap-*

plication, and there is no mention of *a change to something worse*.)

pessimistic did not appear.

philosophy, in part, meant *literally, the love of wisdom.* Notes add: *The objects of philosophy are to ascertain facts or truth, and the causes of things or their phenomena; to enlarge our views of God and his works, and to render our knowledge of both practically useful and subservient to human happiness* (1291). (21st Century: Association or reference is made to *truth.* There is no mention of *love* or *wisdom*, and there is no mention of *God and His works* or of *human happiness*.)

phonographic did not appear.

photographic did not appear.

pitiful, in part, meant *full of pity; tender; compassionate; having a heart to feel sorrow and sympathy for the distressed.* It also meant *to be pitied for littleness or meanness; paltry; contemptible; despicable* (1303). (21st Century: Associations and references made to *compassionate* are considered archaic. There is no mention of being *tender*, and there is no mention of *feel sorrow and sympathy for the distressed*.)

polygamist meant *a person who maintains the lawfulness of polygamy;*

polygamy, in part, meant *having a plurality of wives or husbands at the same time* (1322). (21st Century: *Polygynous* and *polyandrous* are distinguished from *polygamous.* There is no mention of maintaining *the lawfulness of* a plurality of wives, even though the practice was not unlawful in 1828 America and even though it remains lawful in some countries at the present time.)

pontifical, in part, meant *belonging to a high priest*; **pontificate** was a noun that meant *the state or dignity of a high priest* (1324). (21st Century: A verb definition has crept in meaning to be arrogantly dogmatic and pretentiously pompous. There is no mention of *high priest*.)

pornographic did not appear.

prenuptial did not appear.

prestigious meant *practicing tricks; juggling* (1352).

pretentious did not appear.

priestcraft meant *the stratagems and frauds of priests; fraud or impositions in religious concerns; management of selfish and ambitious priests to gain wealth and power, or to impose on the credulity of others* (1356). (21st Century: Association or reference has been severely shifted and limited to having the necessary attributes to be a *priest*. There is no mention of *fraud, imposition, selfishness, ambition, gain, wealth, power* or the *credulity of others*.)

proactive did not appear.

pro-choice did not appear.

pro-life did not appear.

psyched did not appear.

psychic did not appear.

psyching did not appear.

psycho did not appear.

psychoanalytical did not appear.

psychological, in part, meant *the study of the soul of man* (1383). (21st Century: Association or reference is made to behavior and to mental states and processes. There is no mention of *the soul of man*.)

psychopathic did not appear.

psychotherapeutic did not appear.

psychotic did not appear.

Q

quibble, in part, meant *to evade the point in question, or plain truth, by artifice* (1404). (21st Century: There is no mention of *truth*.)

R

racist did not appear.

racketeering did not appear.

reactionary did not appear.

realistic did not appear.

reality, in part, meant *actual being or existence of anything; truth; fact; in distinction from mere appearance* (1424).

recalcitrant did not appear.

reconcile, in part, meant *to call back into union and friendship the affections which have been alienated; to restore to friendship or favor after estrangement*; Notes under **reconciliation** add: *the means by which sinners are reconciled and brought into a state of favor with God* (1433). (21st Century: There is no mention of *God*.)

rectitude, in part, meant *rightness of principle or practice; uprightness of mind; exact conformity to truth, or to the rules prescribed for moral conduct, either by divine or human laws* (1435). (21st Century: Association or reference is made to moral virtue. There is no mention of *uprightness, truth,* or *divine laws*.)

reincarnate and **reincarnating** did not appear.

relativistic and **relativizing** did not appear.

reverence meant *to regard with reverence; to regard with fear mingled with respect and affection* (1478). (21st Century: Association or reference is made to *respect*. There is no mention of *fear* or *affection*.)

rewarding meant *making an equivalent return for good or evil; requiting; recompensing or punishing* (1481). (21st Century: Association or reference is made to *recompensing*. There is no mention of *equivalent return*, and there is no mention of *good or evil*.)

right, in part, meant *just, equitable, accordant to the standard of truth and justice or the will of God* (1485). (21st Century: There is no mention of *God*.)

righteous, in part, meant *just; accordant to the divine law. 'Applied to persons' it denotes one who is holy in heart, and observant of the divine commands in practice* and *applied to God, to his testimonies and to his saints* (1486). (21st Century: There is no mention of *divine law, God, His testimonies* or *His saints*. There is no mention of being *holy in heart* or *observant of the divine commands in practice*. The word has been deliberately perverted or twisted by some into an accepted misnomer for such realities as something *truly genuine* or, along with the confusing use of the word *wicked*, something *wonderfully masterful*.)

risqué did not appear.

robotic did not appear.

S

sabotaging did not appear.

sacramental, in part, meant *an outward and visible sign of inward and spiritual grace; or more particularly, a solemn religious ceremony enjoined by Christ, the head of the christian church, to be observed by his followers, by which their special relation to him is created, or their obligations to him renewed and ratified* (1510). (21st Century: Asso-

ciation or reference is made to rites considered to have been instituted by Jesus Christ. There is no mention of any *special relation* to Him or of any *obligation* to Him.)

sadistic did not appear.

sadomasochistic did not appear.

sanitary did not appear.

sassy did not appear.

satire, in part, meant *a discourse or poem in which wickedness or folly is exposed with severity* (1521). (21st Century: There is no mention of *wickedness*.)

schizoid did not appear.

schizophrenic did not appear.

second-guessing did not appear.

seduce, in part, meant to *draw aside or entice from the path of rectitude and duty in any manner* and *to tempt and lead to iniquity; to corrupt; to deprave* and *to entice to a surrender of chastity* (1547). (21st Century: Association or reference is made to inducing or persuading to have sexual intercourse. There is no mention of *chastity, corruption, depravity, duty, iniquity* or *rectitude*.)

self-actualizing did not appear.

self-aware did not appear.

self-berating did not appear.

self-conscious meant only *consciousness within one's self* (1551). (21st Century: Association or reference is also made to excessive awareness of being observed by others.)

self-defeating did not appear.

self-reliant did not appear.

self-serving did not appear.

sensationalizing did not appear.

serious, in part, meant *particularly attentive to religious concerns or one's own religious state* (1560). (21st Century: There is no mention of *religious concerns* or *religious state*.)

sexist did not appear.

sin, in part, meant *to depart voluntarily from the path of duty prescribed by God to man; to violate the divine law in any particular* (1594). (21st Century: Association or reference is made to violation of *divine law*. There is no mention of *God*, and there is no mention of *duty prescribed by God*.)

sissy did not appear.

sleeping around did not appear.

slumming and **slummy** did not appear.

small-minded did not appear.

snobbish did not appear.

socialist and **socialistic** did not appear.

sociocratic did not appear.

sociological did not appear.

sociopathic did not appear.

soothsaying meant *the foretelling of future events by persons without divine aid or authority, and thus distinguished from prophecy* (1622). (21st Century: Association or reference is made to *foretelling*, predicting and *prophecy*. There is no mention of *divine aid or authority*.)

sorry, in part, meant *grieved for the loss of some good; pained for some evil that has happened to one's self or friends or country* (1624). (21st Century: Association or reference is made to tragedy. There is no mention of *loss of some good*, and there is no mention of being *pained for some evil that has happened*.)

soul, in part, meant *the spiritual, rational and immortal substance in man* (1625). (21st Century: There is no mention of *immortal substance*.)

spaced-out did not appear.

spiritual, in part, meant *consisting of spirit; not material; incorporeal; as a*

'spiritual' substance or being (1638). (21st Century: Association or reference is made to *incorporeal*, insubstantial or nonmaterial being. There is no mention of *spiritual substance or being*.)

standoffish did not appear.

star, in part, meant *to set or adorn with stars or bright radiating bodies* (1655). (21st Century: Association or reference is also to celebrated or distinguished people and to prominent actors, performers or singers.)

stoned meant *pelted or killed with stones; freed from stones; walled with stones* (1671). (21st Century: There is only association or reference to being drunk or intoxicated.)

street-smart and **streetwise** did not appear.

stressed-out did not appear.

stripteasing did not appear.

subduing, in part, meant *to tame; to break by conquering a refractory temper or evil passions* (1686). (21st Century: There is no mention of *refractory* or *evil*.)

subverting, in part, meant *to pervert the mind, and turn it from the truth* (1692). (21st Century: There is no mention of *perversion, turning* or *truth*.)

superhuman, in part, meant *divine* (1700). (21st Century: Association or reference is made to a higher nature or greater powers than humans have. There is no mention of *divine*.)

supersensitive did not appear.

swearing meant *affirming upon oath; uttering a declaration, with an appeal to God for the truth of it* (1713). (21st Century: Association or reference is made to a *solemn declaration* by or with some sacred being or object, as a deity or the Bible. There is no mention of *God* or *truth*.)

T

technological, in part, meant *pertaining to the arts* (1735).
telecommunicating did not appear.
telegraphic, in part, meant *communicated by a telegraph* (1736).
telepathic did not appear.
telephonic and **televising** did not appear.
tempt, in part, meant *to incite or solicit to an evil act; to entice to something wrong* (1739). (21st Century: Association or reference is made to doing something regarded as immoral, unwise or wrongful. There is no mention of *evil*.)
terrific meant *dreadful; causing terror; adapted to excite great fear or dread* (1744). (21st Century: Association or reference has shifted to include something good and wonderful.)
theosophic or **theosophical**, in part, meant *divinely wise* (1750). (21st Century: Association or reference is made to philosophical or religious thought based upon a mystical insight into the divine nature. There is no mention of *wise*.)
totalitarian did not appear.
transsexual did not appear.
transvestite did not appear.
trash-talking did not appear.
trigger-happy did not appear.
twisted meant *formed by winding threads or strands round each other* (1810).

U

ultimate, in part, meant *final; being that to which all the rest is directed, as to the main object.* Notes add: *The 'ultimate' end of our actions should be the glory of God, or the display of his exalted excellence. The 'ultimate' end and aim of men is to be happy, and to attain to this end, we must yield that obedience which will honor the law and character of God* (1813). (21st Century: Association or reference is made to something *final*, fundamental, furthest, highest, greatest, maximum, and unsurpassed. All association and reference to the design or object to which those terms point have been removed. There is no mention of *direction, main object, glory of God, exaltation, happiness, obedience, honor, law* or *character of God*.)
ultraconservative did not appear.
ultraliberal did not appear.
ultranationalisitc did not appear.
ultraradical did not appear.

V

venerable, in part, meant *rendered sacred* or *being consecrated to God and to his worship* (1868). (21st Century: There is no mention of *God* or to *worship* of Him.)
vengeance meant *the infliction of pain on another, in return for an offense or injury.* Notes add: *Such infliction, when it proceeds from malice or mere resentment, and is not necessary for the purposes of justice, is revenge, and a most hainous crime. When such infliction proceeds from a mere love of justice, and the necessity of punishing offenders for the support of the laws, it is 'vengeance,' and is warrantable and just. In this case, vengeance is a just retribution, recompense or punishment* (1869). (21st Century: Association or reference is made only to *revenge*. There is no mention of *just retribution, recompense or punishment*.)

vile, in part, meant to be *sinful; depraved by sin; wicked; hateful in the sight of God and of good men* (1878). (21st Century: There is no mention of *sin* or *wickedness*, and there is no mention of *hateful in the sight of God and of good men*.)

virgin, in part, meant *a woman who has had no carnal knowledge of man* (1880); **virginal**, in part, meant *modest* and *pure; chaste* (1881). (21st Century: Association or reference is made to any person who has never had sexual intercourse, regardless of gender. There is no mention of *modest* or *chaste*.)

W

wash, in part, meant *to purify from the pollution of sin* (1898). (21st Century: There is no mention of *purifying, pollution* or *sin*.)

watchful, in part, meant *to be 'watchful' against the growth of vicious habits* (1900). (21st Century: There is no mention of *vicious habits*, and there is no mention of anyone's duty to avoid them.)

weak, in part, meant *not well supported by truth or reason* (1904). (21st Century: Association or reference is made to *reason*. There is no mention of *truth*.)

whistle-blowing did not appear.

wicked, in part, meant *evil in principle or practice; deviating from the divine law; addicted to vice; sinful; immoral*. Notes add: *This is a word of comprehensive signification, extending to every thing that is contrary to the moral law, and both to persons and actions* (1918). (21st Century: Association or reference is made to *evil, immoral*, malevolent, malicious, *sinful* and vicious. There is no men-

tion of *divine law*. The word has been deliberately perverted or twisted by some into an accepted misnomer for such realities as an *awesome adventure* or, along with the confusing use of the word *righteous*, something *wonderfully masterful*.)

witch meant *a woman who by compact with the devil, practices sorcery or enchantment*; **witchcraft**, in part, meant *the practices of witches; sorcery, enchantments; intercourse with the devil* (1925). (21st Century: Association or reference is made to any person who uses black arts or black magic, regardless of gender. There is no mention of *the devil*.)

workaholic did not appear.

worldly-mindedness meant *a predominating love and pursuit of this world's goods, to the exclusion of piety and attention to spiritual concerns* (1932). (21st Century: Association or reference is made to being devoted to the affairs and interests of this world. There is no mention of *exclusion of piety* or *spiritual concerns*.)

wrath, in part, meant *the just punishment of an offense or crime*. This meaning is given without mention of any anger. The meaning is expanded to include God's *holy and just indignation against sin*; **wrathful**, in part, meant *springing from wrath or expressing it* (1934). (21st Century: Associations or references made to *wrath* are exclusively tied to anger. There is no mention of *holy and just indignation against sin* and there is no mention of *just punishment*.)

wrest, in part, meant *to distort; to turn from truth or twist from its natural meaning by violence; to pervert* (1935). (21st Century: There is, most ironically, no mention of *truth, distortion,* or *turning from truth,* and there is no mention of *twisting from natural meaning* or of *perversion.)*

wrong, in part, meant *not morally right; that deviates from the line of rectitude prescribed by God; not just or equitable; not right or proper* and *a 'wrong' course of life.* It also meant *erroneous; not according to truth; as a 'wrong' statement* (1936). (21st Century: Association or reference is made to deviating from *truth.* There is no mention of *rectitude prescribed by God.)*

X

xenophilic and **xenophobic** did not appear.

Y

yellow meant *being of a bright color; reflecting the most light of any, after white. It is one of the simple or primitive colors* (1939). (21st Century: Association or reference is also made to skin-color and to cowardice.)

Z

Zionist and **Zionistic** did not appear.

CHAPTER EIGHT
Glossary of Terms and Defined Numerical Values

This *Glossary* is written in *first-person form* to help the reader more personally examine and evaluate the truthfulness of what is written. Defined characteristics in the author's dictionaries may provide additional or missing insights on the following terms and defined numerical values:

2 is the defined numerical value (or impact value) given each defined **virtue** which *constantly* and *powerfully* produces, preserves or restores true enlightenment, virtue, integrity, liberty, hope, peace and joy within me, my family and society. It is thus powerfully *enlightening, virtuous and integrating* to exercise thoughts of this nature in my words and actions. I should entertain such thoughts within the active thoughts of my mind *as often, as much, and for as long as possible.* Such thoughts should *always* be developed and exercised as part of who I truly am within my heart. *Simple statement:* I will *always* be this, and I will do and teach this as often, as much, and for as long as possible.

Enlightenment	Virtue	Integrity	Liberty	Hope	Peace	Joy

1 is the defined numerical value (or impact value) given each defined characteristic which *generally* produces, preserves or restores a measure of true enlightenment, virtue, integrity, liberty, hope, peace and joy within me, my family and society. It is thus *usually beneficial* to exercise thoughts of this nature in my words and actions. I should entertain such thoughts within the active thoughts of my mind and should exercise them within my heart, *unless* it becomes necessary for me to refrain from doing so to better produce, preserve or restore positive two (2) characteristics (or virtues) within me, my family and society, or unless I am prompted by enlightened conscience and by personal revelation from God to refrain from doing so. *Simple statement:* I will do, be and teach this unless, to serve a better purpose, I should not.

0 is the defined numerical value (or impact value) given each defined characteristic the *positive* value of which (2 or 1) or the *negative* value of which (-1 or -2) can only be determined by my chosen purpose for its use and by the extent and manner of my actual possession or use of it. *Simple statement:* I will do, be and teach this enough for a good purpose;

and I will neither do, nor be nor teach this to any extent or in any manner for any evil purpose.

-1   is the defined numerical value (or impact value) given each defined characteristic which *generally* produces, preserves or restores a measure of darkness, vice, corruption, bondage, despair, turmoil and misery within me, my family and society. It is thus *usually detrimental* to exercise thoughts of this nature in my words or actions. I should not entertain such thoughts within the active thoughts of my mind and should not exercise them within my heart, *unless* it becomes necessary for me to do so to better produce, preserve or restore positive two (2) characteristics (or virtues) within me, my family and society, or unless I am prompted by enlightened conscience and by personal revelation from God to do so. *Simple statement:* I will neither do, nor be nor teach this unless, to serve a better purpose, I should.

Darkness	Vice	Corruption	Bondage	Despair	Turmoil	Misery

-2   is the defined numerical value (or impact value) given each defined **vice** which *constantly* and *powerfully* produces, preserves or restores darkness, vice, corruption, bondage, despair, turmoil and misery within me, my family and society. It is thus powerfully *darkening, vicious and corrupting* to exercise thoughts of this nature in my words or actions. I should entertain such thoughts within the active thoughts of my mind *no longer than is necessary* to see them for what they are. Such thoughts should *never* be developed or exercised as part of who I truly am within my heart. *Simple statement:* I will *never* do nor be this; or, as part of my lasting true repentance, I will *never* do nor be this *again*. I will teach against this as often, as much, and for as long as possible.

Actual refers to any and every past or present being, thing, thought, word, action, deed or work which is true or which exists in truth. The term may also be used to refer to that which is real or to that which exists in reality.

Accountable means to be advanced beyond the mental and physical age of eight full years (eight years of age or older), and to thus be required by God under the eternally binding law of justice to one day answer and be judged under that law for how well my desires and works prove I have personally chosen to live in perfect harmony with the best and highest laws, rules, standards or values of true enlightenment, virtue and integrity of which I have become aware in my education and training and in my own diligent, honest, ongoing and open-minded searching. Without this type of accountability, I am innocent and am therefore virtuous in the sight of God. Otherwise, this type of *accountable* is what I am and must be. In this sense, *accountable* is a *real human condition*, but not a characteristic of choice.

The term also means to be advanced beyond the mental and physical age of adulthood (eighteen years of age or older), or to be otherwise legally competent, and to thus be required by my government under the law of the land to answer and be judged under that law for the extent to which my words and actions do not comply with that law. In this sense, *accountable* is again a *real human condition*, but not a characteristic of choice. (For applications of *accountable* as a characteristic of choice, see definitions of *accountable* in the author's dictionaries.)

Another person refers to one or more other people.

Beliefs refer to all convictions, creeds, customs, doctrines, dogmas, ideologies, notions, opinions, philosophies, religions, teachings, tenets, traditions, views, and all other things which may grow from, embody and represent that composition or set of thoughts which I confidently embrace or hold within the thoughts of my *heart* as being a trustworthy, reliable or truthful composition or set of personal thoughts, whether or not those thoughts are trustworthy, reliable or truthful.

A belief of mine, if true, can be replaced by superseding enlightened certainty, reality or truth within my mind and heart. Until I know a belief of mine has been replaced by superseding enlightened certainty, reality or truth within my mind and heart, I may deem it trustworthy, reliable or truthful when it is not. (For further understanding, see *enlightened certainty, reality* and *truth* in this *Glossary*, and Chapter Two, entitled *Some True Statements about Human Character.*)

Bondage is defined by *bound* and by related characteristics found in the author's book *The Language of Human Character*. When the term appears within all or part of the context chain of *darkness, vice, corruption, bondage, despair, turmoil and misery*, it means to be addicted to receiving the outside influence of darkness, vice and corruption into my mind.

At a worse level, the term means to be addicted, enslaved or possessed by the powers of darkness, vice and corruption within my mind and heart.

This is internal bondage. As long as I am in bondage within my mind and heart, true and lasting liberty cannot exist within me; hence, I cannot obtain true and lasting hope, peace or joy.

Certainty is to know I have an enlightened or sure knowledge of truth. Certainty within me supersedes compatible belief and nullifies all contrary beliefs with a measure of enlightened or sure knowledge which produces, preserves or restores its own characteristics within me.

Character is the aggregate and finite list of all human characteristics. In a person, character is their present finite list of distinctive characteristics in composition, impact value, and degree of strength. Historically, the word *character* is derived from words meaning to *distinctively carve, engrave or inscribe upon or within*. As each of my characteristics is distinctively carved, engraved, inscribed or otherwise recorded upon or within the true character, intellect or nature of my immortal spirit being, it forms part of my character. Hence, character is the present condition of my immortal spirit being. Character is who I truly am within me.

Characteristics refer to all attitudes, attributes, behaviors, dispositions, features, habits, mannerisms, moods, motives, postures, practices, qualities, quirks, sentiments, temperaments, tendencies, traits, vices, virtues, and all other things which are, have been or may be used to describe the true character of a person, family or society. My characteristics grow from, embody and represent my *values*, which grow from, embody and represent my *beliefs*, which grow from, embody and represent the thoughts of my *heart*.

Characteristics can be used to describe all of the thoughtful images, impressions, beliefs, values, characteristics, intentions, desires, motivations, words, actions, deeds or works distinctively carved, engraved, inscribed or otherwise recorded upon or within my immortal spirit being. (For further understanding, see *beliefs, heart* and *values* in this *Glossary*, and Chapter Two, entitled *Some True Statements about Human Character*.)

Confusion is thinking which is so entangled or mixed up with that which is imaginary that it fails to ascertain, discern or distinguish that which is real from that which is imaginary in a mixture. Confusion is also thinking which is so removed from enlightened certainty, reality or truth that it has lost some if not all sense or sight of plain direction, path, purpose or understanding.

Context chain refers to the unbroken context chain of true *enlightenment, virtue, integrity, liberty, hope, peace and joy*. There can be no lasting joy without peace, no lasting peace without hope, no lasting hope without liberty, no lasting liberty without integrity, no lasting integrity without virtue, and no lasting virtue without enlightenment.

The term also refers to the unbroken context chain of *darkness, vice, corruption, bondage, despair, turmoil and misery*. There can be no lasting misery without turmoil, no lasting turmoil without despair, no lasting despair without bondage, no lasting bondage without corruption, no lasting corruption without vice, and no lasting vice without darkness. (For further understanding, see *defined numerical value* in this *Glossary*.)

Corruption is the presence of darkness and vice within someone. Corruption is the absence of true enlightenment, virtue and integrity within someone. To the extent I willfully allow or cause true enlightenment, virtue and integrity to exist within me corruption cannot exist within me; hence, to that same extent true and lasting liberty replaces bondage within me. To the extent I am accountable for my loss of true enlightenment, virtue and integrity from within me I am accountable for any naturally consequent loss of true and lasting liberty from within me. Corruption is intrinsically evil or satanic.

Darkness is all of the powers of confusion, ignorance and uncertainty. Darkness is the power to dispel or remove enlightenment from within the thoughts of my mind and from within my heart. To the extent darkness exists within me true enlightenment cannot exist within me; hence, to that same extent I can neither discern virtue from vice nor obtain virtue. To the extent I am accountable for my loss of true enlightenment I am accountable for any naturally consequent loss of virtue from within me. Darkness is used as a tool by Satan and his followers to tempt humankind to forsake and withstand enlightened certainty, reality, truth, virtue and integrity.

Defined numerical value is any one of five numerical values listed at the beginning of this *Glossary* as positive two (2), positive one (1), zero (0), negative one (-1) and negative two (-2). The number assigned to a human characteristic in *The Human Virtues Dictionary* in this book represents its impact value within me, my family and society. Defined numerical values do not appear in that dictionary because every listed characteristic is a virtue which has been assigned a positive two (2) defined numerical value.

Definition means a statement of the meaning of a word symbol.

Despair is defined by *despairing* and by related characteristics found in the author's book *The Language of Human Character*. As long as I am despairing, true and lasting hope cannot exist within me; hence, I cannot obtain true and lasting peace or joy.

Disintegrated language is any language which has ceased to be integrated. To disintegrate a language is to take all or part of that language out of context with some portion of enlightened certainty, reality or truth. Disintegrated language can accurately convey neither *truth* nor its opposites. Disintegrated language can, therefore, accurately convey neither a clear understanding of that which is *good* nor of its opposites.

Every person, family and society who causes or allows their language to be viciously disintegrated with semantic darkness and corruption can so distort the truth in their own minds and in the minds of others as to allow or cause themselves and others to stumble and to suffer increasing darkness, vice, corruption, bondage, despair, turmoil and misery. This may result in the tragic downfall or destruction of many of us. (For further understanding, see *integrated language* in this *Glossary*.)

Enlightened certainty is absolute personal knowledge of pure enlightenment or of the pure light of truth. To have enlightened certainty is to know I am being enlightened or have been enlightened by an absolute personal knowledge of pure enlightenment or of the pure light of truth. Enlightened certainty within me supersedes compatible belief and nullifies all contrary beliefs with a measure of enlightened or sure knowledge which produces, preserves or restores its own characteristics within me.

Enlightened conscience consists of and is responsive to inner thoughts, feelings and messages of enlightened certainty, reality and truth granted or sent to my mind and heart from God. To exercise enlightened conscience is to willfully strive to sustain within my thoughts, words and actions the integrity of that enlightened certainty, reality and truth I have received from God.

At a higher level, the term refers to that condition of my heart in which I remain completely integrated in thought, speech and behavior with that measure of absolute, perfect and spiritually verified personal knowledge of enlightened certainty, reality or truth I have received and exercised well enough to make it a part of what I do and who I am.

Enlightenment is the possession of a measure of the powerful light of God which fills the immensity of space, which manifests His love to us and for us, which gives life to all things, and which is the law by which all things are governed. Enlightenment is also the pure light of truth. A measure of the pure light of truth is given to every person born into the world. God grants an increasing measure of the pure light of truth to any and every redeemable person who pays the price of obedience to that divinely appointed law upon which receipt of an increasing measure of the pure light of truth is predicated.

True enlightenment is also my God-given power to recognize, comprehend and rely upon that knowledge of the pure light of truth which I possess. True enlightenment, then, is also my power to dispel or remove darkness from within the thoughts of my mind and from within my heart. There can be no virtue and no vice within me without enough true enlightenment and accountability within me.

To the extent true enlightenment exists within me darkness cannot exist within me; hence, to that same extent I can discern virtue from vice and can obtain virtue. Enlightenment within me supersedes compatible belief and nullifies all contrary beliefs with a measure of enlightened or sure knowledge which produces, preserves or restores its own characteristics within me. (For further understanding, see *intelligence* and *truth* in this *Glossary*. See also definitions of *enlightened* and related characteristics found in the author's dictionaries.)

Error is deviation from truth. As such, error is someone's deviation from their personal knowledge of truth. Error is also someone's deviant and mistaken belief that a falsehood is truth, or that a truth is falsehood. Error is also deviation from the truly pure and virtuous path that leads to God's perfect way of life. Darkened and fearful doubt can allow or cause someone's thoughts to deviate from enlightened certainty into error. Delusion and illusion can allow or cause someone's thoughts to mistake what is real for something imaginary and to thus deviate from reality into error. Deviation from faithfully living in harmony with truth results in deviation from truth into error. Error is used as a tool by Satan and his followers to tempt humankind to forsake and withstand enlightened certainty, reality, truth, virtue and integrity.

Ethical refers to living any socially accepted standard of conduct. The term also refers to living any standard of conduct that is being made socially acceptable by effective use of agreement, discipline, persuasion, law or force, or by default for lack of effective opposition or prohibition.

Ethics consist of ethical standards which may or may not be based on what is moral or virtuous. An applied ethical standard may prove to be either virtuous or vicious in nature and consequence. Only truly virtuous thoughts, words and actions can produce, preserve or restore truly virtuous outcomes in me, my family and society. (For further understanding, see *moral* and *virtuous* in this *Glossary*.)

Evil characteristics are all of the human characteristics which are given a negative two (-2), plus all positive one (1) and zero (0) and negative one (-1) characteristics to the extent my vicious thoughtful entertainment or performance of them produces, preserves or restores negative two (-2) characteristics (or vices) within me, my family and society.

Evil person is an accountable and dishonorable person who willfully fails or refuses to continue to wholeheartedly desire and diligently work to become and remain completely chaste, clean, pure and virtuous at heart, while willfully failing or refusing to completely repent of practicing or performing something unchaste, unclean, impure or vicious. An evil person may *feel* invitations from God to avoid and repent of wrongdoing. An evil person may *do* a good thing such as repent of sin. To choose to remain in sin is to *be* an evil person. To receive and retain a remission of sins is to *be* a good person. (For further understanding, see *good person*, *vicious* and *virtuous* in this *Glossary*. See also definitions of *baptized*, *faithful*, *good*, *repenting* and related characteristics found in the author's dictionaries.)

Existence is the condition, fact or state of being or living.

Factual refers to any and every thing, thought, word, action, deed or work which is true and which exists in truth. To be factual is to be aware of, to rely upon, or to openly express pure truth.

Factual knowledge is that powerful personal enlightenment about things which are truly happening in reality, or which have truly happened in reality, or which will truly happen in reality. My factual knowledge includes but is not necessarily limited to my knowledge of things which I personally confirm by my own empirical, physical, or sensory experience are truly happening or have truly happened in reality.

Family values are all of those values or standards which produce, preserve or restore within me, my family and society those characteristics given a positive two (2) in this book.

Falsehood is all thoughts which lie outside the absolute bounds or limits of enlightened certainty, reality or truth. Falsehood is used as a tool by Satan and his followers to tempt humankind to forsake and withstand enlightened certainty, reality, truth, virtue and integrity.

god is a term which may refer to a station or status of godhood defined by someone. The term may also refer to one or more deity that are real as beliefs in someone's mind and heart. The term may also refer to one or more deity that are imaginary.

God is not only real as a belief, concept, idea, notion or spirit in the hearts and minds of people. God lives. He teaches, perfects, rewards and protects those who love and obey Him. Evidence of who He is and what He does abounds throughout integrated language. No amount of reasoning can absolutely prove or disprove the truthfulness of that evidence to any person. Knowing this, God makes His existence, His works, His true attributes, and His true character spiritually verifiable in truth to any and every redeemable person who lives or has ever lived who pays the price of obedience to that divinely appointed law upon which receipt of that absolute verification of truth is predicated.

Much about who God is and what He does can be found in the virtues defined in *The Human Virtues Dictionary*. By their fruits I shall know whether they are virtues. If they are virtues, then by their fruits I shall know Him and His followers.

Good characteristics are all of the human characteristics pertaining to my gender which are given a positive two (2), plus all positive one (1) and zero (0) and negative one (-1) characteristics to the extent my virtuous thoughtful entertainment or performance of them produces, preserves or restores positive two (2) characteristics (or virtues) within me, my family and society.

Good person is an accountable and honorable person who willfully continues to wholeheartedly desire and diligently work to become and remain completely chaste, clean, pure and virtuous at heart, while willfully and completely repenting of practicing or performing anything unchaste, unclean, impure or vicious. A good person may *feel* invitations from Satan to do wrong. A good person may *do* an evil thing such as sin. To receive and retain a remission of sins is to *be* a good person. To choose to remain in sin is to *be* an evil person. (For further understanding, see *evil person, vicious* and *virtuous* in this *Glossary*. See also definitions of *baptized, faithful, good, repenting* and related characteristics found in the author's dictionaries.)

Heart is the physical organ of my body used to symbolically represent the true character, intellect or nature of my immortal spirit being and its enlivening presence within my living physical body. When my physical heart remains stopped in its beating, it is a sure sign my immortal spirit being has departed my physical body in physical death.

The term also refers to all of the thoughtful actions, beliefs, characteristics, commitments, covenants, deeds, desires, ideas, images, impressions, intentions, motivations, promises, values, words, or works which are distinctively carved, engraved, inscribed or otherwise recorded upon or within the true character, intellect or nature of my immortal spirit being. My heart is who I truly am and choose to be in spirit and in truth. The human mind and heart are the ultimate battleground of good and evil. The human heart is their prize. (For further understanding, see *mind* and *soul* in this *Glossary*.)

Holy Ghost is a gloriously exalted male Spirit Personage of enlivened spirit matter who is sometimes called the Spirit of Truth, the Holy Spirit, or the Spirit of God. He is the first Comforter and a revealer, testator and witness of truth to God's children on Earth. Constant virtuous thoughts, words and actions bring His constant revelatory influence and power.

As the Holy Ghost brings enlightened certainty, reality and truth into the mind and heart of a prayerful person of real intent who sincerely asks in faith, believing they will receive, that person learns of the reality and workings of God by the power of the Holy Ghost and realizes the incontrovertible truthfulness of His message. God has manifest or will manifest the truth of all things by the power of the Holy Ghost to any and every redeemable person who lives or has ever lived who pays the price of obedience to that divinely appointed law upon which receipt of that manifestation of truth is predicated.

Much about who the Holy Ghost is and what He does can be found in the virtues defined in *The Human Virtues Dictionary*. By their fruits I shall know whether they are true. If they are true, then by their fruits I shall know Him and the God who has sent Him and His influence into my mind and heart. (For further understanding, see *Spirit* in this *Glossary*.)

Hope is defined by *hoping* and by related characteristics found in the author's dictionaries. As long as I am truly hopeful, despair cannot exist within me; hence, I can obtain true and lasting peace.

Identity is the condition, fact or state of someone being and living exactly who they truly are and exactly who they are truly becoming. Identity is also the condition, fact or state of something being exactly what it truly is and exactly what it is truly becoming or remaining.

Imaginary refers to that which can exist only in someone's imagination. When I imagine someone or something in thought, the thought itself is real within my thoughts, but who or what is imagined may be or become real outside of my imagination only if it is *not* imaginary (or only if it is nonimaginary). What is imagined *cannot* be real and *cannot* become real if it is imaginary. When I share a thought of something imaginary with someone else, the shared thought itself becomes real both within and outside of each of us, but what is imaginary within the thought remains imaginary within our thoughts, whether or not we have come to that realization. (For further understanding, see *nonimaginary* and *real* in this *Glossary*.)

Imaginary human condition means a human condition or state of being which does not have, has never had and cannot have actual, independent and nonimaginary existence, identity and nature within someone. No imaginary human condition can represent or be represented by any portion of enlightened certainty, reality or truth. The definition of a real human characteristic cannot be a descriptive representation of an imaginary human condition. (For further understanding, see *imaginary*, *real* and *real human condition* in this *Glossary*.)

Impact value refers to the value of the impact which the thoughtful entertainment or performance of a human characteristic has within me, my family and society. Impact value is designated by each of the five defined numerical values listed at the beginning of this *Glossary*.

Independent refers to any and every self-contained or separately identifiable thing which is controlled or governed by law. The term also refers to someone who is individually alive, personally aware, self-committing, self-controlling, self-expressive, self-governing, self-reliant, self-supporting and willfully law-abiding.

At a higher level, the term means to be emancipated, freed, liberated or released from receiving the outside influence of darkness, vice and corruption into my mind. At an even higher level, the term means to be entirely emancipated, freed, liberated or released within my mind and heart from the evil or satanic powers of darkness, vice and corruption.

Integrated language is any language with which someone can communicate a true understanding of *enlightened certainty, reality* or *truth* with another person by expressing commonly used word symbols to reconvey and represent commonly defined images or descriptive representations of certain designated portions of enlightened certainty, reality or truth. Hence, definitions of that which is truly good and of God are made and found to be easily recognizable and clearly distinguishable from definitions of that which is evil or satanic.

For example, integrated language will not allow a word symbol like *evil*, and its commonly defined images or descriptive representations of certain designated portions of reality, to represent a designated portion of reality which is commonly known to be *good*, and vice versa. Truth is in harmony with itself. So is integrated language. Integrated language is, therefore, a thesaurus or *treasury* of truth, and should be preserved as such.

Where language pertaining to human character is integrated, someone can also communicate a common understanding of a *real human condition* with another person by expressing commonly used word symbols to reconvey and represent commonly defined images or descriptive representations of certain designated portions of what is real. Where there is integrated language pertaining to human character, all word symbols and definitions representing *imaginary human conditions* are excluded.

An integrated language of human character can be created and tested by the use of defined numerical values. The five defined numerical values (or impact values) referred to in this book are positive two (2), positive one (1), zero (0), negative one (-1) and negative two (-2) (as defined at the beginning of this *Glossary*).

In integrated language, as long as each definition for each named characteristic is a verifiable statement of truth, then the entire integrated language becomes an effective representation of reality and an integrated treasury of truth for us all, and should be preserved as such. (For further understanding, see *disintegrated language* in this *Glossary*, and the chapters of this book entitled *Words as Representations of Reality, Definitions as Statements of Truth, Integrated Language as a Treasury of Truth,* and *An Open Challenge to the World.*)

Integrity is the presence of pure and increasing enlightenment combined with a pure and increasing abundance of virtue within someone. Integrity is the absence of darkness, vice and corruption within someone. To the extent I willfully allow or cause darkness, vice and corruption to exist within me integrity cannot exist within me; hence, to that same extent bondage replaces true and lasting liberty within me. To have true integrity is to have true and lasting liberty within me. Integrity is intrinsically good and of God.

Intelligence is the glory of God, who possesses all light and truth and is the most intelligent of eternal beings. Intelligence is also the pure light of truth. Intelligence is the personal possession and the willful, virtuous use of the power of pure enlightenment and of the knowledge of pure truth. A measure of intelligence is an integral, pre-mortal part of every person born into the world. God grants an increasing measure of intelligence to any and every redeemable person who lives or has ever lived who pays the price of obedience to that divinely appointed law upon which receipt of an increasing measure of intelligence is predicated. (For further understanding, see *enlightenment* and *truth* in this *Glossary.* See also *intelligent* and related characteristics found in the author's dictionaries.)

Intrinsic means in and of itself.

Joy is defined by *joyful* and by related characteristics found in the author's dictionaries. As long as I am truly joyful, misery cannot exist within me.

Lawful refers to that which is equitably allowed or substantially permitted by law, and is neither contrary to nor forbidden by law.

Legal refers to that which is explicitly authorized or sanctioned by constructed law. The term also applies to that which is cognizable as technically complying with the requirements of constructed law. No words or actions which produce any characteristic given a negative two (-2) should ever be officially permitted or legalized.

Liberty is defined by *liberated* and by related characteristics found in the author's dictionaries. When the term appears within all or part of the context chain of true *enlightenment, virtue, integrity, liberty, hope, peace and joy,* it means to be emancipated, freed, liberated or released from receiving the outside influences of darkness, vice and corruption into my mind.

At a higher level, the term means to be entirely emancipated, freed, liberated or released within my mind and heart from the evil or satanic powers of darkness, vice and corruption. As long as I am truly liberated within my mind and heart, bondage cannot exist within me; hence, I can obtain true and lasting hope, peace and joy.

Living things refers to every living thing on Earth, except living people.

Me, my family and society refers to three interrelationships in society. The interrelationships referred to may be compared to a three-legged stool. The health and well-being of me, my family and society can only be sustained when there is healthy interdependence and cooperation among all three legs of the stool. What happens to one has an impact on what happens to the other two. This reference is to be applied wherever this figurative three-legged stool appears in this book in another form, as with *ourselves, our families and society.*

No person is better-off than their present finite list of distinctive characteristics in composition, impact value, and degree of strength. Family character is a reflection of what is happening within all of its members at the same time; therefore, no family is better-off than the present aggregate composition, impact value, and degree of strength of the characteristics of its members. National character is a reflection of what is happening within all of its individuals and families at the same time; therefore, no nation is better-off than the present aggregate composition, impact value, and degree of strength of the characteristics of its individuals and families.

Mind is the living spiritual intellect within my immortal spirit being which enlivens and gives my physical brain its capacities to control my physical body, to actively process and physically store thoughts, and to recall, recollect, remember or retrieve my stored thoughts for further processing or for use in my words or actions. When my physical body dies, that intellect is withdrawn from my body and remains alive and intact as an integral and inseparable part of my immortal spirit being. When I am resurrected, my brain and my intellect become reunited as part of my one-time and everlasting resurrection from the dead. (For further understanding, see *heart* and *soul* in this *Glossary*.)

Misery is defined by *miserable* and by related characteristics found in the author's book *The Language of Human Character*. As long as I am miserable, true and lasting joy cannot exist within me.

Moral refers to being spiritually righteous or godly enough to be made truly chaste, clean, pure and virtuous in the sight of God. Otherwise, the term refers either to living a socially accepted standard of conduct or to living a standard of conduct that is being made socially acceptable by effective use of agreement, discipline, persuasion, law or force, or by default for lack of effective opposition or prohibition.

Morality consists of moral standards which may or may not be based on what is ethical or virtuous. An applied moral standard may prove to be virtuous or vicious in nature and consequence. Only truly virtuous thoughts, words and actions can produce, preserve or restore truly virtuous outcomes in me, my family and society. (For further understanding, see *ethical* and *virtuous* in this *Glossary*.)

Nature is the sum of specific characteristics or parts which basically, essentially, intrinsically or naturally belong to and exist within or as a part of someone or something. A person's nature is generally a reference to their character, which is changeable.

Nonimaginary refers to that which is *not* a part of that which can exist only in someone's imagination. When I imagine something in thought, the thought itself is real within me, but what is imagined may be or become real outside of my imagination only if it is nonimaginary. What is imagined *cannot* be real and *cannot* become real unless it is nonimaginary. (For further understanding, see *imaginary* and *real* in this *Glossary*.)

Peace is defined by *peaceful* and by related characteristics found in the author's dictionaries. As long as I am truly peaceful, turmoil cannot exist within me; hence, I can obtain true and lasting joy.

Personality refers to the person I outwardly appear or present myself to be in the minds of one or more other people. My personality may reflect or represent my true character, or it may not.

Progress is acquiring virtuous characteristics within my heart while becoming dispossessed of opposing vicious characteristics. The term also refers to deepening or intensifying the extent to which virtuous characteristics are distinctively carved, engraved, inscribed or otherwise recorded upon or within my heart. The term also refers to seeking, finding and implementing the best means and methods of doing so.

Real is that which has actual, independent and nonimaginary existence, identity and nature *outside of* or *within* my thoughts. That which is *real* meets all nine of the following ✔ tests *outside of* or *within* my thoughts.

	actual	independent	nonimaginary
existence	✔	✔	✔
identity	✔	✔	✔
nature	✔	✔	✔

Example One: If a person or thing has actual, independent and nonimaginary existence, identity and nature *outside of* my thoughts, then that person or thing is *real*. If a person or thing does not have actual, independent and nonimaginary existence, identity and nature *outside of* my thoughts, then that person or thing is *imaginary*.

Example Two: If another person thinks a thought, then their thought has actual, independent and nonimaginary existence, identity and nature *outside of* my thoughts and is *real outside of* my thoughts. If I think a thought, then my thought has actual, independent and nonimaginary existence, identity and nature *within* my thoughts and is *real within* my thoughts.

Example Three: When I imagine someone or something, the thought itself is *real within* my thoughts, but whom or what I imagine might be real or imaginary *outside of* my thoughts. To accept someone or something which is *imaginary outside of* my thoughts as someone or something *real within* my thoughts is to suffer from a misconception, misidentification, misjudgment, misperception or other mistake within my thoughts, whether or not I have come to that realization. To accept someone or something which is *real outside of* my thoughts as someone or something *imaginary within* my thoughts is also to suffer from a misconception, misidentification, misjudgment, misperception or other mistake within my thoughts, whether or not I have come to that realization.

Real human condition means a human condition or state of being which has, has had or can have actual, independent and nonimaginary existence, identity and nature within someone. The existence of such a condition within someone may be manifested in one or more of their achievements, actions, admissions, behaviors, contracts, covenants, deeds, oaths, performances, promises, statements, testimonies or in their other evidential or known words or works. Or the condition may exist within them without manifestation known to other people, or as part of their intentions known only to God and to them, unless discerned by or revealed to someone else.

The term also refers to a condition or state of being which I can acquire as part of who I am by willfully pondering and performing it enough. The term also refers to a condition or state of being which I can forsake as part of who I am by willfully refusing to ponder or perform it at all.

The term also refers to a spiritually verifiable positive condition or state of being which has been or can be justly made a real part of who I am by the power of God by His justifiable grace or as I accountably obey His laws. The term also refers to a spiritually verifiable negative condition or state of being which has been or can be justly made a real part of who I am by the power of Satan as I accountably fail or refuse to obey God's laws.

Each real human condition represents and is represented by its own designated portion of enlightened certainty, reality or truth. A definition of a real human characteristic must be a descriptive representation of a real human condition. However, a definition of a real human characteristic can describe a real human condition in which someone accepts, mistakes, proclaims or sponsors as reality an *imaginary human condition*. (For further understanding, see *imaginary* and *imaginary human condition* in this *Glossary*.)

Reality is the sum of knowledge of the *truth* about what is *real*. Reality is also a personal knowledge of the truth about what is *real*. For me, reality is the truth about the actual, independent and nonimaginary existence, identity and nature of someone or something real *outside of* my thoughts, which I know or can know is truth *within* my thoughts. Reality is also the truth about the actual, independent and nonimaginary existence, identity and nature of someone or something real *within* my thoughts, which I know or can know is truth *outside of* my thoughts. Whatever I misconceive, misidentify, misjudge, misperceive or otherwise mistake within the thoughts of my mind as reality is confusion, error or falsehood *within* my thoughts, whether or not I have come to that realization.

Take, for example, a small campfire which is real outside of my thoughts. I can know the truthfulness of the actual, independent and nonimaginary existence, identity and nature of that small campfire within my thoughts by seeing the firelight, by feeling the heat of the fire, by smelling and tasting its smoke and by hearing its crackling or other sounds. What I am simultaneously truly seeing, feeling, smelling, tasting and hearing about that small campfire within my thoughts conveys to me the truth about that small campfire as it exists outside of my thoughts. Conversely, if I were under some confusing or deluding influence and were to thus misconceive, misidentify, misjudge, misperceive or otherwise mistake that campfire as a raging forest fire, as only a lighted match, or as no fire at all within the thoughts of my mind, that small campfire would remain what it is, and I would be suffering from confusion, error or falsehood within my thoughts, whether or not I came to that realization.

Reality is verifiable in experience, observation and truth. To receive or to come to an absolute, perfect and spiritually verified personal knowledge of enlightened certainty, reality or truth by personal enlightenment, inspiration or revelation from God is to clearly and distinctly realize I have perfectly experienced or observed receiving from Him into the thoughts of my mind and heart a perfectly clear and accurate revealed image, descriptive representation or understanding of that measure of truth as it exists, has existed, or will yet exist both within and outside of my thoughts. That means the truth about the present, past or future existence of that small campfire outside of my thoughts can be made known to me within the thoughts of my mind and heart, even if I have not physically experienced or observed it. Reality within me supersedes compatible belief and nullifies all contrary beliefs with a measure of enlightened or sure knowledge which produces, preserves or restores its own characteristics within me.

Relative value is the defined numerical value of positive one (1), zero (0), or negative one (-1), as defined at the beginning of this *Glossary*. These three classifications of human characteristics are collectively referred to as *relative value characteristics*. Relative value characteristics can be *virtuously* used to produce, preserve or restore positive two (2) characteristics (or *virtues*) within me, my family and society. Relative value characteristics can also be *viciously* used to produce, preserve or restore negative two (-2) characteristics (or *vices*) within me, my family and society.

Positive One (1) Example: It is *virtuous* of someone to put in to effect a positive one (1) definition of *humoring* to produce, preserve or restore a positive two (2) condition of *laughing* within someone. It is *vicious* of someone to put in to effect a positive one (1) definition of *humoring* to produce, preserve or restore a negative two (-2) condition of *laughing* within someone.

Zero (0) Example: It is *virtuous* of someone to put in to effect a zero (0) definition of *obeying* to produce, preserve or restore a positive two (2) condition of *popular* within someone. It is *vicious* of someone to put in to effect a zero (0) definition of *obeying* to produce, preserve or restore a negative two (-2) condition of *popular* within someone.

Negative One (-1) Example: It is *virtuous* of someone to put in to effect a negative one (-1) definition of *fighting* or *warring* to produce, preserve or restore a positive two (2) condition of *liberated* within someone. It is *vicious* of someone to put in to effect a negative one (-1) definition of *fighting* or *warring* to produce, preserve or restore a negative two (-2) condition of *liberated* within someone.

Some relative value characteristics are not reasonably useful for producing, preserving or restoring virtue or vice. For example, the first definition of *absent-minded* found in the author's books *The Language of Human Virtue* and *The Language of Human Character* is: *to be distracted or preoccupied to the point of being forgetful, heedless or inattentive*. That definition is given the defined numerical value of negative one (-1), but it is most unlikely that definition can be put in to effect to produce, preserve or restore within me, my family and society one or more of the virtues listed in *The Human Virtues Dictionary*. The same kind of limitation may also apply to characteristics given a zero (0) or a positive one (1).

Satan is not only real as a belief, concept, idea, or notion in the hearts and minds of people. Satan lives. God gives his obedient children power to discern and know with enlightened certainty of Satan's existence and of his true attributes, character, desires, designs, purposes and works. Satan is an enemy to God and to all that is good. God allows Satan to oppose what is good with evil so we can prove in our actual desires and works before God and His laws whether we will choose to love and follow God or Satan. With God's help we can resist Satan's power.

Satan is the father of all vicious lies, and a master of deception, disguise and imitation. One of the most effective deceptions used by him and his followers is that he does not exist. As a counterfeit to true enlightenment, Satan peddles darkness in an appealing mixture of truth and error. As a disguised fake to true virtue he promotes the prideful and self-serving use of vicious words and actions for monetary gain. As an imitation to true integrity, he sells the acceptability of corruption accompanied by a hypocritical pretense of true integrity. Instead of true liberty, he extols excessive liberality that leads to addiction and to bondage. Instead of true hope, he entices with empty promises which, when broken, lead to the despair of misplaced hope and betrayal. Instead of true peace, he tempts with excessive personal tolerance that leads to inner turmoil. Instead of true joy, he touts momentary sinful excitement or pleasure which delivers only lasting misery in the end.

Much about Satan's existence as a living male spirit being and about who he is and what he does can be found under *asatanic, devilish, hellish, satanic* and the other vices defined in the author's book *The Language of Human Character.* By their fruits I shall know whether they are vices. If they are vices, then by their fruits I shall know him and his followers.

Society refers to all of the people of the earth. More specifically, the term refers to each and every human affiliation, alliance, assembly, association, band, body, business, caste, city, clan, class, clique, club, community, companionship, company, conclave, confederation, congregation, congress, convention, convocation, corporation, council, country, county, couple, crowd, culture, enclave, establishment, federation, fellowship, fraternity, gathering, government, group, guild, home, institution, league, nation, neighborhood, order, organization, partnership, population, precinct, province, race, religion, school, sorority, state, subculture, town, township, troop, team, tribe or other unit of two or more people other than those in my own immediate family.

Someone can refer to me, to another person, or to other people. For negative one (-1) definitions, the term may have reference to one or more opponents or enemies.

Soul is the temporary mortal combination of someone's human physical body of earthly physical matter and their immortal spirit being or personage of enlivened spirit matter which gives it life until physical death. In my one-time and everlasting resurrection from the dead, my soul becomes the inseparable restoration of my perfectly and permanently restored human physical body of earthly physical matter with my immortal spirit being or personage of enlivened spirit matter, which combination is granted immortal life by God. The term also applies to other mortal or resurrected creatures or creations of God.

Spirit means enlivened spirit matter. The term may refer to someone who consists of only enlivened spirit matter. My existing immortal spirit being or personage of enlivened spirit matter gives my physical body life. All forms of life have their respective immortal spirit beings or forms of enlivened spirit matter which give their physical forms life. God makes the existence of spirit matter spiritually verifiable in truth to any person who pays the price of obedience to that divinely appointed law upon which receipt of that absolute verification of truth is predicated. The term serves as a foundation for such words as: *spirited, spiriting, spiritless, spiritual, spiritualistic, spiritualizing, spiritually-minded,* and their synonyms, as defined in the author's dictionaries. Much about things spiritual can be learned from those definitions.

Spirit of God generally refers to the Holy Ghost. (See *Holy Ghost* in this *Glossary.*) The term may also refer to the enlightening power and influence of God, which is manifest in my innately enlightened sense of that which is truly good and of God. The term may also refer to the Spirit Personage of God inseparably embodied within His glorified, immortal and tangible body of flesh and bones. God makes His existence, His works, His true attributes and His true character spiritually verifiable in truth to any and every redeemable person who lives or has ever lived who pays the price of obedience to that divinely appointed law upon which receipt of that absolute verification of truth is predicated. Much about who God is and what He does can be found in the virtues defined in *The Human Virtues Dictionary.*

The eternally binding law of justice is coeternal with God and with eternal truth. It is one of the unchanging and eternally binding laws by which God chooses to remain bound and governed and by which He rules and reigns as an unchanging God. God cannot be mocked, and the eternally binding law of justice cannot be robbed. The blessings affixed to this law must be justly granted by God to those people who were *not* accountable to this law while on Earth and to those accountable people who were living in righteous harmony with this law at death. Conversely, the punishments affixed to this law must be justly inflicted by God upon those accountable people who knowingly violated it and then willfully remained subject to its penalties until death. (See *accountable* in this *Glossary*.)

As accountable mortal beings on Earth, we are each in a probationary state in which God gives us the agency or mortal power of liberty to prove before this law whether we will choose *for ourselves* to receive His revealed enlightened certainty, reality and truth instead of confusion, error and falsehood, and whether we will also prove before this law whether we will ascertain and choose *for ourselves* to live by that which is truly good and of God instead of that which is evil or satanic. There could be no agency or mortal power of liberty to choose *for ourselves* on Earth without those choices and without the ultimate effects of this law being held in abeyance, as they are for each of us, until our earthly probation is over.

Because God lives in perfect harmony with the eternally binding law of justice, He is perfectly just. Hence, sins against Him are violations of this law. Sins are debts incurred under this law by an accountable person during their mortal probation. This law demands that those debts must be paid for in full by that debtor's own personal suffering, unless that person is redeemed by the personal sacrifice of a savior who is qualified under this law to make a legally binding payment of suffering for the entire balance of payment due, and, in so doing, is qualified to mercifully but conditionally provide that person with a remission of their sins until their righteous death, and, upon fulfillment of that condition, to forever save that sinner from personally suffering the balance of payment due for their sins following the day of God's final judgment.

The eternally binding law of justice is also that law of truth and virtue which dictates that, notwithstanding God's love, power and grace, no accountable person, living or dead, can be forever redeemed from their own sins unto exaltation without that person's faithful, timely and true repentance, obedience and reconciliation to God. Hence, God makes His existence and the existence of the eternally binding law of justice spiritually verifiable in truth to any and every redeemable person who lives or has ever lived who pays the price of obedience to that divinely appointed law upon which receipt of that absolute verification of truth is predicated. (For further understanding, see such terms as *accountable, consequence-oriented, damned, faithful, faithless, optimistic, punishing, redeemed, repenting, sinning, suffering* and *transgressing* in the author's dictionaries.)

True is that which consists of only truth. The term is further defined by *true* and by related characteristics found in the author's dictionaries.

True value refers to the defined numerical value of positive two (2), as defined at the beginning of this *Glossary*. The term also applies to the defined numerical value of negative two (-2), as defined at the beginning of this *Glossary*. Both of these defined numerical values are unchanging in their impact value within me, my family and society.

True value pertains and refers to each of the positive two (2) characteristics (or virtues) in the author's dictionaries, the defined numerical value of which is derived from the fact that my continued thoughtful entertainment or performance of each of them constantly and powerfully produces, preserves or restores true enlightenment, virtue, integrity, liberty, hope, peace and joy within me, my family and society.

True value also pertains and refers to each of the negative two (-2) characteristics (or vices) found in the author's book *The Language of Human Character*, the defined numerical value of which is derived from the fact that my continued thoughtful entertainment or performance of each of them constantly and powerfully produces, preserves or restores darkness, vice, corruption, bondage, despair, turmoil and misery within me, my family and society.

Truth is the enlightened knowledge of all things. All truth is known to God. All truth, without exception, is always in perfect harmony, integrity, oneness or unity with itself and can, therefore, be combined into one clearly and perfectly coherent, integrated and undiluted whole.

A measure of truth independently exists in that sphere in which God has placed it outside of our thoughts. He has made personal knowledge of it available to us, so that it can also exist within our thoughts. Once we acquire it, this knowledge gives each of us the power to clearly discern and distinguish opposites, such as virtue and vice, from one another.

Truth is also the pure light and Spirit of God. From it comes that measure of pure enlightenment which God has placed or will place into my mind and heart as enlightened certainty, as reality, or as factual knowledge of things as they are, and as they were, and as they are to come.

Truth is also the truly pure and virtuous path that leads to God's perfect way of life back home. To help guide us back home, a measure of the pure light of truth is given to every person born into the world. God continues to grant an increasing measure of the pure light of truth to any and every redeemable person who continues to pay the price of obedience to that divinely appointed law upon which receipt of an increasing measure of the pure light of truth is predicated.

Unlike confusion, error and falsehood, the pure light of truth is capable of producing, preserving or restoring virtuous harmony, integrity, oneness and unity within me, my family and society. Truth within me supersedes compatible belief and nullifies all contrary beliefs with a measure of enlightened or sure knowledge which produces, preserves or restores its own characteristics within me. (For further understanding, see *enlightenment* and *intelligence* in this *Glossary*. See also *truthful* and related characteristics found in the author's dictionaries.)

Turmoil is defined by *turmoiling* and by related characteristics found in the author's book *The Language of Human Character*. As long as I am in turmoil, true and lasting peace cannot exist within me; hence, I cannot obtain true and lasting joy.

Values are all of the standards used by humankind to estimate and measure the acceptability, quality or value of human speech and behavior. My values or standards grow from, embody and represent my chosen *beliefs*. People can work alone or together to standardize the performance or practice of any personal, family or social belief, and of any composition or set of such beliefs. Values are found in agreements, codes, commandments, commands, contracts, covenants, declarations, decrees, directives, duties, ethics, fundamentals, goals, guidelines, ideals, injunctions, instructions, laws, limitations, mandates, manners, maxims, missions, models, morals, norms, oaths, obligations, orders, ordinances, policies, polities, precepts, prescriptions, procedures, processes, proclamations, prohibitions, principles, promises, purposes, regulations, restrictions, rules, standards, statutes and ways. (For further understanding, see *beliefs* in this *Glossary*, and Chapter Two, entitled *Some True Statements about Human Character*.)

Vice is the sum of all vices. It is the sum of all *evil characteristics* (as defined in this *Glossary*). Vice is also the willful exercise or performance of one or more vicious characteristics in the thoughts of my heart or in my words or actions. There can be no virtue and no vice within me without enough true enlightenment and accountability within me.

Vice is also the power to dispel or remove virtue or well-being from within me. In this sense, vice has and is the power to harm. To the extent darkness and vice exist within me true enlightenment and virtue cannot exist within me; hence, to that same extent I cannot achieve or maintain integrity. To the extent I am accountable for my loss of true enlightenment and virtue from within me I am accountable for any naturally consequent loss of integrity from within me. Vice is intrinsically evil or satanic.

Vicious is the pondering, performance or teaching of one or more human characteristics with a defined numerical value of positive one (1), zero (0), negative one (-1) or negative two (-2), which results in the production, preservation or restoration of one or more negative two (-2) human vices within me, my family and society. That which is truly vicious cannot produce, preserve or restore any positive two (2) virtue within me, my family or society.

That which is truly vicious is subject to personal discovery but is never subject to personal whim. To knowingly and accountably intend, do, be or teach what is truly vicious is sin. (For further understanding, see *the eternally binding law of justice, evil characteristics, evil person* and *relative value* in this *Glossary,* as well as *sinning, vicious* and related characteristics found in the author's book *The Language of Human Character.*)

Virtue is the sum of all virtues. It is the sum of all *good characteristics* (as defined in this *Glossary*). Virtue is also the willful exercise or performance of one or more virtuous characteristics in the thoughts of my heart or in my words or actions. There can be no virtue and no vice within me without enough true enlightenment and accountability within me.

Virtue is also the power to dispel or remove vice or malady from within me. In this sense, virtue has and is the power to heal. To the extent virtue exists within me vice cannot exist within me; hence, to that same extent I am closer to obtaining integrity. To be truly enlightened and purely virtuous is to achieve or maintain true integrity within me. Virtue is intrinsically good and of God.

Virtuous is the pondering, performance or teaching of one or more human characteristics with a defined numerical value of positive two (2), positive one (1), zero (0), or negative one (-1), which results in the production, preservation or restoration of one or more positive two (2) human virtues within me, my family and society. That which is truly virtuous cannot produce, preserve or restore any negative two (-2) vice within me, my family or society.

That which is truly virtuous is subject to personal discovery but is never subject to personal whim. To knowingly and accountably intend, do, be or teach what is truly virtuous is righteousness. (For further understanding, see *good characteristics*, *good person* and *relative value* in this *Glossary*, as well as *virtuous* and related characteristics found in the author's dictionaries.)

Word Symbol means any *word* and its hearable or spoken sounds. The term also means any tangible, readable, viewable or written word and its tangible, readable, viewable or written alphabetic, numeric, ideographic, pictographic or other characters, figures, letters, numbers, signs, or symbols. The term is used to refer to each human characteristic defined in the dictionary in this book, including those defined words hyphenated or separated by one or more single spaces.

CHAPTER NINE
Explanatory Notes to *The Human Virtues Dictionary*

A Dictionary

A *lexicon* may be defined as a particular or specialized vocabulary. A *thesaurus* may be defined as a *treasury* of words. A *dictionary* may be defined as a classification system of alphabetized words and their meanings in a given language. *The Human Virtues Dictionary* is all three of these things. As a dictionary, however, it is unique in that it assigns a defined numerical value (or impact value) to each listed definition.

Usual Dictionary Parts Missing

The Human Virtues Dictionary is missing (with some exceptions): cross-references, dates, designated antonyms, designated synonyms, etymologies, functional labels, guide phrases, pronunciations, usage quotations, separate listings of related words, stress marks, syllable designations, and usage labels. Other dictionaries may be consulted for these things.

Noun Forms

Human character is often examined using stated principles in noun form. For example, words such as *liberty, hope, peace* and *joy* may readily come to mind. Yet our characters are formed by a combination of what we want, what we do and who we are. One cannot ordinarily see oneself as living or personifying a stated principle unless it is translated into a specific form of *doing* or *being*. For example, the noun *liberty* may not be as useful in the contemplation, definition and exercise of human character as the words *liberal, liberated* or *liberating*. Hence, adjective, verb, and some adverb forms are prevalent in *The Human Virtues Dictionary*.

Included Characteristics and Definitions

The Human Virtues Dictionary lists all defined human characteristics given a defined numerical value (or impact value) of positive two (2) in the language of human character. The positive two (2) designations have been removed from in front of all defined human characteristics in *The Human Virtues Dictionary* because they are all virtues.

Missing Characteristics and Definitions

There are defined words in or absent from *The Human Virtues Dictionary* that have **additional definitions** written by the author that are not included in this book. A definition of a human characteristic will not appear in *The Human Virtues Dictionary* if it has been given a defined numerical value of positive one (1), zero (0), negative one (-1) or negative two (-2).

There are more than thirty common prefixes which can be used to form additional or missing characteristics which are rarely, if ever, formed, needed or used. Such a characteristic may not appear in *The Human Virtues Dictionary* for this reason. A characteristic may not appear for a number of other reasons, such as the following:

- A characteristic may not appear if it is adequately represented by other words or by other forms of the same word.
- A characteristic may not appear if it appears under a different spelling, such as a British spelling.
- A characteristic may not appear if it ends in *ed*, unless it is something which someone can somehow choose to do or be.
- A particular definition of a characteristic may not appear if it cannot be willfully acquired.
- A characteristic may not appear if it is *slang*, and it is better represented by one or more well established words and definitions in the language.

Definition Sources

The English language is universal and belongs to no one. Some of its definitions may have been around as long as the language. Some are new. Dictionary definitions are ordinarily based on precedents established in etymologies and quotations. Etymologies and quotations have powerfully influenced *The Human Virtues Dictionary*, which is written in accordance with many commonly accepted etymologies and quotations. However, no etymologies or quotations are cited within it for reasons given in Chapter Five, entitled *Definitions as Statements of Truth*.

With influence from multiple sources, each defined virtue in *The Human Virtues Dictionary* has been crafted like a definitive or descriptive painting made while viewing all that can be found within every relevant and personally recorded image or impression of the mind and heart. Full credit is eagerly extended to each and every outside source which created, influenced or reinforced those images or impressions, but the images and impressions are personal and so are the paintings. This book is not perfect in its present form. Neither is its author. Full responsibility for the deficiencies of this book is humbly accepted by its author.

The content and organization of the words found in each definition in *The Human Virtues Dictionary* are based upon personal thought derived from more than fifty years of personal examinations of definitions, etymologies, meanings, quotations or usages found in various commonly used editions or versions of **Oxford, Webster's** and other **dictionaries**, and in a great variety of modern and not so modern biographies, documentaries, films, histories, how-to books, magazines, manuscripts, newspapers, photographs, presentations, programs, recordings, reference books, scriptures, speeches, textbooks, thesauruses, websites and other works of fiction and nonfiction pertaining to the human experience.

Definition content and organization have been further influenced by an accumulation of ten years of university study, by twenty-eight years of full-time or part-time labor on this book, by more than forty years of leadership or professional experience in family, humanitarian, education, business, law, military and other day-to-day jobs, and by more than fifty years of personal observation or study of artifacts, artworks, buildings, crafts, creations, cultures, customs, dress, exhibits, galleries, images, languages, memorials, monuments, museums, music, peoples, poetry, products, religions, styles, symbols and traditions, and of other objects, works and phenomena observed or studied in all fifty of the United States of America and in dozens of other nations.

Definition content and organization have been extensively influenced by the personal possession of a measure of absolute, perfect and spiritually verified personal knowledge of enlightened certainty, reality or truth which has come from experiencing or observing the personal reception of clear and distinct personal enlightenment, inspiration or revelation from God of those things of an eternal nature which ultimately exist and will always exist outside of personal thoughts without adulteration, alteration, change, dilution, exception, imperfection, qualification or restriction. Therefore, full credit for anything good in this book belongs to God.

Regardless of the source or sources from which each definition in this book came, each one offers its own proof in reality. Using the tools in this book, you are invited to personally prove them one and all.

Unique Nature of the Definitions

How each human virtue in *The Human Virtues Dictionary* is valued, defined and organized is unique. In it you will see the following patterns:

- Defined human virtues are alphabetized without regard to whether they are hyphenated or separated by one or more single spaces. The first appearance of a defined positive two (2) virtue is in **bold**, *without* a superscript number behind it. If there is a second definition of a virtue, then its word symbol is repeated *with* a superscript number two[2] behind it. A third definition appears with a three[3] behind it, and so forth.

- Definitions are written in *first-person form* so that someone who already possesses the virtue can personally identify with it, and so that someone who does not possess it can personally try it on to see how it feels or fits.

- An effort has been made throughout *The Human Virtues Dictionary* to organize the definitions of each virtue into a *vertical order of definitions* so that the most powerfully beneficial of them appears first in **bold**, the second most powerfully beneficial second, the third most beneficial third, and so forth. For this reason, you may wish to study a human virtue with more than one definition by reading its last definition first and then upwards through its remaining definitions.

- Each definition is preceded by *introductory words of being or intent* to help you more readily see the virtue as a *real human condition*. These introductory words are explained in the next section of this chapter.

- As an aid to further study, other characteristics found *within* a definition appear in alphabetical order, unless an important alternative sequence is purposefully observed.

Introductory Words of Being or Intent

What we want, what we do and who we are include what we intend to do before we have done it or while we are doing it. Therefore, each human virtue in *The Human Virtues Dictionary* is preceded by one selection from the following defined introductory words of *first-person* being or intent:

- **to be** . . . means the defined characteristic is *now* a real human condition and part of who I truly am within my heart. Unless otherwise specified in the definition, these introductory words mean I am fully accountable for allowing or causing the characteristic to remain a part of who I truly am within my heart.

- **to be and to choose to remain** . . . means I have, until now, chosen to *keep* the defined characteristic as a real human condition and part of who I truly am within my heart. Unless otherwise specified in the definition, these introductory words mean I am fully accountable for allowing or causing the characteristic to remain a part of who I truly am within my heart.

- **to be prone to** . . . means it is *now* a real human condition and part of who I truly am within my heart to *consistently and willfully* do or be what is defined. Unless otherwise specified in the definition, these introductory words mean I am fully accountable for allowing or causing the characteristic to remain a part of who I truly am within my heart.

- **to be prone to avoid** . . . means it is *now* a real human condition and part of who I truly am within my heart to *consistently avoid* doing or being what is defined. Unless otherwise specified in the definition, these introductory words mean I am fully accountable for allowing or causing the characteristic to remain a part of who I truly am within my heart.

- **to be prone to fail or refuse to** . . . means it is *now* a real human condition and part of who I truly am within my heart to *consistently avoid or neglect* doing or being what is defined, or to *consistently and willfully refuse* to do or be what is defined. Unless otherwise specified in the definition, these introductory words mean I am fully accountable for allowing or causing the characteristic to remain a part of who I truly am within my heart.

- **to be prone to refuse to** . . . means it is *now* a real human condition and part of who I truly am within my heart to *consistently and willfully refuse* to do or be what is defined. Unless otherwise specified in the definition, these introductory words mean I am fully accountable for allowing or causing the characteristic to remain a part of who I truly am within my heart.

- to intend to . . . means it is *now* my real aim, ambition, aspiration, commitment, desire, goal, intention, plan, purpose or resolution within the thoughts of my heart to do or be what is defined. The introductory words *to intend to* are typically applied to *action* characteristics ending in *ing*.

In the realm of human character, my formation of a certain defined characteristic *intent* means that intent has been formed by me and exists as a real human condition within my heart, whether or not I am now acting or have previously acted upon that intent. Unless otherwise specified in the definition, these introductory words mean I am fully accountable for allowing or causing the characteristic to become or remain a part of who I truly am within my heart.

Each truly *virtuous intent* carries with it the implicit duty to consistently speak and act in harmony with that intent as well as I can and should in order to effectively carve, engrave or inscribe the defined virtue upon my heart as part of what I do and who I am. Under the eternally binding law of justice, to intend but fail to so speak and act when I can and should do so is to lose the reward of that intent. However, any virtuous intent I accountably form within my heart will be proven and rewarded if I am truly unable to fulfill my duty to speak or act upon that intent.

Absent my complete repentance, any *vicious intent* I accountably form within my heart will be proven and condemned under the eternally binding law of justice, even if I did not speak or act upon that intent. By comparison, under the law of the land my words and actions may be used to prove the intent which lies within my mind or heart. In the realm of criminal law it must be proven that I *acted* upon a criminal intent before I can be found guilty of *actually* committing a crime I may have already committed within my mind or heart.

- to intend to avoid . . . means it is *now* my real aim, ambition, aspiration, commitment, desire, goal, intention, plan, purpose or resolution within the thoughts of my heart to *avoid* doing or being what is defined. These introductory words are typically applied to *action* characteristics ending in *ing*. Unless otherwise specified in the definition, these introductory words mean I am fully accountable for allowing or causing the characteristic to become or remain a part of who I truly am within my heart.

- to intend to fail or refuse to . . . means it is *now* my real aim, ambition, aspiration, commitment, desire, goal, intention, plan, purpose or resolution within the thoughts of my heart to *avoid or neglect* doing or being what is defined, or to *willfully refuse* to do or be what is defined. These introductory words are typically applied to *action* characteristics ending in *ing*. Unless otherwise specified in the definition, these introductory words mean I am fully accountable for allowing or causing the characteristic to become or remain a part of who I truly am within my heart.

- to intend to refuse to . . . means it is *now* my real aim, ambition, aspiration, commitment, desire, goal, intention, plan, purpose or resolution within the thoughts of my heart to *willfully refuse* to do or be what is defined. These introductory words are typically applied to *action* characteristics ending in *ing*. Unless otherwise specified in the definition, these introductory words mean I am fully accountable for allowing or causing the characteristic to become or remain a part of who I truly am within my heart.

Studying Opposites

One way to better understand a human characteristic is to learn from its opposites in context with the language of human character as a whole. For example, one can better understand *virtuous* by also studying *vicious*, and vice versa. So it is with *pure* and *impure*, with *judging* and *misjudging*, and so forth. Human vices are excluded from this book to protect eyes and minds from premature or excessive exposure to human vices. To study opposing human virtues and vices, see the dictionary in the author's book *The Language of Human Character.*

Compounded Definitions

To keep the length of *The Human Virtues Dictionary* more manageable and its use more efficient, some definitions are compounded. For example, the first definition of *able* found in *The Human Virtues Dictionary* is: *to be enlightened or intelligent.* The definition could be made into two definitions: *to be enlightened* and *to be intelligent.* By focusing on the word *or*, one can readily divide the two meanings in the mind. Both would have the same defined numerical value of positive two (2) if separated.

Duplicate Definitions

Some human characteristics convey the same meaning. Therefore, some characteristics have the same definition. Some definitions may appear numerous times, sometimes behind human characteristics which may not be considered traditionally synonymous. For example, the definition *to be healthy* appears as one of the definitions for such characteristics as: *alive, balanced, constitutional, OK, sound, vigorous, well* and *well-off*.

Gender-specific Definitions

Some words and definitions of human character are gender specific. If neither gender is specified in a definition, the definition applies to both genders. Some terms are self-evident. Husband, for example, always refers to a male who is lawfully and legally married to a female wife; and wife always refers to a female who is lawfully and legally married to a male husband.

Figurative Usage

Words such as *hearty* or *weak* can be used to describe the physical condition of someone's body, but should also be interpreted to mean hearty or weak in character. Words such as *laughing* should be seen as *real human conditions* which can be found within the mind and heart, as well as words which are or can be outwardly expressed.

Modifying Adverbs and Adjectives

Where a modifying adverb or adjective appears in a definition, it should be thought of as modifying all of the human characteristics which closely follow it in the definition. For example, the first definition of *emancipating* found in *The Human Virtues Dictionary* is: to be *virtuously freeing, liberating or releasing*. In this case, *virtuously* modifies each of the three verbs which follow it. This understanding saves words while allowing the reader to understand the definition to mean: *to be and to choose to remain virtuously freeing, virtuously liberating or virtuously releasing*. Likewise, the word *viciously* modifies each of the human characteristics which follow it.

The following also applies: Where the word *virtuously* appears as part of a definition, it means and refers to any or every positive two (2) definition of the word modified by *virtuously*. So, to be *virtuously scientific* is to be scientific by any or every definition of the word *scientific* given a positive two (2) in *The Human Virtues Dictionary*. Likewise, to be *viciously scientific* is to be scientific by any or every negative two (-2) definition of the word *scientific* found in the author's book *The Language of Human Character*.

Adverse Human Conditions

Ordinarily we do not choose to suffer adverse or trying human conditions we know will be a severe burden to us and to our families. Yet, sometimes we are born with them. Sometimes we accidentally incur them. Sometimes they are intentionally or recklessly inflicted upon us. And sometimes they happen to us from causes or for reasons we do not know or cannot understand.

The adverse human conditions under which we may personally choose to be virtuous (or vicious) cannot be fully described in *The Human Virtues Dictionary*. Still, whatever they may be and however they may come upon us, our own adverse human conditions cannot change what is virtuous (or vicious) for those of us who are accountable (see *accountable* in the *Glossary*).

There are, for example, many among us who are severely: abused, afflicted, autistic, betrayed, blind, crippled, deaf, debilitated, decrepit, defaced, deformed, dim-witted, disabled, diseased, disfigured, dismembered, dumb, feeble, forsaken, harassed, hated, hermaphroditic in body, ill, impaired, impoverished, inapt, incapacitated, incompetent, infirm, injured, invalid, lame, leprous, maimed, marred, misshapen, mocked, molested, mutilated, obese, oppressed, paralyzed, persecuted, rejected, retarded, slow-witted, starving, terrorized, tormented, victimized, violated, weak-minded and so forth. All accountable people can choose to respond to such adverse human conditions in virtuous (or vicious) ways.

An extraordinary *degree of strength* of virtue is usually needed to thrive in such severely adverse human conditions. Those accountable people among us who are prone to humbly, faithfully, hopefully and charitably continue to actively function and truly progress as well as we can and should under such conditions often provide some of the greatest examples of human virtue. Such people can be found in all populated regions of the world. The truths and virtues in this book attest that such people shall receive their *greater* reward; and that those who likewise suffer, but are not accountable, shall in no wise lose their reward.

Treatment of Animals and Other Creatures

Some definitions in *The Human Virtues Dictionary* might be thought of as generally representing someone's treatment of not only one or more people but of one or more animals or other living creatures. For example, when someone is truly *kind* to an animal it is still human kindness at work.

Page Headings as a Search Guide

In *The Human Virtues Dictionary* the *first* word with a full definition on an even-numbered page appears in the heading in **bold** near the page number at the top left. The *last* word defined on the facing odd-numbered page appears in the heading in **bold** near the page number at the top right. These two words serve as a search guide for themselves and for words that lie between them on the two pages.

CHAPTER TEN
An Open Challenge to the World
(Workbook Steps for Testing and Improving upon this Work)

Things being investigated, knowledge became complete. Their knowledge being complete, their thoughts were sincere. Their thoughts being sincere, their hearts were rectified. Their hearts being rectified, their persons were cultivated. Their persons being cultivated, their families were regulated. Their families being regulated, their States were rightly governed. Their States being rightly governed, the whole kingdom was made tranquil and happy.
—Confucius

1. **Honorably Test Whether Use of this Book Helps You to Better** *Understand* **What Is Truly Virtuous.**

How well you expedite and deepen your understanding of what is truly virtuous will determine how expeditiously and how deeply your character can be changed for the better. As step one of this Open Challenge, honestly find out for yourself whether use of this book actually helps you to better understand what is truly virtuous. Do this by **selecting** and **completing enough** of the following **actions** by the end of **each consecutive day** (and by inviting your good spouse, family or friend to help you as needed) until you ascertain you have honorably completed this test:

☐ Today I wrote questions and looked for answers as part of my thorough study of this entire book.

☐ Today I read through *The Human Virtues Dictionary* looking for definitions I might honestly feel are correct, or incorrect. If I found a definition that does not seem to pass the tests found in Chapter Five, entitled *Definitions as Statements of Truth*, then I marked or listed it for more complete personal testing using those tests. Otherwise, I accepted what I read as correct.

☐ Today I honorably tested at least one of the virtues defined in *The Human Virtues Dictionary* by choosing to plant and grow it within the thoughts of my mind and by choosing to nourish and keep it long and well enough within the thoughts of my heart to taste the kind of fruit it actually produces within me. I noted my feelings and impressions as I prayerfully pondered what I experienced today as I thought, spoke and acted in

harmony with it. I sincerely sought to understand whether I
truly need this characteristic to remain a part of what I do and
who I am.

☐ Today, if a definition seemed to be incorrect in my personal
testing results, I withheld my final judgment of it until I fully
considered each of the steps on definition improvement or
removal found in this chapter.

**2.   Honorably Test Whether Use of this Book Helps You to Better _Do, Be_
and _Teach_ What Is Truly Virtuous.**

Progress is the path to perfection. To be more virtuous today is
progress. Those virtues you want will become a part of what you do, who
you are, and what you can teach by example and precept as you ponder and
perform them one correct choice after another day by day. This can only
happen if you want them enough.

As step two of this Open Challenge, honestly find out for yourself
whether use of this book actually helps you to better do, be and teach other
people what is truly virtuous. Do this by **selecting** and **completing enough**
of the following **actions** by the end of **each consecutive day** (and by inviting
your good spouse, family or friend to help you as needed) until you
ascertain you have honorably completed this test:

☐ This morning I humbly and sincerely promised God in prayer
that I would do my very best to learn, build, preserve and
strengthen my needed virtues until they become what I do and
who I am within my heart. I then trusted Him to help me
identify and keep in mind those virtues I need to willfully and
faithfully learn, build, preserve and strengthen within me
today.

☐ Today I prayerfully selected or reviewed the virtues I feel God
wants me to work on from among those found in _The Human
Virtues Dictionary_ in this book.

☐ Today I spent enough focus on prayerfully reading, studying,
writing or otherwise learning something more about my
needed virtues from the most powerful true sources I can find
and verify for myself.

☐ Today I spent enough focus on writing my best ideas, setting
my best goals and calendaring my best plans to help me do my

very best to consistently learn, build, preserve and strengthen my needed virtues.

☐ Today I spent enough focus on confidently and enthusiastically visualizing my success in consistently learning, building, preserving and strengthening within me my needed virtues.

☐ Today I spent enough focus on measuring, reporting progress, rewarding achievements, or making adjustments to help myself and those I lead, serve or teach do our very best to consistently learn, build, preserve and strengthen needed virtues together.

☐ Today I noticed someone's unmet need to flourish, and I prayerfully discerned and charitably performed one or more of the virtues in this book to help them willfully and faithfully meet that need.

☐ Today I noticed the severe adversity or affliction someone is facing, and I prayerfully discerned and charitably performed one or more of the virtues in this book to help them willfully and faithfully overcome that adversity or affliction.

☐ Today I noticed someone's vicious weakness, and I prayerfully discerned and charitably performed one or more of the virtues in this book to help them willfully and faithfully replace that vicious weakness with virtuous strength.

☐ Today I noticed vicious influences are clouding and tempting someone's soul, and I prayerfully discerned and charitably performed one or more of the virtues in this book to help them willfully and faithfully rise above such clouds and temptations.

☐ Today I consistently used statements to praise the virtue shown by others, such as: "You were very *kind* to do that for them."

☐ Today I did my very best to live and teach in harmony with the best thoughts, beliefs, values and characteristics known to me, and I did my very best to seek and learn better ones.

☐ Today I did my very best to actively counter evil or satanic influence with virtuous words and with virtuous works.

☐ Today I did my very best to actively appoint, elect, recruit or select only the most enlightened, virtuous and wise government and other leaders, and to strengthen them.

☐ Today I kept my pledge to join with others, as necessary, to virtuously withstand evil or satanic attacks against our families and against society—however, whenever and wherever we must.

☐ Today I . . . (write another action that works best for you).

☐   This evening I humbly and sincerely thanked God in prayer for His wise and powerful help with my improvement today. I asked Him how well I did and what more I should do. Then I listened well enough within.

This book is not perfect in its present form. If you choose to improve upon this book in English or in your own language, accept the further challenges found in steps three through ten. Otherwise, accept the challenge of continuing to improve yourself, your family and society by using this book as it is.

---

3.   Correct *Glossary* Terms.

As step three of this Open Challenge, correct any and every *Glossary* term you feel you can improve upon, but make no changes in the five defined numerical values found in the *Glossary*, nor in their defined criteria. They must remain as part of this Open Challenge.

Write *in good conscience* what you believe is a better definition for a *Glossary* term. Leave it for a while. Ponder it when it comes to mind. Improve the definition as better wording comes to you and is proven by you. Continue this process until you can honestly say to yourself with complete integrity that your new definition has comfortably settled within both your thoughts and your feelings.

Repeat this process for each *Glossary* term you change. As you complete the remaining seven steps, make sure each of your new *Glossary* terms is comprehensible, compatible and integrated with all other *Glossary* terms and wherever it appears in your work.

4.   Provide a More Complete List of Human Characteristics.

As step four of this Open Challenge, decide which important missing characteristics belong in this book. If a missing characteristic is not already sufficiently represented by a definition from a synonym, then consider adding it in your work. If the missing characteristic is ordinarily labeled *informal* or *slang*, then it is likely covered well enough by characteristics already in this book. If not, then consider adding it in your work.

Add one or more definitions of each new characteristic to provide a clear and comprehensive understanding of *real human conditions* which are or should be represented by the characteristic's word symbol. Add the appropriate defined numerical value to each definition you add.

5. Improve the Definitions of Characteristics.

Enlightened certainty, reality and truth do not cease to exist and do not change when we attempt to hide them or to hide from them. Neither do confusion, error and falsehood. Distorting or removing definitions used to represent *real human conditions* does not extinguish those conditions. Such distortion or removal merely spreads confusion, error and falsehood about those conditions.

As step five of this Open Challenge, use the process described in step three to change definitions of characteristics to make each definition a more clear reflection of enlightened certainty, reality or truth. In doing so, use any reliable source or means you wish. Carefully keep in mind each of the following:

- One or more definitions of a listed characteristic may be added to provide a more clear or more comprehensive understanding of *real human conditions* which are or should be represented by the characteristic's word symbol. For example, if an important definition of *loving* is missing, then add the definition in your work.

- The condition described in the definition must be a *real human condition*. If you know with enlightened certainty that the described condition is not, never was and cannot be a *real human condition* within someone, then the definition may be improved or removed. Otherwise, it should remain.

- The definition of a real human characteristic cannot be a descriptive representation of an *imaginary human condition*. If you know with enlightened certainty that a definition of a characteristic represents an *imaginary human condition*, then that definition should be removed. Otherwise, it should remain.

- The definition may clearly represent a portion of enlightened certainty, reality or truth, even if you have not yet personally ascertained that it does. Unless you have personally ascertained that a definition of a characteristic cannot be such a definition, then neither the word symbol nor the definition associated or connected with it should be changed or removed.

- The definition, if labeled by someone or by some as *archaic* or *obsolete,* may still clearly represent a portion of enlightened certainty, reality or truth. Unless you know with enlightened certainty that a definition of a characteristic has never clearly represented any portion of enlightened certainty, reality or truth, then neither the word symbol nor the definition associated or connected with it should be changed or removed.

- If you have honorably proven to yourself that a particular definition meets the foregoing criteria for change or removal, then that definition should be changed to make it valid, or it should be removed. Every remaining definition should be regarded as valid until it also meets all of the above criteria for change or removal.

6.   More Accurately Assign Defined Numerical Values.

The line separating good and evil passes not through states, nor between political parties either – but right through every human heart. — Aleksandr Solzhenitsyn

As step six of this Open Challenge, use the criteria for the five defined numerical values found in the *Glossary* to decide which defined characteristics should have defined numerical values other than the positive two (2) assigned to them in *The Human Virtues Dictionary* in this book. Write down *in good conscience* what you believe is a better defined numerical value for a valid definition of that characteristic. Leave it for a while. Ponder it when it comes to mind. Repeat this process until you can honestly say to yourself with complete integrity that your new defined numerical value has comfortably settled within both your thoughts and your feelings. Repeat this process for each defined numerical value you change. Carefully keep in mind each of the following:

- If you know or have good enough reason to believe that you are deceiving yourself in the process, then the defined numerical value should not be changed.
- If you know or have good enough reason to believe that you are being deceived by someone's use of confusion, error or

falsehood in the process, then the defined numerical value should not be changed.

- Unless you and others can each personally ascertain that a definition given a positive two (2) in this book does not and cannot constantly and powerfully produce, preserve or restore true enlightenment, virtue, integrity, liberty, hope, peace and joy within us, our families and society, then that defined numerical value should not be changed.

7. **Make Opposing Definitions and Their Defined Numerical Values More Truly Symmetrical.**

As step seven of this Open Challenge, make opposite or opposing definitions and their defined numerical values more truly symmetrical. To complete this step you will likely need the author's book *The Language of Human Character*. In that book, opposing definitions of characteristics appear as antonyms to each other. Some may sit close or even next to each other, as with *senseless* and *sensible*.

If you have added, changed or removed a definition of a characteristic in the foregoing steps, then be sure to maintain symmetry of opposites by adding, changing or removing any corresponding opposite definitions of its antonyms, as needed. For example, any additions to, changes to or removal of definitions of *senseless* may require corresponding additions, changes or removal of opposing definitions of *sensible*, and vice versa.

If you change a defined numerical value of a characteristic, then be sure to maintain symmetry of opposites by changing the defined numerical values of all of its previously corresponding antonyms in your own new work or in the author's book *The Language of Human Character*, as needed. Be sure to also make necessary changes to the defined numerical values of all other characteristics (and their opposites) affected by the changes, such as those with definitions containing a characteristic with a newly assigned defined numerical value.

Opposing definitions may naturally appear in one or more symmetrical lists or patterns. Be sure to maintain symmetry of opposites in these lists or patterns as well. Here are three examples:

Example One: Opposites may closely mirror each other as two lists of opposing definitions, as illustrated in the author's book *The Language of Human Character* by the definitions of *sure* and *unsure*.

Example Two: Opposites may appear as two lists, with positive definitions leaving off on one list where negative definitions begin on the opposite list, and vice versa, as illustrated in the author's book *The Language of Human Character* by current definitions of *true* and *untrue*.

Example Three: Opposites may closely mirror each other as two lists of more complex opposing definitions, with each list having both positive and negative definitions, as illustrated by the definitions of *revolutionary* and *counterrevolutionary* in the author's book *The Language of Human Character*.

8.   Better Integrate the Entire Language of Human Character.

As step eight of this Open Challenge, better integrate the entire language of human character. To complete this step you will likely need the author's book *The Language of Human Character*. While completing the foregoing steps, make sure each definition for each defined characteristic is written in a manner which is accurately related to all other numbered definitions of its kind from A to Z in the English language (or from the first to the last letter of any alternative alphabet required for another language). In other words, complete each of the following five categories of requirements in your work:

☐   **2**   Make sure all of the positive two (2) definitions of characteristics represent *real human conditions* and match the criteria prescribed in the *Glossary* for positive two (2) definitions. Make sure none of the characteristics named *within* a positive two (2) definition has a *solely* negative (-1 or -2) defined numerical value that makes the definition negative. Make sure no *solely* positive two (2) characteristic appears out of character with its definition or with its defined numerical value anywhere in your work. (Here and below, the word *solely* means the characteristic has only one defined numerical value, and there is no definition of the characteristic which has any other defined numerical value.)

☐   **1**   Make sure all of the positive one (1) definitions of characteristics represent *real human conditions* and match the criteria prescribed in the *Glossary* for positive one (1) definitions. Make sure none of the characteristics named *within* a positive one (1) definition has a *solely* negative (-1 or -2) defined numerical value that makes the definition negative. Make sure no *solely* positive one (1) characteristic appears out of character with its definition or with its defined numerical value anywhere in your work.

☐   **0**   Make sure all of the zero (0) definitions of characteristics represent *real human conditions* and match the criteria prescribed in the *Glossary* for definitions given a zero (0). Make sure characteristics named *within* a zero (0) definition all have at least one definition with the defined numerical value of zero (0); or make sure they have definitions with categories of both positive and negative defined numerical values which indicate the equivalent of a zero (0) definition *space* between the two categories.

☐   **-1**   Make sure all of the negative one (-1) definitions of characteristics represent *real human conditions* and match the criteria prescribed in the *Glossary* for negative one (-1) definitions. Make sure none of the characteristics named *within* a negative one (-1) definition has a *solely* positive (1 or 2) defined numerical value that makes the definition positive. Make sure no *solely* negative one (-1) characteristic appears out of character with its definition or with its defined numerical value anywhere in your work.

☐   **-2**   Make sure all of the negative two (-2) definitions of characteristics represent *real human conditions* and match the criteria prescribed in the *Glossary* for negative two (-2) definitions. Make sure none of the characteristics named *within* a negative two (-2) definition has a *solely* positive (1 or 2) defined numerical value that makes the definition positive. Make sure no *solely* negative two (-2) characteristic appears out of character with its definition or with its defined numerical value anywhere in your work.

9. **Publish Your Better Work to the People of the Earth.**

As step nine of this Open Challenge, compile from your new version of the language of human character your new version of the language of human virtue and your new list of human virtues. Then publish your new work.

For you to fulfill or meet this part of the Open Challenge, all that you have changed according to the foregoing steps must allow or cause you, your family and society to experience **greater** true enlightenment, virtue, integrity, liberty, hope, peace and joy than we can by living in virtuous harmony with this book as it is.

For you to fulfill or meet this part of the Open Challenge, all that you have changed according to the foregoing steps must also allow or cause you, your family and society to experience **less** darkness, vice, corruption, bondage, despair, turmoil and misery within ourselves than we can by living in virtuous harmony with this book as it is. As necessary, provide better virtue building steps to help us know how to better achieve and verify this improvement for ourselves.

All copyrights are reserved for this book and all of its parts. Before you publish your manuscript(s) containing any part of this book, honorably obtain license or written permission from the owner of the copyrights to this book. You can, of course, author better definitions, parts and chapters which are your own.

10. **Use Your Better Work to Build a Better You, a Better Family and a Better Society.**

All who deeply care about creating a better society will be grateful you are doing so with your better work. Whether or not I am still alive upon the earth, I will be among them.

M. G. FAGER

Quotations Cited

How could so much true wisdom and virtue endure for so long and generate such unity in so many minds and hearts across the earth without the presence and power of divine nature, communion, devotion and potential within us? They could not. —The Author

Where the words "The Author" appear behind an *italicized* quotation in this book, they denote M. Gregg Fager, the author of this book. Other quotations are cited as follows:

vi.   *The Doctrine and Covenants of the Church of Jesus Christ of Latter-day Saints.* Salt Lake City, Utah: The Church of Jesus Christ of Latter-day Saints, 1981. Section 121:45. Print.

viii.   Dalton, Elaine S. "Cherish Virtue." *New Era.* March 2009. 16-17. Print. © By Intellectual Reserve, Inc. Used by permission.

xxiii.   *Teachings of the Presidents of the Church, David O. McKay.* Salt Lake City, Utah: The Church of Jesus Christ of Latter-day Saints, 2003. 16. Print. © By Intellectual Reserve, Inc. Used by permission.

Textbook

1.   *The Holy Bible, Authorized King James Version.* Salt Lake City, Utah: The Church of Jesus Christ of Latter-day Saints, 1983. New Testament: Matthew 7:16. Print.

2.   Paine, Thomas. *Inspiration and Wisdom from the Writings of Thomas Paine.* Ed. Joseph Lewis. New York: The Freethought Press Association, 1954. 1. Print.

3.   Webster, Daniel. "Daniel Webster Quotes, Quotations, and Sayings from his Speech in Faneuil Hall." *World of Quotes.* N.p., 2011. Web. 5 May 2012. <http://www.worldofquotes.com>.

3.   *The Holy Bible, Authorized King James Version.* Salt Lake City, Utah: The Church of Jesus Christ of Latter-day Saints, 1983. New Testament: Matthew 7:15; 23:27. Print.

3.   *The Holy Bible, Authorized King James Version.* Salt Lake City, Utah: The Church of Jesus Christ of Latter-day Saints, 1983. Old Testament: 1 Samuel 16:7; 1 Chronicles 29:17; Jeremiah 17:10. Print.

6.   *The Holy Bible, Authorized King James Version.* Salt Lake City, Utah: The Church of Jesus Christ of Latter-day Saints, 1983. New Testament: Matthew 7:16. Print.

9.   *The Holy Bible, Authorized King James Version.* Salt Lake City, Utah: The Church of Jesus Christ of Latter-day Saints, 1983. New Testament: 1 Corinthians 10:13. Print.

10.   *The Holy Bible, Authorized King James Version.* Salt Lake City, Utah: The Church of Jesus Christ of Latter-day Saints, 1983. New Testament: John 7:17. Print.

10.   *The Doctrine and Covenants of the Church of Jesus Christ of Latter-day Saints.* Salt Lake City, Utah: The Church of Jesus Christ of Latter-day Saints, 1981. Section 121:45. Print.

11.   Emerson, Ralph Waldo. "Ralph Waldo Emerson Character Quotes, Quotations, and Sayings." *World of Quotes.* N.p., 2011. Web. 5 May 2012. <http://www.worldofquotes.com>.

23.   Newton, Sir Isaac. *Familiar Quotations.* Ed. John Bartlett. Fifteenth edition. Boston: Little, Brown and Company, 1980. 313. Print.

27.   Stael, Madame Germaine de. *Days Collacon: an Encyclopedia of Prose Quotations . . . .* Ed. Edward Parsons Day. New York: Smith and McDougal, 1883. 121. Google eBooks. <http://books.google.com>.

31.   Confucius. *Confucian Analects, The Great Learning and The Doctrine of the Mean.* Tr. James Legge. New York: Dover Publications, Inc., 1971. 264. Print.

32.   Ghandi, Mohandas K. "Mohandas Karamchand Ghandi." *QuotesNSayings.net.* Web. 5 May 2012. <http://www.quotesnsayings.net/quotes/44381>.

89.   Confucius. *Confucian Analects, The Great Learning and The Doctrine of the Mean.* Tr. James Legge. New York: Dover Publications, Inc., 1971. 358-359. Print.

94.   Solzhenitsyn, Aleksandr. *The Gulag Archipelago, 1918 1956.* Part IV Chapter 1. Tr. Thomas P. Whitney. New York: Harper & Row, 1975. 615. Print.

THE HUMAN VIRTUES DICTIONARY
The Character Fruits of All Virtuous Thoughts, Beliefs and Values

Learn, prove, teach and preserve these definitions or better ones. To prayerfully understand, do, be and teach them is to verify them. To verify them is to know truth. To then live them is to be virtuous. —The Author

A

abiding - to intend to await, continue, endure, suffer or tolerate enough unavoidable opposition to prove I am and will remain faithful and steadfast in my devotion to God

abiding[2] - to be existing

able - to be enlightened or intelligent

able[2] - to be resourceful enough to minimize consumption, expense and waste

able-bodied - to be physically fit, healthy and strong in the good service of other people

able-bodied[2] - to be physically fit, healthy and strong enough to work

abolitionary - to be prone to favor doing away with any and every law or practice which produces, preserves or restores darkness, vice and corruption within me, my family and society

abolitionizing - to intend to convert lawmakers or voters to doing away with a law or practice that is harmful to society

aboriginal - to be prone to live in harmony with the ways of aboriginal character or culture which produce, preserve or restore true enlightenment, virtue and integrity within me, my family and society

abreast - to be and to choose to remain aware of the progress or need for progress in me, my family and society

absolute - to be exalted

absolute[2] - to be ascertaining

absolute[3] - to be discerning

absolutist - to be exalted

absolutist[2] - to be in possession of and to come to an absolute, perfect and spiritually verified personal knowledge of enlightened certainty, reality or truth by experiencing or observing within me the reception of powerfully clear, confirming and distinct personal enlightenment, inspiration or revelation from God of those things of an eternal nature which ultimately exist and will always exist outside of my thoughts without adulteration, alteration, change, dilution, exception, imperfection, qualification or restriction

absolutist[3] - to be in possession of and to come to an absolute, perfect and spiritually verified personal knowledge of enlightened certainty, reality or truth by experiencing or observing within me the reception of powerfully clear, confirming and distinct personal enlightenment, inspiration or revelation from God by my believing and honorably exact obedience to that divinely appointed law upon which receipt of that knowledge is predicated

absolutist[4] - to be prone to continuously and wholeheartedly strive to be perfectly clean, pure and integrated-at-heart

absolutist[5] - to be prone to continuously and wholeheartedly strive to completely and exclusively conform to that which is truly good and of God, regardless of circumstance, time or place

absolutist[6] - to be prone to honestly seek to judge righteous judgment regardless of circumstance, time or place

absolutist[7] - to be prone to think, speak and act in harmony with the true constitution and merit of what I know existed or of what I know exists

absolved - to be redeemed unto exaltation

absolved[2] - to be redeemed and released from the bondage, burdens and debts of my sins

absolved[3] - to be and to be found truly innocent

absolving - to be a duly ordained man called of God who righteously uses true higher priesthood authority, power and revelation from God, without pay, to truly declare that another person has received divine forgiveness and remission of punishment for their own sins through the charitable love, cleansing power and redeeming grace of the Atonement of the Lord Jesus Christ unto exaltation by their faithfully repentant and honorably exact obedience to those divinely appointed commandments, covenants, laws and ordinances upon which receipt of that forgiveness and remission is predicated

abstemious - to be prone to completely abstain from drinking harmful and impairing alcoholic beverages

abstemious[2] - to be virtuously sparing or temperate in personal consumption, pleasure or use of any kind

abstinent - to be prone to forbear or refrain from entertaining any thought of corruptly pleasing or sinfully satisfying a biologically inherent and naturally impelling emotional, physical or sexual appetite, craving, desire, drive or passion

abstinent[2] - to be prone to forbear or refrain from excessively pleasing or satisfying a biologically inherent and naturally impelling emotional, physical or sexual appetite, craving, desire, drive or passion

acceptable - to be godly enough to be made truly chaste, clean, pure and virtuous at heart—and to continue to encourage and help other people by charitable love, kindness, invitation and instruction to be godly enough to be made truly chaste, clean, pure and virtuous at heart

acceptable[2] - to be filled with enough true enlightenment, virtue and integrity to produce, preserve or restore true liberty, hope, peace and joy within me, my family and society

acceptable[3] - to be filled with enough true enlightenment, virtue and integrity to strongly attract or appeal to another person of true enlightenment, virtue and integrity

acceptable[4] - to be prone to win the acceptance of other people by doing and being good

accepted - to be exalted

accomplished - to be prone to wisely make actual or real the best that lies within me

accomplished[2] - to be one of those who are most noble in achievements

accomplished[3] - to be gracious, polite and well-mannered

accountable - to be prone to personally ascertain and live in harmony with the discernibly enlightening and spiritually verifiable truth that: when I have advanced to the mental and physical age of eight I am required by God under the eternally binding law of justice to one day answer and be judged under that law for how well my desires and works prove I have personally chosen to live in perfect harmony with the best and highest laws, rules, standards or values of true enlightenment, virtue and integrity of which I have become aware in my education and training and in

my own constantly diligent, honest and open-minded searching

accountable[2] - to be prone to honorably and justly heed a needed warning to repent of all of the corrupt, sinful or vicious wrongdoing within me—by responding with my faithful, timely and true repentance, obedience and reconciliation to God

accountable[3] - to be prone to honorably and justly answer for, explain or report what I have done wrong or what I have failed to do right when good conscience, justice, truth and virtue require me to do so

accountable[4] - to be prone to readily and willingly subject myself to someone's efforts to honorably and justly place blame, fault or guilt against me

accountable[5] - to be aware I have advanced beyond the mental and physical age of adulthood and am thus required by my government under the good law of the land to answer and be judged under that law for the extent to which my words and actions do not comply with that law

accountable[6] - to be prone to account for, answer for, explain or report what I have said or done or what I have failed to say or do when required to do so by the good law of the land

accountable[7] - to be prepared to think, speak and act in harmony with the rights and responsibilities of a citizen under the good law of the land

acculturating - to intend to coalesce or merge into a goodly and predominant cultural society to an extent and in a manner which will allow me to best receive of and best contribute to the virtuously liberating freedom, health, honorable economic prosperity and steady progress of me, my family and society

acculturating[2] - to intend to coalesce or merge into a goodly and predominant cultural society to an extent and in a manner which will allow me to contribute to the removal of divisive linguistic and other barriers to better collaboration, more efficient use of resources and better opportunity in commercial, educational and other public endeavors among all who have chosen to live together within the good laws of that society

acculturizing - to intend to require people of diverse cultural heritage to coalesce or merge into a goodly and predominant cultural society to an extent and in a manner which will allow them to best receive of and best contribute to the virtuously liberating freedom, health, honorable economic prosperity and steady progress of themselves, their families and society

acculturizing[2] - to intend to coalesce or merge into a goodly and predominant cultural society to an extent and in a manner which will allow me to contribute to the removal of divisive linguistic and other barriers to better collaboration, more efficient use of resources and better opportunity in commercial, educational and other public endeavors among all who

have chosen to live together within the good laws of that society

accurate - to be ascertaining

accurate[2] - to be discerning

achieving - to intend to accomplish or produce the very best results I possibly can

acing - to intend to perform in a first-rate manner

acknowledging - to intend to truly confess I have received a sure knowledge of the truth about God's handiwork by personal enlightenment, inspiration or revelation from Him

acknowledging[2] - to intend to necessarily and truly testify I have received a sure knowledge of the characteristic and distinctive differences between that which is truly good and of God and that which is evil or satanic

acknowledging[3] - to intend to necessarily and truly testify I have received a sure knowledge of the characteristic and distinctive differences between that which is enlightened certainty, reality or truth and that which is confusion, error or falsehood

acknowledging[4] - to intend to necessarily and truly testify I have received a sure knowledge of the characteristic and distinctive differences between that which is real and that which is imaginary

acknowledging[5] - to intend, as required in the sight of God, to truly confess to God and to His chosen servants the corrupt, sinful or vicious wrongdoing within me as part of my faithful, timely and true repentance, obedience and reconciliation to God acknowledging[6] - to intend, as required in the sight of God, to truly confess to God, to His chosen servants, and to my victims the corrupt, sinful or vicious wrongdoing I have committed—as part of my faithful, timely and true repentance, obedience and reconciliation to God

acquitted - to be redeemed unto exaltation

acquitted[2] - to be redeemed and released from the bondage, burdens and debts of my sins

acquitted[3] - to be and to be found truly innocent

acquitting - to intend to satisfy or settle my honorable debt, duty or obligation

acting - to intend to do, move or work to express or fulfill my chosen designs, desires, dispositions, intentions or plans to produce, preserve or restore true enlightenment, virtue and integrity within me, my family and society

active - to be prone to use my own effort, labor or power to achieve a better purpose, to cause a better change or to exert a better influence for good

acute - to be deeply aware and truly discerning in intellect, insight or perception

adducing - to intend to bring or introduce truth into true analysis

adequate - to be godly enough to be made truly chaste, clean, pure and virtuous at heart—and to continue to encourage and help other people by charitable love, kindness, invitation and instruction to be godly enough to be made truly chaste, clean, pure and virtuous at heart

adequate[2] - to be filled with enough true enlightenment, virtue and integrity to produce, preserve or restore true liberty, hope, peace and joy within me, my family and society

adequate[3] - to be filled with enough true enlightenment, virtue and integrity to strongly attract or appeal to another person's sense of true enlightenment, virtue and integrity

adjusted - to be conformed to an honorable and virtuous law, rule, standard or value

admirable - to be godly enough to be made truly chaste, clean, pure and virtuous at heart—and to continue to encourage and help other people by charitable love, kindness, invitation and instruction to be godly enough to be made truly chaste, clean, pure and virtuous at heart

admirable[2] - to be filled with enough true enlightenment, virtue and integrity to produce, preserve or restore true liberty, hope, peace and joy within me, my family and society

admirable[3] - to be filled with enough true enlightenment, virtue and integrity to strongly attract or appeal to another person's sense of true enlightenment, virtue and integrity

admirable[4] - to be prone to win the admiration of other people by doing and being good

admonishing - to intend, when necessary, to urgently encourage, exhort or remind someone to do their good and honorable duty or obligation admonishing[2] - to intend, when necessary, to earnestly caution, remind or warn someone against wrongful neglect of their honorable duty or obligation

adorable - to be truly worthy of divine admiration or honor

adorable[2] - to be truly worthy of the utmost love and respect

adroit - to be expertly correct, resourceful and skillful in bringing about that which is charitably loving, just, right and wise in the sight of God

adult - to be aware I have advanced beyond the mental and physical age at which my government requires me under the good law of the land pertaining to adults to answer and be judged under that law for the extent to which my words and actions do not comply with that law, and to then live above that standard

adult[2] - to be prepared to think, speak and act in harmony with the rights and responsibilities of a citizen under the good law of the land

advanced - to be one of the truly better or truly best

advancing - to intend to continue to progress by continuing to improve the enlightenment and virtue of the thoughts I continue to integrate into the thoughts, beliefs, values and characteristics of my heart

advantaged - to be prone to maintain enough means to live

advantaged[2] - to be of better character than one or more other people

advantaged[3] - to be of greater intelligence than one or more other people

adventuring - to intend to take reasonably anticipated risks and to boldly confront unforeseen hazards to produce, preserve or restore true enlightenment, virtue and integrity within me, my family and society

advertent - to be wisely attentive or heedful

advising - to intend to recommend to another person that which is truly good and of God

advising[2] - to intend to lovingly caution or warn another person against that which is evil or satanic

aesthetic - to be prone to possess and cultivate a sensitive awareness and grateful love of uplifting beauty

affected - to be prone to think, speak and act in harmony with a virtue though I have it not, until I can prove in the fire of adversity that it is mine and until I am thus liberated within my mind and heart from opposing vices

affectionate - to be prone to prove my truly charitable love for another person with good words and deeds in their behalf

affiliated - to be of strong unity of mind and heart with one or more other people of true enlightenment, virtue and integrity

affiliating - to intend to be strongly united in mind and heart with one or more other people of true enlightenment, virtue and integrity

affording - to intend to manage and spend wisely in order to avoid serious consequences

afraid - to be apprehensive or uneasy enough about the

impending dreadful consequences of my sinful desires and works as to seek redemption or salvation from the otherwise inescapable demands of the eternally binding law of justice

afraid[2] - to be filled with enough reverential awe or respect toward God, His laws and His righteous judgments to seek and to maintain faithful, timely and true repentance, obedience and reconciliation to Him and to His laws and ordinances

afraid[3] - to be apprehensive or uneasy enough to do all I must do to avoid the naturally consequent penalties or punishments of breaking or changing the commandments, covenants, laws or ordinances of God

afraid[4] - to be apprehensive or uneasy enough to apprehend the true danger, risk or threat of the negative consequences of such things as accident, breach, crime, disobedience, dissent, failure, guilt, liability, opposition, rebellion, violation or violence

afraid[5] - to be apprehensive or uneasy enough to apprehend the true danger, risk or threat of death, destruction, harm, illness, injury, loss, pain, penalty, punishment or suffering

African - to be prone to live in harmony with the ways of African character or culture which produce, preserve or restore true enlightenment, virtue and integrity within me, my family and society

aged - to be diligent, experienced and faithful enough to be virtuously refined

aging - to be diligent, experienced and faithful enough to continue to become more virtuously refined

agitated - to be disturbed or troubled enough by all of the corrupt, sinful or vicious wrongdoing within me to faithfully and immediately seek true and complete repentance, obedience and reconciliation to God

aglow - to be prone to radiate enlightenment, virtue and integrity

aglow[2] - to be prone to radiate elated feelings of good health

agreeable - to be godly enough to be made truly chaste, clean, pure and virtuous at heart—and to continue to encourage and help other people by charitable love, kindness, invitation and instruction to be godly enough to be made truly chaste, clean, pure and virtuous at heart

agreeable[2] - to be filled with enough true enlightenment, virtue and integrity to produce, preserve or restore true liberty, hope, peace and joy within me, my family and society

agreeable[3] - to be filled with enough true enlightenment, virtue and integrity to strongly attract or appeal to another person's sense of true enlightenment, virtue and integrity

agreeable[4] - to be prone to win the agreement of other people by doing and being good

aiming - to intend to think, speak and act in harmony with an aspiration, commitment, desire, goal, intention, plan, purpose or resolution which is truly good and of God

airy - to be virtuously cheerful within my heart

airy^2 - to be vivacious in appearance, manner or movement

alarming - to intend to rouse someone to vigilance against the evil or satanic powers of darkness, vice, corruption, bondage, despair, turmoil and misery

alert - to be awake and watchful enough to quickly respond with intelligent understanding

alive - to be existent in true joy

alive^2 - to be healthy

allied - to be joined together in a good cause with people whose designs, desires, dispositions, intentions, plans, purposes, words, actions, deeds and works are truly good and of God

all-knowing - to be omniscient

all-knowing^2 - to intend to honorably strive to receive enough knowledge to identify, forsake and withstand all that is evil or satanic within me, my family and society

all-powerful - to be omnipotent

all-powerful^2 - to be prone to honorably strive to receive enough of God's power to identify, forsake and withstand all that is evil or satanic within me, my family and society

all right - to be reliably good

all right^2 - to be healthy

all-star - to be prone to do all I can and should to help other people improve their virtuously liberating freedom, health, honorable economic prosperity and steady progress

all-star^2 - to be prone to perform good works which send a good, praiseworthy and virtuous message to other people

alluring - to be filled with enough true enlightenment, virtue and integrity to produce, preserve or restore true liberty, hope, peace and joy within me, my family and society

alluring^2 - to be filled with enough true enlightenment, virtue and integrity to strongly attract or appeal to another person's sense of true enlightenment, virtue and integrity

all-wise - to be prone to personally ascertain and live in harmony with the discernibly enlightening and spiritually verifiable truth that: God the Eternal Father has all wisdom, and desires that His children, heirs, offspring, posterity or seed do all we must do to become perfectly like Him in this characteristic

allying - to intend to formally associate, bind together or unite with one or more other people of true enlightenment, virtue and integrity by mutual agreement, consent or treaty

almsgiving - to intend to offer the needy and poor aid, assistance, concession, forbearance, forgiveness, leniency or tolerance to an extent and in a manner which is charitably loving, just, right and wise in the sight of God

almsgiving^2 - to intend to actively, charitably, generously and wisely provide for the needy and poor to an extent or in a manner which saves their lives, meets their immediate needs for survival, fosters their adequate education, employment, labors, self-reliance and thrift, and which encourages their service to other people

almsgiving[3] - to intend to actively, charitably, generously and wisely give of my substance or other resources to the needy and poor to help them deal with personal needs which they cannot take care of alone—provided they are continuing to demonstrate by their own determined education, training, labors, investments and savings, that they are responsibly striving to become self-reliant net contributors to the virtuously liberating freedom, health, honorable economic prosperity and steady progress of themselves, their families and society

alogical - to be prone to clearly and correctly learn real consequences or true conclusions by means other than logical reasoning

altruistic - to be honestly and unselfishly devoted to helping other people improve their virtuously liberating freedom, health, honorable economic prosperity and steady progress

altruistic[2] - to be prone to lovingly encourage and kindly help someone to be truistic

amazing - to be astonishingly or wonderfully virtuous

ambitious - to be prone to maintain the earnest and loving desire to bring glory, honor and praise to God by wholeheartedly seeking exaltation all the days of my life

ambitious[2] - to be prone to maintain the earnest and loving desire for true personal betterment, improvement or progress within me, my family and society

ambitious[3] - to be prone to eagerly do enough to achieve or receive results which are good, honorable,

praiseworthy or virtuous in the sight of God

ambitious[4] - to be prone to eagerly seek enough authority, influence or power among humankind to do as much good among them and for them as I can

ambitious[5] - to be prone to eagerly desire challenging activity or work which will allow me to personally progress

ameliorating - to intend to improve or make better

ameliorative - to be prone to ameliorating

amending - to intend to correct my defects to improve who I am at heart and who I can become

American - to be prone to live in harmony with the ways of American character or culture which produce, preserve or restore true enlightenment, virtue and integrity within me, my family and society

amiable - to be good-natured

amorous - to be charitably loving

amplifying - to intend to help someone increase their desires and efforts to become better

amusing - to intend to detain or engage someone's attention in enough healthy diversion or recreation to help them sustain their virtuously liberating freedom, health, honorable economic prosperity and steady progress

analyzing - to intend to truly discern the true nature and relationship of component parts or principles in real things

anchored - to be firmly fastened or fixed to a good, secure and solid base, foundation or position

anchoring - to intend to maintain, support or sustain someone by working to help them fasten or fix themselves to a secure and solid base, foundation or position of true enlightenment, virtue, integrity, liberty, hope, peace and joy

ancient - to be aged and venerable

angelic - to be as filled with true enlightenment, virtue and integrity as the angels of heaven

angelic[2] - to be prone to deliver a duly authorized, heaven-sent message to another person

angelic[3] - to be prone to deliver much-needed aid, protection or support to another person to the fullest extent I can and should, and whenever I am prompted to do so by the Spirit of God

angelic[4] - to be prone to think, speak and act in harmony with that which is truly good and of God

anguished - to be prone to courageously continue to faithfully prove my believing and honorably exact obedience to God in the face of necessary or unavoidable distress or pain

anguished[2] - to be filled with enough distress or pain from all of the corrupt, sinful or vicious wrongdoing within me to faithfully and immediately seek true and complete repentance, obedience and reconciliation to God

anhedonic - to be prone to refuse to digress, fall or sink into the evil or satanic arousal, entertainment or satisfaction of hedonistic pleasure

animate - to be animated

animated - to be filled with true enlightenment, virtue, integrity, liberty, hope, peace and joy

animated[2] - to be healthy and full of life

animating - to intend to lovingly encourage and kindly help someone to be animated

animist - to be prone to personally ascertain and live in harmony with the discernibly enlightening and spiritually verifiable truth that: I am a living soul consisting of both a physical body of earthly physical matter and an immortal spirit being or personage of enlivened spirit matter which shall separate at my physical death and shall eventually be inseparably rejoined and perfectly restored by the power of God during my one-time and everlasting resurrection from the dead

animist[2] - to be prone to personally ascertain and live in harmony with the discernibly enlightening and spiritually verifiable truth that: only enlivened spirit matter divinely formed into a living spirit being and embodied in harmony with divine law within a body of earthly physical matter can bring that earthly physical matter to life on Earth

anointed - to be a baptized, confirmed and otherwise qualified adult who voluntarily enters into the initiatory ordinance of anointing administered in a dedicated holy temple of God by one who truly holds the necessary authority and the authorization from God's own called, ordained and authorized priesthood leaders on Earth to officiate in that initiatory ordinance in that revealed manner and mode of symbolic anointing which is valid

in the sight of God—so that I can
then receive the powerful blessings
of that ordinance in harmony with
my faithfulness, and can be further
prepared on Earth to receive the
blessings of a glorious celestial
resurrection and exaltation in the
world to come
anointing - to intend, as one who
truly holds the necessary authority
to officiate and the authorization to
do so from God's own called,
ordained and authorized
priesthood leaders on Earth, to
administer, without pay, to a
baptized, confirmed and otherwise
qualified living adult in a
dedicated holy temple of God the
initiatory ordinance of anointing in
that revealed manner and mode of
symbolic anointing recognized by
Him as valid, so that they can then
receive the powerful blessings of
that ordinance in harmony with
their faithfulness, and can be
further prepared on Earth to
receive the blessings of a glorious
celestial resurrection and exaltation
in the world to come
anointing^2 - to intend, as one who
truly holds the necessary authority
to officiate and the authorization to
do so from God's own called,
ordained and authorized
priesthood leaders on Earth, to
administer, without pay, in a
dedicated holy temple of God the
initiatory ordinance of anointing
upon righteous living proxy who
act in behalf of deceased family
members and other deceased
persons who are accountable to the
laws of God and whose
preliminary temple work has been
done—so that those deceased

persons who are desirous and
righteous enough to receive the
ordinance work done for them can
then receive the powerful blessings
of that ordinance in harmony with
their faithfulness, and can be
further prepared by loving family
or other living proxy on Earth to
receive the blessings of a glorious
celestial resurrection and exaltation
in the world to come
anonymous - to be and to choose
to remain unidentified, unnamed
or unknown as a contributor or
donor of something good
answerable - to be prone to
honorably and justly heed a
needed warning to repent of all of
the corrupt, sinful or vicious
wrongdoing within me—by
responding with my faithful,
timely and true repentance,
obedience and reconciliation to
God
answerable^2 - to be prone to
honorably and justly answer for,
explain or report what I have done
wrong or what I have failed to do
right when good conscience,
justice, truth and virtue require me
to do so
answerable^3 - to be prone to readily
and willingly subject myself to
someone's efforts to honorably and
justly place blame, fault or guilt
against me
answerable^4 - to be prone to
account for, answer for, explain or
report what I have done wrong or
what I have failed to do right when
required to do so by the good law
of the land
answering - to intend to honestly
and willingly suffer the lawfully
and legally affixed penalties of my

choices and decisions as part of my faithful, timely and true repentance
answering² - to be prepared to honestly account for the choices and decisions for which I am responsible
anticipating - to be foreseeing
anticlerical - to be prone to ban or oppose the participation of clerics, clergy or other members of religious organizations from public or secular affairs when their religious disposition, influence and works produce, preserve or restore darkness, vice and corruption within me, my family and society
antidisestablishmentarian - to be prone to favor the continuing use of my government's tax-exempting authority to help minimize the burden of non-fixed or variable costs incurred by registered religious organizations within my country in performing good works which have proven to be beneficial to society
antidisestablishmentarian² - to be prone to oppose the withdrawal of my government's constitutional or legal recognition of a good and law-abiding religious organization established within my country
antievil - to be good
antipolluting - to intend to think, speak and act to an extent or in a manner which empowers me to avoid darkness, vice, corruption, bondage, despair, turmoil and misery
antipolluting² - to intend to refuse to contaminate or taint me, my family and society with harmful impurities
antipolluting³ - to intend to avoid contaminating or tainting the

environment with harmful impurities
antipollution - to be prone to antipolluting
antipornographic - to be prone to refuse to give in, give up or give way to the evil or satanic powers which tempt me to entertain or act out graphically unchaste and viciously sexual abomination, obscenity, perversion, pollution, uncleanness or whoredom
antipornographic² - to be prone to refuse to expose the thoughts of my own mind to something pornographic or sexually graphic which has or which may have enough evil or satanic power to induce or influence me to willfully reject my good conscience, or to defile the active and stored thoughts of my mind with darkness, vice and corruption, or to drive true enlightenment, virtue and integrity out of my mind and heart, or to infect me with evil or satanic desires to lustfully fulfill or sinfully satisfy one or more of my biologically inherent and naturally impelling emotional, physical or sexual appetites, cravings, desires, drives or passions, or to otherwise cause the Spirit of God to withdraw from me
antipornographic³ - to be prone to refuse to continue to act for, pose for, produce, publish, sponsor, officially permit or legalize something pornographic or sexually graphic which produces, preserves or restores an abusive, addictive, corruptive, vicious or satanic impact or impression in an exposed or targeted mind, family or society

antiracist - to be prone to refuse to be racist
antireligious - to be prone to refuse to be religiously asatanic or atheistic
antireligious^2 - to be prone to reject and withstand the influence of any and every religion which truly produces, preserves or restores darkness, vice and corruption within me, my family and society
antisecular - to be prone to virtuously do all I can and should to censure, counteract, stop or withstand worldly practices which produce, preserve or restore darkness, vice and corruption within me, my family and society
antisecularizing - to intend to virtuously do all I can and should to censure, counteract, stop or withstand worldly practices which produce, preserve or restore darkness, vice and corruption within me, my family and society
antisocial - to be prone to fail or refuse to be worldly
antisocial^2 - to be prone to fail or refuse to associate or work with one or more other people to an extent or in a manner which produces, preserves or restores darkness, vice and corruption within me, my family and society
antisocial^3 - to be prone to refuse to associate with one or more other people for the purpose of showing I am or can remain as faddish, fashionable, stylish or trendy as they are
anxious - to be prone to courageously continue to faithfully prove my believing and honorably exact obedience to God in the face of necessary or unavoidable

apprehension, distress, trouble or uneasiness
anxious^2 - to be apprehensive, distressed, troubled or uneasy enough about all of the corrupt, sinful or vicious wrongdoing within me to faithfully and immediately seek true and complete repentance, obedience and reconciliation to God
apocalyptic - to be prone, by divine authority, commandment and revelation from God, to truly prophesy or reveal the truth about things to come
apocalyptic^2 - to be prone, by divine authority, commandment and revelation from God, to truly prophesy or testify of the imminent or final misery, suffering, torment or woe to be poured out upon those who choose to remain sinful, unrepentant and, hence, unsanctified and unworthy of redemption unto exaltation
apocalyptic^3 - to be prone to personally ascertain and live in harmony with the discernibly enlightening and spiritually verifiable prophecy or testimony given by God's ancient and modern prophets that: misery, suffering, torment and woe await those who choose to remain sinful, unrepentant and, hence, unsanctified and unworthy of redemption unto exaltation
apocalyptic^4 - to be prone to personally ascertain and live in harmony with the discernibly enlightening and spiritually verifiable prophecy or testimony given by God's ancient and modern prophets that: the earth will meet a catastrophic fiery

destruction before it is renewed and receives its paradisiacal glory

apodeictic - to be apodictic

apodictic - to be prone to think, speak and act in harmony with what is absolutely or demonstrably certain or true

apologizing - to intend, when called upon by the Spirit and power of God to do so, to contritely express sincere remorse or sorrow to those who erroneously but sincerely believe I have somehow victimized them

apologizing[2] - to intend to honestly acknowledge or confess to my victims the harm or injury which I have viciously imposed upon them, and to contritely express my sincere remorse or sorrow to them for it

apostate - to be prone to abandon, break away, defect, depart, desert, disown, forsake, leave or withdraw from a truly erroneous or vicious belief, covenant, doctrine, faith, law, priesthood, principle, religion, rule, standard or value, and from any organization which upholds it

apostolic - to be a duly ordained man called of God by prophesy to righteously bear that true higher priesthood authority and power, given by the laying on of hands of the Lord Jesus Christ or His duly authorized representative, to act in the higher priesthood office of Apostle or special witness of His name and, in virtuous oneness with other such apostles, to lead His church and kingdom under His ongoing direction

apostolic[2] - to be prone, until my death, to ascertain and live in harmony with the discernibly enlightening and spiritually verifiable laws, ordinances, prophecies, revelations and teachings of God given by those who have truly received the divine calling, the necessary ordination and the true higher priesthood authority and power of the Lord Jesus Christ to act in the higher priesthood office of Apostle or special witness of His name and are worthy to lead His church and kingdom under His ongoing direction

apostolic[3] - to be prone to live in harmony with the teachings of apostles which produce, preserve or restore true enlightenment, virtue and integrity within me, my family and society

appealing - to be filled with enough true enlightenment, virtue and integrity to produce, preserve or restore true liberty, hope, peace and joy within me, my family and society

appealing[2] - to be filled with enough true enlightenment, virtue and integrity to strongly attract or appeal to another person's sense of true enlightenment, virtue and integrity

appealing[3] - to intend to ask higher authority for a just and virtuous result

appeased - to be peaceable or peaceful

appeasing - to intend to bring someone to a peaceable or peaceful state

apperceiving - to be able to consciously perceive something and to comprehend or understand the truth about it due to previous experience and knowledge

apperceptive - to be prone to apperceiving

applaudable - to be prone to do enough good to deserve appreciation, approval, commendation or praise

applauding - to intend to honorably express well-deserved appreciation, approval, commendation or praise

appraising - to intend to honestly seek to accurately estimate or judge condition, quality, significance, value or worth

appreciated - to be actively and truly progressing

appreciating - to intend to improve, increase, progress or rise in true enlightenment, virtue and integrity

appreciating^2 - to intend to clearly detect and recognize good value or high quality by sensitively expressing well-deserved admiration, approval or gratitude

apprehending - to be discerning and perceptive enough to quickly grasp or understand enlightened certainty, reality or truth

apprehending^2 - to intend to attach true meaning or understanding to what I perceive

apprehending^3 - to intend to capably contemplate or ponder believable evidence in search of certainty

approachable - to be prone to make it as easy as possible for other people to meet, deal with and know me

appropriate - to be prone to think, speak and act in harmony with that which is charitably loving, just, right and wise in the sight of God

appropriate^2 - to be prone to think, speak and act in harmony with the good law of the land

approvable - to be godly enough to be made truly chaste, clean, pure and virtuous at heart—and to continue to encourage and help other people by charitable love, kindness, invitation and instruction to be godly enough to be made truly chaste, clean, pure and virtuous at heart

approvable^2 - to be filled with enough true enlightenment, virtue and integrity to produce, preserve or restore true liberty, hope, peace and joy within me, my family and society

approvable^3 - to be filled with enough true enlightenment, virtue and integrity to strongly attract or appeal to another person's sense of true enlightenment, virtue and integrity

approvable^4 - to be prone to win the approval of other people by doing and being good

approved - to be exalted

apt - to be of keen intellect

Arabian - to be prone to live in harmony with the ways of Arabian character or culture which produce, preserve or restore true enlightenment, virtue and integrity within me, my family and society

aristocratic - to be one of those who are superior and exemplary in true enlightenment, virtue and integrity

aristocratic^2 - to be one of those who are most honorable for true intelligence and wisdom

aristocratic^3 - to be one of those who are most noble in achievement

armed - to be worthy to constantly receive within me the constant companionship of the gloriously and powerfully comforting, cleansing, empowering, enlightening, gifting, instructing, justifying, protecting, purifying, refining, revelatory and sanctifying influence or divine presence of the Holy Ghost by my faithfully repentant and honorably exact obedience to those divinely appointed commandments, covenants, laws and ordinances upon which receipt of that divine gift is predicated

armed^2 - to be in possession of enough personal and heavenly power, means and resources with which to produce, preserve or restore that which is charitably loving, just, right and wise in the sight of God

armed^3 - to be in possession of enough personal and heavenly power, means and resources with which to produce, preserve or restore true enlightenment, virtue and integrity within me, my family and society

armed^4 - to be in possession of enough personal and heavenly power, means and resources with which to produce, preserve or restore virtuously liberating freedom, health, honorable economic prosperity and steady progress within me, my family and society

armed^5 - to be in possession of enough personal and heavenly power, means and resources with which to defeat or withstand an attacking, known or wisely suspected criminal, deadly or evil enemy of society

arm's-length - to be prone to keep a healthy distance from people, places and situations which might otherwise induce or influence me to jeopardize my chastity or my virtue

artistic - to be prone to cultivate a sensitive appreciation for good and uplifting art

artistic^2 - to be prone to create, perform or produce good and uplifting works of art

ascending - to intend to continue to progress by continuing to improve the enlightenment and virtue of the thoughts I continue to integrate into the thoughts, beliefs, values and characteristics of my heart

ascertaining - to be in possession of and to be aware I have come to an absolute, perfect and spiritually verified personal knowledge of enlightened certainty, reality or truth by experiencing or observing within me the reception of powerfully clear, confirming and distinct personal enlightenment, inspiration or revelation from God by my believing and honorably exact obedience to that divinely appointed law upon which receipt of that knowledge is predicated

ascertaining^2 - to intend to come to a clearly distinct and sure knowledge of reality or truth

asexual - to be prone to refuse to be ambisexual, androgynous, bisexual, homosexual, transsexual or otherwise sexually dysfunctional

asexual^2 - to be prone to develop close personal relationships which strictly exclude sexual relations outside of honorable familial and legal wedlock with my husband or wife

ashamed - to be filled with enough love of God and enough painful remorse for my falling into darkness, vice, corruption, sin and wrongdoing before Him to immediately and truly repent

ashamed[2] - to be prone to feel enough painful remorse for my loss of true enlightenment, virtue and integrity, and enough true remorse or godly sorrow for my falling into darkness, vice and corruption, to immediately and truly repent

ashamed[3] - to be prone to do all I can and should to restore my own and my family's good name, honor and reputation by feeling enough humble regret or true remorse for having done something disgraceful, dishonorable, vile or wicked to confess my wrongdoing, face justice, make full restitution and completely repent

ashamed[4] - to be prone to feel enough disappointment, embarrassment, humiliation or reproach for personal deficiencies, failures, inadequacies or weaknesses to prayerfully seek enough heavenly power to overcome them

ashamed[5] - to be prone to feel disappointment, embarrassment, humiliation or reproach for personal deficiencies, failures, inadequacies or weaknesses I have refused to overcome

Asian - to be prone to live in harmony with the ways of Asian character or culture which produce, preserve or restore true enlightenment, virtue and integrity within me, my family and society

aspiring - to intend to maintain the earnest and loving desire to bring glory, honor and praise to God by wholeheartedly striving for exaltation all the days of my life

aspiring[2] - to intend to maintain the earnest and loving desire for the greatest betterment, improvement or progress within me, my family and society

aspiring[3] - to intend to maintain the earnest and loving desire to do enough to achieve or receive results which are good, honorable, praiseworthy or virtuous in the sight of God

assaying - to intend to prove truth and virtue by analysis, examination or experiment

asserting - to intend to confidently and consistently think, speak and act in harmony with that measure of absolute, perfect and spiritually verified personal knowledge of the truth which I have received by personal enlightenment, inspiration or revelation from God

assimilating - to intend to seek the full affiliation, compatibility, cooperation, fellowship, integration, privileges, rights, trust and unity of all law-abiding and responsible individuals, social classes and groups who strive to produce, preserve or restore true enlightenment, virtue, integrity, liberty, hope, peace and joy within ourselves, our families and society

assimilating[2] - to intend to coalesce or merge into a goodly and predominant cultural society to an extent and in a manner which will allow me to best receive of and best contribute to the virtuously liberating freedom, health, honorable economic prosperity and steady progress of me, my family and society

assimilating[3] - to intend to coalesce or merge into a goodly and predominant cultural society to an extent and in a manner which will allow me to contribute to the removal of divisive linguistic and other barriers to better collaboration, more efficient use of resources, and better opportunity in commercial, educational and other public endeavors among all who have chosen to live together within the good laws of that society

associated - to be prone to accompany, join, unite or work with one or more other people of true enlightenment, virtue and integrity as their ally, companion or partner

associating - to intend to accompany, join, unite or work with one or more other people of true enlightenment, virtue and integrity as their ally, companion or partner

assuming - to intend to think, speak and act in harmony with a virtue though I have it not, until that virtue becomes such a part of what I do and who I am at heart that I can prove in the fire of adversity that I am liberated within my mind and heart from all opposing vices

assured - to be solidly settled in enlightened thought and in consequent word and action as a result of prayerfully seeking and personally receiving a sure confirmation, verification or witness of enlightened certainty, reality or truth by personal enlightenment, inspiration or revelation from God

assured[2] - to be truly free from all doubt, misperception and misunderstanding about what I accurately and honestly claim has been made known unto me by personal enlightenment, inspiration or revelation from God

assured[3] - to be doubtlessly decided and sure about what I accurately and honestly claim has been made known unto me by personal enlightenment, inspiration or revelation from God

astringent - to be prone to think in a penetrating manner which discerns and sees through all that is superficial

astute - to be acutely discerning

athletic - to be prone to strive for physical health through vigorous physical activity or exercise

athletic[2] - to be prone to build physical ability, agility, skill, speed, stamina, strength or talent

atoning - to intend to seek full personal conversion or transformation to completely virtuous compatibility, oneness, trust, unity and wholeness with God unto exaltation through the charitable love, cleansing power and redeeming grace of the Atonement of the Lord Jesus Christ by my faithfully repentant and honorably exact obedience to those divinely appointed commandments, covenants, laws and ordinances upon which receipt of that blessing is predicated

attacking - to intend to aggressively initiate or produce true personal betterment, improvement or progress within me, my family and society

attending - to be observant and particular in taking care to safely avoid bondage, despair, turmoil and misery

attending^2 - to be courteously considerate and observant of the needs of another person

attending^3 - to be observant and particular in taking care of my good and honorable duty

attitudinizing - to intend to adopt, assume or possess a characteristic which produces, preserves or restores true enlightenment, virtue and integrity within me, my family and society

attracting - to be filled with enough true enlightenment, virtue and integrity to allure, fascinate or appeal to another person's sense of true enlightenment, virtue and integrity

attuned - to be prone to bring myself into conformity, harmony or sympathy with that which I have ascertained is truly the mind and will of God

attuned^2 - to be prone to bring myself into conformity, harmony or sympathy with integrity

attuned^3 - to be prone to bring myself into conformity, harmony or sympathy with virtue

attuned^4 - to be prone to bring myself into conformity, harmony or sympathy with enlightened certainty, reality or truth

auditing - to intend to examine or inspect in order to develop or improve upon what is important

auditing^2 - to intend to examine or inspect in order to confirm, prove or verify for myself what I truly need to know

august - to be eminently venerable

august^2 - to be impressively majestic

auspicious - to be one of those who are highly favorable or promising in the sight of God

austere - to be prone to practice strict abstinence in order to obey virtuous laws, rules, standards or values well enough to experience greater true enlightenment, virtue, integrity liberty, hope, peace and joy

austere^2 - to be prone to deny myself excessive or needless ease or luxury

Australasian - to be prone to live in harmony with the ways of Australasian character or culture which produce, preserve or restore true enlightenment, virtue and integrity within me, my family and society

Australian - to be prone to live in harmony with the ways of Australian character or culture which produce, preserve or restore true enlightenment, virtue and integrity within me, my family and society

autarkical - to be prone to achieve and to support the achievement of enough economic independence or self-reliance to help prepare the righteous, freedom-loving people within my nation to withstand an economic attack from our enemies

autarkical^2 - to be prone to practice independence or self-reliance in my home

authentic - to be in possession of or to ascertain the truth about who I am at heart

authenticating - to intend to confirm, prove or verify authenticity, credibility, genuineness, quality, reliability, trustworthiness or virtue

authoritative - to be prone to righteously wield the true authority I have been given

autobiographical - to be prone to record or write my own experiences or history as a true account that will bear witness to my posterity and to other people of the miraculous hand of God in my life and of my faithful efforts to please Him during my life

autobiographical^2 - to be prone to record or write my own experiences or history so that other people may learn from me how I overcame darkness, vice, corruption, bondage, despair, turmoil and misery, and how I discovered and obtained greater true enlightenment, virtue, integrity, liberty, hope, peace and joy

avant-garde - to be prone to experiment within some arena, forum or field in order to first create or discover better means or methods of producing, preserving or restoring true enlightenment, virtue and integrity within me, my family and society

avowing - to intend to openly and shamelessly defend my given testimony of enlightened certainty, reality or truth

awake - to be filled with true enlightenment, virtue and integrity unto faithful, timely and true repentance, obedience and reconciliation to God

awake^2 - to be enlightened or intelligent

awake^3 - to be aware of existing danger

awakening - to intend to help other people develop true enlightenment, virtue and integrity by preaching, teaching and expounding pure truth unto them and by lovingly exhorting and warning them of their need for faithful, timely and true repentance, obedience and reconciliation to God

awakening^2 - to intend to help other people become more enlightened or intelligent

awaking - to intend to become awake

awarding - to intend to bestow, give or pay to someone what is merited

aware - to be cognizant, informed or knowledgeable of the characteristic and distinctive differences between that which is truly good and of God and that which is evil or satanic

aware^2 - to be cognizant, informed or knowledgeable of the characteristic and distinctive differences between that which is enlightened certainty, reality or truth and that which is confusion, error or falsehood

aware^3 - to be cognizant, informed or knowledgeable of the characteristic and distinctive differences between that which is real and that which is imaginary

aware^4 - to be watchful enough of danger, risk or threat

awesome - to be filled with enough true enlightenment, virtue and integrity to astonish, impress, inspire or restrain one or more other people to likewise adopt reverential admiration or worshipful adoration toward God

axiological - to be prone to identify and then live in harmony with those thoughts which produce those beliefs which produce those values which produce those characteristics which best produce, preserve or restore the greatest true enlightenment, virtue, integrity, liberty, hope, peace and joy within me, my family and society

axiological[2] - to be prone to prayerfully study and ponder the relative value of thinking about, believing in, valuing and practicing human characteristics to determine the extent to which they produce, preserve or restore that which is truly good and of God or else that which is evil or satanic within me, my family and society

B

babying - to intend to feed, nurture and otherwise provide tender care for an infant

babylike - to be as innocent as a baby

Babylonian - to be prone to personally ascertain and live in harmony with the discernibly enlightening and spiritually verifiable truth that: like ancient Babylon, any and every mighty kingdom or nation which has ripened in iniquity in the sight of God can suffer defeat, destruction and desolation in a day

Babylonian[2] - to be prone to live in harmony with the ways of ancient Babylonian character or culture which produce, preserve or restore true enlightenment, virtue and

integrity within me, my family and society

balanced - to be prone to steadily maintain awareness of and harmonious orientation toward that which is truly good and of God

balanced[2] - to be prone to steadily maintain awareness of and harmonious orientation toward that which is true

balanced[3] - to be healthy in every aspect of my life

balanced[4] - to be virtuously just

balancing - to intend to bring into awareness of and harmony with what is best

balancing[2] - to intend to justly keep the powers authorized and exercised by legislative, executive and judicial branches of government within the boundaries or limits constitutionally apportioned

balancing[3] - to intend to make sure expenditures do not exceed income plus reserves

balancing[4] - to intend to estimate or evaluate relative importance, merit or value

banking - to intend to honestly, legally and responsibly use another person's money entrusted to me or my company for savings, investment or other banking purposes in order to actually make a larger amount of money for them and for me while treating their money and the interest they earn on it as I would want them to treat mine

Baptist - to be prone to live in harmony with the teachings of John the Baptist which produce, preserve or restore true enlightenment, virtue and integrity within me, my family and society Baptist[2] - to be prone to live in harmony with the teachings of a specific Baptist church which has broken away or separated in apostasy or protest from an earlier Baptist or Protestant Christian church during or since the 17th Century—to the extent the teachings produce, preserve or restore true enlightenment, virtue and integrity within me, my family and society

baptized - to be an accountable, faithful and fully repentant believer in the Lord Jesus Christ of at least the age of accountability, who has voluntarily entered into the priesthood covenant and ordinance of baptism by being buried or immersed in a watery grave in symbolic death and then brought forth out of water in a symbolic newness, rebirth or resurrection of life by a duly ordained boy or man called of God who bears true priesthood authority from God and has authorization from God's own called, ordained and authorized priesthood leaders on Earth to administer that ordinance of baptism without pay—so that I can justly receive a remission of sins, and can be confirmed by the priesthood ordinance of confirmation in further preparation for my receiving the blessings of a glorious celestial resurrection and exaltation in the world to come baptized[2] - to be one of those who have voluntarily entered into the priesthood covenant and ordinance of baptism by water for remission of sins in a manner, method or mode of baptism recognized by God as authorized and binding on Earth and in heaven

baptized[3] - to be spiritually and symbolically reborn from the grave by water to renewed cleanliness, innocence and life in the sight of God

baptizing - to be a duly ordained man called of God, who then uses my true priesthood authority from God and authorization from God's own called, ordained and authorized priesthood leaders on Earth to administer, without pay, the priesthood covenant and ordinance of baptism for an accountable, faithful and fully repentant believer in the Lord Jesus Christ of the age of accountability—so that they can justly receive a remission of sins, and can be confirmed by the priesthood ordinance of confirmation in further preparation for their receiving the blessings of a glorious celestial resurrection and exaltation in the world to come baptizing[2] - to be a duly ordained man called of God, who then uses my true higher priesthood authority from God and authorization from God's own called, ordained and authorized priesthood leaders on Earth to administer, without pay, in a dedicated holy temple of God the priesthood covenant and ordinance of baptism through righteous living proxy for deceased family members and other deceased persons who are accountable to the laws of God—so that those deceased persons who are desirous and righteous enough to receive the ordinance work done for them can justly receive a remission of sins, and can be confirmed by the priesthood ordinance of confirmation through righteous living proxy in further preparation for their receiving the blessings of a glorious celestial resurrection and exaltation in the world to come

baptizing[3] - to intend to administer, without pay, to a voluntary participant the priesthood covenant and ordinance of baptism by water for remission of sins in a manner, method or mode of baptism recognized by God as authorized and binding on Earth and in heaven

beaming - to be brightly radiant

beamish - to be beaming

beamy - to be prone to beaming

bearable - to be prone to honorably strive to adequately comply with, live by or obey those laws, rules, standards or values which produce, preserve or restore true enlightenment, virtue and integrity within me, my family and society

bearing - to be with and strengthen a friend, neighbor or relative by helping them carry their burdens, pains or trials

bearing[2] - to intend to endure or suffer through burden, pain or trial

beatific - to be beatifying

beatifying - to intend to assist or encourage someone in their desires and efforts to obtain angelic bliss or the blessings of those who are true saints or sanctified ones of God

beautiful - to be prone to radiate true enlightenment, virtue and integrity

beautiful[2] - to be wonderfully noble and pleasing through good works

beautifying - to intend to assist or encourage someone in their desires and efforts to obtain and radiate greater true enlightenment, virtue, integrity, liberty, hope, peace and joy

beautifying[2] - to intend to assist or encourage someone in their desires and efforts to become wonderfully noble and pleasing through their own good works

becalming - to intend to lovingly encourage and kindly help someone to be peaceable or peaceful

becoming - to be progressing in true enlightenment, virtue and integrity

becoming[2] - to be attractively dignified in appearance and manner

begetting - to intend to perpetuate true enlightenment, virtue and integrity in how I think, speak and act

begging - to intend to discern or perceive my total dependence upon God and to call upon Him to provide what I cannot

behaving - to intend to govern and restrain myself from thinking, speaking or acting in a vicious manner

behooving - to intend to think, speak and act in a dutiful, fitting, goodly and necessary manner

being - to intend to personally ascertain and live in harmony with the discernibly enlightening and spiritually verifiable truth that: I am a living soul consisting of both a physical body of earthly physical matter and an immortal spirit being or personage of enlivened spirit matter which shall separate at my physical death and shall eventually be inseparably rejoined and perfectly restored by the power of God during my one-time and everlasting resurrection from the dead

believable - to be prone to consistently speak or act in an honorable and virtuous manner worthy of confident acceptance and trust

believing - to be persuaded to withstand the satanic seizure of my belief, to endure the affliction and persecution of darkened opposition, and to withdraw from the deceitfulness of worldly popularity and temptations well enough to continue to exercise enough confident and faithful acceptance of and trust in the existence, goodness, love, power and wisdom of a true and living God to be eternally redeemed and gloriously exalted by Him by my faithfully repentant and honorably exact obedience to those divinely appointed commandments, covenants, laws and ordinances upon which receipt of those blessings is predicated

believing[2] - to be persuaded to withstand the satanic seizure of my belief, to endure the affliction and persecution of darkened opposition, and to withdraw from the deceitfulness of worldly popularity and temptations well enough to continue to exercise enough confident acceptance, faith and trust in the fulfillment or realization of a righteously desired blessing, gift or reward which I anticipate or hope for through the Lord Jesus Christ, the fulfillment or realization of which is neither immediately susceptible to nor demanding of proof

believing[3] - to be persuaded enough to exercise confident acceptance of and trust in the potential of something being enlightened certainty, reality or truth when it is in harmony with that which has already been proven to me by personal enlightenment, inspiration or revelation from God

believing[4] - to intend to refuse to think, speak or act to an extent or in a manner which is viciously unbelieving

beloved - to be generously and sincerely good enough to other people to be loved by them

bending - to be repenting

bending[2] - to be rectifying

benedictory - to be prone to recognize and thank God today in humble and sincere prayer for His hand in all of the blessings He has given me, my family and society

benedictory[2] - to be grateful enough to honorably express sincere gratitude to another person

benefic - to be prone to produce, preserve or restore good

benefic[2] - to be benevolent

beneficent - to be benevolent

beneficial - to be prone to produce, preserve or restore true enlightenment, virtue and integrity within me, my family and society

benefiting - to intend to bring true enlightenment, virtue, integrity, liberty, hope, peace and joy to me, my family and society

benevolent - to be prone to charitably, diligently, generously and graciously work to increase true enlightenment, virtue and integrity within me, my family and society

benevolent[2] - to be prone to charitably, diligently, generously and graciously work to effectively safeguard and improve the virtuously liberating freedom, health, honorable economic prosperity and steady progress of me, my family and society

benign - to be gentle, good-natured, gracious and kind

benign[2] - to be prone to refuse to be viciously harmful, malignant or pernicious

benignant - to be virtuously benign

best - to be most like unto God by my faithfully repentant and honorably exact obedience to those divinely appointed commandments, covenants, laws and ordinances upon which receipt of that blessing is predicated

best[2] - to be one of those who are most advanced or most progressive in producing, preserving or restoring the greatest true enlightenment, virtue, integrity, liberty, hope, peace and joy within ourselves, our families and society

best[3] - to be prone to do all I possibly can to produce, preserve or restore the highest quality character within me, my family and society

better - to be more like unto God by my faithfully repentant and honorably exact obedience to those divinely appointed commandments, covenants, laws and ordinances upon which receipt of that blessing is predicated

better[2] - to be one of those who are more advanced or more progressive in producing, preserving or restoring higher levels of true enlightenment, virtue, integrity, liberty, hope, peace and joy within ourselves, our families and society

better[3] - to be prone to improve upon my production, preservation or restoration of higher quality character within me, my family and society

bettering - to intend to lovingly encourage and kindly help someone to be better

bighearted - to be charitably loving

biographical - to be prone to record or write the truth about another person's life and character so that other people may learn how they overcame darkness, vice, corruption, bondage, despair, turmoil and misery, and how they discovered and obtained greater true enlightenment, virtue, integrity, liberty, hope, peace and joy

biological - to be prone to discover and implement better proven biological means or methods of producing, preserving or restoring greater true enlightenment, virtue, integrity, liberty, hope, peace and joy within the human body, mind and spirit

biological[2] - to be prone to examine mental and spiritual phenomena to learn the truth about the physical aspects of human existence

biological[3] - to be prone to prayerfully study and ponder that which has living physical existence

black - to be prone to live in harmony with the ways of character or culture of those with naturally dark-colored skin to the extent those ways produce, preserve or restore true enlightenment, virtue and integrity within me, my family and society
black-and-white - to be godly enough to be made truly chaste, clean, pure and virtuous at heart—and to continue to encourage and help other people by charitable love, kindness, invitation and instruction to be godly enough to be made truly chaste, clean, pure and virtuous at heart
black-and-white[2] - to be ascertaining, discerning, decisively true and righteous enough to become or remain virtuously Zionistic with one or more other people who are and do likewise
black-and-white[3] - to be ascertaining, discerning, enlightened and virtuously integrated enough to become or remain virtuously single-minded and single-hearted with one or more other people who are and do likewise
black-and-white[4] - to be prone to personally ascertain and live in harmony with the discernibly enlightening and spiritually verifiable truth that: I cross the line from guilty into innocent the moment I am righteously pardoned, redeemed and released from further payment for violating the laws of God
black-and-white[5] - to be prone to personally ascertain and live in harmony with the discernibly

enlightening and spiritually verifiable truth that: I cross the line from doing evil into doing good the moment I willfully make the slightest attempt to speak or act in a truly virtuous manner
black-and-white[6] - to be prone to personally ascertain and live in harmony with the discernibly enlightening and spiritually verifiable truth that: I cross the line from choosing evil into choosing good the moment I willfully exercise within the thoughts of my heart the slightest good or pure thought, desire or intention
black-and-white[7] - to be prone to personally ascertain and live in harmony with the discernibly enlightening and spiritually verifiable truth that: I cross the line from guilty into innocent the moment I am righteously pardoned and released from further payment for violating the law of the land
black-and-white[8] - to be prone to personally ascertain and live in harmony with the discernibly enlightening and spiritually verifiable truth that: I can see and personally know of true opposites the moment I ascertain or discern such true opposites as darkness from enlightenment, vice from virtue, corruption from integrity, bondage from liberty, despair from hope, turmoil from peace or misery from joy
black-and-white[9] - to be prone to personally ascertain and live in harmony with the discernibly enlightening and spiritually verifiable truth that: I cross the line from innocent into guilty the moment my actual conduct or

speech becomes a violation of the law of the land

black-and-white[10] - to be prone to personally ascertain and live in harmony with the discernibly enlightening and spiritually verifiable truth that: I cross the line from innocent into guilty the moment my actual thought, conduct or speech becomes a violation of the laws of God

black-and-white[11] - to be prone to personally ascertain and live in harmony with the discernibly enlightening and spiritually verifiable truth that: I cross the line from choosing good into choosing evil the moment I willfully exercise within the thoughts of my heart the slightest impure or evil thought, desire or intention

black-and-white[12] - to be prone to personally ascertain and live in harmony with the discernibly enlightening and spiritually verifiable truth that: I cross the line from doing good into doing evil the moment I willfully make the slightest attempt to speak or act in an evil or satanic manner

black-and-white[13] - to be prone to personally ascertain and live in harmony with the discernibly enlightening and spiritually verifiable truth that: I cross the line from being good into being evil the moment I willfully refuse to be redeemed unto exaltation

blamable - to be prone to honorably and justly heed a needed warning to repent of all of the corrupt, sinful or vicious wrongdoing within me—by responding with my faithful, timely and true repentance,

obedience and reconciliation to God

blamable[2] - to be prone to readily and willingly subject myself to someone's efforts to honorably and justly place blame, fault or guilt against me

blameless - to be truly innocent

blessed - to be prone to obtain blessings from God by my believing and honorably exact obedience to those divinely appointed laws upon which receipt of those blessings is predicated

blessing - to intend to virtuously bestow or pronounce heavenly aid, assurance, comfort, forgiveness, prosperity, protection and other needed benefits, gifts or rewards upon another person by exercising in their behalf true higher priesthood authority and power from God according to His revealed will

blessing[2] - to intend to virtuously invoke heavenly aid, assurance, comfort, forgiveness, prosperity, protection and other needed benefits, gifts or rewards upon another person by exercising prayerful faith in their behalf

blessing[3] - to intend to diligently and gratefully give glory, honor, love, praise or worship to God by obediently keeping His commandments, covenants, laws and ordinances and by virtuously serving other people

blessing[4] - to be charitably loving

blissful - to be completely joyful

blithe - to be virtuously cheerful within my heart

blossoming - to intend to continue to progress by continuing to improve the enlightenment and virtue of the thoughts I continue to integrate into the thoughts, beliefs, values and characteristics of my heart

blossoming[2] - to intend to arise, flourish, grow, prosper or thrive in true enlightenment, virtue, integrity, liberty, hope, peace and joy in direct proportion to my believing and honorably exact obedience to those divinely appointed laws upon which receipt of those blessings is predicated

blotting out - to be prone to deserve the destruction, expunging or obliteration of any record of my corrupt, sinful or vicious wrongdoing by making full payment of all justly imposed consequences, debts, demands, obligations, payments, penalties, punishments, reparations or restitutions and through my faithful, timely and true repentance, obedience and reconciliation to God

blue-blooded - to be a noble member of a noble family

boasting - to intend to speak with well-deserved esteem or praise about someone or something other than myself

bodybuilding - to intend to develop strong enough muscles to be fit or healthy in body and mind

bona fide - to be genuine, honest and sincere with myself

bonny - to be filled with enough true enlightenment, virtue and integrity to produce, preserve or restore true liberty, hope, peace and joy within me, my family and society

bonny[2] - to be filled with enough true enlightenment, virtue and integrity to allure, fascinate or appeal to another person's sense of true enlightenment, virtue and integrity

bouncing - to be healthy enough to spring back from adversity or defeat

bowing - to intend to sincerely approach God in humble prayer on bended knee, on bended knees or in a nearly prone or prostrate position

brainstorming - to intend to allow or cause my mind to freely envision, imagine or search for the best ideas or solutions

brainstorming[2] - to intend to allow or cause my mind to freely envision, imagine or search for better ideas or solutions

brainy - to be enlightened or intelligent

branding - to intend to actively, charitably, generously and wisely esteem, regard and treat another person as the more excellent and progressive person they can and should become, and to thus give them the inspiring confidence, the uplifting encouragement and the elevating opportunity to live up to such esteem, regard and treatment as long as they do so

branding[2] - to intend to ascertain and then accurately and clearly state the truly positive character, condition, influence, merit, power, quality, strength, value or worth of someone or something

brave - to be prone to demonstrate truly daring, dauntless, defiant, dignified and intrepid courage and fortitude in opposing or, if necessary, fighting against someone or something truly criminal, darkened, evil, unclean or unjust

breadwinning - to be a boy or man who is competent, diligent and responsible enough to adequately provide myself and my family with enough financial support through honorable means or methods

breadwinning[2] - to be a girl or woman who is competent, diligent and responsible enough to adequately support myself and my dependents through honorable means or methods when I must

bright - to be radiantly animated, cheerful and joyful

bright[2] - to be radiantly enlightened or intelligent

brilliant - to be one of those who are the most bright, outstanding or splendid in thought, speech and behavior who do the most good in producing, preserving or restoring the greatest true enlightenment, virtue, integrity, liberty, hope, peace and joy within ourselves, our families and society

brilliant[2] - to be one of the brightest, most outstanding or most splendid in intelligence, performance or talent, and to put what I have been given to good use

broadcasting - to intend to seek widespread collaboration in widely presenting and sponsoring thought which produces, preserves or restores true enlightenment, virtue and integrity within me, my family and society

broadcasting[2] - to intend to widely present or sponsor thought which produces, preserves or restores true enlightenment, virtue and integrity within me, my family and society

broad-minded - to be prone to strive for a wide breadth, range or scope of experience, knowledge and understanding

brokenhearted - to be prone to humbly, openly and worshipfully manifest to God my awareness of my utter dependence upon the redeeming power of the Atonement of the Lord Jesus Christ by sincerely manifesting my complete willingness to break away from, give up or sacrifice all of my sins and all of my desire to sin by my faithful, timely and true repentance, obedience and reconciliation to God

brokenhearted[2] - to be and to remain humbly and meekly penitent enough before God to never withdraw or withhold from Him my faithful, timely and true repentance, obedience and reconciliation to Him

brokenhearted[3] - to be filled with enough disappointment, grief or sorrow to fully determine or resolve to change for the better the thoughts, beliefs, values and characteristics of my heart

brooding - to intend to persistently meditate in a deeply inward and purely honest effort to obtain a true understanding of the things of God

brooding[2] - to intend to persistently deliberate in a deeply inward and purely honest effort to commune with the Spirit of God over a difficult matter

brotherly - to be prone to personally ascertain and live in harmony with the discernibly enlightening and spiritually verifiable truth that: all boys and men are sons of God and, hence, brothers in spirit

brotherly[2] - to be a boy or man who is truly charitable

brotherly[3] - to be a boy or man who seeks to produce, preserve or restore true enlightenment, virtue and integrity within me, my family and society

brown - to be prone to live in harmony with the ways of character or culture of those with naturally brown-colored skin to the extent those ways produce, preserve or restore true enlightenment, virtue and integrity within me, my family and society

bubbly - to be prone to float upon or rise to the top in a buoyant manner

Buddhist - to be prone to live in harmony with the teachings of Buddhism which produce, preserve or restore true enlightenment, virtue and integrity within me, my family and society

budgeting - to intend to keep the total of debits and payments less than existing and renewable resources

building - to intend to develop or promote that which produces, preserves or restores true enlightenment, virtue and integrity within me, my family and society

building[2] - to intend to develop or promote good and uplifting health, strength, unity or welfare

building[3] - to intend to develop or promote good and uplifting knowledge or skill

buoyant - to be prone to quickly rise above and to then continue to cheerfully, courageously and hopefully float upon any and every

flood of adversity, depression or evil

businesslike - to be prone to make it my business to honorably seek gain or make money for doing good

businesslike[2] - to be virtuously reciprocating and serving in the way I do business

busy - to be constantly and diligently active, employed, engaged or occupied in a good endeavor

buxom - to be a girl or woman who is healthy, cheerful and lively

by-the-book - to be prone to exactly, faithfully and honorably think, speak and act in harmony with the writings in a book which provide the true commandments, covenants, laws and ordinances of God

by-the-book[2] - to be prone to exactly, faithfully and honorably think, speak and act in harmony with the writings in a book which provide the best and highest laws, rules, standards or values for producing, preserving or restoring the greatest true enlightenment, virtue, integrity, liberty, hope, peace and joy within me, my family and society

by-the-book[3] - to be prone to exactly, faithfully and honorably think, speak and act in harmony with the writings in a book which provide good laws, rules, standards or values

by-the-book[4] - to be prone to wisely focus more on adhering exactly or strictly to the wording of a good written standard in a book when I know or have good enough reason to believe no greater good can result from adhering to a more liberal interpretation and application of the standard by-the-book[5] - to be prone to wisely focus more on adhering exactly or strictly to the wording of a good written standard in a book when a more liberal interpretation and application of the standard is prohibited by good authority by-the-book[6] - to be prone to exactly or strictly think, speak and act in harmony with the writings in a book which provide the good law of the land

C

cagey - to be wary

called - to be a man who has been truly called of God to be ordained to the true higher priesthood of God

called[2] - to be a boy or man who has been truly called of God to be ordained to the lesser or preparatory priesthood of God

called[3] - to be truly called of God to serve in a specific calling or office He wants me to fulfill or magnify

calm - to be peaceable or peaceful

canny - to be discerning

canny[2] - to be prudent

canny[3] - to be thrifty

capable - to be in possession of the ability or power to willfully do and be good

capable[2] - to be in possession of the ability or power to willfully think, speak and act for myself

capitalistic - to be prone to strive for an economy in which the competitive, free market exchange, production, pricing and distribution of goods and services is maintained by those filled with enough true enlightenment, virtue

and integrity to maintain in unison the individual rights and freedoms of private ownership of property, investment, and stewardship of wealth—and who charitably, faithfully and patriotically do enough with our collective surplus to help needy and poor law-abiding citizens, legal resident aliens, and legally admitted refugees accumulate enough personally owned capital by their own determined education, training, labors, investments and savings to become self-reliant net contributors to the virtuously liberating freedom, health, honorable economic prosperity and steady progress of themselves, their families and society

captivating - to be filled with enough true enlightenment, virtue and integrity to strongly attract or appeal to another person's sense of true enlightenment, virtue and integrity

careful - to be prone to obey God's commandments, covenants, laws and ordinances with enough faith, exactness and honor to justly receive from Him greater true enlightenment, virtue, integrity, liberty, hope, peace and joy

careful[2] - to be prone to live in close harmony with that which produces, preserves or restores true enlightenment, virtue and integrity within me, my family and society

caressing - to intend to demonstrate kindness

Caribbean - to be prone to live in harmony with the ways of Caribbean character or culture which produce, preserve or restore true enlightenment, virtue and integrity within me, my family and society

caring - to intend to offer the needy and poor aid, assistance, concession, forbearance, forgiveness, leniency or tolerance to an extent and in a manner which is charitably loving, just, right and wise in the sight of God

caring[2] - to intend to actively, charitably, generously and wisely provide for the needy and poor to an extent or in a manner which saves their lives, meets their immediate needs for survival, fosters their adequate education, employment, labors, self-reliance and thrift, and which encourages their service to other people

caring[3] - to intend to actively, charitably, generously and wisely give of my substance or other resources to the needy and poor to help them deal with personal needs which they cannot take care of alone — provided they are continuing to demonstrate by their own determined education, training, labors, investments and savings, that they are responsibly striving to become self-reliant net contributors to the virtuously liberating freedom, health, honorable economic prosperity and steady progress of themselves, their families and society

catching - to be discerning

catholic - to be prone to seek enlightenment and virtue wherever they may be found

catholic[2] - to be prone to seek more available knowledge of living or natural things

Catholic - to be prone to live in harmony with the teachings of the Roman Catholic Church which produce, preserve or restore true enlightenment, virtue and integrity within me, my family and society

Caucasian - to be prone to live in harmony with the ways of Caucasian character or culture which produce, preserve or restore true enlightenment, virtue and integrity within me, my family and society

cautioning - to intend to carefully advise or warn someone against exposure to darkness, vice and corruption

cautious - to be prone to carefully minimize my own chance or risk of exposure to darkness, vice, corruption, bondage, despair, turmoil and misery

cautious[2] - to be wary

cautious[3] - to be prone to carefully minimize my own chance or risk of exposure to harm or injury

celebrating - to intend to publicly proclaim news which is truly good and of God

celestial - to be one of those who are made perfectly qualified through the charitable love, cleansing power and redeeming grace of the Atonement of the Lord Jesus Christ to receive a resurrected and exalted celestial body and to dwell forever with my exalted husband or wife in the highest degree of God's celestial or heavenly glory, kingdom or reward with a glory like that of the sun

celestial[2] - to be one of those who are made perfectly qualified through the charitable love, cleansing power and redeeming grace of the Atonement of the Lord

Jesus Christ to receive a resurrected celestial body and to dwell forever in one of the three degrees of God's celestial or heavenly glory, kingdom or reward with a glory like that of the sun, including all of the living who live in harmony with celestial law until death, all of the dead who would have lived in harmony with celestial law had they received it on Earth, all who die before the age of eight, all who lack mental capacity on Earth, and all who otherwise lack the capability or competence to be held accountable for obeying and keeping the commandments, covenants, laws and ordinances of God during their mortal lives

censoring - to intend to systematically alter, delete or exclude from my mental forum or marketplace any or all materials which produce, preserve or restore darkness, vice and corruption within me, my family and society

censurable - to be prone to honorably and justly heed a needed warning to repent of all of the corrupt, sinful or vicious wrongdoing within me, by responding with my faithful, timely and true repentance, obedience and reconciliation to God

censurable^2 - to be prone to readily and willingly subject myself to someone's efforts to honorably and justly place blame, fault or guilt against me

censuring - to intend to lovingly and mercifully warn the wicked to repent unto faithful, timely and true repentance, obedience and reconciliation to God

certain - to be made decidedly settled in an undeniably sure confirmation, verification or witness of enlightened certainty, reality or truth I have received by personal enlightenment, inspiration or revelation from God

certain^2 - to be and to choose to remain unalterably decided and undeniably sure about what I accurately and honestly claim has been made known unto me by personal enlightenment, inspiration or revelation from God

certain^3 - to be entirely and truly free from all confusion, deception, delusion, misperception and misunderstanding about what I accurately and honestly claim has been made known unto me by personal enlightenment, inspiration or revelation from God

certain^4 - to be decidedly and doubtlessly sure about that which is truly known to me

certifying - to intend to certainly and honestly uphold that which I have truly testified is truth

challenging - to intend to expect myself to do my very best today to live in perfect harmony with the best and highest laws, rules, standards or values of true enlightenment, virtue and integrity of which I have become aware in my education and training and in my own constantly diligent, honest and open-minded searching

champion - to be prone to successfully defend and uphold truth and virtue

changeable - to be prone to honorably and justly heed a needed warning to repent of all of the corrupt, sinful or vicious wrongdoing within me, by responding with my faithful, timely and true repentance, obedience and reconciliation to God

changeable[2] - to be prone to forsake that which is evil or satanic for that which is truly good and of God

changeless - to be and to choose to remain unable or unwilling to change or vary from that which is virtuous

changing - to intend to forsake that which is evil or satanic for that which is truly good and of God

characterizing - to intend to actively, charitably, generously and wisely esteem, regard and treat another person as the more excellent and progressive person they can and should become, and to thus give them the inspiring confidence, the uplifting encouragement and the elevating opportunity to live up to such esteem, regard and treatment as long as they do so

characterizing[2] - to intend to ascertain and then accurately and clearly state the truly positive character, condition, influence, merit, power, quality, strength, value or worth of someone or something

charismatic - to be one of those who have received the gift and power from God to do good, and to constantly exercise that gift and power, come what may

charitable - to be prone, out of a pure heart, good conscience, unselfish love, unwavering hope and true faith—and in the face of incessant or intense adversity, affliction, distress, doubt,

opposition, persecution or tribulation—to continue to faithfully manifest my desire, intent and power to love, serve and worship God with enough faith, hope, obedience and love in the Lord Jesus Christ to receive as an heir and to strive to help other people receive as heirs—through the charitable love, cleansing power and redeeming grace of the Atonement of the Lord Jesus Christ—each and every heavenly blessing, gift and reward

charitable[2] - to be prone, out of a pure heart, good conscience, unselfish love, unwavering hope and true faith, to courageously continue to faithfully, obediently and prayerfully seek to exercise and to add to the growing measures of discernibly true enlightenment, virtue and integrity within me which prompt me to continue to learn all of the truth I can about God, to love, obey, reverence, serve and worship Him with all of the energy, might, power, strength and will of my soul, and to be completely filled with the loving desire, intent and power to obediently sacrifice and consecrate enough of what I have and am to effectively safeguard and improve the virtuously liberating freedom, health, honorable economic prosperity and steady progress of me, my family and society toward exaltation

charitable[3] - to be prone, out of a pure heart, good conscience, unselfish love, unwavering hope and true faith, to allow or cause the pure love of God to flow through me to other people in my corresponding thoughts, words and actions with them

charitable[4] - to be prone, out of a pure heart, good conscience, unselfish love, unwavering hope and true faith—and in a temperate, Christlike manner—to humbly, meekly, honestly and unselfishly extend loving kindness, peaceable forgiveness, long-suffering and generous benevolence toward all humanity

charitable[5] - to be prone, out of a pure heart, good conscience, unselfish love, unwavering hope and true faith, to benevolently or generously sacrifice to help other people when they have little or no courage, faith, hope or means to the fullest extent I can and should, and whenever I am prompted to do so by the Spirit of God

charitable[6] - to be prone, out of a pure heart, good conscience, unselfish love, unwavering hope and true faith, to benevolently or generously sacrifice to sincerely and unselfishly provide good and tender works of kindness and service to other people to the fullest extent I can and should, and whenever I am prompted to do so by the Spirit of God

charitable[7] - to be prone, out of a pure heart, good conscience, unselfish love, unwavering hope and true faith, to benevolently or generously sacrifice to sincerely and unselfishly speak kind, warm and pleasing words of admiration, affection, appreciation, endearment, praise or reverence to other people to the fullest extent I can and should, and whenever I

am prompted to do so by the Spirit of God

charitable[8] - to be prone, out of a pure heart, good conscience, unselfish love, unwavering hope and true faith, to say good things about other people as often as possible and as often as I am prompted to do so by the Spirit of God

charitable[9] - to be prone, out of a pure heart, good conscience, unselfish love, unwavering hope and true faith, to continue to refuse to be covetous, cruel, envious, lustful, maligning, vicious or easily provoked to intense anger

charitable[10] - to be prone, out of a pure heart, good conscience, unselfish love, unwavering hope and true faith, to patiently and persistently seek to kindly and unselfishly understand the behavior and thinking of other people

charming - to be filled with enough true enlightenment, virtue and integrity to be delightfully attractive or appealing to another person's sense of true enlightenment, virtue and integrity

chary - to be discreetly wary

chaste - to be made truly sexually clean, pure and virtuous in the sight of God through the charitable love, cleansing power and redeeming grace of the Atonement of the Lord Jesus Christ by my faithfully repentant and honorably exact obedience to those divinely appointed commandments, covenants, laws and ordinances upon which receipt of those blessings is predicated

chaste[2] - to be obedient to the divine law of chastity by honestly and truly refraining from all sexual relations, except with my husband or wife to whom I am lawfully and legally wedded

chaste[3] - to be obedient to the divine law of chastity by honestly and truly refraining from all evil or satanic sexual relations and from all thoughts of them

chaste[4] - to be honestly and truly decent and modest in dress, grooming and manner as a reflection of my own spiritual cleanliness and purity and of my desire to help others achieve or maintain their own

chastening - to intend, having the proper authority, to necessarily and righteously administer enough pain or suffering in an honorable and virtuous attempt to correct, recall or reclaim someone from impurity

chatting - to intend to engage in friendly, harmless and informal conversation with one or more other people of true enlightenment, virtue and integrity

checking - to intend to discover the truth about God by prayerful and thorough study and by my believing and honorably exact obedience to that divinely appointed law upon which receipt of that truth is predicated

checking[2] - to intend to stop to examine, inspect, inquire or investigate in order to confirm, prove or verify for myself what I truly need to know

cheerful - to be truly hopeful, peaceful and joyful, and to show it in my countenance

cheerful[2] - to be filled with festive and healthy cheerfulness, gaiety, happiness or merriment through healthy association with good company, and to show it in my countenance

cheerful[3] - to be filled with enough delightful gladness or bright happiness to consistently dispel melancholy and pessimistic gloom, and to show it in my countenance

cherishing - to intend to hold my husband, wife, child or other family member dear enough to actively, charitably, generously and wisely nurture them with enough warm affection and tender care to induce or strengthen their desire and their efforts toward true personal betterment, improvement or progress

cherishing[2] - to intend to hold my true and virtuous friend dear enough to actively, charitably, generously and wisely nurture them with enough warm affection and tender care to induce or strengthen their desire and their efforts toward true personal betterment, improvement or progress

chic - to be filled with enough true enlightenment, virtue and integrity to allure, fascinate or appeal to another person's sense of true enlightenment, virtue and integrity

chicken - to be the first to courageously avoid or abandon a contest of courage used to determine which contestant will face greater risk of serious personal harm or death to avoid being the first to quit or to yield

chief - to be prone to humbly and willingly seek to serve the other people within my organization as though I were the least among them

childlike - to be as virtuously humble, meek, submissive and trusting as a little child toward God

childlike^2 - to be as innocent as a little child

chipper - to be cheerful and healthy

chivalrous - to be a boy or man who possesses superior power and virtue and who, like an ideal knight, chastely, generously, honorably and valiantly uses them to bless and protect the lives of children, girls and women

choice - to be elect

choice^2 - to be truly deserving of preference or selection due to most outstanding or superior qualities

choosing - to intend to pick or select that which is truly good and of God—instead of that which is evil or satanic

choosing^2 - to intend to pick or select that which produces, preserves or restores true enlightenment, virtue, integrity, liberty, hope, peace and joy within me, my family and society—instead of that which produces, preserves or restores darkness, vice, corruption, bondage, despair, turmoil and misery within me, my family and society

chosen - to be elect

chosen^2 - to be select

Christian - to be prone to obey and live in harmony with the commandments, covenants, laws and ordinances of the gospel or good news of the Lord Jesus Christ

which produce, preserve or restore true enlightenment, virtue and integrity within me, my family and society

Christlike - to be exalted

Christlike^2 - to be celestial

Christlike^3 - to be godly enough to be made truly chaste, clean, pure and virtuous at heart—and to continue to encourage and help other people by charitable love, kindness, invitation and instruction to be godly enough to be made truly chaste, clean, pure and virtuous at heart

Christlike^4 - to be prone to prayerfully ask God for enough energy, force, power or strength to do His will, and to then do it

Christlike^5 - to be prone to always do my very best to gratefully, lovingly and willingly think, say and do only those things which please God

Christlike^6 - to be prone to obey and live in harmony with the commandments, covenants, laws and ordinances of the gospel or good news of the Lord Jesus Christ which produce, preserve or restore true enlightenment, virtue and integrity within me, my family and society

Christlike^7 - to be prone to refuse to be anti-Christ

chronicling - to intend to keep an accurate account or register of my personal history that will bear witness to my posterity and to other people of the miraculous hand of God in my life and of my faithful efforts to please Him during my life

chronicling^2 - to intend to keep an accurate account or register of my family history and my ancestry that will bear witness to my posterity and to other people of the continuing importance of producing, preserving or restoring true enlightenment, virtue, integrity, liberty, hope, peace and joy within ourselves, our families and society

chronicling[3] - to intend to keep an accurate account, history or record of the valuable lessons of history

churchgoing - to intend to enjoy the many blessings of obediently worshiping God in His designated house of worship each Sabbath day as He commands or directs

churchy - to be prone to live in harmony with the teachings of a Christian religion which produce, preserve or restore true enlightenment, virtue and integrity within me, my family and society

circumspect - to be godly enough to be made truly chaste, clean, pure and virtuous at heart—and to continue to encourage and help other people by charitable love, kindness, invitation and instruction to be godly enough to be made truly chaste, clean, pure and virtuous at heart

circumspect[2] - to be prone to cautiously and prudently observe behavior, circumstances and consequences in order to discover and pursue the best course of personal conduct

circumspective - to be circumspect

citing - to intend to commend another person for their truly outstanding achievement, devotion or performance

civic-minded - to be prone to patriotically take enough personal

responsibility to produce, preserve or restore true enlightenment, virtue and integrity within me, my family and society—so that I might do my part in virtuous oneness with my law-abiding fellow citizens to effectively preserve or safeguard ourselves against darkness, vice, corruption, bondage, despair, turmoil and misery

civic-minded[2] - to be prone to patriotically appoint or elect only the most enlightened, virtuous and wise government leaders

civic-minded[3] - to be prone to patriotically strive to effectively safeguard and improve the virtuously liberating freedom, health, honorable economic prosperity and steady progress of all law-abiding fellow citizens and our law-abiding guests

civic-minded[4] - to be honorably religious or religiously honorable

civic-minded[5] - to be prone to honor, obey and sustain the good law of the land

civil - to be prone to lovingly encourage and kindly help the general public to be filled with true enlightenment, virtue and integrity, and with their naturally consequent liberty, hope, peace and joy

civil[2] - to be honorably religious or religiously honorable

civil[3] - to be respectably benevolent, courteous and polite toward the general public

civil[4] - to be prone to refuse to be discourteous, impolite or vulgar toward the general public

civilized - to be filled with true enlightenment, virtue, integrity, liberty, hope, peace and joy

civilized² - to be polished or refined in manners

civilized³ - to be prone to think, speak and act in harmony with good thoughts, beliefs, values and characteristics

civilized⁴ - to be honorably religious or religiously honorable

civilized⁵ - to be prone to think, speak and act in harmony with the good law of the land

civil rightist - to be prone to patriotically take responsibility to establish and uphold those legal rights which produce, preserve or restore true enlightenment, virtue and integrity within me, my family and society

civil rightist² - to be prone to patriotically take responsibility to establish and uphold those legal rights which produce, preserve or restore the virtuously liberating freedom, health, honorable economic prosperity and steady progress of all law-abiding fellow citizens and our law-abiding guests

civil rightist³ - to be prone to uphold everyone's right to be honorably religious or religiously honorable

civil rightist⁴ - to be prone to do all I should to make sure an antifamilial or otherwise viciously antisocial or uncivil wrong is not granted the status of a civil right

clairvoyant - to be prone to develop or maintain an ability, authority, gift or power to accurately and clearly comprehend, discern, perceive or otherwise see within my mind or heart a verifiable enlightened certainty, reality or truth which cannot be presently seen by my natural eye

clairvoyant² - to be sagacious

clannish - to be prone to build, improve and strengthen the virtuously liberating freedom, health, honorable economic prosperity and steady progress of my clan by thinking, speaking and acting in harmony with that which produces, preserves or restores true enlightenment, virtue and integrity within me, my family and society

clannish² - to be prone to progress as a group of closely related families or households

clarifying - to intend to necessarily and truly testify of the truthfulness of something to an extent or in a manner which leaves no room for doubt, question or misinterpretation of what I intended to say

clarion - to be prone to express something good in a brilliantly clear manner

class - to be classy or first-class

classic - to be prone to author or write thoughts in a pure and refined manner which produces, preserves or restores true enlightenment, virtue and integrity within me, my family and society

classic² - to be first-class

classical - to be prone to adhere to or perform in harmony with an enduring standard which produces, preserves or restores true enlightenment, virtue and integrity within me, my family and society

classless - to be virtuously Zionistic

classy - to be prone to think, speak and act in an elegant and refined manner

clean - to be sanctified unto perfectly virtuous purity, innocence and integrity

clean² - to be prone to prayerfully keep my thoughts, words and actions chaste, pure and virtuous and above satanic or worldly temptation

clean³ - to be prone to keep my thoughts, words and actions in harmony with that which produces, preserves or restores true enlightenment, virtue and integrity within me, my family and society

clean⁴ - to be prone to keep myself, my attire and my surroundings reasonably free from disorder, filth and pollution

clean-cut - to be wholesome in appearance and in reality

clean-handed - to be truly innocent

cleaning - to intend to lovingly encourage and kindly help someone to be clean

clean-minded - to be clean in my thinking

cleansed - to be made clean

cleansing - to be cleaning

clear - to be innocent in the sight of God

clear² - to be and to be found blameless, guiltless or innocent in harmony with the good law of the land

clear³ - to be filled with an absolute, perfect and spiritually verified personal knowledge of enlightened certainty, reality or truth by personal enlightenment, inspiration or revelation from God

clear⁴ - to be prone to discern, perceive, think or understand without ambiguity or uncertainty

clear⁵ - to be completely and honorably free from debt or liability

clear-headed - to be able to discern, perceive, think or understand without ambiguity or uncertainty

clear-minded - to be clear-headed

clear-sighted - to be acutely discerning and righteously visionary

clerical - to be virtuously ordained or virtuously ordaining

clerical² - to be prone to refuse to advocate, favor or seek to preserve worldly influence in public or secular affairs

clever - to be enlightened or intelligent

clever² - to be skilled in contriving or inventing ingenious practical means or results

climbing - to intend to constantly choose to personally progress

climbing² - to intend to ascend or rise above all that is darkened or degrading

closed-hearted - to be prone to refuse to willingly harbor, hold, keep, retain or store within my heart certain active or stored thoughts of my mind which I know or have good enough reason to believe will produce, preserve or restore darkness, vice and corruption within me, my family and society

closed-minded - to be prone to refuse to entertain or retain within the active thoughts of my mind those thoughts which I know or have good enough reason to believe will produce, preserve or restore darkness, vice and corruption within me, my family and society

closeted - to be prone to keep certain of my thoughts, words and actions private or secret for virtuous reasons

closeting - to intend to discreetly or wisely refuse to broadcast, publish or stage specific thoughts, words and actions which produce, preserve or restore darkness, vice and corruption within me, my family and society

clubbing - to intend to combine or join with one or more other people of true enlightenment, virtue and integrity to contribute to or participate in a good cause or purpose

cluing - to intend to give true information which serves to direct or guide one or more other people toward a good solution

coalescing - to intend to ally, grow together or unite for a good and mutually beneficial purpose

coddling - to intend to nurse or treat a helpless person with great care and tenderness

coeternal - to be prone to personally ascertain and live in harmony with the discernibly enlightening and spiritually verifiable truth that: I will eternally exist together with other living beings

coeternal[2] - to be prone to personally ascertain and live in harmony with the discernibly enlightening and spiritually verifiable truth that: I will eternally exist together with such things as law, matter, space and spirit

cognizant - to be prone to collect, process, understand and recognize the characteristic and distinctive differences between that which is truly good and of God and that which is evil or satanic

cognizant[2] - to be prone to collect, process, understand and recognize the characteristic and distinctive differences between that which is enlightened certainty, reality or truth and that which is confusion, error or falsehood

cognizant[3] - to be prone to collect, process, understand and recognize the characteristic and distinctive differences between that which is real and that which is imaginary

cohabitating - to intend to live together with my husband or wife to whom I am lawfully and legally wedded

coherent - to be godly enough to be made truly chaste, clean, pure and virtuous at heart—and to continue to encourage and help other people by charitable love, kindness, invitation and instruction to be godly enough to be made truly chaste, clean, pure and virtuous at heart

coherent[2] - to be prone to personally ascertain and live in harmony with the discernibly enlightening and spiritually verifiable truth that: all truth, without exception, is always in perfect harmony, integrity, oneness or unity with itself and can, therefore, be circumscribed or combined into one clearly and perfectly distinct, integrated and undiluted sphere or whole which, unlike confusion, error or falsehood, is capable of producing, preserving or restoring harmony, integrity, oneness or unity within me, my family and society

cohering - to intend to seek connection or unity in interest, principle, purpose or relationship with one or more other people of true enlightenment, virtue and integrity

collegiate - to be prone to complete an honorable degree of learning at a learned or scholarly academy, college, school, society or university

color-blind - to be able to see past the adopted or imposed coloring or discoloring of another person's identity, image, personality, prestige or reputation to discern their true character

color-blind^2 - to be prone to refuse to regard skin color as an indication of the purity, strength or virtue of someone's character, or as an indication of a lack thereof

coloring - to intend to actively, charitably, generously and wisely esteem, regard and treat another person as the more excellent and progressive person they can and should become, and to thus give them the inspiring confidence, the uplifting encouragement and the elevating opportunity to live up to such esteem, regard and treatment as long as they do so

coloring^2 - to intend to ascertain and then accurately and clearly state the truly positive character, condition, influence, merit, power, quality, strength, value or worth of someone or something

combatant - to be a healthy man who is filled with enough true enlightenment, virtue and integrity

to prayerfully acquire and exercise enough powerful skill from God to righteously prevail in unavoidable and horribly violent military or police combat, bloodshed, death and destruction commenced against my government, as long as my government and its cause are good and honorable and as long as my government strives to safeguard the fundamental right to human life, the fundamental right and control of personal property, equal justice under virtuous law, and the pursuit and preservation of that true enlightenment, virtue and integrity which produce, preserve or restore true liberty, hope, peace and joy within us, our families and society

combatant^2 - to be willing to fight for the preservation of my good and honorable country and its virtuous laws

comely - to be filled with enough true enlightenment, virtue and integrity to produce, preserve or restore true liberty, hope, peace and joy within me, my family and society

comely^2 - to be filled with enough true enlightenment, virtue and integrity to strongly attract or appeal to another person's sense of true enlightenment, virtue and integrity

comforted - to be worthy to be visited by the Lord Jesus Christ

comforted^2 - to be worthy to constantly receive within me the constant companionship of the gloriously and powerfully comforting, cleansing, empowering, enlightening, gifting, instructing, justifying, protecting, purifying, refining, revelatory and sanctifying influence or divine presence of the Holy Ghost by my faithfully repentant and honorably exact obedience to those divinely appointed commandments, covenants, laws and ordinances upon which receipt of that divine gift is predicated

comforted[3] - to be filled with enough charity and enough other virtues to faithfully and prayerfully receive an absolute, perfect and spiritually verified personal knowledge of the truth by personal enlightenment, inspiration or revelation from God through the glorious influence or divine presence of the Holy Ghost

comforted[4] - to be prone to obtain true enlightenment, virtue and integrity within me, my family and society

comforting - to intend to offer or provide someone with the means for obtaining true enlightenment, virtue, integrity, liberty, hope, peace and joy

commendable - to be competent, of good report, praiseworthy and virtuous

commending - to intend to give or extend well-deserved favor, good report and special praise

commercial - to be prone to cultivate a sensitive appreciation for good and beneficial goods and services

commercial[2] - to be prone to create, perform or produce good and beneficial goods or services

commiserating - to intend to offer the needy and poor aid, assistance, concession, forbearance, forgiveness, leniency or tolerance to an extent and in a manner which is charitably loving, just, right and wise in the sight of God

commiserating[2] - to intend to actively, charitably, generously and wisely provide for the needy and poor to an extent or in a manner which saves their lives, meets their immediate needs for survival, fosters their adequate education, employment, labors, self-reliance and thrift, and which encourages their service to other people

commiserating[3] - to intend to actively, charitably, generously and wisely give of my substance or other resources to the needy and poor to help them deal with personal needs which they cannot take care of alone—provided they are continuing to demonstrate by their own determined education, training, labors, investments and savings, that they are responsibly striving to become self-reliant net contributors to the virtuously liberating freedom, health, honorable economic prosperity and steady progress of themselves, their families and society

committed - to be constantly bound, dedicated and determined to diligently and faithfully keep a covenant or promise which is holy or sacred in the sight of God

common-sense - to be common-sensible

common-sensible - to be prone to rely upon fundamentally sound intelligence and generally practical judgment in seeking a good conclusion or result

commonsensical - to be common-sensible

communal - to be virtuously Zionistic

communicating - to intend to receive increasing true enlightenment by worthily communing with God

communicating[2] - to be enlightening

communing - to intend to seek and respond to close, familiar or intimate communication or conversation with God in true conversation, dream, meditation, prayer, revelation, vision or other means of communication from Him

companionable - to be prone to associate with another person to an extent or in a manner which brings joy to both of us

comparing - to intend to systematically examine in order to discern, discriminate or identify important differences or similarities

compassionate - to be prone to offer the needy and poor aid, assistance, concession, forbearance, forgiveness, leniency or tolerance to an extent and in a manner which is charitably loving, just, right and wise in the sight of God

compassionate[2] - to be prone to actively, charitably, generously and wisely provide for the needy and poor to an extent or in a manner which saves their lives, meets their immediate needs for survival, fosters their adequate education, employment, labors, self-reliance and thrift, and which encourages their service to other people

compassionate[3] - to be prone to actively, charitably, generously and wisely give of my substance or other resources to the needy and poor to help them deal with personal needs which they cannot take care of alone—provided they are continuing to demonstrate by their own determined education, training, labors, investments and savings, that they are responsibly striving to become self-reliant net contributors to the virtuously liberating freedom, health, honorable economic prosperity and steady progress of themselves, their families and society

compelling - to intend to speak or act with such an overwhelming power of true enlightenment, virtue and integrity as to arouse or evoke the healthy admiration and respect of other people of true enlightenment, virtue and integrity

competent - to be able to take good care of people and things

competing - to intend to constantly fight to overcome my sins and weaknesses in order to continue to achieve true personal betterment, improvement or progress

competing[2] - to intend to lay down my life, if necessary, in order to defeat or withstand an attacking, known or wisely suspected criminal, deadly or evil enemy of society who seeks to impose darkness, vice, corruption, bondage, despair, turmoil and misery upon me, my family and society

complaisant - to be socially courteous, mannerly or polite

complementary - to be prone to cooperatively act in harmony with one or more other people to boost, empower or lift each other toward becoming more pure-in-heart or

more filled with that liberating
integrity which comes from
increasing true enlightenment and
from an increasing abundance of
truly virtuous thoughts, words,
actions, deeds or works
complete - to be whole
complimentary - to be prone to
complimenting
complimenting - to intend to
sincerely express well-deserved
admiration, congratulations, praise
or respect
complimenting[2] - to intend to
reciprocate kindness
composed - to be peaceable or
peaceful
composed[2] - to be dignified
composed[3] - to be controlled,
deliberate, disciplined or poised in
thinking, speaking and acting in
harmony with only good thoughts
comprehending - to be enlightened
or intelligent
comprehending[2] - to intend to
grasp or understand the true and
valuable meaning, nature or
significance of a specific
composition or set of things
comprehensive - to be prone to
personally ascertain and live in
harmony with the discernibly
enlightening and spiritually
verifiable truth that: all truth,
without exception, is always in
perfect harmony, integrity, oneness
or unity with itself and can,
therefore, be circumscribed or
combined into one clearly and
perfectly distinct, integrated and
undiluted sphere or whole which,
unlike confusion, error or
falsehood, is capable of producing,
preserving or restoring harmony,

integrity, oneness or unity within
me, my family and society
comprehensive[2] - to be prone to
grasp full, inclusive or thorough
understanding of a specific
composition or set of things at once
compunctious - to be prone to
avoid potential negligent or willful
wrongdoing by obeying the
sharply painful pricking or
warnings of my conscience
compunctious[2] - to be prone to
hearken unto my pained
conscience by faithfully, timely and
truly repenting of the negligent or
willful wrongdoing I have
committed
compunctious[3] - to be filled with
enough painful guilt for the
corrupt, sinful or vicious
wrongdoing I have committed
compunctive - to be prone to heed
a revealed commandment from
God to lovingly prick or warn
another person's conscience
enough to help them find enough
humble regret or true remorse to
immediately and truly repent of
their negligent or willful
wrongdoing
compunctive[2] - to be prone to
honorably use practical or punitive
means to lovingly prick or warn
another family member's
conscience enough to help them
find enough humble regret or true
remorse to immediately and truly
repent of their negligent or willful
wrongdoing
concealing - to intend to refuse to
viciously disclose or say more than
should be disclosed or said
concealing[2] - to intend to refuse to
excessively or needlessly disclose

confidential, personal, private, proprietary or secret information

concealing[3] - to intend to truly do more good than harm by refusing to make something generally known

conceiving - to intend to certainly hold, interpret, maintain or understand truth

concerned - to be prone to discern or perceive that I am affected by, connected to or involved in a matter which can have a negative impact upon me, my family and society

conciliated - to be fully reconciled to God unto exaltation through the charitable love, cleansing power and redeeming grace of the Atonement of the Lord Jesus Christ by my faithfully repentant and honorably exact obedience to those divinely appointed commandments, covenants, laws and ordinances upon which receipt of that reconciliation is predicated

conciliated[2] - to be one of those who have received divine favor from God by my believing and honorably exact obedience to that divinely appointed law upon which receipt of that divine favor is predicated

conciliated[3] - to be in complete harmony, integrity, oneness or unity with another person of true enlightenment, virtue and integrity

conciliated[4] - to be at peace with another person

concluding - to intend to resolve or settle a debate or question by discovering irrefutable proof using the same means by which it can be verified by others

concrete - to be prone to coalesce my thoughts into righteous thinking

concrete[2] - to be prone to coalesce my thoughts into practical thinking

condemning - to intend, in response to that true divine command or instruction I have ascertained by personal enlightenment, inspiration or revelation from God, to dutifully notify and warn another person that their evil and sinful misbehavior is, at the moment, under God's just condemnation and, absent their faithful, timely and true repentance, obedience and reconciliation to God, shall eventually result in God justly declaring that person damned or exposed to the agonizing suffering and miserable torment of hell as long as it takes them to pay for their own sins

condescending - to intend to esteem and treat those of lesser or lower power, prestige, property, privilege, rank, status or wealth as better than I am

condescending[2] - to intend to willingly esteem and treat those of lesser or lower power, prestige, property, privilege, rank, status or wealth as equal to myself

conditional - to be prone to carefully select and entertain virtuous thoughts, knowing that my resulting words and actions will produce, preserve or restore true enlightenment, virtue and integrity within me, my family and society

conditional[2] - to be prone to recognize that my thoughts, words and actions produce specific

consequential events or results within me, my family and society
conditional[3] - to be prone to recognize that the actual being, existence or occurrence of one thing can produce the actual being, existence or occurrence of another
conditional[4] - to be prone to recognize that my actual personal productivity and progress are dependent upon the condition or character of my body, mind and spirit
conditioned - to be of virtuous character, behavior and moral disposition
conditioned[2] - to be healthy
conditioning - to intend to make someone virtuously conditioned
conditioning[2] - to intend to increase the frequency and reliability of someone's positive response by offering them immediate reward and by withholding punishment from them as often as their positive response needs to be reinforced
condoling - to intend to express sincere and sympathetic grief or mourning to a friend, neighbor or relative to help them deal with their grief or mourning
confederating - to intend to enter into a contract or covenant to join or unite in allegiance or league with one or more other people of true enlightenment, virtue and integrity to virtuously cooperate as allies
confessing - to intend to fully, honestly and willingly acknowledge, admit, declare or disclose my significant wrongdoing to those I have wronged, to those in authority who should know, and to God

confident - to be convinced of and to feel secure trust in the goodness, love, power and wisdom of God and in my likelihood of success, knowing or having good enough reason to believe that the course I am now faithfully and prayerfully pursuing is pleasing unto Him and that my consistently virtuous thinking and my persistently charitable desires and works toward humankind are deserving of His perfect grace
confident[2] - to be filled with the charitable works and the virtuous integrity necessary to remain convinced of, to feel secure trust in, and to boldly exhibit my individual worth, my personal abilities, and my likelihood of success
confidential - to be prone to refuse to viciously disclose or say more than should be disclosed or said
confidential[2] - to be prone to refuse to excessively or needlessly disclose confidential, personal, private, proprietary or secret information
confidential[3] - to be prone to truly do more good than harm by refusing to make something generally known
confirmed - to be a faithful, fully repentant, newly baptized believer in the Lord Jesus Christ, who has voluntarily participated in the priesthood ordinance of confirmation performed by a duly ordained man called of God who bears true higher priesthood authority from God and has authorization from God's own called, ordained and authorized priesthood leaders on Earth to administer the ordinance by the

laying on of hands—so that I can justly receive confirmation of my membership into His church and kingdom, along with the gift of the constant companionship of the Holy Ghost, and can be further prepared on Earth to receive the blessings of a glorious celestial resurrection and exaltation in the world to come

confirmed[2] - to be entitled by the priesthood ordinance of confirmation to receive and to retain from day to day by my faithfulness the gift of the constant companionship of the glorious influence when not the divine presence of the Holy Ghost, who shall bring into my increasingly charitable and virtuous soul manifestations of God's love, and an increasing knowledge and remembrance of truth, and liberty from darkness, vice and corruption, and spiritual cleansing, and greater power to personally progress toward justly receiving a greater gifted measure of true enlightenment, virtue, integrity, liberty, hope, peace and joy, and all of the other blessings which come from my faithfully repentant and honorably exact obedience to the commandments, covenants, laws and ordinances of God

confirmed[3] - to be one of those who have voluntarily entered into the priesthood ordinance of confirmation in a manner, method or mode of confirmation recognized by God as authorized and binding on Earth and in heaven

confirmed[4] - to be reborn by the Spirit of God

confirming - to be a duly ordained man called of God, who then uses my true higher priesthood authority from God and authorization from God's own called, ordained and authorized priesthood leaders on Earth to administer, without pay, the priesthood ordinance of confirmation by the laying on of hands upon a desirous, repentant, newly baptized believer in the Lord Jesus Christ—so that they can justly receive confirmation of their membership into His church and kingdom, along with the gift of the constant companionship of the Holy Ghost, and can be further prepared on Earth to receive the blessings of a glorious celestial resurrection and exaltation in the world to come

confirming[2] - to be a duly ordained man called of God, who then uses my true higher priesthood authority from God and authorization from God's own called, ordained and authorized priesthood leaders on Earth to administer, without pay, in a dedicated holy temple of God the priesthood ordinance of confirmation by the laying on of hands upon living proxy who act in behalf of deceased family members and other deceased persons who are accountable to the laws of God and for whom the work of baptism has been vicariously performed—so that they can justly receive confirmation of their membership into His church and kingdom, along with the gift of the constant companionship of the Holy Ghost, and can be further prepared by loving family or other living proxy on Earth to receive the blessings of a glorious celestial resurrection and exaltation in the world to come

confirming[3] - to intend to administer, without pay, the priesthood ordinance of confirmation in a manner, method or mode of confirmation recognized by God as authorized and binding on Earth and in heaven

confirming[4] - to intend to indisputably establish or verify for myself that something is accurate, correct, genuine, true or valid

confirming[5] - to intend to necessarily and truly testify to one or more other people that something is accurate, correct, genuine, true or valid

confronting - to intend to face and deal with one or more other people who must be dealt with, in an effort to produce an acceptable result for everyone involved

confronting[2] - to intend to face and deal with something which must be dealt with, in an effort to produce an acceptable result

Confucianist - to be prone to live in harmony with the teachings of Confucianism which produce, preserve or restore true enlightenment, virtue and integrity within me, my family and society

congratulating - to intend to feel and to wish someone heartfelt joy for their joyous event or success

congratulatory - to be prone to feel and to wish someone heartfelt joy for their joyous event or success

congruent - to be prone to live in perfect agreement or harmony with

that which is truly good and of God

congruent[2] - to be prone to live in perfect agreement or harmony with enlightened certainty, reality or truth

conjoining - to intend to associate, join or unite together with one or more other people of true enlightenment, virtue and integrity for a good purpose

connected - to be and to choose to remain part of a celestial, exalted or sealed family relationship

connected[2] - to be and to choose to remain part of a healthy and unified family relationship

connecting - to intend to develop celestial, exalted or sealed family relationships

connecting[2] - to intend to develop healthy and unified family relationships

conquerable - to be prone to become or remain virtuously self-controlled

conquered - to be virtuously self-controlled

conquering - to intend to keep the covenants and promises I have made with God to faithfully keep His commandments, covenants, laws and ordinances well enough to receive from Him the power I need to progress

conquering[2] - to intend to keep the pleasure and satisfaction of all of my biologically inherent and naturally impelling emotional, physical or sexual appetites, cravings, desires, drives and passions integrated within the safe and discernibly enlightened boundaries of chastity, cleanliness, purity and virtue which God has justly set by law and commandment

conquering[3] - to intend to control, subdue, overcome or overpower darkness, vice and corruption within myself

conscientious - to be prone to remain completely integrated in thought, speech and behavior with the dictates of that measure of absolute, perfect and spiritually verified personal knowledge of enlightened certainty, reality or truth which I know I have received from God and which induces or influences me to be made truly chaste, clean, pure and virtuous at heart and to continue to encourage and help other people by charitable love, kindness, invitation and instruction to be godly enough to be made truly chaste, clean, pure and virtuous at heart

conscientious[2] - to be prone to honestly pay enough careful and thorough attention to the dictates of that inherent measure of innate enlightenment with which I was born, to my innately enlightened knowledge and sense of that which is truly good and of God, and to my innately enlightened feelings of personal duty and love toward God, myself, my family and society to willfully think, speak and act in harmony with the commandments, covenants, laws and ordinances of God

conscientious[3] - to be prone to honestly pay enough careful and thorough attention to the dictates of my innately enlightened sense of that which is truly good and of God, and to my innately enlightened feelings of personal duty and love toward God, myself, my family and society to willfully think, speak and act in harmony with that which produces, preserves or restores true enlightenment, virtue and integrity within me, my family and society

conscientious[4] - to be prone to honestly pay enough careful and thorough attention to the dictates of my innately enlightened sense of that which is truly good and of God, and to my innately enlightened feelings of personal duty and love toward God, myself, my family and society to willfully think, speak and act in harmony with that which produces, preserves or restores the virtuously liberating freedom, health, honorable economic prosperity and steady progress of me, my family and society

conscientious[5] - to be prone to honestly and willfully conform my thoughts, words and actions to my best understanding of what is truly good

conscientious[6] - to be prone to willfully strive to sustain within my thoughts, words and actions the integrity of that measure of truth which I know I possess

conscientious[7] - to be prone to alleviate the plain uneasiness, the warning distress or the alarming anguish of my enlightened conscience by immediately repenting toward doing and being what it takes to preserve its welcome powers of protection within me, to avoid violating its saving dictates, and to avoid becoming conscienceless conscientious[8] - to be virtuously scientific

conscionable - to be virtuously conscientious

conscious - to be newly aware of or to recognize from memory the characteristic and distinctive differences between that which is truly good and of God and that which is evil or satanic

conscious[2] - to be newly aware of or to recognize from memory that which is enlightened certainty, reality or truth and that which is confusion, error or falsehood

conscious[3] - to be newly aware of or to recognize that which is real and that which is imaginary

conscious[4] - to be aware or perceptive enough to clearly evaluate and effectively plan my impact upon, my interaction with or my response to reality

consecrated - to be dedicated or devoted to faithfully and honorably serving God's sacred purposes

consecrating - to intend to voluntarily appropriate, dedicate or devote all worthy means I possess and may ever possess to God's sacred purposes

consequence-oriented - to be prone to personally ascertain and live in harmony with the discernibly enlightening and spiritually verifiable truth that: God is bound by the eternally binding law of justice, which law demands that certain rewards must eventually be granted to me in harmony with proof of my believing and honorably exact obedience to the commandments, covenants, laws and ordinances of God

consequence-oriented[2] - to be prone to personally ascertain and live in harmony with the discernibly enlightening and spiritually verifiable truth that: God is bound by the eternally binding law of justice, which law prohibits His condemnation of any person who has heard nothing and hence understands nothing of His divinely enlightening commandments, covenants, laws and ordinances, and hence cannot knowingly disobey them, and hence cannot be brought under their condemnation, and hence cannot repent of any disobedience to them, and hence is saved from the negative effects of Adam's and Eve's fall through the Atonement of the Lord Jesus Christ

consequence-oriented[3] - to be prone to personally ascertain and live in harmony with the discernibly enlightening and spiritually verifiable truth that: notwithstanding His perfect love for me, God is bound by the eternally binding law of justice to be no unjust respecter of persons, and He is thus bound to justly condemn my proven willful rejection of Him by withdrawing or withholding a measure of His enlightenment and other blessings from me to the extent I willfully reject greater enlightened certainty, reality or truth about Him and His divinely enlightening commandments, covenants, laws and ordinances

consequence-oriented[4] - to be prone to personally ascertain and live in harmony with the discernibly enlightening and spiritually verifiable truth that: God is bound by the eternally binding law of justice, which law demands that certain consequences, debts, demands, obligations, payments, penalties, punishments, reparations or restitutions must eventually be justly imposed upon and required of me to the proven extent I fail or refuse to repent of my willful violations of the commandments, covenants, laws and ordinances of God

consequence-oriented[5] - to be prone to think, speak and act in harmony with the naturally obvious truth that certain natural rewards are justly granted to me when I obey in certain ways the natural or physical laws established for this earth

consequence-oriented[6] - to be prone to think, speak and act in harmony with the naturally obvious truth that certain consequences, debts, demands, obligations, payments, penalties, punishments, reparations or restitutions justly befall me when I disobey in certain ways the natural or physical laws established for this earth

consequence-oriented[7] - to be prone to think, speak and act in harmony with the self-evident truth that certain benefits can justly come to me because of my obedience to definite man-made laws, regulations or rules

consequence-oriented[8] - to be prone to think, speak and act in harmony with the self-evident truth that certain man-made consequences, debts, demands, obligations,

payments, penalties, punishments, reparations or restitutions may be justly imposed upon and required of me because of my disobedience to definite man-made laws, regulations or rules

consequential - to be prone to make an important, significant or valuable contribution to someone's virtuously liberating freedom, health, honorable economic prosperity and steady progress

conservative - to be prone to honorably and justly preserve truth and virtue from damage, decay, destruction, disintegration, loss, injury or waste

conservative[2] - to be prone to limit freedom enough to safeguard true enlightenment, virtue and integrity within me, my family and society

conservative[3] - to be prone to execute, judge or legislate to an extent or in a manner which is enlightened, virtuous and wise enough to preserve the virtuously liberating freedom, health, honorable economic prosperity and steady progress of me, my family and society

conservative[4] - to be prone to avoid wasting resources by responsibly giving or spending enough to fill immediate needs while preserving diligence, self-reliance and thrift

conservative[5] - to be practical

conservative[6] - to be prone to follow and preserve the best-known and time-proven means and methods of caution, discretion, moderation and thrift

conserving - to intend to wisely manage or preserve resources

conserving[2] - to intend to prevent or stop misuse or waste

considerate - to be prone to kindly and thoughtfully respond to the feelings, needs and rights of other people

considering - to intend to carefully contemplate, deliberate, discuss or evaluate, before reaching or rendering a good and honorable conclusion, decision or judgment

consistent - to be prone to refuse to falter or waver from the condition, course, place or position I have ascertained is most pleasing unto God

consistent[2] - to be prone to fail or refuse to be capricious or volatile

consolidating - to intend to bring together or unify people of true enlightenment, virtue and integrity

consorting - to intend to accompany, agree, associate or unite with one or more other people of true enlightenment, virtue and integrity

conspicuous - to be obviously filled with true enlightenment, virtue and integrity

constant - to be consistently and persistently faithful or loyal to that which is charitably loving, just, right and wise in the sight of God

constitutional - to be prone to create, establish or form good character within me

constitutional[2] - to be healthy

constitutional[3] - to be prone, as a law-abiding citizen of my nation, to defend, honor, obey and sustain my nation's constitution as long as its administration, application or use consistently defends, honors and sustains true enlightenment, virtue and integrity within me, my family and society

constitutional[4] - to be prone, as a law-abiding citizen of my nation, to defend, honor, obey and sustain my good nation's good constitution against all domestic and foreign enemies who attempt to powerfully impose darkness, vice and corruption within me, my family and society

constructive - to be prone to construct or promote true personal betterment, improvement or progress within me, my family and society

construing - to intend to correctly understand the true character, identity or meaning of something

consulting - to intend to seek advice, direction, guidance or information from God

consulting[2] - to intend to seek advice, direction, guidance or information from those who are truly authorized and worthy to receive inspiration from God concerning me

consulting[3] - to intend to provide or seek the best advice, direction, guidance, information or services from the best people in order to make the best choices or decisions or to achieve optimum results

consulting[4] - to intend to provide or seek better advice, direction, guidance, information or services from better people in order to make better choices or decisions or to achieve better results

contemplating - to intend to deliberately consider, observe or ponder spiritual things

content - to be satisfied with doing the very best I can to progress

content[2] - to be gratified, pleased and satisfied with receiving sufficient for my needs

contextualizing - to intend to seek better understanding of someone by striving to accurately, comprehensively and realistically observe or realize how well their words and actions are truly woven together with, interact with, relate to or result from true enlightenment, virtue, integrity, liberty, hope, peace and joy

contextualizing[2] - to intend to seek better understanding of someone by striving to accurately, comprehensively and realistically observe or realize how their words and actions are truly woven together with the thoughts, words and actions of other people and with their collective circumstances, experiences, focus, labors, needs, resources and so forth

contextualizing[3] - to intend to seek better understanding of something by striving to accurately, comprehensively and realistically observe or realize how it is truly woven together, interacts with, relates to or results from other things

continent - to be chaste in thought, speech and behavior

continent[2] - to be prone to exercise enough moderation, self-control, self-discipline, self-restraint or temperance to keep my thoughts, words and actions integrated within the safe and discernibly enlightened boundaries of chastity, cleanliness, purity and virtue which God has justly set by law and commandment

continuous - to be prone to maintain unceasing devotion to God by my believing and honorably exact obedience to the divinely appointed commandments, covenants, laws and ordinances of God

continuous[2] - to be prone to consistently or constantly refuse to be evil or satanic

contradistinguishing - to intend to distinguish any contrasting or dissimilar qualities

contrasting - to intend to compare and discern differences

contrite - to be prone to feel so worn down within my heart by godly sorrow or remorse for offending God with my sins as to humbly and submissively commit myself to turn away from them and to permanently throw them off through my faithful, timely and true repentance, obedience and reconciliation to God

contrite[2] - to be prone to feel so worn down within my heart by deep and humble regret for my wrongdoing toward other people as to do all I can and should to make full confession, apology and restitution for the injury I have caused them in order to seek full reconciliation with them

contrite[3] - to be prone to feel so worn down within my heart by deep and humble regret for my weaknesses or vices as to do all I can and should to replace them with strengths or virtues

controlled - to be prone to possess and maintain liberty, hope, peace, joy and other heavenly blessings by my believing and honorably exact obedience to those divinely

appointed laws upon which receipt of those blessings is predicated
controlled[2] - to be prone to powerfully govern or restrain myself to an extent or in a manner which produces, preserves or restores true enlightenment, virtue and integrity within me, my family and society
controlled[3] - to be prone to powerfully govern or restrain myself to an extent or in a manner which produces, preserves or restores the virtuously liberating freedom, health, honorable economic prosperity and steady progress of me, my family and society
controlled[4] - to be prone to keep my thoughts, words and actions within the safe and discernibly enlightened boundaries of chastity, cleanliness, purity and virtue which God has justly set by law and commandment
controlled[5] - to be prone to powerfully govern or restrain the pleasure and satisfaction of all of my biologically inherent and naturally impelling emotional, physical or sexual appetites, cravings, desires, drives and passions enough to keep them safely integrated within the discernibly enlightened boundaries of chastity, cleanliness, purity and virtue which God has justly set by law and commandment
controlled[6] - to be prone to repress or suppress darkness, vice and corruption from entering into the thoughts, beliefs, values and characteristics of my heart
controlled[7] - to be prone to readily and willingly submit to those who exercise their duly authorized powers of direction, dominion, government, restraint or rule to an extent or in a manner which produces, preserves or restores true enlightenment, virtue and integrity within me, my family and society
controlled[8] - to be prone to readily and willingly submit to those who exercise their duly authorized powers of direction, dominion, government, restraint or rule to an extent or in a manner which produces, preserves or restores the virtuously liberating freedom, health, honorable economic prosperity and steady progress of me, my family and society
controlling - to intend to honorably and justly use my authority and power to direct, dominate, govern, guide, regulate, restrain or rule to an extent or in a manner which produces, preserves or restores true enlightenment, virtue and integrity within me, my family and society
controlling[2] - to intend to honorably and justly use my authority and power to direct, dominate, govern, guide, regulate, restrain or rule to an extent or in a manner which produces, preserves or restores the virtuously liberating freedom, health, honorable economic prosperity and steady progress of me, my family and society
convalescing - to intend to gradually recover health and strength over darkness, vice and corruption
convalescing[2] - to intend to gradually recover health and strength over illness or sickness

converted - to be prone to add more good to the good I already have and am

converted[2] - to be changed, reborn, renewed or transformed into someone filled with greater true enlightenment, virtue, integrity, liberty, hope, peace and joy

converted[3] - to be changed, reborn, renewed or transformed into a better religion or way of life

converting - to intend to lovingly encourage and kindly help someone to add more good to the good they already have and are

converting[2] - to intend to lovingly encourage and kindly help someone to be changed, reborn, renewed or transformed into someone filled with greater true enlightenment, virtue, integrity, liberty, hope, peace and joy

converting[3] - to intend to lovingly encourage and kindly help someone to be changed, reborn, renewed or transformed into a better religion or way of life

converting[4] - to intend to lovingly encourage and kindly help someone to exchange something for something better

convicted - to be so overcome by recognition of personal guilt and remorse within my personal conscience as to willingly confess and repent of all of the corrupt, sinful or vicious wrongdoing within me

convicting - to intend to find enough recognition of guilt and remorse by my enlightened conscience to freely choose to confess and repent of all of the corrupt, sinful or vicious wrongdoing within me

convicting[2] - to intend to help a guilty person find enough recognition of guilt and remorse of conscience to freely choose to confess and repent of their vice, corruption, sin and wrongdoing

convivial - to be filled with festive and healthy cheerfulness, gaiety, happiness or merriment through healthy association with good company

cool - to be unflappable

coolheaded - to be unflappable

cooperating - to intend to operate or work well with one or more other good people to accomplish a good purpose

coordinating - to intend to bring into or join in good operation or order

co-parenting - to intend to share with my lawfully and legally wedded husband or wife the care and custody of our children

coping - to intend to persistently seek to effectively deal with unavoidable challenges, difficulties, problems or responsibilities

cordial - to be courteous and gracious enough to be uplifting

corporative - to be prone to join, unite or work with other company directors, officers, employees or shareholders of true enlightenment, virtue and integrity in bringing to market that which produces, preserves or restores true enlightenment, virtue and integrity within me, my family and society

corporative[2] - to be prone to join, unite or work with other directors, officers, employees or shareholders of a company in which enough emphasis is placed on creating and maintaining a working culture or environment which produces, preserves or restores true enlightenment, virtue and integrity within me, my family and society

correct - to be prone to accurately identify, evaluate, interpret, judge, understand or otherwise think, speak or act in harmony with that which is charitably loving, just, right and wise in the sight of God

correcting - to intend to become cleansed or sanctified from my sins through my faithful, timely and true repentance, obedience and reconciliation to God—so I can then progress toward greater true enlightenment, virtue, integrity, liberty, hope, peace and joy

correcting^2 - to intend to lovingly encourage and kindly help other people to become cleansed from their sins through their faithful, timely and true repentance, obedience and reconciliation to God—so they can then progress toward greater true enlightenment, virtue, integrity, liberty, hope, peace and joy

correcting^3 - to intend to rectify or otherwise bring something into harmony with that which is charitably loving, just, right and wise in the sight of God

correcting^4 - to intend to rectify or otherwise bring something into harmony with truly chaste, clean, pure and virtuous thoughts, beliefs, values and characteristics

correcting^5 - to intend to rectify or otherwise bring into harmony with the good law of the land

correlating - to intend to join in establishing a mutually complementary connection, order or relationship between or among people of true enlightenment, virtue and integrity

corresponding - to intend to participate with one or more other people of true enlightenment, virtue and integrity in complementary relationships

corrigible - to be prone to readily and willingly submit to personal progress or personal improvement

cosmological - to be prone to study and to accurately portray the realities of the origin, nature or structure of the universe or of one or more of its parts

cosmological^2 - to be prone to study and to accurately portray the realities of astronomy

cosmopolitan - to be prone to demonstrate or seek a broad knowledge of the truth that is free from local, provincial, national or regional biases or prejudices and that encompasses a sophisticated understanding of many parts of the world

cosmopolitanizing - to intend to lovingly encourage and kindly help someone to be cosmopolitan

counseling - to intend to prayerfully seek advice, direction, guidance or information from God

counseling^2 - to intend to seek advice, direction, guidance or information from those who are truly authorized and worthy to receive personal inspiration or revelation from God about me

counseling^3 - to intend to consult on important decisions and other matters with good parents, family members and leaders

countercultural - to be prone to strive to counteract, defeat or

withstand a lifestyle, path or way of character or culture which produces, preserves or restores darkness, vice and corruption within me, my family and society
counterrevolutionary - to be prone to resist or overthrow radical change toward that which produces, preserves or restores darkness, vice, corruption, bondage, despair, turmoil and misery within me, my family and society
counterrevolutionary[2] - to be prone to resist or overthrow radical change away from that which produces, preserves or restores greater true enlightenment, virtue, integrity, liberty, hope, peace and joy within me, my family and society
counting - to intend to know and recognize the true character, condition, influence, merit, power, quality, strength, value or worth of someone or something
courageous - to be prone—while I am faithfully doing that which is truly good and of God—to boldly encounter unavoidable adversity, failure, hardship, harm, opposition, pain or persecution with a calm and firm resolve to faithfully vanquish it
courageous[2] - to be prone to boldly encounter evil or satanic opposition with a faithful, heroic-at-heart, intrepid or valiant resolve to do and be only that which is truly good and of God
courageous[3] - to be prone, with all of the powers of my heart, might, mind and strength, to refuse to be enslaved or oppressed by depressing or intimidating

darkness, vice, corruption, bondage, despair, turmoil and misery
courageous[4] - to be prone to boldly encounter uncertainty with a calm, fearless and unwavering resolve to faithfully obtain a sure knowledge of enlightened certainty, reality or truth
courteous - to be prone to use good, well-polished manners to show gracious consideration and respect worthy of a dignified company or court
courting - to intend to steadily use courteous dating in order to steadily induce, influence or persuade growth and improvement in the truly virtuous love I share with my lawfully and legally wedded husband or wife
courting[2] - to be courteous enough to win the courtesy of another person
courtly - to be elegantly courteous, dignified and polished in manner
couth - to be polished in manners and speech
covenanting - to intend, as God requires, to pledge before God and His authorized witnesses to uphold my part of a good and true covenant, promise or vow entered into with God in exchange for His promised blessings, with a solemn promise to personally answer for its fulfillment with all that I possess, even with my own life if necessary
covenanting[2] - to intend, as God requires, to place my personal honor at stake or to give my word of honor to faithfully and honorably fulfill, keep or uphold the sacred covenants or promises I

make with God to obey and keep His commandments, covenants, laws and ordinances in exchange for His promised blessings

covenanting[3] - to intend, as God requires, to enter into and sustain virtuous married status

covenanting[4] - to intend, as God requires, to exercise enough faith to immediately and truly repent and to enter into a true covenant of baptism and with God so that, as I continue to exactly, faithfully and honorably manifest adherence to my promise to live up to my baptism covenant, I can receive and retain a remission of my sins, the right to receive the priesthood ordinance of confirmation, and the assurance of promised everlasting redemption from the bondage and burdens of sin, from the agonizing suffering and miserable torment of hell, and from everlasting separation from the glorious celestial presence of God in spiritual death—unto spiritual rebirth and salvation through the charitable love, cleansing power and redeeming grace of the Atonement of His Son, the Lord Jesus Christ

covenant-keeping - to intend, as God requires, to continue to do all I must do to fulfill, keep or uphold a good and true covenant, promise or vow I know I have made before God and His authorized witnesses to obey and keep one or more of His commandments, covenants, laws and ordinances

coveting - to intend to eagerly, earnestly or intensely crave or desire to attain or obtain that which produces, preserves or

restores true enlightenment, virtue and integrity within me, my family and society

creating - to intend to newly organize my personal progress in order to do all I can and should to produce, preserve or restore the greatest true enlightenment, virtue, integrity, liberty, hope, peace and joy within me, my family and society

creating[2] - to intend to invent better ways of doing better things

creationist - to be prone to personally ascertain and live in harmony with the discernibly enlightening and spiritually verifiable truth that: the world and all of its original life forms were created or organized by God from existing matter, and were placed here by Him

creationist[2] - to be prone to personally ascertain and live in harmony with the discernibly enlightening and spiritually verifiable truth that: only enlivened spirit matter divinely formed into a living spirit being and embodied in harmony with divine law within a body of earthly physical matter can bring that earthly physical matter to life on Earth

creationistic - to be creationist

credentialed - to be prone to obtain a good character worthy of belief, confidence, credibility and trust

credible - to be prone to live up to the full confidence and trust God has placed in me to learn and do His will with His help, so that by His grace, love and power I can justly receive all earthly and heavenly blessings, gifts or rewards He wants me to receive

credible[2] - to be prone to consistently speak or act in an honorable and virtuous manner worthy of confident acceptance and trust

creditable - to be prone to produce, preserve or restore admirable, commendable, honorable or praiseworthy actions, deeds or works in the sight of God by my believing and honorably exact obedience to the divinely appointed commandments, covenants, laws and ordinances of God

creditable[2] - to be prone to live up to the good, uplifting and well-deserved belief, confidence, reliance or trust someone has placed in me

creditable[3] - to be prone to live up to the good, uplifting and well-deserved admiration, commendation, esteem or praise someone has placed in me

crediting - to intend to acknowledge or recognize with admiration, commendation, esteem or praise another person's truly admirable, commendable, honorable or praiseworthy actions, deeds or works

crediting[2] - to intend to demonstrate or show my belief, confidence or trust in someone or something truly good and of God

crediting[3] - to intend to demonstrate or show my belief, confidence or trust in someone or something true

creditworthy - to be truly worthy of credit because I pay my honorable debts on time

criminalizing - to intend to justly and wisely prescribe or lawfully and legally impose criminal consequences, debts, demands, obligations, payments, penalties or restrictions against someone's spoken words and actions which produce, preserve or restore darkness, vice and corruption within me, my family and society

criticizing - to intend to accurately and clearly discern or distinguish between that which is truly good and of God and that which is evil or satanic

criticizing[2] - to intend to carefully and skillfully analyze and evaluate in a sincere effort to accurately and fairly judge the relative importance, merit or value of someone or something

cultish - to be religiously virtuous or virtuously religious

cultivated - to be virtuously refined

cultivated[2] - to be improved

cultivating - to intend to lovingly encourage and kindly help someone to be cultivated

cultivating[2] - to intend to labor, nurture or study to foster or promote improvement toward something better

cultured - to be prone to welcome, enjoy and live in harmony with the academic, dancing, dress, food, graphic, intellectual, literary, musical or other socially recognized human characteristics or products found among various social classes, groups, nations or other factions of society which produce, preserve or restore true enlightenment, virtue and integrity within me, my family and society

cultured[2] - to be prone to enjoy learning more about and living more in harmony with the beneficial elements and virtuous qualities of the arts, sciences and humanities from one or more social classes, groups, nations or other factions of society

cultured[3] - to be prone to enjoy learning more about and living more in harmony with the beneficial elements and virtuous qualities of academic, dancing, dress, food, graphic, intellectual, literary, musical or other socially recognized human characteristics or products found among various social classes, groups, nations or other factions of society

cultured[4] - to be prone to enjoy learning more about and living more in harmony with the beneficial elements and virtuous qualities of the social beliefs, behaviors, forms, manners, traits and ways of one or more social classes, groups, nations or other factions of society

cultured[5] - to be prone to live in harmony with a lifestyle, path or way of character or culture which produces, preserves or restores true enlightenment, virtue and integrity within me, my family and society

curable - to be prone to readily and willingly submit to healing, recovery or restoration from disease, harm, illness or trouble

curing - to intend to justly and kindly provide means for healing, recovery or restoration from disease, harm, illness or trouble

cursing - to intend, by true higher priesthood authority, commandment, and power from God, to bind, imprecate or invoke His condemning curse upon another person or thing

D

dainty - to be a girl or woman who is of such delicate, diminutive, elegant, gracious and pure inward beauty, acute sensibility and goodly manners as to forbid harsh or rough handling

dainty[2] - to be prone to avoid what is coarse

damning - to intend, in response to that true divine command or instruction I have ascertained by personal enlightenment, inspiration or revelation from God, to obediently notify and warn another person that their evil and sinful misbehavior is, at the moment, under God's just condemnation and, absent their faithful, timely and true repentance, obedience and reconciliation to God, shall eventually result in God justly declaring that person damned or exposed to the agonizing suffering and miserable torment of hell as long as it takes them to pay for their own sins

dancing - to intend to cultivate a sensitive appreciation for good and uplifting dance

dancing[2] - to intend to compose, create, make, perform or produce good and uplifting dance

dandy - to be first-rate

darling - to be truly worthy to be cherished or dearly beloved by someone dear to me

dashing - to be a boy or man who is elegant and gallant in manner

dating - to intend to agree with my lawfully and legally wedded husband or wife to meet each week at an appointed time and place to enjoy sharing positive interaction, loving partnership, romantic togetherness and marital rejuvenation

dating[2] - to intend, as a chaste and virtuous unmarried man, to initiate agreement with a reputedly chaste and virtuous unmarried woman to meet at an appointed time and place to enjoy sharing positive interaction and to explore the prospects of lasting romantic togetherness and loving partnership in courteous courtship and in lasting honorable familial marriage

dating[3] - to intend, as a chaste and virtuous unmarried boy sixteen years old or older, to initiate agreement with a reputedly chaste and virtuous unmarried girl sixteen years old or older to meet at an appointed time and place to enjoy sharing good, clean interaction and enjoyable togetherness which will give us valuable experience for when it comes time to seek honorable familial marriage to an adult member of the opposite gender who is eligible for lawful and legal marriage

dauntless - to be prone to refuse to be excessively or needlessly disheartened, dismayed or intimidated by fear

dazzling - to be brilliant

dealing - to intend to conduct bargaining, business or trade to an extent or in a manner which produces, preserves or restores true enlightenment, virtue and integrity within me, my family and society

dear - to be truly worthy of great esteem and love

debating - to intend to consider or evaluate opposing viewpoints

debonair - to be prone to exercise elegant and gracious courtesy

debtless - to be prone to honorably and justly discharge all of my need or obligation to repent

debtless[2] - to be prone to finally and honorably discharge all of my indebtedness, liability or obligation to repay

decent - to be prone to conform to those laws, rules, standards or values which produce, preserve or restore cleanliness, modesty or other forms of true enlightenment, virtue and integrity within me, my family and society

decent[2] - to be prone to refuse to conform to those laws, rules, standards or values which produce, preserve or restore filthiness, immodesty or other forms of darkness, vice and corruption within me, my family and society

decent[3] - to be respectably generous and kind

decided - to be prone to knowingly stick to the right decision with determination and resolve

decided[2] - to be prone to refuse to needlessly delay, postpone or procrastinate making a decision

decisive - to be prone to make decisions which are charitably loving, just, right and wise in the sight of God

declaring - to intend to make an honorable accounting or disclosure when necessary

declining - to intend to refuse to accept anyone's invitation to think, say or do that which produces, preserves or restores darkness, vice and corruption within me, my family and society

decontaminating - to intend to remove that which is evil or satanic from me

decorating - to intend to graciously acknowledge another person with well-deserved honors

decorous - to be prone to think, speak and act to an extent or in a manner which shows respect for social customs of good taste and propriety

defeatist - to be prone to personally ascertain and live in harmony with the discernibly enlightening and spiritually verifiable truth that: by God's matchless power and wisdom shall come the inevitable and ultimate defeat, subjection and abolition of all darkness, vice, corruption, bondage, despair, turmoil and misery from the earth

defederalizing - to intend to refuse to viciously exercise, enforce or impose the supreme authority or power of my nation's central government

defederalizing^2 - to intend to refuse to allow or cause a central government to take excessive authority or power unto itself

defended - to be prone to defend, protect or secure myself against everything which has or which may have enough evil or satanic power to induce or influence me to willfully reject my good conscience, or to defile the active and stored thoughts of my mind with darkness, vice and corruption, or to drive true enlightenment, virtue and integrity out of my mind and heart, or to infect me with evil or satanic desires to lustfully fulfill or sinfully satisfy one or more of my

biologically inherent and naturally impelling emotional, physical or sexual appetites, cravings, desires, drives or passions, or to otherwise cause the Spirit of God to withdraw from me

defending - to intend to deter or protect against a potentially deadly attack against me, my family and society

defending^2 - to intend to deter or protect against the production, preservation or restoration of darkness, vice and corruption within me, my family and society

defending^3 - to intend to defeat or withstand a harmful attack from an attacking, known or wisely suspected criminal, deadly or evil enemy of society

defending^4 - to be prepared and ready to meet a potentially harmful attack

defiant - to be prone to bravely and contemptuously strive to defeat or withstand the courageous attack or daring opposition of an attacking, known or wisely suspected criminal, deadly or evil enemy of society

defiant^2 - to be prone to boldly and openly resist darkness, vice and corruption

defining - to intend to attach or associate words or word symbols with clear and distinctive meanings by which they act or work together to accurately carry, convey, disclose, explain, present or represent a portion of enlightened certainty, reality or truth

defining^2 - to intend to fully identify the true and valuable meaning, nature, qualities or limits of something

definite - to be conclusively and precisely committed to being exalted

definite[2] - to be conclusively and precisely committed to being redeemed

definite[3] - to be conclusively and precisely committed to optimum personal progress

definite[4] - to be able to clearly define something in harmony with enlightened certainty, reality or truth

definite[5] - to be absolutely certain, positive or sure of the truthfulness of something

deflated - to be made virtuously humble or lowly-of-heart

deflating - to intend to lovingly encourage and kindly help myself to be virtuously humble or lowly-of-heart

deflecting - to intend to turn darkness, vice and corruption aside or away from me, my family and society

defrocking - to intend to divest someone of authority to function in an office or position which they have stripped or attempted to strip of its dignity, honor or respectability

defying - to intend to bravely and contemptuously strive to defeat or withstand the courageous attack or daring opposition of an attacking, known or wisely suspected criminal, deadly or evil enemy of society

defying[2] - to intend to boldly and openly resist darkness, vice and corruption

deglamorizing - to intend to ignore or remove the impact of apparently alluring enchantment, fascination or other forms of glamor in order to interact with someone as they really are

deglamorizing[2] - to intend to ignore or remove the impact of apparently alluring enchantment, fascination or other forms of glamor in order to see something as it really is

deisitic - to be prone to believe in God on the basis of personal experience, natural evidence and sound reason

deliberating - to intend to carefully and slowly balance, consider, evaluate, examine, study or weigh possible choices and their possible consequences within the thoughts of my mind and within the feelings of my heart, and to then make that choice which is most likely to best produce, preserve or restore the greatest true enlightenment, virtue, integrity, liberty, hope, peace and joy within me, my family and society

deliberating[2] - to intend to carefully and slowly balance, consider, evaluate, examine, study or weigh evidence within the thoughts of my mind, and to then render a decision which logically upholds the good law of the land

delicate - to be a girl or woman who maintains and exhibits my inherently fine sense of charitably loving gentleness and tenderness

delicate[2] - to be a girl or woman who maintains and exhibits my inherently fine sense of decency, humility, purity, refinement and tact

delicate[3] - to be a girl or woman who refuses to harbor or exhibit a viciously arrogant, hardened and tactless manner

delicate[4] - to be prone to handle so as to avoid excessive or needless harm or injury

delighted - to be joyfully enlightened and virtuous

delightful - to be enlightened and virtuous enough to produce, preserve or restore true enlightenment, virtue and integrity within me, my family and society

delightful[2] - to be prone to share pure enlightenment and virtue through good works

delighting - to intend to share pure enlightenment and virtue through good works

delighting[2] - to intend to produce, preserve or restore joy or rejoicing

delightsome - to be enlightened and virtuous enough to produce, preserve or restore true enlightenment, virtue and integrity within me, my family and society

delightsome[2] - to be prone to share pure enlightenment and virtue through good works

delivered - to be exalted

delivered[2] - to be redeemed unto exaltation

delivered[3] - to be redeemed and released from the bondage, burdens and debts of my sins

delivering - to intend to lovingly encourage and kindly help someone to be redeemed unto exaltation

delivering[2] - to intend to rescue or save someone from darkness, vice and corruption

delivering[3] - to intend to rescue or save from all of the evil or satanic powers of binding addiction, compulsion, impulsion, obsession, occupation and possession

delivering[4] - to intend to rescue or save someone from the darkness of confusion

demeaning - to intend to behave or conduct myself to an extent or in a manner which is truly good and of God

democratic - to be prone to advocate, favor or seek to preserve government of the people, by the people and for the people, as long as the majority prove themselves in conduct and by vote to be so filled with true enlightenment, virtue and integrity that God can justly intervene to protect and preserve them as a government and as a nation

democratic[2] - to be prone to favor or seek the equal individual burden, liberty, privilege, right and responsibility of all law-abiding citizens to constitute, share and exercise supreme government authority and power by the plenary rule and will of a majority of virtuous people and by their freely and honorably elected virtuous representatives

democratizing - to intend to establish a virtuously democratic government

demonizing - to intend to warn my family and society against those whom I have truly discerned are evil or satanic by their evil or satanic works

demure - to be modest

demurring - to intend to honorably object to something on the basis of virtuously conscientious personal inhibition and self-restraint

demystifying - to intend to remove or resolve a mystery in order to discover the truth for myself

demythologizing - to intend to personally seek to verify the attributes ascribed or given to someone or something, in order to learn the truth for myself

dependable - to be prone to live up to the full confidence and trust God has placed in me to learn and to do His will with His help, so that by His grace, love and power I can justly receive all earthly and heavenly blessings, gifts and rewards He wants me to receive

dependable[2] - to be capable, consistent, responsible and trustworthy enough to produce the level of virtuous judgment, outcome, performance or support I have agreed to produce

dependent - to be prone to prayerfully, righteously and wisely rely upon God for help and salvation

dependent[2] - to be virtuously self-reliant

dependent[3] - to be prone to willingly share virtuous commitment or obligation with my dependents or family

deprecating - to intend to pray for deliverance from darkness, vice and corruption

deprecating[2] - to intend to express a strong desire that evil influence be removed

depriving - to intend to deny or divest myself of excessive pleasure or possession

desegregated - to be godly enough to be made truly chaste, clean, pure and virtuous at heart—and to continue to encourage and help other people by charitable love, kindness, invitation and instruction to be godly enough to be made truly chaste, clean, pure and virtuous at heart

desegregating - to be integrating-at-heart

desegregating[2] - to intend to seek the full affiliation, compatibility, cooperation, fellowship, integration, privileges, rights, trust and unity of all law-abiding and responsible individuals, social classes and groups who strive to produce, preserve or restore true enlightenment, virtue, integrity, liberty, hope, peace and joy within ourselves, our families and society

desirable - to be godly enough to be made truly chaste, clean, pure and virtuous at heart—and to continue to encourage and help other people by charitable love, kindness, invitation and instruction to be godly enough to be made truly chaste, clean, pure and virtuous at heart

desirable[2] - to be filled with enough true enlightenment, virtue and integrity to produce, preserve or restore true liberty, hope, peace and joy within me, my family and society

desirable[3] - to be filled with enough true enlightenment, virtue and integrity to strongly attract or appeal to another person's sense of true enlightenment, virtue and integrity

desirable[4] - to be prone to win the acceptance, attraction, pleasure or satisfaction of other people by doing and being good

destined - to be prone to personally ascertain and live in

harmony with the discernibly
enlightening and spiritually
verifiable truth that: my final
condition or state will ultimately
depend upon whether I chose on
Earth to love, obey and serve God
unto liberty, hope, peace and joy,
or Satan unto bondage, despair,
turmoil and misery

destined^2 - to be prone to
personally ascertain and live in
harmony with the discernibly
enlightening and spiritually
verifiable truth that: my final
condition or state will ultimately
depend upon those specific laws I
chose to obey, those specific laws I
chose to disobey, and the
everlasting consequences affixed to
those laws

detail-oriented - to be meticulous

detecting - to intend to discover,
notice or perceive the truth about
people and things through
personal enlightenment,
inspiration or revelation from God

detecting^2 - to intend to seek valid
evidence of the truth about people
or things

determinate - to be prone to
positively identify, locate or reach a
clear and precise understanding of
enlightened certainty, reality or
truth

determinate^2 - to be resolutely firm,
fixed or settled in a good opinion
or purpose

determining - to intend to
ascertain a clear and precise
understanding of enlightened
certainty, reality or truth

determining^2 - to intend to reach a
conclusion, decision or resolution
in harmony with enlightened
certainty, reality or truth

dethroning - to intend to
undertake the extreme difficulty of
working to depose or remove a
despot or tyrant from sovereign
authority

detoxifying - to intend to
counteract the effects of being
poisoned

developed - to be prone to achieve
and maintain greater personal
progress

developing - to intend to assist or
encourage someone in their desires
and efforts to personally progress

deviating - to intend to diverge or
turn aside from pursuing that
which is evil or satanic

devising - to intend to compose,
contrive, create, design, form or
invent something good

devout - to be prone to reverently
worship God

die-hard - to be prone to dispel or
withstand evil, come what may

dietary - to be more fit, healthy and
immune from illness by eating and
drinking of those things provided
by God for my use

dietary^2 - to be more fit, healthy
and immune from illness by
refraining from eating and
drinking those things currently
forbidden by God from my use

dietary^3 - to be prone to eat and
drink to improve my fitness, health
or immunity

dietary^4 - to be virtuously
temperate in my eating and
drinking

differentiating - to intend to
accurately and clearly discern,
distinguish or perceive difference,
diversity or variety

dignified - to be prone to truly
demonstrate honorable, humble

and noble allegiance to the best and highest laws, rules, standards or values of true enlightenment, virtue and integrity of which I have become aware in my education and training and in my own constantly diligent, honest and open-minded searching

dignified[2] - to be prone to honorably and justly avoid that which is not compatible with true enlightenment, virtue, integrity, liberty, hope, peace and joy

dignified[3] - to be prone to rise above darkness, vice, corruption, bondage, despair, turmoil and misery

dignified[4] - to be prone to refuse to viciously harm or injure another person

dignifying - to intend to lovingly encourage and kindly help someone to be dignified

diligent - to be prone to find great hope, peace and joy in carefully, earnestly, energetically and persistently doing all I can and should to effectively, efficiently and steadily achieve or produce good works

diligent[2] - to be prone to work hard enough to honorably complete a worthwhile job

diluting - to intend to weaken the negative energy, force, power or strength of misery by replacing it with joy

diluting[2] - to intend to weaken the negative energy, force, power or strength of turmoil by replacing it with peace

diluting[3] - to intend to weaken the negative energy, force, power or strength of despair by replacing it with hope

diluting[4] - to intend to weaken the negative energy, force, power or strength of bondage by replacing it with liberty

diluting[5] - to intend to weaken the negative energy, force, power or strength of corruption by replacing it with integrity

diluting[6] - to intend to weaken the negative energy, force, power or strength of vice by replacing it with virtue

diluting[7] - to intend to weaken the negative energy, force, power or strength of darkness by replacing it with enlightenment

diminutive - to be endearingly humble and devoid of self-importance

diplomatic - to be peacemaking

disabused - to be liberated within my mind and heart from self-abuse

disabused[2] - to be liberated within my mind and heart from darkness, vice, corruption, bondage, despair, turmoil and misery

disabusing - to intend to lovingly encourage and kindly help someone to be disabused

discerning - to be able to clearly or realistically detect, bring out and build upon the best within me

discerning[2] - to be able to clearly detect and get rid of error and evil from within me

discerning[3] - to be able to clearly or realistically detect and charitably, generously and wisely help other people bring out and build upon the best within them

discerning[4] - to be able to spiritually detect and clearly distinguish between the revealed influence and presence of spirit beings who are good and of God from those who are evil or satanic

discerning[5] - to be able to clearly or realistically perceive and distinguish between that which is truly good and of God and that which is evil or satanic

discerning[6] - to be able to clearly or realistically perceive and distinguish between that which is enlightened certainty, reality or truth and that which is confusion, error or falsehood

discerning[7] - to be able to clearly or realistically perceive and distinguish between that which is real and that which is imaginary

discerning[8] - to be able to clearly or realistically perceive and distinguish between what is important and what is unimportant

discerning[9] - to be able to clearly or realistically perceive and distinguish between what is relevant and what is irrelevant

discerning[10] - to be able to clearly or realistically perceive and distinguish one thing from another in harmony with true differences

discerning[11] - to be able to clearly distinguish the distinctive real form and true nature of someone from all dissemblers, imposters and pretenders

discerning[12] - to be able to clearly distinguish the distinctive real form or true nature of something from all counterfeits and imitations

discharging - to intend to honorably and justly pay an honorable debt, expense, fee, liability or obligation

discharging[2] - to intend to fulfill my good and honorable duty, obligation or responsibility

discipled - to be so educated, instructed, taught or trained as to willingly conform and obey as a true disciple, follower or pupil of the commandments, covenants, laws and ordinances of the gospel of the Lord Jesus Christ

disciplined - to be prone to conform or obey as a true disciple or follower of that which is truly good and of God

disciplined[2] - to be prone to refuse to conform or obey as a disciple or follower of Satan and of that which is evil or satanic

disciplined[3] - to be prone to conform or obey as a true disciple or follower of a person or standard of enlightenment, virtue and integrity

disciplined[4] - to be prone to refuse to conform or obey as a disciple or follower of any person or standard of darkness, vice and corruption

discipling - to intend to lovingly administer some combination of righteous admonition, education, exhortation, instruction, preaching and teaching in order to assist or encourage someone in their desires and efforts to explore conversion to the level of conformity and obedience required of a true disciple, follower or pupil of the commandments, covenants, laws and ordinances of the gospel of the Lord Jesus Christ

discipling[2] - to intend to lovingly use righteous discipline to train up someone to the level of conformity and obedience required of a true disciple, follower or pupil of the commandments, covenants, laws and ordinances of the gospel of the Lord Jesus Christ

disciplining - to intend to lovingly administer some combination of righteous chastening, control, correction, dominion, government, penalty, punishment, regulation, reproof, reward or subordination in order to effectively train up someone to the level of conformity and obedience of a true disciple, follower or pupil of the commandments, covenants, laws and ordinances of the gospel of the Lord Jesus Christ

discomforted - to be prone to abandon or dispose of my complacency

discoursing - to intend to formally convey good and uplifting thoughts with spoken or written words

discrediting - to intend to withdraw or withhold a measure of belief, confidence or trust from someone who chooses to remain evil or satanic

discreet - to be prone to adjudicate or handle sensitive matters with accurate discernment, righteous judgment and wisdom

discretionary - to be discreet

discretionary[2] - to be prone to maintain and rely upon my power or right to freely choose or judge

discriminating - to intend to accurately distinguish and virtuously favor that which is truly good and of God over that which is evil or satanic

discriminating[2] - to intend to accurately distinguish and virtuously favor that which is truth over that which is confusion, error or falsehood

discriminating[3] - to intend to accurately distinguish and

virtuously favor the righteous over the wicked

discriminating[4] - to intend to accurately distinguish and virtuously favor who or what is more deserving or praiseworthy

discriminating[5] - to intend to virtuously favor responsible humanitarian care for the needy and the poor over the excessive or selfish interests of the rich

disenchanted - to be emancipated, freed, liberated or released from every influence or power which directly or subtly attempts to corruptly, malevolently, maliciously or viciously seize control of my mind and will so as to drag my thoughts captive into darkness, vice, corruption, bondage, despair, turmoil and misery

disgusted - to be filled with aversion toward that which is offensive in the sight of God

disgusted[2] - to be filled with aversion toward darkness, vice and corruption

disgusted[3] - to be filled with aversion toward that which assaults or violates good taste

disillusioned - to be enlightened or intelligent

disillusioned[2] - to be able to clearly see and understand reality

disillusioning - to be enlightening

disillusioning[2] - to intend to identify and understand what clouds reality

disintegrating - to intend—as necessity and honorable justice demand, and pending their full repentance—to deny or withhold some degree or measure of affiliation, compatibility, cooperation, fellowship, integration, privilege, right, trust or unity from an individual, social class, group, organization, population, nation or other faction of society found guilty of attempting to produce, preserve or restore darkness, vice and corruption within me, my family and society

disintegrating^2 - to intend—as necessity and honorable justice demand, and pending their full rehabilitation or repayment—to deny or withhold some degree or measure of affiliation, compatibility, cooperation, fellowship, integration, privilege, right, trust or unity from an individual, social class, group, organization, population, nation or other faction of society found guilty of striving to circumvent, ignore, overthrow or subvert the good law of the land

disintegrating^3 - to intend—as necessity and honorable justice demand, and pending their full rehabilitation or repayment—to deny or withhold some degree or measure of affiliation, compatibility, cooperation, fellowship, integration, privilege, right, trust or unity from an individual, social class, group, organization, population, nation or other faction of society found guilty of failing or refusing to obey, honor and sustain the good law of the land

disintegrating^4 - to intend to refuse to be viciously desegregating or integrating

dispassionate - to be prone to refuse to be lustful

dispassionate^2 - to be prone to refuse to allow or cause myself to be easily aroused or moved to negative desires, emotions, feelings or passions

dispelling - to intend to drive out misery with joy

dispelling^2 - to intend to drive out turmoil with peace

dispelling^3 - to intend to drive out despair with hope

dispelling^4 - to intend to drive out bondage with liberty

dispelling^5 - to intend to drive out corruption with integrity

dispelling^6 - to intend to drive out vice with virtue

dispelling^7 - to intend to drive out darkness with enlightenment

dispirited - to be prone to allow or cause myself to be dispossessed of or dissuaded from the energy, enthusiasm and optimism to oppose or resist that which is truly good and of God

dispirited^2 - to be prone to allow or cause myself to be dispossessed of or dissuaded from the energy, enthusiasm and optimism to oppose or resist true enlightenment, virtue and integrity within me, my family and society

displeased - to be annoyed or offended enough by that which is evil or satanic within me to forsake and repent of that which is evil or satanic within me

displeased^2 - to be annoyed or offended enough by the darkness, vice and corruption within me to forsake and repent of that darkness, vice and corruption

disposed - to be and to choose to remain godly

disposed[2] - to be and to choose to remain healthy
disposed[3] - to be and to choose to remain well-mannered
disposed[4] - to be prone to knowingly stick to the right decision with determination and resolve
distinct - to be prone to accurately and clearly discern, distinguish or perceive
distinguishable - to be truly worthy of being distinguished
distinguished - to be truly worthy of conspicuous honor and praise for truly charitable works
distinguished[2] - to be truly worthy of conspicuous honor and praise for producing, preserving or restoring true enlightenment, virtue and integrity within me, my family and society
distinguished[3] - to be truly worthy of conspicuous honor and praise for works of excellence
distinguished[4] - to be dignified and eminent
distinguishing - to intend to widely honor or praise another person's truly charitable works
distinguishing[2] - to intend to widely honor or praise another person's efforts to produce, preserve or restore true enlightenment, virtue and integrity within me, my family and society
distinguishing[3] - to intend to widely honor or praise another person's works of excellence
distinguishing[4] - to intend to accurately and clearly discern discriminating or identifiable differences
distinguishing[5] - to intend to lovingly encourage and kindly

help someone to be dignified and eminent
distressed - to be prone to courageously continue to faithfully prove my believing and honorably exact obedience to God in the face of necessary or unavoidable extreme hardship, misfortune, pressure, strain or stress
distressed[2] - to be prone to recognize enough acute suffering from all of the corrupt, sinful or vicious wrongdoing within me to faithfully and immediately seek true and complete repentance, obedience and reconciliation to God
distrustful - to be prone to cease from being credulous
disturbed - to be prone to courageously continue to faithfully prove my believing and honorably exact obedience to God in the face of necessary or unavoidable anxiety, bother, distress or trouble
disturbed[2] - to be agitated, anxious, bothered, distressed or troubled enough by all of the corrupt, sinful or vicious wrongdoing within me to faithfully and immediately seek true and complete repentance, obedience and reconciliation to God
disunited - to be prone to refuse to be viciously united
disunited[2] - to be prone to cease from being viciously united
disuniting - to intend to lovingly encourage and kindly help one or more people to be virtuously disunited from one or more other people
divided - to be prone to detach, disintegrate, disunite, divorce, segregate or otherwise separate

myself from that which is evil or satanic

divided[2] - to be prone to detach, disintegrate, disunite, divorce, segregate or otherwise separate myself from darkness, vice, corruption, bondage, despair, turmoil and misery

dividing - to intend to detach, disintegrate, disunite, divorce, segregate or otherwise separate myself, my family and society from that which is evil or satanic

dividing[2] - to intend to detach, disintegrate, disunite, divorce, segregate or otherwise separate myself, my family and society from that which produces, preserves or restores darkness, vice and corruption within us—by refusing to accommodate, entertain, produce, preserve, restore, tolerate or uphold darkness, vice and corruption within me

dividing[3] - to intend to constantly discern and differentiate that which is truly good and of God from that which is evil or satanic

dividing[4] - to intend to constantly discern and differentiate true opposites in my thinking

dividing[5] - to intend to constantly discern and differentiate enlightened certainty, reality or truth from confusion, error and falsehood

divine - to be exalted

divine[2] - to be celestial

divine[3] - to be godly enough to be made truly chaste, clean, pure and virtuous at heart—and to continue to encourage and help other people by charitable love, kindness, invitation and instruction to be godly enough to be made truly

chaste, clean, pure and virtuous at heart

divine[4] - to be prone to produce, preserve or restore the greatest true enlightenment, virtue, integrity, liberty, hope, peace and joy within me, my family and society

divining - to intend to foreknow, foresee or perceive the enlightened certainty, reality or truth of things to come, by divine insight, inspiration or revelation from God

do-good - to be prone to actively strive to do good

do-good[2] - to be prone to maintain the best intentions to do good, regardless of my effectiveness or misunderstanding

do-it-yourself - to be prone, by my own education, training, labors, investments and savings, to become a self-reliant net contributor to the virtuously liberating freedom, health, honorable economic prosperity and steady progress of me, my family and society

doctoring - to be virtuously medical or medicating as a doctor

dogmatic - to be prone to courageously, humbly and kindly assert, teach or write true doctrine or true principles by authority and commandment received from God

domesticated - to be prone to enjoy life at home

domesticated[2] - to be prone to enjoy familiarity or proficiency in homemaking

donating - to intend to anonymously and lovingly present valuable property or service as a contribution or gift to someone in need

down-to-earth - to be practical and sensible

dreaming - to intend to successfully actualize or enact something envisioned or imagined which is truly good and of God

dreaming[2] - to intend to constantly choose to think, speak and act in harmony with that revealed instruction or knowledge which the Spirit of God confirms to me was revealed to me by a vision from God while I was asleep

dreaming[3] - to intend to be truly worthy to receive and see things as they truly are, were or will be by personal enlightenment, inspiration or revelation from God, while I am asleep

dreaming[4] - to intend to be truly worthy to receive memorable revelation from God by vision, while I am asleep

dreaming[5] - to intend to prayerfully seek memorable revelation from God by vision while I am asleep

dreaming[6] - to intend to truly envision and act to realize the true state of eternal bliss promised to the righteous

dreaming[7] - to intend to truly envision and act to realize true personal betterment, improvement or progress within me, my family and society

dreaming[8] - to intend to personally ascertain and live in harmony with the discernibly enlightening and spiritually verifiable truth that: even when I willfully keep my thoughts clean and above satanic or worldly temptation while I am awake, my sleeping and thus unrestrained brain may manifest within some dreams or imaginations of my mind while I am asleep my then unrestrained stored thoughts or my then unrestrained biologically inherent and naturally impelling emotional, physical or sexual appetites, cravings, desires, drives or passions, but I remain innocent of accountability for any such dreams or imaginations which are unclean or reproachable provided I willfully remain devoid of the desire or intent to entertain them or to act upon them if and when I become wakefully aware of them

drinking - to intend to drink enough liquids healthy to my body

driving - to intend to vigorously impel someone to fight for true personal betterment, improvement or progress for the good of all

driving[2] - to intend, if necessary, to force my own will toward my own true personal betterment, improvement or progress for the good of all

dry - to be liberated within my mind and heart from the use of harmful and impairing alcoholic drink

dual - to be dualist

dualist - to be prone to ascertain or discern the characteristic and distinctive differences between that which is truly good and of God and that which is evil or satanic

dualist[2] - to be in possession of or to honestly seek a correct knowledge of both physical and spirit matter

dualistic - to be dualist

dying - to intend to think, speak and act in harmony with the indisputable reality that I am now aging, deteriorating or fading toward my physical death

dynamic - to be prone to effectively develop, maintain or enhance true personal betterment, improvement or progress within me, my family and society

dynamite - to be prone to have a dynamic and uplifting impact on other people

E

eagle-eyed - to be discerning

earning - to intend to seek enough gain or income from honest labor or service

earthy - to be down-to-earth

Eastern - to be prone to live in harmony with the ways of Eastern character or culture which produce, preserve or restore true enlightenment, virtue and integrity within me, my family and society

Eastern Orthodox - to be prone to live in harmony with the teachings of the Eastern Church, of the Eastern Orthodox Church or of the Orthodox Church which produce, preserve or restore true enlightenment, virtue and integrity within me, my family and society

Eastern Orthodox[2] - to be prone to live in harmony with the teachings of the Greek Orthodox Church—or of another Christian church which broke away or separated in apostasy or protest from the Eastern Church, from the Eastern Orthodox Church or from the Orthodox Church—to the extent the teachings produce, preserve or restore true enlightenment, virtue and integrity within me, my family and society

Eastern Orthodox[3] - to be prone to live in harmony with the teachings

of a Christian church which broke away or separated in apostasy or protest from an earlier Eastern Christian church—to the extent the teachings produce, preserve or restore true enlightenment, virtue and integrity within me, my family and society

ecclesiastical - to be a duly ordained man called of God who righteously uses true higher priesthood authority, power and revelation from God, without pay, to direct the administration of God's works on Earth among a congregation of His church and kingdom

eclectic - to be prone to seek after greater knowledge of that which is good, lovely, praiseworthy or virtuous wherever it may be found

eclectic[2] - to be prone to combine or integrate the best elements or parts from various sources or systems into something better

ecological - to be prone to manage the physical environment of the earth in order to enhance or protect the physical interaction and well-being of the living things of the earth

economic - to be prone to economizing

economical - to be prone to economizing

economizing - to be debt free and to keep household expenditures less than household income

economizing[2] - to intend to minimize consumption, expense and waste of resources while maintaining adequate reserves

ecstatic - to be joyful

ecumenical - to be prone to join with those of other religious denominations in cooperative, unified efforts to seek the greatest true enlightenment, virtue, integrity, liberty, hope, peace and joy for ourselves, our families and society

ecumenical[2] - to be prone to join with those of other religious denominations in cooperative, unified efforts to foster, promote, restore or safeguard the virtuously liberating freedom, health, honorable economic prosperity and steady progress of the individual, the family and society

ecumenical[3] - to be prone to live in peace with all other honorable and law-abiding members of various religious denominations

edifying - to intend to build up, enlighten, improve or uplift another person

educable - to be prone to seek greater true enlightenment, intelligence or wisdom

educated - to be prone to successfully continue to make actual or real the best that lies within me

educated[2] - to be prone to successfully obtain greater true enlightenment, intelligence or wisdom

educated[3] - to be prone to successfully continue to obtain enough edifying learning, knowledge or skill to continue to enhance the quality of my life and thus the lives of other people within my family and society

educating - to intend to successfully assist or encourage someone in their personal desires and efforts to actualize or realize the best that lies within them

educating[2] - to intend to successfully impart learning, knowledge or skill which will continue to enhance the quality of a willing recipient's life and thus the lives of other people within their family and society

educating[3] - to intend to successfully transfer a better way of life to one or more willing recipients

educating[4] - to intend to successfully assist or encourage someone in their personal desires and efforts to successfully obtain greater true enlightenment, intelligence or wisdom

effacing - to be modest

effective - to be prone to produce virtuous results

effeminate - to be a girl or woman who is feminine

effeminate[2] - to be a girl or woman who is wonderfully delicate, mild and tender

effervescent - to be effervescing

effervescing - to intend to metaphorically boil or rise to the top in a buoyant, bubbly and vivacious manner

effortful - to be prone to personally exert and expend enough energy, force, power or strength to achieve my very best today

effulgent - to be brilliantly radiant

egalitarian - to be prone to advocate or seek a collectivist society of people of true enlightenment, virtue and integrity in which there are no poor or needy and everyone has enough

egalitarian[2] - to be prone to advocate or seek for myself and for other fellow law-abiding residents the legal rights necessary to

lawfully pursue true enlightenment, virtue, integrity, liberty, hope, peace and joy within ourselves, our families and society
elated - to be joyful
elating - to intend to lovingly encourage and kindly help someone to do what it takes to be joyful
elect - to be chosen, favored or selected to receive some great blessing from God by my believing and honorably exact obedience to that divinely appointed law upon which receipt of that blessing is predicated
electing - to intend to obtain the liberty to choose, pick or select my government or my government's action by vote
electing^2 - to intend to exercise my right to choose, pick or select my government or my government's action by vote
electrifying - to be successful in helping another person be joyful
electrifying^2 - to be filled with enough true enlightenment, virtue and integrity to be extremely pleasing to another person's sense of true enlightenment, virtue and integrity
electrifying^3 - to be truly animating
elegant - to be gracefully and tastefully dignified, poised and refined
elevated - to be most like unto God by my faithfully repentant and honorably exact obedience to those divinely appointed commandments, covenants, laws and ordinances upon which receipt of that blessing is predicated
elevated^2 - to be drawing closer to God by my faithfully repentant

and honorably exact obedience to those divinely appointed commandments, covenants, laws and ordinances upon which receipt of that blessing is predicated
elevating - to intend to cheer, edify, educate, improve or lift someone to a better and higher condition
elite - to be one of those who are the best in true enlightenment, virtue and integrity
elitist - to be prone to advocate, favor or seek to preserve government by those who are among the best in true enlightenment, virtue and integrity
emancipated - to be exalted
emancipated^2 - to be redeemed unto exaltation
emancipated^3 - to be redeemed and released from the bondage, burdens and debts of my sins
emancipated^4 - to be prone to humbly and prayerfully allow the heavenly power which comes from virtuous forgiving to free, liberate or release me from the self-consuming bitterness and festering pain I might otherwise viciously continue to wish upon someone else
emancipated^5 - to be virtuously freed, liberated or released
emancipating - to be virtuously freeing, liberating or releasing
embellishing - to intend to improve the true character, nature or quality of something
eminent - to be truly worthy of a distinguished or meritorious reputation
eminent^2 - to be prone to honorably hold public position or rank

emoting - to be so proficient in perceptive and sensitive understanding of another person's feelings, passions or sensitivities as to kindly react with enough benevolent and edifying compassion, empathy or sympathy, as needed

empathizing - to intend to vicariously experience or undertake with another person what that person should not be left to experience or undertake without comforting companionship or help

empirical - to be prone to rely upon my own personal experience, experimentation and observation to aid my perception, discernment or verification of truth and virtue

employable - to be qualified for gainful and honorable employment by someone

employed - to be ambitiously, diligently and responsibly engaged in a good cause as a valuable worker

empowered - to be prone to competently use my available power to produce, preserve or restore true enlightenment, virtue and integrity within me, my family and society

emulating - to intend to imitate another person's truly charitable or virtuous works

emulating[2] - to intend to imitate another person's praiseworthy or virtuous achievements in an attempt to bring out the best in me

enabled - to be prone to exercise my personal abilities, powers, resources, skills, strengths or talents for good

enchanting - to be filled with enough true enlightenment, virtue

and integrity to strongly attract or appeal to another person's sense of true enlightenment, virtue and integrity

encouraged - to be so good, faithful, soft-hearted and repentant as to be possessed of or persuaded to obtain true hope

encouraged[2] - to be inspired or stimulated to enough confidence, courage or resolve to think, say or do something good

encyclopedic - to be prone to seek learning about those things which will better empower me to produce, preserve or restore greater true enlightenment, virtue, integrity, liberty, hope, peace and joy within me, my family and society

encyclopedic[2] - to be prone to grasp or to teach with a broad understanding of many things

endearing - to intend to evoke another person's great esteem or love with kind and loving service

endowed - to be a baptized, confirmed and otherwise qualified adult who voluntarily enters into the priesthood covenant and ordinance of endowment administered in a dedicated holy temple of God by one who truly holds the necessary authority and the authorization from God's own called, ordained and authorized priesthood leaders on Earth to officiate in that preparatory ordinance in that revealed manner and mode of priesthood covenant, instruction and further preparation necessary for my salvation and my return to God's presence—which priesthood covenants then justly bind me on Earth and in heaven to receive all of the powerful blessings pertaining to those covenants in harmony with my faithfulness, which qualifies me to be further prepared on Earth to receive the blessings of a glorious celestial resurrection and exaltation in the world to come

endowing - to intend, as one who truly holds the necessary authority to officiate and the authorization to do so from God's own called, ordained and authorized priesthood leaders on Earth, to administer, without pay, to a baptized, confirmed and otherwise qualified living adult in a dedicated holy temple of God the priesthood covenant and ordinance of endowment in that revealed manner and mode of priesthood covenant, instruction and further preparation necessary for their salvation and their return to God's presence—which priesthood covenants then justly bind them on Earth and in heaven to receive all of the powerful blessings pertaining to those covenants in harmony with their faithfulness, which qualifies them to be further prepared on Earth to receive the blessings of a glorious celestial resurrection and exaltation in the world to come

endowing^2 - to intend, as one who truly holds the necessary authority to officiate and the authorization to do so from God's own called, ordained and authorized priesthood leaders on Earth, to administer, without pay, in a dedicated holy temple of God the priesthood covenant and ordinance of endowment upon righteous

living proxy who act in behalf of deceased family members and other deceased persons who are accountable to the laws of God and whose preliminary temple work has been done—so that those deceased persons who are desirous and righteous enough to receive the ordinance work done for them are then justly bound by priesthood covenants on Earth and in heaven to receive all of the powerful blessings pertaining to those covenants in harmony with their faithfulness, and can be further prepared by loving family or other living proxy on Earth to receive the blessings of a glorious celestial resurrection and exaltation in the world to come

endowing^3 - to intend to willingly furnish or provide a good and honorable person or entity with a source of income or with other resources which they put to good use

energetic - to be prone to exert and expend abundant energy, force, power or strength in doing and being that which is truly good and of God

energetic^2 - to be prone to exert and expend abundant energy, force, power or strength in producing, preserving or restoring true enlightenment, virtue and integrity within me, my family and society

enforcing - to intend to receive and apply enough personal energy, force, power or strength to remain godly, by my faithfully repentant and honorably exact obedience to those divinely appointed commandments, covenants, laws and ordinances upon which receipt of that energy, force, power or strength is predicated

enforcing[2] - to intend to receive and apply enough personal energy, force, power or strength to produce, preserve or restore that which is truly good and of God within me, my family and society, by my faithfully repentant and honorably exact obedience to those divinely appointed commandments, covenants, laws and ordinances upon which receipt of that energy, force, power or strength is predicated

enforcing[3] - to intend to receive and apply enough personal energy, force, power or strength to produce, preserve or restore true enlightenment, virtue and integrity within me, my family and society, by my believing and honorably exact obedience to that divinely appointed law upon which receipt of that energy, force, power or strength is predicated

enforcing[4] - to intend to vote with and openly support enough enlightened, virtuous and wise civic and government leaders, legislators, judges and other fellow citizens in our combined efforts to willfully apply enough virtuous energy, force, power or strength to produce, preserve or restore that which is truly good and of God within our minds, hearts and borders

enforcing[5] - to intend to vote with and openly support enough enlightened, virtuous and wise civic and government leaders, legislators, judges and other fellow citizens in our combined efforts to willfully apply enough virtuous energy, force, power or strength to produce, preserve or restore true enlightenment, virtue and integrity within our minds, hearts and borders

enforcing[6] - to intend to vote with and openly support enlightened, virtuous and wise civic and government leaders, legislators, judges and other fellow citizens to advocate, favor and seek to uphold good laws backed by the willful application of enough virtuous energy, force, power or strength to stop or expel those who would produce, preserve or restore that which is evil or satanic within our minds, hearts and borders

enforcing[7] - to intend to vote with and openly support enlightened, virtuous and wise civic and government leaders, legislators, judges and other fellow citizens to advocate, favor or seek to preserve good laws backed by the willful application of enough virtuous energy, force, power or strength to stop or expel those who would produce, preserve or restore darkness, vice and corruption within our minds, hearts and borders

enforcing[8] - to intend to uphold the good law of the land by lawfully and legally bringing its violators to just punishment

enfranchising - to intend to give each law-abiding citizen the right to vote

engaging - to be filled with enough true enlightenment, virtue and integrity to strongly attract or appeal to another person's sense of true enlightenment, virtue and integrity

enhancing - to intend to edify, magnify or uplift someone in true enlightenment, virtue and integrity
enhancing[2] - to intend to lovingly encourage and kindly help someone to improve or progress
enjoyable - to be prone to produce, preserve or restore joy or rejoicing
enjoying - to intend to experience or find joy or rejoicing
enlightened - to be prone, following my divinely recognized faith, repentance, baptism and confirmation, to personally receive the gift of the constantly enlightening and joyous influence or presence of the Holy Ghost to be with me so He can help me comprehend and share God's love, and constantly reveal spiritually verified personal knowledge of truth to my soul, and enlighten and quicken my intellect, and purify my biologically inherent and naturally impelling emotional, physical or sexual appetites, cravings, desires, drives and passions to their lawful uses, and justly cleanse or sanctify my soul of all sin and of all disposition to commit sin, and inspire refined development of virtuous feelings, thoughts and sympathies, and instill more and greater power of true enlightenment, virtue, integrity, liberty, hope, peace and joy into my soul, eye and feature, and thereby steadily build, enliven and strengthen a healthier body, mind and spirit within me unto exaltation
enlightened[2] - to be prone, in harmony with my faithful and prayerful seeking, my increasingly virtuous thoughts, my increasingly charitable works, and what is expedient in God for me, to personally receive divine guidance or revealed truth directly from God, or by the power of the Holy Ghost, or through God's holy angels, or through His holy apostles and prophets, or by His written word when its truthfulness is personally confirmed to me by the power of the Holy Ghost
enlightened[3] - to be prone, in harmony with my faithful and prayerful seeking, my increasingly virtuous thoughts, my increasingly charitable works, and what is expedient in God for me, to be personally visited within my mind and within my heart by the directing, inspiring, manifesting or prompting power of the Holy Ghost to know by the revealed light of certainty what God would have me do
enlightened[4] - to be in possession of or to receive enough intelligence or the pure light of truth by my personal experience, by my prayerful and thorough study, by my believing and honorably exact obedience to God, and by revelation from Him to continue to righteously judge and to humbly do that which is charitably loving, just, right and wise in the sight of God
enlightened[5] - to be prone to faithfully and prayerfully increase my initial endowment or measure of guiding personal intelligence or the pure light of truth from God enough to continue to accurately and clearly discern between that which is truly good and of God and that which is evil or satanic

enlightened[6] - to be prone to faithfully and prayerfully increase my initial endowment or measure of guiding personal intelligence or the pure light of truth from God enough to continue to accurately and clearly discern between that which is enlightened certainty, reality or truth and that which is confusion, error or falsehood

enlightened[7] - to be prone to faithfully and prayerfully increase my initial endowment or measure of guiding personal intelligence or the pure light of truth from God enough to continue to accurately and clearly discern between that which is real and that which is imaginary

enlightened[8] - to be made aware that the presence of a portion of bright, clear, illuminating knowledge of enlightened certainty, reality or truth within me has come to me from God by my believing and honorably exact obedience to that divinely appointed law upon which receipt of that knowledge is predicated

enlightening - to intend to help rescue someone else from darkness by teaching them with true enlightenment or the pure light of truth I possess

enlightening[2] - to intend to lovingly encourage and kindly help someone to be enlightened or intelligent

enlivened - to be filled with true enlightenment, virtue, integrity, liberty, hope, peace and joy

enlivened[2] - to be healthy and full of life

enlivening - to intend to lovingly encourage and kindly help someone to be enlivened

ennobling - to intend to lovingly encourage and kindly help someone to be more noble

enriched - to be improved

enriching - to intend to aid, assist or encourage someone in their desires and efforts to personally progress

entertaining - to intend to implant or present within the thoughts of an audience selected actions, characters, descriptions, ideas, images, impressions, representations, scenes, situations, sounds, stories or symbols which produce, preserve or restore true enlightenment, virtue, integrity, liberty, hope, peace and joy within ourselves, our families and society

entertaining[2] - to intend to willingly harbor, hold, keep, retain or store truly chaste, clean, pure and virtuous thoughts in my mind often and long enough for them to enter into and liberate the thoughts, beliefs, values and characteristics of my heart from darkness, vice and corruption

entertaining[3] - to intend to receive and treat guests in my home with courtesy, warmth and generosity

enthralling - to be filled with enough true enlightenment, virtue and integrity to strongly attract or appeal to another person's sense of true enlightenment, virtue and integrity

enthusiastic - to be animated

entrepreneurial - to be prone to create jobs, income and wealth for others and for myself by succeeding in a personally initiated and personally owned business which produces or provides goods or services which are good for me, my family and society

environmentalistic - to be prone to advocate or work for the wise preservation or restoration of that certain balanced use of available natural resources which will maximize the quality of life on Earth for humankind and for all other species of life which are of benefit and use to humankind

environmentalistic^2 - to be prone to advocate or work for the wise preservation or restoration of the earth's air, water and other beneficial natural resources from harmful pollution and its detrimental effects

environmentalistic^3 - to be prone to advocate or work for the wise preservation or restoration of certain living things within a particular environment, or of a certain balance of living things within that particular environment, to an extent and in a manner which has a positive impact upon what is and will be best for humankind within that particular environment

epic - to be heroic-at-heart

epigrammatic - to be prone to use evident and obvious truths to adjudge, evaluate or identify a particular circumstance, event or thought

epistemological - to be prone to honestly investigate how I can ascertain that which is truth

epistemological^2 - to be prone to honestly investigate the origin, nature, limits or validity of human knowledge

equal - to be prone to personally ascertain and live in harmony with the discernibly enlightening and spiritually verifiable truth that: all accountable people who have ever lived and will yet live upon the earth and who are neither murderous nor perdition may be redeemed unto exaltation by our faithfully repentant and honorably exact obedience to those divinely appointed commandments, covenants, laws and ordinances upon which receipt of that exaltation is predicated

equal^2 - to be prone to esteem or regard all other people as being just as intrinsically important and valuable as I am

equal^3 - to be prone to treat each other person as I would be treated if their words or actions were mine

equalitarian - to be prone to advocate or seek a collectivist society of people of true enlightenment, virtue and integrity in which there are no poor or needy and everyone has enough

equalitarian^2 - to be prone to advocate or seek for myself and for other fellow law-abiding residents the legal rights necessary to lawfully pursue true enlightenment, virtue, integrity, liberty, hope, peace and joy within ourselves, our families and society

equitable - to be prone to treat all other people to an extent or in a manner which produces, preserves or restores true enlightenment, virtue and integrity within me, my family and society

equitable^2 - to be prone to consistently render good and righteous judgment in harmony with truly chaste, clean, pure and virtuous thoughts, beliefs, values and characteristics

equitable[3] - to be prone to refuse to viciously rely exclusively upon prejudiced or unreasoned judgment in favoring one person or thing over another

equitable[4] - to be prone to refuse to think, speak or act in an excessive manner

equitable[5] - to be prone to consistently render dispassionate, impartial and well-reasoned judgment in harmony with the good law of the land

ergonomic - to be prone to arrange, design, engineer, manage or produce things to make them more physically effective, fitting, healthy and safe for human use and work

erudite - to be learned and scholarly enough to wisely live in harmony with that which I have ascertained is truly the mind and will of God

escaping - to intend to avoid or flee from that which produces, preserves or restores darkness, vice and corruption within me, my family and society

eschatological - to be concerned enough about death, life after death and final judgment to prepare myself and my family to be made truly chaste, clean, pure and virtuous at heart prior to our deaths

eschatological[2] - to be concerned about the conditions, consequences, effects or results of death, life after death and final judgment

established - to be proven firmly settled upon the sure foundation of enlightenment, virtue and integrity

established[2] - to be proven firmly settled upon the sure foundation of enlightened certainty, reality or truth

esthetic - to be prone to possess and cultivate a sensitive awareness and grateful love of beauty

estimable - to be prone to do enough good to remain worthy of admiration, esteem or respect

estimating - to intend to fairly and honestly seek to approximate or calculate a good and wise esteem, opinion or judgment when certainty cannot be obtained

estranging - to intend to turn against or away from serving Satan to serving God

estranging[2] - to intend to turn against or away from evil to good

eternal - to be exalted

eternal[2] - to be celestial

eternal[3] to be prone to personally ascertain and live in harmony with the discernibly enlightening and spiritually verifiable truth that: my existence was without beginning prior to my birth, has continued during this life, and shall be endless, enduring, everlasting or perpetual, following my physical death

etherealizing - to be spiritually-minded

ethical - to be prone to think, speak, act, judge, lead and teach in virtuous oneness with God, with my family and with society

ethical[2] - to be prone to think, speak, act, judge, lead and teach in virtuous oneness with the dictates of my enlightened conscience

ethical[3] - to be prone to think, speak, act, judge, lead and teach in a practical manner which I have ascertained is charitably loving, just, right and wise in the sight of God

ethical[4] - to be spiritually-minded

ethical[5] - to be prone to think, speak, act, judge, lead and teach in harmony with truly chaste, clean, pure and virtuous thoughts, beliefs, values and characteristics of good and right conduct which produce, preserve or restore true enlightenment, virtue and integrity within me, my family and society

ethical[6] - to be prone to refuse to think, believe, evaluate, judge, speak or act in accordance with impure, unchaste, unclean or vicious principles of conduct which produce, preserve or restore darkness, vice and corruption within me, my family and society

ethical[7] - to be prone to think, speak, act, judge, lead and teach as though my own virtuously liberating freedom, health, honorable economic prosperity and steady progress are tied to the virtuously liberating freedom, health, honorable economic prosperity and steady progress of my family and society

etymological - to be prone to better clarify and hence improve the true meanings and values of words pertaining to truth and virtue

etymological[2] - to be prone to preserve the true meanings and values of words pertaining to truth and virtue

etymological[3] - to be prone to correct and hence restore the true meanings and values of words pertaining to truth and virtue

etymological[4] - to be prone to study the true meanings and values of words pertaining to truth and virtue

Eucharistic - to be prone to spiritually commune with and to gratefully offer thanks unto God

Eucharistic[2] - to be prone, to an extent or in a manner which is pleasing unto God, to use emblems of the body and blood of the Lord Jesus Christ to commemorate in solemn ceremony or ordinance His redeeming sacrifice for sin

Eucharistical - to be Eucharistic

eulogizing - to intend to greatly or highly commend, extol or praise someone or something good

euphoric - to be joyful

European - to be prone to live in harmony with the ways of European character or culture which produce, preserve or restore true enlightenment, virtue and integrity within me, my family and society

evaluating - to intend to ascertain or truly discern true character, quality, significance, value or worth

evangelical - to be prone to live in harmony with the proclaimed gospel of a Christian church which has broken away or separated in apostasy or protest from an earlier Protestant church—to the extent the teachings produce, preserve or restore true enlightenment, virtue and integrity within me, my family and society

everlasting - to be eternal

evidencing - to intend, as necessary, to clearly or plainly prove that which is allegedly good and of God is truly good and of God by use of that true evidence or enlightening information which can prove it

evidencing[2] - to intend, as necessary, to clearly or plainly prove that which is allegedly evil or satanic is truly evil or satanic by use of that true evidence or enlightening information which can prove it

evidencing[3] - to intend, as necessary, to clearly or plainly prove that which is evil or satanic is not truly good and of God — or that which is truly good and of God is not evil or satanic — by use of that true evidence or enlightening information which can prove it

evidencing[4] - to intend, as necessary, to clearly or plainly prove that which is allegedly truth is truth by use of that true evidence or enlightening information which can prove it

evidencing[5] - to intend, as necessary, to clearly or plainly prove that which is allegedly reality is reality by use of that true evidence or enlightening information which can prove it

evidencing[6] - to intend, as necessary, to clearly or plainly prove that which is allegedly enlightened certainty is enlightened certainty by use of that true evidence or enlightening information which can prove it

evidencing[7] - to intend, as necessary, to clearly or plainly prove what is allegedly confusion is confusion by use of that true

evidence or enlightening information which can prove it

evidencing[8] - to intend, as necessary, to clearly or plainly prove what is allegedly error is error by use of that true evidence or enlightening information which can prove it

evidencing[9] - to intend, as necessary, to clearly or plainly prove what is allegedly falsehood is falsehood by use of that true evidence or enlightening information which can prove it

evidencing[10] - to intend, as necessary, to clearly or plainly prove that which is confusion, error or falsehood is not enlightened certainty, reality or truth — or that which is enlightened certainty, reality or truth is not confusion, error or falsehood — by use of that true evidence or enlightening information which can prove it

evidencing[11] - to intend, as necessary, to clearly or plainly prove that which is imaginary is not real — or that which is real is not imaginary — by use of that true evidence or enlightening information which can prove it

evidencing[12] - to intend to disprove or prove something with true evidence or enlightening information

evolutionary - to be prone to advance, change, develop or progress by improving the true enlightenment, virtue and integrity of the thoughts I continue to entertain within the thoughts of my mind and to exercise within the thoughts of my heart evolutionary[2] - to be prone to strive for steady improvement in the conditions experienced by me, my family and society

evolutionary[3] - to be prone to honestly seek a true knowledge of real and changing interactions of interrelated natural or universal phenomena

evolutionary[4] - to be prone to personally ascertain and live in harmony with the discernibly enlightening and spiritually verifiable truth that: God is capable of originating forms of life and is capable of naturally causing them to make whatever beneficial adaptations, changes, developments, modifications or variations are necessary to allow or cause them to continue to survive, thrive and multiply in changing environments and conditions over successive generations

evolutionary[5] - to be prone to think, speak and act in harmony with the scientifically proven fact that successive generations of some tested biological life forms have shown beneficial adaptations, changes, developments, modifications or variations which have allowed them to survive, thrive and propagate in changing environments and conditions over time

exact - to be prone to think, speak and act with enough cautious, precise or strict obedience to God's commandments, covenants, laws and ordinances to honorably and justly receive His greatest blessings, gifts and rewards

exact[2] - to be prone to think, speak and act in close harmony with those thoughts, beliefs, values and characteristics which produce, preserve or restore the greatest true enlightenment, virtue, integrity, liberty, hope, peace and joy within me, my family and society

exact[3] - to be correct, precise and punctual enough in performance to avoid causing undue delay, harm, injury or waste to myself or to other people

exacting - to intend to necessarily make a truly honorable and just demand

exalted - to be made worthy to be made like unto God in the highest degree or kingdom of celestial glory, and to there receive—along with my worthy resurrected husband or wife to whom I have been duly sealed on Earth and in heaven by divinely recognized priesthood authority—an everlasting fulness of supreme peace and joy and all other celestial blessings, gifts and rewards through the charitable love, cleansing power and redeeming grace of the Atonement of the Lord Jesus Christ by my faithfully repentant and honorably exact obedience to those divinely appointed commandments, covenants, laws and ordinances upon which receipt of those eternal blessings is predicated

exalted[2] - to be made worthy to inherit, along with my worthy resurrected husband or wife to whom I have been duly sealed on Earth and in heaven by divinely recognized priesthood authority, every celestial blessing, gift and reward with each other in the presence of God in the highest celestial degree or kingdom of glory through the charitable love, cleansing power and redeeming grace of the Atonement of the Lord Jesus Christ by our faithfully repentant and honorably exact obedience to those divinely appointed commandments, covenants, laws and ordinances upon which receipt of those eternal blessings is predicated

exalted[3] - to be made worthy to receive from God the power to acquire every virtue in its fulness by my faithfully repentant and honorably exact obedience to those divinely appointed commandments, covenants, laws and ordinances upon which receipt of that virtue is predicated

exalted[4] - to be made worthy to receive from God a perfect knowledge of all truth by my faithfully repentant and honorably exact obedience to those divinely appointed commandments, covenants, laws and ordinances upon which receipt of that knowledge is predicated

exalted[5] - to be prone to become completely finished, fulfilled or perfected with the help of God in the full measure of His highest desires and purposes for me as one of His children, heirs, offspring, posterity or seed

exalted[6] - to be uplifted

exalting - to intend to bring as much glory and honor to God as I possibly can

exalting[2] - to intend to help elevate or raise someone toward being exalted

exalting[3] - to intend to elevate or raise someone toward purely

virtuous character and ultimate well-being

exalting[4] - to be uplifting

examining - to be virtuously conscientious, diligent and faithful in striving to discover the truth about God by prayerful and thorough study and by my believing and honorably exact obedience to that divinely appointed law upon which receipt of that truth is predicated

examining[2] - to intend to inspect, investigate, observe, question or test in order to confirm, prove or verify for myself what I truly need to know

excellent - to be remarkably and truly chaste, clean, pure and virtuous

exceptional - to be remarkably and truly chaste, clean, pure and virtuous

exchanging - to intend to replace evil with good

exchanging[2] - to intend to replace confusion, error or falsehood with enlightened certainty, reality or truth

excusable - to be prone to think, speak or act to an extent or in a manner which can be legally and virtuously excused

excusing - to intend to completely repent

excusing[2] - to intend to offer apology and adequate redress or restitution for my wrongdoing or for my failure to do something right

exemplary - to be a good example or role model

exercising - to intend to condition, develop, discipline or train myself well enough to be healthy in every way

exhausted - to be completely drained of personal resources or strength for a good purpose, when necessary

exhilarated - to be joyful

existent - to be existing

existential - to be existing

existing - to intend to personally ascertain and live in harmony with the discernibly enlightening and spiritually verifiable truth that: regardless of time and space, and independent of human awareness or choice, I am experiencing endless existence, I have endless being and I will always be alive as an immortal spirit being either temporarily separated from my physical body of flesh and bones following my physical death, or as a resurrected being following my eventual and inevitable one-time resurrection

exonerated - to be redeemed unto exaltation

exonerated[2] - to be redeemed and released from the bondage, burdens and debts of my sins

exonerated[3] - to be and to be found truly innocent

exonerating - to intend to emancipate, free, liberate or release an innocent person from accountability to a judicial system infected or polluted by darkness, vice and corruption

exorcising - to be a man who righteously uses true higher priesthood authority and power from God to actually cast out or expel Satan or one or more of his spirit followers from a person or place

exorcising[2] - to intend to receive power from God by the prayer of faith unto the casting out or expulsion of Satan and his spirit followers from my thoughts, from my being, from my presence and from my home

expecting - to intend to patiently await a truly prophesied event or outcome, having received an absolute, perfect and spiritually verified personal knowledge by personal enlightenment, inspiration or revelation from God that it will come to pass

expecting[2] - to intend to patiently pray to God for the anticipated fulfillment of a desirable event or outcome with confident belief or trusting hope that He will bless me with what is best by my believing and honorably exact obedience to that divinely appointed law upon which receipt of that blessing is predicated

expedient - to be prone to exercise enough faith in the Lord Jesus Christ to receive power from Him to do and be that which is charitably loving, just, right and wise in the sight of God

expedient[2] - to be prone to advise or choose in harmony with what is immediately practical and prudent

expendable - to be prone to spend my life in a praiseworthy cause in the sight of God

experienced - to be familiar enough with the consequences of applied thought

experiencing - to intend to safely seek enough familiarity with the consequences of applied thought

experientialistic - to be prone to personally ascertain and live in

harmony with the discernibly
enlightening and spiritually
verifiable truth that: personal
experience with personal
enlightenment, inspiration or
revelation from God provides a
solid foundation of absolute,
perfect and spiritually verified
personal knowledge
experimenting - to intend to
personally discover the truth about
God by my prayerful study and by
my believing and honorably exact
obedience to that divinely
appointed law upon which receipt
of that truth is predicated
expiated - to be restored to
appeasement, atonement,
conciliation or harmony with God
expiating - to intend, by my
faithful, timely and true repentance
and by my believing and
honorably exact obedience to all of
the other commandments,
covenants, laws and ordinances of
the gospel of the Lord Jesus Christ,
to be restored to that full
appeasement, atonement, harmony
and reconciliation with God made
available to me by the charitable
love, cleansing power and
redeeming grace of the Lord Jesus
Christ's atoning suffering to satisfy
the demands of the eternally
binding law of justice
exploiting - to intend to regularly
perform small charitable acts or
deeds of kindness for other people
exploiting[2] - to intend to perform a
great and heroically virtuous deed
of renown
exporting - to intend to carry,
convey or ship a certain measure of
goods or services out of my
country and into another country,

thus bringing a commensurate
measure of business, jobs, money
and economic self-reliance or self-
sustainability from that country
into my country
expurgating - to intend to cleanse
or purge from darkness, vice and
corruption
expurgatorial - to be prone to
expurgating
exquisite - to be exalted
exquisite[2] - to be celestial
exquisite[3] - to be godly enough to
be made truly chaste, clean, pure
and virtuous at heart—and to
continue to encourage and help
other people by charitable love,
kindness, invitation and instruction
to be godly enough to be made
truly chaste, clean, pure and
virtuous at heart
exquisite[4] - to be most ascertaining
and intelligent
exquisite[5] - to be elegantly refined
and sensitive in manners
exquisite[6] - to be prone to produce
rare and very fine
accomplishments, performances or
works
extant - to be existent
extenuating - to intend to lessen or
lighten either the degree of
seriousness of a crime, offense or
vice alleged or charged, or the
degree of the perpetrator's
culpability, by pointing not to
excuse or justification, but to
circumstances which should, in
equity, fairness and mercy, be
considered in righteous judgment
externalizing - to be extroverted
extraordinary - to be remarkably
and truly chaste, clean, pure and
virtuous
extravert - to be extrovert

extreme - to be prone to achieve what is best

extrovert - to be extroverted

extroverted - to be prone to work hard enough on improving the virtuously liberating freedom, health, honorable economic prosperity and steady progress of my family and society to improve my own

exulting - to intend to experience the exultation or great joy of rising above darkness, vice, corruption, bondage, despair, turmoil and misery into true enlightenment, virtue, integrity, liberty, hope, peace and joy

exulting^2 - to be joyously successful or gloriously triumphant in personal progress

eye-opening - to be enlightening

F

fabulous - to be heroically virtuous

fabulous^2 - to be extraordinarily or remarkably good

face-saving - to intend to avoid the further acknowledging of any wrongdoing I have committed for which I have honorably completed all of the steps of true repentance in the sight of God

fact-finding - to intend to ascertain what truly existed or exists

fact-finding^2 - to intend to ascertain that which truly happened or is happening

factional - to be prone to promote partisan disintegration when necessary to produce, preserve or restore true enlightenment, virtue and integrity within me, my family and society

factual - to be aware of and to rely upon pure truth

factualistic - to be prone to gather and rely upon pure truth

fair - to be redeemed unto exaltation

fair^2 - to be redeemed and released from the bondage, burdens and debts of my sins

fair^3 - to be truly chaste, clean, pure and virtuous at heart

fair^4 - to be truly honorable

fair^5 - to be prone to refuse to allow or cause my true enlightenment, virtue and integrity to be compromised or lost

fair^6 - to be prone to refuse to allow or cause something which produces, preserves or restores true enlightenment, virtue and integrity within me, my family and society to be compromised or lost

fair^7 - to be prone to consistently render good and righteous judgment in harmony with truly chaste, clean, pure and virtuous thoughts, beliefs, values and characteristics

fair^8 - to be prone to refuse to allow or cause the good law of the land to be compromised or violated

fair-minded - to be prone to consistently render good and righteous judgment in harmony with truly chaste, clean, pure and virtuous thoughts, beliefs, values and characteristics

faithful - to be prone, in the face of incessant or intense adversity, affliction, distress, doubt, opposition, persecution or tribulation, to continue to patiently prove—by my faithful, timely and true repentance, by the reality of my intent and the sincerity of my desire, by my steady exercise of my entire belief, confidence, hope and trust in God, by the constant virtuous integrity of my thoughts, by the humility and meekness of my daily prayers to God, by my diligent and loving works of truly charitable service to my family and to society, and by my patient obedience to all of the commandments, covenants, laws and ordinances of God—that I seek to love, serve and worship God with all of the energy, might, power, strength and will of my soul and with enough faith in the Lord Jesus Christ to become an heir and to charitably strive to help other people become heirs to exaltation through the charitable love, cleansing power and redeeming grace of the Atonement of the Lord Jesus Christ

faithful[2] - to be prone, come what may, to continue to patiently prove—by my faithful, timely and true repentance, by the reality of my intent and the sincerity of my desire, by my steady exercise of my entire belief, confidence, hope and trust in God, by the constant virtuous integrity of my thoughts, by the humility and meekness of my daily prayers to God, by my diligent and loving works of truly charitable service to my family and to society, and by my patient obedience to all of the commandments, covenants, laws and ordinances of God—that I anticipate, expect or hope for the fulfillment or realization of a righteously desired blessing or gift that is expedient in the Lord Jesus Christ, the fulfillment or realization of which is neither immediately susceptible to nor demanding of proof

faithful[3] - to be prone to add to the growing measures of discernibly true enlightenment, virtue and integrity within me until God justly fulfills and lovingly replaces a portion of my gift and power of faithful belief with an absolute, perfect and spiritually verified personal knowledge of enlightened certainty, reality or truth by personal enlightenment, inspiration or revelation from Him by the power of the Holy Ghost that God the Eternal Father and His Only Begotten Son in the flesh, the Lord Jesus Christ, are two distinctly separate, gloriously exalted Spirit Personages who are each inseparably embodied within His own gloriously exalted, immortal body of flesh and bones, the Holy Ghost is a gloriously exalted male Spirit Personage of enlivened spirit matter, and these three distinctly separate divine Beings are members of a Godhead who function and speak as one in purpose to bring to pass the immortality and exaltation of humankind by our faithfully repentant and honorably exact obedience to those divinely appointed commandments, covenants, laws and ordinances upon which receipt of those blessings is predicated

faithful[4] - to be prone to add to the growing measures of discernibly true enlightenment, virtue and integrity within me until God justly fulfills and lovingly replaces a portion of my gift and power of faithful belief with an absolute, perfect and spiritually verified personal knowledge of enlightened certainty, reality or truth by personal enlightenment, inspiration or revelation from Him by the power of the Holy Ghost that God the Eternal Father lives, that I am His child, that He loves me, that no unclean thing can dwell in His glorious celestial presence, that He yearns for my return to His presence in cleanliness following my death, that He has provided a way for me to overcome physical death by resurrection and a way for me, unless I am murderous or perdition, to be cleansed or sanctified from my sins to overcome spiritual death by the charitable love, cleansing power and redeeming grace of the Atonement of the Lord Jesus Christ unto exaltation by my faithfully repentant and honorably exact obedience to those divinely appointed commandments, covenants, laws and ordinances upon which receipt of that knowledge is predicated

faithful[5] - to be prone to add to the growing measures of discernibly true enlightenment, virtue and integrity within me which prompt me to continue to learn all of the truth I can about God, to love, obey, reverence, serve and worship Him with all of the energy, might, power, strength and will of my soul, and to be completely filled with the truly charitable desire, intent and power to obediently sacrifice and consecrate enough of what I have and am to effectively safeguard and improve the virtuously liberating freedom, health, honorable economic prosperity and steady progress of me, my family and society toward exaltation

faithful[6] - to be prone to grow in true enlightenment, virtue and integrity and to continue to prayerfully exercise my entire belief, confidence, hope and trust in God until He replaces faithful belief with knowledge within me that He shall justly save all little children and all other people who are not spiritually accountable or mentally competent before His law, and shall mercifully make it possible for each and every one of His accountable children who has ever lived or will ever live on Earth to hear His plan of salvation during life or after death, to choose to fully obey His commandments, covenants, laws and ordinances of salvation when we hear of them, to consequently resurrect or rise in triumph from the grave, and, provided we are neither murderous nor perdition, to consequently live together forever in His glorious celestial presence as righteous, exalted families in perfect love and with a fulness of everlasting true enlightenment, virtue, integrity, liberty, hope, peace and joy

faithful[7] - to be prone to grow in true enlightenment, virtue and integrity and to continue to prayerfully exercise my entire belief, confidence, hope and trust in God until He replaces faithful belief with knowledge within me that in His own due time He shall mercifully and tenderly lift the burdens, wipe away the tears, heal the wounds and eternally, commensurately and justly compensate each person who, in their innocence, has suffered horrible abuse, adversity, atrocity, bloodshed, bondage, brutality, calamity, captivity, corruption, disaster, genocide, murder, rape, slavery, torture, tyranny or violence from whatever cause, or for whatever reason, or from whatever source

faithful[8] - to be prone to grow in true enlightenment, virtue and integrity and to continue to prayerfully exercise my entire belief, confidence, hope and trust in God until He replaces faithful belief with knowledge within me that although I have been called upon by Him, along with others, to gain from agonizing personal experience the greater personal rewards of proving more patient belief, more refined hope, and more pure obedience to Him, He shall, in His own due time, mercifully and tenderly lift the burdens, wipe away the tears, heal the wounds and eternally, commensurately and justly reward each person who has overcome the world by being faithfully, timely and truly repentant and righteous in the face of awful physical death, harm, illness, injury, pain, suffering, torment or torture from whatever cause, or for whatever reason, or from whatever source

faithful[9] - to be prone to grow in true enlightenment, virtue and integrity and to continue to prayerfully exercise my entire belief, confidence, hope and trust in God until He replaces faithful belief with knowledge within me that He shall continue to manifest truth unto me by the power of the Holy Ghost, empower me to be more virtuous, deliver me from all evil temptation, give me power to have and to do what is expedient in Him, and enlighten me with His revealed will, by my believing and honorably exact obedience to those divinely appointed laws upon which receipt of those blessings is predicated

faithful[10] - to be prone to grow in true enlightenment, virtue and integrity and to continue to prayerfully exercise my entire belief, confidence, hope and trust in God until He can justly begin to replace my gift and power of faithful belief line upon line and portion by portion with an absolute, perfect and spiritually verified personal knowledge of enlightened certainty, reality or truth by personal enlightenment, inspiration or revelation from Him by the power of the Holy Ghost about such things as His true character, attributes and perfections, and His designs, intentions, plans, purposes, words and works, and what it means to truly worship Him, and the workings of the Spirit of God within me, and whether the course of life I am now pursuing is pleasing unto Him, and what more I must do to receive the blessings, gifts and rewards He delights in giving to those who obey His commandments, covenants, laws and ordinances

faithful[11] - to be prone to seek to replace a portion of my gift and power of faithful belief with a portion of spiritually verified personal knowledge of truth by charitably, diligently, hopefully, humbly, obediently, lovingly, meekly and patiently asking of God with real intent in sincere and heartfelt prayer, with my entire and steady belief, confidence, hope and trust in God that I shall receive the spiritually verified personal enlightenment, inspiration or revelation I need from Him by the power of the Holy Ghost

faithful[12] - to be prone to seek to replace a portion of my gift and power of faithful belief with a portion of spiritually verified personal knowledge of truth by honorably conducting the experiment of softening and planting within the thoughts, beliefs, values and characteristics of my heart what appears to be the best unique religious doctrine about God of which I have become aware in my education and training and in my own constantly diligent, honest and open-minded searching, and to desire to believe in that doctrine to some degree, and to then think, speak and act in harmony with that doctrine to some degree, and to then honorably observe whether it begins to enlarge, enlighten, integrate and uplift my understanding, and whether it begins to feel or taste delicious within me, and whether it begins to fill me with the desire to seek complete liberty from darkness, vice and corruption through my

true repentance and true obedience to the commandments, covenants, laws and ordinances of God, and whether it begins to produce greater true enlightenment, virtue, integrity, liberty, hope, peace and joy within me as I continue to do my very best to think, speak and act in harmony with it, and whether such obedience begins to produce more charitable love and greater liberty, hope, peace and joy within me and my family

faithful[13] - to be prone to increase my discernibly enlightening and spiritually verifiable gift and power of faith by continuing to confidently believe, hope and trust that God shall continue to give me power to prayerfully cast out, dispel or forsake all tempting darkness, doubt and fear within me and to replace them with His perfect hope, light and love, by my faithfully repentant and honorably exact obedience to those divinely appointed commandments, covenants, laws and ordinances upon which receipt of that power is predicated

faithful[14] - to be prone to increase my discernibly enlightening and spiritually verifiable gift and power of faith by continuing to confidently believe, hope and trust that God is a perfectly just, loving, omnipotent, omniscient and unchanging eternal Being who shall eventually answer my prayers by helping me personally ascertain whether He has revealed, now reveals or will yet reveal His enlightening word to known apostles, prophets or other special witnesses duly authorized, called, empowered, ordained and set apart by Him or by His authorized servants, by my believing and honorably exact obedience to that divinely appointed law upon which receipt of that answer is predicated faithful[15] - to be prone to increase my discernibly enlightening and spiritually verifiable gift and power of faith by continuing to confidently believe, hope and trust that God is a perfectly just, loving, omnipotent, omniscient and unchanging eternal Being who shall eventually answer my prayers by helping me personally ascertain whether He has revealed to humankind His mind and will in enlightening words of scripture, what those scriptures truly are, were or will be, and whether those scriptures are or have been taught, preached, interpreted or translated correctly, by my believing and honorably exact obedience to that divinely appointed law upon which receipt of that answer is predicated faithful[16] - to be prone to increase my discernibly enlightening and spiritually verifiable gift and power of faith by continuing to confidently believe, hope and trust that God is a perfectly just, loving, omnipotent, omniscient and unchanging eternal Being who shall eventually send or help me find His true messengers and His truth to help me come to a correct understanding of His character, attributes and perfections, and to a correct understanding of His designs, intentions and purposes for this earth, its inhabitants and

for me personally, by my believing and honorably exact obedience to that divinely appointed law upon which receipt of that understanding is predicated faithful[17] - to be prone to increase my discernibly enlightening and spiritually verifiable gift and power of faith by continuing to confidently believe, hope and trust that God is a perfectly just, loving, omnipotent, omniscient and unchanging eternal Being who shall continue to justly liberate, redeem or rescue me from all darkness, vice, corruption, bondage, despair, turmoil and misery, by my faithfully repentant and honorably exact obedience to those divinely appointed commandments, covenants, laws and ordinances upon which receipt of that blessing is predicated faithful[18] - to be prone to increase my discernibly enlightening and spiritually verifiable gift and power of faith by continuing to confidently believe, hope and trust that living the commandments, covenants, laws and ordinances of God will empower me to abandon or forsake my unworthy appetites, comforts, cravings, desires, drives, passions, pleasures and unwillingness so that I can learn, build, preserve and strengthen greater true enlightenment, virtue, integrity, liberty, hope, peace and joy in me, my family and society faithful[19] - to be prone to increase my discernibly enlightening and spiritually verifiable gift and power of faith by continuing to confidently believe, hope and trust that living the commandments, covenants, laws and ordinances of God will empower me to abandon or forsake that which is viciously faddish, fashionable, stylish or trendy so that I can learn, build, preserve and strengthen greater true enlightenment, virtue, integrity, liberty, hope, peace and joy in me, my family and society

faithful[20] - to be prone to increase my discernibly enlightening and spiritually verifiable gift and power of faith by continuing to confidently believe, hope and trust that each person on Earth is an eternal being created or organized in the image and by the power of God with a divine heritage and a just opportunity to receive a divine inheritance, by our faithfully repentant and honorably exact obedience to those divinely appointed commandments, covenants, laws and ordinances upon which receipt of that divine inheritance is predicated

faithful[21] - to be prone to increase my discernibly enlightening and spiritually verifiable gift and power of faith by continuing to confidently believe, hope and trust that God shall continue to grant me a measure of the power of faith to receive that which is truly good and of God, a measure of the power of faith to continue to do only good, and a measure of the power of faith to do and be that which He wants of me, to the extent of my faithfully repentant and honorably exact obedience to those divinely appointed commandments, covenants, laws and ordinances upon which receipt of that power is predicated

faithful[22] - to be prone to recognize and sincerely think, speak and act in harmony with that measure of discernible light within me which prompts me to receive the gift and power of faith by continuing to confidently believe, hope and trust that God is bound by the eternally binding law of justice, and He is thus bound to grant me the power to justly receive and exercise the heavenly gift and power of enough faith to be perfected in Him, by my faithfully repentant and honorably exact obedience to those divinely appointed commandments, covenants, laws and ordinances upon which receipt of that gift and power of faith is predicated

faithful[23] - to be prone to recognize and sincerely think, speak and act in harmony with that measure of discernible light within me which prompts me to unceasingly exercise my entire belief, confidence, hope and trust that God is bound by the eternally binding law of justice and is a perfectly just, loving, omnipotent, omniscient and unchanging eternal Being whose blessings, gifts and rewards are incomprehensibly great, and He is thus bound to bless me with every needed blessing, gift and reward here and hereafter, by my faithfully repentant and honorably exact obedience to those divinely appointed commandments, covenants, laws and ordinances upon which receipt of those blessings, gifts and rewards is predicated

faithful[24] - to be prone to recognize and sincerely think, speak and act in harmony with that measure of discernible light within me which prompts me to unceasingly exercise my entire belief, confidence, hope and trust that, notwithstanding His perfect love for me, God is bound by the eternally binding law of justice to be no unjust respecter of persons, and He is thus bound to justly condemn my proven willful rejection of Him by withdrawing or withholding a measure of His enlightenment and other blessings from me to the extent I willfully reject greater enlightened certainty, reality or truth about Him and His divinely enlightening commandments, covenants, laws and ordinances

faithful[25] - to be prone to recognize and sincerely think, speak and act in harmony with that measure of discernible light within me which prompts me to unceasingly exercise my entire belief, confidence, hope and trust that God is bound by the eternally binding law of justice, which law prohibits His condemnation of any person who has heard nothing and hence understands nothing of His divinely enlightening commandments, covenants, laws and ordinances, and hence cannot knowingly disobey them, and hence cannot be brought under their condemnation, and hence cannot repent of any disobedience to them, and hence is saved from the negative effects of Adam's and Eve's fall through the Atonement of the Lord Jesus Christ

faithful[26] - to be prone to recognize and sincerely think, speak and act in harmony with that measure of discernible light within me which prompts me to unceasingly exercise my entire belief, confidence, hope and trust that when our first parents, Adam and Eve, chose to obey Satan and transgress the commandment of God not to partake of the forbidden fruit, they each fell by God's just design and foreknowledge from His presence and brought upon this earth, upon themselves and upon their posterity the just consequences of their fall, which consequences include such things as telestial conditions of opposition, enmity, pestilence and suffering on Earth, our spiritual death or physical separation from God's presence, mortal bodies and our separation from them in physical death, the power to produce posterity, the power to discern and know truth from error, and the power to choose between good and evil—along with which came to them and to each of us who are not perdition the promise of redemption from our own sins and from the negative effects of the fall through the Atonement of the Lord Jesus Christ to receive, following our physical deaths, a glorious and everlasting physical resurrection, the glory of which He shall justly determine by our individual accountability for our own choices, decisions, desires and works, and not by Adam's and Eve's transgression

faithful[27] - to be prone to recognize and sincerely think, speak and act in harmony with that measure of discernible light within me which prompts me to unceasingly exercise my entire belief, confidence, hope and trust that God formed this life-sustaining earth, that He set in order, controls, and sustains its intergalactic, galactic, solar system, interplanetary and lunar distances, relationships, revolution and rotation speeds, and its forces of gravity, and the patterns, limitations and consistencies of its atmospheres, electrical balances, lights, pressures, seasons, temperatures, humidity levels and weather, and its land masses, mountains, hills, soils, minerals, and inorganic chemical compositions and balances, and its rainfall, snowfall, streams, rivers, oceans, currents and tides, and all of the other numerous complex and interrelated variables necessary to sustain all of the forms of life here, and that He created, organized and gave life to the first mortal man and woman, and to their children, offspring, posterity or seed, and to all of the other untold numbers and varieties of newly enlivened, reproducing, aging and dying plants, flowers, grasses, herbs, shrubs, trees, animals, birds, fishes, insects, microorganisms and other forms of life which have existed and which now exist upon the face of this earth

faithful[28] - to be prone to recognize and sincerely think, speak and act in harmony with that measure of discernible light within me which prompts me to unceasingly exercise my entire belief, confidence, hope and trust that God has provided an abundance of witnesses and, according to my faith in Him, shall continue to pour out an abundance of discernibly enlightening and spiritually verifiable evidence of His existence, goodness, love, power and wisdom in the form of good and miraculous blessings, revelations, healings, the casting out of evil spirits, spiritual gifts, spiritual impressions or promptings, signs, visions, warnings and other wonders—without removing the faithless opposition which must exist on this earth in its present telestial condition or state

faithful[29] - to be prone to recognize and sincerely think, speak and act in harmony with that measure of discernible light within me which prompts me to unceasingly exercise my entire belief, confidence, hope and trust that all of the prophesies and promises spoken of by God's apostles, prophets or other special witnesses since the world began have been or will yet be fulfilled

faithful[30] - to be prone to recognize and sincerely think, speak and act in harmony with that measure of discernible light within me which prompts me to unceasingly exercise my entire belief, confidence, hope and trust that God did and can again call, ordain and set apart apostles, prophets or other special witnesses and give them authority and power to reveal His will and to truly prophesy among humankind of things to come

faithful[31] - to be prone to recognize and sincerely think, speak and act in harmony with that measure of discernible light within me which prompts me to unceasingly exercise my entire belief, confidence, hope and trust that God the Eternal Father still has and shall always have the desire, the love, the need and the power to reveal absolute, perfect and verifiable knowledge of the truth about Himself and about His mind and will to His inquiring, believing and obedient children on Earth

faithful[32] - to be prone to recognize and sincerely think, speak and act in harmony with that measure of discernible light within me which prompts me to unceasingly exercise my entire belief, confidence, hope and trust that God the Eternal Father is perfectly aware of and perfectly compassionate toward the true conditions and needs of each of His children on Earth, and that He consistently hears and shall justly answer the prayers of the faithful, repentant and righteous soul in His own due time, in His own way, and in harmony with His own will for our best good

faithful[33] - to be prone to recognize and sincerely think, speak and act in harmony with that measure of discernible light within me which prompts me to unceasingly exercise my entire belief, confidence, hope and trust that God *never* lies and He must and shall *always* fulfill His rewarding promises to me when I contritely, humbly and meekly continue to do and endure whatsoever thing He may require for my good

faithful[34] - to be prone to recognize and sincerely think, speak and act in harmony with that measure of discernible light within me which prompts me to unceasingly exercise my entire belief, confidence, hope and trust that God is, was and shall always be a perfectly just, loving, omnipotent, omniscient and unchanging eternal Being who is and must be the same yesterday, today and forever, or He would cease to be God

faithful[35] - to be prone to recognize and sincerely think, speak and act in harmony with that measure of discernible light within me which prompts me to unceasingly exercise my entire belief, confidence, hope and trust that God lives, and that He is all-powerful, all-wise, and the source of all that is good

faithful[36] - to be prone, in the face of wavering doubt, fearful apprehension, sinking despair and questioning suspicion, to unceasingly exercise my entire belief, confidence, hope and trust that God will neither censure nor reproach me but will justly and liberally reward me in His own due time and in His own way as I diligently come unto Him in sincere prayer and as I diligently strive to obey His will as well as I know it

faithful[37] - to be prone to think, speak and act in harmony with the self-evident truth that entire and steady belief, confidence, hope and trust in God could not exist as choices without enough opposing evidence, grounds or reasons for both firm belief and wavering doubt, for both full confidence and fearful apprehension, for both buoyant hope and sinking despair, and for both complete trust and questioning suspicion

faithful[38] - to be prone to refuse to remain evil or satanic, but to desire to be redeemed unto exaltation

faithful[39] - to be prone to refuse to remain sinful, unrepentant and, hence, unsanctified and unworthy of redemption unto exaltation

faithful[40] - to be prone to refuse to remain spiritually and unconscionably unbelieving, faithless, fallen, lost or dead

faithful[41] - to be religiously virtuous or virtuously religious

faithful[42] - to be perfectly chaste in refraining from all sexual relations, except with my husband or wife to whom I am lawfully and legally wedded

faithful[43] - to be perfectly chaste in refraining from all tempting thoughts of evil or satanic sexual relations

faithful[44] - to be carefully and constantly dependable, reliable and trustworthy in the performance of my good and honorable duty

faithful[45] - to be prone to live in harmony with that measure of enlightenment I have received

fallen - to be separated from the presence of God because my immortal spirit being has, in harmony with His plan, left His presence to enter into a physical body which is subject to physical death in a state of earthly mortality, procreation, opposition and choice brought about by the fall of Adam and Eve, and to live in harmony with celestial law in order to make the best of my earthly probation to be redeemed from

both physical and spiritual death through the Atonement of the Lord Jesus Christ to receive, following my physical death, a glorious and everlasting celestial resurrection, the glory of which He shall justly determine by my individual accountability for my own choices, decisions, desires and works, and not by Adam's and Eve's transgression

familial - to be and to choose to remain part of a celestial, exalted or sealed family relationship which grows, endures and extends from generation to generation forever

familial[2] - to be and to choose to remain part of a godly family relationship which grows, endures and extends from generation to generation

familial[3] - to be and to choose to remain part of a charitably loving family relationship which grows, endures and extends from generation to generation

familial[4] - to be and to choose to remain part of a healthy and unified family relationship which grows, endures and extends from generation to generation

familial[5] - to be and to choose to remain virtuously patriarchal or matriarchal

familial[6] - to be grandfatherly or grandmotherly

familial[7] - to be prone to please God in bringing enough worthy admiration, praise, respect or veneration to my parents and to my other ancestors to whom I belong by adoption, by blood, by lineage or by marriage

familial[8] - to be prone to enable and encourage my spouse to please

God in bringing enough worthy admiration, praise, respect or veneration to my spouse's parents and to my spouse's ancestors

familial[9] - to be prone, as a parent, to be virtuously parenting

familial[10] - to be prone to honorably perpetuate, through children naturally born to my spouse and to me, the healthy ancestral identity, blood lineage, genealogy, genetics and other blessings of healthy mortal life which my parents and other progenitors have given to me through and since my birth in preparation for eternal life with them and with our collective posterity

familial[11] - to be fatherly or motherly

familial[12] - to be prone to create and build upon a mutually beneficial, complementary and interdependent relationship with my lawfully and legally wedded husband or wife

familial[13] - to be a girl or woman who is virtuously homemaking

familial[14] - to be prone, as an unavoidably single adult who is part of an institutional family of birth-related and blood-related ancestry and relatives, to continue to prepare myself for those greater family blessings which shall come to be by my believing and honorably exact obedience to those divinely appointed laws upon which receipt of those blessings is predicated

familial[15] - to be prone to regularly spend enough meal times, play times, sharing times, teaching times, together times, work times and other times building and strengthening healthy and unified family relationships

familial[16] - to be prone, as a child, to accept correction from, to honor, to learn from and to obey my goodly parents

familial[17] - to be charitably loving toward my family enough for them to miss my presence when we are apart for a while

familial[18] - to be virtuously familiar and serving toward others who are not closely related to me by birth, blood or marriage as though they are my family

familial[19] - to be prone to build, improve and strengthen the virtuously liberating freedom, health, honorable economic prosperity and steady progress of me, my family and society by thinking, speaking and acting in harmony with that which produces, preserves or restores true enlightenment, virtue and integrity within me, my family and society

familial[20] - to be prone to preserve as an institutional family the divinely authorized natural form and order of one chaste and virtuous man and his lawfully and legally wedded chaste and virtuous wife, along with any children born to them or adopted by them

familial[21] - to be prone to preserve and record as an institutional family the natural form and order of birth-related and blood-related ancestry, relatives and posterity

familial[22] - to be prone to reject every form and function of a so-called institutional family that is contrary, destructive or otherwise offensive to the designs and purposes of God the Eternal Father for the exalted, glorious and joyful eternal fulfillment of His children

familial[23] - to be prone to reject every form and function of a so-called institutional family that is based upon, includes or institutionalizes evil or satanic sexual relations

familial[24] - to be prone to reject every form and function of a so-called institutional family which produces, preserves or restores darkness, vice and corruption within me, in my family and in society

familial[25] - to be prone to refuse to be antifamilial

familiar - to be familial or familistic

familiar[2] - to be charitably loving and kind

familistic - to be familial

familistic[2] - to be prone to think, speak and act as though the virtuously liberating freedom, health, honorable economic prosperity and steady progress of society are tied to the virtuously liberating freedom, health, honorable economic prosperity and steady progress of each of its families

familistic[3] - to be prone to think, speak and act as though the virtuously liberating freedom, health, honorable economic prosperity and steady progress of my family are tied to the virtuously liberating freedom, health, honorable economic prosperity and steady progress of each of its members

familistic[4] - to be prone to refuse to be antifamilial

famous - to be truly deserving of a widespread and well-deserved

reputation of distinguished praise and celebrated renown

fancying - to intend to envision or imagine what is or could be truly good and of God in reality

fantasizing - to intend to tell, write, publish, sell or sponsor good, praiseworthy, virtuous and uplifting fictional, unreal or untrue accounts of things as someone chooses to envision, fancy, fantasize, feign, imagine, imitate, pretend or simulate them to be

fantastic - to be extraordinarily or remarkably good

farsighted - to be sagacious or wise enough to foresee potential developments

farsighted[2] - to be prone to prudently prepare or provide for things likely to come

fascinating - to be filled with enough true enlightenment, virtue and integrity to captivate or enthrall another person's sense of true enlightenment, virtue and integrity

fasting - to intend, when age, circumstance and health will allow, to merit the blessings affixed to proving the firmness of my devotion to God and the sincerity of my prayers to Him by abstaining from drink and food for at least one full day each month while donating an offering equivalent to the cost of the two meals I would ordinarily consume during that period, or an even more generous donated offering, to bring relief to the needy and the poor

fasting[2] - to intend to use a healthy period of self-imposed hunger to help me suppress thoughts of corruptly pleasing or sinfully satisfying any of my biologically inherent and naturally impelling emotional, physical or sexual appetites, cravings, desires, drives or passions

fathering - to be a man who is fatherly

fatherly - to be a virtuous man who does the very best I can to understand, do, be and teach that which produces, preserves or restores the greatest true enlightenment, virtue, integrity, liberty, hope, peace and joy within me, my family and society, and to do my very best to help my sons and daughters understand, do, be and teach the same

fatherly[2] - to be a virtuous man who does the very best I can to avoid doing or being that which produces, preserves or restores darkness, vice and corruption within me, my family and society, and to do my very best to help my sons and daughters avoid the same

fatherly[3] - to be a virtuous man worthy of dignity, esteem or reverence due to the loving care, discipline, guidance, provision, instruction and protection I offer to children, especially my own

fatigued - to be tired or weary from performing good works

faultfinding - to intend to search for and overcome my own defects, failings, imperfections, mistakes or weaknesses by increasing the enlightenment and virtue of the thoughts I continue to integrate into the thoughts, beliefs, values and characteristics of my heart

faultless - to be redeemed unto exaltation

faultless[2] - to be redeemed and released from the bondage, burdens and debts of my sins

faultless[3] - to be prone to perform without defect or flaw

favorable - to be godly enough to be made truly chaste, clean, pure and virtuous at heart — and to continue to encourage and help other people by charitable love, kindness, invitation and instruction to be godly enough to be made truly chaste, clean, pure and virtuous at heart

favorable[2] - to be filled with enough true enlightenment, virtue and integrity to produce, preserve or restore true liberty, hope, peace and joy within me, my family and society

favorable[3] - to be filled with enough true enlightenment, virtue and integrity to strongly attract or appeal to another person's sense of true enlightenment, virtue and integrity

favorable[4] - to be prone to win the favor of other people by doing and being good

favored - to be prone to willingly receive and work to retain blessings from God by my believing and honorably exact obedience to those divinely appointed laws upon which receipt of those blessings is predicated

favored[2] - to be prone to willingly receive and work to retain that which produces, preserves or restores true enlightenment, virtue and integrity within me, my family and society

favored[3] - to be prone to willingly receive and work to retain benevolent, gracious and kind regard from another person

favoring - to intend to seek God's approval and blessings by lovingly keeping His commandments, covenants, laws and ordinances

favoring[2] - to intend to choose or decide to produce, preserve or restore true enlightenment, virtue and integrity within me, my family and society

favoring[3] - to intend to offer the needy and poor aid, assistance, concession, forbearance, forgiveness, leniency or tolerance to an extent and in a manner which is charitably loving, just, right and wise in the sight of God

favoring[4] - to intend to actively, charitably, generously and wisely provide for the needy and poor to an extent or in a manner which saves their lives, meets their immediate needs for survival, fosters their adequate education, employment, labors, self-reliance and thrift, and which encourages their service to other people

favoring[5] - to intend to actively, charitably, generously and wisely give of my substance or other resources to the needy and poor to help them deal with personal needs which they cannot take care of alone—provided they are continuing to demonstrate by their own determined education, training, labors, investments and savings, that they are responsibly striving to become self-reliant net contributors to the virtuously liberating freedom, health, honorable economic prosperity and steady progress of themselves, their families and society

fearing - to be apprehensive or uneasy enough about the impending dreadful consequences of my sinful desires and works as to seek redemption or salvation from the otherwise inescapable demands of the eternally binding law of justice

fearing[2] - to be filled with enough reverential awe or respect toward God, His laws and His righteous judgments to seek and to maintain faithful, timely and true repentance, obedience and reconciliation to Him and to His laws and ordinances

fearing[3] - to be apprehensive or uneasy enough to do all I must do to avoid the naturally consequent penalties or punishments of breaking or changing the commandments, covenants, laws or ordinances of God

fearing[4] - to be apprehensive or uneasy enough to apprehend the true danger, risk or threat of the negative consequences of such things as accident, breach, crime, disobedience, dissent, failure, guilt, liability, opposition, rebellion, violation or violence

fearing[5] - to be apprehensive or uneasy enough to apprehend the true danger, risk or threat of death, destruction, harm, illness, injury, loss, pain, penalty, punishment or suffering

feasting - to intend to please or satisfy myself in freely partaking of a delicious abundance of enlightenment

featuring - to intend to introduce someone or something virtuous as an especially valuable attraction

federal - to be virtuously uniting as a nation

federal^2 - to be prone to refuse to be viciously dividing as a nation

federalizing - to intend to virtuously exercise, enforce or impose the supreme authority or power of my nation's central government when necessary to actively defeat or withstand the attack of a criminal, deadly or evil enemy of society against the fundamental right to human life, against the fundamental right and control of personal property, against equal justice under virtuous law, or against the pursuit and preservation of that true enlightenment, virtue and integrity which produce, preserve or restore true liberty, hope, peace and joy within me, my family and society

federalizing^2 - to intend to virtuously exercise, enforce or impose the supreme authority or power of my nation's central government when necessary to defend virtuously liberating freedom, health, honorable economic prosperity and steady progress against our domestic or foreign enemies

federating - to intend to favor the joining or uniting of sovereign governments into a league or union established to pursue together an honorable and virtuous purpose while each continues to control their own internal affairs

feeding - to be nourishing

feeling - to be sensitively and spiritually aware, discerning or perceptive of spiritual manifestations or revelations made available to me from God

feeling^2 - to intend to refuse to be emotionally or mentally callous and hard-hearted

feeling^3 - to be realistically aware, perceptive or sensitive to the biologically inherent and naturally impelling emotional, physical or sexual appetites, cravings, desires, drives and passions which arise within me

feeling^4 - to be realistically aware, perceptive or sensitive to or with physical touch in reality

felicitating - to intend to pleasantly compliment or congratulate another person upon the occurrence, celebration or commemoration of a joyful event

female - to be a girl or woman who is feminine

feminine - to be a charitable, pure, strong and tenderly benevolent woman of refined and powerful true enlightenment, virtue and integrity who is married to a leading, presiding, protecting and providing husband, and who accepts my God-given family role of acting in full partnership with my husband, of conceiving by or adopting our young with my husband, of giving birth to or adopting our young, of warmly enriching, feeding and nurturing our young, and of building good character within them in our home

feminine^2 - to be a charitable, pure, strong and tenderly benevolent girl or woman of refined and powerful true enlightenment, virtue and integrity who develops characteristics or qualities which are naturally becoming and naturally fulfilling to a woman because they match my God-given family role and because they bring the greatest true enlightenment, virtue, integrity, liberty, hope, peace and joy to me and through me to my family and to society

feminine[3] - to be a charitable, pure, strong and tenderly benevolent girl or woman of refined and powerful true enlightenment, virtue and integrity who is endowed with a marvelous measure of inherent power to righteously bless, enrich, feed, fortify, heal and otherwise nurture or strengthen my family and society, particularly with the positive two (2) virtues in this dictionary—rather than to use my agency to forsake that endowment for something defeminized, something different or something less

feminine[4] - to be a competent girl or woman who accepts my natural efficacy, role, power and strength, and my natural ability to procreate

feminine[5] - to be a girl or woman who accepts my natural identity as a girl or woman born to the female sex

feminine[6] - to be a girl or woman who refuses to be defeminized, gender-confused, masculinized, transsexual, transvestite or viciously unisexual

feminist - to be prone to strive to eliminate the abuse of girls and women by human males and females

feminized - to be a girl or woman who is feminine

feminizing - to intend to help a girl or woman be feminine

ferreting - to intend to discover truth

festive - to be prone to joyously celebrate for good reason

fetterless - to be redeemed unto exaltation

fetterless[2] - to be redeemed and released from the bondage, burdens and debts of my sins

fictionalizing - to intend to tell, write, publish or sponsor good, praiseworthy and uplifting fictional, unreal or untrue accounts of things as someone chooses to envision, fancy, fantasize, feign, imagine, imitate, pretend or simulate them to be

field-testing - to intend to live in harmony with seemingly good thoughts, beliefs, values and characteristics in order to prove or test them by personal experience

fighting - to be filled with enough true enlightenment, virtue and integrity to prayerfully acquire and exercise enough powerful skill from God to righteously prevail in any and every inner personal battle, conflict or war against Satan and his followers in my daily efforts to do and be only that which is truly good and of God

fighting[2] - to be filled with enough true enlightenment, virtue and integrity to prayerfully acquire and exercise enough powerful skill from God to righteously prevail in any and every inner personal battle, conflict or war against Satan and his followers in my daily efforts to do my very best to produce, preserve or restore true enlightenment, virtue and integrity within me, my family and society

fighting[3] - to be filled with enough true enlightenment, virtue and integrity to prayerfully acquire and exercise enough powerful skill from God to righteously cast out, dispel or withstand all evil or satanic powers of darkness, vice, corruption, bondage, despair, turmoil and misery from within me

fighting[4] - to be filled with enough true enlightenment, virtue and integrity to prayerfully acquire and exercise enough powerful skill from God to righteously prevail in any and every inner personal battle, conflict or war against that which produces, preserves or restores darkness, vice and corruption within me, my family and society

fighting[5] - to be filled with enough true enlightenment, virtue and integrity to faithfully, hopefully and prayerfully seek enough power from God to righteously defeat or withstand the power of an attacking, known or wisely suspected criminal, deadly or evil enemy of society

fighting[6] - to be filled with enough true enlightenment, virtue and integrity to faithfully, hopefully and prayerfully seek enough power from God to righteously prevail in unavoidable deadly single combat necessary to the preservation of my life or the life of another person I am bound to protect

figuring - to intend to calculate or reason consequences, effects, outcomes or results

filial - to be prone to show my goodly parents enough honor, obedience and respect to be a righteous child in the sight of God

filial[2] - to be prone to prove to my goodly parents my natural affection as a grateful and loving child

filial[3] - to be prone to treat the goodly people among the preceding generation as though I were their own goodly daughter or son

filibustering - to intend, in a democracy, to honorably apply delay tactics allowed under legislative rules to strive to hinder, impede or obstruct the adoption of a measure until I am satisfied my fellow legislators who are or may be likely to pass it have given me enough opportunity to clearly raise any new facts I honestly believe are relevant and important enough to be considered before the final vote is taken

filled - to be enlightened

filled[2] - to be richly supplied with that which produces, preserves or restores true enlightenment, virtue and integrity within me, my family and society

filled[3] - to be satisfied with receiving enough of what I need to survive

filling - to intend to lovingly encourage and kindly help someone to be fulfilled

filtering - to intend to keep my thoughts, words and actions clean by removing impurities and keeping them out

finding - to intend to identify that which best produces, preserves or restores the greatest true enlightenment, virtue, integrity, liberty, hope, peace and joy within me, my family and society

finding[2] - to intend to ascertain or discern truth

finding[3] - to intend to judiciously reach a good decision or render a righteous judgment
fine - to be truly clean, healthy and well
fine[2] - to be fully repentant
fine[3] - to be elegant, gracious, polished or refined in manners
finished - to be fulfilled
finished[2] - to be polished or refined
first - to be first-class or first-rate
first[2] - to be first-line, first-string or first-team
first-class - to be celestial
first-class[2] - to be one of those who are the most honorable in quality of character
first-class[3] - to be one of those who are the most productive or skilled in good performance
first-line - to be first-team
first-rate - to be first-class
first-string - to be first-line or first-team
first-team - to be one of those who are best prepared to start in an honorable team competition or contest, and to then make sure I am producing the best efforts I can to the success of my team
fit - to be redeemed unto exaltation
fit[2] - to be redeemed and released from the bondage, burdens and debts of my sins
fit[3] - to be extraordinarily or remarkably good
fit[4] - to be prone to maintain good health and strength
fitting - to intend to think, speak and act in harmony with that which is charitably loving, just, right and wise in the sight of God
fitting[2] - to intend to think, speak and act in harmony with the good law of the land

fixed - to be established, grounded or settled upon the sure foundation of enlightenment, virtue and integrity
fixed[2] - to be established, grounded or settled upon the sure foundation of enlightened certainty, reality or truth
flattering - to intend to please or satisfy someone with sincerely expressed and well-deserved praise
fleeing - to intend to quickly or rapidly abandon or turn away from corrupt, sinful or vicious wrongdoing
fleeing[2] - to intend to quickly or rapidly abandon or turn away from all of the evil or satanic powers of binding addiction, compulsion, impulsion, obsession, occupation and possession
flourishing - to intend to continue to progress by continuing to improve the enlightenment and virtue of the thoughts I continue to integrate into the thoughts, beliefs, values and characteristics of my heart
flourishing[2] - to intend to arise, blossom, grow, prosper or thrive in true enlightenment, virtue, integrity, liberty, hope, peace and joy in direct proportion to my believing and honorably exact obedience to those divinely appointed laws upon which receipt of those blessings is predicated
flowing - to intend to cautiously, smoothly and steadily make good progress
following - to be Christlike
following[2] - to intend to become like one or more other people in producing, preserving or restoring

one or more virtues within me, my family and society

forceful - to be prone to exert and expend enough energy, force, power or strength to say and do enough good to be a powerful influence for good

forcing - to intend to exert and expend enough energy, force, power or strength to say and do enough good to be a powerful influence for good

foreknowing - to be foreseeing

foremost - to be preeminent, prominent or superior in purity and virtue

foreordained - to be prone to personally ascertain and live in harmony with the discernibly enlightening and spiritually verifiable truth that: I am one of those who received God's authority and power before I came to earth to fulfill a specific mission or purpose on Earth by my believing and honorably exact obedience to that divinely appointed law upon which receipt of that blessing is predicated

foreordained[2] - to be prone to personally ascertain and live in harmony with the discernibly enlightening and spiritually verifiable truth that: because of the agency or mortal power of liberty I have been given to make choices of my own while on Earth, I cannot be justly controlled, disciplined, governed or restrained by destiny or by fate, but I can ascertain the truth about any earthly purpose or mission to which I was called and ordained before my birth

foreseeing - to be foresighted

foresighted - to be one of those who have received by personal enlightenment, inspiration or revelation from God a knowledge of how to avoid or guard against any evil which will surely come to pass

foresighted[2] - to be one of those who have received by personal enlightenment, inspiration or revelation from God a knowledge of that which will surely come to pass

foresighted[3] - to be prone to wisely prepare or provide for the future

foresightful - to be foresighted

forgetting - to intend to fail to remember or to refuse to entertain thoughts of the wrongdoing someone has inflicted upon me, as part of my own virtuous repentance and forgiveness process

forgivable - to be redeemable

forgivable[2] - to be virtuous and virtuously forgiving

forgiven - to be redeemed

forgiving - to intend to completely, permanently and unconditionally give away and forget all personally enforceable or imposable consequences, debts, payments, penalties and punishments, all other demands, obligations, reparations and restrictions, and all anger, resentment, revenge and reviling I might otherwise think to personally enforce or impose upon another person who faithfully, timely and truly repents each time they have viciously imposed personal harm, injury or offense upon me

forgiving[2] - to intend to completely, permanently and unconditionally give away and forget all personally enforceable or imposable consequences, debts, payments, penalties and punishments, all other demands, obligations, reparations and restrictions, and all anger, resentment, revenge and reviling I might otherwise think to personally enforce or impose upon myself after I have faithfully, timely and truly repented of viciously imposing personal harm, injury or offense upon someone

forgiving[3] - to intend to completely, permanently and unconditionally give away and forget all personally enforceable or imposable consequences, debts, payments, penalties and punishments, all other demands, obligations, reparations and restrictions, and all anger, resentment, revenge and reviling I might otherwise think to personally enforce or impose upon another person who fails or refuses to completely repent for all of the bearable or tolerable harm, injury or offense they have viciously imposed upon me once, twice or three times

forgiving[4] - to intend, without imposing any measure of personal retaliation or vengeance, to cry unto God for His vengeance against another person who fails or refuses to repent for all of the personal harm, injury or offense they have viciously imposed upon me four or more times, and to then leave matters in God's hands as I pray for them and as I do that good which I have been personally prompted by His Spirit to do unto them—and to then wholeheartedly absolve or pardon them after they completely repent and make four

times the restitution to me before God, knowing He will repay me a hundred times over if they do not

forgiving[5] - to intend, as a citizen of a nation and in cooperation with any allies we may have, to withhold horribly violent bloodshed, death and destruction from those of one or more other nations who have declared or proclaimed horribly violent bloodshed, death or destruction against us, until they have rejected at least three offerings of peace from us

fortified - to be securely strengthened in good health and true safety

fortifying - to intend to securely strengthen someone in good health and true safety

fortitudinous - to be emotionally and mentally firm and strong in courageously dispelling, forsaking, overcoming or withstanding darkness, vice and corruption

fortitudinous[2] - to be emotionally and mentally firm and strong in courageously dispelling, forsaking, overcoming or withstanding unavoidable danger or trial

forward-thinking - to intend to plan well for a good future

founded - to be established, fixed or settled upon the sure foundation of enlightenment, virtue and integrity

founded[2] - to be established, fixed or settled upon the sure foundation of enlightened certainty, reality or truth

free - to be exalted

free[2] - to be redeemed unto exaltation

free[3] - to be redeemed and released from the bondage, burdens and debts of my sins

free[4] - to be filled with enough true enlightenment, virtue and integrity, and with enough of the spirit of virtuously liberating freedom or the Spirit of God to become or remain entirely emancipated, freed, liberated or released within my mind and heart from the evil or satanic powers of darkness, vice, corruption, bondage, despair, turmoil and misery, and to thus maintain complete personal control over the thoughts of my mind and heart, and to thus maintain my personal liberty or power to choose to live in harmony with the Spirit of God, and to thus be protected against all of the evil or satanic powers of addiction, bondage or slavery and against their naturally consequent bondage, despair, turmoil and misery

free[5] - to be prone to join with other members of my family and society to continue to live in harmony with the spirit of virtuously liberating freedom or the Spirit of God well enough to produce, preserve or restore emancipation, immunity or liberty from the ever threatening evil or satanic powers of darkness, vice, corruption, bondage, despair, turmoil and misery wielded by our vicious domestic and foreign enemies

free[6] - to be prone to join with other members of my family to continue to live in harmony with the spirit of virtuously liberating freedom or the Spirit of God well enough to produce, preserve or restore emancipation, immunity or liberty from the ever threatening evil or satanic powers of darkness, vice, corruption, bondage, despair, turmoil and misery wielded by our vicious family enemies

free[7] - to be prone to live in harmony with the spirit of virtuously liberating freedom or the Spirit of God well enough to continue to enjoy the emancipating or liberating power to dispel or withstand the evil or satanic powers of darkness, vice, corruption, bondage, despair, turmoil and misery

free[8] - to be prone to maintain my personal freedom, liberty or power to choose and to act for myself for good, and to thus protect myself against evil or satanic addiction, bondage, captivity, slavery and tyranny

free[9] - to be prone to refuse to regard my individual liberty of choosing or deciding for myself as being more important than the harm its abuse or misuse can do to me, my family and society

free[10] - to be prone to enjoy enough of the civil liberty, religious liberty and political liberty afforded by good government

free[11] - to be prone to emancipate, free, liberate or release myself from those who would viciously use beguiling charm or flattery to ensnare my affection or love for their own selfish purposes

freed - to be exalted

freed[2] - to be redeemed unto exaltation

freed[3] - to be redeemed and released from the bondage, burdens and debts of my sins freed[4] - to be prone to humbly and prayerfully allow the heavenly power which comes from virtuous forgiving to emancipate, liberate or release me from the self-consuming bitterness and festering pain I might otherwise viciously continue to wish upon someone else

freed[5] - to be emancipated, liberated or released from the evil or satanic powers of addiction, bondage or slavery

freedom-loving - to intend to love the spirit of virtuously liberating freedom or the Spirit of God enough to seek to be redeemed and released from the bondage, burdens and debts of my sins

freedom-loving[2] - to intend to love the spirit of virtuously liberating freedom or the Spirit of God enough to seek freedom or liberty from the evil or satanic powers of darkness, vice, corruption, bondage, despair, turmoil and misery

freedom-loving[3] - to intend to love the spirit of virtuously liberating freedom or the Spirit of God enough to seek freedom or liberty from addiction, bondage, captivity, oppression, slavery and tyranny

freedom-loving[4] - to be patriotic enough to refuse to abandon or surrender my freedom and power to choose the authority, control, dominion, government, influence, power or rule that is exerted or wielded over me

freedom-loving[5] - to intend to cherish and defend liberty and political independence

freedom-loving[6] - to intend to refuse to abandon or surrender my freedom and power to honorably control the pleasure and satisfaction of my biologically inherent and naturally impelling emotional, physical or sexual appetites, cravings, desires, drives and passions

free-handed - to be generous or liberal in giving of my substance to those in need

freeing - to be virtuously emancipating, liberating or releasing

freethinking - to intend to honestly rely upon my own thinking ability in honorably questioning all thoughts, beliefs, values and characteristics in order to discover and select for myself those which produce, preserve or restore the greatest true enlightenment, virtue, integrity, liberty, hope, peace and joy within me, my family and society

fresh - to be animated or enlivened

friendly - to be gratefully, humbly, lovingly and meekly obedient to the commandments, covenants, laws and ordinances of God, come what may

friendly[2] - to be prone to encourage and to seek faithful, timely and true repentance, obedience and reconciliation to God

friendly[3] - to be prone to affectionately share clean personal attachment, well-founded confidence, well-deserved respect, and complete trust with another person of true enlightenment, virtue and integrity

friendly[4] - to be prone to actively, charitably, generously and wisely help other people build, preserve and strengthen their virtuously liberating freedom, health, honorable economic prosperity and steady progress

friendly[5] - to be prone to judge righteous judgment by looking for the good in other people and by striving to build on it as often as possible

friendly[6] - to be prone to mercifully give other people unconditional forgiveness as often as possible

friendly[7] - to be slow to take offense, to refuse to seek personal revenge, and to seek reconciliation with other people as often as possible

friendly[8] - to be prone to disagree, differ or dissent in a courteous, kind, neighborly, soft-spoken and understanding manner

frightened - to be virtuously afraid or fearing

frugal - to be prone to consume, save and spend in an economical, prudent, temperate or thrifty manner

fruitful - to be prone to produce truly virtuous designs, desires, dispositions, intentions, plans, purposes, words, actions, deeds and works for the glory and honor of God

fruitful[2] - to be godly enough to be made truly chaste, clean, pure and virtuous at heart—and to continue to encourage and help other people by charitable love, kindness, invitation and instruction to be godly enough to be made truly chaste, clean, pure and virtuous at heart

fulfilled - to be exalted

fulfilled[2] - to be redeemed unto exaltation

fulfilled[3] - to be redeemed and released from the bondage, burdens and debts of my sins

fulfilled[4] - to be prone to actualize, realize or satisfy the full measure of my best potential

fulfilled[5] - to be filled with true enlightenment, virtue, integrity, liberty, hope, peace and joy

fulfilling - to intend to lovingly encourage and kindly help someone to be fulfilled

functional - to be prone to act, behave or operate to an extent or in a manner which is truly good and of God

fundamental - to be prone to think, speak and act in harmony with a foundation of beliefs which integrates basic principles or values, the living of which produces, preserves or restores true enlightenment, virtue and integrity within me, my family and society

fundamentalist - to be prone to invite all to come unto the Lord Jesus Christ and be perfected in Him by thinking, speaking and acting in harmony with the discernibly enlightening and spiritually verifiable basic truths found in His correctly translated and understood words and those of His apostles and prophets past and present

fundamentalist[2] - to be prone to personally ascertain and live in harmony with the discernibly enlightening and spiritually verifiable basic truths found in writings which are truly holy or sacred as scripture in the sight of God

fussy - to be prone to pay enough exact, precise and thorough attention to those details by which or through which I can produce, preserve or restore the greatest true enlightenment, virtue, integrity, liberty, hope, peace and joy within me, my family and society

fussy[2] - to be prone to pay enough attention to details

futuristic - to be actively and truly progressing

G

gainful - to be prone to do honest work for honest pay

gaining - to intend to continue to progress by continuing to improve the enlightenment and virtue of the thoughts I continue to integrate into the thoughts, beliefs, values and characteristics of my heart

gaining[2] - to intend to earn honest advantage, increase or profit by honest effort, labor or work

gainly - to be comely or handsome in true enlightenment, virtue and integrity

gallant - to be a chivalrous, noble and stately boy or man who is kindly attentive and courteous toward children, girls and women and who is known to be brave, courageous and spirited in defense of truth and virtue

garnering - to intend to collect or gather into my home storage for future use the resources my immediate family needs to survive for one or more years

garnering[2] - to intend to store enough food

gay - to be filled with jolly gaiety or festive merriment in healthy association or companionship with other people during respectable social activities

gay[2] - to be homosexless

generous - to be benevolently consecrating, donating, sacrificing or serving in the sight of God

generous[2] - to be welfarist to an extent or in a manner which is charitably loving, just, right and wise in the sight of God

generous[3] - to be prone to kindly, liberally, nobly, unselfishly and wisely give, serve or share as much or as well as I can and should for the virtuously liberating freedom, health, honorable economic prosperity and steady progress of me, my family and society

generous[4] - to be prone to directly, regularly and voluntarily deliver, impart or present a more than expected, necessary or usual portion of my substance to the needy and the poor, without compensation, expectation or notoriety

genial - to be as cheerful, cordial and warm toward another person as possible

genteel - to be prone to truly embody refined elegance, gentleness, grace, politeness and style

genteel[2] - to be prone to utterly avoid evil or satanic amusement, comedy, entertainment, fun, game, humor, play or sport

gentle - to be prone to peaceably treat other people with as much polite kindness and quiet tenderness as possible

gentlemanly - to be a pure and virtuous boy or man who is masculine, polite, well-educated, well-mannered and well-spoken enough to convince pure and virtuous girls and women to accept or desire my honorable attention and devotion

gentlemanly[2] - to be a boy or man who lives in harmony with the best and highest laws, rules, standards or values of true enlightenment, virtue and integrity of which I have become aware in my education and training and in my own constantly diligent, honest and open-minded searching

gentlemanly[3] - to be a boy or man who is prone to peaceably treat other people with polite kindness and quiet tenderness

gentlemanly[4] - to be a boy or man who is honorably genteel

gentlewomanly - to be a pure and virtuous girl or woman who is feminine, polite, well-educated, well-mannered and well-spoken enough to attract the honorable attention and devotion of pure and virtuous boys and men

gentlewomanly[2] - to be a girl or woman who lives in harmony with the best and highest laws, rules, standards or values of true enlightenment, virtue and integrity of which I have become aware in my education and training and in my own constantly diligent, honest and open-minded searching

gentlewomanly[3] - to be a girl or woman who is prone to peaceably treat other people with polite kindness and quiet tenderness

gentlewomanly[4] - to be a girl or woman who is honorably genteel

genuflecting - to intend to bow the knee in prayerful and reverent worship of God

genuine - to be prone to possess a truly chaste, clean, pure and

virtuous character without affectation, hypocrisy or pretense

genuine[2] - to be prone to honestly and sincerely think, speak and act in harmony with true enlightenment, virtue and integrity

geopolitical - to be prone to think, speak and act as though the virtuously liberating freedom, health, honorable economic prosperity and steady progress of one political faction are tied to the virtuously liberating freedom, health, honorable economic prosperity and steady progress of all of the political factions of the world

geopolitical[2] - to be prone to learn enough about the geographical and political factors pertaining to the government of nations

gifted - to be exalted

gifted[2] - to be worthy to constantly receive within me the constant companionship of the gloriously and powerfully comforting, cleansing, empowering, enlightening, gifting, instructing, justifying, protecting, purifying, refining, revelatory and sanctifying influence or divine presence of the Holy Ghost by my faithfully repentant and honorably exact obedience to those divinely appointed commandments, covenants, laws and ordinances upon which receipt of that divine gift is predicated

gifted[3] - to be prone to develop and put to good use the valuable abilities, knowledge, skills or talents with which I have been blessed or endowed by God

gifting - to intend to confer, donate, offer or present something

good and valuable to another person as a favor, with no expectation of anything in return
gilding - to intend to improve the appearance of something
ginger - to be gingering
gingering - to be enlivening
giving - to be benevolently consecrating, donating, sacrificing or serving in the sight of God
giving² - to be welfarist to an extent or in a manner which is charitably loving, just, right and wise in the sight of God
giving³ - to intend to directly, regularly and voluntarily deliver, impart or present a generous portion of my substance to the needy and the poor, without compensation, expectation or notoriety
glad - to be gratefully delighted or elated
glamorous - to be filled with enough true enlightenment, virtue and integrity to charm or fascinate another person's sense of true enlightenment, virtue and integrity
gleeful - to be full of exuberant joy
glittering - to be brilliant
globalist - to be prone to encourage my nation to place the unmet needs of the rest of the world above our own excessive, needless or selfish wants
glorified - to be exalted
glorified² - to be celestial
glorifying - to intend to cast bright, magnificent or splendid light upon God or to elevate Him to supremely distinguished or honored reputation within the thoughts of other people through my virtuous adoration, praise, service and worship of Him

glorious - to be worthy to be exalted as a sanctified, redeemed and resurrected being in God's highest celestial kingdom of glory through the charitable love, cleansing power and redeeming grace of the Atonement of the Lord Jesus Christ by my faithfully repentant and honorably exact obedience to those divinely appointed commandments, covenants, laws and ordinances upon which receipt of that blessing is predicated
glorious² - to be godly enough to be made truly chaste, clean, pure and virtuous at heart—and to continue to encourage and help other people by charitable love, kindness, invitation and instruction to be godly enough to be made truly chaste, clean, pure and virtuous at heart
glorious³ - to be worthy to constantly receive within me the constant companionship of the gloriously and powerfully comforting, cleansing, empowering, enlightening, gifting, instructing, justifying, protecting, purifying, refining, revelatory and sanctifying influence or divine presence of the Holy Ghost by my faithfully repentant and honorably exact obedience to those divinely appointed commandments, covenants, laws and ordinances upon which receipt of that divine gift is predicated
glorious⁴ - to be filled with enough truly virtuous thoughts and with enough truly charitable works to faithfully and prayerfully receive an absolute, perfect and spiritually verified personal knowledge of the

truth by personal enlightenment, inspiration or revelation from God through the glorious influence or divine presence of the Holy Ghost

glorious[5] - to be filled with bright, magnificent or splendid true enlightenment, virtue and integrity by my believing and honorably exact obedience to those divinely appointed laws upon which receipt of those blessings is predicated

glorious[6] - to be prone to personally ascertain and live in harmony with the discernibly enlightening and spiritually verifiable truth that: God is humanity's source of perfect liberty, hope, peace and joy

glorious[7] - to be prone to personally ascertain and live in harmony with the discernibly enlightening and spiritually verifiable truth that: God is humanity's source of perfect glory, intelligence, knowledge, life, love, power, truth, virtue and wisdom

glorious[8] - to be prone to develop my mental capacity for quick comprehension, sound reasoning, enlightened understanding and righteous judgment

glorious[9] - to be enlightened or intelligent by living in harmony with light and truth

glorious[10] - to be prone to personally ascertain and live in harmony with the discernibly enlightening and spiritually verifiable truth that: I was born with a certain endowment of enlightenment and with the freedom to increase that endowment by choosing that which is truly good and of God — or to lose that endowment

by choosing that which is evil or satanic

glorying - to be filled with triumphant joy or rejoicing by my believing and honorably exact obedience to that divinely appointed law upon which receipt of that joy is predicated

glowing - to be radiant

glowing[2] - to intend to radiate true enlightenment, virtue and integrity

glowing[3] - to intend to radiate elated emotions, feelings or passions of good health and true safety

gnostic - to be spiritually-minded

goal-oriented - to be prone to aim for and strive toward achieving the best level, objective, purpose, result or standard possible

God-fearing - to be so deeply respectful and reverent toward God as to piously offer Him my wholehearted devotion

godlike - to be exalted

godlike[2] - to be celestial

godlike[3] - to be godly enough to be made truly chaste, clean, pure and virtuous at heart—and to continue to encourage and help other people by charitable love, kindness, invitation and instruction to be godly enough to be made truly chaste, clean, pure and virtuous at heart

godly - to be exalted

godly[2] - to be celestial

godly[3] - to be Christlike

godly[4] - to be prone to bring as much glory and honor to God as I possibly can by most faithfully and willingly maximizing my honorable designs, desires, dispositions, intentions, works and characteristics of truly charitable

love for Him and for my family and society out of a pure heart, good conscience, unselfish love, unwavering hope and true faith
godly[5] - to be worthy to be exalted as a sanctified, redeemed and resurrected being in God's highest celestial kingdom of glory through the charitable love, cleansing power and redeeming grace of the Atonement of the Lord Jesus Christ by my faithfully repentant and honorably exact obedience to those divinely appointed commandments, covenants, laws and ordinances upon which receipt of that blessing is predicated
godly[6] - to be purchased or redeemed from the bondage and burdens of sin, from the agonizing suffering and miserable torment of hell, and from everlasting separation from the glorious celestial presence of God in spiritual death—unto spiritual rebirth and salvation through the charitable love, cleansing power and redeeming grace of the Atonement of the Lord Jesus Christ by my faithfully repentant and honorably exact obedience to those divinely appointed commandments, covenants, laws and ordinances upon which receipt of that rebirth and salvation are predicated
godly[7] - to be made truly chaste, clean, pure and virtuous in the sight of God through the charitable love, cleansing power and redeeming grace of the Atonement of the Lord Jesus Christ by my faithfully repentant and honorably exact obedience to those divinely appointed commandments,

covenants, laws and ordinances upon which receipt of those blessings is predicated
godly[8] - to be prone, after coming to know with an absolute, perfect and spiritually verified personal knowledge of enlightened certainty, reality or truth by personal enlightenment, inspiration or revelation from God of His actual being, nonimaginary existence, independent identity and true character, to then follow the direction of His Spirit in testifying of His actual being, existence, identity, nature or character and of how other people can come to the same knowledge of enlightened certainty, reality or truth
godly[9] - to be worthy to constantly receive within me the constant companionship of the gloriously and powerfully comforting, cleansing, empowering, enlightening, gifting, instructing, justifying, protecting, purifying, refining, revelatory and sanctifying influence or divine presence of the Holy Ghost by my faithfully repentant and honorably exact obedience to those divinely appointed commandments, covenants, laws and ordinances upon which receipt of that divine gift is predicated
godly[10] - to be filled with enough truly virtuous thoughts and with enough truly charitable works to faithfully and prayerfully receive an absolute, perfect and spiritually verified personal knowledge of the truth by personal enlightenment, inspiration or revelation from God

through the glorious influence or divine presence of the Holy Ghost

godly[11] - to be filled with enough true enlightenment, virtue and integrity to remain at liberty to be hopeful, peaceful and joyful and to be delivered from the bondage, despair, turmoil and misery which inevitably result from darkness, vice and corruption

godly[12] - to be made charitably loving, just, right and wise in the sight of God by my faithfully repentant and honorably exact obedience to those divinely appointed commandments, covenants, laws and ordinances upon which receipt of those blessings is predicated

godly[13] - to be prone to become or remain one of the many pure-in-heart who are filled with that liberating integrity which comes from increasing true enlightenment and from an increasing abundance of truly virtuous thoughts, words, actions, deeds or works

godly[14] - to be prone to refuse to be vicious

godly[15] - to be prone to refuse to be evil or satanic

golden - to be radiant

good - to be made truly chaste, clean, pure and virtuous in the sight of God through the charitable love, cleansing power and redeeming grace of the Atonement of the Lord Jesus Christ by my faithfully repentant and honorably exact obedience to those divinely appointed commandments, covenants, laws and ordinances upon which receipt of those blessings is predicated

good[2] - to be prone to always follow that discernible light within me which invites and entices me to confidently believe, hope and trust Jesus is the Christ, Messiah, Redeemer and Savior of all humankind and to courageously and faithfully follow His perfect example of loving and serving God by exactly, faithfully and honorably obeying and keeping His commandments, covenants, laws and ordinances in all I think, say and do

good[3] - to be godly enough to be made truly chaste, clean, pure and virtuous at heart—and to continue to encourage and help other people by charitable love, kindness, invitation and instruction to be godly enough to be made truly chaste, clean, pure and virtuous at heart

good[4] - to be prone to continue, to the best of my ability, to better understand, do, be and teach that which is godly

good[5] - to be prone to produce, preserve or restore true enlightenment, virtue and integrity within me, my family and society by willfully thinking, speaking and acting in harmony with one or more positive two (2) virtues in this dictionary—or with one or more relative value characteristics to the extent my virtuous pondering, performance or teaching of them produces, preserves or restores one or more of the virtues within me, my family and society

good[6] - to be prone to vanquish darkness, vice and corruption within me, my family and society by willfully thinking, speaking and

acting in harmony with one or
more positive two (2) virtues in this
dictionary—or with one or more
relative value characteristics to the
extent my virtuous pondering,
performance or teaching of them
produces, preserves or restores one
or more of the virtues within me,
my family and society

good[7] - to be prone to refuse to
produce, preserve or restore
consequences, effects, results or
works of darkness, vice and
corruption within me, my family
and society

good-hearted - to be good at heart

good-hearted[2] - to be truly chaste,
clean, pure and virtuous at heart

good-hearted[3] - to be charitably
loving, benevolent, generous and
kind

good-humored - to be good-
natured and kind in disposition or
mood

good-humored[2] - to be buoyant

goodly - to be good

good-natured - to be prone to show
a kind and pleasant disposition or
temperament

good-tempered - to be good-
natured

goody-goody - to be righteous

gorgeous - to be a girl or woman
who is filled with enough true
enlightenment, virtue and integrity
to be magnificently beautiful in
character and manner

gorgeous[2] - to be a boy or man who
is filled with enough true
enlightenment, virtue and integrity
to be magnificently handsome in
character and manner

governable - to be prone to
virtuously govern myself

governable[2] - to be prone to readily
and willingly submit to a publicly
authorized exercise of social power
exercised in behalf of me and the
rest of the governed for the
betterment, improvement or
progress of the governed

governed - to be prone to possess
and maintain liberty, hope, peace,
joy and other heavenly blessings
by my believing and honorably
exact obedience to those divinely
appointed laws upon which receipt
of those blessings is predicated

governed[2] - to be prone to
powerfully control or restrain
myself to an extent or in a manner
which produces, preserves or
restores true enlightenment, virtue
and integrity within me, my family
and society

governed[3] - to be prone to
powerfully control or restrain
myself to an extent or in a manner
which produces, preserves or
restores the virtuously liberating
freedom, health, honorable
economic prosperity and steady
progress of me, my family and
society

governed[4] - to be prone to keep my
thoughts, words and actions within
the safe and discernibly
enlightened boundaries of chastity,
cleanliness, purity and virtue
which God has justly set by law
and commandment

governed[5] - to be prone to
powerfully control or restrain the
pleasure and satisfaction of all of
my biologically inherent and
naturally impelling emotional,
physical or sexual appetites,
cravings, desires, drives and
passions enough to keep them

safely integrated within the discernibly enlightened boundaries of chastity, cleanliness, purity and virtue which God has justly set by law and commandment

governed[6] - to be prone to repress or suppress darkness, vice and corruption from entering into the thoughts, beliefs, values and characteristics of my heart

governed[7] - to be prone to readily and willingly submit to those who exercise their duly authorized powers of control, direction, dominion, restraint or rule to an extent or in a manner which produces, preserves or restores the greatest true enlightenment, virtue, integrity, liberty, hope, peace and joy within me, my family and society

governed[8] - to be prone to readily and willingly submit to those who exercise their duly authorized powers of control, direction, dominion, restraint or rule to an extent or in a manner which produces, preserves or restores the virtuously liberating freedom, health, honorable economic prosperity and steady progress of me, my family and society

governed[9] - to be prone to readily and willingly submit to those who exercise their duly authorized powers of control, direction, dominion, restraint or rule to an extent or in a manner which produces, preserves or restores the fundamental right to human life, the fundamental right and control of personal property, equal justice under virtuous law, and the pursuit and preservation of that true enlightenment, virtue and integrity which produce, preserve or restore true liberty, hope, peace and joy within us, our families and society

governed[10] - to be prone to avoid being misgoverned

governing - to be virtuously sovereign

governing[2] - to intend to faithfully continue to wield government authority and political power in harmony with the discernibly enlightening and spiritually verifiable truth that: notwithstanding His perfect love for us, God is bound by the eternally binding law of justice to be no unjust respecter of persons, and He is thus bound to withdraw or withhold His protective power from my nation and to abandon us to our enemies and to destruction *when* we refuse to keep His commandments, covenants, laws and ordinances, and *when* we refuse to hearken to His loving warnings unto faithful, timely and true repentance, obedience and reconciliation to Him, and *when* the agency or mortal power of liberty of the rising generation to choose good instead of evil is seriously jeopardized or destroyed, and *when* it is time to curtail the just demands, penalties and judgments we are heaping upon our own heads, or *when* we have otherwise become ripened in iniquity in the sight of God

governing[3] - to intend to faithfully continue to wield government authority and political power in harmony with the dictates of my enlightened conscience

governing[4] - to intend to faithfully continue to wield government authority and political power to an extent or in a manner which produces, preserves or restores the greatest true enlightenment, virtue, integrity, liberty, hope, peace and joy within me, within my family and within a consequently and increasingly integrated, liberated and united society

governing[5] - to intend to faithfully continue to wield government authority and political power to an extent or in a manner which produces, preserves or restores the virtuously liberating freedom, health, honorable economic prosperity and steady progress of me, my family and society

governing[6] - to intend to faithfully continue to wield government authority and political power to an extent or in a manner which produces, preserves or restores the fundamental right to human life, the fundamental right and control of personal property, equal justice under virtuous law, and the pursuit and preservation of that true enlightenment, virtue and integrity which produce, preserve or restore true liberty, hope, peace and joy within us, our families and society

governing[7] - to intend to faithfully continue to wield government authority and political power to an extent or in a manner which neither suppresses the freedom of the soul to think and believe nor binds the free inward exercise of conscience in the process

governing[8] - to intend to faithfully continue to wield government authority and political power to an extent or in a manner which does not seek to proscribe any personally held thought or belief

governing[9] - to intend to faithfully continue to wield government authority and political power to an extent or in a manner which does not attempt to dictate or enforce any prescribed form of personal devotion or worship

governing[10] - to intend to faithfully continue to wield government authority and political power to an extent or in a manner which adequately and effectively restrains corruption and crime while equitably and justly punishing those guilty of committing or perpetrating corruption or crime

governing[11] - to intend to faithfully continue to wield government authority and political power to an extent or in a manner which brings violators of good laws to equal and honorable justice, especially those guilty of stirring up dissent, rebellion or sedition against a good government which seeks to enforce good laws in order to protect the good rights of its law-abiding citizens, legal resident aliens, and legally admitted refugees

governing[12] - to intend to faithfully continue to wield government authority and political power to an extent or in a manner which grants and preserves to all law-abiding citizens the right under the law of the land to carry or keep arms or weapons and to use whatever force is necessary to defend ourselves, our families and society against any unlawful assault or attack against any person or against any unlawful encroachment upon our property, whenever and wherever our government cannot be appealed to for timely protection or has not yet placed adequate protection in force

governing[13] - to intend to faithfully exercise my duly authorized powers of control, direction, dominion, restraint or rule to an extent or in a manner which produces, preserves or restores true enlightenment, virtue and integrity within me, my family and society

governing[14] - to intend to avoid misgoverning

graceful - to be prone to receive the unmerited and saving grace of God through the charitable love, cleansing power and redeeming grace of the Atonement of the Lord Jesus Christ by my faithfully repentant and honorably exact obedience to those divinely appointed commandments, covenants, laws and ordinances upon which receipt of that grace is predicated

graceful[2] - to be truly chaste, clean, pure and virtuous at heart

graceful[3] - to be filled with true enlightenment, virtue and integrity

graceful[4] - to be elegantly dignified in action, appearance, manner, motion or speech

gracious - to be truly beneficent, benevolent or charitable

gracious[2] - to be elegantly dignified in the courteous and kindly use of polished and virtuous social manners

graduating - to intend to constantly choose to continue to progress by continuing to improve the enlightenment and virtue of the thoughts I continue to integrate into the thoughts, beliefs, values and characteristics of my heart

graduating[2] - to intend to complete a higher and better level of learning

graduating[3] - to intend to achieve an officially recognized degree of learning on the way to reaching a higher and better level of learning

grand - to be esteemed great and noble in the sight of God by my faithfully repentant and honorably exact obedience to those divinely appointed commandments, covenants, laws and ordinances upon which receipt of those blessings is predicated

grand[2] - to be grandfatherly or grandmotherly

grand[3] - to be aged and venerable

grandfatherly - to be a virtuous man worthy of great dignity, esteem or reverence due to the refined fatherly example and treatment I offer to children two or more generations descendant from me, especially my own

grandmotherly - to be a virtuous woman worthy of great dignity, esteem or reverence due to the refined motherly example and treatment I offer to children two or more generations descendant from me, especially my own

graphic - to be prone to use strikingly clear imagination or perception to envision or see a lifelike image, picture, presentation or representation of something good and uplifting

graphic[2] - to be prone to use strikingly clear description to evoke or plant in someone's imagination or thoughts an image, picture, presentation or representation of something good and uplifting

grateful - to be prone to feel enough loving and sincere appreciation to God to be made truly chaste, clean, pure and virtuous at heart and to continue to encourage and help other people by charitable love, kindness, invitation and instruction to be godly enough to be made truly chaste, clean, pure and virtuous at heart

grateful[2] - to be prone to feel and to express enough sincere appreciation to God, and to give Him all credit, glory, honor and praise for the charitable love, saving grace and tender mercy He has given to me, my family and society

grateful[3] - to be prone to feel and to express enough sincere appreciation to God, and to give Him all credit, glory, honor and praise for all of the true enlightenment, virtue, integrity, liberty, hope, peace and joy He has given to me, my family and society

grateful[4] - to be prone to express enough sincere appreciation or gratitude to God, and to give Him all credit, glory, honor and praise for all of the good, honorable or noble achievements, advantages, associations, learning, possessions, power, wealth and wisdom He has given to me, my family and society

grateful[5] - to be prone to feel and to extend heartfelt pleasure and rewarding acknowledgment, recognition or service to God by wisely sharing enough with the needy and the poor of the valuable

advantage, benefit, blessing, favor or kindness He has given me

grateful[6] - to be prone to feel and to extend heartfelt pleasure and rewarding acknowledgment, recognition or service toward those who have given me good and honorable advantage, benefit, blessing, favor or kindness

grateful[7] - to be prone to appreciate and live in harmony with the fact that having enough in my family is as good as having more than enough

gratifying - to intend to please God by being godly enough to be made truly chaste, clean, pure and virtuous at heart—and by continuing to encourage and help other people by charitable love, kindness, invitation and instruction to be godly enough to be made truly chaste, clean, pure and virtuous at heart

gratifying[2] - to be filled with enough true enlightenment, virtue and integrity to produce, preserve or restore true liberty, hope, peace and joy within me, my family and society

gratifying[3] - to be filled with enough true enlightenment, virtue and integrity to strongly attract or appeal to another person's sense of true enlightenment, virtue and integrity

gratifying[4] - to intend to win the good pleasure of other people by doing and being good unto them

great - to be exalted

great[2] - to be celestial

great[3] - to be godly enough to be made truly chaste, clean, pure and virtuous at heart—and to continue to encourage and help other people by charitable love, kindness, invitation and instruction to be godly enough to be made truly chaste, clean, pure and virtuous at heart

great[4] - to be eminently, notably or remarkably superior in commonplace good works and everyday service to other people

gregarious - to be prone to obtain or maintain good association with good people in my family and in society

grieved - to be prone to recognize enough afflicting distress, pain, remorse or sorrow from all of the corrupt, sinful or vicious wrongdoing within me to faithfully and immediately seek true and complete repentance, obedience and reconciliation to God

groping - to intend to feel, search or seek for enlightened certainty, reality or truth while in confusion, error or falsehood

groping[2] - to intend to feel, search or seek for enlightenment while in darkness

grounded - to be established, fixed or settled upon the sure foundation of enlightenment, virtue and integrity

grounded[2] - to be established, fixed or settled upon the sure foundation of enlightened certainty, reality or truth

growing - to intend to continue to progress by continuing to improve the enlightenment and virtue of the thoughts I continue to integrate into the thoughts, beliefs, values and characteristics of my heart

growing[2] - to intend to arise, blossom, flourish, prosper or thrive in true enlightenment, virtue,

integrity, liberty, hope, peace and joy in direct proportion to my believing and honorably exact obedience to those divinely appointed laws upon which receipt of those blessings is predicated

guarded - to be prone to defend, protect or secure myself against everything which has or which may have enough evil or satanic power to induce or influence me to willfully reject my good conscience, or to defile the active and stored thoughts of my mind with darkness, vice and corruption, or to drive true enlightenment, virtue and integrity out of my mind and heart, or to infect me with evil or satanic desires to lustfully fulfill or sinfully satisfy one or more of my biologically inherent and naturally impelling emotional, physical or sexual appetites, cravings, desires, drives or passions, or to otherwise cause the Spirit of God to withdraw from me

guarded[2] - to be circumspect and prudent

guileless - to be prone to refuse to viciously deceive or disguise in an artful manner

guiltless - to be truly innocent

guilty - to be prone to honorably and justly acknowledge and willingly accept full responsibility to immediately and truly repent of my sins

guilty[2] - to be prone to honorably and justly acknowledge and willingly accept full responsibility to pay full penalty and to make full restitution for my wrongdoing

gumptious - to be practical and wise

gumptious[2] - to be prone to
minimize consumption, expense
and waste
gymnastic - to be prone to develop
my physical agility, balance and
strength
gymnastical - to be gymnastic

H

habitual - to be prone to
consistently practice or repetitively
follow the very best thought,
expression and behavior patterns
known to me
hale - to be whole
hallowed - to be virtuously holy
hallowed[2] - to be venerable
handsome - to be a boy or man
who is attractively gracious and
refined in character and manner
handy - to be resourceful enough
to minimize consumption, expense
and waste
happy - to be exceedingly joyful
happy[2] - to be filled with true
enlightenment, virtue, integrity,
liberty, hope, peace and joy
happy[3] - to be humbly mindful of
and gratefully delighted or elated
for all good things
happy[4] - to be humbly and
gratefully delighted or elated when
someone is emancipated, freed,
liberated or released from
unavoidable pain, harm or injury
happy[5] - to be humbly and
gratefully delighted or elated with
the virtuously liberating freedom,
health, honorable economic
prosperity and steady progress of
me, my family and society
hard - to be carefully or strictly
determined, fixed and immovable
in exactly, faithfully and honorably
thinking, saying and doing that

which is charitably loving, just,
right and wise in the sight of God
hard[2] - to be prone to maintain
good fitness, health and strength
hard-and-fast - to be prone to
strongly bind myself to fulfill, keep
or uphold a virtuous standard
hard-boiled - to be tough enough
to dispel or withstand evil or
satanic adversity, affliction, defeat
or hardship
hard-headed - to be prone to
stubbornly or willfully adhere to a
virtuous purpose or course of
action
hard-line - to be godly enough to
be made truly chaste, clean, pure
and virtuous at heart—and to
continue to encourage and help
other people by charitable love,
kindness, invitation and instruction
to be godly enough to be made
truly chaste, clean, pure and
virtuous at heart, come what may
hard-line[2] - to be prone to choose
only that which produces,
preserves or restores true
enlightenment, virtue and integrity
within me, my family and society
hard-line[3] - to be prone to
stubbornly refuse to think, speak or
act in accordance with a law, rule,
standard or value which produces,
preserves or restores darkness, vice
and corruption within me, my
family and society
hard-line[4] - to be black-and-white
hard-to-please - to be prone to do
the very best I can to do whatever
it takes to bring out the very best
within me until the day I die
hard-working - to intend to work
in a diligent manner for a good
purpose

harmonizing - to be godly enough to be made truly chaste, clean, pure and virtuous at heart—and to continue to encourage and help other people by charitable love, kindness, invitation and instruction to be godly enough to be made truly chaste, clean, pure and virtuous at heart

harmonizing[2] - to intend to constantly choose to progress in unison toward greater mutual forgiveness, reconciliation, agreement, cooperation, unity, friendship and peacemaking with other people of true enlightenment, virtue and integrity

harmonizing[3] - to be peacemaking

healing - to be worthy to receive from God the full healing of my body, mind and spirit from the effects of my sins through the charitable love, cleansing power and redeeming grace of the Atonement of the Lord Jesus Christ by my faithfully repentant and honorably exact obedience to those divinely appointed commandments, covenants, laws and ordinances upon which receipt of that healing is predicated

healing[2] - to be worthy to faithfully ask a worthy man who exercises true higher priesthood authority and power from God and enough faith to pronounce upon me a heavenly inspired and powerfully effective blessing of new or renewed health or well-being to me by the laying on of hands, as needed

healing[3] - to be a worthy man who exercises true higher priesthood authority and power from God, without pay, and with enough faith to pronounce a heavenly inspired and powerfully effective blessing of new or renewed health or well-being upon another person by the laying on of hands, as requested

healing[4] - to intend to restore good health and true safety to me, my family and society

healing[5] - to intend to use medical and scientific remedy to strive to enhance the ability of a human body to cure, heal or strengthen itself

healthful - to be healthy

healthy - to be exalted

healthy[2] - to be redeemed unto exaltation

healthy[3] - to be redeemed and released from the bondage, burdens and debts of my sins

healthy[4] - to be made whole and wholesome and to lovingly encourage and kindly help other people to be made whole and wholesome

healthy[5] - to be healed from and immune to all of the evil or satanic powers of binding addiction, compulsion, impulsion, obsession, occupation and possession

healthy[6] - to be healed from and immune to darkness, vice and corruption

healthy[7] - to be prone to enhance the ability of a human body to cure, heal or strengthen itself

hearing - to intend to obey the mind, voice, will or word of God when it comes to me

hearing[2] - to intend to entertain, harbor, hold or pay attention to the still, small voice of the Spirit of God within me long enough and well enough within my mind and heart to hear the mind, voice, will or word of God

hearing[3] - to intend to examine, learn or pay attention to what I am hearing and feeling, following my righteous prayers to God

hearing[4] - to intend to live in harmony with those voices which tell me of that which produces, preserves or restores greater true enlightenment, virtue, integrity, liberty, hope, peace and joy within me, my family and society

hearing[5] - to be perceptively aware of sounds or voices which come to me in reality

heartbroken - to be and to choose to remain humbly and meekly penitent before God so He can continue to help me improve

heartwarming - to intend to evoke or inspire warmly grateful and tender sentiments of goodness

hearty - to be nourishing

hearty[2] - to be durably healthy, strong and vigorous

heavenly - to be exalted

heavenly[2] - to be celestial

heavenly[3] - to be godly enough to be made truly chaste, clean, pure and virtuous at heart—and to continue to encourage and help other people by charitable love, kindness, invitation and instruction to be godly enough to be made truly chaste, clean, pure and virtuous at heart

heavenly[4] - to be prone to produce, preserve or restore the greatest true enlightenment, virtue, integrity, liberty, hope, peace and joy within me, my family and society

heavenly[5] - to be prone to deserve or qualify to be admitted into a better condition or state

heeding - to intend to implement and exercise the best known means of producing, preserving or restoring true enlightenment, virtue and integrity within me, my family and society

heeding[2] - to intend to implement and exercise the best known means of dispelling, forsaking, overcoming or withstanding darkness, vice and corruption within me, my family and society

hegemonistic - to be predominant in the truly virtuous use of authority, influence, leadership or power

helping - to be charitable

heroic-at-heart - to be exalted

heroic-at-heart[2] - to be celestial

heroic-at-heart[3] - to be godly enough to be made truly chaste, clean, pure and virtuous at heart—and to continue to encourage and help other people by charitable love, kindness, invitation and instruction to be godly enough to be made truly chaste, clean, pure and virtuous at heart, come what may

heroic-at-heart[4] - to be prone to continuously and faithfully strive with all of the energy, might, power, strength and will of my soul to keep my thoughts, words and actions truly chaste, clean, pure and virtuous in the sight of God

heroic-at-heart[5] - to be a girl or woman heroine who, in the face of horrible affliction or powerful opposition, boldly acts toward or produces honorable and noble deeds of feminine or motherly valor—primarily in bearing and nurturing life and in ambitiously, diligently and responsibly producing, preserving and restoring true enlightenment, virtue and integrity within me, my family and society

heroic-at-heart[6] - to be a boy or man hero who, in the face of horrible affliction or powerful opposition, boldly acts toward or produces honorable and noble deeds of masculine or fatherly valor—primarily in ambitiously, diligently and responsibly providing for and preserving the virtuously liberating freedom, health, honorable economic prosperity and steady progress of me, my family and society

herolike - to be like someone who is heroic-at-heart

heterogeneous - to be prone to establish, join or maintain a social class, group, organization, population, nation or other faction of society who welcomes and remains open to all law-abiding people who are virtuous

heterogeneous[2] - to be prone to establish, join or maintain a social class, group, organization, population, nation or other faction of society who welcomes and remains open to all law-abiding people who work together to produce, preserve or restore true enlightenment, virtue and integrity within that social class, group, organization, population, nation or other faction of society

heterogeneous[3] - to be prone to establish, join or maintain a social class, group, organization, population, nation or other faction of society who welcomes and remains open to all law-abiding

people who work together to produce, preserve or restore the virtuously liberating freedom, health, honorable economic prosperity and steady progress of that social class, group, organization, population, nation or other faction of society

heterosexist - to be heterosexual and to forsake or shun homosexuality

heterosexual - to be prone to righteously exercise and fulfill my naturally impelling, procreative sexual appetites, cravings, desires, drives and passions and my corresponding bodily functions by directing them towards and by engaging in sexual relations only with my husband or wife to whom I am lawfully and legally wedded

heterosexual[2] - to be prone to enjoy truly healthy and truly loving sexual relations with a person of the opposite gender, but only after we are lawfully and legally wedded to each other

heterosexual[3] - to be prone to develop good personal relationships with members of the opposite gender which absolutely exclude sexual relations and any thought of them outside of honorable familial and legal wedlock

heterosexual[4] - to be prone to personally ascertain and live in harmony with the discernibly enlightening and spiritually verifiable truth that: chastity is an indispensable and integral part of God's commandments to become or remain chaste, clean, pure and virtuous in His sight heterosexual[5] - to be prone to personally ascertain and live in harmony with the discernibly enlightening and spiritually verifiable truth that: the natural, procreative sexual appetites, cravings, desires, drives and passions and the naturally interdependent, symmetrical and harmonious sexual interactions of the two genders are biologically inherent and naturally impelling and, when exercised within His commandments, covenants or laws of chastity, are of God

hiding - to intend to refuse to viciously disclose or say more than should be disclosed or said

hiding[2] - to intend to refuse to excessively or needlessly disclose confidential, personal, private, proprietary or secret information

hiding[3] - to intend to truly do more good than harm by refusing to make something generally known

high - to be exalted

high[2] - to be celestial

high[3] - to be godly enough to be made truly chaste, clean, pure and virtuous at heart—and to continue to encourage and help other people by charitable love, kindness, invitation and instruction to be godly enough to be made truly chaste, clean, pure and virtuous at heart

high[4] - to be one of the truly better or truly best

highbrowed - to be virtuously intelligent

high-class - to be one of those who are most honorable

highflying - to intend to energetically pursue noble aims

high-level - to be prone to achieve or perform with the best

high-minded - to be prone to absorb and to transmit noble and uplifting messages

high-spirited - to be spiritually-minded

high-spirited[2] - to be highly animated with the power of God by my faithfully repentant and honorably exact obedience to those divinely appointed commandments, covenants, laws and ordinances upon which receipt of that power is predicated

high-spirited[3] - to be filled with the influence or presence of the Spirit of God by my believing and honorably exact obedience to that divinely appointed law upon which receipt of that influence or presence is predicated

high-spirited[4] - to be prone to boldly, courageously, energetically, enthusiastically and optimistically oppose that which is evil or satanic

high-spirited[5] - to be greatly or highly uplifting in disposition or mood

high-spirited[6] - to be prone to boldly exude courageous and energetic enthusiasm in a good cause

hilarious - to be virtuously cheerful or merry

Hindu - to be prone to live in harmony with the teachings of Hinduism which produce, preserve or restore true enlightenment, virtue and integrity within me, my family and society

Hispanic - to be prone to live in harmony with the ways of Hispanic character or culture which produce, preserve or restore true enlightenment, virtue and integrity within me, my family and society

holy - to be exalted

holy^2 - to be celestial

holy^3 - to be godly enough to be made truly chaste, clean, pure and virtuous at heart—and to continue to encourage and help other people by charitable love, kindness, invitation and instruction to be godly enough to be made truly chaste, clean, pure and virtuous at heart

homemaking - to intend to help make life at home a bit of heaven for my family, for our guests, for our visitors and for myself

homemaking^2 - to be a married girl or woman who cares for, feeds and otherwise nurtures family members, keeps a clean and orderly home and effectively manages its day-to-day business to an extent or in a manner which lovingly encourages and kindly helps family members do the very best we can to progress day by day

homesick - to be prone to yearn for the presence of my good family when we are apart for a while

homesick^2 - to be prone to yearn to be back in my good home or community when I am away for a while

homogeneous - to be prone to establish, join or maintain a law-abiding social class, group, organization, population, nation or other faction of society consisting of only virtuous people

homogeneous^2 - to be prone to establish, join or maintain a social class, group, organization, population, nation or other faction of society consisting of only law-abiding people who work together to produce, preserve or restore true enlightenment, virtue and integrity within that social class, group, organization, population, nation or other faction of society

homogeneous^3 - to be prone to establish, join or maintain a social class, group, organization, population, nation or other faction of society consisting of only law-abiding people who work together to produce, preserve or restore the virtuously liberating freedom, health, honorable economic prosperity and steady progress of that social class, group, organization, population, nation or other faction of society

homosexless - to be prone to abstain from both same gender marriage and same gender sexual relations despite any and all of the homosexual appetites, cravings, desires, drives or passions I may suffer toward one or more members of my same gender

homosexless^2 - to be prone, whenever I am tempted by thoughts or invitations of homosexual attraction, behavior or pleasure, to refuse to entertain or retain those thoughts or invitations within my mind or heart, and to refuse to engage in any sodomizing or other abusive, dysfunctional, perverse or unnatural sexual acts or relations with one or more members of my same gender

homosexless^3 - to be prone to refuse to entertain or suffer from the discernibly domineering and vicious thinking disorder or problem of misdirecting my sexual appetites, cravings, desires, drives or passions toward one or more members of my same gender

honest - to be prone to live, love, speak and tell the truth enough to consistently keep the commandments, covenants, laws and ordinances of God in a truly virtuous manner, understanding that the quality of my dealings with other people depends upon it and can be no better than my true level of personal virtue

honest^2 - to be prone to live, love, speak and tell the truth enough to consistently deal with other people in a truly honorable and just manner

honest^3 - to be prone to live, love, speak and tell the truth enough to consistently think, speak and act in a truly honorable and just manner

honest^4 - to be prone to refuse to lie or to accept lying as though someone is or can be honorably justified in whimsically using lies at their convenience and for no virtuous purpose

honorable - to be heroically virtuous

honorable^2 - to be truly worthy of the high admiration, praise, respect, reverence or veneration of other people by doing or being something good

honorable^3 - to be prone to hold office or rank in a distinguished manner

honored - to be exalted

honoring - to intend to please God in bringing enough worthy admiration, glory, praise, respect or veneration to God

honoring^2 - to intend to please God in bringing enough worthy admiration, praise, respect or veneration to my parents and to my other ancestors to whom I belong by adoption, by blood, by lineage or by marriage

honoring^3 - to intend to enable and encourage my spouse to please God in bringing enough worthy admiration, praise, respect or veneration to my spouse's parents and to my spouse's ancestors

honoring^4 - to intend to please God in bringing enough worthy admiration, praise, respect or veneration to me, my family and society

honoring^5 - to intend to lovingly encourage and kindly help someone to be honorable

hopeful - to be prone to hoping

hoping - to intend to faithfully and patiently persevere in the completely confident, enthusiastic, joyful, optimistic and peaceful anticipation and trust that I shall be redeemed unto salvation from the bondage and burdens of sin, from the agonizing suffering and miserable torment of hell, and from everlasting separation from the glorious celestial presence of God in spiritual death, through the charitable love, cleansing power and redeeming grace of the Atonement of the Lord Jesus Christ by my faithfully repentant and honorably exact obedience to those divinely appointed commandments, covenants, laws and ordinances upon which receipt of that salvation is predicated

hoping^2 - to intend to faithfully and patiently persevere in the completely confident, enthusiastic, joyful, optimistic and peaceful anticipation and trust that God will justly bless me by my believing and honorably exact obedience to that divinely appointed law upon which receipt of that blessing is predicated

hoping[3] - to intend to faithfully and patiently persevere in the completely confident, enthusiastic, joyful, optimistic and peaceful anticipation and trust that God will justly give me power to do His will by my faithfully repentant and honorably exact obedience to those divinely appointed commandments, covenants, laws and ordinances upon which receipt of that power is predicated

hoping[4] - to intend to confidently trust in and to think, speak and act in harmony with the positive thoughts of my mind and to invite them into the thoughts, beliefs, values and characteristics of my heart

hoping[5] - to intend to confidently work hard to fulfill my positive desires and to meet my positive expectations

hospitable - to be prone to receive and treat welcome guests in my home with courtesy, warmth and generosity

hospitable[2] - to be prone to receive and treat welcome guests in my community or country with courtesy, warmth and generosity

hospitable[3] - to be prone to compassionately, safely and wisely offer another person truly needed assistance

housekeeping - to intend to keep a house clean and in good order

human - to be a truly virtuous person

humane - to be prone to reverently regard the worth of every human being's divine origin, purpose and potential

humane[2] - to be prone to provide as many truly charitable works of tender benevolence, kindness and mercy as possible to all humankind

humane[3] - to be prone to produce, preserve or restore true enlightenment, virtue and integrity within me, my family and society

humane[4] - to be prone to build, improve and strengthen the virtuously liberating freedom, health, honorable economic prosperity and steady progress of all people

humane[5] - to be prone to peaceably treat other people with as much polite kindness and quiet tenderness as possible

humane[6] - to be virtuously compassionate, merciful or sympathetic

humane[7] - to be prone to treat all life as well as I can and should

humanist - to be humane and to lovingly encourage and kindly help other people to be humane

humanist[2] - to be prone to promote the virtuously liberating freedom, health, honorable economic prosperity and steady progress of me, my family and society

humanist[3] - to be prone to observe and learn from human nature how I can and should progress

humanitarian - to be prone to offer the needy and poor aid, assistance, concession, forbearance, forgiveness, leniency or tolerance to an extent and in a manner which is charitably loving, just, right and wise in the sight of God

humanitarian[2] - to be prone to actively, charitably, generously and wisely provide for the needy and poor to an extent or in a manner which saves their lives, meets their immediate needs for survival, fosters their adequate education, employment, labors, self-reliance and thrift, and which encourages their service to other people

humanitarian[3] - to be prone to actively, charitably, generously and wisely give of my substance or other resources to the needy and poor to help them deal with personal needs which they cannot take care of alone—provided they are continuing to demonstrate by their own determined education, training, labors, investments and savings, that they are responsibly striving to become self-reliant net contributors to the virtuously liberating freedom, health, honorable economic prosperity and steady progress of themselves, their families and society

humanizing - to intend to perceive and treat a fellow human being as a brother or sister and as a fellow child of God

humanizing[2] - to intend to share with another person true enlightenment, virtue, integrity, liberty, hope, peace and joy

humanizing[3] - to intend to lovingly encourage and kindly help someone to be humane

humanizing[4] - to intend to refuse to misperceive or mistreat any fellow human being as a commodity, object or thing

humble - to be as submissive and obedient to God as the dust of the earth which He organized, and to lower myself in esteem or posture toward or upon the ground as an outward symbol of my entire desire and reverent willingness to hold open my heart to His charitable love and guiding revelations, to submit to His perfect testing of me and to faithfully obey His perfecting will for me toward my exaltation

humble[2] - to be spiritually-minded

humble[3] - to be penitent enough to be repenting

humble[4] - to be prone to express grateful appreciation to God, and to give Him all credit, glory, honor and praise for the good achievements, advantages, associations, learning, possessions, power, wealth or wisdom which are mine, acknowledging before Him that I could not have achieved or received them without His gracious and loving blessing or help

humble[5] - to be prone to place more respect and trust in God than in myself

humble[6] - to be condescending or lowly-of-heart enough to esteem or regard other people as being above myself

humble[7] - to be prone to refuse to indulge in a conceited or exaggerated estimate of my importance or power

humble[8] - to be willingly modest

humbled - to be made virtuously humble or lowly-of-heart

humbling - to intend to lovingly encourage and kindly help someone to be virtuously humble or lowly-of-heart

humiliated - to be made virtuously humble or lowly-of-heart

humiliating - to intend to lovingly encourage and kindly help someone to be virtuously humble or lowly-of-heart

humiliating[2] - to intend to embarrass, mortify, reprove or shame myself enough to rid myself of my excessive pride or self-importance

humiliating[3] - to intend to lovingly cry faithful, timely and true repentance, obedience and reconciliation to God unto those who produce, preserve or restore darkness, vice and corruption within me, my family and society

humiliating[4] - to intend, when inspired of God to do so, to strive to pull down the pride and bring down to ignominious defeat those who produce, preserve or restore darkness, vice and corruption within me, my family and society

humored - to be filled with truly joyful laughter

humored[2] - to be filled with jolly gaiety or festive merriment in healthy association or companionship with other people during respectable social activities

humoring - to intend to edify or enliven someone by working to draw out or evoke from them truly joyful laughter

humoring[2] - to intend to edify or enliven someone by working to draw out or evoke from them jolly gaiety or festive merriment in healthy association or companionship with other people during respectable social activities

hunting - to intend to diligently search for and forcefully pursue members of secret criminal or terrorist groups in order to capture them and bring them to equal and honorable justice, if not to repentance

hustling - to intend to aggressively and energetically hasten or push for true personal betterment, improvement or progress within me, my family and society

hygienic - to be prone to maintain good health by practicing cleanliness and sanitation

hypothesizing - to intend to honestly seek knowledge by using available facts to form a reasonable assumption, proposition or provisional theory of conjecture or explanation which may reasonably be used to guide or limit further investigation or testing

I

iconoclastic - to be prone to refuse to worship false deities or gods

ideal - to be exalted

ideal[2] - to be celestial

ideal[3] - to be godly enough to be made truly chaste, clean, pure and virtuous at heart—and to continue to encourage and help other people by charitable love, kindness, invitation and instruction to be godly enough to be made truly chaste, clean, pure and virtuous at heart

ideal[4] - to be prone to perfectly conform to the best and highest laws, rules, standards or values of true enlightenment, virtue and integrity of which I have become aware in my education and training and in my own constantly diligent, honest and open-minded searching

idealizing - to intend to lovingly encourage and kindly help

someone to be made truly chaste, clean, pure and virtuous at heart
idealizing[2] - to intend to perfectly conform to the best and highest laws, rules, standards or values of true enlightenment, virtue and integrity of which I have become aware in my education and training and in my own constantly diligent, honest and open-minded searching
idealizing[3] - to intend to think, speak and act in harmony with those thoughts, words and actions which best produce, preserve or restore true enlightenment, virtue and integrity within me, my family and society
identified - to be blessed with an absolute, perfect and spiritually verified personal knowledge of enlightened certainty, reality or truth by personal enlightenment, inspiration or revelation from God about who I was before I came to earth, who I now am, and who I can become following my death
identified[2] - to be blessed with an absolute, perfect and spiritually verified personal knowledge of enlightened certainty, reality or truth by personal enlightenment, inspiration or revelation from God that no other person can be the selfsame person I truly am, was and will become in body, mind and spirit
identifying - to intend to ascertain or discern the characteristic and distinctive differences between that which is truly good and of God and that which is evil or satanic
identifying[2] - to intend to ascertain or discern the characteristic and distinctive differences between that

which is enlightened certainty, reality or truth and that which is confusion, error or falsehood
identifying[3] - to intend to maintain and increase my initial endowment or measure of guiding personal enlightenment from God enough to continue to accurately and clearly discern between that which is real and that which is imaginary
idyllic - to be naturally simple and virtuous to an extent or in a manner which is typical of those who live in provincial or open country areas who are relatively unaccustomed to more darkened influences and more worldly lifestyles
idyllic[2] - to be prone to appreciate pleasant and natural simplicity
illiberal - to be prejudiced against and intolerant of another person's freedom to help produce, preserve or restore darkness, vice and corruption within me, my family and society
illuminant - to be illuminated and illuminating
illuminated - to be enlightened or intelligent
illuminating - to intend to enlighten one or more other people
illuminative - to be prone to enlighten one or more other people
illustrating - to be enlightening
illustrious - to be gloriously distinguished and eminent
imagining - to be virtuously envisioning, fanciful, fantasizing, pretending or visualizing in order to realize something better
imitable - to be filled with enough true enlightenment, virtue and integrity to be truly worthy of imitation

immaculate - to be virtuous enough to be made spotlessly chaste, clean, pure and undefiled in the sight of God through the charitable love, cleansing power and redeeming grace of the Atonement of the Lord Jesus Christ unto exaltation

immaculate[2] - to be prone to perfectly conform to an errorless, faultless or flawless standard of pure enlightenment and virtue

immortal - to be prone to personally ascertain and live in harmony with the discernibly enlightening and spiritually verifiable truth that: I am a living soul consisting of both a physical body of earthly physical matter and an immortal spirit being or personage of enlivened spirit matter which shall separate at my physical death and shall eventually be inseparably rejoined and perfectly restored by the power of God during my one-time and everlasting resurrection from the dead

immortal[2] - to be prone to personally ascertain and live in harmony with the discernibly enlightening and spiritually verifiable truth that: my physical body is alive because it contains a living spirit being or personage of enlivened spirit matter which can be separated from the glorious celestial presence of God in spiritual death, but can never cease to live

immortal[3] - to be prone to personally ascertain and live in harmony with the discernibly enlightening and spiritually verifiable truth that: only enlivened spirit matter divinely formed into a living spirit being and embodied in harmony with divine law within a body of earthly physical matter can bring that earthly physical matter to life on Earth

immune - to be protected against the bondage and burdens of sin, the agonizing suffering and miserable torment of hell, and against everlasting separation from the glorious celestial presence of God in spiritual death

immune[2] - to be filled with enough true enlightenment, virtue and integrity to be protected against darkness, vice and corruption

immune[3] - to be filled with enough enlightened certainty, reality or truth to be protected against confusion, error or falsehood

impartial - to be prone to refuse to viciously rely exclusively upon prejudiced or unreasoned judgment in favoring or respecting one person or thing over another

impeachable - to be prone to honorably and justly heed a needed warning to repent of all of the corrupt, sinful or vicious wrongdoing within me, by responding with my faithful, timely and true repentance, obedience and reconciliation to God

impeachable[2] - to be prone to readily and willingly subject myself to someone's efforts to honorably and justly place blame, fault or guilt against me

imperial - to be prone to exercise sovereign authority in a dignified, noble or majestic manner

imperialistic - to be prone to kindly share the means of

acquiring greater true
enlightenment, virtue, integrity,
liberty, hope, peace and joy with
the people of another sovereign
nation who, by the true majority
voice of those people, are willing to
receive it

imperialistic[2] - to be prone to use
government or other
organizational authority, power
and resources to seek the
virtuously liberating freedom,
health, honorable economic
prosperity and steady progress of
all humankind

imperturbable - to be prone to
refuse to be worried

imperturbable[2] - to be prone to
refuse to despair in the face of
agitation or disturbance

important - to be prone to first
exercise my most influential and
most powerful resources on
bringing about the best and most
valuable consequences, outcomes
or results for me, my family and
society

importing - to intend to advocate,
favor or seek to preserve a
government which orders or
provides the necessary means to
successfully help law-abiding and
hard-working citizens make
necessary life-sustaining transitions
to adequate jobs when they suffer
loss of employment in industries
damaged or destroyed by my
country's balance of trade or by its
bargain-priced imports

importing[2] - to intend to advocate,
favor or seek to preserve a
government which defends and
promotes the general welfare by
requiring large importers to help
replace domestic jobs lost with

equivalent jobs in domestic
business sectors they have severely
damaged due to their large
bargain-priced imports

importing[3] - to intend to advocate,
favor or seek to preserve a
government which maintains
tolerable trade practices by paying
close enough attention to
maintaining a wise and affordable
balance of equity between how
much in total human costs the
citizens of my country are giving,
losing or paying for our imports,
including such costs as diminished
business, jobs, money, monetary
exchange rates, security, economic
self-reliance and self-sustainability,
when compared to how much our
foreign trading partners are giving,
losing or paying for their imports
from us

imposing - to intend to be truly
worthy of admirable or respectable
esteem or reverence

impregnable - to be filled with
enough true enlightenment, virtue
and integrity to dispel, resist or
withstand darkness, vice and
corruption

impressive - to be godly enough to
be made truly chaste, clean, pure
and virtuous at heart—and to
continue to encourage and help
other people by charitable love,
kindness, invitation and instruction
to be godly enough to be made
truly chaste, clean, pure and
virtuous at heart

impressive[2] - to be filled with
enough true enlightenment, virtue
and integrity to be honorable

improved - to be exalted

improved[2] - to be celestial

improved[3] - to be godly enough to be made truly chaste, clean, pure and virtuous at heart—and to continue to encourage and help other people by charitable love, kindness, invitation and instruction to be godly enough to be made truly chaste, clean, pure and virtuous at heart

improved[4] - to be raised to a more beneficial, healthy or profitable condition or quality of true enlightenment, virtue, integrity, liberty, hope, peace and joy

improving - to intend to constantly choose to advance, ascend, grow, increase, progress or rise toward an exalted character or condition of heart by my faithfully repentant and honorably exact obedience to those divinely appointed commandments, covenants, laws and ordinances upon which receipt of that blessing is predicated

improving[2] - to intend to constantly choose to change, reform or repent in order to continue to advance, ascend, grow, increase, progress or rise toward producing, preserving or restoring greater true enlightenment, virtue, integrity, liberty, hope, peace and joy within me, my family and society

improving[3] - to intend to think, speak and act in more perfect harmony with one or more positive two (2) virtues in this dictionary—or with one or more relative value characteristics to the extent my virtuous pondering, performance or teaching of them produces, preserves or restores one or more of the virtues within me, my family and society

improving[4] - to intend to constantly choose to advance, ascend, grow, increase, progress or rise toward a purely virtuous character or condition of heart one good word, action or deed at a time

improving[5] - to intend to constantly choose to advance, ascend, grow, increase, progress or rise toward a purely virtuous character or condition of heart one good thought, belief or value at a time

improving[6] - to intend to constantly choose to advance, ascend, grow, increase, progress or rise toward a purely virtuous character or condition of heart one good choice or decision at a time

improving[7] - to intend to constantly choose to advance, ascend, grow, increase, progress or rise toward a purely virtuous character or condition of heart one good lesson at a time

improving[8] - to intend to lovingly encourage and kindly help someone to be improved

incandescent - to be brilliantly, intensely or lucidly aglow with true enlightenment, virtue and integrity

incendiary - to be prone to promote factional or partisan disintegration when necessary to produce, preserve or restore true enlightenment, virtue and integrity within me, my family and society

incisive - to be prone to think in a penetrating manner which avoids all that is superficial

including - to intend to build, improve and strengthen the virtuously liberating freedom, health, honorable economic prosperity and steady progress of all people

incomparable - to be prone to personally ascertain and live in harmony with the discernibly enlightening and spiritually verifiable truth that: no other person can be the selfsame person I truly am, was and will become in body, mind and spirit

inconspicuous - to be prone to refuse to be infamous or notorious

inconspicuous[2] - to be prone to refuse to be ostentatious, vainglorious or worldly

inconspicuous[3] - to be prone to refuse to selfishly seek excessive personal attention or notice

incontrovertible - to be and to choose to remain unquestionably straight and unalterably true in conforming to that which is truly good and of God

incontrovertible[2] - to be unquestionably straight and unalterably true in a necessary expression of indisputable fact or truth

incorruptible - to be prone to refuse to expose myself to or to suffer from corrupting activities, influences or temptations

increasing - to be actively and truly progressing

incredulous - to be prone to refuse to be easily deceived by false or unverifiable evidence

incredulous[2] - to be prone to refuse to believe or trust in insufficient, unsubstantiated or unverified evidence

incredulous[3] - to be prone to refuse to impetuously believe or trust in slight or uncertain evidence

indebted - to be prone to acknowledge my debt of gratitude to God with my faithful, timely and true repentance, obedience and reconciliation to Him

indelicate - to be so unaccustomed to ease, self-indulgence, pleasure and luxury as to not be fragile or squeamish

indelicate[2] - to be prone to refuse to be fastidious

indemnifying - to intend to secure myself against the stain of corrupt and grievous injustice by acting to fully compensate, reimburse or restore another person who would otherwise be required to act alone to pay for the economic or financial cost, damage, harm or loss I have viciously caused them to suffer

independent - to be entirely emancipated, freed, liberated or released from being viciously bound or possessed

independent[2] - to be entirely emancipated, freed, liberated or released from being addicted or enslaved

independent[3] - to be entirely emancipated, freed, liberated or released within my mind and heart from the evil or satanic powers of darkness, vice, corruption, bondage, despair, turmoil and misery

independent[4] - to be emancipated, freed, liberated or released from the flow of darkness, vice and corruption into my mind and heart

independent[5] - to be filled with enough true enlightenment, virtue and integrity to join with enough other like-minded people in paying the price which we must continue to dependably pay in unison in order to progress as a society toward greater true enlightenment, virtue, integrity, liberty, hope, peace and joy

independent[6] - to be filled with enough true enlightenment, virtue and integrity to join with enough other like-minded people in paying the price which we must continue to dependably pay in unison in order to preserve the liberty of self-government for ourselves, our families and society from the ever threatening evil or satanic powers of darkness, vice, corruption, bondage, despair, turmoil and misery wielded by our vicious domestic and foreign enemies

independent[7] - to be a law-abiding and self-reliant net contributor to the virtuously liberating freedom, health, honorable economic prosperity and steady progress of me, my family and society

independent[8] - to be prone to personally ascertain and live in harmony with the discernibly enlightening and spiritually verifiable truth that: enough true independence cannot be produced, preserved or restored by my excessive habitual dependence

independent[9] - to be prone to refuse to be a parasitic drain upon my family and society

independent[10] - to be a boy or man who is competent, diligent and responsible enough to adequately support myself and my dependents when I can

independent[11] - to be a girl or woman who is competent, diligent and responsible enough to adequately support myself and my dependents when I must

independent[12] - to be prone to adequately support myself and my dependents, as necessary

indestructible - to be redeemable

indeterminist - to be indeterministic

indeterministic - to be prone to refuse to be deterministic

indisputable - to be unquestionably straight and true in conforming to or expressing incontrovertible fact or truth

individual - to be prone to become the best person I can possibly become

individualistic - to be prone to obtain and preserve the right to willfully think, speak and act as an independent, responsible and self-reliant person

individualistic[2] - to be prone to refuse to regard what I want as more important than the harm its abuse or misuse can do to me, my family and society

indivisible - to be prone to do all I need to do to prevent Satan and his followers from dividing or separating me from the glorious celestial presence of God the Eternal Father, from the charitable love, cleansing power and redeeming grace of the Atonement of the Lord Jesus Christ, and from the glorious influence and divine presence of the Holy Ghost

indivisible[2] - to be godly enough to be made truly chaste, clean, pure and virtuous at heart—and to continue to encourage and help other people by charitable love, kindness, invitation and instruction to be godly enough to be made truly chaste, clean, pure and virtuous at heart, and to thus make it impossible for my enemies to induce or influence me to be infected or polluted by darkness, vice, corruption, bondage, despair, turmoil and misery

indivisible[3] - to be prone to do my part to maintain enough true enlightenment, virtue and integrity within my family to make our family disintegration, disunity or division impossible to our vicious family enemies

indivisible[4] - to be prone to do my part to maintain enough true enlightenment, virtue and integrity within society to make our social disintegration, disunity or division impossible to our vicious domestic and foreign enemies

indivisible[5] - to be prone to do my part to maintain enough unity with people of true enlightenment, virtue and integrity to avoid being detached, disintegrated, disunited, divorced, segregated or otherwise separated from them

indomitable - to be inviolable

indubitable - to be prone to possess and express unquestionably virtuous character, ethics, morality, politics or religion without affectation, hypocrisy or pretense

industrial - to be prone to develop or support good and honorable organized systems of productive labor and manufacturing which are commercially powerful enough to provide needy and poor law-abiding citizens, legal resident aliens, and legally admitted refugees the jobs, the benefits, the income and the training which will empower them, by their own determined education, training,

labors, investments and savings, to become self-reliant net contributors to the virtuously liberating freedom, health, honorable economic prosperity and steady progress of themselves, their families and society

industrial[2] - to be prone to develop or support good and honorable organized systems of productive labor and manufacturing which are commercially powerful enough to preserve the honorable economic prosperity and self-reliance of a nation whose citizens do good in the world

industrious - to be prone to work in a diligent manner for a good purpose

ineligible - to be a married person who is not available for flirting, dating, courtship, intimate relationship or sexual relationship, except with the person of the opposite gender to whom I am lawfully and legally wedded

infallible - to be prone to faithfully continue to do my very best to personally progress in godliness

infallible[2] - to be constantly effective in dispelling, forsaking, overcoming or withstanding that which is evil or satanic

infallible[3] - to be ascertaining

infallible[4] - to be discerning

inferior - to be prone to think, speak and act in a humble, meek, respectful and subservient manner toward God

influenceable - to be prone to allow or cause someone else's example or teachings of true enlightenment, virtue and integrity to flow into me with enough power to convince or move me to retain and practice them as part of what I do and who I am at heart until they produce, preserve or restore their naturally consequent liberty, hope, peace and joy within me, my family and society

influencing - to intend to exemplify and teach true enlightenment, virtue and integrity with enough power to convince or move another person to retain and practice them as part of who they are and what they think, say and do until they produce, preserve or restore their naturally consequent liberty, hope, peace and joy within them, their family and society

informed - to be enlightened or intelligent

informed² - to be learned or knowledgeable in the characteristic and distinctive differences between that which is truly good and of God and that which is evil or satanic

informed³ - to be learned or knowledgeable in the characteristic and distinctive differences between that which is enlightened certainty, reality or truth and that which is confusion, error or falsehood

informed⁴ - to be learned or knowledgeable in the characteristic and distinctive differences between that which is real and that which is imaginary

informing - to intend to assist or encourage someone in their desires and efforts to become more enlightened or intelligent

informing² - to intend to assist or encourage someone in their desires and efforts to learn or know more about the characteristic and distinctive differences between that

which is truly good and of God and that which is evil or satanic

informing³ - to intend to assist or encourage someone in their desires and efforts to learn or know more about the characteristic and distinctive differences between that which is enlightened certainty, reality or truth and that which is confusion, error or falsehood

informing⁴ - to intend to assist or encourage someone in their desires and efforts to learn or know more about the characteristic and distinctive differences between that which is real and that which is imaginary

ingenious - to be prone to resourcefully create or invent better ways of doing better things

ingenuous - to be virtuously sincere

inhabiting - to be existing

inheriting - to intend to accept or timely exercise the right to succeed to ownership of the blessings of heaven passed on to me by God by my faithfully repentant and honorably exact obedience to those divinely appointed commandments, covenants, laws and ordinances upon which receipt of those blessings is predicated

inhibited - to be prone to arrest, check, prohibit, restrain or suppress away from my heart all evil or satanic thoughts, beliefs, values and characteristics, and their consequences

inhibited² - to be prone to arrest, check, prohibit, restrain or suppress my words and actions enough to avoid breaking the good law of the land

inhuman - to be prone to refuse to be evil or satanic

initiating - to intend to take the lead to introduce or originate what is best

initiating[2] - to intend to take the lead to introduce or originate something better

innervated - to be animated or enlivened

innocent - to be celestial

innocent[2] - to be redeemed

innocent[3] - to be devoid of evil or satanic desire, guile or intent

innocent[4] - to be and to be found blameless or guiltless in harmony with the good law of the land

innocent[5] - to be so devoid of wrongdoing as to be harmlessly ignorant, naive or unsophisticated regarding wrongdoing

inquiring - to intend to personally ascertain whether God will reveal knowledge of the truth about Himself to me by my believing and honorably exact obedience to that divinely appointed law upon which receipt of that knowledge is predicated

inquiring[2] - to intend, through righteous prayer, study and obedience, to faithfully, honestly and sincerely seek verified personal knowledge of the truth about God

inquiring[3] - to intend, through righteous prayer, study and obedience, to faithfully, honestly and sincerely seek verified personal knowledge of the truth about who I am at heart, where I came from before birth, why I am here, and where I am going after my death

inquiring[4] - to intend to become better informed

inscrutable - to be prone to keep my thoughts, words and actions clean and above the need for serious examination, observation, inspection or scrutiny by any person other than myself

insensitive - to be prone to refuse to be excessively or needlessly hurt or offended

insightful - to be prone to deeply or thoroughly discern, recognize or understand enlightened certainty, reality or truth

insouciant - to be prone to avoid and remain undisturbed by despair

inspecting - to intend to carefully audit, examine or scrutinize to look for ways to personally progress

inspecting[2] - to intend to audit, examine or scrutinize in order to confirm, prove or verify what I truly need to know

inspired - to be enlightened

inspired[2] - to be animated or enlivened by uplifting thought, word or action

inspiring - to intend to speak or write truth by the power of the Holy Ghost so that those who are prepared can hear and feel of the truthfulness of what I say by that same power

inspiring[2] - to intend to actively, charitably, generously and wisely esteem, regard and treat another person as the more excellent and progressive person they can and should become, and to thus give them the motivating confidence, the uplifting encouragement and the elevating opportunity to live up to such esteem, regard and treatment as long as they do so

inspiring[3] - to intend to lovingly encourage and kindly help someone to be uplifted

instrumental - to be prone to humbly and prayerfully obtain from God the inspiration and power to serve Him and others in cheerfully doing and being good in harmony with His mind and will

instrumentalist - to be prone to receive enlightened certainty, reality or truth by examining or tasting the fruits of various harmless thoughts, beliefs or values in an honest and pragmatic effort to discover which ones, if thoughtfully exercised or put into practice in daily life, are most useful in the progress of me, my family and society

instrumentalist[2] - to be prone to receive enlightened certainty, reality or truth by examining or tasting the fruits of various harmless thoughts, beliefs or values in an honest and pragmatic effort to discover which ones, if thoughtfully exercised or put into practice in daily life, are most useful in solving existing problems

insubordinate - to be prone to refuse to obey and serve Satan and his followers

insuring - to intend to take affordable and reasonable precaution to be indemnified for any serious economic or financial cost, damage, harm or loss I may suffer

insuring[2] - to intend to take affordable and reasonable precaution to be able to indemnify another person for any serious economic or financial cost, damage, harm or loss for which I am liable

integrated - to be godly enough to be made truly chaste, clean, pure and virtuous at heart—and to continue to encourage and help other people by charitable love, kindness, invitation and instruction to be godly enough to be made truly chaste, clean, pure and virtuous at heart

integrated[2] - to be familial or familistic

integrated[3] - to be integrated-at-heart

integrated[4] - to be prone to keep my thoughts, words and actions in complete harmony with enlightenment and virtue

integrated[5] - to be committed to remaining indivisibly united with the other members of a particular group of people who are filled with true enlightenment, virtue and integrity

integrated[6] - to be as good as my honorable word

integrated-at-heart - to be so faithfully, humbly and prayerfully righteous, true and unflinching in keeping the commandments, covenants, laws and ordinances of God as to become one with God within the thoughts, beliefs, values and characteristics of my heart

integrated-at-heart[2] - to be godly enough to be made truly chaste, clean, pure and virtuous at heart

integrated-at-heart[3] - to be pure-in-heart by successfully keeping all of the thoughts, beliefs, values and characteristics of my heart truly chaste, clean, pure and virtuous

integrated-at-heart[4] - to be prone to successfully keep darkness, vice and corruption out of the thoughts, beliefs, values and characteristics of my heart

integrated-at-heart[5] - to be prone to improve and preserve my integrity by refusing to be broken, corrupted, defective, dishonest, divided, fractional, incomplete, impaired, impure, insincere or partial in my thoughtful designs, desires, dispositions, intentions, plans and purposes to become or remain completely, perfectly or wholly good, sound or upright

integrated-at-heart[6] - to be prone to personally ascertain and live in harmony with the discernibly enlightening and spiritually verifiable truth that: all truth, without exception, is always in perfect harmony, integrity, oneness or unity with itself and can, therefore, be circumscribed or combined into one clearly and perfectly distinct, integrated and undiluted sphere or whole which, unlike confusion, error or falsehood, is capable of producing, preserving or restoring harmony, integrity, oneness or unity within me, my family and society

integrating - to be integrating-at-heart

integrating[2] - to intend to seek the full affiliation, compatibility, cooperation, fellowship, integration, privileges, rights, trust and unity of all law-abiding and responsible individuals, social classes and groups who strive to produce, preserve or restore true enlightenment, virtue, integrity, liberty, hope, peace and joy within ourselves, our families and society

integrating-at-heart - to intend to lovingly encourage and kindly help someone to be integrated-at-heart

integrating-at-heart[2] - to intend to refuse to corrupt or pervert someone's integrity

integrating-at-heart[3] - to intend to refuse to induce or influence someone to be disintegrated-at-heart

integrity-minded - to be prone to successfully keep my thoughts, words and actions truly chaste, clean, pure and virtuous in the sight of God

integrity-minded[2] - to be godly enough to be made truly chaste, clean, pure and virtuous at heart—and to continue to encourage and help other people by charitable love, kindness, invitation and instruction to be godly enough to be made truly chaste, clean, pure and virtuous at heart

intellective - to be enlightened or intelligent

intellectual - to be enlightened and virtuously conscientious within my heart

intellectual[2] - to be prone to increase in intelligence

intelligent - to be prone to become exalted

intelligent[2] - to be prone to become redeemed unto exaltation

intelligent[3] - to be prone to become godly enough to be made truly chaste, clean, pure and virtuous at heart—and to continue to encourage and help other people by charitable love, kindness, invitation and instruction to be godly enough to be made truly chaste, clean, pure and virtuous at heart intelligent[4] - to be and to choose to remain worthy to constantly receive within me the constant companionship of the gloriously and powerfully comforting, cleansing, empowering, enlightening, gifting, instructing, justifying, protecting, purifying, refining, revelatory and sanctifying influence or divine presence of the Holy Ghost by my faithfully repentant and honorably exact obedience to those divinely appointed commandments, covenants, laws and ordinances upon which receipt of that divine gift is predicated

intelligent[5] - to be and to choose to remain filled with enough truly virtuous thoughts and with enough truly charitable works to faithfully and prayerfully receive an absolute, perfect and spiritually verified personal knowledge of the truth by personal enlightenment, inspiration or revelation from God through the glorious influence or divine presence of the Holy Ghost

intelligent[6] - to be prone to produce, preserve or restore the greatest true enlightenment, virtue, integrity, liberty, hope, peace and joy within me, my family and society

intelligent[7] - to be and to choose to remain filled with bright, magnificent or splendid true enlightenment, virtue and integrity by my believing and honorably exact obedience to those divinely appointed laws upon which receipt of those blessings is predicated

intelligent[8] - to be prone to personally ascertain and live in harmony with the discernibly enlightening and spiritually verifiable truth that: God is humanity's source of perfect liberty, hope, peace and joy

intelligent[9] - to be prone to personally ascertain and live in harmony with the discernibly enlightening and spiritually verifiable truth that: God is humanity's source of perfect glory, intelligence, knowledge, life, love, power, truth, virtue and wisdom

intelligent[10] - to be prone to develop my mental capability for quick comprehension, sound reasoning, enlightened understanding and righteous judgment

intelligent[11] - to be prone to increase in enlightenment by continuing to live in harmony with light and truth

intelligent[12] - to be prone to personally ascertain and live in harmony with the discernibly enlightening and spiritually verifiable truth that: I was born with a certain endowment of enlightenment and with the freedom to increase that endowment by choosing that which is truly good and of God—or to lose that endowment by choosing that which is evil or satanic

intelligent[13] - to be virtuously mathematical and scientific in my pursuit of greater light and knowledge

intending - to be disposed or inclined to think, speak and act in harmony with those specific thoughts, beliefs, values and characteristics which produce, preserve or restore the greatest true enlightenment, virtue, integrity, liberty, hope, peace and joy within me, my family and society

intentional - to be prone to think, speak and act in harmony with that which produces, preserves or restores true enlightenment, virtue and integrity within me, my family and society

interacting - to intend to build honorable and virtuous familial and other interpersonal relationships

intercultural - to be prone to personally select, adopt and live in harmony with those academic, dancing, dress, food, graphic, intellectual, literary, musical or other socially recognized human characteristics or products found among various social classes, groups, nations or other factions of society which produce, preserve or restore the greatest true enlightenment, virtue, integrity, liberty, hope, peace and joy within me, my family and society

intercultural[2] - to be prone to personally select, adopt and live in harmony with the most socially beneficial elements and the most virtuous qualities of the arts, sciences and humanities from one or more social classes, groups, nations or other factions of society

intercultural[3] - to be prone to personally select, adopt and live in harmony with the most socially beneficial elements and the most virtuous qualities of academic, dancing, dress, food, graphic, intellectual, literary, musical or other socially recognized human characteristics or products found among various social classes,

groups, nations or other factions of society

intercultural[4] - to be prone to personally select, adopt and live in harmony with the most socially beneficial elements and the most virtuous qualities of the social beliefs, behaviors, forms, manners, traits and ways of one or more social classes, groups, nations or other factions of society

intercultural[5] - to be prone to exchange or share with people of other cultures that which produces, preserves or restores true enlightenment, virtue, integrity, liberty, hope, peace and joy within ourselves, our families and society

intercultural[6] - to be prone to learn enough about the cultural background or heritage of other people to determine that which produces, preserves or restores true enlightenment, virtue and integrity within them, within their families and within society

intercultural[7] - to be prone to refuse to abuse, malign or persecute another person because of their cultural background or heritage

interdependent - to be prone to personally ascertain and live in harmony with the discernibly enlightening and spiritually verifiable truth that: the virtuously liberating freedom, health, honorable economic prosperity and steady progress of me, my family and of society are and can be enhanced by the virtuous choices and decisions I make and by the virtuous choices and decisions they make

interdependent[2] - to be familial or familistic

interdependent[3] - to be socially-minded

interesting - to be filled with enough true enlightenment, virtue and integrity to arouse, evoke or stimulate another person's sense of true enlightenment, virtue and integrity

interethnic - to be prone to personally select, adopt and live in harmony with the ethnic backgrounds, origins or traditions of other people which produce, preserve or restore the greatest true enlightenment, virtue, integrity, liberty, hope, peace and joy within me, my family and society

interethnic[2] - to be prone to personally select, adopt and live in harmony with the most socially beneficial elements and the most virtuous qualities of the ethnic backgrounds, origins or traditions of other people

interethnic[3] - to be prone to exchange or share with people of other ethnic backgrounds, origins or traditions that which produces, preserves or restores true enlightenment, virtue, integrity, liberty, hope, peace and joy within ourselves, our families and society

interethnic[4] - to be prone to learn enough about the ethnic backgrounds, origins or traditions of other people to determine that which produces, preserves or restores true enlightenment, virtue and integrity within them, within their families and within society

interethnic[5] - to be prone to refuse to abuse, malign or persecute another person because of the particular national or social

background, origin or tradition into which they were born

interfering - to intend, whenever necessary, to legally and forcefully intervene or take part in the affairs or concerns of other people without invitation, permission or welcome in order to honorably and justly prevent or stop their attempts to produce, preserve or restore darkness, vice and corruption within me, my family and society

intermingling - to intend to associate, combine, interact, integrate, mix or unite with one or more people of true enlightenment, virtue and integrity

international - to be godly enough to be made truly chaste, clean, pure and virtuous at heart—and to continue to encourage and help all other people by charitable love, kindness, invitation and instruction to be godly enough to be made truly chaste, clean, pure and virtuous at heart

international[2] - to be humane and to invite all other people to be humane

interpersonal - to be godly enough to be made truly chaste, clean, pure and virtuous at heart—and to continue to encourage and help other people by charitable love, kindness, invitation and instruction to be godly enough to be made truly chaste, clean, pure and virtuous at heart

interpersonal[2] - to be charitably loving

interpersonal[3] - to be prone to produce, preserve or restore true enlightenment, virtue and integrity within me, my family and society

interpersonal[4] - to be skilled at bringing out the best in other people

interpreting - to intend to define, explain, construe, expound, judge, portray or translate in harmony with what I know is charitably loving, just, right and wise in the sight of God

interpreting[2] - to intend to define, explain, construe, expound, judge, portray or translate something in harmony with the commandments, covenants, laws and ordinances of God

interpreting[3] - to intend to define, explain, construe, expound, judge, portray or translate something in harmony with the good law of the land

interracial - to be prone to join with people of other races to produce, preserve or restore true enlightenment, virtue, integrity, liberty, hope, peace and joy within ourselves, our families and society

interracial[2] - to be prone to develop and maintain pleasant and mutually enjoyable relationships with other people of true enlightenment, virtue and integrity who are members of other races

interracial[3] - to be prone to refuse to be racist

interrelating - to intend to develop and maintain pleasant and mutually enjoyable relationships with other people of true enlightenment, virtue and integrity

interreligious - to be prone to join with people of other religions to produce, preserve or restore true enlightenment, virtue, integrity, liberty, hope, peace and joy within ourselves, our families and society

interreligious[2] - to be prone to develop and maintain pleasant and mutually enjoyable relationships with other people of true enlightenment, virtue and integrity who belong to other religions

intervening - to intend, whenever necessary, to legally and forcefully interfere in the affairs or concerns of other people without invitation, permission or welcome in order to honorably and justly prevent or stop them from viciously harming or injuring themselves or other people

intervening[2] - to intend, whenever necessary, to forcefully stand between opposing sides without invitation, permission or welcome in order to honorably and justly prevent or stop them from viciously harming or injuring themselves or other people

intimate - to be virtuously sexual

intimate[2] - to be prone to enjoy a warm friendship of well-deserved and unreserved trust with another person

in-touch - to be prone to receive personal enlightenment, inspiration or revelation from God by my believing and honorably exact obedience to that divinely appointed law upon which receipt of that blessing is predicated

intrepid - to be prone to fearlessly and resolutely endure or persist against darkness, vice and corruption

introspective - to be prone to monitor the condition of the thoughts of my mind and the condition of the thoughts, beliefs, values and characteristics of my heart, and to then constantly do the

best I can to make improvements in
them
intruding - to intend—having
willfully undertaken and having
been entrusted with the patriarchal
or parental authority, duty,
jurisdiction and power to do so—to
forcefully push my way into the
private affairs, concerns,
conversations or property of my
minor children without invitation,
permission or welcome in order to
honorably and justly prevent or
stop their attempts to produce,
preserve or restore darkness, vice
and corruption within them, our
family and society
intruding² - to intend, whenever
necessary, to use the necessary
civic, governmental, military or
police authority to forcefully push
my way into the private affairs,
concerns, conversations or
property of other people without
invitation, permission or welcome
in order to honorably and justly
prevent or stop their attempts to
produce, preserve or restore
darkness, vice and corruption
within me, my family and society
intruding³ - to intend, whenever
necessary, to use the necessary
civic, governmental, military or
police authority to forcefully push
my way into the private affairs,
concerns, conversations or
property of other people without
invitation, permission or welcome
in order to enforce the good law of
the land
intuitive - to be discerning
intuitive² - to be prone, in harmony
with my initial endowments of
childlike prayerful faith in God,
purity of heart, and clarity of
enlightened conscience, to seek
more available enlightenment,
inspiration or revelation from God
intuitive³ - to be endowed with and
in possession of an initial measure
of guiding and personally
enlightening certainty,
comprehension, conscience,
discernment, instinct, intuition,
spirit, vision or understanding
from God, by which I then strive to
personally identify and verify
additional complementary or
harmonious enlightenment,
inspiration or revelation from God
inured - to be accustomed to
effectively dealing with
unavoidable affliction, difficulty,
pain, hardship, suffering or
tribulation
invading - to be virtuously
intruding
invaluable - to be prone to
personally ascertain and live in
harmony with the discernibly
enlightening and spiritually
verifiable truth that: my soul is of
infinite worth in the sight of God
invaluable² - to be prone to
personally ascertain and live in
harmony with the discernibly
enlightening and spiritually
verifiable truth that: to develop a
character of true enlightenment,
virtue and integrity is and will
ultimately be of greater worth to
me and my family than any
monetary amount in excess of our
needs
invaluable³ - to be prone to make
my contribution, influence or work
of greater worth to me, my family
and society than any monetary
amount in excess of my needs

inventing - to intend to create better ways of doing better things

inventorying - to intend to carefully and regularly evaluate, list or summarize achievements, progress and resources in order to better account for and manage what has been done and what can be done

investigating - to be virtuously conscientious, diligent and faithful in striving to discover the truth about God by prayerful and thorough study and by my believing and honorably exact obedience to that divinely appointed law upon which receipt of that truth is predicated

investigating[2] - to intend to personally discover truth by prayerful and thorough study and by faithful and prayerful inquiry

investigating[3] - to intend to discover for myself the truth about how to improve or progress

investigating[4] - to intend to inspect, observe, question or test in order to confirm, prove or verify what I truly need to know

investing - to intend to wisely entrust money I cannot afford to lose to someone of true enlightenment, virtue and integrity whose business practices are enlightened, virtuous and wise, and to pay them a reasonable amount to safeguard it and to use it to make a reasonable amount of gain, profit or return for me

invigorated - to be animated or enlivened

invincible - to be inviolable

inviolable - to be enlightened, virtuous and pure enough within my heart to remain liberated

within my mind and heart from the evil or satanic powers of darkness, vice and corruption

inviolable[2] - to be powerful enough to keep my thoughts, words and actions integrated within the safe and discernibly enlightened boundaries of chastity, cleanliness, purity and virtue which God has justly set by law and commandment

inviolate - to be truly chaste, clean, pure and virtuous at heart, and to stay that way

inviolate[2] - to be unadulterated, uncorrupted, undefiled, unpolluted or unprofaned, and to stay that way

invoking - to be virtuously praying

involved - to be committed to or engaged in truly virtuous participation

invulnerable - to be healthy and powerful enough to be inviolable

irenic - to be prone to obtain or maintain peaceful reconciliation and tranquility with other people

irenical - to be irenic

irradiating - to be obviously filled with beaming, illuminating or shining intelligence or the pure light of truth

irradiative - to be prone to irradiating

irrationalistic - to be prone to refuse to be viciously rationalistic

irreconcilable - to be prone to refuse to compromise that which is charitably loving, just, right and wise in the sight of God to achieve reconciliation with one or more other people

irreconcilable[2] - to be prone to refuse to compromise my true enlightenment, virtue and integrity in order to achieve reconciliation with one or more other people

irrefutable - to be truly honest

irreligious - to be prone to refuse to be religiously asatanic or atheistic

irreligious[2] - to be prone to personally reject and withstand the influence of any and every religion which truly produces, preserves or restores darkness, vice and corruption within me, my family and society

irreproachable - to be truly innocent

Islamic - to be prone to live in harmony with the teachings of Islam which produce, preserve or restore true enlightenment, virtue and integrity within me, my family and society

J

Jainist - to be prone to live in harmony with the teachings of Jainism which produce, preserve or restore true enlightenment, virtue and integrity within me, my family and society

jaunty - to be animated or vivacious

jealous - to be prone to vigilantly strive to safeguard truth and virtue by defeating or withstanding the depraving, diminishing or destructive designs of all those who would take them from me

jealous[2] - to be prone to vigilantly strive to safeguard the truly virtuous progress of me, my family and society by defeating or withstanding the depraving, diminishing or destructive designs of all those who would hinder or destroy it

jealous[3] - to be prone to vigilantly strive to safeguard the fundamental right to human life, the fundamental right and control of personal property, equal justice under virtuous law, and the pursuit and preservation of that true enlightenment, virtue and integrity which produce, preserve or restore true liberty, hope, peace and joy within me, my family and society by defeating or withstanding the depraving, diminishing or destructive designs of all who would take them from me

Jewish - to be prone to live in harmony with the teachings of Judaism which produce, preserve or restore true enlightenment, virtue and integrity within me, my family and society

joining - to intend to associate, participate or unite with one or more other people of true enlightenment, virtue and integrity

joining[2] - to intend to enlist one or more other people of true enlightenment, virtue and integrity to associate, participate or unite together

jollying - to intend to enjoy cheerful or merry association in good company

journalizing - to intend to keep for the future benefit of my family and posterity a written personal history containing evidence and personal testimony of the enlightened certainty, reality or truth of the grace, love and power of God manifested in my life

journalizing[2] - to intend to publicly broadcast, publish or otherwise represent verified and newsworthy events or facts, along with carefully distinguished and honorable editorial conclusions or opinions to an extent or in a manner which produces, preserves or restores true enlightenment, virtue and integrity within me, my family and society

jovial - to be prone to naturally exert a joyous influence while associating with other people

joyful - to be prone to actively receive and be filled with a measure of that exhilarating delight, heavenly elation or jubilant gladness which comes from knowing with an absolute, perfect and spiritually verified personal knowledge of enlightened certainty, reality or truth by personal enlightenment, inspiration or revelation from God that I am sanctified and redeemed unto exaltation, and from knowing that I am leaving the world a legacy of righteous posterity who will obediently continue to strive until death to faithfully, lovingly and unselfishly sacrifice to effectively safeguard and improve the virtuously liberating freedom, health, honorable economic prosperity and steady progress of themselves, their families and society, and who will otherwise obediently continue to serve God, to keep all of His commandments, covenants, laws and ordinances, and to become exalted heirs to every heavenly blessing, gift and reward

joyful[2] - to be prone to actively receive and be filled with a great measure of that exhilarating delight, heavenly elation or jubilant gladness which comes from a good conscience and a pure heart filled with liberating true enlightenment, virtue and integrity

joyful[3] - to be prone to actively receive and be filled with a great measure of that exhilarating delight, heavenly elation or jubilant gladness which comes from knowing with an absolute, perfect and spiritually verified personal knowledge of enlightened certainty, reality or truth by personal enlightenment, inspiration or revelation from God that the course I am now faithfully and prayerfully pursuing toward exaltation is pleasing unto Him

joyful[4] - to be prone to actively receive and be filled with a great measure of that exhilarating delight, heavenly elation or jubilant gladness which comes from knowing with an absolute, perfect and spiritually verified personal knowledge of truth by personal enlightenment, inspiration or revelation from God the Eternal Father that He lives, that I am His child, that He loves me, that no unclean thing can dwell in His glorious celestial presence, that He yearns for my return to His presence in cleanliness following my death, that He has provided a way for me to overcome physical death by resurrection and a way for me to be cleansed or sanctified from my sins to overcome spiritual death by the charitable love, cleansing power and redeeming grace of the Atonement of His Son, the Lord Jesus Christ, and that He is bound to fill me with increasing liberty, hope, peace and joy by my faithfully repentant and honorably exact obedience to those divinely appointed commandments, covenants, laws and ordinances upon which receipt of those blessings is predicated

joyful[5] - to be prone to actively receive and be filled with a great measure of that exhilarating delight, heavenly elation or jubilant gladness which comes from knowing with an absolute, perfect and spiritually verified personal knowledge of enlightened certainty, reality or truth by personal enlightenment, inspiration or revelation from God the Eternal Father that He is a just, loving, omnipotent and omniscient Being who will justly continue to manifest truth unto me by the power of the Holy Ghost, empower me to be more virtuous, deliver me from all evil temptation, give me power to have and to do what is expedient in Him, and enlighten me with His revealed will, by my believing and honorably exact obedience to those divinely appointed laws upon which receipt of those blessings is predicated

joyful[6] - to be prone to actively receive and be filled with a great measure of that exhilarating delight, heavenly elation or jubilant gladness which comes from worthily receiving personal enlightenment, inspiration or revelation from God noticeably placed within the thoughts of my mind and noticeably confirmed within my heart as His by the enlightening and simultaneous presence of the glorious power of the Holy Ghost within me

joyful[7] - to be prone to actively receive and be filled with a great measure of that exhilarating delight, heavenly elation or jubilant gladness which comes to those who faithfully do what is required to be justly liberated, redeemed or rescued by God from all that produces, preserves or restores darkness, vice, corruption, bondage, despair, turmoil and misery within ourselves, our families and society

joyous - to be prone to lovingly encourage and kindly help someone to do what it takes to be joyful

jubilating - to intend to receive, exult in and shout out triumphant joy

judging - to intend to accurately and clearly discern and righteously judge that which is truly best

judging[2] - to intend to exercise and uphold the true patriarchal, parental, ecclesiastical or higher priesthood authority, jurisdiction, power and trust given to me by forming, administering and enforcing those judgments justly demanded or required by the commandments, covenants, laws and ordinances of God, to an extent or in a manner which is not prohibited by the good law of the land

judging[3] - to intend to exercise and uphold the true patriarchal, parental, ecclesiastical or higher priesthood authority, duty, jurisdiction, power and trust given to me, by refusing to form, reach or render judgments which are beyond or outside the scope of that authority, duty, jurisdiction, power or trust

judging[4] - to intend to form, administer and enforce only those discriminatory decisions, estimates, evaluations, judgments or opinions which produce, preserve or restore the greatest true enlightenment, virtue, integrity, liberty, hope, peace and joy within me, my family and society, to an extent or in a manner which is not prohibited by the good law of the land

judging[5] - to intend to accurately and clearly discern, distinguish or judge between that which is truly good and of God and that which is evil or satanic

judging[6] - to intend to accurately and clearly discern, distinguish or judge between that which is enlightened certainty, reality or truth and that which is confusion, error or falsehood

judging[7] - to intend to accurately and clearly discern, distinguish or judge between that which is real and that which is imaginary

judging[8] - to intend to acquire or reach an accurate or true perception

judging[9] - to intend to cautiously analyze, test and interpret the testimony of witnesses or other evidence in a sincere effort to form or reach a truly honorable and just discriminatory decision, estimate, evaluation, judgment or opinion

judging[10] - to intend to ensure that my judicial decisions do not abuse, circumvent or usurp the combined voice of a goodly citizenry or the constitutional powers of their duly elected legislative and executive officials

judging[11] - to intend to uphold the actual civic, governmental, military or police authority, duty, jurisdiction, power and trust given to me by refusing to form, reach or render judicial decisions which are clearly beyond or outside the scope of that authority, duty, jurisdiction, power or trust

judging[12] - to intend to avoid forming or reaching an erroneous, incorrect or mistaken discriminatory decision, estimate, evaluation or opinion

judging[13] - to intend to uphold the civic, governmental, military or police authority, jurisdiction, power and trust given to me by forming, administering and enforcing judicial decisions demanded or required by the good law of the land

judging[14] - to intend to form or reach a discriminatory decision, estimate, evaluation, judgment or opinion that is in harmony with the good law of the land

judgmatic - to be judicious

judgmatical - to be judicious

judgmental - to be prone to exercise judgment to an extent or in a manner which is charitably loving, just, right and wise in the sight of God

judgmental[2] - to be prone to judge and, if necessary, seek to honorably and justly censure, counteract, stop or withstand someone's expression or behavior when they speak or act to an extent or in a manner which produces, preserves or restores darkness, vice and corruption within me, my family and society

judgmental[3] - to be prone to judge the character, conduct or speech of another person as mercifully as I would have them judge my character, conduct or speech
judgmental[4] - to be prone to refuse to be viciously nonjudgmental
judicative - to be capable of righteous judgment
judicious - to be prone to exercise judgment which is charitably loving, just, right and wise in the sight of God by my believing and honorably exact obedience to that divinely appointed law upon which receipt of that judgment is predicated
judicious[2] - to be discreet, practical and prudent in judgment
judicious[3] - to be prone to advocate, favor or seek to preserve government which limits the terms of service of all local, state and federal justices, judges, executives and legislators to election periods of no more than six years each and totaling no more than three terms, or until their willful retirement, or until they are removed from office for lack of good behavior or virtuous judgment, whichever comes first
judicious[4] - to be prone to advocate, favor or seek to preserve government which requires a body of less than ten lower judges to gather to sit in judgment of whether one or more higher or highest judges will be removed from office for lack of good behavior or virtuous judgment, or whether they will have one of their decisions dismissed or overruled when it is regarded as lacking virtuous judgment by the voice of

the majority of people otherwise subject to the higher or highest judge or judges or their decision
juridic - to be prone to administer equal and honorable justice in a truly just manner
jurisprudent - to be knowledgeable, skilled and wise in the righteous administration of that which is charitably loving, just, right and wise in the sight of God
jurisprudent[2] - to be knowledgeable, skilled and wise in keeping, making, interpreting or enforcing good laws when it is my duty to do so
jurisprudent[3] - to be prone to refuse to be litigious
jurisprudential - to be jurisprudent
just - to be exalted
just[2] - to be redeemed from the bondage, burdens and debts of my sins unto exaltation by my faithfully repentant and honorably exact obedience to those divinely appointed commandments, covenants, laws and ordinances upon which receipt of that exaltation is predicated
just[3] - to be godly enough to be made truly chaste, clean, pure and virtuous at heart—and to continue to encourage and help other people by charitable love, kindness, invitation and instruction to be godly enough to be made truly chaste, clean, pure and virtuous at heart
just[4] - to be prone, having the necessary patriarchal, parental or social authority and jurisdiction, to faithfully and diligently fulfill my duty to God, to my family and to society to firmly enforce good laws and to deter or prevent their

violation by administering to an accountable and guilty wrongdoer that commensurately painful condemnation, penalty, punishment, retribution or revenge which is charitably loving, just, right and wise in the sight of God, to an extent or in a manner which is not prohibited by the good law of the land

just[5] - to be prone to consistently render judgment which produces, preserves or restores true enlightenment, virtue and integrity within me, my family and society

just[6] - to be prone to use equal and honorable justice to faithfully sustain and defend truth and virtue, rather than to perpetuate contrary legal precedent

just[7] - to be prone to consistently render discerning and righteous judgment in harmony with the dictates of my enlightened conscience

just[8] - to be prone to consistently render the kind of righteous judgment with which I would like to be judged

just[9] - to be prone to treat another person as well as I would have them treat me if their words or actions were mine

just[10] - to be prone to consistently render righteous judgment in harmony with truly chaste, clean, pure and virtuous thoughts, beliefs, values and characteristics

just[11] - to be prone to refuse to be corrupted, infected or polluted by darkness, vice and corruption

just[12] - to be prone to refuse to be filled with the evil or satanic powers of binding addiction, compulsion, impulsion, obsession, occupation and possession

just[13] - to be prone to consistently render dispassionate, impartial and well-reasoned judgment in harmony with the good law of the land

just[14] - to be truly innocent

justifiable - to be prone to honorably and justly heed a needed warning to repent of all of the corrupt, sinful or vicious wrongdoing within me, by responding with my faithful, timely and true repentance, obedience and reconciliation to God

justifiable[2] - to be prone to honorably and justly answer for, explain or report what I have done wrong or what I have failed to do right when good conscience, justice, truth and virtue require me to do so

justifiable[3] - to be prone to readily and willingly subject myself to someone's efforts to honorably and justly place blame, fault or guilt against me

justifiable[4] - to be prone to account for, answer for, explain or report what I have done wrong or what I have failed to do right when required to do so by the good law of the land

justified - to be prone, in harmony with my faithful, timely and true repentance, obedience and reconciliation to God, to receive a confirming witness by revelation from Him by the power of the Holy Ghost that I am justly pardoned and sanctified unto spotless innocence by the Atoning blood of the Lord Jesus Christ

justified² - to be prone to think, speak and act in virtuous oneness with the dictates of my enlightened conscience

justified³ - to be prone to think, speak and act in harmony with truly chaste, clean, pure and virtuous thoughts, beliefs, values and characteristics

justified⁴ - to be prone to think, speak and act in harmony with the good law of the land

justifying - to intend to offer another person the means of obtaining positive proof that someone or something is charitably loving, just, right and wise in the sight of God

justifying² - to intend to obtain the means of obtaining positive proof that someone or something is charitably loving, just, right and wise in the sight of God

justifying³ - to intend to virtuously legalize something

K

keen - to be sharply alert, acutely perceptive and wise

kind - to be prone to actively assist another person in distress, supply their unmet needs, or otherwise contribute to their good health and true safety as cheerfully, mercifully, tenderly, thoughtfully and wisely as possible

kind² - to be honorably and justly reciprocating

kindhearted - to be kind at heart

kindly - to be kind

kingly - to be a married boy or man who powerfully personifies the most dignified, handsome, noble and masculine characteristics of godly manhood by my faithfully repentant and honorably exact

obedience to those divinely appointed commandments, covenants, laws and ordinances upon which receipt of that power is predicated

kingly² - to be a boy or man monarch who powerfully personifies the most dignified, handsome, noble and masculine characteristics of godly manhood by my faithfully repentant and honorably exact obedience to those divinely appointed commandments, covenants, laws and ordinances upon which receipt of that power is predicated

kingly³ - to be a boy or man who prevails by distinguished performance

knightly - to be a boy or man who is chivalrous and noble

knowing - to be in possession of and to be aware I have clearly and distinctly experienced or observed within the resulting enlightened thoughts of my mind and within the resulting joyous feelings within my heart the reception of an absolute, perfect and spiritually verified personal knowledge of the truth about God by personal enlightenment, inspiration or revelation from God by my believing and honorably exact obedience to that divinely appointed law upon which receipt of that knowledge is predicated

knowing² - to intend to maintain and build upon my personally verified, perfectly clear and distinctly certain enlightenment, realistic awareness or truthful understanding of the characteristic and distinctive differences between that which is truly good and of

God and that which is evil or satanic

knowing[3] - to be in possession of and to be aware I have clearly and distinctly experienced or observed within the resulting enlightened thoughts of my mind and within the resulting joyous feelings within my heart the reception of an absolute, perfect and spiritually verified personal knowledge of that which is truly good and of God by personal enlightenment, inspiration or revelation from God by my believing and honorably exact obedience to that divinely appointed law upon which receipt of that knowledge is predicated

knowing[4] - to intend to maintain and build upon my personally verified, perfectly clear and distinctly certain enlightenment, realistic awareness or truthful understanding of the characteristic and distinctive differences between that which is enlightened certainty, reality or truth and that which is confusion, error or falsehood

knowing[5] - to be in possession of and to be aware I have clearly and distinctly experienced or observed within the resulting enlightened thoughts of my mind and within the resulting joyous feelings within my heart the reception of an absolute, perfect and spiritually verified personal knowledge of that which is truth by personal enlightenment, inspiration or revelation from God by my believing and honorably exact obedience to that divinely appointed law upon which receipt of that knowledge is predicated

knowing[6] - to intend to maintain and build upon my personally verified, perfectly clear and distinctly certain enlightenment, realistic awareness or truthful understanding of the characteristic and distinctive differences between that which is real and that which is imaginary

knowing[7] - to be in possession of and to be aware I have clearly and distinctly experienced or observed within the resulting enlightened thoughts of my mind and within the resulting joyous feelings within my heart the reception of an absolute, perfect and spiritually verified personal knowledge of that which is reality by personal enlightenment, inspiration or revelation from God by my believing and honorably exact obedience to that divinely appointed law upon which receipt of that knowledge is predicated

knowing[8] - to be in possession of and to be aware I have clearly and distinctly experienced or observed within the resulting enlightened thoughts of my mind and within the resulting joyous feelings within my heart the reception of an absolute, perfect and spiritually verified personal knowledge of that which is enlightened certainty by personal enlightenment, inspiration or revelation from God by my believing and honorably exact obedience to that divinely appointed law upon which receipt of that knowledge is predicated

knowing[9] - to be endowed with and in possession of an initial measure of guiding personal enlightenment from God enough to accurately and clearly discern between that which is real and that which is imaginary

knowing[10] - to be endowed with and in possession of an initial measure of guiding personal enlightenment from God, by which certainty, comprehension, conscience, discernment, instinct, intuition, spirit, vision or understanding I can personally identify and verify additional complementary or harmonious enlightenment, inspiration or revelation from God

knowing[11] - to intend to maintain and build upon my personal awareness by using my mental powers of clarity, cognition, collection, distinction, learning, perception, viewpoint and so forth to continue to learn to more clearly and more perfectly distinguish, learn, perceive, recognize, recollect or seek the most perfectly valuable awareness available

knowing[12] - to be endowed with and in possession of an initial measure of personal awareness from God, by which I can willfully become more clearly aware of or more perfectly acquainted or familiar with certain learned information

knowledgeable - to be in possession of and to be aware I have come to an absolute, perfect and spiritually verified personal knowledge of enlightened certainty, reality or truth by experiencing or observing within me the reception of powerfully clear, confirming and distinct personal enlightenment, inspiration or revelation from God

of those things He would have me think, say and do

knowledgeable[2] - to be prone to come to an absolute, perfect and spiritually verified personal knowledge of enlightened certainty, reality or truth by experiencing or observing within me the reception of powerfully clear, confirming and distinct personal enlightenment, inspiration or revelation from God by my believing and honorably exact obedience to that divinely appointed law upon which receipt of that knowledge is predicated

knowledgeable[3] - to be prone to achieve or acquire general awareness, experience, education, information or training

known - to be prone to obtain or maintain association or familiarity with people whose designs, desires, dispositions, intentions, plans, purposes, words, actions, deeds and works are truly good and of God

kosher - to be prone to wisely eat and drink only what is healthy for my body in the sight of God

L

labeling - to intend to actively, charitably, generously and wisely esteem, regard and treat another person as the more excellent and progressive person they can and should become, and to thus give them the inspiring confidence, the uplifting encouragement and the elevating opportunity to live up to such esteem, regard and treatment as long as they do so

labeling[2] - to intend to ascertain and then accurately and clearly state the truly positive character, condition, influence, merit, power, quality, strength, value or worth of someone or something

ladylike - to be a pure and virtuous girl or woman

ladylike² - to be a girl or woman who lives in harmony with the best and highest laws, rules, standards or values of true enlightenment, virtue and integrity of which I have become aware in my education and training and in my own constantly diligent, honest and open-minded searching

ladylike³ - to be a girl or woman who is attractively feminine, polite, well-educated, well-mannered and well-spoken

laissez-faire - to be prone to respect the rights of other people and to allow or cause them to freely make choices and to conduct their affairs without interference from me so long as their choices and their conduct produce, preserve or restore true enlightenment, virtue and integrity within me, my family and society

laissez-faire² - to be prone to advocate, favor or seek to preserve government which promotes but intervenes as little as possible in the honorable business, commercial and economic affairs of those subject to its laws

lamenting - to be penitent

Latin American - to be prone to live in harmony with the ways of Latin American character or culture which produce, preserve or restore true enlightenment, virtue and integrity within me, my family and society

laudable - to be truly worthy of honorable acclaim, commendation or praise

laughing - to intend to express great joy with a smile and sounds which ordinarily represent great joy

laughing² - to intend to express grateful delight or elation with a smile and with sounds which ordinarily represent happiness

laughing³ - to intend to express gaiety or merriment with a smile and sounds which ordinarily represent jolly gaiety or festive merriment from healthy association or companionship with other people

laughing⁴ - to intend to share pleasant laughter with another person often enough to maintain good health

laureate - to be truly deserving of special recognition for prominently good achievement, as traditionally represented by the presentation of a wreath of laurel

law-abiding - to intend to faithfully think, speak, act, judge, lead and teach in harmony with the commandments, covenants, laws and ordinances of God well enough to justly inherit or receive all earthly and heavenly blessings, gifts and rewards which God would have me receive

law-abiding² - to intend to faithfully think, speak, act, judge, lead and teach in harmony with divine law well enough to justly receive absolute, perfect and spiritually verified personal knowledge of enlightened certainty, reality or truth by personal enlightenment, inspiration or revelation from God

law-abiding[3] - to intend to honor, obey and sustain the commandments, covenants, laws and ordinances of God

law-abiding[4] - to intend to honor, obey and sustain the good law of the land

lawful - to be prone to think, speak and act to an extent or in a manner which is equitably allowed or substantially permitted by the commandments, covenants, laws and ordinances of God, and is neither contrary to nor forbidden by them

lawful[2] - to be prone to think, speak and act to an extent or in a manner which is equitably allowed or substantially permitted by the good law of the land, and is neither contrary to nor forbidden by it

leading - to be Christlike

leading[2] - to be godly enough to be made truly chaste, clean, pure and virtuous at heart—and to continue to encourage and help other people by charitable love, kindness, invitation and instruction to be godly enough to be made truly chaste, clean, pure and virtuous at heart

leading[3] - to intend, by my words and actions, to personally conduct, direct, guide, induce, influence or inspire other people toward greater true enlightenment, virtue, integrity, liberty, hope, peace and joy

leading[4] - to intend, by my words and actions, to honorably fulfill my responsibility to effectively safeguard and improve the virtuously liberating freedom, health, honorable economic prosperity and steady progress of me, my family and society

leading[5] - to be of noble, honorable or valiant achievement, character or merit

leading-edge - to be prone to introduce what is best

leading-edge[2] - to be prone to introduce something better

leading-edge[3] - to be prone to introduce something good

lean - to be hardy and hard-working enough to be healthy

lean[2] - to be economical, frugal, providential, thrifty or resourceful

learned - to be intelligent or knowing enough to wisely live in harmony with the mind and will of God

learned[2] - to be intelligent or knowing enough to wisely live in harmony with that which produces, preserves or restores true enlightenment, virtue and integrity within me, my family and society

learned[3] - to be prone to learn and live in harmony with edifying true enlightenment

learned[4] - to be prone to obtain enough good education, knowledge or skill to be a law-abiding and self-reliant net contributor to the virtuously liberating freedom, health, honorable economic prosperity and steady progress of me, my family and society

learning - to be ascertaining

learning[2] - to be discerning

least - to be virtuously serving

least[2] - to be prone to suppose my personal wants are less important than the personal needs of other people

legal - to be prone to think, speak and act in harmony with the requirements of the commandments, covenants, laws and ordinances of God

legal[2] - to be prone to think, speak and act in harmony with the requirements of the good law of the land

legendary - to be connected to and known for the verified and heroically virtuous deeds I did

legislating - to intend to help enact, form, make or pass good laws needed to produce, preserve or restore true enlightenment, virtue and integrity, along with their naturally consequent liberty, hope, peace and joy, within me, my family and society

legislating[2] - to intend to help enact, form, make or pass good laws needed to protect me, my family and society against darkness, vice and corruption, and against their naturally consequent bondage, despair, turmoil and misery

legislating[3] - to intend to help enact, form, make or pass good laws needed to protect me, my family and society in our combined efforts to form a society more perfectly united in virtue, to establish equal and honorable justice under virtuous law, to exercise enough peacemaking at home and abroad, to sustain our common defense, to promote our shared progress and well-being, and to thereby secure the blessings of liberty to ourselves, our families and our posterity

legislating[4] - to intend to help enact, form, make or pass good laws needed to uphold the virtuously liberating freedom, health, honorable economic prosperity and steady progress of me, my family and society

legitimate - to be prone to refuse to be hypocritical or schizophrenic to any degree

legitimate[2] - to be prone to refuse to be viciously deceptive or false

legitimate[3] - to be prone to think, speak and act in harmony with the good law of the land

legitimist - to be prone to advocate, favor or seek to preserve government by those holding legitimate or rightful authority

legitimistic - to be legitimist

lettered - to be skilled in reading and writing

levelheaded - to be of practical judgment in making choices and decisions

leveraging - to intend to use available resources in an honorable manner to produce far more valuable resources

liable - to be prone to personally ascertain and live in harmony with the discernibly enlightening and spiritually verifiable truth that: I shall one day be justly required to pay for my own sins, unless I honorably seek faithful, timely and true repentance, obedience and reconciliation to God in this life

liable[2] - to be prone to assume full accountability and responsibility to faithfully, timely and truly repent and make full restitution for all of the affliction, damage, distress, harm, injury, loss or pain I have viciously caused me, my family and society liable[3] - to be prone to assume full legal accountability and responsibility to see that all of my honorable debts, obligations or penalties are paid for the affliction, damage, distress, harm, injury, loss or pain I have viciously caused me, my family and society

liable[4] - to be prone to accept full legal accountability and responsibility for fulfillment of all of my good and honorable duties required by the good law of the land

liaising - to intend to establish or maintain communications with other people of true enlightenment, virtue and integrity in order to preserve mutual understanding and to ensure cooperative interaction

liberal - to be charitably religious or religiously charitable

liberal[2] - to be prone to refuse to be selfish

liberal[3] - to be prone to refuse to be malicious

liberal[4] - to be prone to advocate or tolerate another person's freedom to help produce, preserve or restore true enlightenment, virtue and integrity within me, my family and society

liberal[5] - to be prone to respectfully and rightfully consider the interests, sentiments or views of other people in changing or making decisions which can impact them

liberated - to be exalted

liberated[2] - to be redeemed unto exaltation

liberated[3] - to be redeemed and released from the bondage, burdens and debts of my sins

liberated[4] - to be prone to humbly and prayerfully allow the heavenly power which comes from virtuous forgiving to emancipate, free or release me from the self-consuming bitterness and festering pain I might otherwise viciously continue to wish upon someone else

liberated[5] - to be filled with enough true enlightenment, virtue and integrity, and with enough of the spirit of virtuously liberating freedom or the Spirit of God to become or remain entirely emancipated, freed, liberated or released within my mind and heart from the evil or satanic powers of darkness, vice, corruption, bondage, despair, turmoil and misery, and to thus maintain complete personal control over the thoughts of my mind and heart, and to thus maintain my personal liberty or power to choose to live in harmony with the Spirit of God, and to thus be protected against all of the evil or satanic powers of addiction, bondage or slavery and against their naturally consequent bondage, despair, turmoil and misery

liberated[6] - to be prone to join with other members of my family and society to continue to live in harmony with the spirit of virtuously liberating freedom or the Spirit of God well enough to produce, preserve or restore emancipation, immunity or liberty from the ever threatening evil or satanic powers of darkness, vice, corruption, bondage, despair, turmoil and misery wielded by our vicious domestic and foreign enemies liberated[7] - to be prone to join with other members of my family to continue to live in harmony with the spirit of virtuously liberating freedom or the Spirit of God well enough to produce, preserve or restore emancipation, immunity or liberty from the ever threatening evil or satanic powers of darkness, vice, corruption, bondage, despair, turmoil and misery wielded by our vicious family enemies

liberated[8] - to be prone to live in harmony with the spirit of virtuously liberating freedom or the Spirit of God well enough to continue to enjoy the emancipating or liberating power to dispel or withstand the evil or satanic powers of darkness, vice, corruption, bondage, despair, turmoil and misery

liberated[9] - to be prone to maintain my personal freedom, liberty or power to choose and to act for myself, and to thus protect myself against addiction, bondage or slavery under the power of an oppressing or destroying tyrant

liberated[10] - to be prone to refuse to regard my individual freedom of choosing or deciding for myself as being more important than the harm its abuse or misuse can do to me, my family and society

liberated[11] - to be prone to enjoy enough of the civil liberty, religious liberty and political liberty afforded by good government

liberated[12] - to be prone to emancipate, free or release myself from those who would viciously use beguiling charm or flattery to ensnare my affection or love for their own selfish purposes

liberating - to be virtuously emancipating, freeing or releasing

liberating[2] - to intend to emancipate, free, liberate or release from the evil or satanic powers of addiction, bondage or slavery

licit - to be prone to obey the commandments, covenants, laws and ordinances of God

licit[2] - to be prone to refuse to digress, fall or sink into what is forbidden by the commandments, covenants, laws and ordinances of God

licit[3] - to be prone to do what is required by the good law of the land

licit[4] - to be prone to refuse to do what is forbidden or prohibited by the good law of the land

lifting - to be edifying

light - to be prone to lovingly encourage and kindly help someone to become enlightened or intelligent

light[2] - to be enlightened or intelligent

light[3] - to be filled with enough delightful gladness or bright happiness to consistently dispel melancholy and pessimistic gloom

lightening - to be enlightening

lighthearted - to be filled with true enlightenment, virtue, integrity, liberty, hope, peace and joy

lighthearted[2] - to be virtuously cheerful or humorous within my heart

lightsome - to be virtuously cheerful or humorous

likable - to be filled with enough true enlightenment, virtue and integrity to find favor in the sight of God

likable² - to be filled with enough true enlightenment, virtue and integrity to produce, preserve or restore true liberty, hope, peace and joy within me, my family and society

likable³ - to be filled with enough true enlightenment, virtue and integrity to strongly attract or appeal to another person's sense of true enlightenment, virtue and integrity

likable⁴ - to be prone, as a true reflection of the charitable love and kindness within me, to treat other people as well as possible

likable⁵ - to be prone to strive to project a personality which accurately portrays to other people the best that is within the thoughts, beliefs, values and characteristics of my heart

limited - to be self-subdued

lionhearted - to be exceptionally brave or courageous for a good cause

lionized - to be truly worthy of exceptionally high regard for being greatly influential for good

lionizing - to intend to highly regard someone for being greatly influential for good

listening - to intend to entertain, harbor, hold or pay attention to what I am hearing long enough and well enough within my mind and heart to hear the mind, voice, will or word of God

listening² - to intend to entertain, harbor, hold or pay attention to those voices I am hearing long enough and well enough to discover which ones will produce, preserve or restore greater true enlightenment, virtue, integrity,

liberty, hope, peace and joy within the thoughts, beliefs, values and characteristics of my heart

literal - to be prone to use those clearly defined and consistently understood meanings or translations of words which best convey a clear and consistent understanding of enlightened certainty, reality or truth

literary - to be prone to cultivate a sensitive appreciation for good, praiseworthy and uplifting literature

literary² - to be prone to write, publish or sponsor good, praiseworthy and uplifting literature

literary³ - to be sufficiently informed through reading

literate - to be lucid and polished in writing

literate² - to be well-read

literate³ - to be skilled in reading and writing

lively - to be buoyant

lively² - to be animated or vivacious

living - to be existent in true joy

living² - to be healthy

lofty - to be prone to build and maintain eminently elevated or excellent levels of true enlightenment, virtue and integrity within the thoughts, beliefs, values and characteristics of my heart

lofty² - to be edifying or elevating in speech or behavior

lofty³ - to be dignified or eminent

logical - to be prone to clearly and correctly reason real consequence or true conclusion

long-suffering - to intend to diligently and patiently persevere in faithful righteousness long

enough for my sincere exercise of
faith in God, for my faithful, timely
and true repentance, and for my
strict obedience to His
commandments, covenants, laws
and ordinances to bear their fruits
of virtuous character within me
long-suffering[2] - to be charitable
and divinely instrumental enough
to calmly and patiently bear,
endure or tolerate without reprisal
another person's mistaken and not
too serious misbehavior or
wrongdoing against me, while I
lovingly admonish, exhort, teach or
warn them to undertake faithful,
timely and true repentance,
obedience and reconciliation to
God
long-suffering[3] - to be charitable
and divinely instrumental enough
to calmly and patiently bear,
endure or tolerate another person's
not too serious frailties or
weaknesses as we each work on
overcoming our own
loose - to be free enough to
willfully think, speak and act for
myself
lordly - to be dignified and noble
lovable - to be prone to unselfishly
express or show the kind of truly
charitable love for other people
that God would have them show to
me
loved - to be prone to feel and
know of God's perfect love for me
loved[2] - to be prone to willingly
receive and work to retain the kind
of affection or love from other
people that God would have me
show to them
lovely - to be of true
enlightenment, virtue and integrity

lovely[2] - to be a good girl or
woman who is charmingly
beautiful and pleasing to the soul
as well as to the eye
loving - to intend, in the face of
incessant or intense adversity,
affliction, distress, doubt,
opposition, persecution or
tribulation, to continue to patiently
manifest—by my faithful, timely
and true repentance, by the reality
of my intent and the sincerity of
my desire, by my steady exercise of
my entire belief, confidence, hope
and trust in God, by the constant
virtuous integrity of my thoughts,
by the humility and meekness of
my daily prayers to God, by my
diligent and loving works of truly
charitable service to my family and
to society, and by my patient
obedience to all of the
commandments, covenants, laws
and ordinances of God—that I seek
to love, serve and worship God
with all of the energy, might,
power, strength and will of my
soul and with enough faith in the
Lord Jesus Christ to become an heir
and to charitably strive to help
other people become heirs to
exaltation through the charitable
love, cleansing power and
redeeming grace of the Atonement
of the Lord Jesus Christ
loving[2] - to intend to constantly
choose to faithfully, obediently and
prayerfully exercise and strive to
add to the growing measures of
discernibly true enlightenment,
virtue and integrity within me
which prompt me to continue to
learn all of the truth I can about
God, to love, obey, reverence, serve
and worship Him with all of the

energy, might, power, strength and will of my soul, and to be completely filled with the truly charitable desire, intent and power to obediently sacrifice and consecrate enough of what I have and am to effectively safeguard and improve the virtuously liberating freedom, health, honorable economic prosperity and steady progress of me, my family and society

loving[3] - to intend to actively, charitably and generously allow the charitable and unifying love of God to flow through me to my husband, wife, child or other person enough to give my life, if it is taken from me, in vigorously and virtuously defending or safeguarding them against an imminent threat of bloodshed or death

loving[4] - to intend to actively, charitably and generously allow the charitable and unifying love of God to flow through me to my husband, wife, child or other person enough to give my life, if it is taken from me, in vigorously and virtuously defending or safeguarding them against an imminent threat of evil or satanic defilement of their chastity they want to prevent

loving[5] - to intend to actively, charitably and generously allow the charitable and unifying love of God to flow through me to my husband, wife, child or other family member enough to nurture them with enough warm affection and tender care to induce or strengthen their desire and their efforts toward true personal betterment, improvement or progress for our happiness sake, rather than dwelling on what they should be doing to pleasantly serve me for my happiness sake

loving[6] - to intend to hold my true and virtuous friend dear enough to actively, charitably, generously and wisely nurture them with enough warm affection and tender care to induce or strengthen their desires and their works toward true personal betterment, improvement or progress for our happiness sake, rather than dwelling on what they should be doing to pleasantly serve me for my happiness sake

loving[7] - to intend to actively, charitably and generously allow the charitable and unifying love of God to flow through me to other people by sincerely and unselfishly providing good and tender works of kindness and service to them to the fullest extent I can and should, and whenever I am prompted to do so by the Spirit of God

loving[8] - to intend to actively, charitably and generously allow the charitable and unifying love of God to flow through me to other people by sincerely and unselfishly speaking kind, warm and pleasing words of admiration, affection, appreciation, endearment, praise or reverence to them to the fullest extent I can and should, and whenever I am prompted to do so by the Spirit of God

loving[9] - to intend to actively, charitably and generously allow the charitable and unifying love of God to flow through me to other people by constantly thinking, speaking and acting with the pure

desire and intent to produce, preserve or restore true enlightenment, virtue and integrity within me, my family and society
loving[10] - to intend to actively, charitably and generously allow the charitable and unifying love of God to flow through me to other people by consistently doing that which is charitably loving, just, right and wise in the sight of God to the fullest extent I can and should, and whenever I am prompted to do so by the Spirit of God
loving[11] - to intend to actively and persistently serve and sustain that which is truly good and of God instead of that which is evil or satanic
loving[12] - to intend to actively and persistently serve and sustain enlightened certainty, reality and truth rather than confusion, error or falsehood
loving[13] - to intend to actively, charitably and generously allow the charitable and unifying love of God to flow through me to other people by refusing to produce, preserve or restore darkness, vice and corruption within me, my family and society
loving[14] - to intend to actively, charitably and generously allow the charitable and unifying love of God to flow through me to other people by thinking, speaking and acting with the pure desire and intent to kindly caution, notify or warn them of their need to repent of all their sins and to exactly, faithfully and honorably keep the commandments, covenants, laws and ordinances of God in order to

help them avoid or escape the bondage and burdens of sin, the agonizing suffering and miserable torment of hell, and everlasting separation from the glorious celestial presence of God in spiritual death for failing or refusing to do so
loving[15] - to intend to actively, charitably and generously allow the charitable and unifying love of God to flow through me to other people by thinking, speaking and acting with the pure desire and intent to kindly caution, notify or warn them of their need to repent of all their sins and to exactly, faithfully and honorably keep the commandments, covenants, laws and ordinances of God in order to help them avoid or escape darkness, vice, corruption, bondage, despair, turmoil and misery
loving[16] - to intend to actively, charitably and generously allow the charitable and unifying love of God to flow through me to other people by striving today to help them produce, preserve or restore as much true liberty, hope, peace and joy in their lives as possible through the acquisition of true enlightenment, virtue and integrity and through the consequent and simultaneous forsaking of darkness, vice and corruption
loving[17] - to intend to actively, charitably and generously allow the charitable and unifying love of God to flow through me to other people by thinking, speaking and acting with the pure desire and intent to kindly caution, notify or warn them of the destructive

power of evil or wickedness and of the truth that darkness, vice and corruption can never produce, preserve or restore true liberty, hope, peace or joy in anyone's life loving[18] - to intend to actively and willingly love and serve God and the good of society instead of Satan by fully repenting for the harm, injury or offense I have brought upon myself, upon my family and upon society in the sight of God loving[19] - to intend—having willfully undertaken and having been entrusted with the honorable civic, governmental, military or police authority, duty, jurisdiction and power to so act—to actively and willingly love and serve God and the good of society instead of Satan by personally satisfying the demands of equal and honorable justice for the harm, injury or offense I have brought upon myself, my family and society in violation of good laws, rules, standards or values loving[20] - to intend—having willfully undertaken and having been entrusted with the patriarchal or parental authority, duty, jurisdiction and power to so act—to actively and willingly love and serve God and the good of society instead of Satan by refusing to viciously emancipate, free, liberate or release my accountable child, who can and should do better, from fully repenting for the harm, injury or offense they have brought upon me, upon my family and upon society in the sight of God loving[21] - to intend—having willfully undertaken and having been entrusted with the patriarchal or parental authority, duty, jurisdiction and power to so act—to actively and willingly love and serve God and the good of society instead of Satan by refusing to viciously emancipate, free, liberate or release my accountable child, who can and should do better, from satisfying the demands of equal and honorable justice for the harm, injury or offense they have brought upon them, upon our family and upon society in violation of good laws, rules, standards or values loving[22] - to intend—having willfully undertaken and having been entrusted with the honorable civic, governmental, military or police authority, duty, jurisdiction and power to so act—to actively and willingly love and serve God and the good of society instead of Satan by refusing to viciously emancipate, free, liberate or release other people from satisfying the demands of equal and honorable justice for the harm, injury or offense they have caused themselves, their families and society in violation of good laws, rules, standards or values loving[23] - to intend—having willfully undertaken and having been entrusted with the honorable civic, governmental, military or police authority, duty, jurisdiction and power to so act—to actively and willingly love and serve God and the good of society rather than Satan by doing all that is within my power to actively defeat or withstand the attack of a criminal, deadly or evil enemy of society

against the fundamental right to human life, against the fundamental right and control of personal property, against equal justice under virtuous law, or against the pursuit and preservation of that true enlightenment, virtue and integrity which produce, preserve or restore true liberty, hope, peace and joy within me, my family and society
low - to be modest
lowly-of-heart - to be humble, meek and modest toward God
lowly-of-heart[2] - to be modest
loyal - to be true to God by keeping His commandments, come what may
loyal[2] - to be virtuously faithful and true to my true and virtuous husband, wife, child or other family member, come what may
loyal[3] - to be virtuously faithful and true to my true and virtuous friend, come what may
loyal[4] - to be prone to faithfully execute or perform a good and honorable allegiance, commitment, contract, covenant, duty, oath, obligation, promise or vow into which I have entered
lucid - to be prone to accurately and clearly discern, perceive or understand
luminary - to be prone to provide an illuminating example of true enlightenment, virtue and integrity
luminary[2] - to be enlightening
luminary[3] - to be eminent
luminous - to be prone to radiate or reflect brilliant intelligence or the pure light of truth
luminous[2] - to be prone to accurately and clearly discern,

perceive or understand intelligence or the pure light of truth
lustrous - to be brilliant or luminous
lusty - to be vigorous

M

macho - to be a boy or man who feels and exhibits enough assertiveness, aggressiveness, defiance or power to be masculine
magnanimous - to be prone to prove my honorably courageous and noble forgiveness and generosity
magnificent - to be prone to think, speak and act in an enlightened, brilliant, glorious or splendid manner
magnificent[2] - to be virtuously fine, noble or outstanding
maidenly - to be an unmarried girl or woman who is truly chaste, clean, modest, pure and virtuous
majestic - to be prone to exercise sovereign authority in a dignified, noble and stately manner
majestical - to be majestic
male - to be a boy or man who is masculine
malleable - to be prone to repent and progress in response to the pressure of sore affliction or trial
manful - to be a noble boy or man who is masculine
manly - to be a boy or man who is masculine
mannerly - to be prone to think, speak and act in harmony with enlightened, polished and refined laws, rules, standards or values of courtesy and decency
mannerly[2] - to be well-mannered
mannerly[3] - to be prone to care enough about the pleasantness of personal circumstances and

feelings for everyone present to kindly avoid needlessly causing unpleasant distraction, disruption or disturbance

mannish - to be a boy or man who is manly

marketable - to be prone to develop good working abilities, knowledge and skills worthy of good appointment, employment or hire in a virtuous market which is of keen interest to me

marking - to intend to actively, charitably, generously and wisely esteem, regard and treat another person as the more excellent and progressive person they can and should become, and to thus give them the inspiring confidence, the uplifting encouragement and the elevating opportunity to live up to such esteem, regard and treatment as long as they do so

marking[2] - to intend to ascertain and then accurately and clearly state the truly positive character, condition, influence, merit, power, quality, strength, value or worth of someone or something

marriageable - to be an unmarried adult who is mature and prepared enough for honorable familial marriage to an adult member of the opposite gender who is eligible for lawful and legal marriage

married - to be virtuously faithful and true in living in harmony with the priesthood covenant and ordinance of eternal marriage of husband and wife lawfully and legally performed in a dedicated holy temple of God by a duly ordained man called of God who actually holds true higher priesthood authority from God and authorization from God's own called, ordained and authorized priesthood leaders on Earth—by which ordinance my worthy husband or wife and I covenant to be married and sealed together for eternity to inherit celestial glory and exaltation in the highest kingdom of God as husband and wife, in harmony with our willing acceptance of that covenant and ordinance of eternal marriage of husband and wife and our faithfully repentant and honorably exact obedience to those divinely appointed commandments, covenants, laws and ordinances upon which receipt of those blessings is predicated

married[2] - to be virtuously faithful and true to my lawfully and legally wedded husband or wife, as long as that husband or wife is virtuously faithful and true to God and to me, and until death do us part or as long as we both shall live

marrying - to intend to enter into and sustain virtuous married status

marrying[2] - to be a duly ordained man called of God, who then uses my true higher priesthood authority from God and authorization from God's own called, ordained and authorized priesthood leaders on Earth, along with any necessary public authorization to perform marriage, who administers, without pay, in a dedicated holy temple of God the priesthood ordinance of eternal marriage of husband and wife who have necessary public license to marry—by which ordinance a worthy man and woman covenant to be married and sealed together for eternity to inherit celestial glory and exaltation in the highest kingdom of God as husband and wife, in harmony with their willing acceptance of the priesthood covenant and ordinance and their faithfully repentant and honorably exact obedience to those divinely appointed commandments, covenants, laws and ordinances upon which receipt of those blessings is predicated

marrying[3] - to be a duly ordained man called of God, who then uses my true higher priesthood authority from God and authorization from God's own called, ordained and authorized priesthood leaders on Earth to administer, without pay, in a dedicated holy temple of God the priesthood ordinance of eternal marriage of husband and wife through righteous living proxy who act in behalf of deceased husbands and their wives who were lawfully and legally wedded during mortal life and whose preliminary temple work has been done—so that those deceased couples who are desirous and righteous enough to receive the ordinance work done for them can be justly married and sealed together for eternity to inherit celestial glory and exaltation in the highest kingdom of God as husband and wife forever, in harmony with their faithfully repentant and honorably exact obedience to those divinely appointed commandments, covenants, laws and ordinances upon which receipt of those blessings is predicated

martyring - to intend to willingly suffer unavoidable and vicious discrimination, rejection, persecution or death at the hands of one or more other people, rather than deny my true testimony or witness of enlightened certainty, reality or truth

martyring[2] - to intend to willingly suffer unavoidable and vicious discrimination, rejection, persecution or death at the hands of one or more other people, rather than compromise the enlightened and virtuous integrity of my heart

martyring[3] - to intend to willingly suffer unavoidable and vicious discrimination, rejection, persecution or death at the hands of one or more other people, rather than renounce my pure and virtuous thoughts, beliefs, values and characteristics

martyring[4] - to intend to willingly suffer unavoidable and vicious discrimination, rejection, persecution or death at the hands of one or more other people, rather than fail or refuse to do what my enlightened mind, pure heart and good conscience tell me is the right thing to do

martyring[5] - to intend to willingly suffer unavoidable and vicious discrimination, rejection, persecution or death at the hands of one or more other people, rather than do what my enlightened mind, pure heart and good conscience tell me is the wrong thing to do

marvelous - to be godly enough to be made truly chaste, clean, pure and virtuous at heart—and to continue to encourage and help other people by charitable love, kindness, invitation and instruction to be godly enough to be made truly chaste, clean, pure and virtuous at heart

marvelous[2] - to be astonishingly or wonderfully virtuous

masculine - to be a clean, discerning, strong and valiant man of powerful true enlightenment, virtue and integrity who accepts my God-given family role of presiding in the home, of acting in full partnership with my wife, of naturally producing offspring, posterity or seed by my wife and of ambitiously, diligently and responsibly protecting and providing for her and our young, while humbly showing enough kindly favor, generosity and service toward all children, girls and women

masculine[2] - to be a clean, discerning, strong and valiant boy or man of powerful true enlightenment, virtue and integrity who develops characteristics or qualities which are naturally becoming and naturally fulfilling to a boy or man because they match my God-given family role and because they bring the greatest true enlightenment, virtue, integrity, liberty, hope, peace and joy to me and through me to my family and to society

masculine[3] - to be a clean, discerning, strong and valiant boy or man of powerful true enlightenment, virtue and integrity who is endowed with a marvelous measure of inherent power to righteously lead, preside, protect and provide for my family and

society, particularly by powerfully defending and safeguarding truth and the positive two (2) virtues in this dictionary—rather than to use my agency to forsake that endowment for something demasculinized, something different or something less

masculine[4] - to be a competent boy or man who accepts my natural efficacy, role, power and strength, and my natural ability to procreate

masculine[5] - to be a boy or man who accepts my natural identity as a boy or man born to the male sex

masculine[6] - to be a boy or man who refuses to be demasculinized, feminized, gender-confused, transsexual, transvestite or viciously unisexual

masculinized - to be a boy or man who is masculine

masculinizing - to intend to help a boy or man be masculine

matching - to intend to refuse to be mismating

matchless - to be prone to personally ascertain and live in harmony with the discernibly enlightening and spiritually verifiable truth that: no other person can be the selfsame person I truly am, was and will become in body, mind and spirit

material - to be prone to gather enough material or physical resources to meet my material or physical needs

maternal - to be a woman who is motherly

mathematical - to be familiar enough with advanced numeric axioms, calculations, coefficients, diagrams, functions, formulas, interactions, models, operations, parameters, postulates, principles, procedures, properties, propositions, relationships, rules and theorems to enable me to look for and to strive to implement better proven ways to help human beings produce, preserve or restore greater true enlightenment, virtue, integrity, liberty, hope, peace and joy within the human body, mind and spirit

mathematical[2] - to be familiar enough with advanced numeric axioms, calculations, coefficients, diagrams, functions, formulas, interactions, models, operations, parameters, postulates, principles, procedures, properties, propositions, relationships, rules and theorems to enable me to scientifically seek knowledge of truth about things material or physical

mathematical[3] - to be knowledgeable and skilled enough in the calculation or treatment of figures, forms, measurements, numbers or other symbols of quantity to creatively solve problems and accurately answer questions pertaining to area, dimension, direction, distance, energy, expanse, figure, form, quantity, light, location, magnitude, mass, matter, measurement, motion, number, size, shape, speed, time, volume or weight

mathematical[4] - to be skilled enough in the use of addition, subtraction, multiplication, division, fractions, decimals and percentages to function well in the everyday business of life

matriarchal - to be the worthy wife of the exemplary and oldest living son of the lineage of his fathers and a man who holds the true higher priesthood of God and faithfully exercises his God-given authority and jurisdiction to righteously preside in our family, and, along with that husband to whom I am sealed, to forever spiritually govern or rule in faithful righteousness over our worthy unmarried sons and daughters and over our worthy married sons, grandsons, great-grandsons and so forth, by our faithfully repentant and honorably exact obedience to those divinely appointed commandments, covenants, laws and ordinances upon which receipt of that blessing is predicated

matriarchal[2] - to be the worthy wife of a man who holds the true higher priesthood of God and who faithfully exercises his God-given authority and jurisdiction to righteously preside in our family, and, along with that husband to whom I am sealed, to forever spiritually govern or rule in faithful righteousness over our worthy unmarried sons and daughters and over our worthy married sons, grandsons, great-grandsons and so forth, by our faithfully repentant and honorably exact obedience to those divinely appointed commandments, covenants, laws and ordinances upon which receipt of that blessing is predicated

matriarchal[3] - to be a wife who exercises my God-given authority and full partnership with my husband within our family in faithful righteousness

matriarchal[4] - to be a woman who is motherly

matronal - to be matronly

matronly - to be an older, dignified and motherly woman or widow who handles well my position of responsibility in my home or over one or more human female groups in society

matter-of-fact - to be prone to live in strict harmony with enlightened certainty, reality or truth

matter-of-fact[2] - to be prone to live in strict harmony with a practical application of known facts

mature - to be exalted

mature[2] - to be celestial

mature[3] - to be godly enough to be made truly chaste, clean, pure and virtuous at heart—and to continue to encourage and help other people by charitable love, kindness, invitation and instruction to be godly enough to be made truly chaste, clean, pure and virtuous at heart

mature[4] - to be ripened in righteousness

mature[5] - to be aged and venerable

mature[6] - to be virtuously refined

mature[7] - to be virtuously humble or lowly-of-heart

mature[8] - to be grateful enough

meaningful - to be prone to produce, preserve or restore the greatest true enlightenment, virtue, integrity, liberty, hope, peace and joy within me, my family and society

meaningful[2] - to be prone to choose for myself a good aim, ambition, aspiration, commitment, desire, goal, intention, plan, purpose or resolution

media-healthy - to be prone to use media to a virtuous extent and in a virtuous manner, while refusing to become or remain media-sick

medical - to be prone to effectively enhance healing, restore health or preserve life using curative, immunizing, medicating, natural, preventive, reconstructive, surgical, therapeutic or other effective means and methods of physical health care

medicating - to intend to administer duly authorized drugs or medications to someone to relieve or eliminate their otherwise unavoidable and unbearable suffering

medicating[2] - to intend to administer duly authorized drugs or medications to someone to build, safeguard or sustain their better health

meditating - to intend to calm my thoughts and remove them from distraction so that I can prayerfully commune with the Spirit of God within the thoughts of my mind and heart—in a faithful, honorable, intentional and sincere effort to receive personal enlightenment, inspiration or revelation from God

meditating[2] - to intend to calm my thoughts and remove them from distraction so that I can carefully, deeply and thoroughly evaluate or weigh something potentially virtuous within the thoughts of my mind and heart—in a faithful, honorable, intentional and sincere effort to evaluate or weigh for myself whether it is truly virtuous

meditating[3] - to intend to calm my thoughts and remove them from distraction so that I can carefully, deeply and thoroughly evaluate or weigh something potentially true within the thoughts of my mind and heart—in a faithful, honorable, intentional and sincere effort to evaluate or weigh for myself whether it is true

Mediterranean - to be prone to live in harmony with the ways of Mediterranean character or culture which produce, preserve or restore true enlightenment, virtue and integrity within me, my family and society

meek - to be prone to prove my genuinely gentle, mild, patient, peaceable and long-suffering willingness to gratefully and righteously submit or yield to the known mind and will of God in all things, rather than to peevishly, proudly or stubbornly complain or murmur against Him

meek[2] - to be prone to bear or suffer unavoidable pain, strain, stress or trial in a gentle, mild, patient, peaceable and long-suffering manner

Melanesian - to be prone to live in harmony with the ways of Melanesian character or culture which produce, preserve or restore true enlightenment, virtue and integrity within me, my family and society

meliorating - to intend to improve or make better

meliorative - to be prone to meliorating

mellow - to be virtuously mature

mellow[2] - to be prone to become more and more perfected, polished or refined

mellow[3] - to be prone to avoid discord and tension with gentleness and sympathy

memorable - to be good enough to be truly worthy of mention, note or remembrance for some time to come

mending - to be repenting and progressing

mental - to be enlightened or intelligent

merciful - to be prone to charitably and compassionately extend to another person that measure of benevolence, concession, forbearance, forgiveness, leniency or tolerance I am prompted by the Spirit of God to extend as that which is charitably loving, just, right and wise in the sight of God

merciful[2] - to be prone to charitably and compassionately extend as much tender concession, forbearance, leniency or tolerance to another person as righteous judgment can allow under righteous law

merciful[3] - to be prone to charitably and compassionately extend as much tender concession, forbearance, leniency or tolerance to another person as equal and honorable justice can allow under virtuous law

merciful[4] - to be prone to charitably and compassionately extend as much tender concession, forbearance, leniency or tolerance to another person as can be allowed without robbing equal and honorable justice under virtuous law

merciful[5] - to be prone to charitably and compassionately extend as much tender concession, forbearance, leniency or tolerance to another person as I would have them extend to me if their words or actions were mine

merciful[6] - to be prone to refuse to be abusive, cruel and hard-hearted

merciless - to be prone, in harmony with good conscience and righteous judgment, to refuse to be corruptly or grievously unjust in emancipating, freeing, liberating or releasing someone

merciless[2] - to be prone, in harmony with good conscience and righteous judgment, to refuse to be corruptly or grievously unjust in absolving, acquitting, exonerating, forgiving, palliating, pardoning or vindicating someone

merciless[3] - to be prone, in harmony with good conscience and righteous judgment, to refuse to be corruptly or grievously unjust in excusing, expiating, extenuating or justifying someone

mercurial - to be animated or vivacious

meritorious - to be truly worthy of high esteem, honor, praise or reward

merry - to be filled with festive and healthy cheerfulness, gaiety, happiness or merriment through healthy association with good company

merrymaking - to intend to arouse, evoke or participate in festive and healthy cheerfulness, gaiety, happiness or merriment through healthy association with good company

Messianist - to be prone to personally ascertain and live in harmony with the discernibly enlightening and spiritually verifiable promises, prophecies or testimonies given by God's ancient and modern prophets that the Lord Jesus Christ is the divine Anointed One who will return to the earth in glory to justly deliver the repentant righteous, to justly destroy the unrepentant wicked, and to personally reign in righteous glory upon this renewed and paradisiacally glorified earth

Messianist[2] - to be prone to personally ascertain and live in harmony with the discernibly enlightening and spiritually verifiable promises, prophecies or testimonies given by God's ancient prophets that a divine Anointed One shall come to personally reign in righteous glory upon the earth

messianist - to be virtuously Messianist

metaethical - to be prone to personally ascertain and live in harmony with the mind and will of God

metaethical[2] - to be prone to identify and then willfully think, speak and act in harmony with those thoughts, beliefs, values and characteristics which produce, preserve or restore the greatest true enlightenment, virtue, integrity, liberty, hope, peace and joy within me, my family and society

meticulous - to be prone to pay enough precise and thorough attention to those details by which I can produce, preserve or restore the greatest true enlightenment, virtue, integrity, liberty, hope, peace and joy within me, my family and society

meticulous[2] - to be prone to pay enough attention to details

mettlesome - to be valiant
Micronesian - to be prone to live in harmony with the ways of Micronesian character or culture which produce, preserve or restore true enlightenment, virtue and integrity within me, my family and society
Middle Eastern - to be prone to live in harmony with the ways of Middle Eastern character or culture which produce, preserve or restore true enlightenment, virtue and integrity within me, my family and society
mild - to be peaceable
militaristic - to be prepared for and skilled in warfare against the evil or satanic powers of darkness, vice, corruption, bondage, despair, turmoil and misery
militaristic^2 - to be prepared for and skilled in warfare against that which destroys the virtuously liberating freedom, health, honorable economic prosperity and steady progress of me, my family and society
mind-expanding - to intend to impart or seek greater intelligence
miraculous - to be prone to prayerfully invoke wonderfully good blessings or works beyond the human power of faithless duplication, which justly and mercifully come to me by the perfect grace, love, power and will of God by my faithfully repentant and honorably exact obedience to those divinely appointed commandments, covenants, laws and ordinances upon which the bringing forth of those blessings or works is predicated

miraculous^2 - to be a man who faithfully uses true priesthood authority and power from God to worthily bring forth in behalf of other faithful people wonderfully good blessings or works of God which are expedient in Him, which are beyond the human power of faithless duplication
miraculous^3 - to be prone to faithfully, prayerfully and worthily receive wonderfully good blessings or works of God which people might otherwise seek to imitate but are otherwise powerless to produce
mirthful - to be prone to enjoy enough of the high excitement and merriment of good and joyful company
missionary - to be called of God and given His authority to lovingly encourage and kindly help other people to honorably investigate for themselves whether God will manifest and verify to their minds and hearts an absolute, perfect and spiritually verified personal knowledge of the truthfulness of His message by personal enlightenment, inspiration or revelation from Him, by using the same means I have used to do so
missionary^2 - to be called of God and given His authority to lovingly encourage and kindly help other people to honorably investigate for themselves whether God will manifest to their minds and hearts by the power of the Holy Ghost which religious organization they should join, by using the same means I have used to do so
missionary^3 - to be called of God and given His authority to assist in His work of charitably, justly,

rightly and wisely serving the needs of humankind on Earth
missionary[4] - to be called of God and given His authority to assist in His work for a certain time and in a certain place
missionary[5] - to be prone to share or teach a belief, ideology, philosophy or religion which truly produces, preserves or restores greater true enlightenment, virtue, integrity, liberty, hope, peace and joy within me, my family and society
mitigating - to intend to alleviate, diminish, moderate, reduce or soften pain, penalty or punishment in harmony with circumstances which should, in equity, fairness and mercy, be considered as part of righteous judgment
modeling - to intend, without being paid to do so, to provide an excellent example or pattern of good character worthy of imitation
moderate - to be prone to keep my thoughts, words and actions integrated within the safe and discernibly enlightened boundaries of chastity, cleanliness, purity and virtue which God has justly set by law and commandment
moderate[2] - to be satisfied with receiving enough
moderate[3] - to be well-balanced
modern - to be virtuously up-to-date
modest - to be prone to keep my thoughts, words and actions integrated within the safe and discernibly enlightened boundaries of chastity, cleanliness, purity and virtue which God has justly set by law and commandment

modest[2] - to be prone to exercise honorable humility, reserve and self-restraint
modest[3] - to be reasonably and wisely discreet or moderate
mollifying - to be a girl or woman who is more delicate and soft rather than more hard or tough in disposition or temperament
monocultural - to be godly enough to be made truly chaste, clean, pure and virtuous at heart—and to continue to encourage and help other people by charitable love, kindness, invitation and instruction to be godly enough to be made truly chaste, clean, pure and virtuous at heart
monocultural[2] - to be prone to live in harmony with the one best culture known to me
monotonous - to be prone to refuse to falter or waver from a condition, course, place or position I have ascertained is most pleasing unto God
monotonous[2] - to be prone to choose to do and be that which is truly good and of God and to refuse to erratically swing between that which is truly good and of God and that which is evil or satanic
moral - to be godly or spiritually righteous enough to be made truly chaste, clean, pure and virtuous in the sight of God
moral[2] - to be virtuously ethical
Mormon - to be prone to live in harmony with the teachings of The Church of Jesus Christ of Latter-day Saints (or LDS Church) which produce, preserve or restore true enlightenment, virtue and integrity within me, my family and society

mortal - to be prone to prepare myself to meet God in His final judgment of my earthly works and desires following my physical death and one-time resurrection

mortifying - to intend to rely upon faithful, timely and true repentance, healthy abstinence, humble prayer, believing and honorably exact obedience to God, and willing fasting and sacrifice in order to effectively subdue or subjugate all thoughts of corruptly pleasing or sinfully satisfying any of my biologically inherent and naturally impelling emotional, physical or sexual appetites, cravings, desires, drives or passions

Mosaic - to be prone to live in harmony with the teachings of the prophet Moses which produce, preserve or restore true enlightenment, virtue and integrity within me, my family and society

Mosaic^2 - to be prone to live in harmony with the teachings of Judaism which produce, preserve or restore true enlightenment, virtue and integrity within me, my family and society

mothering - to be a woman who is motherly

motherly - to be a virtuous woman who does the very best I can to understand, do, be and teach that which produces, preserves or restores the greatest true enlightenment, virtue, integrity, liberty, hope, peace and joy within me, my family and society, and to do my very best to help my sons and daughters understand, do, be and teach the same

motherly^2 - to be a virtuous woman who does the very best I can to avoid doing or being that which produces, preserves or restores darkness, vice and corruption within me, my family and society, and to do my very best to help my sons and daughters avoid the same

motherly^3 - to be a virtuous woman worthy of dignity, esteem or reverence due to the loving and tender care, good character development, discipline, guidance, instruction, nurturing and protection I offer to children, especially my own

mourning - to be penitent

mourning^2 - to be with and strengthen a friend, neighbor or relative to help them deal with the death, harm, illness, injury, pain or suffering of a loved one

movable - to be and to choose to remain excited, inspired, motivated or stirred by that which is truly good and of God

movie-making - to intend to compose, create, make, perform or produce good and uplifting motion pictures

movie-watching - to intend to cultivate a sensitive appreciation for good and uplifting motion pictures

moving - to intend to actively express or fulfill my chosen designs, desires, dispositions, intentions or plans to produce, preserve or restore true enlightenment, virtue and integrity within me, my family and society

mulling - to be meditating or pondering about spiritual things

multifarious - to be universal

mundane - to be down-to-earth

munificent - to be prone to kindly, liberally, nobly, unselfishly and wisely give, serve or share as much or as well as I can and should for the virtuously liberating freedom, health, honorable economic prosperity and steady progress of me, my family and society

murmurless - to be prone to refuse to be grumbling or murmuring

muscular - to be prone to develop and maintain strong enough muscles to remain fit or healthy in body and mind

musical - to be prone to cultivate a sensitive appreciation for good and uplifting music

musical[2] - to be prone to compose, create, make, perform or produce good and uplifting music

musing - to intend to contemplate, meditate or ponder spiritual things

mutual - to be mutualistic

mutualistic - to be prone to associate with one or more other people to an extent or in a manner which produces improvement in both or all of us, our families and society

mystical - to be spiritually-minded

N

narrow-minded - to be prone to narrowly limit or restrict the active thoughts of my mind and the thoughts, beliefs, values and characteristics of my heart to those which produce, preserve or restore true enlightenment, virtue and integrity within me, my family and society

narrow-minded[2] - to be prone to narrowly limit or restrict from the active thoughts of my mind and from the thoughts, beliefs, values and characteristics of my heart

those which produce, preserve or restore darkness, vice and corruption within me, my family and society

nationalistic - to be prone to live in harmony with the ways of my nation's character or culture which produce, preserve or restore true enlightenment, virtue and integrity within me, my family and society

nationalistic[2] - to be virtuously patriotic within and toward my good and honorable nation

nationalistic[3] - to be prone to honor, obey and sustain the good law of my nation

native - to be prone to live in harmony with the ways of indigenous or native character or culture which produce, preserve or restore true enlightenment, virtue and integrity within me, my family and society

natural - to be prone to live in virtuous harmony with natural law or the laws of God which govern nature

negotiating - to intend to creatively and honestly seek an agreement or settlement of good and mutually beneficial terms with one or more other people

neighborly - to be prone to do good to my fellow human beings

neighborly[2] - to be prone to do good to those who live in my neighborhood

neighborly[3] - to be prone to treat other people in the same manner in which I would like them to treat me if their words or actions were mine

nerdy - to be intelligently devoted to less popular interests or pursuits

nervous - to be anxious or distressed enough about all of the corrupt, sinful or vicious wrongdoing within me to faithfully and immediately seek true and complete repentance, obedience and reconciliation to God

networking - to intend to build and share honorable working relationships with other people of true enlightenment, virtue and integrity

newsworthy - to be virtuously notable

nice - to be virtuous

nice[2] - to be courteous, kind and mannerly

nifty - to be remarkably good

nimble - to be enlightened or intelligent enough to alertly perceive and quickly understand

noble - to be exalted

noble[2] - to be celestial

noble[3] - to be godly enough to be made truly chaste, clean, pure and virtuous at heart—and to continue to encourage and help other people by charitable love, kindness, invitation and instruction to be godly enough to be made truly chaste, clean, pure and virtuous at heart

noble[4] - to be one of those who are most dignified and honorable in thought, speech and behavior

noble-minded - to be noble in my thinking

nominalistic - to be prone to personally ascertain and live in harmony with the discernibly enlightening and spiritually verifiable truth that: facts, life, people, objects and other realities continue to exist with or without the names, words or word symbols

people use to characterize, describe or represent them

nominating - to intend to propose only enlightened, virtuous and wise people for appointment or election to public office

noncombatant - to be prone to refuse to kill other people in forceful or physical military battle—in a truly conscientious effort to retain a remission of my sins or complete reconciliation with God

noncombatant[2] - to be prone to refuse to viciously initiate deadly battle

noncombatant[3] - to be prone to refuse to be viciously combatant

nonsecular - to be prone to refuse to be viciously secular

North American - to be prone to live in harmony with the ways of North American character or culture which produce, preserve or restore true enlightenment, virtue and integrity within me, my family and society

nostalgic - to be prone to ponder people, places or things dear to my memory

notable - to be distinguished

notable[2] - to be prone to produce, preserve or restore enough true enlightenment, virtue and integrity within me, my family and society to unintentionally draw admiring attention or observation from other people

notable[3] - to be prone to perform in such an outstanding, remarkable or memorable manner as to unintentionally draw admiring attention or observation from other people

noteworthy - to be virtuously notable

nourished - to be prone to maintain the necessary spiritual enlightenment, strength or support to sustain my spiritual life, health or improvement

nourished[2] - to be prone to maintain the necessary physical nutriment, strength or support to sustain my physical life and health as long as I can

nourishing - to intend to share with another person the care, confidence, education, encouragement, enlightenment, love, strength or support necessary to sustain their progress or improvement toward purely virtuous character and ultimate well-being

nourishing[2] - to intend to feed, foster, keep alive or nurture another person by imparting to them from my supply or surplus the necessary physical nutriment, strength or support to sustain their physical life and health to the fullest extent I can and should, and whenever I am prompted to do so by the Spirit of God

numerical - to be knowledgeable and skilled enough with numbers to accurately observe their application in reality and to put them to good use in daily life

nursing - to be a girl or woman who provides care, education or nourishment to one or more children

nursing[2] - to be a girl or woman who breast feeds my milk to an infant in need of my nourishment

nursing[3] - to intend to care for, nourish or otherwise minister to someone who is ill or otherwise in need

nursing[4] - to be virtuously medical or medicating as a nurse

nursing[5] - to intend to foster, influence or manage true personal betterment, improvement or progress within me, my family and society

nurturing - to intend to build, develop, encourage, nourish, support or sustain purely virtuous character in myself

nurturing[2] - to be warmly nourishing toward another person

nymphal - to be a girl or woman who strives to be beautifully and graciously ladylike

O

obedient - to be prone to willingly conform to, comply with, follow, keep, observe and remember the commandments, covenants, laws and ordinances of God

obedient[2] - to be prone to prove—by the abundance of my righteous desires and my abundant labors of sacrifice to produce, preserve or restore good works of faith in the Lord Jesus Christ—that my will is to conform to, comply with, follow, keep, observe and remember the commandments, covenants, laws and ordinances of God

obedient[3] - to be prone to willingly conform to, comply with, follow, keep, observe and remember the admonitions, commandments and teachings of goodly parents

obedient[4] - to be prone to willingly conform to, comply with, follow, keep, observe and remember the teachings of God's duly appointed,

authorized and empowered
servants on Earth
obedient[5] - to be prone to prove I
am willing to conform to, comply
with, follow, keep, observe and
remember a good standard by the
sacrifices I make to do so
obedient[6] - to be prone to conform
to, comply with, follow, keep or
observe the good law of the land
objective - to be prone to render a
truly honorable and just decision or
judgment by deciding or judging in
harmony with the personal
enlightenment, inspiration,
prompting or revelation which has
previously come to me from God
into the stored thoughts of my
mind and into the thoughts, beliefs,
values and characteristics of my
heart
objective[2] - to be prone to decide or
judge the truthfulness or value of
what is presented to the active
thoughts of my mind by recalling
and relying upon those truly
virtuous thoughts which have
previously come into the stored
thoughts of my mind and into the
thoughts, beliefs, values and
characteristics of my heart, and
which induce me to reach a truly
honorable and just decision or
judgment
objective[3] - to be prone to decide or
judge the truthfulness or value of
what is presented to the active
thoughts of my mind by forsaking
and withstanding the influence of
those vicious thoughts which have
previously come into the stored
thoughts of my mind or into the
thoughts, beliefs, values and
characteristics of my heart, and

which induce me to reach a vicious
decision or judgment
objective[4] - to be prone to decide or
judge in harmony with legal
precedent or with another standard
or value, provided that precedent,
standard or value produces,
preserves or restores true
enlightenment, virtue, integrity,
liberty, hope, peace and joy within
me, my family and society
objective[5] - to be prone to decide or
judge in accordance with a legal
precedent, standard or value while
attempting to ascertain the virtue
of my decision or judgment, and
while deliberately allowing my
decision or judgment to be
reviewed by my good conscience
observant - to be prone to take care
to alertly and quickly notice,
perceive and understand spiritual
things
observing - to intend to constantly
choose to pay close enough
attention to manifestations of
spiritual things
Occidental - to be prone to live in
harmony with the ways of
American or European character or
culture which produce, preserve or
restore true enlightenment, virtue
and integrity within me, my family
and society
occult - to be prone to conceal or
hide from the public those good,
true and sacred things which could
otherwise be viciously abused,
defiled, desecrated, destroyed or
ridiculed by other people
Oceanian - to be prone to live in
harmony with the ways of
Oceanian character or culture
which produce, preserve or restore
true enlightenment, virtue and

integrity within me, my family and society

OK - to be reliably good

OK^2 - to be healthy

old-fashioned - to be virtuously mature

old-fashioned^2 - to be polished

old-fashioned^3 - to be practical

old-fashioned^4 - to be prone to follow and preserve the best-known and time-proven means and methods of caution, discretion, moderation and thrift

old-school - to be practical

old-school^2 - to be prone to follow and preserve the best-known and time-proven means and methods of caution, discretion, moderation and thrift

omnific - to be omnificent

omnificent - to be prone to personally ascertain and live in harmony with the discernibly enlightening and spiritually verifiable truth that: God the Eternal Father has complete or universal creative power which He wields upon principles of righteousness and within the bounds of eternal law, and desires that His children, heirs, offspring, posterity or seed do all we must do to become perfectly like Him in this characteristic

omnipotent - to be prone to personally ascertain and live in harmony with the discernibly enlightening and spiritually verifiable truth that: God the Eternal Father has complete or universal power which He wields upon principles of righteousness and within the bounds of eternal law, and desires that His children, heirs, offspring, posterity or seed do all we must do to become perfectly like Him in this characteristic

omnipresent - to be prone to personally ascertain and live in harmony with the discernibly enlightening and spiritually verifiable truth that: God the Eternal Father has the capability of projecting His spiritual awareness or influence into all places at all times, and desires that His children, heirs, offspring, posterity or seed do all we must do to become perfectly like Him in this characteristic

omniscient - to be prone to personally ascertain and live in harmony with the discernibly enlightening and spiritually verifiable truth that: God the Eternal Father has an absolute and perfect knowledge of all things, and desires that His children, heirs, offspring, posterity or seed do all we must do to become perfectly like Him in this characteristic

one - to be as one with God by being godly enough to be made truly chaste, clean, pure and virtuous at heart—and by continuing to encourage and help other people by charitable love, kindness, invitation and instruction to be godly enough to be made truly chaste, clean, pure and virtuous at heart

one^2 - to be as one with God by being one of the many pure-in-heart who are filled with that liberating integrity which comes from increasing true enlightenment and from an increasing abundance of truly virtuous thoughts, words, actions, deeds or works

one[3] - to be as one with God by thinking, speaking and acting without darkness, vice and corruption

one[4] - to be as one with God by thinking, speaking and acting in harmony with the dictates of my enlightened conscience

one[5] - to be ascertaining, discerning, enlightened and virtuously integrated enough to become or remain virtuously Zionistic with one or more other people who are and do likewise

one[6] - to be ascertaining, discerning, enlightened and virtuously integrated enough to become or remain virtuously single-minded and single-hearted with one or more other people who are and do likewise

one-upping - to intend to seek a better personal achievement or performance than I have previously attained

open-eyed - to be carefully discerning and vigilant

open-handed - to be prone to actively, charitably, generously and wisely give, serve or share as much or as well as I can and should for the virtuously liberating freedom, health, honorable economic prosperity and steady progress of other people

open-hearted - to be prone to willingly harbor, hold, keep, retain or store within my heart certain active or stored thoughts of my mind which I know or have good enough reason to believe will produce, preserve or restore greater true enlightenment, virtue, integrity, liberty, hope, peace and joy within me, my family and society

open-hearted[2] - to be prone to actively, charitably, generously and wisely give, serve or share as much or as well as I can and should for the virtuously liberating freedom, health, honorable economic prosperity and steady progress of me, my family and society

open-minded - to be prone to eagerly seek greater true enlightenment, intelligence or wisdom

open-minded[2] - to be prone to entertain, harbor, hold or pay attention to active thoughts of my mind long enough and well enough to discover which ones will likely produce, preserve or restore greater true enlightenment, virtue, integrity, liberty, hope, peace and joy within the thoughts, beliefs, values and characteristics of my heart

open-minded[3] - to be prone to pay enough careful and impartial attention to arguments, evidence, ideas, information, opinions or other thoughts to accurately and clearly discern and reason their true value

open-minded[4] - to be prone to refuse to be bigoted

open-minded[5] - to be prone to refuse to be selfish

optimistic - to be prone to personally ascertain and live in harmony with the discernibly enlightening and spiritually verifiable truth that: God is bound by the eternally binding law of justice, and He is thus bound to eventually grant me exaltation with its everlasting and glorious

rewards by my faithfully repentant and honorably exact obedience to those divinely appointed commandments, covenants, laws and ordinances upon which receipt of those blessings is predicated
optimistic[2] - to be prone to personally ascertain and live in harmony with the discernibly enlightening and spiritually verifiable truth that: good shall ultimately triumph over evil, and true enlightenment, virtue and integrity shall ultimately be rewarded
optimistic[3] - to be prone to confidently perform in an honorable and virtuous manner which will likely improve my praiseworthy success
optimizing - to intend to constantly choose to bring out and build upon the best within me
optimizing[2] - to intend to constantly choose to actively, charitably, generously and wisely do all I can and should to help other people build upon and bring out the best within them
optimizing[3] - to intend to make the best use of resources
ordained - to be a baptized, confirmed and worthy man who has been truly called of God by prophecy to receive by my covenant with God true higher priesthood authority and office from God by the laying on of hands of one or more of God's own called, ordained and authorized priesthood leaders, and to then use my true higher priesthood authority from God and authorization from those priesthood leaders to serve in a

faithfully righteous manner which divinely empowers me to do God's binding work of blessing and preparing His willing and obedient children for exaltation in the world to come, and which divinely empowers me to receive fulfillment of God's oath to me of all of the blessings of heaven for doing so
ordained[2] - to be a man who is one of those who has received the true higher priesthood of God and, with it, the promise of eternal blessings which shall come to those of us who faithfully and righteously continue to keep our covenant to wield our priesthood authority and power in the name of Jesus Christ to uphold truth and virtue, to bless the lives of our wives, our posterity, our ancestors, and all other people, to preach the commandments, covenants, laws and ordinances of the gospel of the Lord Jesus Christ, to administer, as authorized, in its holy ordinances on Earth, and to thus help God prepare His willing and obedient children for exaltation in the world to come
ordained[3] - to be a man who has worthily received true higher priesthood ordination, office and authority from God through God's true priesthood representatives on Earth
ordained[4] - to be a boy or man who has worthily received true lesser or preparatory priesthood ordination, office and authority from God through God's true priesthood representatives on Earth
ordained[5] - to be foreordained to receive God's authority and power to fulfill a specific mission or

purpose on Earth by my faithfully repentant and honorably exact obedience to those divinely appointed commandments, covenants, laws and ordinances upon which receipt of that blessing is predicated

ordaining - to be a duly ordained man called of God who, by the laying on of hands, uses true priesthood authority from God and authorization from God's own called, ordained and authorized priesthood leaders on Earth to give true priesthood authority and office from God, without pay, to another baptized, confirmed and worthy boy or man called of God by prophesy—so that he who is ordained can then receive enough authority and power from God in faithful righteousness to do God's binding work of blessing and preparing God's willing and obedient children for exaltation in the world to come, and can then receive the blessings of heaven which can come to him from doing so

ordaining[2] - to be a duly ordained man called of God, who then uses my true higher priesthood authority from God and authorization from God's own called, ordained and authorized priesthood leaders on Earth to administer, without pay, in a dedicated holy temple of God the priesthood ordinance of higher priesthood ordination by the laying on of hands upon living male proxy who act in behalf of deceased men whose preliminary temple work of baptism and confirmation has been done—so

that those deceased men who are desirous and righteous enough to receive the ordinance work done for them can then receive enough authority and power from God in faithful righteousness to do God's binding work of blessing and preparing for exaltation in the world to come all of His willing and obedient children who are deceased, and can then receive the blessings of heaven which can come to them from doing so

ordaining[3] - to be a duly ordained man called of God, who then uses my true priesthood authority from God and authorization from God's own called, ordained and authorized priesthood leaders on Earth to administer, without pay, priesthood ordination and to pronounce its office and authority upon a worthy boy or man using a manner, method or mode of ordination which I have ascertained by personal enlightenment, inspiration or revelation from God is recognized by God as authorized and binding on Earth and in heaven

ordering - to intend to methodically or systematically produce, preserve or restore true enlightenment, virtue and integrity within me, my family and society

ordering[2] - to intend to methodically or systematically remove darkness, vice, corruption, bondage, despair, turmoil and misery from within me, my family and society

ordering[3] - to intend to methodically or systematically overcome chaos and confusion

orderly - to be prone to carefully speak or act in harmony with that which produces, preserves or restores true enlightenment, virtue and integrity within me, my family and society
orderly[2] - to be prone to carefully resist darkness, vice and corruption
orderly[3] - to be prone to carefully resist anarchy, chaos, confusion and darkness
Oriental - to be prone to live in harmony with the ways of Asian character or culture which produce, preserve or restore true enlightenment, virtue and integrity within me, my family and society
oriented - to be fully aware of my direction, condition, location and time
orienting - to intend to better adjust my direction, condition, location or time
original - to be prone to personally ascertain and live in harmony with the discernibly enlightening and spiritually verifiable truth that: no other person can be the selfsame person I truly am, was and will become in body, mind and spirit
original[2] - to be prone to use clever imagination and skill to independently devise, invent, organize or produce new and better means or methods of producing, preserving or restoring greater true enlightenment, virtue, integrity, liberty, hope, peace and joy within me, my family and society
orthodox - to be prone to live in harmony with the commandments, covenants, laws and ordinances of God

orthodox[2] - to be prone to think, speak and act in harmony with those religious thoughts, beliefs, values and characteristics which produce, preserve or restore the greatest true enlightenment, virtue, integrity, liberty, hope, peace and joy within me, my family and society
ostracizing - to intend to banish, exclude, reject or separate from power every person who is justly found guilty of striving to leverage or translate a renowned reputation or a position of power into a selfish seizure of tyrannical power or into the destruction of true enlightenment, virtue and integrity within me, my family and society
ostracizing[2] - to intend to banish, exclude, reject or separate another person from confidence, esteem, friendship, honor, leadership or trust whose works produce, preserve or restore darkness, vice and corruption within me, my family and society, and who fails or refuses to repent
outdoing - to intend to progress by improving upon my best previous performance
outgoing - to intend to think, speak and act well enough to be one of those who are filled with true enlightenment, virtue and integrity
outliving - to intend to constantly choose to dispel or withstand evil, come what may
outshining - to be more shining than I was before
outsmarting - to intend to surpass the mental performance of a criminal, deadly or evil enemy of society in order to defeat or withstand them

out-sourcing - to intend to advocate, favor or seek to preserve a government which orders or provides the necessary means to successfully help law-abiding and hard-working citizens make necessary life-sustaining transitions to adequate jobs when they suffer loss of employment in industries damaged or destroyed by my country's bargain-priced foreign labor purchases

outstanding - to be prominently good

overachieving - to intend to accomplish or produce more good results than expected

overcoming - to intend to persist in my struggle against darkness, vice and corruption until I absolutely conquer, defeat, overpower, overwhelm, prevail or win

overjoyed - to be extremely joyful

overqualified - to be accomplished, competent and educated enough to meet honorable limits, requirements or restrictions of eligibility, fitness or qualification, and then some

overrating - to intend to actively, charitably, generously and wisely assign a capable and responsible person a position or ranking within a particular class, grade, job or rank which is better or higher than is truly earned in order to give them the opportunity to live up to the good, uplifting and probably deserved belief, confidence, reliance or trust I have placed in them

overrating[2] - to intend to actively, charitably, generously and wisely esteem, regard and treat another person as the more excellent and progressive person they can and should become, and to thus give them the inspiring confidence, the uplifting encouragement and the elevating opportunity to live up to such esteem, regard and treatment as long as they do so

overthrowing - to intend to terminate or throw down the evil or satanic powers of darkness, vice and corruption within me, my family and society

owning - to intend to accept, acknowledge or confess responsibility for something I said or did wrong, when I have not yet made it right

P

pacesetting - to intend to consistently progress by improving the enlightenment and virtue of the thoughts I continue to integrate into the thoughts, beliefs, values and characteristics of my heart

pained - to be prone to courageously continue to faithfully prove my believing and honorably exact obedience to God in the face of necessary or unavoidable mental, physical or spiritual distress, grief or suffering

pained[2] - to be prone to experience or recognize enough acute mental, physical or spiritual distress, grief or suffering from all of the corrupt, sinful or vicious wrongdoing within me to faithfully and immediately seek true and complete repentance, obedience and reconciliation to God

painstaking - to intend to make careful and diligent effort to do good

painting - to intend to actively, charitably, generously and wisely esteem, regard and treat another person as the more excellent and progressive person they can and should become, and to thus give them the inspiring confidence, the uplifting encouragement and the elevating opportunity to live up to such esteem, regard and treatment as long as they do so

painting[2] - to intend to ascertain and then accurately and clearly state the truly positive character, condition, influence, merit, power, quality, strength, value or worth of someone or something

pampering - to intend to generously coddle and feed an infant until the infant is delightfully gratified

paradisiacal - to be exalted

paradisiacal[2] - to be celestial

paradisiacal[3] - to be bound for the realm of righteous spirits awaiting the resurrection

paradisiacal[4] - to be prone to strive for an everlasting condition of true enlightenment, virtue and integrity within me, my family and society

paradisiacal[5] - to be prone to establish or reach a terrestrial place of true beauty, happiness, peace and plenty

paradoxical - to be prone to think, speak and act to an extent or in a manner which seems in popular thinking to be contrary to that which is charitably loving, just, right and wise in the sight of God, but is not

pardonable - to be made worthy of redemption unto exaltation

pardonable[2] - to be made worthy of redemption and release from the bondage, burdens and debts of my sins

pardonable[3] - to be and to be found blameless, guiltless or innocent in harmony with the good law of the land

pardoned - to be redeemed unto exaltation

pardoned[2] - to be redeemed and released from the bondage, burdens and debts of my sins

pardoned[3] - to be and to be found truly innocent

parenting - to intend to cooperate with my lawfully and legally wedded husband or wife in doing my very best to discipline, educate, nurture and train our lawfully and legally adopted or naturally born child or children toward becoming a family of redeemed and exalted beings

parenting[2] - to intend to cooperate with my lawfully and legally wedded husband or wife in doing my very best to discipline, educate, nurture and train our lawfully and legally adopted or naturally born child or children toward greater true enlightenment, virtue, integrity, liberty, hope, peace and joy

parenting[3] - to intend to cooperate with my lawfully and legally wedded husband or wife in doing my very best to discipline, educate, nurture and train our lawfully and legally adopted or naturally born child or children into capable, responsible and self-reliant net contributors to the virtuously liberating freedom, health, honorable economic prosperity and steady progress of me, my family and society

parenting[4] - to intend, as someone forced to be a single parent or guardian, to do my very best to adequately clothe, discipline, educate, enrich, feed, house, nurture and train up my children

parliamentary - to be prone to advocate, favor or seek to preserve government which consists of a democratically elected and virtuous supreme legislative body which grants executive power to a cabinet composed of some of the good, wise and honest members of that body

particular - to be prone to pay enough careful attention to important details

partisan - to be prone to promote factional disintegration, division or divisiveness when necessary to produce, preserve or restore greater true enlightenment, virtue and integrity within me, my family and society

partnering - to intend, once I am lawfully and legally wedded to my husband or wife, to combine and share all we have or may yet have for the mutually beneficial purpose of producing, preserving or restoring the greatest true enlightenment, virtue, integrity, liberty, hope, peace and joy within both of us, within our family and within society

partnering^2 - to intend, once I am lawfully and legally wedded to my husband or wife, to treat them to an extent or in a manner which recognizes the equally important and complimentary God-given family roles of a husband and a wife who both remain fully dedicated to the virtuously liberating freedom, health, honorable economic prosperity and

steady progress of one another, our family and society

party-line - to be prone to adhere to political party policies, practices or principles which produce, preserve or restore greater true enlightenment, virtue, integrity, liberty, hope, peace and joy within me, my family and society

passionate - to be prone to allow or cause myself to be easily aroused or moved to desires, emotions, feelings or passions which are truly good and of God

passionate^2 - to be prone to allow or cause myself to be easily aroused or moved to positive desires, emotions, feelings or passions

pastoral - to be prone, as a teacher, to fulfill my responsibility for the enlightenment of my students

paternal - to be a man who is fatherly

pathfinding - to intend to locate and follow the path which leads to redemption and exaltation

patient - to be prone to diligently, faithfully and hopefully persevere toward and to calmly await good, achievable results, while facing adversity, delay, disappointment, opposition, pain, suffering and the temptation to give up

patient^2 - to be prone to calmly and meekly bear, endure or suffer necessary or unavoidable pain, strain, stress or trial without murmuring

patient^3 - to be prone to refuse to be excessively or needlessly hasty or uneasy under adversity, delay, disappointment, opposition, pain, suffering or the temptation to give up patient[4] - to be prone to deal with or handle pain, strain, stress or trial without becoming excessively or needlessly distressed or disturbed

patriarchal - to be the exemplary and oldest living son of the lineage of my fathers and a married man who holds the true higher priesthood of God and faithfully exercises my God-given authority and jurisdiction to righteously preside in my family, and, along with my wife to whom I am sealed, to forever spiritually govern or rule in faithful righteousness over our worthy unmarried sons and daughters and over our worthy married sons, grandsons, great-grandsons and so forth, by our faithfully repentant and honorably exact obedience to those divinely appointed commandments, covenants, laws and ordinances upon which receipt of that blessing is predicated

patriarchal[2] - to be a married man who holds the true higher priesthood of God and who faithfully exercises my God-given authority and jurisdiction to righteously preside in my family, and, along with my wife to whom I am sealed, to forever spiritually govern or rule in faithful righteousness over our worthy unmarried sons and daughters and over our worthy married sons, grandsons, great-grandsons and so forth, by our faithfully repentant and honorably exact obedience to those divinely appointed commandments, covenants, laws and ordinances upon which receipt of that blessing is predicated

patriarchal[3] - to be a husband who exercises my God-given authority and full partnership with my wife within our family in faithful righteousness

patriarchal[4] - to be a man who is fatherly

patriarchal[5] - to be a duly ordained man called of God by prophesy to receive true higher priesthood authority by the laying on of hands of one of God's own called, ordained and authorized priesthood leaders to act in the higher priesthood office of patriarch and to pronounce by the laying on of hands and by enlightenment, inspiration or revelation from God the actual spiritual lineage of another person and a blessing containing guidelines and revelations which can help that person fulfill their foreordained purposes and pursue their righteous journey home to the glorious celestial presence of God

patriotic - to be virtuously governing

patriotic[2] - to be prone to honor, revere and sustain government officials who seek to enact, enforce and interpret good laws for the virtuously liberating freedom, health, honorable economic prosperity and steady progress of ourselves, our families and society

patriotic[3] - to be prone to grant government authority or political power to that group, organization, party or person who is good, honest, knowledgeable, skilled and wise enough in human conditions, economies, events, governments, histories, laws and values to wield government authority and political power to an extent or in a manner which produces, preserves or restores the greatest true enlightenment, virtue, integrity, liberty, hope, peace and joy within me, within my family and within a consequently and increasingly integrated, liberated and united society

patriotic[4] - to be prone to faithfully continue to exercise my personal freedom and my right to wield personal civic authority and political power to defend, protect, preserve and sustain the constitutional right of all law-abiding citizens to equal access to the decent and orderly expression of their personal religious views in or on property owned by our local, state and national governments, while recognizing that a government prohibited by its own constitution from prohibiting the free exercise of religion cannot and must not fail or refuse to permanently allow its law-abiding citizens at least some recurrent form of decent and orderly expression or worship in or on such property wherever that constitution is lawfully and legally binding

patriotic[5] - to be prone to refuse to attempt to entirely cut off or eliminate a particular law-abiding antireligious, irreligious, nonreligious, religious or unreligious congregation, organization or person from wielding influence or persuasion in the public forum when they form no conspiracy and make no attempt to infringe upon the natural rights of other people, no

attempt to exert, seize or wield exclusive or sovereign power to govern or rule, and no attempt to destroy duly elected representative government, and especially when their influence or persuasion calls for the production, preservation or restoration of true enlightenment, virtue and integrity within me, my family and society

patriotic[6] - to be prone to faithfully continue to exercise my personal freedom and my right to wield personal civic authority and political power to make provision for every fellow law-abiding citizen's decent and orderly expression of their personal influence or persuasion in the public forum

patriotic[7] - to be prone to maintain my loyalty to my local, state and national governments and to honor, obey and sustain their laws as long as those laws protect me, my family and society in our combined efforts to form a society more perfectly united in virtue, to establish equal and honorable justice under virtuous law, to exercise enough peacemaking at home and abroad, to sustain our common defense, to promote our shared progress and well-being, and to thereby secure the blessings of liberty to ourselves, our families and our posterity

patriotic[8] - to be prone to faithfully continue to exercise my personal freedom and my right to wield personal civic authority and political power to defend, protect, preserve and sustain my good local, state and national governments against those who

would destroy the freedom, independence or liberty of its law-abiding citizens to produce, preserve or restore true enlightenment, virtue, integrity, liberty, hope, peace and joy within ourselves, our families and society
patriotic[9] - to be prone to faithfully continue to exercise my personal freedom and my right to wield personal civic authority and political power to defend, protect, preserve and sustain my good local, state and national governments against those who might otherwise heap some form of persecution upon one or more law-abiding residents
patriotic[10] - to be prone to faithfully continue to exercise my personal freedom and my right to wield personal civic authority and political power to defend, protect, preserve and sustain my good local, state and national governments against those who demand either the exclusive, permanent and unlimited expression of their own choice of religious or other views in the public forum or the denial of some or all of their fellow law-abiding citizens' equal access to the decent and orderly expression of their religious or other views in the public forum
patriotic[11] - to be prone to faithfully continue to exercise my personal freedom and my right to wield personal civic authority and political power to defend, protect, preserve and sustain my good local, state and national governments against those who seek an unconstitutional

government endorsement or establishment of a particular state religion that gives a particular church, congregation, group, organization, party or person—alone—the supreme right of exclusive, permanent and unlimited expression of their own choice of antireligious, irreligious, nonreligious, religious or unreligious views in or on property owned by our local, state or national governments
patriotic[12] - to be prone to faithfully continue to exercise my personal freedom and my right to wield personal civic authority and political power to defend, protect, preserve and sustain my good local, state and national governments against believers in any one religious authority, denomination, hierarchy or organization from seizing exclusive or sovereign power to impose evil favoritism toward believers, evil discrimination against unbelievers, evil exoneration of believers who are wrongdoers, misjudgment against unbelievers who are innocent, the destruction of duly elected representative government, or any other conditions or consequences which produce, preserve or restore darkness, vice, corruption, bondage, despair, turmoil and misery within me, my family and society
patriotic[13] - to be prone to withhold government authority or political power from any and every group, organization, party or person who is so dishonest, evil, ignorant, unskilled or unwise in human events, governments, histories,

laws and values as to wield government authority and political power to an extent or in a manner which produces, preserves or restores darkness, vice, corruption, bondage, despair, turmoil and misery within me, within my family and within a consequently and increasingly disintegrated, divided and enslaved society

patriotic[14] - to be prone to faithfully continue to exercise my personal freedom and my right to wield personal civic authority and political power to defend, protect, preserve and sustain my good local, state and national governments against the contention, persecution and crime which inevitably arise from the erosion or destruction of the civil, political, religious and secular independence, liberty and rights afforded by good government, and which inevitably result in darkness, vice, corruption, bondage, despair, turmoil and misery within me, my family and society

patriotic[15] - to be prone to faithfully refuse to abandon or surrender the freedom, the political power or the legal authority granted back to me by local, state and national governments to defend, protect, preserve and sustain my good local, state and national governments against evil or satanic enemies of society who seek to powerfully impose abuse, addiction, chaos, crime, drunkenness, idleness, idolatry, iniquity, lasciviousness, perversion, pornography, profanity, promiscuity, tyranny, wickedness or any other form of darkness, vice, corruption, bondage, despair, turmoil and misery upon me, my family and society

patriotic[16] - to be prone to faithfully continue to exercise my personal freedom and my right to wield personal civic authority and political power to defend, protect, preserve and sustain my good local, state and national governments by helping them bring violators of good laws to equal and honorable justice

patriotic[17] - to be prone to refuse to abandon or surrender the freedom, the political power or the legal authority granted back to me by local, state and national governments to defend, protect, preserve and sustain my good local, state and national governments against darkness, vice, corruption, bondage, despair, turmoil and misery

patriotic[18] - to be prone to refuse to abandon or surrender the freedom, the political power or the legal authority granted back to me by local, state and national governments to help choose the governmental authority, control, dominion, influence, power or rule that is to be exerted or wielded over me and my family

patriotic[19] - to be prone to honor, obey and sustain the good law of the land

patronal - to be an older, dignified and fatherly man or widower who handles well my position of responsibility in my home and in society

patronal[2] - to be prone to favor, protect or sustain with resources that which produces, preserves or restores true enlightenment, virtue and integrity within me, my family and society

paying - to intend to honorably do all I can and should to make full restitution as part of my faithful, timely and true repentance for all of the corrupt, sinful or vicious wrongdoing I have committed

paying^2 - to intend to honorably suffer the just consequences, penalties, punishment or retribution for all of the corrupt, sinful or vicious wrongdoing I have committed

paying^3 - to intend to do my very best to honorably settle every honorable claim against me

paying^4 - to intend to honorably recompense one or more other people for all actual interest I owe them on their loan to me

paying^5 - to intend to honorably compensate someone for goods and services satisfactorily delivered to me, or for work satisfactorily completed for me

paying^6 - to intend to honorably recompense one or more other people for all actual yield on their investment, less any agreed upon compensation I am entitled to receive

paying^7 - to intend to fulfill my good and honorable duty

peaceable - to be prone to wholeheartedly strive to become or remain peaceful

peaceful - to be prone to actively receive and be filled with a great measure of that wonderfully quiet serenity and tranquility of soul which comes from knowing with an absolute, perfect and spiritually verified personal knowledge of enlightened certainty, reality or truth by personal enlightenment, inspiration or revelation from God that I am sanctified and redeemed unto exaltation, and from knowing that I am leaving the world a legacy of righteous posterity who will obediently continue to strive until death to faithfully, lovingly and unselfishly sacrifice to effectively safeguard and improve the virtuously liberating freedom, health, honorable economic prosperity and steady progress of themselves, their families and society, and who will otherwise obediently continue to serve God, to keep all of His commandments, covenants, laws and ordinances, and to become exalted heirs to every heavenly blessing, gift and reward

peaceful^2 - to be prone to actively receive and be filled with a great measure of that wonderfully quiet serenity and tranquility of soul which comes from a good conscience and a pure heart filled with liberating true enlightenment, virtue and integrity

peaceful^3 - to be prone to actively receive and be filled with a great measure of that wonderfully quiet serenity and tranquility of soul which comes from knowing with an absolute, perfect and spiritually verified personal knowledge of enlightened certainty, reality or truth by personal enlightenment, inspiration or revelation from God that the course I am now faithfully and prayerfully pursuing toward exaltation is pleasing unto Him

peaceful[4] - to be prone to actively receive and be filled with a great measure of that wonderfully quiet serenity and tranquility of soul which comes from knowing with an absolute, perfect and spiritually verified personal knowledge of truth by personal enlightenment, inspiration or revelation from God the Eternal Father that He lives, that I am His child, that He loves me, that no unclean thing can dwell in His glorious celestial presence, that He yearns for my return to His presence in cleanliness following my death, that He has provided a way for me to overcome physical death by resurrection and a way for me to be cleansed or sanctified from my sins to overcome spiritual death by the charitable love, cleansing power and redeeming grace of the Atonement of His Son, the Lord Jesus Christ, and that He is bound to fill me with increasing liberty, hope, peace and joy by my faithfully repentant and honorably exact obedience to those divinely appointed commandments, covenants, laws and ordinances upon which receipt of those blessings is predicated

peaceful[5] - to be prone to actively receive and be filled with a great measure of that wonderfully quiet serenity and tranquility of soul which comes from knowing with an absolute, perfect and spiritually verified personal knowledge of enlightened certainty, reality or truth by personal enlightenment, inspiration or revelation from God the Eternal Father that He is a just, loving, omnipotent and omniscient Being who will justly continue to manifest truth unto me by the power of the Holy Ghost, empower me to be more virtuous, deliver me from all evil temptation, give me power to have and to do what is expedient in Him, and enlighten me with His revealed will, by my believing and honorably exact obedience to those divinely appointed laws upon which receipt of those blessings is predicated

peaceful[6] - to be prone to actively receive and be filled with a great measure of that wonderfully quiet serenity and tranquility of soul which comes from worthily receiving personal enlightenment, inspiration or revelation from God noticeably placed within the thoughts of my mind and noticeably confirmed within my heart as His by the enlightening and simultaneous presence of the glorious power of the Holy Ghost within me

peaceful[7] - to be prone to actively receive and be filled with a great measure of that wonderfully quiet serenity and tranquility of soul which comes to those who faithfully do what is required to be justly liberated, redeemed or rescued by God from all that produces, preserves or restores darkness, vice, corruption, bondage, despair, turmoil and misery within ourselves, our families and society

peaceful[8] - to be prone to achieve a pure state of mind and heart that is wonderfully calm, composed, mild, pacific, quiet, still, tranquil or undisturbed peaceful[9] - to be filled with that great measure of relief which comes to those who are liberated within the mind and heart from anguish, despair, doubt, fear, misery, turmoil and uncertainty

peaceful[10] - to be filled with that great measure of relief which comes to those who are liberated from chaos, commotion, conflict, discord, enmity, feuding, hostility, quarreling, rivalry, strife or variance

peaceful[11] - to be filled with that great measure of relief which comes to those who are liberated from the threat and the effects of horrible abuse, adversity, atrocity, bloodshed, bondage, brutality, calamity, captivity, corruption, disaster, genocide, murder, rape, slavery, torture, tyranny or violence from whatever cause, or for whatever reason, or from whatever source

peaceful[12] - to be filled with that great measure of relief which comes to those who are liberated from the threat and the effects of drought, earthquake, eruption, famine, fire, flood, hurricane, lightning, pestilence, sword, tempest, thunder, tsunami, upheaval, whirlwind and so forth

peacekeeping - to intend to advocate, favor or seek to preserve government which generously provides every freedom, liberty and right necessary for its citizens to preserve true enlightenment, virtue, integrity, liberty, hope, peace and joy within themselves, their families and society

peacekeeping[2] - to intend to wholeheartedly act with other good and law-abiding citizens, including those given military or police power, to pay the price we must pay in unison to preserve the fundamental right to human life, the fundamental right and control of personal property, equal justice under virtuous law, and the pursuit and preservation of that true enlightenment, virtue and integrity which produce, preserve or restore true liberty, hope, peace and joy within us, our families and society

peacekeeping[3] - to intend to wholeheartedly act with other good and law-abiding citizens, including those given military or police power, to pay the price we must pay in unison to protect ourselves against the darkened, corrupted, vicious or tyrannical power of any and every attacking, known or wisely suspected criminal, deadly or evil enemy of society, domestic or foreign

peacekeeping[4] - to intend to do my good and honorable duty to actively help arrest and bring violators of good laws to equal and honorable justice

peacekeeping[5] - to intend, when necessary, to do my good and honorable duty to warn one or more other people against violating good laws

peacekeeping[6] - to intend to preserve or restore reconciliation or unity with one or more other people of true enlightenment, virtue and integrity

peacemaking - to be peaceful and to continue to lovingly encourage and kindly help other people to be peaceful

peacemaking^2 - to intend to do all I can and should to peaceably calm and reconcile the chaos, commotion, conflict, discord, enmity, feuding, hostility, quarreling, rivalry, strife or variance that arises between or among us

peacemaking^3 - to be virtuously peacekeeping

peacemaking^4 - to intend to refuse to be contentious or quarrelsome

peachy - to be wonderfully fine

peaking - to intend to do my very best to achieve the best within me

peart - to be vivacious

peering - to be discerning

penetrating - to intend to acquire and exercise enough acute awareness, penetrating discernment and enlightened understanding with which to bore through or pierce confusion and darkness

penitent - to be prone, having truly repented, to continue to lovingly place my salvation from corrupt, sinful or vicious wrongdoing into the hands of God by remaining brokenhearted and spiritually contrite enough to retain a remission of my sins from day to day by my faithfully repentant and honorably exact obedience to those divinely appointed commandments, covenants, laws and ordinances upon which receipt of that remission is predicated—essential requirements of which include entirely forsaking my sinful and vicious wrongdoing, ministering enough to the relief of the needy and the poor, imparting enough of my substance to them

and visiting them enough on a regular basis

penitent^2 - to be prone to feel enough true contrition, painful remorse and godly sorrow to fully repent of all of the corrupt, sinful or vicious wrongdoing I have committed

penitent^3 - to be prone to feel enough true contrition, painful remorse and godly sorrow to fully repent of all of the darkness, vice and corruption within me

penny-pinching - to intend to consume, save and spend in an economical, prudent, temperate or thrifty manner

perceiving - to be able to truly ascertain, discern, experience, grasp or observe by manifest personal enlightenment, inspiration or revelation from God within my mind and heart an absolutely and perfectly true awareness, comprehension, identification, knowledge, realization or understanding of that which is enlightened certainty, reality or truth

perceiving^2 - to be able to accurately or realistically interpret sensation within the thoughts of my mind and within the feelings of my heart in order to correctly experience, grasp or observe a true awareness, comprehension, identification, knowledge, realization or understanding of true information about the characteristic and distinctive differences between that which is enlightened certainty, reality or truth and that which is confusion, error or falsehood

perceiving[3] - to be able to accurately or realistically interpret sensation within the active thoughts of my mind in order to correctly experience, grasp or observe a true awareness, comprehension, identification, knowledge, realization or understanding of true information about the characteristic and distinctive differences between that which is real and that which is imaginary

peremptory - to be incontrovertible in goodness

peremptory[2] - to be incontrovertible in expression

perfect - to be exalted

perfect[2] - to be redeemed unto exaltation

perfect[3] - to be redeemed and released from the bondage, burdens and debts of my sins

perfect[4] - to be godly enough to be made truly chaste, clean, pure and virtuous at heart—and to continue to encourage and help other people by charitable love, kindness, invitation and instruction to be godly enough to be made truly chaste, clean, pure and virtuous at heart

perfect[5] - to be prone to continuously and faithfully strive with all of the energy, might, power, strength and will of my soul to keep my thoughts, words and actions truly chaste, clean, pure and virtuous in the sight of God

perfect[6] - to be prone to continuously and faithfully strive with all of the energy, might, power, strength and will of my soul to keep my thoughts, words

and actions in harmony with the commandments, covenants, laws and ordinances of God

perfect[7] - to be prone to personally ascertain and live in harmony with the discernibly enlightening and spiritually verifiable truth that: God the Eternal Father is perfect, and desires that His children, heirs, offspring, posterity or seed do all we must do to become like Him

perfected - to be made perfect in the sight of God

perfectible - to be prone to obediently continue to do the very best I can to willfully continue to invite and permit God to completely finish or fulfill within me the full measure of His glorious celestial purposes for me

perfectible[2] - to be prone to continue until the day I die to do the very best I can to personally progress

perfecting - to intend to lovingly encourage and kindly help someone to be redeemed unto exaltation

perfectionistic - to be prone to personally ascertain and live in harmony with the discernibly enlightening and spiritually verifiable truth that: as a child of God, He has given me the agency or mortal power of liberty to choose to exactly and honorably live by faith in Him in a realm of opposition so that, by my believing and honorably exact obedience to His commandments, covenants, laws and ordinances, He can justly exercise power within me to completely finish or fulfill within me the full measure of His purposes for me

perforating - to intend to acquire and exercise enough acute awareness, penetrating discernment and enlightened understanding with which to bore through or pierce confusion and darkness

perishing - to intend to think, speak and act in harmony with the indisputable reality that I am now aging, deteriorating or fading toward my physical death

perky - to be vivacious

permanent - to be prone to personally ascertain and live in harmony with the discernibly enlightening and spiritually verifiable truth that: my actual being, existence and identity are eternal, everlasting or never ending

personable - to be filled with enough true enlightenment, virtue and integrity to find favor in the sight of God

personable[2] - to be filled with enough true enlightenment, virtue and integrity to produce, preserve or restore true liberty, hope, peace and joy within me, my family and society

personable[3] - to be filled with enough true enlightenment, virtue and integrity to strongly attract or appeal to another person's sense of true enlightenment, virtue and integrity

personable[4] - to be prone, as a true reflection of the charitable love and kindness within me, to treat other people as well as possible

personable[5] - to be prone to strive to project a personality which accurately portrays to other people the best that is within the thoughts, beliefs, values and characteristics of my heart

perspicacious - to be acutely discerning

pert - to be healthy

petite - to be a girl or woman who is diminutive

phenomenal - to be sensorial

philanthropic - to be prone to demonstrate truly charitable love toward humankind

philanthropic[2] - to be prone to lovingly donate benevolent and generous means of support in advancing the virtuously liberating freedom, health, honorable economic prosperity and steady progress of me, my family and society

philanthropical - to be philanthropic

philanthropistic - to be philanthropic

philanthropizing - to intend to lovingly encourage and kindly help someone to be philanthropic

philogynous - to be prone to like girls and women who are filled with true enlightenment, virtue and integrity

philologic - to be philological

philological - to be prone to love to prayerfully study and ponder the origin, history, language and meanings of the words and writings of all humankind which best produce, preserve or restore the greatest true enlightenment, virtue, integrity, liberty, hope, peace and joy within me, my family and society

philological[2] - to be prone to love to evaluate the extent to which certain words, used as representations of that which is real or of that which is imaginary, can readily present to the reader or hearer the precise ideas which are intended to be expressed

philological[3] - to be prone to love to seek verified personal knowledge of the affinity and consistency of word definitions used to represent common ideas among diverse languages, tongues and populations

philosophical - to be prone to rationally and spiritually ascertain and live in harmony with the commandments, covenants, laws and ordinances of God by which I can be exalted

philosophical[2] - to be prone to rationally and spiritually ascertain and live in harmony with the commandments, covenants, laws and ordinances of God by which I can be redeemed

philosophical[3] - to be prone to rationally and spiritually ascertain and live in harmony with the commandments, covenants, laws and ordinances of God by which I am and will be judged by Him

philosophical[4] - to be prone to rationally and spiritually ascertain and live in harmony with those thoughts which produce those beliefs which produce those values which produce those characteristics which produce, preserve or restore the greatest true enlightenment, virtue, integrity, liberty, hope, peace and joy within me, my family and society

philosophical[5] - to be prone to rationally and spiritually discover how to personally ascertain enlightened certainty, reality or truth, and to then continue to

ascertain and live in harmony with enlightened certainty, reality or truth

philosophical[6] - to be prone to calmly rationalize and accept unavoidable affliction, defeat or loss

picky - to be prone to pay enough careful attention to important details

piercing - to intend to acquire and exercise enough acute awareness, penetrating discernment and enlightened understanding with which to bore through or penetrate confusion and darkness

pioneering - to intend to take the initiative to go before to discover the best route, to clear obstructions and to envision and initiate improvements in order to prepare a better way for other people to follow

pious - to be prone to consistently and honestly demonstrate an earnest, pure, virtuous and worthy spirit of devoted, respectful or reverent obedience to God

pitiable - to be one of the distressed, the needy or the poor who unavoidably needs to seek and who seeks truly charitable, merciful and tender assistance from other people to help me deal with personal needs which are most difficult if not impossible for me to take care of alone, until I can and should become, by my own education, training, labors, investments and savings, a self-reliant net contributor to the virtuously liberating freedom, health, honorable economic prosperity and steady progress of me, my family and society

pitying - to intend to offer the needy and poor aid, assistance, concession, forbearance, forgiveness, leniency or tolerance to an extent and in a manner which is charitably loving, just, right and wise in the sight of God

pitying^2 - to intend to actively, charitably, generously and wisely provide for the needy and poor to an extent or in a manner which saves their lives, meets their immediate needs for survival, fosters their adequate education, employment, labors, self-reliance and thrift, and which encourages their service to other people

pitying^3 - to intend to actively, charitably, generously and wisely give of my substance or other resources to the needy and poor to help them deal with personal needs which they cannot take care of alone—provided they are continuing to demonstrate by their own determined education, training, labors, investments and savings, that they are responsibly striving to become self-reliant net contributors to the virtuously liberating freedom, health, honorable economic prosperity and steady progress of themselves, their families and society

placable - to be peaceable

placable^2 - to be prone to maintain my power to forgive

placable^3 - to be prone to maintain my power to appease or pacify my passions

placid - to be peaceful

placing - to intend to wisely bestow or invest confidence, trust or something else of value

plain - to be modest

plain^2 - to be plain dealing

plain dealing - to be as honestly or honorably artless, direct, open, simple, sincere and unreserved as I can be in communications, relations and transactions with another person

plain-spoken - to be as honestly or honorably artless, direct, open, simple, sincere and unreserved as I can be in expressing myself to another person

planning - to intend to prepare a method, process, schedule or system for the orderly achievement of a good consequence, outcome or result

planting - to intend to broadcast, disseminate or sow thoughts, beliefs or values of true enlightenment, virtue and integrity into someone's thoughts so that they will take them to heart and act on them in order to gather, glean or harvest naturally consequent liberty, hope, peace and joy for them, their family and society

platonic - to be prone to exercise a more chaste, clean, pure and virtuous love with another person of the same or opposite gender by eliminating all evil or satanic sexual appetite, craving, desire, drive or passion from the relationship

plausive - to be truly worthy of applause, approval or praise without seeking it

playing - to intend to engage in enough healthy amusement, comedy, entertainment, frolic, fun, game, humor, play or sport to produce, preserve or restore virtuously liberating freedom, health, honorable economic

prosperity and steady progress within me, my family and society
playing[2] - to intend to engage in enough healthy diversion or recreation to produce, preserve or restore my good health
playing[3] - to intend to engage in enough mental or physical exercise to produce, preserve or restore my good health
play-writing - to intend to compose, create or write for presentation or sale good and uplifting artistic, literary or theatric manuscripts
pleasant - to be virtuously pleasing
pleased - to be joyfully grateful for that which is truly good and of God
pleased[2] - to be joyfully grateful for true enlightenment, virtue and integrity, and for their naturally consequent liberty, hope, peace and joy
pleased[3] - to be delighted or joyfully elated
pleasing - to intend to please God by being godly enough to be made truly chaste, clean, pure and virtuous at heart—and by continuing to encourage and help other people by charitable love, kindness, invitation and instruction to be godly enough to be made truly chaste, clean, pure and virtuous at heart
pleasing[2] - to be filled with enough true enlightenment, virtue and integrity to produce, preserve or restore true liberty, hope, peace and joy within me, my family and society
pleasing[3] - to be filled with enough true enlightenment, virtue and integrity to strongly attract or

appeal to another person's sense of true enlightenment, virtue and integrity
pleasing[4] - to intend to win the good pleasure of other people by doing and being good
pleasure-seeking - to intend to seek the company of good, praiseworthy and virtuous people
plodding - to intend to diligently and steadily labor to pay the price of godliness
plodding[2] - to intend to diligently and steadily labor to pay the price of pondering and performing enough true enlightenment, virtue and integrity to produce, preserve or restore true liberty, hope, peace and joy within me, my family and society
pluralist - to be dualist
pluralist[2] - to be prone to allow, enfranchise or empower the law-abiding citizens of a minority faction of a community or nation to fully function or perform within that community or nation, while maintaining their healthy and virtuously unifying differences
pluralist[3] - to be prone to wield government authority or political power to ensure the fundamental rights of citizenship held by the people of a minority faction of a community or nation are not fewer than or less than the fundamental rights of citizenship held by the people of the dominant, majority or prevalent faction of that community or nation
poised - to be balanced enough to steadily maintain awareness of and proper orientation toward what is best

poised[2] - to be composed and dignified

polarizing - to intend to sharply divide, segregate or separate myself and my minor children from all that produces, preserves or restores darkness, vice and corruption within me, my family and society

polarizing[2] - to intend to sharply divide, segregate or separate myself and my minor children from corrupt, sinful or vicious wrongdoing

polarizing[3] - to intend to sharply divide, segregate or separate myself and my minor children from all sources of the evil or satanic powers of binding addiction, compulsion, impulsion, obsession, occupation and possession

polarizing[4] - to intend to sharply divide, segregate or separate myself and my minor children from all sources of confusion

polarizing[5] - to intend to sharply divide, segregate or separate myself and my minor children from all those who continue to speak or act in accordance with darkness, vice and corruption, and who fail or refuse to repent

polished - to be made perfect in the sight of God through the charitable love, cleansing power and redeeming grace of the Atonement of the Lord Jesus Christ by my faithfully repentant and honorably exact obedience to those divinely appointed commandments, covenants, laws and ordinances upon which receipt of that blessing is predicated

polished[2] - to be made truly chaste, clean, pure and virtuous in the sight of God through the charitable love, cleansing power and redeeming grace of the Atonement of the Lord Jesus Christ by my faithfully repentant and honorably exact obedience to those divinely appointed commandments, covenants, laws and ordinances upon which receipt of those blessings is predicated

polished[3] - to be wonderfully courteous, dignified, gracious and refined

polishing - to intend to lovingly encourage and kindly help someone to be more polished

polite - to be prone to treat another person in a thoughtfully courteous, generous and respectful manner

political - to be virtuously governing

political[2] - to be virtuously patriotic

political[3] - to be prone to honor, revere and sustain government officials who strive to enact, enforce and interpret good laws for the virtuously liberating freedom, health, honorable economic prosperity and steady progress of ourselves, our families and society

political[4] - to be prone to grant government authority or political power to that group, organization, party or person who is good, honest, knowledgeable, patriotic, skilled and wise enough in human conditions, economies, events, governments, histories, laws and values to wield government authority and political power to an extent or in a manner which produces, preserves or restores the greatest true enlightenment, virtue, integrity, liberty, hope, peace and joy within me, within my family and within a consequently and increasingly integrated, liberated and united society

political[5] - to be prone to withhold government authority or political power from any and every group, organization, party or person who is so dishonest, evil, ignorant, unpatriotic, unskilled or unwise in human events, governments, histories, laws and values as to wield government authority and political power to an extent or in a manner which produces, preserves or restores darkness, vice, corruption, bondage, despair, turmoil and misery within me, within my family and within a consequently and increasingly disintegrated, divided and enslaved society

political[6] - to be prone to use my government authority to favor political appointment or nomination of my truthful, virtuous, wise and otherwise well-qualified personal friends for public office

polling - to intend to exercise or seek the right of shared government of the people by openly expressing or secretly casting the voice or voting power of my own political judgment at the voting polls as a competent citizen who is qualified to vote

Pollyannaish - to be prone to personally ascertain and live in harmony with the discernibly enlightening and spiritually verifiable truth that: good shall ultimately triumph over evil

Pollyannaish[2] - to be prone to faithfully look for blessings and goodness wherever they may be found, but especially in the midst of inescapable or unavoidable adversity, affliction or trial

polygynous - to be a righteous man who willingly obeys a commandment from God to enter into or to sustain lawful and legal marriage to more than one righteous and willing wife at a time

polygynous[2] - to be a righteous woman who willingly obeys a commandment from God to enter into or to sustain lawful and legal marriage to a righteous and willing husband who seeks to obey a commandment from God to be polygynous

Polynesian - to be prone to live in harmony with the ways of Polynesian character or culture which produce, preserve or restore true enlightenment, virtue and integrity within me, my family and society

polytheistic - to be prone to worship and serve God the Eternal Father in the name of the Lord Jesus Christ, as prompted by the Holy Ghost, while thinking, speaking and acting in harmony with the discernibly enlightening and spiritually verifiable truth that: God the Eternal Father and His Only Begotten Son in the flesh, the Lord Jesus Christ, are two distinctly separate, gloriously exalted Spirit Personages who are each inseparably embodied within His own gloriously exalted, immortal body of flesh and bones, the Holy Ghost is a gloriously exalted male Spirit Personage of enlivened spirit matter, and these three distinctly separate divine Beings are members of a Godhead who function and speak as one in purpose to bring to pass the immortality and exaltation of humankind by our faithfully repentant and honorably exact obedience to those divinely appointed commandments, covenants, laws and ordinances upon which receipt of those blessings is predicated

polytheistic^2 - to be prone to personally ascertain and live in harmony with the discernibly enlightening and spiritually verifiable truth that: God the Eternal Father has the plan and the power to help His faithful and righteous children, offspring, posterity or seed progress until we inherit all He has, enjoy the life He enjoys and become as our Heavenly Parents are by our faithfully repentant and honorably exact obedience to those divinely appointed commandments, covenants, laws and ordinances upon which receipt of those blessings is predicated

pondering - to intend to seek communion with God in deeply sincere and prayerful deliberation or meditation

pondering^2 - to intend to deeply and thoroughly evaluate or weigh something potentially virtuous within the thoughts of my mind and heart—in a faithful, honorable, intentional and sincere effort to learn for myself whether it is truly virtuous

pondering^3 - to intend to deeply and thoroughly evaluate or weigh

something potentially true within the thoughts of my mind and heart—in a faithful, honorable, intentional and sincere effort to learn for myself whether it is true

pontificating - to intend to function or officiate as a virtuously ordained high priest or other religious leader to an extent or in a manner which produces, preserves or restores true enlightenment, virtue and integrity within me, my family and society

poor - to be poor-in-spirit

poor-in-spirit - to be prone to willfully think, speak and act in a brokenhearted, contrite and penitent manner before God which demonstrates my unfeigned realization of my utter dependence upon Him for all good things which come to me

popular - to be godly enough to be made truly chaste, clean, pure and virtuous at heart—and to continue to encourage and help other people by charitable love, kindness, invitation and instruction to be godly enough to be made truly chaste, clean, pure and virtuous at heart

popular^2 - to be filled with enough true enlightenment, virtue and integrity to attract or appeal to every other good person's sense of true enlightenment, virtue and integrity

popular^3 - to be prone to do enough common good to win the acceptance, approval or favor of many good and common people

popular^4 - to be prone, in my efforts to win acceptance, approval or favor from one or more other people, to obediently, submissively or willingly meet their truly virtuous expectations

popularizing - to be godly enough to be made truly chaste, clean, pure and virtuous at heart—and to continue to encourage and help other people by charitable love, kindness, invitation and instruction to be godly enough to be made truly chaste, clean, pure and virtuous at heart

popularizing[2] - to intend to lovingly encourage and kindly help my family and society to conform to and pay for that which produces, preserves or restores truly virtuous progress within us

popularizing[3] - to intend to lovingly encourage and kindly help many or most of a particular population to accept, approve or favor that person or thing which produces, preserves or restores true enlightenment, virtue and integrity within us, our families and society

positive - to be prone to confidently and consistently live in harmony with that measure of absolute, perfect and spiritually verified personal knowledge of enlightened certainty, reality or truth I have received by personal enlightenment, inspiration or revelation from God

positive[2] - to be prone to honestly encourage, emphasize, harbor and practice true enlightenment, virtue, integrity, liberty, hope, peace and joy—while refusing to encourage, emphasize, harbor or practice darkness, vice, corruption, bondage, despair, turmoil and misery

positive[3] - to be prone to honestly encourage, emphasize, harbor and

practice true beliefs, values and characteristics of pure and virtuous belief, faith, hope and charity

positive[4] - to be prone to confidently and consistently live in harmony with personally verified and incontrovertible proof

positive[5] - to be prone to refuse to deny, doubt, oppose or resist personally verified and incontrovertible proof

positive[6] - to be prone to solve problems in a constructive, helpful and optimistic manner, rather than in a destructive, harmful or pessimistic manner

positive[7] - to be prone to think, speak and act in harmony with the positive two (2) virtues in this dictionary

possessing - to be made a rightful heir to the highest eternal blessings of God through the charitable love, cleansing power and redeeming grace of the Atonement of the Lord Jesus Christ by my faithfully repentant and honorably exact obedience to those divinely appointed commandments, covenants, laws and ordinances upon which receipt of those blessings is predicated

possessing[2] - to intend to retain a remission of my sins through the charitable love, cleansing power and redeeming grace of the Atonement of the Lord Jesus Christ by my faithfully repentant and honorably exact obedience to those divinely appointed commandments, covenants, laws and ordinances upon which receipt of that remission is predicated—essential requirements of which include entirely forsaking my sinful and vicious wrongdoing, ministering enough to the relief of the needy and the poor, imparting enough of my substance to them and visiting them enough on a regular basis

possessing[3] - to intend to retain a godly and progressive character by my faithfully repentant and honorably exact obedience to those divinely appointed commandments, covenants, laws and ordinances upon which receipt of that blessing is predicated

possessing[4] - to intend to retain true enlightenment, virtue and integrity by my believing and honorably exact obedience to those divinely appointed laws upon which receipt of those blessings is predicated

powerful - to be exalted

powerful[2] - to be celestial

powerful[3] - to be godly enough to be made truly chaste, clean, pure and virtuous at heart

powerful[4] - to be prone to faithfully request and worthily receive by the laying on of hands a blessing of divine power from a duly ordained and righteous man who bears true higher priesthood authority and power from God and who is authorized and inspired of God to give me that blessing and that power

powerful[5] - to be a man who authoritatively exerts or wields true higher priesthood authority and power from God to truly bless the lives of other people following my divinely authorized calling and ordination, by my faithfully repentant and honorably exact obedience to those divinely

appointed commandments, covenants, laws and ordinances upon which receipt of that power is predicated

powerful[6] - to be a boy or man who authoritatively exerts or wields true lesser or preparatory priesthood authority and power from God to truly bless the lives of other people following my divinely authorized calling and ordination, by my faithfully repentant and honorably exact obedience to those divinely appointed commandments, covenants, laws and ordinances upon which receipt of that power is predicated

powerful[7] - to be prone to personally ascertain and live in harmony with the discernibly enlightening and spiritually verifiable truth that: all of my power to do and be good originated with and came to me from God, and I can increase that power within me by my faithfully repentant and honorably exact obedience to those divinely appointed commandments, covenants, laws and ordinances upon which receipt of that power is predicated

powerful[8] - to be prone to personally ascertain and live in harmony with the discernibly enlightening and spiritually verifiable truth that: all who are faithful, obedient and prayerful disciples or servants of God are and can always be saved from the powerful temptations of Satan and his followers by faithfully praying for and receiving the supreme power of God

powerful[9] - to be prone to faithfully continue to join with enough other good people to exert or wield in unison an amount, degree or measure of power to actually produce, preserve or restore true enlightenment, virtue, integrity, liberty, hope, peace and joy within ourselves, our families and society—that is greater than the power exerted or wielded by those who are striving to actually produce, preserve or restore darkness, vice, corruption, bondage, despair, turmoil and misery within us, our families and society

powerful[10] - to be prone to exert or wield enough authority, dominion, energy, faith, force, heart, influence, might, mind, persuasion, potency, resources, strength, talent or will to actually produce, preserve or restore true enlightenment, virtue and integrity within me, my family and society

practical - to be intelligent

practical[2] - to be prone to actually adopt those thoughtful practices which best produce, preserve or restore the greatest true enlightenment, virtue, integrity, liberty, hope, peace and joy within me, my family and society

practical[3] - to be prone to actually produce, preserve or restore the best possible consequences or the most socially beneficial results for me, my family and society

practical[4] - to be prone to actually plan the best use of available resources to achieve the best possible consequences or the most socially beneficial results for me, my family and society

practical[5] - to be prone to actually put useful experience, knowledge or practice to good use

pragmatic - to be prone to think, speak and act in harmony with those thoughts, beliefs, values and characteristics which actually produce, preserve or restore the greatest true enlightenment, virtue, integrity, liberty, hope, peace and joy within me, my family and society

pragmatic[2] - to be prone to seek a greater knowledge of enlightened certainty, reality or truth about the characteristic and distinctive differences between that which is truly good and of God and that which is evil or satanic by examining, observing or tasting the fruits of various thoughts, and their consequent beliefs, and their consequent values in a faithful, honorable, intentional and sincere effort to discover which ones, if thoughtfully exercised or put into practice in daily life, actually produce the best consequent characteristics within me, my family and society

pragmatic[3] - to be prone to learn wisdom from the lessons of accurately observed or recorded history

pragmatist - to be pragmatic

pragmatistic - to be pragmatic

praiseworthy - to be truly worthy of admiration, approval, commendation, homage, honor or praise for doing and being good

praiseworthy[2] - to be truly worthy of admiration, approval, commendation, homage, honor or praise for producing, preserving or restoring true enlightenment, virtue and integrity within me, my family and society

praising - to intend to express admiration, approval, commendation, homage, honor or praise when it is due

praying - to intend to truly and faithfully qualify myself to receive from God the power to prayerfully ask of God in harmony with the revelatory Spirit of God, and to therefore ask for that which is according to the will of God, and to thereby have it done by His power as I have asked

praying^2 - to intend to truly and faithfully stay in open and heartfelt communication with God through constantly maintained, momentary and silent heartfelt prayers and by my believing and honorably exact obedience to that divinely appointed law upon which receipt of answers to my prayers is predicated

praying^3 - to intend—at morning and night and throughout the day, aloud or silently, and alone or taking turns each time as directed by the one presiding over our kneeling family—to deeply, faithfully, humbly, meekly and reverently address God the Eternal Father in prayer to sincerely express grateful and worshipful remembrance for blessings received from Him, before wholeheartedly crying or pleading for the grace, love and power of His divine enlightenment, guidance, power, protection, provision and other needed blessings, with unfeigned faith I will receive in harmony with His timing, my worthiness, my needs, my righteous desires, and what He knows is best, to close in the name of the Lord Jesus Christ before listening for any immediate response, and to then move ahead believing He will justly bless me by my believing and honorably exact obedience to those divinely appointed laws upon which receipt of those blessings is predicated

praying^4 - to intend to continually give God enough joyful and sincere gratitude in my heartfelt prayers for past or present blessings such as activity, body, breath, challenges, children, choices, clothing, discernment, education, enlightenment, faith, family, food, freedom, growth, health, healing, hearing, heart, hope, improvement, intellect, intelligence, joy, knowledge of truth and error, knowledge of good and evil, liberty, life, light, love, marriage, means, mind, mortality, movement, opportunities, parents, peace, power, progress, prophesy, prosperity, protection, redemption, repentance, revelation, resources, salvation, service, shelter, smell, spirit, spiritual gifts, strengths, talents, taste, touch, testimony, true friends, vision, voice, wealth and every other good thing I enjoy, and to constantly demonstrate that gratitude by serving Him and humankind, especially the needy and the poor

praying^5 - to intend to faithfully and sincerely ask God often enough and well enough in my heartfelt prayers for enough power to withstand Satan and his followers and their evil or satanic powers of darkness, vice, corruption, bondage, despair, turmoil and misery, and to then move ahead believing He will give me that power by my faithfully repentant and honorably exact obedience to those divinely appointed commandments, covenants, laws and ordinances upon which receipt of that power is predicated

praying[6] - to intend to faithfully and sincerely ask God often enough and well enough in my heartfelt prayers about continued blessings for which I am grateful, and about such things as my afflictions, assignments, calamities, character, charity, children, crops, decisions, desires, disasters, enemies, enlightenment, faith, faithfulness, family, feelings, forgiveness, freedom, goals, health, heartache, herds, hope, household, integrity, investments, liberty, job, joy, judgment, leaders, livelihood, love, marriage, mercy, needs, pain, parents, peace, performance, power, progress, prosperity, protection, righteousness, strength, success, suffering, testimony, trials, troubles, understanding, virtue, wants, weaknesses, wisdom, and worthiness, and about the dispelling of darkness, vice and corruption from me, my family and society, and about the opening of minds and nations to a knowledge of God and His will, and about the success of His prophets, apostles, missionaries and other servants, and about the well-being and wisdom of leaders in authority, and about the well-being of those around us, especially the afflicted, injured, needy, poor and sick, and about every other good and needful thing

precautional - to be precautious

precautionary - to be precautious

precautious - to be prone to pay enough careful attention ahead of time, in advance or beforehand to preserving true enlightenment, virtue and integrity within me, my family and society

precautious[2] - to be prone to pay enough careful attention ahead of time, in advance or beforehand to preventing the exposure of me, my family and society to darkness, vice, corruption, bondage, despair, turmoil and misery

precautious[3] - to be prone to pay enough careful attention ahead of time, in advance or beforehand to avoiding the exposure of me, my family and society to avoidable harm or injury

precious - to be prone to personally ascertain and live in harmony with the discernibly enlightening and spiritually verifiable truth that: my soul is of infinite worth in the sight of God

precious[2] - to be prone to live in harmony with the highest and best values of which I have become aware in my education and training and in my own constantly diligent, honest and open-minded searching

precious[3] - to be prone to think, speak and act in a goodly manner which is beloved or cherished by goodly people

precise - to be prone to think, speak and act with enough honorably exact obedience to God's commandments, covenants, laws and ordinances to justly receive

from Him the greatest true enlightenment, virtue, integrity, liberty, hope, peace and joy within me, my family and society
precise[2] - to be prone to think, speak and act in distinctly accurate, clear and exactly measured harmony with those thoughts, beliefs, values and characteristics which produce, preserve or restore the greatest true enlightenment, virtue, integrity, liberty, hope, peace and joy within me, my family and society
precise[3] - to be prone to think, speak and act in distinctly accurate, clear and exactly measured harmony with those thoughts, beliefs, values and characteristics which consequently exclude or preclude the production, preservation or restoration of darkness, vice and corruption within me, my family and society
precise[4] - to be prone to think, speak and act in distinctly accurate, clear and exactly measured standards which exclude or preclude avoidable delay, harm, illness, injury or waste
predeterminate - to be prone to positively identify, locate or reach ahead of time, in advance or beforehand a clear and precise understanding of the truth
predominating - to intend to exercise controlling authority, dominion, influence or power over myself
predominating[2] - to intend to exercise righteous authority, dominion, influence or power to an extent or in a manner which produces, preserves or restores the virtuously liberating freedom,

health, honorable economic prosperity and steady progress of me, my family and society
preeminent - to be outstanding, superior or supreme in truth and virtue among people
prefiguring - to intend to accurately recognize the signs of something which is about to occur
prejudging - to intend to carefully rely upon all available evidence to form a reasonable inference, presumption, speculation, supposition or theory which I then honorably seek to prove before relying upon it to form or render a final judgment or opinion
premonitory - to be prone to rely upon an unmistakable forewarning or presentiment of danger, risk or threat to forewarn
prepared - to be worthy to be redeemed unto exaltation
prepared[2] - to be worthy to be redeemed and released from the bondage, burdens and debts of my sins
prepared[3] - to be properly motivated, qualified and otherwise made ready ahead of time, in advance or beforehand to do only good, come what may
prepared[4] - to be properly motivated, qualified and otherwise made ready ahead of time, in advance or beforehand to vanquish that which produces, preserves or restores darkness, vice and corruption within me, my family and society
preparing - to intend to lovingly encourage and kindly help someone to be virtuously prepared

preppy - to be prone to ambitiously pursue a good formal education to prepare for a better life

prescient - to be prone to receive and rely upon impressions which teach or warn me of things to come, verification of which I know I have received by enlightenment, inspiration or revelation from God

prescribing - to intend to designate a guiding course, regulation, remedy or rule of action to be followed to achieve greater true enlightenment, virtue, integrity, liberty, hope, peace and joy within me, my family and society

present - to be existent

presentable - to be prone to present myself in an honorable, praiseworthy or venerable manner

presentimental - to be prone to receive and rely upon impressions which teach or warn me of things to come, verification of which I know I have received by enlightenment, inspiration or revelation from God within my mind and heart

preserving - to intend to protect, safeguard or sustain that which produces, preserves or restores true enlightenment, virtue and integrity within me, my family and society

presiding - to be a married boy or man who righteously exercises my God-given familial or patriarchal authority and jurisdiction to preside over my family and, along with my wife, to govern, judge or rule over our family in faithful righteousness

presiding[2] - to be a man who has been called and ordained of God who righteously exercises my God-given ecclesiastical or higher priesthood authority and jurisdiction to preside over a religious organization in faithful righteousness

presiding[3] - to intend to exert or wield my legitimate authority or power of presidency to an extent or in a manner which produces, preserves or restores true enlightenment, virtue and integrity within me, my family and society

prestigious - to be truly worthy of an honorable reputation based upon truly virtuous achievement

pretending - to intend to adopt or assume a virtuous characteristic by imagining it is a part of me and by practicing or simulating it until it is a part of what I do and who I am at heart

pretty - to be a girl or woman who is attractively gracious and refined in character and manner

prevailing - to intend to effectively and persistently exercise belief, influence, persuasion or power until greater true enlightenment, virtue, integrity, liberty, hope, peace and joy are achieved within me, my family and society

priceless - to be invaluable

prideless - to be virtuously humble or lowly-of-heart and in no way viciously proud

priestly - to be a boy or man who is a duly called and ordained priesthood bearer of God who truly bears God's priesthood authority to righteously fulfill the duties of the office of a priest

primary - to be prone to deal first with what is most important and most urgent

prime - to be first-rate in quality of character

princely - to be an unmarried boy or man who is learning and working to powerfully personify the most dignified, handsome and masculine characteristics of godly manhood by my faithfully repentant and honorably exact obedience to those divinely appointed commandments, covenants, laws and ordinances upon which receipt of that power is predicated

princely^2 - to be a royal boy or man who is learning and working to powerfully personify the most dignified, handsome and masculine characteristics of godly manhood by my faithfully repentant and honorably exact obedience to those divinely appointed commandments, covenants, laws and ordinances upon which receipt of that power is predicated

princely^3 - to be a boy or man who prevails by distinguished performance

princessly - to be an unmarried girl or woman who is learning and working to powerfully personify the most beautiful, feminine, gracious and noble characteristics of godly womanhood by my faithfully repentant and honorably exact obedience to those divinely appointed commandments, covenants, laws and ordinances upon which receipt of that power is predicated

princessly^2 - to be a royal girl or woman who is learning and working to powerfully personify the most beautiful, feminine, gracious and noble characteristics of godly womanhood by my

faithfully repentant and honorably exact obedience to those divinely appointed commandments, covenants, laws and ordinances upon which receipt of that power is predicated

princessly^3 - to be a girl or woman who prevails by distinguished performance

principled - to be prone to think, speak and act in an enlightened, virtuous and dignified manner

prioritizing - to intend to pay attention to people and things in a *most-important-and-most-urgent-first-to-least-important-and-least-urgent-last* sequence which produces, preserves or restores the greatest true enlightenment, virtue, integrity, liberty, hope, peace and joy within me, my family and society

prioritizing^2 - to intend to cooperate with other members of my family in paying attention to people and things in a *most-important-and-most-urgent-first-to-least-important-and-least-urgent-last* sequence which produces, preserves or restores the greatest true enlightenment, virtue, integrity, liberty, hope, peace and joy within ourselves, our families and society

prioritizing^3 - to intend to cooperate with other people in society in paying attention to people and things in a *most-important-and-most-urgent-first-to-least-important-and-least-urgent-last* sequence which produces, preserves or restores the greatest true enlightenment, virtue, integrity, liberty, hope, peace and joy within ourselves, our families and society

pristine - to be as innocent, pure and uncorrupted as the day I was born

privatist - to be prone to pursue what is best for me, my family and society ahead of or instead of what is considered or esteemed by someone or by some to be popular

prizing - to intend to greatly or highly esteem, rate or value someone or something found or known to be good

proactive - to be prone to direct or initiate activity or participation to produce, preserve or restore good consequences, effects, outcomes or results

probationary - to be prone to personally ascertain and live in harmony with the discernibly enlightening and spiritually verifiable truth that: mortal life on Earth is both a God-given condition of opposing choices and a period of time given to me to prepare to be judged by Him in harmony with my personally chosen and personally proven desires and works while I am here

pro-choice - to be prone to advocate, maintain or support the right of a pregnant girl or woman to choose the legalized killing of a viable or potentially viable human fetus within her body to preserve her own life, or to rid herself of a pregnancy imposed upon her by incest or rape, or to stop a pregnancy when competent medical authority determines the fetus has physical defects which will not allow the fetus to survive

productive - to be prone to continue to progress by continuing to improve the enlightenment and virtue of the thoughts I continue to integrate into the thoughts, beliefs, values and characteristics of my heart

productive[2] - to be prone to maintain the means or power to personally progress

professional - to be prone, by the way I speak and act, to openly or publicly affirm, avow, claim, declare or teach my true faith in God and my sincere desire to please Him

professional[2] - to be prone, by the way I speak and act, to openly or publicly affirm, avow, claim, declare or teach that which produces, preserves or restores true enlightenment, virtue and integrity within me, my family and society

professorial - to be prone, by the way I speak and act, to openly or publicly affirm, avow, claim, declare or teach my true faith in God and my sincere desire to please Him

professorial[2] - to be prone to openly or publicly affirm, avow, claim, declare or teach that which produces, preserves or restores true enlightenment, virtue and integrity within me, my family and society

professorial[3] - to be prone to teach another person how to truly discern or distinguish between that which is truly good and of God and that which is evil or satanic

professorial[4] - to be prone to teach another person how to truly discern or distinguish between that which is enlightened certainty, reality or truth and that which is confusion, error or falsehood

professorial[5] - to be prone to teach another person how to truly discern or distinguish between that which is real and that which is imaginary

profiling - to intend to accurately describe or truly identify the prevalent positive characteristics of an individual, social class, group, organization, population, nation or other faction of society in order to duplicate or emulate what they are doing for the good of society

profitable - to be exalted

profitable[2] - to be redeemed unto exaltation

profitable[3] - to be redeemed and released from the bondage, burdens and debts of my sins

profitable[4] - to be godly enough to be made truly chaste, clean, pure and virtuous at heart—and to continue to encourage and help other people by charitable love, kindness, invitation and instruction to be godly enough to be made truly chaste, clean, pure and virtuous at heart

profitable[5] - to be prone to continue to progress by continuing to improve the enlightenment and virtue of the thoughts I continue to integrate into the thoughts, beliefs, values and characteristics of my heart

profitable[6] - to be prone to spend less than I earn

profitable[7] - to be prone to virtuously add positive value to the valuable things I have been given

profitable[8] - to be prone to produce, preserve or restore as many good works as I can

profiting - to intend to continue to progress by continuing to improve the enlightenment and virtue of the thoughts I continue to integrate into the thoughts, beliefs, values and characteristics of my heart

profound - to be deeply humble, lowly, meek and submissive toward God

profound[2] - to be deeply and thoroughly honest, insightful and intelligent

progressing - to intend to constantly choose to advance, ascend, grow, increase, improve or rise toward an exalted character or condition of heart by my faithfully repentant and honorably exact obedience to those divinely appointed commandments, covenants, laws and ordinances upon which receipt of that blessing is predicated

progressing[2] - to intend to constantly choose to change, reform or repent in order to continue to advance, ascend, grow, increase, progress or rise toward producing, preserving or restoring greater true enlightenment, virtue, integrity, liberty, hope, peace and joy within me, my family and society

progressing[3] - to intend to think, speak and act in more perfect harmony with one or more positive two (2) virtues in this dictionary—or with one or more relative value characteristics to the extent my virtuous pondering, performance or teaching of them produces, preserves or restores one or more of the virtues within me, my family and society

progressing[4] - to intend to
constantly choose to advance,
ascend, grow, increase, progress or
rise toward a purely virtuous
character or condition of heart one
good word, action or deed at a time
progressing[5] - to intend to
constantly choose to advance,
ascend, grow, increase, progress or
rise toward a purely virtuous
character or condition of heart one
good thought, belief or value at a
time
progressing[6] - to intend to
constantly choose to advance,
ascend, grow, increase, progress or
rise toward a purely virtuous
character or condition of heart one
good choice or decision at a time
progressing[7] - to intend to
constantly choose to advance,
ascend, grow, increase, progress or
rise toward a purely virtuous
character or condition of heart one
good lesson at a time
progressional - to be actively and
truly progressing
progressive - to be prone to
lovingly encourage and kindly
help someone to be actively and
truly progressing
progressivist - to be progressive
proletarian - to be prone to sell my
labor as I can and must to earn my
daily bread
pro-life - to be a girl or woman
who refuses to condone or practice
the legalized killing of a viable or
potentially viable human fetus
within my body as a form of birth
control, or in an attempt to avoid
the consequences of my adultery,
fornication, promiscuity or
prostitution, or for any other
reason other than to preserve my
own life, or to rid myself of a
pregnancy imposed upon me by
incest or rape, or to stop a
pregnancy when competent
medical authority determines the
fetus has physical defects which
will not allow the fetus to survive
prominent - to be truly worthy of a
distinguished or meritorious
reputation
prominent[2] - to be prone to
honorably hold public position or
rank
promising - to intend to think,
speak and act in an honorable
manner which gives someone
reason to expect I will produce,
preserve or restore praiseworthy
achievement, improvement or
success
promoting - to intend to advance,
develop or further true personal
betterment, improvement or
progress within me, my family and
society
proper - to be prone to think, speak
and act in harmony with that
which is charitably loving, just,
right and wise in the sight of God
proper[2] - to be prone to think,
speak and act in harmony with the
good law of the land
proper[3] - to be prone to fulfill my
good and honorable duty or
responsibility
prophesying - to be authorized and
commanded of God to certainly
foretell the occurrence of one or
more future events the truthfulness
of which I have ascertained by
personal enlightenment,
inspiration or revelation from God
prophesying[2] - to intend to
personally ascertain and then truly
preach, teach and testify by

authority and revelation from God that: the Lord Jesus Christ, the only begotten son of God the Eternal Father in the flesh, is the Anointed One foreordained to be the Savior of all humankind and the Redeemer of the world
prophesying[3] - to intend to truly declare, exhort, preach, teach or testify by authority and revelation from God
prophylactic - to be prone to preserve, protect or safeguard against disease
propitious - to be kind
prospective - to be foresighted
prospering - to intend to continue to progress by continuing to improve the enlightenment and virtue of the thoughts I continue to integrate into the thoughts, beliefs, values and characteristics of my heart
prospering[2] - to intend to arise, blossom, flourish, grow or thrive in true enlightenment, virtue, integrity, liberty, hope, peace and joy in direct proportion to my believing and honorably exact obedience to those divinely appointed laws upon which receipt of those blessings is predicated
prospering[3] - to be breadwinning and provident
prostrating - to intend to throw myself face down in humble adoration and prayerful submission to God
protected - to be prone to defend, protect or secure myself against everything which has or which may have enough evil or satanic power to induce or influence me to willfully reject my good conscience, or to defile the active and stored

thoughts of my mind with darkness, vice and corruption, or to drive true enlightenment, virtue and integrity out of my mind and heart, or to infect me with evil or satanic desires to lustfully fulfill or sinfully satisfy one or more of my biologically inherent and naturally impelling emotional, physical or sexual appetites, cravings, desires, drives or passions, or to otherwise cause the Spirit of God to withdraw from me
Protestant - to be prone to live in harmony with the teachings of a Christian church which has broken away or separated in apostasy or protest from an earlier Christian church—to the extent the teachings produce, preserve or restore true enlightenment, virtue and integrity within me, my family and society
Protestant[2] - to be prone to live in harmony with the teachings of the Hussite Church, of the Lutheran Church or of another Christian church which broke away or separated in apostasy or protest from the Roman Catholic Church during or since the Reformation—to the extent the teachings produce, preserve or restore true enlightenment, virtue and integrity within me, my family and society
Protestant[3] - to be prone to live in harmony with the teachings of the Eastern Church, of the Eastern Orthodox Church, of the Orthodox Church or of another Christian church which broke away or separated in apostasy or protest from the Roman Catholic Church before the Reformation—to the extent the teachings produce,

preserve or restore true enlightenment, virtue and integrity within me, my family and society

proud - to be deeply pleased or satisfied about the distinguished, grand, honorable, magnificent, majestic, noble or splendid achievements, advantages, associations, learning, possessions, power, wealth or wisdom with which someone has been blessed by the miraculous hand of God

proven - to be prone to continue to consistently confirm, demonstrate, establish or verify my genuine, true or valid faith in and love for God by my faithfully repentant and honorably exact obedience to His commandments, covenants, laws and ordinances, come what may

provident - to be economical, frugal or thrifty enough in spending to live within my means and to resourcefully store a surplus of clothing, food, money and other needed items for emergency use by my immediate family for one or more years

provident^2 - to be prone to prudently anticipate, prepare or provide for the future needs of me, my family and society

providential - to be provident

providing - to be a boy or man who is competent, diligent and responsible enough to adequately supply myself and my family with enough financial support through honorable means or methods

providing^2 - to be a girl or woman who is competent, diligent and responsible enough to adequately support myself and my dependents through honorable means or methods when I must

providing^3 - to intend to prepare with due foresight to furnish, equip, protect, support or sustain myself and my family

provincial - to be naturally simple and virtuous to an extent or in a manner which is typical of those who live in provincial or open country areas who are relatively unaccustomed to more darkened influences and more worldly lifestyles

proving - to intend to consistently confirm, demonstrate, establish or verify my genuine, true or valid faith in God by my believing and honorably exact obedience to His commandments, covenants, laws and ordinances

proving^2 - to be virtuously conscientious, diligent and faithful in striving to discover the truth about God by prayerful and thorough study and by my believing and honorably exact obedience to that divinely appointed law upon which receipt of that truth is predicated

proving^3 - to intend to personally ascertain and live in harmony with the discernibly enlightening and spiritually verifiable truth that: no deception, lie or pretense can permanently change the consequences of my tested and true desires, intentions and works on Earth

proving^4 - to intend to ascertain and distinguish that which is truly good and of God from that which is evil or satanic in order to choose that which is truly good and of God

proving^5 - to intend to ascertain and distinguish enlightened certainty, reality or truth from confusion, error and falsehood in order to choose enlightened certainty, reality or truth

proving[6] - to intend to analyze, evaluate, test or try the genuineness, quality, value or validity of all things in order to hold fast to the best instead of the rest

prowessed - to be intrepid and valiant in fighting against the evil or satanic powers of darkness, vice, corruption, bondage, despair, turmoil and misery

prudent - to be prone to choose that which is charitably loving, just, right and wise in the sight of God

prudent[2] - to be prone to cautiously and discreetly make providential and wise decisions in practical matters

prudent[3] - to be wise

pruning - to intend to refuse to be excessive

pruning[2] - to intend to cut, eliminate or remove that which is excessive

prying - to intend, whenever necessary, to honorably and justly search into the affairs or concerns of other people in order to safeguard me, my family and society from darkness, vice, corruption, bondage, despair, turmoil and misery

psyched - to be determined and enthused to do, be and give my very best

psychic - to be spiritually-minded

psychic[2] - to be discerning or perceptive of unseen reality

psychoanalytic - to be prone to effectively diagnose and treat

mental illness to an extent or in a manner which actually improves mental health

psychological - to be prone to discover and implement better proven mental means or methods of producing, preserving or restoring greater true enlightenment, virtue, integrity, liberty, hope, peace and joy within the human body, mind and spirit

psychological[2] - to be prone to examine physical and spiritual phenomena to learn the truth about human thinking and behavior

psychological[3] - to be prone to prayerfully study and ponder thinking and behavior

psychotherapeutic - to be prone to use valid cures or remedies which effectively promote healing or restoration to good emotional or mental health

public - to be virtuously patriotic

public[2] - to be virtuously civic-minded and social

public[3] - to be prone to honor, obey and sustain the good law of the land

public-spirited - to be virtuously patriotic

public-spirited[2] - to be virtuously public or social

publishing - to intend to seek widespread collaboration in announcing, declaring, proclaiming, stating or otherwise making a material public communication of thought which produces, preserves or restores true enlightenment, virtue and integrity within me, my family and society

publishing[2] - to intend to make a material public announcement, declaration, proclamation, statement or other material public communication of edifying or uplifting thought through or within an item publicly distributed, issued or sold

punctilious - to be prone to exactly, precisely or strictly observe the details or fine points in fulfilling my good and honorable agreements, commitments, covenants or debts

puncturing - to intend to acquire and exercise enough acute awareness, penetrating discernment and enlightened understanding with which to bore through or pierce confusion and darkness

punishing - to be virtuously just in dutifully administering by rightful authority that penalizing equal and honorable justice which is charitably loving, just, right and wise in the sight of God, to an extent or in a manner which is not prohibited by the good law of the land

purchased - to be redeemed

pure - to be sanctified unto perfectly virtuous cleanliness, innocence and integrity

pure[2] - to be prone to prayerfully keep my thoughts, words and actions chaste, clean, virtuous and above satanic or worldly temptation

pure[3] - to be godly enough to be made truly chaste, clean, pure and virtuous at heart—and to continue to encourage and help other people by charitable love, kindness, invitation and instruction to be godly enough to be made truly chaste, clean, pure and virtuous at heart

purehearted - to be sanctified unto perfectly virtuous cleanliness, innocence and integrity

purehearted[2] - to be pure-in-heart

pure-in-heart - to be virtuously Zionistic

pure-in-heart[2] - to be integrated-at-heart or purehearted

pure-in-heart[3] - to be prone to prayerfully and effectively keep the thoughts of my heart chaste, clean, virtuous and above satanic or worldly temptation

pure-in-heart[4] - to be filled with enough true enlightenment, virtue and integrity to see and reverence God and His chosen servants for who they are

purged - to be pure

purificatory - to be prone to purifying

purified - to be sanctified unto perfectly virtuous cleanliness, innocence and integrity

purified[2] - to be prone to prayerfully keep my thoughts, words and actions clean and above satanic or worldly temptation

purifying - to intend to lovingly encourage and kindly help someone to be pure

puristic - to be prone to strictly adhere to true enlightenment, virtue and integrity

puritanical - to be godly enough to be made truly chaste, clean, pure and virtuous at heart—and to continue to encourage and help other people by charitable love, kindness, invitation and instruction to be godly enough to be made truly chaste, clean, pure and virtuous at heart

puritanical[2] - to be prone to live in pure harmony with the

commandments, covenants, laws
and ordinances of God
purposeful - to be prone to do all
that I have ascertained by personal
enlightenment, inspiration or
revelation from God is truly
required by Him to receive from
Him all of the heavenly blessings,
gifts or rewards He wants me to
receive
purposeful² - to be resolved to
continue to do my very best to
think, speak and act in harmony
with each personal aim, ambition,
aspiration, commitment, desire,
goal, intention, plan, procedure or
resolution I have been commanded
to fulfill by personal
enlightenment, inspiration or
revelation from God
purposeful³ - to be prone to
produce, preserve or restore true
enlightenment, virtue and integrity
within me, my family and society
purposing - to intend to adopt,
form, make or set a good aim,
ambition, aspiration, commitment,
desire, goal, intention, plan,
procedure or resolution
pushing - to intend to exert
ambitious and energetic enterprise
or initiative toward something
which is truly better

Q

quality - to be of virtuous
character, disposition or
temperament
qualmish - to be prone to alleviate
the plain uneasiness, the warning
distress or the alarming anguish
within my enlightened conscience
by faithfully repenting and by
turning toward thinking, speaking
and acting in harmony with the

commandments, covenants, laws
and ordinances of God
qualmish² - to be prone to alleviate
the plain uneasiness, the warning
distress or the alarming anguish
within my enlightened conscience
by faithfully repenting and by
turning toward thinking, speaking
and acting in harmony with that
which produces, preserves or
restores true enlightenment, virtue
and integrity within me, my family
and society
quantitative - to be skilled in the
use of amounts, magnitudes,
mathematics, measurements or
numbers
queenly - to be a married girl or
woman who powerfully
personifies the most beautiful,
feminine, gracious and noble
characteristics of godly
womanhood by my faithfully
repentant and honorably exact
obedience to those divinely
appointed commandments,
covenants, laws and ordinances
upon which receipt of that power is
predicated
queenly² - to be a girl or woman
monarch who powerfully
personifies the most beautiful,
feminine, gracious and noble
characteristics of godly
womanhood by my faithfully
repentant and honorably exact
obedience to those divinely
appointed commandments,
covenants, laws and ordinances
upon which receipt of that power is
predicated
queenly³ - to be a girl or woman
who prevails by distinguished
performance

questioning - to intend to personally ascertain whether God will reveal knowledge of the truth about Himself to me by my believing and honorably exact obedience to that divinely appointed law upon which receipt of that knowledge is predicated

questioning[2] - to intend, through righteous prayer, study and obedience, to faithfully, honestly and sincerely seek verified personal knowledge of the truth about God

questioning[3] - to intend to honestly seek verified personal knowledge of the truth about who I am at heart, where I came from before birth, why I am here, and where I am going after my death

questioning[4] - to intend to honestly seek verified personal knowledge of the truth through personal and prayerful examination, inquiry, investigation or research into which personal thoughts, beliefs, values and characteristics can best produce, preserve or restore the greatest true enlightenment, virtue, integrity, liberty, hope, peace and joy within me, my family and society

questioning[5] - to intend to honestly seek verified personal knowledge of the truth through personal and prayerful examination, inquiry, investigation or research into which form of religion can actually empower me to best unite with others to best produce, preserve or restore the greatest true enlightenment, virtue, integrity, liberty, hope, peace and joy within ourselves, our families and society

questioning[6] - to intend to honestly seek verified personal knowledge of the truth through personal and prayerful examination, inquiry, investigation or research into which condition, form and practice of government can actually empower me to best unite with others to best produce, preserve or restore virtuously liberating freedom, health, honorable economic prosperity and steady progress within ourselves, our families and society

quickened - to be enlightened or glorified

quickened[2] - to be animated or enlivened

quickened[3] - to be healthy

quick-witted - to be keenly and quickly judicious

quick-witted[2] - to be vigilant, perceptive and prepared enough to quickly respond with understanding

quiet to be peaceful

quotable - to be prone to say good things worth repeating

R

race-blind - to be prone to refuse to regard race as an indication of the purity, strength or virtue of someone's character, or as an indication of a lack thereof

radiant - to be radiating

radiating - to be brightly aglow with beaming true enlightenment, virtue and integrity

radiating[2] - to intend to openly express my heartfelt hope, peace and joy in my countenance

radiative - to be prone to radiating

radiatory - to be prone to radiating

radical - to be rooted in that which is truly good and of God, and to advocate reform toward it or toward more of it

radical[2] - to be rooted in that which produces, preserves or restores enlightenment, virtue and integrity within me, my family and society, and to advocate reform toward it or toward more of it

raising - to be cultivating

raising[2] - to be elevating or uplifting

rallying - to intend to bounce back to mental, physical or spiritual health with renewed focus and strength

ransoming - to intend to pay or sacrifice enough to help deliver, discharge, redeem, release, rescue or save someone from darkness, vice, corruption, bondage, despair, turmoil and misery

rapturous - to be joyful

rare - to be exceptionally or uncommonly exemplary

rarefying - to intend to lovingly encourage and kindly help someone to be more spiritual

rarefying[2] - to intend to lovingly encourage and kindly help someone to be more refined

rating - to intend to be truly worthy to be esteemed remarkably good in the value of my actual performance

rational - to be prone to honorably, reasonably and sensibly think, speak, act, judge, lead and teach in harmony with a sure basis or foundation of thoughts, beliefs, values and characteristics which I have ascertained by personal enlightenment, inspiration or revelation from God are charitably loving, just, right and wise in the sight of God

rational[2] - to be prone to honorably, reasonably and sensibly seek to know whether something is firmly established upon or is in harmony with enlightened certainty, reality or truth by my believing and honorably exact obedience to that divinely appointed law upon which receipt of that knowledge is predicated

rationalistic - to be prone to personally ascertain and live in harmony with the discernibly enlightening and spiritually verifiable truth that: reasoning with true information and without erroneous information is prerequisite to coming to a true conclusion

rationing - to intend to dispense so as to minimize consumption, expense and waste

reaching - to intend to achieve that which is truly good and of God

reactionary - to be prone to react with enough strong opposition against change or reform that is evil or satanic

reactionary[2] - to be prone to react with enough strong opposition against change or reform which will produce, preserve or restore darkness, vice and corruption within me, my family and society

reactionary[3] - to be prone to react with enough strong opposition against change or reform which will destroy the virtuously liberating freedom, health, honorable economic prosperity and steady progress of me, my family and society

reading - to intend to truly ascertain, discern, experience, grasp or observe by personal enlightenment, inspiration or revelation from God within my mind and heart an absolutely and perfectly true awareness, comprehension, identification, knowledge, recognition or understanding of enlightened certainty, reality or truth, and to use it to correctly apprehend, interpret, learn, perceive or understand other things of which I become aware, including things written or otherwise recorded

reading[2] - to intend to correctly apprehend, interpret, learn, perceive or understand the true and valuable meaning and significance of things of which I become aware, including things written or otherwise recorded

real - to be prone to accept as real that which I know or have good enough reason to believe is real

real[2] - to be prone to refuse to accept as real that which I know or have good enough reason to believe is imaginary

realistic - to be in possession of and aware I have ascertained, discerned, experienced, observed, perceived or recognized within me the reception of an absolute, perfect and spiritually verified personal knowledge of the truth by personal enlightenment, inspiration or revelation from God that He has empowered me to know the truth about Him and about those good things He would have me think, say and do—along with those evil or satanic things I must avoid thinking, saying or doing—to receive His greatest blessings, gifts and rewards

realistic[2] - to be in possession of and aware I have ascertained, discerned, experienced, observed, perceived or recognized within me the reception of an absolute, perfect and spiritually verified personal knowledge of the truth by personal enlightenment, inspiration or revelation from God that He has empowered me to ascertain such realities as true enlightenment, virtue, integrity, liberty, hope, peace and joy—along with their opposites of darkness, vice, corruption, bondage, despair, turmoil and misery

realistic[3] - to be in possession of and aware I have ascertained, discerned, experienced, observed, perceived or recognized within me the reception of an absolute, perfect and spiritually verified personal knowledge of the truth by personal enlightenment, inspiration or revelation from God that He has empowered me to think and choose for myself

realistic[4] - to be in possession of and aware I have ascertained, discerned, experienced, observed, perceived or recognized within me the reception of an absolute, perfect and spiritually verified personal knowledge of the truth by personal enlightenment, inspiration or revelation from God about my existence, identity and nature as an immortal spirit being whose presence within my physical body gives my physical body life

realistic[5] - to be in possession of and aware I have ascertained, discerned, experienced, observed, perceived or recognized within me the reception of an absolute, perfect and spiritually verified personal knowledge of the truth by personal enlightenment, inspiration or revelation from God that He has empowered me to ascertain or discern truth by my believing and honorably exact obedience to that divinely appointed law upon which receipt of that knowledge is predicated

realistic[6] - to be prone to accept as reality the truth about someone or something real outside of my thoughts, which I know or can know by enlightened reasoning is truth within my thoughts

realistic[7] - to be prone to refuse to accept as reality that which I have ascertained is confusion, error or falsehood

realistic[8] - to be prone to come to an accurate factual knowledge of things as they are or as they were through the accurate processing and correct interpretation of perceived sensation within my thoughts

realizing - to intend to think, say and do all that I know God would have me think, say and do

realizing[2] - to be aware I have ascertained, discerned, experienced, observed, perceived or recognized within me the reception of an absolute, perfect and spiritually verified personal knowledge of enlightened certainty, reality or truth by personal enlightenment, inspiration or revelation from God of those things He would have me think, say and do

realizing[3] - to intend to come to an absolute, perfect and spiritually verified personal knowledge of

enlightened certainty, reality or truth by experiencing or observing within me the reception of powerfully clear, confirming and distinct personal enlightenment, inspiration or revelation from God by my believing and honorably exact obedience to that divinely appointed law upon which receipt of that knowledge is predicated

realizing[4] - to intend to clearly recall, recognize or understand the pure truth about someone or something

rearing - to intend to bring up or raise up a child in true enlightenment, virtue, integrity, liberty, hope, peace and joy

reasonable - to be prone to refuse to speak or act in a vicious manner

reasoning - to intend to clearly understand, correctly organize, accurately interpret and consistently apply what I have ascertained is truly good and of God

reasoning[2] - to intend to clearly understand, correctly organize, accurately interpret and consistently apply what I have ascertained is truth

reasoning[3] - to intend to accurately deduce, clearly derive and correctly organize verified or verifiably true relationships between and among the people and things I have experienced or observed

reasoning[4] - to intend to honorably rely upon what I honestly believe to be true in my efforts to logically reach sound conclusions, decisions or judgments from given facts or evidence

reasoning[5] - to intend to deduce or induce logical conclusions, decisions, propositions or judgments in harmony with earlier legal conclusions, decisions, precedents or judgments which are the good law of the land

reborn - to be redeemed unto exaltation

reborn[2] - to be redeemed and released from the bondage, burdens and debts of my sins

reborn[3] - to be prone, as a baptized believer in the charitable love, cleansing power and redeeming grace of the Atonement of the Lord Jesus Christ, to justly receive by the priesthood ordinance of confirmation and through my faithful righteousness the gift of the constant companionship of the divine influence or divine presence of the Holy Ghost, who, in harmony with my faithfulness, brings into my body, mind and spirit manifestations of God's love and a newness of life characterized by my sanctification from the consequences and effects of sin, by my liberation from darkness, vice and corruption, by my having no more disposition to do evil, by my increase in hope, peace and joy, by my reception of greater power to personally progress toward exaltation, and by my reception of additional blessings which come from my faithfully repentant and honorably exact obedience to the commandments, covenants, laws and ordinances of God

reborn[4] - to be prone, as a faithful and repentant believer in the charitable love, cleansing power and redeeming grace of the Atonement of the Lord Jesus Christ, to be buried or immersed in a watery grave in symbolic death and then brought forth out of water in a symbolic newness, rebirth or resurrection of life by a duly ordained boy or man called of God who bears true priesthood authority from God and has authorization from God's own called, ordained and authorized priesthood leaders on Earth to administer that ordinance of baptism without pay—so that I can justly receive a remission of sins, and can be confirmed by the priesthood ordinance of confirmation in further preparation for my receiving the blessings of a glorious celestial resurrection and exaltation in the world to come

reborn[5] - to be prone to change or convert myself to a better way of life by adopting and then willfully thinking, speaking and acting in harmony with those religious thoughts, beliefs, values and characteristics which produce, preserve or restore the greatest true enlightenment, virtue, integrity, liberty, hope, peace and joy within me, my family and society

rebounding - to intend to spring back into better health

recalcitrant - to be prone to somehow obstinately kick or rebel against evil or satanic authority, control, influence or power

receiving - to intend to acquire from God and to retain within my soul from day to day the gift of the Holy Ghost by my faithfully repentant and honorably exact obedience to those divinely appointed commandments, covenants, laws and ordinances upon which receipt of that gift is predicated

receiving[2] - to intend to openly embrace, greet or welcome the Spirit of God into my mind and heart

reciprocating - to intend to kindly offer in exchange truly charitable love, virtuous service and true enlightenment to those who defame, persecute or otherwise despitefully abuse me, so that we might become reconciled with one another well enough to enjoy greater true enlightenment, virtue, integrity liberty, hope, peace and joy together

reciprocating[2] - to intend to kindly offer in exchange truly charitable love, virtuous service and true enlightenment to those who curse or revile me, so that we might become reconciled with one another well enough to enjoy greater true enlightenment, virtue, integrity liberty, hope, peace and joy together

reciprocating[3] - to intend to kindly offer in exchange truly charitable love, virtuous service and true enlightenment to those who hate me, so that we might become reconciled with one another well enough to enjoy greater true enlightenment, virtue, integrity liberty, hope, peace and joy together

reciprocating[4] - to intend to kindly offer that truly charitable love, virtuous service and true enlightenment to other people that I would have them give to me

reciprocating[5] - to intend to pray for those who defame, persecute or otherwise despitefully abuse me

for being truly chaste, clean, pure and virtuous at heart or for encouraging and helping other people by charitable love, kindness, invitation and instruction to be godly enough to be made truly chaste, clean, pure and virtuous at heart

reciprocating[6] - to intend to pray for those who defame, persecute or otherwise despitefully abuse me

reciprocating[7] - to intend to do unto other people the good I would have them do unto me if their words or actions were mine

reciprocating[8] - to intend to desire for other people the good I desire for myself

reciprocating[9] - to intend to avoid the despiteful abuse of other people by refusing to despitefully abuse them

reciprocating[10] - to intend to refuse to do unto other people what I would not like myself

reciprocating[11] - to intend to refuse to behave toward other people to an extent or in a manner which is disagreeable to me

reciprocating[12] - to intend to return sincere kindness with sincere kindness

recking - to intend to carefully and responsibly regard the consequences or risks of actions to be taken or of decisions to be made

recognizing - to intend to accurately recollect or reprocess true knowledge or understanding of the characteristic and distinctive differences between that which is truly good and of God and that which is evil or satanic

recognizing[2] - to intend to accurately recollect or reprocess

true knowledge or understanding
of the characteristic and distinctive
differences between that which is
enlightened certainty, reality or
truth and that which is confusion,
error or falsehood

recognizing[3] - to intend to
accurately recollect or reprocess
true knowledge or understanding
of the characteristic and distinctive
differences between that which is
real and that which is imaginary

recognizing[4] - to intend to recollect
or reprocess knowledge or
understanding of truth

recognizing[5] - to intend to formally
and willingly accept or
acknowledge reality for what it is

recommendable - to be truly
worthy to be endorsed, introduced,
presented or referred to as
commendable or recommended

recommended - to be prone to
willingly receive and work to
retain commendation,
endorsement, introduction,
presentation or referral as being
truly favorable, of good report,
praiseworthy and virtuous

recommending - to intend to truly
endorse, introduce, present or refer
to someone or something with
well-deserved favor, good report
and special praise

reconcilable - to be able and
willing to immediately and truly
repent and obey the
commandments, covenants, laws
and ordinances of God well
enough to be reconciled to God
through the charitable love,
cleansing power and redeeming
grace of the Atonement of the Lord
Jesus Christ

reconcilable[2] - to be and to choose
to remain reconciled with another
person in a mutually beneficial
manner through our honorable and
virtuous forgiving of one another
and our faithful, timely and true
repentance, obedience and
reconciliation to God

reconciled - to be sanctified and
made virtuously one in mind and
heart with God through the
charitable love, cleansing power
and redeeming grace of the
Atonement of the Lord Jesus Christ
by my faithfully repentant and
honorably exact obedience to those
divinely appointed
commandments, covenants, laws
and ordinances upon which receipt
of that virtuous oneness is
predicated

reconciled[2] - to be made virtuously
one, unified or whole with another
person through our complete
reconciliation and through our
faithful, timely and true
repentance, obedience and
reconciliation to God

reconciling - to intend to seek full
restoration to virtuous oneness in
mind and heart with God by
faithfully, timely and truly
repenting, by obeying His
commandments, covenants, laws
and ordinances, and by calling
upon Him in fasting and prayer
until I receive by the Spirit of God
a healing manifestation or witness
that my sins are remitted and I am
restored to virtuous oneness with
Him

reconciling[2] - to intend to
virtuously and wisely seek full
compatibility, oneness, trust, unity
or wholeness with a person who

claims I have abused or injured them, by conversing or meeting with them alone to seek a clear understanding of any actual abuse or injury I have actually caused them and to then complete all repenting necessary for me to become or to remain one with God and with them

reconciling[3] - to intend to unconditionally forgive and virtuously reciprocate in an effort to seek full compatibility, oneness, trust, unity or wholeness with another person who fails or refuses to completely repent for all of the bearable or tolerable harm, injury or offense they have viciously imposed upon me once, twice or three times

reconciling[4] - to intend to unconditionally forgive and virtuously reciprocate in an effort to seek full compatibility, oneness, trust, unity or wholeness with another person who is completely repentant of the personal harm or injury they have inflicted upon me

reconciling[5] - to intend to seek full restoration to compatibility, oneness, trust, unity or wholeness with an unrepentant person who has personally inflicted vicious harm, injury or offense upon me four or more times, after that person completely repents

reconsidering - to intend to again contemplate, deliberate, discuss or evaluate something which must be taken care of as part of faithful, timely and true repentance, obedience and reconciliation to God

reconsidering[2] - to intend to again contemplate, deliberate, discuss or evaluate something which must be taken care of for equal and honorable justice to be served in harmony with the good law of the land

reconsidering[3] - to intend to again contemplate, deliberate, discuss or evaluate something which can and should be changed and improved

recording - to intend to make and keep an accurate account or register of my personal history that will bear witness to my posterity and to other people of the miraculous hand of God in my life and of my faithful efforts to please Him during my life

recording[2] - to intend to make an accurate account or register of my family history and my ancestry that will bear witness to my posterity and to other people of the continuing importance of producing, preserving or restoring true enlightenment, virtue, integrity, liberty, hope, peace and joy within ourselves, our families and society

recording[3] - to intend to make an accurate account, history or record of the valuable lessons of history

record-keeping - to intend to keep for my posterity an accurate account or register of my personal life, my family and our ancestry which will teach them the importance of producing, preserving or restoring true enlightenment, virtue, integrity, liberty, hope, peace and joy within ourselves, our families and society

recouping - to intend to indemnify, pay or make restitution to one or more other people as well as I can and should for damages, injuries or losses which I have viciously caused them

recreating - to intend to recover, refresh, renew or revive my good health with enough healthy indoor or outdoor activities

rectifying - to be repenting

rectifying^2 - to intend to make things right by correcting what is erroneous, false or wrong

rectifying^3 - to intend to compensate, recompense or restore enough to make things right

rectitudinous - to be made charitably loving, just, right and wise in the sight of God by my faithfully repentant and honorably exact obedience to those divinely appointed commandments, covenants, laws and ordinances upon which receipt of those blessings is predicated

rectitudinous^2 - to be prone to think, say and do what is right in harmony with the commandments, covenants, laws and ordinances of God

rectitudinous^3 - to be prone to think, say and do what is right in harmony with the good law of the land

recuperating - to intend to seek recovery or restoration from loss of health and strength to my body, mind or spirit

recusing - to intend to officially challenge or disqualify someone from forming or passing judgment to prevent their exercise of bias, favoritism or partiality toward sustaining that which produces, preserves or restores darkness, vice and corruption within me, my family and society

recusing^2 - to intend to officially challenge or disqualify someone from forming or passing judgment in order to prevent the risk of corruptly unjust treatment of one of the parties subject to that judgment

recusing^3 - to intend to officially challenge or disqualify someone from forming or passing judgment due to the possibility they might viciously act in their own self-interest

red - to be prone to live in harmony with the ways of character or culture of those with naturally reddish-brown-colored skin to the extent those ways produce, preserve or restore true enlightenment, virtue and integrity within me, my family and society

redeemable - to be found worthy in the sight of God to be redeemed unto exaltation

redeemable^2 - to be prone to successfully avoid being irredeemable

redeemed - to be purchased or ransomed from physical death and from separation from God by the charitable love, cleansing power and redeeming grace of the Atonement of the Lord Jesus Christ unto a glorious celestial resurrection by the gift and power of God because of my innocence in the sight of God as a child who dies before reaching the age of accountability or as another person who is not spiritually accountable or mentally competent to choose to commit sin on Earth

redeemed^2 - to be purchased or ransomed from physical death and from separation from God by the charitable love, cleansing power and redeeming grace of the Atonement of the Lord Jesus Christ unto a glorious celestial resurrection by the gift and power of God because of my innocence in the sight of God as one who dies without knowing the commandments, covenants, laws and ordinances of the gospel of the Lord Jesus Christ, who would have otherwise received and obeyed them before my physical death

redeemed[3] - to be desirous and righteous enough to receive the commandments, covenants, laws and ordinances of the gospel of the Lord Jesus Christ well enough when I am dead to be purchased or ransomed from physical death and from the effects of my transgressions by the charitable love, cleansing power and redeeming grace of the Atonement of the Lord Jesus Christ unto a glorious celestial resurrection by the gift and power of God because of my innocence in the sight of God as one who has ignorantly sinned and then dies without knowing the truth of my rebellion against the will of God

redeemed[4] - to be one of those who are neither murderous nor perdition who are justly purchased or ransomed from physical death and from the just demands, liabilities and penalties imposed upon me by the eternally binding law of justice for my own sins, and to be sanctified and reconciled to God unto a glorious celestial resurrection through the charitable love, cleansing power and

redeeming grace of the Atonement of the Lord Jesus Christ

redeemed[5] - to be a partaker of the charitable love, cleansing power and redeeming grace of the Atonement of the Lord Jesus Christ, by which He justly and graciously applies His own perfect and everlasting mortal sacrificial payment of suffering for the sins of all humankind, both the living and the dead, including mine, when I have brought forth the fruits of faithfully repentant and honorably exact obedience to those divinely appointed commandments, covenants, laws and ordinances upon which receipt of that redeeming grace is predicated

redeemed[6] - to be justly purchased or ransomed from all of the evil or satanic powers of binding addiction, compulsion, impulsion, obsession, occupation and possession through the charitable love, cleansing power and redeeming grace of the Atonement of the Lord Jesus Christ by my faithfully repentant and honorably exact obedience to those divinely appointed commandments, covenants, laws and ordinances upon which receipt of that redeeming grace is predicated

redeemed[7] - to be purchased or ransomed by the gift and power of the Lord Jesus Christ from physical death and the grave unto resurrection into the highest kingdom of glory I have qualified myself to receive

redeemed[8] - to be purchased or ransomed by the charitable love, cleansing power and redeeming grace of the Atonement of the Lord

Jesus Christ from the just liabilities and penalties demanded by the eternally binding law of justice for the transgression and fall of Adam and Eve

redeemed[9] - to be purchased or ransomed from all bewilderment, confusion and perplexity of confusion, error and falsehood by my believing and honorably exact obedience to that divinely appointed law upon which receipt of that blessing is predicated

redeeming - to intend to lovingly encourage and kindly help someone to be redeemed unto exaltation

redefining - to intend to again attach or associate words or word symbols with clear and distinctive meanings by which they once acted or worked together to accurately carry, convey, disclose, explain, present or represent a portion of enlightened certainty, reality or truth previously explained or known but lost

redefining[2] - to intend to again fully identify the true and valuable meaning, nature, qualities or limits of something

redressing - to intend to set things right or straight by justly providing enough amends, compensation, correction, recompense, relief or remedy

referential - to be a source of enlightenment

refined - to be redeemed unto exaltation

refined[2] - to be redeemed and released from the bondage, burdens and debts of my sins

refined[3] - to be godly enough to be made truly chaste, clean, pure and

virtuous at heart—and to continue to encourage and help other people by charitable love, kindness, invitation and instruction to be godly enough to be made truly chaste, clean, pure and virtuous at heart

refined[4] - to be so polished and pure in true enlightenment, virtue and integrity as to be liberated within my mind and heart from all that is evil or satanic

refined[5] - to be polished in the sensitive and subtle use of good manners

refined[6] - to be prone to enjoy learning more about and living in harmony with the beneficial elements and virtuous qualities of the arts, sciences and humanities from one or more social classes, groups, nations or other factions of society

refined[7] - to be prone to enjoy learning more about and living more in harmony with the beneficial elements and virtuous qualities of academic, dancing, dress, food, graphic, intellectual, literary, musical or other socially recognized human characteristics or products found among various social classes, groups, nations or other factions of society

refined[8] - to be prone to enjoy learning more about and living more in harmony with the beneficial elements and virtuous qualities of the social beliefs, behaviors, forms, manners, traits and ways of one or more social classes, groups, nations or other factions of society

refining - to intend to lovingly encourage and kindly help someone to be refined

reforming - to intend to continue to progress by continuing to improve the enlightenment and virtue of the thoughts I continue to integrate into the thoughts, beliefs, values and characteristics of my heart

reforming[2] - to be repenting

reforming[3] - to be rectifying

refreshed - to be newly animated or enlivened

refulgent - to be prone to radiate brilliant enlightenment

regenerating - to intend to produce or submit to complete improvement

registered - to be one of those accurately listed or recorded as being filled with good works and righteous desires

regretting - to be filled with sincere remorse or sorrow for my corrupt, sinful or vicious wrongdoing of which I have not yet completely repented

rehabilitating - to intend, as part of my faithful, timely and true repentance, to do all I can and should to reestablish or restore the good name or reputation of each person I have victimized by my backbiting, defaming, denigrating, discrediting, evil-speaking or maligning

rehabilitating[2] - to intend to reform or restore to good health

reinforcing - to intend to strengthen or support truly virtuous behavior by rewarding it

reinforcing[2] - to intend to strengthen or support positive behavior by rewarding it

rejoicing - to be joyful

rejoicing[2] - to intend to experience or express true feelings of exhilarating gladness or joy

rejoining - to intend to renew association, enlistment, membership, participation, relationship or unity with one or more other people of true enlightenment, virtue and integrity

relating - to intend to seek better relations with God

relating[2] - to intend to seek better family relations

relating[3] - to intend to seek better human relations

relational - to be prone to seek a better relationship with God

relational[2] - to be prone to seek a better marriage relationship with my lawfully and legally wedded husband or wife

relational[3] - to be prone to seek a better relationship with my child or children

relational[4] - to be prone to seek a better relationship with those who are my relatives by blood or by marriage

relational[5] - to be prone to obtain or maintain good human relations

released - to be redeemed unto exaltation

released[2] - to be redeemed and liberated from the bondage, burdens and debts of my sins

released[3] - to be prone to humbly and prayerfully allow the heavenly power which comes from virtuous forgiving to emancipate, free or liberate me from the self-consuming bitterness and festering pain I might otherwise viciously continue to wish upon someone else

released[4] - to be virtuously emancipated, freed or liberated

releasing - to be virtuously emancipating, freeing or liberating

releasing[2] - to intend to lovingly encourage and kindly help someone to be virtuously released

relevant - to be virtuously realistic

reliable - to be prone to live up to the full confidence and trust God has placed in me to learn and do His will with His help, so that by His grace, love and power I can justly receive all earthly and heavenly blessings, gifts or rewards He wants me to receive

religionistic - to be religious to an extent or in a manner which produces, preserves or restores true enlightenment, virtue and integrity within me, my family and society

religious - to be virtuously conscientious in giving all that I have and am to doing my very best day by day to inherit or receive the greatest eternal blessings of knowing, loving, reverencing, serving and worshiping God by my faithfully repentant and honorably exact obedience to those divinely appointed commandments, covenants, laws and ordinances upon which receipt of those blessings is predicated

religious[2] - to be prone to bind myself to continue to faithfully strive to do all I can and should to discover and then live by that form of religion which best empowers me to best unite with others to best produce, preserve or restore the greatest true enlightenment, virtue, integrity, liberty, hope, peace and joy within ourselves, our families and society

religious[3] - to be prone to bind myself to continue to faithfully strive to do all I can and should to discover and then live by that form of religion which best empowers me to best add to that measure of true enlightenment, virtue, integrity, liberty, hope, peace and joy already found within me

religious[4] - to be prone to bind myself to continue to faithfully strive to do all I can and should to discover and then live in harmony with those religious anointings, ceremonies, confirmations, covenants, endowments, formalities, oaths, observances, orders, ordinances, ordinations, pledges, practices, rites, rituals, sacraments, sealings, services or washings which best empower me to receive the greatest true enlightenment, virtue, integrity, liberty, hope, peace and joy of which I have become aware in my education and training and in my own constantly diligent, honest and open-minded searching

religious[5] - to be prone to bind myself to continue to faithfully strive to do all I can and should to diligently, persistently and wholeheartedly live in harmony with the best and highest doctrines, laws, precepts, principles, rules, standards or values of truth and virtue of which I have become aware in my education and training and in my own constantly diligent, honest and open-minded searching

religious[6] - to be prone to think, speak and act in harmony with the self-evident truth that each accountable person habitually

binds or fastens the conduct and outcome of our own life to our own personal form of religion by willfully choosing to rely on the practice of complying with and conforming to one particular system of devotion, faith, reverence, veneration or worship, or to one particular form of ideology or ideological constraint, obligation or restraint, or to one particular lifestyle or way of life, or to one particular set of thoughts, beliefs, values and characteristics—any one of which can be a personal form of religion
relishing - to be grateful
remediable - to be prone to accept correction, cure, healing or removal from that which is evil or satanic
remedying - to be repenting
remedying[2] - to intend to correct, cure, heal or remove from that which is evil or satanic
remorseful - to be prone to deeply feel painfully biting anguish, regret or sorrow for my corrupt, sinful or vicious wrongdoing of which I have not yet completely repented
repairing - to intend to reconcile, remedy, renew or restore someone to good and sound condition
reparable - to be and to choose to remain reconciled, remedied, renewed or restored to good and sound condition
repentant - to be repenting
repenting - to intend to personally ascertain and live in harmony with the discernibly enlightening and spiritually verifiable truth that: while the truly repentant may not be able to make up all of the naturally consequent losses to ourselves or to the other victims of

our corrupt, sinful or vicious wrongdoing, the heavenly gift of repentance, the miracle of the forgiveness of God, a cleansing rebirth to a new and better lifestyle, and the hope of exaltation are nevertheless available to all people who are neither murderous nor perdition, through the charitable love, cleansing power and redeeming grace of the Atonement of the Lord Jesus Christ by our faithfully repentant and honorably exact obedience to those divinely appointed commandments, covenants, laws and ordinances upon which receipt of those blessings is predicated
repenting[2] - to intend to lovingly place my salvation from my corrupt, sinful or vicious wrongdoing into the hands of God by remaining brokenhearted and spiritually contrite enough before God to willfully retain a remission of my sins from day to day by my faithfully repentant and honorably exact obedience to those divinely appointed commandments, covenants, laws and ordinances upon which receipt of that remission is predicated—essential requirements of which include entirely forsaking my sinful and vicious wrongdoing, ministering enough to the relief of the needy and the poor, imparting enough of my substance to them and visiting them enough on a regular basis
repenting[3] - to intend to lovingly place my salvation from my corrupt, sinful or vicious wrongdoing into the hands of God by remaining brokenhearted and spiritually contrite enough before

God to consistently do all I can and should to successfully and wholeheartedly complete all of the requirements of faithful, timely and true repentance—so that I can worthily receive a remission of my sins through divinely authorized baptism and confirmation and through the charitable love, cleansing power and redeeming grace of the Atonement of the Lord Jesus Christ—so that I can now experience a conversion, healing or rebirth of my soul into a heavenly state of liberty, hope, peace and joy—so that I can enjoy a better life as a better person, as a better family member and as a law-abiding and self-reliant net contributor to the virtuously liberating freedom, health, honorable economic prosperity and steady progress of me, my family and society now and forever

repenting[4] - to intend to lovingly place my salvation from my corrupt, sinful or vicious wrongdoing into the hands of God by seeking necessary atonement, peace and reconciliation with God, with other people and with myself by successfully and wholeheartedly completing every element, requirement and step of the process of true repentance, including: consciously recognizing and honestly admitting guilt to myself for all of my corrupt, sinful or vicious wrongdoing—and then humbly and willfully suffering transforming godly sorrow—and then achieving enough change of heart to completely forsake my wrongdoing—and then humbly, willfully and personally confessing my wrongdoing to God and to each of my victims (and to ecclesiastical and public authorities for major sins and serious violations of law)—and then humbly and sincerely apologizing to my victims—and then honorably doing the best I can to make full compensation, payment or restitution to my victims—and then virtuously forgiving myself and others—and then humbly and prayerfully continuing to do my very best to live a new and better life by my believing and honorably exact obedience to the divinely appointed commandments, covenants, laws and ordinances of God

repenting[5] - to intend to constantly choose to personally progress by consistently turning my mind and heart back and toward thoughts, beliefs, values and characteristics which produce, preserve or restore true enlightenment, virtue and integrity within me, my family and society

repenting[6] - to intend to constantly choose to personally progress by consistently turning my mind and heart back and away from those thoughts, beliefs, values and characteristics which produce, preserve or restore darkness, vice and corruption within me, my family and society

repenting[7] - to intend to refuse to be terrestrial or telestial when God's gift of repentance and His miracle of forgiveness are available to help me become celestial

repenting[8] - to intend to do all I can and should to repent as a murderer as long as I live

reposed - to be dignified
reprehensible - to be prone to honorably and justly heed a needed warning to repent of all of the corrupt, sinful or vicious wrongdoing within me, by responding with my faithful, timely and true repentance, obedience and reconciliation to God
reprehensible[2] - to be prone to readily and willingly subject myself to someone's efforts to honorably and justly place blame, fault or guilt against me
representative - to be a duly elected legislative representative who is virtuously governing and patriotic
representing - to intend to again express, perform or present thoughts, words or actions which are truly good and of God
repressing - to intend to restrain or keep darkness, vice and corruption from entering into the thoughts, beliefs, values and characteristics of my heart
reproachable - to be prone to honorably and justly heed a needed warning to repent of all of the corrupt, sinful or vicious wrongdoing within me, by responding with my faithful, timely and true repentance, obedience and reconciliation to God
reproachable[2] - to be prone to readily and willingly subject myself to someone's efforts to honorably and justly place disapproval, blame, fault or guilt against me
reproaching - to intend to honorably and justly seek to bring

someone to enough disgrace or shame with enough censure, rebuke or reproof to awaken within them the remorse essential to their faithful, timely and true repentance, obedience and reconciliation to God
reproving - to intend, as prompted by the Spirit of God, to charitably, gently, kindly, patiently, persuasively and necessarily correct someone in order to help them ascertain, discern or certainly prove that which is truly good and of God from that which is evil or satanic in order to help them value and choose the good
reproving[2] - to intend, as prompted by the Spirit of God, to charitably, gently, kindly, patiently, persuasively and necessarily correct someone in order to help them ascertain, discern or certainly prove enlightened certainty, reality or truth from confusion, error and falsehood in order to help them value and choose the truth
reproving[3] - to intend, as prompted by the Spirit of God, to strive in a non-abusive manner to somehow abruptly, intensely, painfully and severely cut, pierce or otherwise wound a viciously recalcitrant person to the depth of their soul in a reproaching test of integrity to see if they will find enough true remorse or godly sorrow to prove again their faithfulness to God by immediately and truly repenting of their corrupt, sinful or vicious wrongdoing, followed by my demonstration of increased love designed to reassure them I have acted as their true friend and not as an enemy

reputable - to be godly enough to be made truly chaste, clean, pure and virtuous at heart—and to continue to encourage and help other people by charitable love, kindness, invitation and instruction to be godly enough to be made truly chaste, clean, pure and virtuous at heart

reputable^2 - to be filled with enough true enlightenment, virtue and integrity to produce, preserve or restore true liberty, hope, peace and joy within me, my family and society

reputable^3 - to be filled with enough true enlightenment, virtue and integrity to strongly attract or appeal to another person's sense of true enlightenment, virtue and integrity

reputable^4 - to be prone to win favorable consideration or reputation from other people by doing and being good

rescued - to be exalted

rescued^2 - to be redeemed unto exaltation

rescued^3 - to be redeemed and released from the bondage, burdens and debts of my sins

rescuing - to intend to lovingly encourage and kindly help someone to be redeemed unto exaltation

rescuing^2 - to intend to deliver or save someone from becoming infected or polluted by darkness, vice and corruption

rescuing^3 - to intend to deliver or save someone from all of the evil or satanic powers of binding addiction, compulsion, impulsion, obsession, occupation and possession

rescuing^4 - to intend to deliver or save someone from the darkness of confusion

researching - to intend to effectively and virtuously experiment, inquire, investigate or study ways and means for bringing about a result which is truly good and of God

researching^2 - to intend to effectively and virtuously experiment, inquire, investigate or study ways and means for bringing about a better result

researching^3 - to intend to effectively and virtuously experiment, inquire, investigate or study in order to discover the characteristic and distinctive differences between that which is truly good and of God and that which is evil or satanic

researching^4 - to intend to effectively and virtuously experiment, inquire, investigate or study in order to discover that which is enlightened certainty, reality or truth and that which is confusion, error or falsehood

researching^5 - to intend to effectively and virtuously experiment, inquire, investigate or study in order to discover that which is real and that which is imaginary

reserved - to be prone to restrain all of my thoughts, words and actions enough to keep them safely integrated within the discernibly enlightened boundaries of chastity, cleanliness, purity and virtue which God has justly set by law and commandment

resilient - to be prone to quickly rise above and to then continue to cheerfully, courageously and hopefully float upon darkened and submerging depression, doubt or discouragement

resolute - to be decisively determined, firm, fixed or steady in righteous thought, word and action

resolute[2] - to be prone to refuse to indecisively hesitate, vacillate or waver from righteous thought, word and action

resolving - to intend to think, say and do that which is charitably loving, just, right and wise in the sight of God

resourceful - to be prone to promptly and skillfully deal with unexpected difficulty or emergency while conserving or preserving available means

resourceful[2] - to be economical, frugal or thrifty enough in spending to live within my means and to providently store a surplus of clothing, food, money and other needed items for emergency use by my immediate family for one or more years

resourceful[3] - to be prone to minimize consumption, expense and waste

respectable - to be filled with enough true enlightenment, virtue and integrity to be honorable, praiseworthy or venerable in the sight of God

respecting - to intend to reverence the worth of a person's divine origin, purpose and potential

respecting[2] - to intend to abstain from abusing or mistreating a human being in any way

respecting[3] - to intend to regard someone as possessing great worth as a human being

resplendent - to be prone to brilliantly radiate or shine with true enlightenment, virtue and integrity

responsible - to be prone to do my very best to be my very best

responsible[2] - to be prone to honorably and justly heed a needed warning to repent of all of the corrupt, sinful or vicious wrongdoing within me, by responding with my faithful, timely and true repentance, obedience and reconciliation to God

responsible[3] - to be prone to honorably and justly answer for, explain or report what I have done wrong or what I have failed to do right when good conscience, justice, truth and virtue require me to do so

responsible[4] - to be prone to readily and willingly subject myself to someone's efforts to honorably and justly place blame, fault or guilt against me

responsible[5] - to be prone to discharge or pay my honorable debts in a timely manner

responsible[6] - to be prone to fulfill my good and honorable duties or obligations in a timely manner

responsible[7] - to be prone to account for, answer for, explain or report what I have done wrong or what I have failed to do right when required to do so by the good law of the land

resting - to be peaceful

resting[2] - to intend to keep my mind at ease with a clean conscience

restless - to be disquieted or distressed enough about my

thoughts, beliefs, values and characteristics of corrupt, sinful or vicious wrongdoing to faithfully and immediately seek true and complete repentance, obedience and reconciliation to God
restrained - to be prone to possess and maintain liberty, hope, peace, joy and other heavenly blessings by my believing and honorably exact obedience to those divinely appointed laws upon which receipt of those blessings is predicated
restrained[2] - to be prone to powerfully control or govern myself to an extent or in a manner which produces, preserves or restores true enlightenment, virtue and integrity within me, my family and society
restrained[3] - to be prone to powerfully control or govern myself to an extent or in a manner which produces, preserves or restores the virtuously liberating freedom, health, honorable economic prosperity and steady progress of me, my family and society
restrained[4] - to be prone to keep my thoughts, words and actions within the safe and discernibly enlightened boundaries of chastity, cleanliness, purity and virtue which God has justly set by law and commandment
restrained[5] - to be prone to powerfully control or govern the pleasure and satisfaction of all of my biologically inherent and naturally impelling emotional, physical or sexual appetites, cravings, desires, drives and passions enough to keep them safely integrated within the

discernibly enlightened boundaries of chastity, cleanliness, purity and virtue which God has justly set by law and commandment
restrained[6] - to be prone to repress or suppress darkness, vice and corruption from entering into the thoughts, beliefs, values and characteristics of my heart
restrained[7] - to be prone to readily and willingly submit to those who exercise their duly authorized powers of control, direction, dominion, government or rule to an extent or in a manner which produces, preserves or restores true enlightenment, virtue and integrity within me, my family and society
restrained[8] - to be prone to readily and willingly submit to those who exercise their duly authorized powers of control, direction, dominion, government or rule to an extent or in a manner which produces, preserves or restores the virtuously liberating freedom, health, honorable economic prosperity and steady progress of me, my family and society
restrictionist - to be prone to legally enact and enforce binding or confining limitations, prohibitions, restraints or restrictions against that which produces, preserves or restores darkness, vice and corruption within me, my family and society
resurgent - to be buoyant
resurrecting - to intend to personally ascertain and live in harmony with celestial law so that, following my physical death, the elements of my physical body of flesh and bones will, in the due time and by the powers of the

redemption and resurrection of the Lord Jesus Christ, be once and forever reformed and reunited with my immortal spirit being in a celestial glorified, prime and tangible form of myself that is no more subject to physical death, defect, deformity, disability or sickness, to justly inherit an everlasting realm of glory like that of the sun as compared to the moon and stars—and to dwell in the celestial presence of God the Eternal Father and to receive of His celestial blessings forever

resuscitated - to be reawakened or revived away from darkness, vice and corruption

resuscitated^2 - to be reawakened or revived away from all of the evil or satanic powers of binding addiction, compulsion, impulsion, obsession, occupation and possession

resuscitated^3 - to be reawakened or revived away from the darkness of confusion

resuscitating - to intend to reawaken or revive someone from darkness, vice and corruption

resuscitating^2 - to intend to reawaken or revive someone from all of the evil or satanic powers of binding addiction, compulsion, impulsion, obsession, occupation and possession

resuscitating^3 - to intend to reawaken or revive someone from the darkness of confusion

retrenching - to intend to cut down, cut off, cut out or cut short that which produces, preserves or restores the flow of darkness, vice and corruption into me, my family and society

retrospective - to be prone to wisely continue to apply the true lessons I have learned about that which is truly good and of God

retrospective^2 - to be prone to wisely continue to apply the true lessons I have learned about truth

returning - to be repenting

reunifying - to intend to again combine, harmonize, join or unite with one or more other people of true enlightenment, virtue and integrity

reunifying^2 - to intend to lovingly encourage and kindly help people of true enlightenment, virtue and integrity to again be united

reunited - to be united again with one or more other people of true enlightenment, virtue and integrity

revelational - to be truly enlightened or inspired of God by one or more messages revealed audibly to me by God the Eternal Father, or by His Son, the Lord Jesus Christ, or by Their angelic messengers, or by the dreams, visions or deeply inspirational impressions of a still, small voice—all of which are clearly and undeniably confirmed as truth within my mind and heart by the power of the Holy Ghost by my believing and honorably exact obedience to that divinely appointed law upon which receipt of that revelation is predicated

revelational^2 - to be prone to personally ascertain and live in harmony with the discernibly enlightening and spiritually verifiable truth that: God is a living God who is empowered to reveal the truth about Himself and about His mind and will to His prayerfully seeking children on Earth in His own time, in His own way and according to His own will, and by our believing and honorably exact obedience to that divinely appointed law upon which receipt of that revelation is predicated

revelational[3] - to be prone to personally ascertain and live in harmony with the discernibly enlightening and spiritually verifiable truth that: God the Eternal Father has never ceased to be a god of personal revelation to His inquiring, believing and obedient children on Earth, but we, in accordance with our God-given agency or mortal power of liberty, can choose and have chosen at times to cut ourselves off from all personal revelation from God by our sinful disobedience and unbelief

revelational[4] - to be prone to personally ascertain and live in harmony with the discernibly enlightening and spiritually verifiable truth that: God willingly and regularly reveals His secrets unto His servants, the prophets, in His own time, in His own way and according to His own will, and by their faithfully repentant and honorably exact obedience to those divinely appointed commandments, covenants, laws and ordinances upon which receipt of that revelation is predicated

revered - to be so virtuously awesome as to be truly worthy of profoundly affectionate, deferential and fearful respect

reverent - to be prone to sincerely feel and sincerely demonstrate profoundly affectionate, deferential and fearful awe, honor and respect toward God

reverent[2] - to be prone to sincerely feel and sincerely demonstrate profoundly affectionate, deferential and fearful awe, honor and respect toward goodly parents

reverent[3] - to be prone to sincerely feel and sincerely demonstrate profoundly affectionate, deferential and fearful awe, honor and respect toward all who are good and honorable people of the earth

reverent[4] - to be prone to sincerely feel and sincerely demonstrate respect toward truly sacred places or things

reverifying - to intend to use valid evidence or testimony to confirm, establish or substantiate again the enlightened certainty, reality or truthfulness of something for someone

reversing - to intend to turn again, turn back or repent toward true enlightenment, virtue and integrity

revising - to intend to carefully review or revisit what I think, say or do in order to make important corrections or improvements

revisionist - to be prone to evaluate and alter what has been recorded or taught in the past in order to bring it back into complete harmony with enlightened certainty, reality or truth

revived - to be reborn or redeemed to a new and better life or lifestyle

revived[2] - to be renewed, restored or returned to virtuous conscientiousness

revived[3] - to be renewed, restored or returned to vigorous health

revolutionary - to be prone to strive for radical change toward that which produces, preserves or restores greater true enlightenment, virtue, integrity, liberty, hope, peace and joy within me, my family and society

revolutionary^2 - to be prone to strive for radical change away from that which produces, preserves or restores darkness, vice and corruption within me, my family and society

rewarding - to intend to lovingly encourage and kindly help someone to receive the blessings of a glorious celestial resurrection and exaltation

rewarding^2 - to intend to lovingly encourage and kindly help someone to merit the greater heavenly rewards of remaining faithful to God in tribulation

rewarding^3 - to intend to notice the good my spouse says and does and to then give them enough positively reinforcing benefit, blessing, payment, praise or other reward for their good words and works to encourage and strengthen them in their rightful course

rewarding^4 - to intend to notice the good my children say and do and to then justly administer enough positively reinforcing benefit, blessing, payment, praise or other reward upon that child to encourage and strengthen them in their rightful course—then to use the reward experienced by the child to discipline, teach, train or remind them of right from wrong, of the commensurate payments which must always be made to the righteous to satisfy the naturally consequent demands of the eternally binding law of justice, and of the blessings of a glorious celestial resurrection and exaltation which await each member of our family by our faithfully repentant and honorably exact obedience to those divinely appointed commandments, covenants, laws and ordinances upon which receipt of those blessings is predicated

rewarding^5 - to intend to lovingly encourage and kindly help someone to merit the liberty, hope, peace and joy which shall inevitably come to them from living in harmony with true enlightenment, virtue and integrity

rewarding^6 - to intend to notice the good things other people say and do and to then give them enough positively reinforcing benefit, blessing, payment, praise or other reward for their good words and works to help them experience and then strive for more of the same

rewarding^7 - to be virtuously reciprocating

rewarding^8 - to intend to make compensation, payment or other return of equivalent amount, measure or value for good work performed in my behalf

rhapsodic - to be joyful

rich - to be exalted

rich^2 - to be celestial

rich^3 - to be godly enough to be made truly chaste, clean, pure and virtuous at heart—and to continue to encourage and help other people by charitable love, kindness, invitation and instruction to be godly enough to be made truly chaste, clean, pure and virtuous at heart

rich[4] - to be fruitful enough to produce an abundance of good works

rich[5] - to be married to a faithful and righteous person of the opposite gender

rich[6] - to be blessed with a numerous and righteous posterity

rich[7] - to be prone to use my wealth to contribute to, pay for or otherwise financially support truly virtuous purposes

rich[8] - to be prone to use my wealth to contribute to, pay for or otherwise financially support that which produces, preserves or restores true enlightenment, virtue and integrity within me, my family and society

rich[9] - to be prone to use my wealth to actively, charitably, generously and wisely provide for the needy and poor to an extent or in a manner which saves their lives, meets their immediate needs for survival, fosters their adequate education, employment, labors, self-reliance and thrift, and which encourages their service to other people

rich[10] - to be prone to use my wealth to contribute to, pay for or otherwise financially support the virtuously liberating freedom, health, honorable economic prosperity and steady progress of me, my family and society

rich[11] - to be in possession of enough wealth to satisfy the needs of me and my spouse for the rest of our lives

rich[12] - to be prone to live on less than household income each year while conserving, preserving, saving or storing enough to satisfy the needs of my immediate family for one or more years

rich[13] - to be prone to appreciate and live in harmony with the fact that having enough in my family is as good as having more than enough

rich[14] - to be prone to refuse to allow myself to be defined by the things I accumulate, consume or own

rich[15] - to be very generously blessed or gifted by God with honorable or noble achievements, possessions, power, wealth or wisdom by my believing and honorably exact obedience to those divinely appointed laws upon which receipt of those blessings is predicated

right - to be prone to think, speak and act in virtuous oneness with the dictates of my enlightened conscience

right[2] - to be prone to think, speak and act in harmony with the commandments, covenants, laws and ordinances of God

right[3] - to be prone to think, speak and act in harmony with truly chaste, clean, pure and virtuous thoughts, beliefs, values and characteristics

right[4] - to be prone to judge and treat another person as honorably and justly as I would have them judge and treat me

right[5] - to be prone to judge righteously

right[6] - to be prone to refuse to excessively or needlessly harm or injure

right[7] - to be prone to think, speak and act in harmony with the good law of the land right[8] - to be prone to refuse to violate the law of the land without truly honorable and just cause, excuse or provocation

right[9] - to be prone to refuse to violate another person's legal rights without truly honorable and just cause, excuse or provocation

righteous - to be exalted

righteous[2] - to be redeemed unto exaltation

righteous[3] - to be redeemed and released from the bondage, burdens and debts of my sins

righteous[4] - to be godly enough to be made truly chaste, clean, pure and virtuous at heart—and to continue to encourage and help other people by charitable love, kindness, invitation and instruction to be godly enough to be made truly chaste, clean, pure and virtuous at heart

righteous[5] - to be prone to continuously and faithfully strive with all of the energy, might, power, strength and will of my soul to keep my thoughts, words and actions truly chaste, clean, pure and virtuous in the sight of God

righteous[6] - to be prone to continuously and faithfully strive with all of the energy, might, power, strength and will of my soul to continue to keep the pleasure and satisfaction of all of my biologically inherent and naturally impelling emotional, physical or sexual appetites, cravings, desires, drives and passions truly chaste, clean, pure and virtuous in the sight of God

righteous[7] - to be prone to faithfully continue to meekly submit to the authority, power and influence of God and His chosen servants and to humbly and willfully continue to follow them in doing and being good

righteous[8] - to be virtuously just

righteous[9] - to be prone to courageously continue to faithfully refuse to expose myself to the evil or satanic powers of addiction, bondage or slavery and to their naturally consequent despair, turmoil and misery

righteous[10] - to be prone to faithfully continue to refuse to be corrupted, infected or polluted by darkness, vice and corruption

righteous[11] - to be prone to faithfully continue to refuse to be adulterated or defiled by what is filthy, impure, unchaste or unclean

righting - to intend to bring my thoughts, words and actions into harmony with the mind and will of God by my believing and honorably exact obedience to His commandments, covenants, laws and ordinances

righting[2] - to intend to do all I can and should to fully repent of each wrong I have caused or committed, as I continue to do my very best to think, speak and act honorably and justly

righting[3] - to intend to honorably and justly compel an accountable and guilty wrongdoer to cease their wrongdoing

righting[4] - to intend to bring truly honorable and just relief to someone suffering from corrupt and grievous injustice

righting[5] - to intend to honorably and justly impute corrupt, sinful or vicious wrongdoing to someone

righting[6] - to intend to refuse to misjudge or mistreat another person

righting[7] - to intend to bring relief to someone suffering from the darkness of confusion

right-minded - to be prone to think, speak and act in harmony with righteous thoughts, beliefs, values and characteristics

right-thinking - to be right-minded

rigorous - to be scrupulously exact, precise or strict in performing my duty to God in order to justly receive all earthly and heavenly blessings, gifts and rewards He wants me to receive

ripened - to be so developed, matured or prepared in righteousness as to be saved from the bondage and burdens of sin, from the agonizing suffering and miserable torment of hell, and from everlasting separation from the glorious celestial presence of God in spiritual death

ripened[2] - to be so developed, matured or prepared in true enlightenment, virtue and integrity as to be integrated-at-heart or pure-in-heart

rising - to intend to continue to progress by continuing to improve the enlightenment and virtue of the thoughts I continue to integrate into the thoughts, beliefs, values and characteristics of my heart

ritzy - to be elegant

robust - to be as metaphorically healthy and vigorous as a live oak tree

romantic - to be prone to regularly, deeply and lovingly arouse healthy, biologically inherent and naturally impelling emotional, physical or sexual appetite, craving, desire, drive or passion in courting or wooing a person of the opposite gender who is my lawfully and legally wedded husband or wife

romantic[2] - to be a girl or woman who is most ladylike

romantic[3] - to be a boy or man who is most chivalrous

royal - to be a righteous child of God who is worthy to receive as an heir with God's other children all earthly and heavenly blessings, gifts and rewards He has promised to those who are faithful in keeping His commandments, covenants, laws and ordinances

royal[2] - to be a truly charitable and godly monarch or sovereign

royal[3] - to be a good and honorable monarch or sovereign

rudimentary - to be prone to rely upon basic and solid principles of true enlightenment, virtue and integrity

rugged - to be enduring, healthy, strong and vigorous

rural - to be naturally simple and virtuous to an extent or in a manner which is typical of those who live in provincial or open country areas who are relatively unaccustomed to more darkened influences and more worldly lifestyles

rustic - to be naturally simple and virtuous to an extent or in a manner which is typical of those who live in provincial or open country areas who are relatively unaccustomed to more darkened influences and more worldly lifestyles

ruthful - to be humane

S

Sabbath-keeping - to intend to reap the influence or presence of the Spirit of God and the other delightful and powerful heavenly blessings which come to me and to my family from keeping God's law and commandment to keep the Sabbath day holy as a day of virtuous worship, a day for doing good and a day of rest

sacramental - to be prone to weekly and worthily partake of the sacred symbolic emblems of the atoning body and blood of the Lord Jesus Christ administered by a boy or man holding true priesthood authority from God—in order to renew my baptismal covenants to live worthy of His name, to always remember Him, and to carefully keep His commandments, covenants, laws and ordinances—in order to retain the divine gift of the constant companionship of the glorious influence when not the divine presence of the Holy Ghost to be with me

sacramental[2] - to be prone to participate in a sacred ordinance recognized by God as authorized and binding on Earth and in heaven

sacred - to be exalted

sacred[2] - to be celestial

sacred[3] - to be godly enough to be made truly chaste, clean, pure and virtuous at heart—and to continue to encourage and help other people by charitable love, kindness, invitation and instruction to be godly enough to be made truly chaste, clean, pure and virtuous at heart

sacred[4] - to be totally consecrated, dedicated or devoted to what God would have me do

sacrificing - to intend to stand ready to obediently give up or surrender all of my possessions and my life, if necessary, to fulfill God's known will—once I have ascertained His will

sacrificing[2] - to intend to constantly choose to worshipfully offer my brokenhearted and contrite spirit to God as a measure of my willingness to faithfully fulfill His known will, come what may

sacrificing[3] - to intend to give up or surrender the evil or satanic thoughts of my mind and heart in order to make room for true enlightenment, virtue and integrity

sacrificing[4] - to intend to give up or surrender the selfish thoughts of my mind and heart in order to adopt or contribute to something better

sacrificing[5] - to intend to offer animal life, fruits, grains or other plants as offerings to God in the symbolic manner He prescribes when He gives a commandment to do so or until He revokes a commandment He has given to do so

sacrificing[6] - to intend to give up or surrender what is personally cherished, precious or valuable in order to adopt or contribute to something better

safe - to be faithful enough in keeping the commandments, covenants, laws and ordinances of God to receive His promise of exaltation

safe[2] - to be delivered, freed, liberated, redeemed or saved from the bondage and burdens of sin, from the agonizing suffering and miserable torment of hell, and from everlasting separation from the glorious celestial presence of God in spiritual death—unto spiritual rebirth and salvation through the charitable love, cleansing power and redeeming grace of the Atonement of the Lord Jesus Christ by my faithfully repentant and honorably exact obedience to those divinely appointed commandments, covenants, laws and ordinances upon which receipt of that rebirth and salvation are predicated

safe³ - to be delivered, freed, liberated, redeemed or saved from corrupt, sinful or vicious wrongdoing

safe⁴ - to be delivered, freed, liberated, redeemed or saved from all of the evil or satanic powers of binding addiction, compulsion, impulsion, obsession, occupation and possession

safe⁵ - to be delivered, freed, liberated, redeemed or saved from the darkness of confusion

safe⁶ - to be filled with enough true enlightenment, virtue and integrity to deserve the protective power of God over my enemies

safe⁷ - to be prone to refuse to expose the thoughts of my own mind to anything which has or which may have enough evil or satanic power to induce or influence me to willfully reject my good conscience, or to defile the active and stored thoughts of my mind with darkness, vice and corruption, or to drive true enlightenment, virtue and integrity

out of my mind and heart, or to infect me with evil or satanic desires to lustfully fulfill or sinfully satisfy one or more of my biologically inherent and naturally impelling emotional, physical or sexual appetites, cravings, desires, drives or passions, or to otherwise cause the Spirit of God to withdraw from me

safekeeping - to intend to keep myself virtuously safe

safekeeping² - to intend to lovingly encourage and kindly help other people to remain virtuously safe

sagacious - to be made acutely discerning and wise in the sight of God by my faithfully repentant and honorably exact obedience to those divinely appointed commandments, covenants, laws and ordinances upon which receipt of those blessings is predicated

sagacious² - to be discerning and practical

sage - to be prudent or wise enough to righteously judge and humbly do that which is charitably loving, just, right and wise in the sight of God

saintly - to be sanctified unto perfectly virtuous cleanliness, innocence and integrity

salty - to be enhancing, exemplary or savory in true enlightenment, virtue and integrity

salty² - to be prone to improve quality

salubrious - to be prone to promote good health and true safety

salubrious² - to be prone to enjoy good health and true safety

salutary - to be prone to benefit, improve or promote what is healthy or wholesome
salutatory - to be prone to ceremoniously or formally express greeting or welcome at commencement or graduation exercises as the person with the second highest academic ranking in an academic class
saluting - to intend to express well-deserved commendation, honor or praise
sanctified - to be prone to obtain and retain a complete remission of all personal burden, guilt or stain of sin through faith in the Lord Jesus Christ, through my true repentance, through duly authorized baptism and confirmation, through my reception of the Holy Ghost, and through my enduring faithfulness until—through the charitable love, cleansing power and redeeming grace of the Atonement of the Lord Jesus Christ—I am admitted following my death and resurrection into the glorious celestial presence of God, where no unclean thing can dwell
sanctified[2] - to be made completely cleansed from the spot or stain of sin and liberated within my mind and heart from any disposition to commit sin and from any disposition to do evil, by the Atoning blood of the Lord Jesus Christ and by the sanctifying power of the Holy Ghost following my faithfully repentant and honorably exact obedience to those divinely appointed commandments, covenants, laws

and ordinances upon which receipt of those blessings is predicated
sanctifying - to intend to lovingly encourage and kindly help someone to be sanctified
sane - to be prone to maintain enlightened, healthy and orderly thinking
sane[2] - to be prone to maintain sensible thinking
sane[3] - to be prone to refuse to be avoidably crazed or insane
sanitary - to be prone to sanitizing
sanitizing - to intend to preserve physical health with healthy cleanliness
sanitizing[2] - to be cleaning
sapient - to be sagacious
satirical - to be prone to use clear language and factual literary expression to truly expose corrupt, sinful or vicious wrongdoing
satisfactory - to be godly enough to be made truly chaste, clean, pure and virtuous at heart—and to continue to encourage and help other people by charitable love, kindness, invitation and instruction to be godly enough to be made truly chaste, clean, pure and virtuous at heart
satisfactory[2] - to be filled with enough true enlightenment, virtue and integrity to produce, preserve or restore true liberty, hope, peace and joy within me, my family and society
satisfactory[3] - to be filled with enough true enlightenment, virtue and integrity to strongly attract or appeal to another person's sense of true enlightenment, virtue and integrity

satisfactory[4] - to be prone to win the satisfaction of other people by doing and being good

satisfying - to intend to please God by being godly enough to be made truly chaste, clean, pure and virtuous at heart—and by continuing to encourage and help other people by charitable love, kindness, invitation and instruction to be godly enough to be made truly chaste, clean, pure and virtuous at heart

satisfying[2] - to be filled with enough true enlightenment, virtue and integrity to produce, preserve or restore true liberty, hope, peace and joy within me, my family and society

satisfying[3] - to be filled with enough true enlightenment, virtue and integrity to strongly attract or appeal to another person's sense of true enlightenment, virtue and integrity

satisfying[4] - to intend to win the satisfaction of other people by doing and being good

savant - to be prone to testify that my extraordinary intellectual gifts are from God, and to use them for His purposes

savant[2] - to be enlightened or intelligent

savant[3] - to be wise

saved - to be exalted

saved[2] - to be redeemed unto exaltation

saved[3] - to be redeemed and released from the bondage, burdens and debts of my sins

saving - to intend to lovingly encourage and kindly help someone to be redeemed unto exaltation

saving[2] - to intend to compensate, deliver, preserve or redeem myself from want by being economical, frugal or thrifty enough to live within my means and to providently store a surplus of clothing, food, money and other needed items for emergency use by my immediate family for one or more years

savoring - to intend to appreciate and enjoy something good

savory - to be filled with true enlightenment, virtue and integrity

savvy - to be sagacious

Scandinavian - to be prone to live in harmony with the ways of Scandinavian character or culture which produce, preserve or restore true enlightenment, virtue and integrity within me, my family and society

scavenging - to intend to cleanse from filth

schismatic - to be prone to abandon, break away, defect, depart, desert, disown, forsake, leave or withdraw from a previously chosen belief, religion, set of values or way of life in order to embrace one which I have ascertained or discerned is better

scholarly - to be motivated and skilled enough at learning to wisely live in harmony with that which I have ascertained is truly the mind and will of God

scientific - to be prone to use experimental means and methods to strive to discover and implement better proven ways of producing, preserving or restoring greater true enlightenment, virtue, integrity, liberty, hope, peace and joy within the human body, mind and spirit

scientific[2] - to be prone to use experimental means and methods to strive to discover and implement better proven ways of producing, preserving or restoring the virtuously liberating freedom, health, honorable economic prosperity and steady progress of me, my family and society

scientific[3] - to be prone to accept or embrace as truth a personally verified knowledge of things material or physical which have been and can be logically, mathematically and statistically verified from hypotheses, premises or propositions which are logically, mathematically or statistically verified from a valid methodical gathering and analysis of measurable relevant data

scientific[4] - to be prone to seek knowledge of truth about things material or physical by logically, mathematically and statistically striving to prove hypotheses, premises or propositions which are logically, mathematically or statistically derived from a methodical gathering and analysis of measurable relevant data

scintillant - to be prone to scintillating

scintillating - to be animated and sparkling

scouring - to be sanctifying

scrambling - to intend to effectively and quickly respond to an alert or warning of imminent danger or harm

scraping - to intend to strive to make my income equal or exceed my necessary expenses

screening - to be ascertaining

screening[2] - to be discerning

screen-writing - to intend to compose, create or write for presentation or sale good and uplifting artistic, literary or theatric manuscripts

scrimping - to intend to practice frugality or thrift by limiting spending to what is necessary and by limiting consumption to what can be set aside for sparing use from supplies at hand

scriptural - to be prone to remember and live in harmony with the enlightening power of the words of God revealed or spoken by Him and by His Holy Spirit to my mind and heart to enable me to pursue a course which I know is pleasing unto Him

scriptural[2] - to be prone to remember and live in harmony with every word which proceeds forth from the mouth of God to humankind on Earth by His own voice or by the voice of His chosen apostles and prophets, ancient and modern, when that word has been established as holy writ under the divine law of witnesses by the mouths of two more witnesses testifying of its truthfulness, and when the truthfulness of their testimonies has been unmistakably verified within my mind and heart by the power of the Holy Ghost

scriptural[3] - to be prone to obediently and prayerfully study holy writ daily, alone and when possible with my family, in order to allow the Holy Ghost to powerfully teach, remind and bear witness to me of the truths of the things of God the Eternal Father and of the charitable love, cleansing power and redeeming grace of the Atonement of His Son, the Lord Jesus Christ

scriptural[4] - to be prone to obediently and prayerfully study holy writ daily, alone and when possible with my family, in order to allow the power of the Holy Ghost to guide my thoughts into more perfect harmony with the enlightening power, mind and will of God found in the revealed or spoken word of God as truly recorded or written by His chosen apostles and prophets, ancient and modern

scriptural[5] - to be prone to earnestly search for, ponder and pray about finding the enlightening power of the words of God which He has revealed, which He does now reveal and which He will yet reveal to humankind on Earth whenever and wherever such holy scripture may be found

scriptural[6] - to be prone to rely upon the enlightening power of the words of God to resist or withstand the evil or satanic powers of darkness, vice, corruption, bondage, despair, turmoil and misery

scriptural[7] - to be prone to personally ascertain and live in harmony with the discernibly enlightening and spiritually verifiable truth that: all good words of true enlightenment given to humankind by God as scripture are the mind, voice and will of God unto us as long as His words have not been mistranslated, misinterpreted, mistaught or misunderstood by us or by those who pass them on to us

script-writing - to intend to compose, create or write for presentation or sale good and uplifting documents, scripts or manuscripts

scrupled - to be prone to live by good laws, rules, standards or values which induce or influence me to restrain myself from thinking, saying or doing that which is truly evil or wrong

scrupulous - to be prone to exactly and honorably live by good laws, rules, standards or values which induce or influence me to restrain myself from doing that which is truly evil or wrong

scrutinizing - to intend to thoroughly examine, observe or inspect in order to confirm, prove or verify what I truly need to know

scumming - to intend to remove what is dirty, foul or vicious from within me

sealed - to be virtuously faithful and true in living in harmony with the priesthood covenant and ordinance of eternal marriage of husband and wife lawfully and legally performed in a dedicated holy temple of God by a duly ordained man called of God who actually holds true higher priesthood authority from God and authorization from God's own called, ordained and authorized priesthood leaders on Earth—by which ordinance my worthy husband or wife and I covenant to be married and sealed together for eternity to inherit celestial glory and exaltation in the highest kingdom of God as husband and wife, in harmony with our willing acceptance of that covenant and ordinance of eternal marriage of husband and wife and our faithfully repentant and honorably exact obedience to those divinely appointed commandments, covenants, laws and ordinances upon which receipt of those blessings is predicated

sealed[2] - to be virtuously faithful and true in living in harmony with the priesthood covenant and ordinance of sealing performed in a dedicated holy temple of God by a duly ordained man called of God who actually holds true higher priesthood authority from God and authorization from God's own called, ordained and authorized priesthood leaders on Earth—by which ordinance I, as a worthy child, am sealed to my worthy and eternally married parents and am thereby linked to my worthy and eternally married ancestors for eternity to inherit all of the glorious celestial blessings of God as family, in harmony with our willing acceptance of the ordinance and our faithfully repentant and honorably exact obedience to the those divinely appointed commandments, covenants, laws and ordinances upon which receipt of those blessings is predicated

sealed[3] - to be one of those who have voluntarily entered into the priesthood covenant and ordinance of sealing in a manner, method or mode of sealing recognized by God as authorized and binding on Earth and in heaven

sealing - to be a duly ordained man called of God, who then uses my true higher priesthood authority from God and

authorization from God's own called, ordained and authorized priesthood leaders on Earth, along with any necessary public authorization to perform marriage, who administers, without pay, in a dedicated holy temple of God the priesthood ordinance of eternal marriage of husband and wife who have necessary public license to marry—by which ordinance a worthy man and woman covenant to be married and sealed together for eternity to inherit celestial glory and exaltation in the highest kingdom of God as husband and wife, in harmony with their willing acceptance of the priesthood covenant and ordinance and their faithfully repentant and honorably exact obedience to those divinely appointed commandments, covenants, laws and ordinances upon which receipt of those blessings is predicated

sealing[2] - to be a duly ordained man called of God, who then uses my true higher priesthood authority from God and authorization from God's own called, ordained and authorized priesthood leaders on Earth to administer, without pay, in a dedicated holy temple of God the priesthood ordinance of eternal marriage of husband and wife through righteous living proxy who act in behalf of deceased husbands and their wives who were lawfully and legally wedded during mortal life and whose preliminary temple work has been done—so that those deceased couples who are desirous and righteous enough to receive the ordinance work done for them can be justly married and sealed together for eternity to inherit celestial glory and exaltation in the highest kingdom of God as husband and wife forever, in harmony with their faithfully repentant and honorably exact obedience to those divinely appointed commandments, covenants, laws and ordinances upon which receipt of those blessings is predicated

sealing[3] - to be a duly ordained man called of God who administers, without pay, in a dedicated holy temple of God a priesthood ordinance with true higher priesthood authority from God and authorization from God's own called, ordained and authorized priesthood leaders on Earth—by which ordinance worthy living children are sealed to their worthy and eternally married parents and are thereby linked to their worthy and eternally married ancestors for eternity to inherit all of the glorious celestial blessings of God as family, in harmony with their acceptance of the ordinance and, if accountable, in harmony with their faithfully repentant and honorably exact obedience to those divinely appointed commandments, covenants, laws and ordinances upon which receipt of those blessings is predicated

sealing[4] - to be a duly ordained man called of God who administers, without pay, in a dedicated holy temple of God a priesthood ordinance with true higher priesthood authority from God and authorization from God's

own called, ordained and authorized priesthood leaders on Earth—by which ordinance deceased children are sealed through righteous living proxy to their worthy and eternally married parents and are thereby linked to their worthy and eternally married ancestors for eternity to inherit all of the glorious celestial blessings of God as family, in harmony with their acceptance of the ordinance and, if accountable, in harmony with their faithfully repentant and honorably exact obedience to those divinely appointed commandments, covenants, laws and ordinances upon which receipt of those blessings is predicated

sealing[5] - to intend to administer, without pay, the priesthood covenant and ordinance of sealing in a manner, method or mode of sealing recognized by God as authorized and binding on Earth and in heaven

searching - to intend to find the truth about God

second-class - to be one of those who have risen from what is considered third-class productivity or performance to become more productive or skilled in good performance

second-team - to be one of those who are well prepared to relieve or support first-string teammates in an honorable team competition or contest, when that is the best team contribution my best efforts can achieve

secret - to be prone to refuse to viciously disclose or say more than should be disclosed or said secret[2] - to be prone to refuse to excessively or needlessly disclose confidential, personal, private, proprietary or secret information

secret[3] - to be prone to truly do more good than harm by refusing to make something generally known

secure - to be faithful enough in keeping the commandments, covenants, laws and ordinances of God to receive His promise of exaltation

secure[2] - to be delivered, freed, liberated, redeemed or saved from the bondage and burdens of sin, from the agonizing suffering and miserable torment of hell, and from everlasting separation from the glorious celestial presence of God in spiritual death—unto spiritual rebirth and salvation through the charitable love, cleansing power and redeeming grace of the Atonement of the Lord Jesus Christ by my faithfully repentant and honorably exact obedience to those divinely appointed commandments, covenants, laws and ordinances upon which receipt of that rebirth and salvation are predicated

secure[3] - to be delivered, freed, liberated, redeemed or saved from corrupt, sinful or vicious wrongdoing

secure[4] - to be delivered, freed, liberated, redeemed or saved from all of the evil or satanic powers of binding addiction, compulsion, impulsion, obsession, occupation and possession

secure[5] - to be delivered, freed, liberated, redeemed or saved from the darkness of confusion

secure[6] - to be filled with enough true enlightenment, virtue and integrity to deserve the protective power of God over my enemies

secure[7] - to be prone to refuse to expose the thoughts of my own mind to anything which has or which may have enough evil or satanic power to induce or influence me to willfully reject my good conscience, or to defile the active and stored thoughts of my mind with darkness, vice and corruption, or to drive true enlightenment, virtue and integrity out of my mind and heart, or to infect me with evil or satanic desires to lustfully fulfill or sinfully satisfy one or more of my biologically inherent and naturally impelling emotional, physical or sexual appetites, cravings, desires, drives or passions, or to otherwise cause the Spirit of God to withdraw from me

secure[8] - to be prone to refuse to be excessively or needlessly unsafe

securing - to be ascertaining

securing[2] - to be discerning

securing[3] - to intend to make virtuously secure

seeing - to intend to ascertain or foresee enlightened certainty, reality or truth by personal enlightenment, inspiration or revelation from God

seeing[2] - to be spiritually aware, discerning or inspired

seeking - to intend to ascertain or discern enlightened certainty, reality or truth by personal enlightenment, inspiration or revelation from God by my believing and honorably exact obedience to that divinely

appointed law upon which receipt
of that knowledge is predicated
seemly - to be virtuously attractive
and decent
segregating - to intend—as
necessity and honorable justice
demand, and pending their full
repentance—to deny or withhold
some degree or measure of
affiliation, compatibility,
cooperation, fellowship,
integration, privilege, right, trust or
unity from an individual, social
class, group, organization,
population, nation or other faction
of society found guilty of
attempting to produce, preserve or
restore darkness, vice and
corruption within me, my family
and society
segregating^2 - to intend—as
necessity and honorable justice
demand, and pending their full
rehabilitation or repayment—to
deny or withhold some degree or
measure of affiliation,
compatibility, cooperation,
fellowship, integration, privilege,
right, trust or unity from an
individual, social class, group,
organization, population, nation or
other faction of society found
guilty of striving to circumvent,
ignore, overthrow or subvert the
good law of the land
segregating^3 - to intend—as
necessity and honorable justice
demand, and pending their full
rehabilitation or repayment—to
deny or withhold some degree or
measure of affiliation,
compatibility, cooperation,
fellowship, integration, privilege,
right, trust or unity from an
individual, social class, group,

organization, population, nation or
other faction of society found
guilty of failing or refusing to obey,
honor and sustain the good law of
the land
segregating^4 - to intend to refuse to
be viciously desegregating or
integrating
select - to be truly worthy of
preferred selection due to excellent
or outstanding performance or
qualities
self-abasing - to intend to bring
down, humble or lower myself in
prestige, rank or status
self-accusing - to intend to blame
or charge myself with corrupt,
sinful or vicious wrongdoing I
have committed in order to bring a
violator of good laws to equal and
honorable justice and to complete
repentance—namely, myself
self-accusing^2 - to intend to blame
or charge myself with a crime I
have committed in order to bring a
violator of good law to equal and
honorable justice—namely, myself
self-actualizing - to intend to
achieve or bring my best self into
fruition or reality through action
self-asserting - to intend to
confidently and consistently think,
speak and act in harmony with that
measure of absolute, perfect and
spiritually verified personal
knowledge of truth I have received
by personal enlightenment,
inspiration or revelation from God
self-assured - to be solidly settled
in enlightened thought and in
consequent word and action as a
result of prayerfully seeking and
personally receiving a sure
confirmation, verification or
witness of enlightened certainty,

reality or truth by personal enlightenment, inspiration or revelation from God

self-assured[2] - to be truly free from all doubt, misperception and misunderstanding about what I accurately and honestly claim has been made known unto me by personal enlightenment, inspiration or revelation from God

self-assured[3] - to be doubtlessly decided and sure about what I accurately and honestly claim has been made known unto me by personal enlightenment, inspiration or revelation from God

self-confident - to be convinced of and to feel secure trust in the goodness, love, power and wisdom of God and in my likelihood of success, knowing or having good enough reason to believe that the course I am faithfully and prayerfully pursuing is pleasing unto Him and that my desires and works are deserving of His perfect grace

self-confident[2] - to be filled with the charitable works and the virtuous integrity necessary to remain convinced of, to feel secure trust in, and to boldly exhibit my individual worth, my personal abilities, and my likelihood of success

self-conscious - to be presently aware of and to necessarily correct my thoughts, words and actions in order to keep myself on course to become the best person I can be

self-conscious[2] - to be presently aware of and to recognize the reality or truth about myself

self-conscious[3] - to be presently aware of and to recognize from memory the reality of my thoughts, words and actions

self-conscious[4] - to be aware or perceptive enough to clearly evaluate and effectively plan my impact upon, my interaction with or my response to reality

self-controlled - to be liberated and powerful enough to willfully control my mind and will in harmony with the mind and will of God

self-controlled[2] - to be liberated and powerful enough to willfully choose for myself

self-controlled[3] - to be prone to refuse to surrender control or possession of my mind, will or choices to Satan or his followers

self-controlled[4] - to be prone to refuse to allow darkness, vice and corruption to control me

self-controlled[5] - to be prone to refuse to be addicted by or to anyone or anything

self-controlled[6] - to be prone to refuse to entertain or be controlled by thoughts of corruptly pleasing or sinfully satisfying one or more of my biologically inherent and naturally impelling emotional, physical or sexual appetites, cravings, desires, drives or passions

self-controlled[7] - to be prone to refuse to allow any measure of my self-control to be impaired by means of alcoholic drink, abuse of drugs, or other harmful and impairing substances

self-defeating - to intend to refuse to be carnal, sensual, devilish or worldly

self-denying - to intend to deny or refuse myself all evil or satanic thoughts, words and actions

self-denying[2] - to intend to deny or refuse myself all thoughts of corruptly pleasing or sinfully satisfying any of my biologically inherent and naturally impelling emotional, physical or sexual appetites, cravings, desires, drives or passions

self-determining - to intend to ascertain for myself a clear and precise understanding of the truth

self-disciplined - to be prone to independently and willfully conform or obey as a true disciple or follower of that which is truly good and of God

self-disciplined[2] - to be prone to independently and willfully refuse to conform or obey as a true disciple or follower of any person or standard of darkness, vice and corruption

self-effacing - to be modest

self-examining - to be virtuously conscientious, diligent and faithful in striving to personally discover the truth about myself by my believing and honorably exact obedience to that divinely appointed law upon which receipt of that truth is predicated

self-examining[2] - to intend to inspect, investigate, observe, question or test in order to confirm, prove or verify what I truly need to know about myself

self-governed - to be governed by myself to an extent and in a manner which is truly good and of God

self-governing - to intend to faithfully exercise my authority or power of control, direction, dominion, restraint or rule over myself to an extent or in a manner which is truly good and of God

self-governing[2] - to intend to faithfully exercise my authority or power of control, direction, dominion, restraint or rule over myself to an extent or in a manner which produces, preserves or restores true enlightenment, virtue and integrity within me, my family and society

self-governing[3] - to intend to faithfully refuse to exercise my authority or power of control, direction, dominion, restraint or rule over myself to an extent or in a manner which produces, preserves or restores darkness, vice and corruption within me, my family and society

self-improving - to intend to constantly choose to personally progress by constantly improving the enlightenment and virtue of the thoughts I continue to integrate into the thoughts, beliefs, values and characteristics of my heart

self-improving[2] - to intend to see that I am improving

selfless - to be charitably loving

selfless[2] - to be prone to refuse to be selfish

self-made - to be prone to willingly assume full responsibility to do all I can and should to continue to progress by consistently continuing to improve the enlightenment and virtue of the thoughts I consistently continue to integrate into the thoughts, beliefs, values and characteristics of my heart

self-made[2] - to be prone to willingly assume full responsibility to do all I can and should to achieve, attain or obtain what is best in life

self-possessed - to be prone to do all that is required of me to successfully avoid being viciously possessed

self-punitive - to be prone to honorably and justly complete all aspects of necessary, faithful, timely and true repentance

self-reliant - to be prone to live up to God's confidence in my real ability, integrity, sincerity and willingness to serve Him, my family and society by producing, preserving or restoring as much good as He expects of me

self-reliant^2 - to be prone to acquire and maintain enough true enlightenment, virtue, integrity and liberty to care for, contribute to, labor for, or otherwise effectively safeguard and improve the virtuously liberating freedom, health, honorable economic prosperity and steady progress of me, my family and society

self-reliant^3 - to be prone to think, speak and act as a person who is capable, confident, consistent, diligent, reliable, responsible and trustworthy enough to care for, contribute to, labor for, or otherwise effectively safeguard and improve the virtuously liberating freedom, health, honorable economic prosperity and steady progress of me, my family and society

self-reliant^4 - to be prone to acquire and maintain enough competent aptitude, learning or skill to care for, contribute to, labor for, or otherwise effectively safeguard and

improve the virtuously liberating freedom, health, honorable economic prosperity and steady progress of me, my family and society

self-reproaching - to intend to honorably and justly seek to bring myself to enough disgrace or shame with enough censure, rebuke or reproof to evoke that remorse which is essential to my faithful, timely and true repentance, obedience and reconciliation to God

self-respecting - to intend to reverence the worth of my divine origin, purpose and potential

self-respecting^2 - to intend to abstain from abusing or mistreating myself in any way

self-respecting^3 - to intend to regard myself as possessing great worth as a human being

self-sacrificing - to intend to stand ready to obediently give up or surrender all of my possessions and my life, if necessary, to fulfill God's known will—once I have ascertained His will

self-sacrificing^2 - to intend to constantly choose to worshipfully offer my brokenhearted and contrite spirit to God as a measure of my willingness to faithfully fulfill His known will, come what may

self-sacrificing^3 - to intend to give up or surrender the evil or satanic thoughts of my mind and heart in order to make room for true enlightenment, virtue and integrity

self-sacrificing^4 - to intend to give up or surrender the selfish thoughts of my mind and heart in order to adopt or contribute to something better

self-starting - to intend to habitually take the initiative to improve, progress or repent toward perfection

self-starting^2 - to intend to habitually take the initiative to get my highest priority work done without being directed, encouraged, reminded or supervised by another person

self-subdued - to be prone to conquer, control or repress all of my thoughts, words and actions enough to keep them safely integrated within the discernibly enlightened boundaries of chastity, cleanliness, purity and virtue which God has justly set by law and commandment

self-subdued^2 - to be prone to conquer, control or repress the pleasure and satisfaction of all of my biologically inherent and naturally impelling emotional, physical or sexual appetites, cravings, desires, drives and passions enough to keep them safely integrated within the discernibly enlightened boundaries of chastity, cleanliness, purity and virtue which God has justly set by law and commandment

self-subduing - to intend to be self-subdued

self-sufficient - to be prone to do every necessary and reasonable thing I can to sufficiently provide for my own needs

self-supporting - to intend to care for, contribute to, labor for, or otherwise effectively safeguard and improve the virtuously liberating freedom, health, honorable

economic prosperity and steady progress of me, my family and society

self-taught - to be prone to diligently undertake the virtuous educational cultivation of my mind and heart

self-taught^2 - to be prone to assume full responsibility to learn what I truly need to know

self-willed - to be prone to demand the freedom or liberty to think, speak and act for myself in a harmless, lawful and legal manner, along with the responsibility to account for what I say and do

self-willed^2 - to be prone to demand the freedom or liberty to speak or act in a deliberate, intentional, volitional or voluntary manner, along with the responsibility to account for what I say and do

semantic - to be prone to recognize in the study of historical and sacred writings recorded in various integrated languages or tongues the discernibly enlightening and spiritually verifiable truth that: God has helped preserve for the people of the earth a measure of enlightened awareness or common knowledge of the characteristic and distinctive differences between that which is real and that which is imaginary, of the characteristic and distinctive differences between that which is enlightened certainty, reality or truth and that which is confusion, error or falsehood, and also of the characteristic and distinctive differences between that which is truly good and of God and that which is evil or satanic—while preventing one nation's confusion, corruption, disintegration, distortion or perversion of one or more of its own languages or tongues from resulting in the simultaneous confusion, corruption, disintegration, distortion or perversion of all languages and tongues

semantic[2] - to be prone to personally ascertain and live in harmony with the discernibly enlightening and spiritually verifiable truth that: God has given the people of the earth enough true enlightenment and the personally verifiable means of ascertaining and sharing a common knowledge of enlightened certainty, reality or truth by the spiritually verified communication of common word symbols and their commonly defined images or representations which reconvey and represent certain designated portions of enlightened certainty, reality or truth

semantic[3] - to be prone to communicate a common understanding of enlightened certainty, reality or truth with another person by expressing commonly used words or word symbols to reconvey and represent commonly defined images or representations of certain designated portions of enlightened certainty, reality or truth

semantic[4] - to be prone to seek a more perfect understanding of human thought by studying words, the corroboration of their various language etymologies, their various quoted uses and their various definitions in my own or in another language or tongue

senatorial - to be a duly elected senator who is virtuously governing and patriotic

sensational - to be extraordinarily or surprisingly good

senseful - to be sensible

sensible - to be prone to exercise righteous judgment based upon accurate awareness, clear discernment, sound reasoning and pure wisdom

sensitive - to be spiritually attuned and responsive to enlightened awareness, discernment or revelation from God

sensitive[2] - to be prone to readily perceive, comprehend, discern and understand enlightened certainty, reality or truth

sensitive[3] - to be prone to handle touchy matters in a prudent manner

sensitive[4] - to be prone to handle touchy matters in a virtuously diplomatic manner

sensorial - to be healthy enough to remain physically attuned and mentally perceptive to hearing, seeing, smelling, tasting or touching

sensory - to be sensorial

sententious - to be prone, when called upon by the Spirit and power of God to do so, to humbly make polished true statements about that which is truly good and of God or about that which is evil or satanic

sentient - to be prone to effectively use my powers of conscious perception and sensation

sentimental - to be maturely and passionately grateful

separable - to be able to disunite or separate myself from someone or something when I wish

separating - to intend to divide, segregate or withdraw myself and my minor children from the evil power and influence of Satan and his followers

separating^2 - to intend to divide, segregate or withdraw myself and my minor children from the corrupting power and influence of unclean or vicious friends

separating^3 - to intend to divide, segregate or withdraw myself and my minor children from that which produces, preserves or restores darkness, vice and corruption within me, my family and society

serene - to be peaceable or peaceful

serene^2 - to be redeemed and released from the agonizing suffering and miserable torment of hell

serene^3 - to be liberated within my mind and heart from the evil or satanic powers of darkness, vice, corruption, bondage, despair, turmoil and misery

serious - to be prone to ascertain whether the course I am now pursuing is pleasing unto God

serious^2 - to be prone to pay due respect or reverence toward holy beings, places and things

serious^3 - to be prone to earnestly and sincerely move my thoughts, words and actions toward greater true enlightenment, virtue, integrity, liberty, hope, peace and joy—and away from darkness, vice, corruption, bondage, despair, turmoil and misery

serious^4 - to be prone to deeply and sedately concentrate on resolving perplexing questions

serious^5 - to be prone to pay careful attention to what is critical, important, significant or weighty

serious^6 - to be prone to abstain from excessive or light-minded laughter, merrymaking or mirth

serious^7 - to be prone to refuse to be volatile in disposition or temperament

serving - to intend to constantly choose to charitably, faithfully, hopefully, lovingly, meekly and reverently gift my whole-souled and unreserved adoration, devotion, honor, obedience, praise, respect, service and will to God so that He can help me and the other people I serve to be exalted

serving^2 - to intend to humbly and prayerfully obtain from God the inspiration and power to serve Him and others in cheerfully doing and being good in harmony with His mind and will

serving^3 - to intend to constantly choose to give my whole-souled and unreserved adoration, devotion, honor, obedience, praise, respect, service and will to God in harmony with the dictates of my enlightened conscience

serving^4 - to intend to produce, preserve or restore greater true enlightenment, virtue, integrity, liberty, hope, peace and joy within me, my family and society

serving^5 - to be familial or familistic

serving^6 - to be virtuously civic-minded or patriotic

serving^7 - to intend to build, improve and strengthen the virtuously liberating freedom, health, honorable economic prosperity and steady progress of all people

serving[8] - to intend to offer the needy and poor aid, assistance, concession, forbearance, forgiveness, leniency or tolerance to an extent and in a manner which is charitably loving, just, right and wise in the sight of God

serving[9] - to intend to actively, charitably, generously and wisely provide for the needy and poor to an extent or in a manner which saves their lives, meets their immediate needs for survival, fosters their adequate education, employment, labors, self-reliance and thrift, and which encourages their service to other people

serving[10] - to intend to actively, charitably, generously and wisely give of my substance or other resources to the needy and poor to help them deal with personal needs which they cannot take care of alone—provided they are continuing to demonstrate by their own determined education, training, labors, investments and savings, that they are responsibly striving to become self-reliant net contributors to the virtuously liberating freedom, health, honorable economic prosperity and steady progress of themselves, their families and society

settled - to be established, founded or grounded upon a sure foundation of enlightenment, virtue and integrity

settled[2] - to be established, founded or grounded upon a sure foundation of enlightened certainty, reality or truth

settled[3] - to be debtless

settling - to intend to replace enmity with truly charitable and peaceful reconciliation

settling[2] - to intend to replace dispute with truly honorable and just resolution

settling[3] - to intend to replace confusion, error or falsehood with enlightened certainty, reality or truth

sexist - to be prone to distinguish God-given or natural family roles based upon gender

sexless - to be prone to completely abstain from all evil or satanic sexual relations

sexual - to be prone to righteously exercise and fulfill my naturally impelling, procreative sexual appetites, cravings, desires, drives and passions and my corresponding bodily functions by directing them towards and by engaging in sexual relations only with my husband or wife to whom I am lawfully and legally wedded

sexual[2] - to be prone to enjoy truly healthy and truly loving sexual relations with a person of the opposite gender, but only after we are lawfully and legally wedded to each other

sexual[3] - to be prone to develop good personal relationships with members of the opposite gender which absolutely exclude sexual relations and any thought of them outside of honorable familial and legal wedlock

sexual[4] - to be prone to personally ascertain and live in harmony with the discernibly enlightening and spiritually verifiable truth that: chastity is an indispensable and integral part of God's commandments to become or remain chaste, clean, pure and virtuous in His sight

sexual[5] - to be prone to personally ascertain and live in harmony with the discernibly enlightening and spiritually verifiable truth that: the natural, procreative sexual appetites, cravings, desires, drives and passions and the naturally interdependent, symmetrical and harmonious sexual interactions of the two genders are biologically inherent and naturally impelling and, when exercised within His commandments, covenants or laws of chastity, are of God

shamefaced - to be modest

shaping - to intend to carve, cast, form or mold a purely virtuous character or condition of heart one good word, action or deed at a time

shaping[2] - to intend to carve, cast, form or mold a purely virtuous character or condition of heart one good thought, belief or value at a time

shaping[3] - to intend to carve, cast, form or mold a purely virtuous character or condition of heart one good choice or decision at a time

shaping[4] - to intend to carve, cast, form or mold a purely virtuous character or condition of heart one good lesson at a time

sharing - to be charitably loving

sharp - to be astutely discerning

sharp-witted - to be acutely discerning

shielded - to be virtuously safeguarded from the bondage and burdens of sin, from the agonizing suffering and miserable torment of hell, and from everlasting

separation from the glorious celestial presence of God in spiritual death

shining - to be brilliant, gleaming, radiant or resplendent in truth and virtue

shining[2] - to be remarkably fine or splendid

Shintoist - to be prone to live in harmony with the teachings of Shintoism which produce, preserve or restore true enlightenment, virtue and integrity within me, my family and society

showy - to be filled with enough true enlightenment, virtue and integrity to be strikingly attractive or impressive

shrewd - to be sagacious

shy - to be virtuously humble or lowly-of-heart

significant - to be prone to produce, preserve or restore true enlightenment, virtue and integrity within me, my family and society

significant[2] - to be prone to exercise my power to influence or produce good and precious consequences, outcomes or results

Sikh - to be prone to live in harmony with the teachings of Sikhism which produce, preserve or restore true enlightenment, virtue and integrity within me, my family and society

simple - to be integrated-at-heart or pure-in-heart

simple[2] - to be modest

simplifying - to intend to understand a complex unknown by attempting to understand the true nature, operations and interactions of its most basic or most simple component parts

sincere - to be integrated-at-heart in all I think, say and do

sincere[2] - to be prone to refuse to be hypocritical or schizophrenic to any degree

sincere[3] - to be prone to refuse to be viciously deceptive or false

singing - to intend to think or vocalize melodic or musical sound that allows me to maintain hopeful, peaceful or joyful thoughts

singing[2] - to intend to think or vocalize melodic or musical sound that allows me to entertain only enlightening, enlivening and edifying thoughts

single-hearted - to be ascertaining, discerning, enlightened and virtuously integrated enough to become or remain godly within my heart and to lovingly encourage and kindly help others to do the same within their hearts

single-hearted[2] - to be ascertaining, discerning, enlightened and virtuously integrated enough to become or remain virtuously Zionistic within my heart with one or more other people who are and do likewise within their hearts

single-hearted[3] - to be ascertaining, discerning, enlightened and virtuously integrated enough to become or remain virtuously one within my heart with one or more other people who are and do likewise within their hearts

single-minded - to be ascertaining, discerning, enlightened and virtuously integrated enough to become or remain godly in mind and to lovingly encourage and kindly help others to be godly in mind

single-minded[2] - to be ascertaining, discerning, enlightened and virtuously integrated enough to become or remain virtuously Zionistic in mind with one or more other people who are and do likewise in their minds

single-minded[3] - to be ascertaining, discerning, enlightened and virtuously integrated enough to become or remain virtuously one in mind with one or more other people who are and do likewise in their minds

sinless - to be purchased or redeemed from the bondage and burdens of sin, from the agonizing suffering and miserable torment of hell, and from everlasting separation from the glorious celestial presence of God in spiritual death—unto spiritual rebirth and salvation through the charitable love, cleansing power and redeeming grace of the Atonement of the Lord Jesus Christ by my faithfully repentant and honorably exact obedience to those divinely appointed commandments, covenants, laws and ordinances upon which receipt of that rebirth and salvation are predicated

sinless[2] - to be redeemed and liberated from the penalties of the eternally binding law of justice by my faithfully repentant and honorably exact obedience to those divinely appointed commandments, covenants, laws and ordinances upon which receipt of that redemption and liberation is predicated

sisterly - to be prone to personally ascertain and live in harmony with the discernibly enlightening and spiritually verifiable truth that: all girls and women are daughters of God and, hence, sisters in spirit

sisterly[2] - to be a girl or woman who is truly charitable

sisterly[3] - to be a girl or woman who seeks to produce, preserve or restore true enlightenment, virtue and integrity within me, my family and society

situational - to be prone to choose that which is charitably loving, just, right and wise in the sight of God—in every set of conditions or circumstances I am in

situational[2] - to be prone to forsake or reject what is cruel, unjust, unwise or wrong in the sight of God—in every set of conditions or circumstances I am in

situational[3] - to be prone to produce, preserve or restore true enlightenment, virtue and integrity within me, my family and society—in every set of conditions or circumstances I am in

situational[4] - to be prone to refuse to produce, preserve or restore darkness, vice and corruption within me, my family and society—in every set of conditions or circumstances I am in

sleeping - to intend to get enough regularly recurring sleep to remain healthy

slick - to be first-class or first-rate

small-time - to be modest

smart - to be enlightened, quick or sharp in intelligence

smart[2] - to be socially elegant and refined

smashing - to be extremely, impressively or wonderfully virtuous

smelling - to be discerning

smiling - to intend to openly express my heartfelt hope, peace and joy in my countenance, usually with joyful expression of eyes and highly upturned cheeks and mouth

smiling[2] - to intend to openly express my heartfelt good cheer or grateful happiness in my countenance, usually with happy expression of eyes and highly upturned cheeks and mouth

smitten - to be filled with romantic love toward my lawfully and legally wedded husband or wife

smooth - to be polished

smooth[2] - to be elegant

smothering - to intend to repress, stifle or suppress that which is evil or satanic

sober - to be prone to pay due respect or reverence to God

sober[2] - to be sensible

sober[3] - to be modest

sober[4] - to be liberated within my mind and heart from addiction

sober[5] - to be liberated within my mind and heart from intoxication

sober[6] - to be prone to pay close enough attention to what is critical, important, significant or weighty

social - to be charitable

social[2] - to be familial or familistic

social[3] - to be virtuously patriotic

social[4] - to be prone to enjoy good and uplifting companionship with friends who are truly good and of God

social[5] - to be prone to take personal responsibility to produce, preserve or restore true enlightenment, virtue and integrity within me, my family and society

social[6] - to be prone to take personal responsibility to

effectively safeguard and improve the virtuously liberating freedom, health, honorable economic prosperity and steady progress of me, my family and society against darkness, vice, corruption, bondage, despair, turmoil and misery

social[7] - to be prone to personally ascertain and live in harmony with the discernibly enlightening and spiritually verifiable truth that: the virtuously liberating freedom, health, honorable economic prosperity and steady progress of me, my family and of society are and can be enhanced by the virtuous choices and decisions I make and by the virtuous choices and decisions they make

social[8] - to be prone to honor, obey and sustain the good law of the land

socialist - to be prone to advocate, favor or seek to preserve an economic system or form of government under which the power to lawfully and legally determine the ownership and control of the means of production and distribution of goods and services is collectively held by and upheld within all capable and socially responsible citizens

socialist[2] - to be prone to advocate, favor or seek to preserve an economic system or form of government that is virtuously social

socially-minded - to be prone to personally ascertain and live in harmony with the discernibly enlightening and spiritually verifiable truth that: the virtuously liberating freedom, health,

honorable economic prosperity and steady progress of me, my family and of society are and can be enhanced by the virtuous choices and decisions I make and by the virtuous choices and decisions they make

socially-minded[2] - to be prone to produce, preserve or restore greater true enlightenment, virtue, integrity, liberty, hope, peace and joy within me, my family and society

socially-minded[3] - to be prone to help build, improve and strengthen the virtuously liberating freedom, health, honorable economic prosperity and steady progress of all people

social-minded - to be socially-minded

societal - to be prone to personally ascertain and live in harmony with the discernibly enlightening and spiritually verifiable truth that: the virtuously liberating freedom, health, honorable economic prosperity and steady progress of me, my family and of society are and can be enhanced by the virtuous choices and decisions I make and by the virtuous choices and decisions they make

societal[2] - to be familial or familistic

societal[3] - to be socially-minded

sociocratic - to be socially-minded

sociological - to be prone to discover and implement better proven sociological means or methods of producing, preserving or restoring greater true enlightenment, virtue, integrity, liberty, hope, peace and joy within the human body, mind and spirit

sociological[2] - to be prone to examine important factors and phenomena pertaining to the actual progress of me, my family and society

sociological[3] - to be prone to prayerfully study and ponder how to best achieve progress within the human family and society

soft - to be soft-hearted or warm-hearted

soft-hearted - to be humane

soft-hearted[2] - to be as generously kind and sympathetically tender as possible

soft-spoken - to be soft-hearted or warm-hearted in speech

solacing - to be with and to strengthen a friend, neighbor or relative to help them deal with the death, harm, illness, injury, pain or suffering of a loved one

solemn - to be prone to formally, seriously and sincerely give my word of honor to faithfully and honorably fulfill, keep or uphold the sacred covenants or promises I make with God to obey and keep His commandments, covenants, laws and ordinances in exchange for His promised blessings

solemn[2] - to be prone to humbly, obediently and reverently appeal, cry or plead unto God

solemn[3] - to be dignified

solemn[4] - to be prone to abstain from excessive or light-minded laughter, merrymaking or mirth

solid - to be firmly united with one or more other people of true enlightenment, virtue and integrity in a good attitude, cause, effort or purpose

solvent - to be able to dissolve or pay all of my honorable debts

sophisticated - to be filled with enough enlightened wisdom to avoid thinking, speaking or acting in accordance with the ways of subtle and worldly people

sophisticated[2] - to be filled with enough enlightened wisdom to effectively avoid the pitfalls and snares laid for me by subtle and worldly people

sorrowing - to intend, as I deeply ponder the truly charitable and unifying love of God for me, to be filled with enough painful remorse for my own corrupt, sinful or vicious wrongdoing before Him to immediately and truly repent so that I can be reconciled to Him and to those I have victimized

sorrowing[2] - to intend to feel enough painful remorse for my loss of true enlightenment, virtue and integrity—along with enough true remorse or godly sorrow for my simultaneous fall into darkness, vice and corruption—to faithfully, timely and truly repent

sorrowing[3] - to be filled with deep anguish, distress or grief over the loss of a true source of true enlightenment, virtue, integrity, liberty, hope, peace and joy

sorrowing[4] - to intend to feel deep anguish, distress or grief for viciously attempting to destroy the virtuously liberating freedom, health, honorable economic prosperity and steady progress of me, my family and society

sorrowing[5] - to be filled with deep anguish, distress or grief over falling into darkness, vice, corruption, bondage, despair, turmoil and misery sorrowing[6] - to intend to compassionately and kindly grieve or mourn with another person who is grieving or mourning

sorry - to be prone, as I deeply ponder the truly charitable and unifying love of God for me, to be filled with enough painful remorse for my own corrupt, sinful or vicious wrongdoing before Him to immediately and truly repent so that I can be reconciled to Him and to those I have victimized

sorry[2] - to be prone to feel enough painful remorse for my wrongdoing to faithfully, timely and truly repent

sorry[3] - to be prone to offer the needy and poor aid, assistance, concession, forbearance, forgiveness, leniency or tolerance to an extent and in a manner which is charitably loving, just, right and wise in the sight of God

sorry[4] - to be prone to actively, charitably, generously and wisely provide for the needy and poor to an extent or in a manner which saves their lives, meets their immediate needs for survival, fosters their adequate education, employment, labors, self-reliance and thrift, and which encourages their service to other people

sorry[5] - to be prone to actively, charitably, generously and wisely give of my substance or other resources to the needy and poor to help them deal with personal needs which they cannot take care of alone—provided they are continuing to demonstrate by their own determined education, training, labors, investments and savings, that they are responsibly striving to become self-reliant net contributors to the virtuously liberating freedom, health, honorable economic prosperity and steady progress of themselves, their families and society

sound - to be made charitably loving, just, right and wise in the sight of God by my faithfully repentant and honorably exact obedience to those divinely appointed commandments, covenants, laws and ordinances upon which receipt of those blessings is predicated

sound[2] - to be prone to think, speak and act in harmony with the commandments, covenants, laws and ordinances of God

sound[3] - to be pure-in-heart

sound[4] - to be healthy

sound[5] - to be enlightened or intelligent

sound[6] - to be sensible

sound[7] - to be prone to think, speak and act in harmony with the good law of the land

South American - to be prone to live in harmony with the ways of South American character or culture which produce, preserve or restore true enlightenment, virtue and integrity within me, my family and society

sovereign - to be accountable and prone to willfully choose to solely govern my thoughts, words and actions in harmony with the mind and will of God, having ascertained that I shall someday stand before God to be judged by Him for those thoughts, words and actions and for the resulting true character I have developed during the time of my earthly probation

sovereign[2] - to be prone to wield whatever personal power I have to uphold a form of government under which the highest governing authority is held and wielded by the manifest majority will of a self-governing people of true enlightenment, virtue and integrity who establish and sustain good constitutional law in harmony with the exercise of good personal conscience enhanced by the reception of powerfully clear, confirming and distinct personal enlightenment, inspiration or revelation from God, and who thereby afford equal protection under the good law of the land to all who are subject to that law

sovereign[3] - to be prone to advocate, favor or seek to preserve a form of government which is truly good and of God

sowing - to intend to broadcast, disseminate, plant or implant thoughts of true enlightenment, virtue and integrity within someone's mind, so that they will take them to heart and act on them in order to gather, glean or harvest naturally consequent liberty, hope, peace and joy within them, their family and society

sparing - to intend to minimize consumption, expense and waste

sparkling - to be brilliant

sparkling[2] - to be effervescent

sparkling[3] - to be vivacious

speaking - to intend to use words or word symbols to give sound or voice to thoughts which produce, preserve or restore true enlightenment, virtue and integrity within me, my family and society

special - to be valued because of my virtuous character

speculating - to intend to ponder, meditate or reflect with curiosity or wonder

spellbinding - to be filled with enough true enlightenment, virtue and integrity to strongly attract or appeal to another person's sense of true enlightenment, virtue and integrity

spent - to be exhausted for a good purpose, when necessary

spinsterish - to be a pure and virtuous woman who is eligible for honorable familial marriage, who has not married before the normal age for marrying has past, and who chooses to remain unmarried until I can be blessed with an honorable familial marriage to a good and loving husband

spirited - to be spiritually-minded

spirited[2] - to be animated with the power of God by my faithfully repentant and honorably exact obedience to those divinely appointed commandments, covenants, laws and ordinances upon which receipt of that power is predicated

spirited[3] - to be filled with the influence or presence of the Spirit of God by my believing and honorably exact obedience to that divinely appointed law upon which receipt of that influence or presence is predicated

spirited[4] - to be prone to energetically, enthusiastically and optimistically oppose that which is evil or satanic with that which is truly good and of God

spirited[5] - to be uplifting in disposition or mood

spiritual - to be prone to courageously continue to faithfully and reverently worship God within my heart and in truth

spiritual² - to be prone to courageously continue to faithfully seek greater intelligence or the pure light of truth by personal enlightenment, inspiration or revelation from God

spiritual³ - to be prone to willfully invite and permit God to direct and improve my life by exactly, faithfully and honorably living in harmony with that which my good conscience tells me is charitably loving, just, right and wise in the sight of God

spiritual⁴ - to be prone to courageously continue to faithfully allow God to direct and improve my life by faithfully, timely and truly repenting of everything within me which my troubled conscience tells me is cruel, unjust, unwise or wrong in the sight of God

spiritual⁵ - to be virtuously conscientious

spiritualistic - to be prone to personally ascertain and live in harmony with the discernibly enlightening and spiritually verifiable truth that: some righteous angels or spirits have been, can be and may be sent from God to communicate with the living

spiritualistic² - to be prone to personally ascertain and live in harmony with the discernibly enlightening and spiritually verifiable truth that: God can help me ascertain, detect, discern or

identify whether an angel or spirit manifested to me is sent from Him

spiritualizing - to intend to lovingly encourage and kindly help someone to be spiritually-minded

spiritually-minded - to be spiritual in thought, speech and behavior

splendent - to be prone to brilliantly radiate or shine with true enlightenment, virtue and integrity

splendid - to be exalted

splendid² - to be celestial

splendid³ - to be godly enough to be made truly chaste, clean, pure and virtuous at heart—and to continue to encourage and help other people by charitable love, kindness, invitation and instruction to be godly enough to be made truly chaste, clean, pure and virtuous at heart

splendid⁴ - to be heroic-at-heart, sublime or superb in thought, speech or behavior

splendid⁵ - to be brightly distinguished or eminent

sponsoring - to be fatherly or motherly toward children

sponsoring² - to intend to bind or pledge myself to accountably or responsibly ensure and vouch for the adequate education and proper upbringing of a child who would otherwise lack that help

spoon-feeding - to intend to feed another person who is incapable of taking care of their need to be fed with a spoon

sporting - to be sportsmanlike or sportsmanly

sportsmanlike - to be prone to keep my thoughts, words and actions honorably clean and virtuous while coaching, officiating, playing or otherwise attending, following or participating in an honorable contest, game or sport

sportsmanlike[2] - to be consistently and graciously fair-minded, courteous and kind while coaching, officiating, playing or otherwise attending, following or participating in an honorable contest, game or sport

sportsmanlike[3] - to be prone to use honorable contest, game or sport to do my very best to build and improve my own character and skills, rather than to disprove, taunt or tear down another person's achievement, record or reputation

sportsmanlike[4] - to be prone to refuse to coach, officiate, play or otherwise attend, follow or participate in any vicious contest, game or sport

sportsmanlike[5] - to be prone to refuse to attempt to cheat in any way as I coach, officiate, play or otherwise attend, follow or participate in a contest, game or sport

sportsmanlike[6] - to be prone to refuse to viciously use or abuse any chemical or other substance on or within my body which could allow or cause me to cheat against my fellow competitors while I am preparing for or participating in a contest, game or sport

sportsmanlike[7] - to be prone to refuse to fix or racketeer the outcome of an otherwise honorable contest, game or sport

sportsmanlike[8] - to be prone to refuse to viciously disrupt,

interfere or tamper with another person's ability to coach, officiate or play their very best within the rules of an honorable contest, game or sport

sportsmanlike[9] - to be prone to refuse to coach, officiate, play or otherwise participate in an honorable contest, game or sport to an extent or in a manner which is less than my very best when I have allowed someone else to count on me or to pay to see me do my very best

sportsmanlike[10] - to be prone to refuse to viciously coach, officiate or play outside the rules of an honorable contest, game or sport

sportsmanlike[11] - to be prone to refuse to be excessively competitive while coaching, observing or participating in an honorable contest, game or sport

sportsmanly - to be sportsmanlike

spotless - to be sanctified unto perfectly virtuous cleanliness, innocence and integrity

spotless[2] - to be prone to prayerfully keep my thoughts, words and actions clean and above satanic or worldly temptation

sprightly - to be animated or vivacious

springing - to be buoyant

square - to be prone to keep my thoughts, words, and actions in exact harmony with that which is charitably loving, just, right and wise in the sight of God

squeaky-clean - to be completely clean

squeaky-clean[2] - to be innocent

stable - to be firmly established or steadily resolved in one condition, course, place or position I have ascertained is most pleasing unto God

staid - to be prone to refuse to be volatile

stalwart - to be valiant

standard - to be prone to possess or uphold a conspicuously excellent and well-established character as an example toward which other people should work in order to produce, preserve or restore greater true enlightenment, virtue, integrity, liberty, hope, peace and joy within themselves, their families and society

starring - to be godly enough to be made truly chaste, clean, pure and virtuous at heart—and to continue to encourage and help other people by charitable love, kindness, invitation and instruction to be godly enough to be made truly chaste, clean, pure and virtuous at heart

starring[2] - to intend to do all I can and should to effectively safeguard and improve the virtuously liberating freedom, health, honorable economic prosperity and steady progress of me, my family and society

starring[3] - to intend to perform to an extent or in a manner which sends a good, praiseworthy and virtuous message to other people

starting - to intend to begin to improve, progress or repent toward perfection

stately - to be humbly and truly majestic

stately[2] - to be humbly and truly dignified, elegant or poised

statesmanlike - to be statesmanly

statesmanly - to be virtuously diplomatic, governing, patriotic and political

statesmanly[2] - to be prone to sincerely seek the virtuously liberating freedom, health, honorable economic prosperity and steady progress of society whether I am in or out of government

statesmanly[3] - to be prone to exercise wise political leadership untainted by vicious partisanship

statistical - to be prone to accept or embrace as truth a personally verified knowledge of things material or physical which have been verified and can be logically, mathematically and statistically reverified from hypotheses, premises or propositions which are logically, mathematically or statistically verifiable using a valid methodical gathering and analysis of measurable relevant data

statistical[2] - to be prone to seek knowledge of truth about things material or physical by logically, mathematically and statistically striving to prove hypotheses, premises or propositions with numeric conclusions or results which are logically, mathematically or statistically derived from a methodical gathering and analysis of measurable relevant numeric data

steady - to be prone to consistently refuse to falter, wander or waver from a condition, course, place or position I have ascertained is most pleasing unto God

stellar - to be brilliant

stellar[2] - to be outstanding

sterling - to be genuinely pure in truth and virtue

sterling² - to be excellent, fine or superior in something good
stickling - to intend to restrain myself from violating good laws, rules, standards or values
still - to be prone to quietly maintain a peaceful serenity of soul
stinting - to be frugal and thrifty
stirred - to be animated
storytelling - to intend to tell, write, publish or sponsor good, praiseworthy and uplifting nonfictional accounts of truly chaste, clean, pure and virtuous people, places and things as they truly are or truly were
storytelling² - to intend to tell, write, publish or sponsor good, praiseworthy and uplifting fictional accounts of things as someone chooses to envision, fantasize or imagine them to be
stowing - to intend to put things into proper condition and where they belong when not in use
straight - to be thoroughly devoted to clean and righteous living
straight² - to be liberated within my mind and heart from addiction
straight³ - to be fully repentant
straight⁴ - to be heterosexual
straight⁵ - to be practical
straight-arrow - to be thoroughly devoted to clean and righteous living
strait - to be prone to confine or restrict my thoughts, words and actions within the narrow boundaries or limits of righteousness set forth in God's commandments, covenants, laws and ordinances
straitening - to intend to confine or restrict my thoughts, words and actions within the narrow

boundaries or limits of righteousness set forth in God's commandments, covenants, laws and ordinances
straitening² - to intend, having the proper authority, to necessarily and righteously administer enough correction, discipline, punishment or reward to induce one or more other people toward confining or restricting themselves within the narrow boundaries or limits set forth in God's commandments, covenants, laws and ordinances
strait-laced - to be consistently, firmly and scrupulously cautious, exact or precise about living in perfect harmony with honorable, pure and virtuous character, ethics, morality, politics or religion
strapping - to intend to develop a healthy, powerful and sturdy body
streamlining - to intend to design, organize or simplify in order to produce desired or expected results in a more efficient and resourceful manner
street-smart - to be prone to acquire enough true enlightenment, virtue and integrity to help myself and my family escape corrupt and slummy thoughts, words and actions so we can escape our corrupt and slummy environment
strengthened - to be prone to maintain more true enlightenment, virtue and integrity
strengthening - to intend to acquire more true enlightenment, virtue and integrity
stressless - to be filled with enough true enlightenment, virtue, integrity, liberty and hope to be peaceable or peaceful under intense

pressure, strain or stress—trusting that, inasmuch as I shall faithfully and humbly believe, obey and put my wholehearted trust in God, I shall, to that extent, be delivered out of my afflictions, trials and troubles

stressless[2] - to be prone to refuse to be excessively or needlessly anxious, distressed, disturbed, pained or vexed under intense pressure, strain or stress

strict - to be prone to think, speak and act with enough faithfully repentant and honorably exact obedience to God's commandments, covenants, laws and ordinances to justly receive all earthly and heavenly blessings, gifts and rewards He wants me to receive

strict[2] - to be prone to think, speak and act in close harmony with those thoughts, beliefs, values and characteristics which produce, preserve or restore the greatest true enlightenment, virtue, integrity, liberty, hope, peace and joy within me, my family and society

strict[3] - to be prone to refuse to be excessively indulgent, permissive or tolerant

stripping - to intend to deprive, dispossess or divest myself of all darkness, vice and corruption by removing them from within the thoughts, beliefs, values and characteristics of my heart

strong - to be prone to humbly do what is required to receive from God the blessings of power I need to be redeemed unto exaltation

strong[2] - to be prone to humbly do what is required to receive from God the blessings of power I need

to continue to endure in virtuous integrity until my death

strong[3] - to be prone to humbly do what is required to receive from God the blessings of power I need to continue to receive from Him increasing true enlightenment, virtue and integrity within me, my family and society

strong[4] - to be prone to humbly do what is required to receive from God the blessings of power I need to continue to do and be that which is truly good and of God and to consequently continue to prosper spiritually and temporally in harmony with His will

strong[5] - to be prone to humbly do what is required to receive from God the blessings of power I need to repent and to continue to conquer and regulate all of my biologically inherent and naturally impelling emotional, physical or sexual appetites, cravings, desires, drives and passions enough to keep them safely integrated within the discernibly enlightened boundaries of chastity, cleanliness, purity and virtue which God has justly set by law and commandment

strong[6] - to be prone to humbly do what is required to receive from God the blessings of power I need to vanquish my enemies and to gain or preserve my liberty from darkness, vice and corruption

strong[7] - to be filled with enough true enlightenment, virtue and integrity to be well-grounded

strong[8] - to be determined, firm or steady in holding to a good decision or resolve strong[9] - to be able to exert great intellectual or mental ability

strong[10] - to be able to exert great bodily or physical force

strong-minded - to be prone to seek increasing true enlightenment, virtue, integrity, liberty, hope, peace and joy for me, my family and society

strong-minded[2] - to be prone to refuse to entertain unclean thoughts

strong-minded[3] - to be of powerful intellectual or mental ability

studying - to intend to examine, investigate, observe, read or scrutinize ways and means for bringing about a good plan, purpose or result

stunning - to intend to astonish or bedazzle with good works

stunting - to intend to hinder, slow or stop someone's regressing

stylish - to be prone to newly create or popularize a virtuous social standard or value of appearance, behavior, capability, character, expression, performance, possession or lifestyle within me, my family and society

suave - to be informed and polished in good social graces and manners

subcultural - to be prone to think, speak and act in harmony with a distinguishable cultural class or group within a culture whose thoughts, beliefs, values and characteristics produce, preserve or restore true enlightenment, virtue and integrity within me, my family and society

subdued - to be self-subdued

subduing - to intend to conquer, control, dominate, oppress, repress or subject myself to an extent or in a manner which produces, preserves or restores true enlightenment, virtue and integrity within me, my family and society

subduing[2] - to intend to conquer, control, dominate, oppress, repress or subject myself to an extent or in a manner which produces, preserves or restores the virtuously liberating freedom, health, honorable economic prosperity and steady progress of me, my family and society

subduing[3] - to intend to conquer, control, dominate, oppress, repress or subject all of my thoughts, words and actions enough to keep them safely integrated within the discernibly enlightened boundaries of chastity, cleanliness, purity and virtue which God has justly set by law and commandment

subduing[4] - to intend to conquer, control, dominate, oppress, repress or subject the pleasure and satisfaction of all of my biologically inherent and naturally impelling emotional, physical or sexual appetites, cravings, desires, drives and passions enough to keep them safely integrated within the discernibly enlightened boundaries of chastity, cleanliness, purity and virtue which God has justly set by law and commandment

subduing[5] - to intend, by righteous use of legal and powerful means, to conquer, control, dominate, oppress, repress or subject darkness, vice, corruption, bondage, despair, turmoil and misery in order to minimize or eliminate their impact upon me, my family and society

subjective - to be prone to render a truly honorable and just decision or judgment in harmony with the dictates of my enlightened conscience

subjective[2] - to be prone to decide or judge the truthfulness or value of what is presented to the active thoughts of my mind by relying upon the influence of those virtuous thoughts and feelings I have stored within my mind and heart which induce me to reach a truly honorable and just decision or judgment

sublime - to be exalted

sublime[2] - to be celestial

sublime[3] - to be godly enough to be made truly chaste, clean, pure and virtuous at heart—and to continue to encourage and help other people by charitable love, kindness, invitation and instruction to be godly enough to be made truly chaste, clean, pure and virtuous at heart

sublime[4] - to be prone to think, speak and act in a lofty and noble manner

submitting - to intend to humbly subject or yield myself to the authority, power and will of God

subordinate - to be prone to willingly obey and serve God

subordinate[2] - to be prone to virtuously obey and serve another person

subsisting - to intend to do all I can and should to honorably obtain enough means to allow or cause me and my family to continue to live

substantial - to be firm, solid and strong in good quality character

substantiating - to intend to lovingly encourage and kindly help someone to be enduringly, firmly and independently good

substantiating[2] - to intend to adequately confirm, prove or verify what I truly need to know

substantive - to be enduringly, firmly and independently good

substantive[2] - to be prone to rely upon enlightened certainty, reality or truth

subtle - to be mentally acute and discerning

succeeding - to be actively and truly progressing

successful - to be exalted

successful[2] - to be redeemed unto exaltation

successful[3] - to be redeemed and released from the bondage, burdens and debts of my sins

successful[4] - to be actively and truly progressing

successful[5] - to be prone to faithfully, patiently and persistently overcome opposition to accomplish, achieve, attain or obtain that which produces, preserves or restores the greatest true enlightenment, virtue, integrity, liberty, hope, peace and joy within me, my family and society

succoring - to intend to eagerly and charitably rush to timely offer the needy and poor aid, assistance, concession, forbearance, forgiveness, leniency or tolerance to an extent and in a manner which is charitably loving, just, right and wise in the sight of God

succoring[2] - to intend to eagerly and charitably rush to timely provide for the needy and poor to

an extent or in a manner which saves their lives, meets their immediate needs for survival, fosters their adequate education, employment, labors, self-reliance and thrift, and which encourages their service to other people
succoring[3] - to intend to eagerly and charitably rush to timely give of my substance or other resources to the needy and poor to help them deal with personal needs which they cannot take care of alone—provided they are continuing to demonstrate by their own determined education, training, labors, investments and savings, that they are responsibly striving to become self-reliant net contributors to the virtuously liberating freedom, health, honorable economic prosperity and steady progress of themselves, their families and society
suckling - to be a girl or woman who breast feeds my milk to an infant in need of my nourishment
suffering - to intend to constantly choose to faithfully prove my believing and honorably exact obedience to God in the face of necessary or unavoidable affliction, damage, distress, harm, injury, loss or pain
suffering[2] - to intend to recognize enough affliction, damage, distress, harm, injury, loss or pain from all of the corrupt, sinful or vicious wrongdoing within me to faithfully and immediately seek true and complete repentance, obedience and reconciliation to God
sunny - to be celestial
super - to be first-rate in goodness or virtue

superb - to be virtuously refined
superb[2] - to be majestic
supercharged - to be eager, enthused or excited enough to be virtuously victorious
supereminent - to be truly worthy of a distinguished, meritorious, prominent or outstanding reputation that is unsurpassed
superhuman - to be exalted
superhuman[2] - to be virtuously immortal
superior - to be one of those who are above average in true enlightenment, virtue and integrity
superlative - to be supernal
superlative[2] - to be prone to produce, preserve or restore the greatest true enlightenment, virtue, integrity, liberty, hope, peace and joy within me, my family and society
supernal - to be exalted
supernal[2] - to be celestial
supernal[3] - to be godly enough to be made truly chaste, clean, pure and virtuous at heart—and to continue to encourage and help other people by charitable love, kindness, invitation and instruction to be godly enough to be made truly chaste, clean, pure and virtuous at heart
supernal[4] - to be prone to think, speak and act in a lofty and noble manner
supernatural - to be spiritually-minded
supporting - to intend to give or offer aid, assistance or cooperation in order to perpetuate, maintain, sustain or uphold that which is charitably loving, just, right and wise in the sight of God

supporting[2] - to intend to give or offer aid, assistance and cooperation to those who produce, preserve or restore true enlightenment, virtue and integrity within me, my family and society

suppressible - to be able to subject myself to self-control or self-restraint

suppressing - to intend to join with other people of true enlightenment, virtue and integrity in dispelling, forsaking, overcoming or withstanding that which produces, preserves or restores darkness, vice and corruption within us, our families and society

suppressing[2] - to intend to subdue and vanquish darkness, vice and corruption from entering into the thoughts, beliefs, values and characteristics of my heart

suprarational - to be prone to recognize and properly deal with that which cannot be comprehended by reason alone

supreme - to be exalted

sure - to be made solidly settled in an absolute confirmation, verification or witness of enlightened certainty, reality or truth made known unto me by personal enlightenment, inspiration or revelation from God

sure[2] - to be truly free from all doubt, misperception and misunderstanding about what I accurately and honestly claim has been made known unto me by personal enlightenment, inspiration or revelation from God

sure[3] - to be certainly decided about what I accurately and honestly claim has been made known unto me by personal

enlightenment, inspiration or revelation from God

sure[4] - to be prone to think, speak and act in an unerringly and unfailingly loyal, reliable and trustworthy manner in the sight of God

sure-fired - to be charitable, faithful and virtuous enough to be fully assured, confident, convinced or persuaded of successful results

sure-footed - to be firmly and virtuously established in that which I have ascertained is truly the mind and will of God

surmounting - to intend to excel in true enlightenment, virtue and integrity

surrendering - to intend to actively, faithfully, humbly and meekly submit or yield my mind and will to believing and honorably exact obedience to that which I have ascertained is truly the mind and will of God

surrendering[2] - to intend to give up, give in or give way to that which produces, preserves or restores true enlightenment, virtue and integrity within me, my family and society

surviving - to intend to constantly choose to dispel or withstand evil, come what may

sustaining - to intend to aid, assist, support or uphold that which is charitably loving, just, right and wise in the sight of God

sustaining[2] - to intend to give or offer enough aid, assistance, cooperation and support to preserve or uphold that which produces, preserves or restores true enlightenment, virtue and integrity within me, my family and society

swanky - to be elegant

swearing - to intend, as required by God and in a manner He prescribes, to make a good and true covenant, declaration, oath, promise, statement, testimony or vow before God and His authorized witnesses, with a solemn promise to personally answer for, uphold or witness its truthfulness with all that I possess, even with my own life if necessary

sweating - to intend to constantly choose until my retirement to put forth enough labor to become or remain a self-reliant net contributor to the economic well-being of me, my family and society

sweeping - to be cleaning

sweet - to be kind, mild and wholesome enough in service to be dearly beloved

sweet^2 - to be wonderfully noble and pleasing through good works

sweet^3 - to be prone to radiate true enlightenment, virtue and integrity

sweet^4 - to be prone to avoid excessive or needless harm or injury

sweet-tempered - to be kind and pleasant in disposition or temperament

swell - to be virtuously lovable

swerving - to intend to depart, diverge or turn away from that which is evil or satanic

swimming - to be actively and truly progressing in order to avoid digressing or sinking into despair or destruction

swimming^2 - to be buoyant, especially in water

swinging - to be animated or vivacious

symbiotic - to be prone to create and build upon a mutually beneficial, complementary and interdependent relationship with my lawfully and legally wedded husband or wife

sympathizing - to intend to allow or cause myself to be so deeply affected by a person of true enlightenment, virtue and integrity as to willfully entertain the influence of their true enlightenment, virtue and integrity within my heart

sympathizing^2 - to intend to offer the needy and poor aid, assistance, concession, forbearance, forgiveness, leniency or tolerance to an extent and in a manner which is charitably loving, just, right and wise in the sight of God

sympathizing^3 - to intend to actively, charitably, generously and wisely provide for the needy and poor to an extent or in a manner which saves their lives, meets their immediate needs for survival, fosters their adequate education, employment, labors, self-reliance and thrift, and which encourages their service to other people

sympathizing^4 - to intend to actively, charitably, generously and wisely give of my substance or other resources to the needy and poor to help them deal with personal needs which they cannot take care of alone—provided they are continuing to demonstrate by their own determined education, training, labors, investments and savings, that they are responsibly striving to become self-reliant net contributors to the virtuously liberating freedom, health,

honorable economic prosperity and
steady progress of themselves,
their families and society

sympathizing[5] - to intend to kindly
commiserate or mourn with
another person who has cause to
mourn

synchronizing - to be realistic
enough to realize the miraculous
and simultaneous coexistence,
coincidence, concurrence and
cooperation of people and things
over time

syndicating - to intend to combine
or unite with groups or
organizations of people of true
enlightenment, virtue and integrity
to conduct business

synergetic - to be prone to increase
the production, preservation or
restoration of greater true
enlightenment, virtue, integrity,
liberty, hope, peace and joy within
me, my family and society by
energetically working together
with one or more other people to
produce more enlightenment,
virtue and integrity than we could
produce individually

synoptic - to be prone to see or
understand separate things
comprehensively

T

tactful - to be sagacious or wise in
all I think, say and do

tactful[2] - to be skilled in tactically
avoiding the giving of excessive or
needless irritation or offense to
another person

tactical - to be prone to prudently
or wisely move ahead or proceed

tactile - to be realistically aware,
perceptive or sensitive to or with
physical touch in reality

taking - to intend to refuse to be
viciously mistaking

talented - to be endowed, gifted or
skilled with valuable abilities
which I increase in value by
putting them to good use

talismanic - to be prone to
recognize the actual or potential
influence or power which human
awareness, identification,
knowledge or perception of a
certain object can evoke in the
human mind or heart

talking - to intend to do what is
necessary to truly commune or
speak with God

talking[2] - to intend to use words or
word symbols to lecture, signal,
speak or write good things to
someone

tame - to be converted, reclaimed
or reformed from overindulging
the pleasure and satisfaction of any
of my biologically inherent and
naturally impelling emotional,
physical or sexual appetites,
cravings, desires, drives or
passions

Taoist - to be prone to live in
harmony with the teachings of
Taoism which produce, preserve or
restore true enlightenment, virtue
and integrity within me, my family
and society

tasteful - to be godly enough to be
made truly chaste, clean, pure and
virtuous at heart—and to continue
to encourage and help other people
by charitable love, kindness,
invitation and instruction to be
godly enough to be made truly
chaste, clean, pure and virtuous at
heart

tasteful[2] - to be prone to prefer and select that which is truly good and of God

tasting - to intend to personally experience or partake of that which produces, preserves or restores true enlightenment, virtue and integrity within me, my family and society

tasting[2] - to be realistically aware, perceptive or sensitive to flavors in reality

tattling - to intend to help bring violators of good laws to equal and honorable justice by reporting their known or wisely suspected corrupt, sinful or vicious wrongdoing to patriarchal, parental or other good authority having rightful jurisdiction

tattling[2] - to intend to faithfully continue to exercise my personal freedom and my right to patriotically wield personal civic authority and political power to defend, protect, preserve and sustain my good local, state and national governments by informing them of known or wisely suspected violators of their good laws

taught - to be cultivated

taxing - to intend to honorably and wisely exert myself to the point where I am a self-reliant net contributor to the virtuously liberating freedom, health, honorable economic prosperity and steady progress of me, my family and society

taxing[2] - to intend to honorably and wisely exert myself to the point where I can learn, earn, invest and save enough to avoid placing an excessive or needless burden or demand upon the resources of my family or upon the resources of society

taxing[3] - to intend to use or condone the legal use of government taxing and spending authority to offer to needy and poor law-abiding citizens, legal resident aliens, and legally admitted refugees aid, assistance, concession, forbearance, forgiveness, leniency or tolerance to an extent and in a manner which is charitably loving, just, right and wise in the sight of God

taxing[4] - to intend to use or condone the legal use of government taxing and spending authority to actively, charitably, generously and wisely provide for needy and poor law-abiding citizens, legal resident aliens, and legally admitted refugees to an extent or in a manner which saves their lives, meets their immediate needs for survival, fosters their adequate education, employment, labors, self-reliance and thrift, and which encourages their service to other people

taxing[5] - to intend to use or condone the legal use of government taxing and spending authority to actively, charitably, generously and wisely give taxpayer substance or other resources to needy and poor law-abiding citizens, legal resident aliens, and legally admitted refugees to help them deal with personal needs which they cannot take care of alone—provided they are continuing to demonstrate by their own determined education, training, labors, investments and savings, that they are responsibly striving to become self-reliant net contributors to the virtuously liberating freedom, health, honorable economic prosperity and steady progress of themselves, their families and society

taxing[6] - to intend to condone the legal use of government taxing and spending authority to legally collect enough money to pay for the justly and wisely established needs of its law-abiding citizens, legal resident aliens, and legally admitted refugees in harmony with a justly and wisely established percentage of the value of capital, money or property which changes hands within its geographical boundaries or upon the occurrence of certain legally taxable events or over a specified period of time

taxpaying - to intend to pay the taxes I owe in harmony with my government's lawful authority to legally collect enough money to pay for the justly and wisely established needs of its law-abiding citizens, legal resident aliens, and legally admitted refugees in harmony with a justly and wisely established percentage of the value of capital, money or property which changes hands within its geographical boundaries, or upon the occurrence of certain legally taxable events or over a specified period of time

taxpaying[2] - to intend to pay taxes in harmony with the good law of the land

teachable - to be prone to seek greater true enlightenment, intelligence or wisdom

technological - to be prone to produce, own, use or otherwise take advantage of the latest artfully crafted useful objects, inventions or techniques in order to better fulfill the purposes of God

technological[2] - to be prone to produce, own, use or otherwise take advantage of the latest artfully crafted useful objects, inventions or techniques in order to produce, preserve or restore greater true enlightenment, virtue, integrity, liberty, hope, peace and joy within me, my family and society

teleological - to be prone to seek after and to prayerfully study and ponder the evidence of God's design and purpose in nature

teleological[2] - to be prone to seek after and to prayerfully study and ponder evidence of the truth about the existence, reality and sources of natural causes

televising - to intend to compose, create, make, perform or produce good and uplifting television shows

television-watching - to intend to cultivate a sensitive appreciation for good and uplifting television shows

temperable - to be prone to moderate, mitigate, soften or tone down my thoughts, words and actions enough to keep them safely integrated within the discernibly enlightened boundaries of chastity, cleanliness, purity and virtue which God has justly set by law and commandment

temperable[2] - to be prone to moderate, mitigate, soften or tone down the pleasure and satisfaction of my biologically inherent and naturally impelling emotional, physical or sexual appetites, cravings, desires, drives and passions enough to keep them safely integrated within the discernibly enlightened boundaries of chastity, cleanliness, purity and virtue which God has justly set by law and commandment

temperate - to be prone to keep all of my thoughts, words and actions integrated within the safe and discernibly enlightened boundaries of chastity, cleanliness, purity and virtue which God has justly set by law and commandment

temperate[2] - to be prone to keep the pleasure and satisfaction of all of my biologically inherent and naturally impelling emotional, physical or sexual appetites, cravings, desires, drives and passions integrated within the safe and discernibly enlightened boundaries of chastity, cleanliness, purity and virtue which God has justly set by law and commandment

temperate[3] - to be prone to refuse to viciously indulge any of my biologically inherent and naturally impelling emotional, physical or sexual appetites, cravings, desires, drives or passions

temperate[4] - to be prone to refuse to excessively indulge any of my biologically inherent and naturally impelling emotional, physical or sexual appetites, cravings, desires, drives or passions

temperate[5] - to be prone to refuse to exceed the degree, limit or measure of what is decent, good and honorable

temperate[6] - to be prone to refuse to indulge in the drinking of harmful and impairing alcoholic beverages

temperate[7] - to be prone to refuse to indulge in the harmful use of substances such as tobacco

temperate[8] - to be prone to refuse to indulge in the abuse of drugs

temperate[9] - to be prone to refuse to indulge in too much pleasure

temperate[10] - to be prone to refuse to indulge in too much physical inactivity or leisure

temperate[11] - to be prone to refuse to indulge in too much consumption or spending

temperate[12] - to be prone to refuse to indulge in eating too much food

temperate[13] - to be prone to refuse to exceed the limits of enough

tempering - to intend to assist or encourage someone in their desires and efforts to restrain their thoughts, words and actions within good and reasonable limits in order to avoid darkness, vice and corruption

temporal - to be prone to accumulate or seek ownership of enough property to sustain me and the necessarily dependent members of my family while I am alive

temporal[2] - to be prone to accumulate or seek ownership of enough property with which to bless the lives of the needy and the poor while I am alive

temporal[3] - to be prone to live in the world without being worldly

tenderhearted - to be a girl or woman who is wonderfully and virtuously delicate, feminine and soft-hearted

tenderhearted[2] - to be prone to treat another person as kindly as I would have them treat me
tenderhearted[3] - to be as anxious for the well-being of other people as I would have them be for mine
tenderhearted[4] - to be as compassionate about the pain or suffering of other people as I would have them be for mine
tenderhearted[5] - to be easily sensitive to and expressive of virtue
tenseless - to be filled with enough true enlightenment, virtue, integrity, liberty and hope to be peaceable or peaceful under intense pressure, strain or stress—trusting that, inasmuch as I shall faithfully and humbly believe, obey and put my wholehearted trust in God, I shall, to that extent, be delivered out of my afflictions, trials and troubles
tenseless[2] - to be prone to refuse to be high-strung
tenseless[3] - to be prone to refuse to be excessively or needlessly strained, stretched, stressed or tight
tensionless - to be peaceable or peaceful
tentative - to be prone to hesitate long enough to personally ascertain or discern that which is truly good and of God from that which is evil or satanic
tentative[2] - to be prone to hesitate long enough to necessarily ascertain or truly discern enlightened certainty, reality or truth from confusion, error and falsehood
territorial - to be prone to personally ascertain and live in harmony with the discernibly

enlightening and spiritually verifiable truth that: all land and waters on Earth, however previously or presently claimed, possessed or used by humankind belong to God, who has the ultimate sovereign right to grant claim, possession or use of all or any portion of them to whomever He will for as long as He will
territorial[2] - to be prone to virtuously safeguard the personal area, domain or space of my mind, person and property against corruptly unjust influence, intrusion, invasion, occupation or possession
territorial[3] - to be prone to help my family virtuously safeguard our minds, persons and property against corruptly unjust influence, intrusion, invasion, occupation or possession
territorial[4] - to be prone to patriotically join with the people of my country to virtuously safeguard our minds, persons and property against corruptly unjust influence, intrusion, invasion, occupation or possession
terrorless - to be prone to refuse to be terrorizing
terrorless[2] - to be filled with enough true enlightenment, virtue and integrity to maintain enough faith in God to remain liberated within my mind and heart from another person's evil or satanic efforts to demoralize or terrorize me into surrendering or yielding to darkness, vice and corruption
testamentary - to be prone to keep those sacred covenants I have entered into before or with God

testamentary[2] - to be virtuously covenant-keeping

testifying - to intend, when I am called upon by God or by His Spirit to do so, to boldly, humbly and solemnly affirm, attest or bear in His name my personal declaration, statement, testimony or witness of absolute, perfect and spiritually verified personal knowledge of truth I have received by personal enlightenment, inspiration or revelation from Him

testifying[2] - to intend, when necessary, to freely choose to honestly and solemnly bear a purely factual personal testimony or witness which is absolutely reliable as valid evidence of that which it claims is true

testimonializing - to intend to gratefully give someone well-deserved admiration, esteem or recognition in writing

testing - to be discerning

thankful - to be prone to feel enough loving and sincere appreciation to God to be made truly chaste, clean, pure and virtuous at heart and to continue to encourage and help other people by charitable love, kindness, invitation and instruction to be godly enough to be made truly chaste, clean, pure and virtuous at heart

thankful[2] - to be prone to feel and to express enough sincere appreciation to God, and to give Him all credit, glory, honor and praise for the charitable love, saving grace and tender mercy He has given to me, my family and society

thankful[3] - to be prone to feel and to express enough sincere appreciation to God, and to give Him all credit, glory, honor and praise for all of the true enlightenment, virtue, integrity, liberty, hope, peace and joy He has given to me, my family and society

thankful[4] - to be prone to express enough sincere appreciation or gratitude to God, and to give Him all credit, glory, honor and praise for all of the good, honorable or noble achievements, advantages, associations, learning, possessions, power, wealth and wisdom He has given to me, my family and society

thankful[5] - to be prone to feel and to extend heartfelt pleasure and rewarding acknowledgment, recognition or service to God by wisely sharing enough with the needy and the poor of the valuable advantage, benefit, blessing, favor or kindness He has given me

thankful[6] - to be prone to feel and to extend heartfelt pleasure and rewarding acknowledgment, recognition or service toward those who have given me good and honorable advantage, benefit, blessing, favor or kindness

thankful[7] - to be prone to appreciate and live in harmony with the fact that having enough in my family is as good as having more than enough

thanking - to be thanksgiving

thanksgiving - to be thankful enough to truly give thanks

thankworthy - to be truly deserving of gratitude from another person for some good thing I have done for them

thearchic - to be prone to willingly subject myself to the government or will of God

thearchic^2 - to be prone to learn enough about religious belief, discourse or doctrine pertaining to the government or will of deity, as part of my efforts to ascertain that which is of God and that which is not

theatrical - to be prone to cultivate a sensitive appreciation for good and uplifting theatric works presented on screen or stage

theatrical^2 - to be prone to compose, create, make, perform or produce good and uplifting theatric works presented on screen or stage

theistic - to be godly and to continue to encourage and help other people by charitable love, kindness, invitation and instruction to be godly

theistic^2 - to be prone to learn enough about religious belief, discourse or doctrine pertaining to belief in or worship of deity, as part of my efforts to ascertain that which is of God and that which is not

theocratic - to be prone to willingly subject myself to the government or will of God

theocratic^2 - to be prone to advocate, favor or seek to preserve government by those who worthily receive divine direction or guidance from God

theocratic^3 - to be prone to learn enough about religious belief, discourse or doctrine pertaining to government by divine direction or guidance from deity, as part of my efforts to ascertain that which is of God and that which is not

theological - to be prone to seek personal revelation of the truth from and about God by my believing and honorably exact obedience to that divinely appointed law upon which receipt of that revelation is predicated

theological^2 - to be prone to carefully, faithfully, honestly and prayerfully examine, study and practice living in harmony with the most compelling personal or scriptural testimonies or witnesses about God in a wholehearted effort to learn for myself which ones are truly sent from Him and hence contain the truth about His true character and attributes and His workings among humankind

theological^3 - to be prone to prayerfully study and ponder the evident presence of truth in another religion in a wholehearted effort to learn for myself whether it has more truth than I already possess

theophanic - to be worthy to experience or witness an appearance, vision or other manifestation of God to me

theophanic^2 - to be prone to personally ascertain by revelation from God whether He has appeared or otherwise manifested Himself to His apostles and prophets past or present

theophanic^3 - to be prone to personally ascertain by revelation from God whether He has appeared or otherwise manifested Himself to one or more other people theophanic[4] - to be prone to learn enough about religious belief, discourse or doctrine about divine appearances or manifestations to one or more other people

theosophical - to be prone to seek after and to receive enough personal enlightenment, inspiration or revelation from God to be able to truly teach or testify of truth

therapeutic - to be prone to use valid cures or remedies which effectively promote healing or restoration to good health

therapeutic[2] - to be prone to seek after valid cures or remedies which effectively promote healing or restoration to good health

thick - to be profound

thinking - to intend to choose to continue to faithfully entertain within the thoughts of my mind and to exercise within the thoughts of my heart that absolute, perfect and spiritually verified personal knowledge of truth which has come to me by personal enlightenment, inspiration or revelation from God

thinking[2] - to intend to choose to continue to entertain within the thoughts of my mind and to exercise within the thoughts of my heart those virtuous thoughts, beliefs, values and characteristics which produce, preserve or restore the greatest true enlightenment, virtue, integrity, liberty, hope, peace and joy within me, my family and society

thinking[3] - to intend to refuse to entertain within the thoughts of my mind or to exercise within the thoughts of my heart those vicious thoughts, beliefs, values and characteristics which produce, preserve or restore darkness, vice and corruption within me, my family and society

thinking[4] - to intend to be virtuously conscientious

third-class - to be one of those who have risen from what is considered less than third-class productivity or performance to become more productive or skilled in good performance

third-team - to be one of those who are well prepared to relieve or support first-string and second-string teammates in an honorable team competition or contest, when that is the best team contribution my best efforts can achieve

thorough - to be prone to pay enough precise and thorough attention to those details by which I can produce, preserve or restore the greatest true enlightenment, virtue, integrity, liberty, hope, peace and joy within me, my family and society

thorough[2] - to be prone to pay enough attention to details

thoughtful - to be prone to contemplate, deliberate, meditate or think enough to choose wisely

thoughtful[2] - to be prone to demonstrate carefully attentive and kindly considerate concern for someone else

thrifty - to be wisely conservative and provident

thrifty[2] - to be resourceful enough to minimize consumption, expense and waste

thrilled - to be overjoyed

thrilled[2] - to be animated

thrilling - to be successful in helping another person be joyful
thrilling^2 - to be filled with enough true enlightenment, virtue and integrity to be extremely pleasing to another person's sense of true enlightenment, virtue and integrity
thrilling^3 - to be truly animating
thriving - to intend to continue to progress by continuing to improve the enlightenment and virtue of the thoughts I continue to integrate into the thoughts, beliefs, values and characteristics of my heart
thriving^2 - to intend to arise, blossom, flourish, grow or prosper in true enlightenment, virtue, integrity, liberty, hope, peace and joy in direct proportion to my believing and honorably exact obedience to those divinely appointed laws upon which receipt of those blessings is predicated
ticklish - to be tactile
tidy - to be prone to refuse to selfishly force other people to suffer the cost of cleaning up what is mine to clean up, or to otherwise force them to unwillingly compensate for, work around or work with my unnecessarily dirty, disorderly or messy way of discarding, storing, functioning or living
tidy^2 - to be prone to refuse to unnecessarily leave or scatter things in a confused or disorderly mess as an unpleasant eyesore to other people
tight - to be honorably exact and firm in obeying and keeping the commandments, covenants, laws and ordinances of God

tight-lipped - to be prone to refuse to viciously disclose or say more than should be disclosed or said
tight-lipped^2 - to be prone to refuse to excessively or needlessly disclose confidential, personal, private, proprietary or secret information
tight-lipped^3 - to be prone to truly do more good than harm by refusing to make something generally known
timely - to be prone to faithfully complete my own true repentance, obedience and reconciliation to God without delay
timely^2 - to be prone to faithfully complete my own true repentance, obedience and reconciliation to God before I become so infected or polluted by darkness, vice and corruption as to lose all desire and all power to escape the binding despair, turmoil and misery of Satan and his followers
timely^3 - to be prone to faithfully complete my own true repentance, obedience and reconciliation to God before my death
timely^4 - to be prone to think, speak and act to an extent or in a manner which is sufficiently early or in good time in the performance of my good and honorable duty
timesaving - to intend to minimize waste of time
tireless - to be prone to refuse to surrender to boredom
tithing - to intend to obey God's commandment to repay one tenth of my annual increase into His storehouse to be used by those men called, ordained and authorized of Him to hold His higher priesthood

authority and to use that tenth to build up His kingdom on Earth

tolerable - to be prone to honorably strive to adequately comply with, live by or obey those good laws, rules, standards or values which produce, preserve or restore true enlightenment, virtue and integrity within me, my family and society

tolerating - to intend to constantly choose to accept, allow, bear, endure, forgive, respect, suffer or support someone who continues to honorably strive to adequately comply with, live by or obey those laws, rules, standards or values which produce, preserve or restore true enlightenment, virtue and integrity within me, my family and society

tolerating² - to intend to constantly choose to accept, allow, bear, endure, forgive, respect, suffer or support someone who continues to honorably strive to adequately comply with, live by or obey a good composition or set of laws, rules, standards or values to a degree which can be justly accepted, allowed, endured, forgiven, respected or supported

top-notch - to be one of those who are the best and most honorable in quality of character

topping - to intend to be better than I have been

topping² - to intend to do better than I have done

touching - to intend to interact with or relate to another person to an extent or in a manner which produces, preserves or restores true enlightenment, virtue and integrity within us, our families and society

touching² - to be realistically aware, perceptive or sensitive to what is, was or will be true

tough - to be prone to do what it takes to remain clean, healthy and strong within the thoughts, beliefs, values and characteristics of my heart

tough² - to be prone to do what it takes to remain filled with true enlightenment, virtue, integrity, liberty, hope, peace and joy

tough³ - to be prone to do what it takes to vanquish darkness, vice, corruption, bondage, despair, turmoil and misery from within me

tough⁴ - to be enduring or persevering enough to dispel or withstand evil or satanic adversity, affliction, defeat or hardship

tough⁵ - to be determined to remain powerfully practical

tough-minded - to be determined to remain virtuously tough

tracing - to intend to investigate and record facts pertaining to my personal ancestry or family history

trading - to intend to advocate, favor or seek to preserve a government which produces, preserves or restores honorable and prosperous trade practices within the international community

trading² - to intend to advocate, favor or seek to preserve a government which orders or provides the necessary means to successfully help law-abiding and hard-working citizens make necessary life-sustaining transitions to adequate jobs when they suffer loss of employment in industries damaged or destroyed by my country's balance of trade or by its bargain-priced imports

trading[3] - to intend to advocate, favor or seek to preserve a government which defends and promotes the general welfare by requiring large importers to help replace domestic jobs lost with equivalent jobs in domestic business sectors they have severely damaged due to their large bargain-priced imports

trading[4] - to intend to advocate, favor or seek to preserve a government which maintains tolerable trade practices by paying close enough attention to maintaining a wise and affordable balance of equity between how much in total human costs the citizens of my country are giving, losing or paying for our imports, including such costs as diminished business, jobs, money, monetary exchange rates, security, economic self-reliance and self-sustainability, when compared to how much our foreign trading partners are giving, losing or paying for their imports from us

traditional - to be prone to think, speak and act in harmony with thoughts, beliefs, values and characteristics known to produce, preserve or restore true enlightenment, virtue and integrity within me, my family and society over time or through successive generations

traditionalist - to be prone to personally ascertain and live in harmony with the discernibly enlightening and spiritually verifiable truth that: an absolute, perfect and spiritually verified personal knowledge of truth has come, has always come and shall continue to come by personal enlightenment, inspiration or revelation from God to each and every person by their believing and honorably exact obedience to that divinely appointed law upon which receipt of that knowledge is predicated

trainable - to be prone to seek greater true enlightenment, intelligence or wisdom

trained - to be experienced, knowledgeable and practiced enough to be disciplined, educated, proficient and qualified in thinking, speaking and acting in harmony with pure and virtuous thoughts, beliefs, values and characteristics

training - to intend to use instruction and practice to help develop or form in someone a specific level of discipline, education, proficiency and quality of thought, word or action in harmony with pure and virtuous thoughts, beliefs, values and characteristics

tranquil - to be peaceable or peaceful

tranquil[2] - to be redeemed and released from the agonizing suffering and miserable torment of hell

tranquil[3] - to be liberated within my mind and heart from the evil or satanic powers of darkness, vice, corruption, bondage, despair, turmoil and misery

transcendent - to be supreme or unsurpassed in true enlightenment, virtue and integrity

transcendental - to be prone to think, speak and act in harmony with thoughts, beliefs, values and characteristics which produce, preserve or restore more true enlightenment, virtue, integrity, liberty, hope, peace and joy than anything which material possessions or worldly pleasures have to offer

transcendental[2] - to be spiritually-minded enough to honestly seek superior learning which rises above, surpasses or transcends the learning of things material or worldly

transformed - to be changed or converted to a purely virtuous character or condition of heart

tremendous - to be so extraordinarily virtuous as to arouse grateful trembling in another person I have served

trenchant - to be prone to think and communicate with sharply perceptive intelligence and penetrating clarity

trendy - to be prone to newly create or popularize better means of truly virtuous progress within me, my family and society

tribal - to be prone to build, improve and strengthen the virtuously liberating freedom, health, honorable economic prosperity and steady progress of my tribe by thinking, speaking and acting in harmony with that which produces, preserves or restores true enlightenment, virtue and integrity within me, my family and society

tribal[2] - to be prone to progress as a group of closely related families or households

tried - to be tried-and-true

tried[2] - to be of better and stronger character from dispelling, forsaking, overcoming or withstanding adversity, hardship, opposition, persecution, tribulation or trouble

tried-and-true - to be virtuously faithful and true in keeping the commandments, covenants, laws and ordinances of God in a test or trial against evil or satanic adversity, hardship, opposition, persecution, tribulation or trouble

trim - to be of healthy physical condition

trimming - to intend to lovingly encourage and kindly help someone to be of healthy physical condition

triumphant - to be prone to join one or more other people in uniting our desires and efforts to experience the great liberty, hope, peace and joy which come from using our true enlightenment, virtue and integrity to victoriously rise above and completely overcome darkness, vice and corruption, and their naturally consequent bondage, despair, turmoil and misery, anywhere and everywhere we can

triumphant[2] - to be prone to experience the great liberty, hope, peace and joy which come from using my true enlightenment, virtue and integrity to victoriously rise above and completely overcome darkness, vice and corruption, and their naturally consequent bondage, despair, turmoil and misery, anywhere and everywhere I can

troubled - to be prone to courageously continue to faithfully prove my believing and honorably exact obedience to God in the face of necessary or unavoidable anxiety, distress, disturbance, pain or vexation

troubled[2] - to be anxious, distressed, disturbed, pained or vexed enough about all of the corrupt, sinful or vicious wrongdoing within me to faithfully and immediately seek true and complete repentance, obedience and reconciliation to God

true - to be made truly chaste, clean, pure and virtuous in the sight of God through the charitable love, cleansing power and redeeming grace of the Atonement of the Lord Jesus Christ by my faithfully repentant and honorably exact obedience to those divinely appointed commandments, covenants, laws and ordinances upon which receipt of those blessings is predicated

true[2] - to be firmly and virtuously established in obeying and keeping the commandments, covenants, laws and ordinances of God

true[3] - to be perfectly chaste

true[4] - to be filled with enough true enlightenment, virtue and integrity to produce, preserve or restore true liberty, hope, peace and joy within me, my family and society

true[5] - to be filled with enough true enlightenment, virtue and integrity to be truly liberated within my mind and heart from the evil or satanic powers of darkness, vice, corruption, bondage, despair, turmoil and misery

true[6] - to be prone to exactly, faithfully and honorably think, speak, act, judge, lead and teach in harmony with my own sure knowledge of enlightened certainty, reality or truth

true[7] - to be prone to refuse to be viciously perfidious

true[8] - to be prone to refuse to viciously counterfeit, deceive, defraud, falsify, lie, misrepresent or pretend

true[9] - to be prone to refuse to be viciously disloyal, faithless and unsteady in agreement or allegiance

true[10] - to be prone to refuse to be viciously disloyal, faithless and unsteady in what I practice or profess

true-blue - to be true

truehearted - to be true

truistic - to be prone to exactly, faithfully and honorably think, speak, act, judge, lead and teach in harmony with obvious reality or self-evident truth

truistical - to be truistic

trusting - to intend to wholeheartedly believe in God and unconditionally trust in Him to perform or produce as He has agreed, assured or promised when I am doing my very best to do and be all He has required of me

trusting[2] - to intend to confidently believe in and rely upon my own trustworthy ability, integrity, sincerity and willingness to perform or produce as I have agreed, assured or promised

trustworthy - to be prone to faithfully demonstrate my wholehearted belief in God and my unconditional trust in Him by my believing and honorably exact obedience to His commandments, covenants, laws and ordinances

trustworthy[2] - to be prone to produce, preserve or restore as much good as God expects of me

trusty - to be prone to live up to God's confidence in my real ability, integrity, sincerity and willingness to serve Him, my family and society by producing, preserving or restoring as much good as He expects of me

truthful - to be prone to faithfully think, speak, act, judge, lead and teach in harmony with divine law well enough to be justly filled with an absolute, perfect and spiritually verified personal knowledge of enlightened certainty, reality or truth by personal enlightenment, inspiration or revelation from God

truthful[2] - to be prone to absolutely and perfectly ascertain, discern, perceive, realize, receive or recognize an absolute, perfect and spiritually verified personal knowledge of enlightened certainty, reality or truth by personal enlightenment, inspiration or revelation from God by my believing and honorably exact obedience to that divinely appointed law upon which receipt of that knowledge is predicated

truthful[3] - to be prone to accept as truth that which I know with an absolute, perfect and spiritually verified personal knowledge is that powerful personal enlightenment which comes from a sure knowledge of reality or from a factual knowledge of things as they are, and as they were, and as they are to come

truthful[4] - to be prone to absolutely and perfectly ascertain, discern, perceive or recognize reality by personal enlightenment, inspiration or revelation from God by my believing and honorably exact obedience to that divinely appointed law upon which receipt of that blessing is predicated

truthful[5] - to be prone to honestly and willfully conform my thoughts, words and actions to my best understanding of enlightened certainty, reality and truth

truthful[6] - to be prone to refuse to accept as truth that which I know with an absolute, perfect and spiritually verified personal knowledge is confusion, error or falsehood

truth seeking - to intend to strive to personally ascertain, discern, perceive, realize, receive or recognize an absolute, perfect and spiritually verified personal knowledge of enlightened certainty, reality or truth by personal enlightenment, inspiration or revelation from God by my believing and honorably exact obedience to that divinely appointed law upon which receipt of that knowledge is predicated

truth seeking[2] - to intend to explore, inquire or investigate in order to discover and learn for myself that absolute duplicable and verifiable formula, pattern or recipe which I too must lawfully obey or follow to personally ascertain, discern, perceive, realize, receive or recognize for myself a measure of personal knowledge of enlightened certainty, reality or truth

truth seeking[3] - to be virtuously obedient to the commandments, covenants, laws and ordinances of God, come what may

truth seeking[4] - to be virtuously prayerful, come what may truth seeking[5] - to be virtuously scriptural, come what may

trying - to be discerning

trying[2] - to be virtuously conscientious, diligent and faithful in my examining, experiencing, experimenting, proving or testing for that which is truly good and of God and for that which is evil or satanic

trying[3] - to be virtuously conscientious, diligent and faithful in my examining, experiencing, experimenting, proving or testing for that which is enlightened certainty, reality or truth and for that which is confusion, error or falsehood

turning - to be repenting

turning[2] - to intend to convert and reverse away from that which is evil or satanic

turning[3] - to intend to convert and reverse away from that which produces, preserves or restores darkness, vice and corruption within me, my family and society

typological - to be prone to seek verified personal knowledge of any truth to be found in messages which are written in figurative or metaphorical shadows, symbols or types and which are communicated to me by those who may have known and spoken of things yet to come

U

ultimate - to be exalted

ultranationalistic - to be patriotic enough to actually help achieve what is best for the people of my good nation

unabashed - to be prone to refuse to be bewildered, confused, perplexed, uncertain or otherwise darkened

unadulterated - to be sanctified unto perfectly virtuous cleanliness, innocence and integrity

unadulterated[2] - to be prone to prayerfully keep my thoughts, words and actions clean and above satanic or worldly temptation

unambiguous - to be prone to refuse to viciously deceive or mislead by being clear in action or expression

unbiased - to be prone to refuse to viciously rely upon predisposed, prejudiced or unreasoned judgment to influence or reach a decision

unblemished - to be sanctified unto perfectly virtuous cleanliness, innocence and integrity

unblemished[2] - to be prone to prayerfully keep my thoughts, words and actions clean and above satanic or worldly temptation

unchanging - to intend to refuse to forsake that which is truly good and of God for that which is evil or satanic

uncomfortable - to be prone to avoid being complacent

uncompromised - to be truly innocent

uncompromising - to intend to refuse to accept or offer vicious concession or deviation

unconcerned - to be prone to refuse to be worried

unconquerable - to be inviolable

unconquered - to be prone to refuse to be viciously conquered

uncontrolled - to be prone to refuse to suffer corrupt and grievous injustice, bondage, despair, turmoil, misery and other hellish

suffering by refusing to submit my thoughts and my will to the control, direction, domination, government, restraint or rule of Satan and his followers
uncontrolled[2] - to be prone to refuse to remain directed, dominated, governed, restrained or ruled to an extent or in a manner which destroys the virtuously liberating freedom, health, honorable economic prosperity and steady progress of me, my family and society
uncorrupted - to be prone to refuse to be corrupted
undaunted - to be prone to refuse to be excessively or needlessly disheartened, dismayed or intimidated by fear
undaunting - to intend to refuse to viciously dishearten, dismay or intimidate someone with fear
undaunting[2] - to intend to refuse to excessively or needlessly dishearten, dismay or intimidate someone with fear
undefiled - to be prone to refuse to be defiled
underrated - to be and to choose to remain necessarily unpopular in the eyes of other people in order to become or remain worthy in the sight of God
understanding - to intend to comprehend or take hold of a sure knowledge of enlightened certainty, reality or truth
undeviating - to intend to refuse to diverge or turn aside from pursuing that which is truly good and of God
undeviating[2] - to intend to refuse to erratically diverge or turn aside from righteousness to sin

undeviating[3] - to intend to refuse to erratically diverge or turn aside from doing my good and honorable duty
uneasy - to be anxious or restless enough about all of the corrupt, sinful or vicious wrongdoing within me to faithfully and immediately seek true and complete repentance, obedience and reconciliation to God
unemotional - to be prone to virtuously control, bridle or restrain my negative feelings, passions or sensitivities
unemotional[2] - to be prone to refuse to exaggerate my feelings, passions or sensitivities to other people in any selfish attempt to evoke self-serving sympathy
unequal - to be prone to correctly think, speak and act as though all things are not one and the same thing
unequal[2] - to be prone to correctly think, speak and act as though opposites are not the same
unequal[3] - to be prone to refuse to attempt to make all things equal for all people
unequaled - to be matchless
unfailing - to intend to constantly choose to strive or work to personally progress
unfailing[2] - to intend to constantly choose to strive or work to produce, preserve or restore true enlightenment, virtue and integrity within me, my family and society
unfeigning - to be honest
unfeigning[2] - to be virtuously sincere
unflappable - to be imperturbably calm, clear-headed and self-controlled in crisis or disaster

unflinching - to intend to refuse to falter, pause, shrink or withdraw from my own true enlightenment, virtue and integrity in the face of darkness, vice and corruption

unflinching[2] - to intend to refuse to falter, pause, shrink or withdraw from fulfilling my good and honorable duty

unforgettable - to be good enough to be truly worthy of mention, note or remembrance

uniform - to be integrated-at-heart or pure-in-heart

unifying - to intend to combine, harmonize, join or unite with one or more other people of true enlightenment, virtue and integrity

unifying[2] - to intend to lovingly encourage and kindly help people of true enlightenment, virtue and integrity to be united with one another

unimpeachable - to be prone to keep my thoughts, words and actions clean and above valid blame, reproach or suspicion

uninhibited - to be prone to refuse to continue to suffer from self-destroying self-restraint

uninhibited[2] - to be prone to refuse to continue to suffer from abusive or excessive self-restraint

unique - to be prone to personally ascertain and live in harmony with the discernibly enlightening and spiritually verifiable truth that: no other person can be the selfsame person I truly am, was and will become in body, mind and spirit

united - to be made of one heart and one mind with God by my faithfully repentant and honorably exact obedience to those divinely appointed commandments, covenants, laws and ordinances upon which receipt of that virtuous oneness is predicated

united[2] - to be prone to collaborate and progress in godliness with one heart and one mind with my lawfully and legally wedded husband or wife and with our ancestors and posterity

united[3] - to be prone to collaborate and progress in godliness with one heart and one mind with my parents and with my siblings

united[4] - to be integrated-at-heart or pure-in-heart

united[5] - to be prone to join together with enough other good and like-minded people working in unison to effectively form a society more perfectly united in virtue, and to establish equal and honorable justice under virtuous law, exercise enough peacemaking at home and abroad, sustain our common defense, promote our shared progress and well-being, and to thereby secure the blessings of liberty to ourselves, our families and our posterity

united[6] - to be prone to adhere, combine, integrate, merge or join together with one or more other people to produce, preserve or restore true enlightenment, virtue, integrity, liberty, hope, peace and joy within ourselves, our families and society

uniting - to intend to lovingly encourage and kindly help one or more people to be virtuously united with one or more other people

universal - to be integrated-at-heart or pure-in-heart

universal[2] - to be prone to seek enlightenment and virtue wherever they may be found

universal[3] - to be prone to seek more available knowledge of living or natural things

unnatural - to be prone to avoid the lower qualities of human nature by refusing to be viciously natural

unperturbed - to be prone to refuse to be greatly confused

unperturbed[2] - to be prone to refuse to be excessively or needlessly disturbed

unpolluted - to be prone to refuse to be polluted

unpretentious - to be prone to refuse to falsely assume, claim or demand exaggerated attention, dignity, distinction, importance or honor

unpretentious[2] - to be prone to fail or refuse to be self-important

unprofaned - to be prone to refuse to be profaned

unquestionable - to be trustworthy in the sight of God

unreserved - to be prone to refuse to be bashful or retarded in personal development or progress

unrestrained - to be prone to refuse to be viciously restrained

unselfish - to be prone to refuse to be selfish

unsophisticated - to be prone to refuse to be worldly

unsophisticated[2] - to be prone to refuse to be viciously deceptive, falsifying or lying

unsophisticated[3] - to be prone to refuse to be viciously artful, faking and complex

unspotted - to be sanctified unto perfectly virtuous cleanliness, innocence and integrity

unspotted[2] - to be prone to prayerfully keep my thoughts, words and actions clean and above satanic or worldly temptation

unspotted[3] - to be accurate, consistent or perfect

unswerving - to intend to refuse to depart, diverge or turn away from that which is truly good and of God

unswerving[2] - to intend to refuse to depart, diverge or turn away from obeying the good law of the land

unwavering - to intend to constantly choose that which is truly good and of God without doubt, hesitation or indecision

unwavering[2] - to intend to constantly choose enlightened certainty, reality or truth without doubt, hesitation or indecision

unwilling - to intend to refuse to choose, control, decide or determine in accordance with that which I have ascertained is the mind and will of Satan

unwilling[2] - to intend to refuse to choose, control, decide or determine in accordance with that which is evil or satanic

up-and-coming - to intend to prove I am bright, hard-working and capable of extraordinary progress

upbeat - to be hopeful

upbeat[2] - to be filled with enough humble gratitude, delightful gladness, bright happiness, pleasant liveliness or hearty willingness to consistently dispel melancholy and pessimistic gloom

uplifted - to be edified, elevated or raised in greater true enlightenment, virtue, integrity, liberty, hope, peace and joy

uplifting - to intend to edify, elevate or raise someone to greater true enlightenment, virtue, integrity, liberty, hope, peace and joy

upright - to be righteous

upstanding - to be upright or righteous

up-to-date - to be prone to think, speak and act in harmony with that which best produces, preserves or restores true enlightenment, virtue and integrity within me, my family and society at the present time

urbane - to be informed and polished in good social graces and manners

useful - to be prone to exercise my power to produce, preserve or restore good effects or results

utilitarian - to be prone to adopt and to live in harmony with whatever source of religion I can honestly discover and prove to be of greatest power and usefulness in bringing exaltation in the presence of God to me and my family

utilitarian[2] - to be prone to adopt and to live in harmony with whatever source of thoughts, beliefs, values and characteristics I can honestly prove to be of greatest power and usefulness in producing, preserving or restoring the greatest true enlightenment, virtue, integrity, liberty, hope, peace and joy within me, my family and society

utilitarian[3] - to be practical

utopian - to be exalted

utopian[2] - to be celestial

utopian[3] - to be godly enough to be made truly chaste, clean, pure and

virtuous at heart—and to continue to encourage and help other people by charitable love, kindness, invitation and instruction to be godly enough to be made truly chaste, clean, pure and virtuous at heart

utopian[4] - to be prone to seek ideal, perfect, ultimate or supreme goodness and righteousness

utopian[5] - to be virtuously Zionistic

V

vacationing - to intend to spend enough time away from work to gain enough recreation, rejuvenation, rest or relaxation to produce, preserve or restore good health within me and my family

valedictory - to be prone to ceremoniously or formally express farewell at commencement or graduation exercises as the person with the highest academic ranking in an academic class

valedictory[2] - to be prone to ceremoniously or formally express the wish that one or more other people fare well as we part ways

valiant - to be prone, in the face of great and powerful darkness, vice and corruption, to demonstrate strict and persevering faithfulness, bold and powerful courage and most honorable and noble virtue in producing, preserving or restoring true enlightenment, virtue, integrity, liberty, hope, peace and joy within me, my family and society

valid - to be powerfully fixed or founded upon that which is charitably loving, just, right and wise in the sight of God

valid[2] - to be powerfully fixed or founded upon that which is lawful or legal under the good law of the land

validating - to intend to credit, uphold and strengthen that which is charitably loving, just, right and wise in the sight of God

validating[2] - to intend to credit, uphold and strengthen that which is lawful or legal under the good law of the land

valorous - to be valiant

valorous[2] - to be prone to encounter unavoidable darkness, vice and corruption with conquering and heroic-at-heart courage, determination, prowess, resolve and strength

valuable - to be prone to personally ascertain and live in harmony with the discernibly enlightening and spiritually verifiable truth that: I am one of God's children who has divine potential and can receive divine power to do and be only good by my faithfully repentant and honorably exact obedience to those divinely appointed commandments, covenants, laws and ordinances upon which receipt of that power is predicated

valuable[2] - to be prone to produce, preserve or restore true enlightenment, virtue and integrity within me, my family and society

valuable[3] - to be prone to help remove darkness, vice, corruption, bondage, despair, turmoil and misery from within me, my family and society

valuable[4] - to be and to choose to remain commendable or praiseworthy

valuing - to intend to accurately appraise, judge or rate the relative importance, merit, value or worth of something

venerable - to be godly enough to be made truly chaste, clean, pure and virtuous at heart—and to continue to encourage and help other people by charitable love, kindness, invitation and instruction to be godly enough to be made truly chaste, clean, pure and virtuous at heart

venerable[2] - to be prone to consecrate myself and all I possess in faithfully and honorably serving and worshiping God in harmony with His mind and will

venerable[3] - to be prone to serve other people with such truth and virtue as to be truly worthy of their deference, honor, respect or reverence

venerating - to intend to lovingly encourage and kindly help someone to be venerable

venting - to intend to skillfully rely upon healthy and necessary dialogue to strive to develop with one or more other people an ongoing exchange of compassionate understanding, mutual appreciation, respectful cooperation, kindly support, peaceful coexistence and truly virtuous love

venting[2] - to intend to openly discuss or express important issues in healthy and necessary dialogue

veracious - to be true

veracious[2] - to be honest

verbal - to be knowledgeable and skilled enough in the use of a definite word language to help another person who is at least equally familiar with the language come to a clear understanding of the thoughts I seek to express to them

verbal[2] - to be knowledgeable and skilled enough in the use of words or word symbols to help another person increase their knowledge and skill in the use of them

verbal[3] - to be familiar with both commonly used words or word symbols and the definitions or descriptions of realities they are each commonly understood to represent

verbalistic - to be knowledgeable and skilled in the clear use of the appropriate words or word symbols

verifying - to be ascertaining

verifying[2] - to be discerning

verifying[3] - to intend to use valid evidence or testimony to confirm, establish or substantiate the enlightened certainty, reality or truthfulness of something

veritable - to be true

veritable[2] - to be unquestionably authentic or genuine in integrity

vested - to be worthily clothed in divinely prescribed garments, robes or vestments worn to truly signify or symbolize the actual presence of authority or power from God within me as I wear them

vexed - to be prone to courageously continue to faithfully prove my believing and honorably exact obedience to God in the face of necessary or unavoidable annoyance, distress or pain

vexed[2] - to be annoyed, distressed or pained enough about all of the corrupt, sinful or vicious wrongdoing within me to faithfully and immediately seek true and

complete repentance, obedience and reconciliation to God

vibrant - to be animated, enlivened and buoyant

vigilant - to be awake and watchful enough to defend, protect or secure someone against corrupt, sinful or vicious wrongdoing

vigilant[2] - to be awake and watchful enough to defend, protect or secure someone against all of the evil or satanic powers of binding addiction, compulsion, impulsion, obsession, occupation and possession

vigilant[3] - to be awake and watchful enough to defend, protect or secure someone against confusion, error or falsehood

vigorous - to be healthy

vilifying - to intend to warn my family and society against those whom I have truly discerned are vile by their vile works

villainizing - to intend to warn my family and society against those whom I have truly discerned are villainous by their villainous works

virgin - to be an unmarried girl or woman who is a truly chaste, clean, pure and virtuous maiden who has never had sexual relations with another person and who willfully and wisely refrains from all sexual relations prior to honorable familial and legal wedlock with my husband

virgin[2] - to be an unmarried girl or woman who has never allowed or caused myself to have sexual relations with another person prior to honorable familial and legal wedlock with my husband

virginal - to be a girl or woman who is virgin

virginal[2] - to be and to choose to remain truly chaste, clean, pure and virtuous

virginal[3] - to be made sexually chaste, clean, pure and virtuous in the sight of God through the charitable love, cleansing power and redeeming grace of the Atonement of the Lord Jesus Christ by my faithfully repentant and honorably exact obedience to those divinely appointed commandments, covenants, laws and ordinances upon which receipt of those blessings is predicated

virile - to be a boy or man who possesses such desirable masculine qualities as manly strength and the manly natural ability to procreate

virtuosic - to be prone to cultivate a sensitive appreciation for good and uplifting art, literature or music

virtuosic[2] - to be prone to compose, create, make, perform or produce good and uplifting works of art, literature or music

virtuous - to be exalted

virtuous[2] - to be redeemed unto exaltation

virtuous[3] - to be redeemed and released from the bondage, burdens and debts of my sins

virtuous[4] - to be godly and to continue to encourage and help other people by charitable love, kindness, invitation and instruction to be godly

virtuous[5] - to be prone to think, speak and act in harmony with one or more positive two (2) virtues in this dictionary—or with one or more relative value characteristics to the extent my virtuous pondering, performance or teaching of them produces,

preserves or restores one or more of the virtues within me, my family and society

virtuous[6] - to be prone to become and remain completely chaste, clean and pure

virtuous[7] - to be prone to refuse to be vicious

visceral - to be virtuously conscientious

visceral[2] - to be prone, within the thoughts of my mind and within the feelings of my heart, to be sensitively and spiritually aware, discerning or perceptive of spiritual manifestations or revelations made available to me from God

visceral[3] - to be sensible

visionary - to be prone to constantly choose to think, speak and act in harmony with that revealed instruction or knowledge which the Spirit of God confirms to me has been revealed to me by a vision from God

visionary[2] - to be prone to receive and see things as they truly are, were or will be by personal enlightenment, inspiration or revelation from God

visionary[3] - to be truly worthy to receive revelation from God by vision

visionary[4] - to be prone to prayerfully seek revelation from God by vision

visionary[5] - to be prone to accurately foresee what will truly be best

visiting - to intend to go to the home of the widow, the fatherless, the needy or the poor to make sure needed uplifting aid, comfort and encouragement are consistently provided

visiting[2] - to intend to honorably complete a mutually uplifting stay with another person as a guest in their home, and to thus improve personal or social relations with them

vivacious - to be animated or enlivened

vivid - to be enlivened

vivifying - to intend to build or impart animating or enlivening vivacity

vocational - to be prone to pursue the occupational guidance, instruction or training I need to pursue an honorable career or profession for which I have both the capability and the passionate interest to hold down a good job

volitional - to be prone to independently and intentionally control, choose, decide, determine, form or will my own thoughts, words and actions

voluntaristic - to be prone to give of my labor, money and other resources to support unselfish institutions which care for the needy and the poor, foster self-reliance and encourage service to other people

voluntary - to be prone to independently and intentionally form and exercise conscious choice, control, decision, determination, intent, purpose or will to an extent or in a manner which produces, preserves or restores true enlightenment, virtue and integrity within me, my family and society

volunteering - to intend to do, make, produce or undertake that which is truly good and of God, without recompense or expectation of recompense

voting - to intend to exercise my right of shared government of the people by openly expressing or secretly casting the voice or voting power of my own political judgment in order to help produce, preserve or restore the greatest true enlightenment, virtue, integrity, liberty, hope, peace and joy within me, my family and society

voting[2] - to intend to exercise my right of shared government of the people by openly expressing or secretly casting the voice or voting power of my own political judgment in order to help elect only the most enlightened, virtuous and wise government leaders

voting[3] - to intend to exercise my right of shared government of the people by openly expressing or secretly casting the voice or voting power of my own political judgment in a virtuously civic-minded, electing, nominating and patriotic manner

vouching - to intend to affirm, prove, substantiate, verify or witness the truth for myself

vowing - to intend to solemnly commit, dedicate, pledge or promise to obey God and to carefully keep His commandments, covenants, laws and ordinances

vowing[2] - to intend to solemnly consecrate who I am at heart and what I possess to producing, preserving or restoring true enlightenment, virtue and integrity within me, my family and society

W

waiting - to intend to faithfully and patiently anticipate or expect good results while praying, preparing and working for them

wanting - to intend to desire what is needful

warm - to be prone to demonstrate or prove my kindly affection, cheerfulness, respect and sympathy as much as possible

warm[2] - to be animated or vivacious

warm-hearted - to be prone to demonstrate or prove my kindly affection, cheerfulness, respect and sympathy as much as possible

warning - to intend to kindly caution or notify another person of their need to repent of all their sins and to exactly, faithfully and honorably keep the commandments, covenants, laws and ordinances of God in order to help them avoid or escape the bondage and burdens of sin, the agonizing suffering and miserable torment of hell, and everlasting separation from the glorious celestial presence of God in spiritual death for failing or refusing to do so

warning[2] - to intend to kindly caution or notify another person of their need to repent of all their sins and to exactly, faithfully and honorably keep the commandments, covenants, laws and ordinances of God in order to help them avoid or escape darkness, vice, corruption, bondage, despair, turmoil and misery

warning[3] - to intend to kindly caution or notify another person against the impending, potential or present destructive power of evil

warning[4] - to intend to caution or notify another person to help them avoid suffering the consequences of their failing or refusing to obey the good law of the land

warring - to be filled with enough true enlightenment, virtue and integrity to prayerfully acquire and exercise enough powerful skill from God to righteously prevail in any and every inner personal battle, conflict or war against Satan and his followers in my daily efforts to do and be only that which is truly good and of God

warring[2] - to be filled with enough true enlightenment, virtue and integrity to prayerfully acquire and exercise enough powerful skill from God to righteously prevail in any and every inner personal battle, conflict or war against Satan and his followers in my daily efforts to do my very best to produce, preserve or restore true enlightenment, virtue and integrity within me, my family and society

warring[3] - to be filled with enough true enlightenment, virtue and integrity to prayerfully acquire and exercise enough powerful skill from God to righteously cast out, dispel or withstand all evil or satanic powers of darkness, vice, corruption, bondage, despair, turmoil and misery from within me

warring[4] - to be filled with enough true enlightenment, virtue and integrity to prayerfully acquire and exercise enough powerful skill from God to righteously prevail in any and every inner personal battle, conflict or war against that which produces, preserves or restores darkness, vice and corruption within me, my family and society

warring[5] - to be filled with enough true enlightenment, virtue and integrity to faithfully, hopefully and prayerfully seek enough power from God to righteously defeat or withstand the power of an attacking, known or wisely suspected criminal, deadly or evil enemy of society

warring[6] - to be filled with enough true enlightenment, virtue and integrity to faithfully, hopefully and prayerfully seek enough power from God to righteously prevail in unavoidable deadly single combat necessary to the preservation of my life or the life of another person I am bound to protect

wary - to be prone to prudently guard against the evil or satanic powers of darkness, vice, corruption, bondage, despair, turmoil and misery

wary[2] - to be prone to prudently guard against deception

wary[3] - to be prone to prudently guard against danger

washed - to be a baptized, confirmed and otherwise qualified adult who voluntarily enters into the initiatory ordinance of washing administered in a dedicated holy temple of God by one who truly holds the necessary authority and the authorization from God's own called, ordained and authorized priesthood leaders on Earth to officiate in that initiatory ordinance in that revealed manner and mode of symbolic washing which is valid

in the sight of God — so that I can then receive the powerful blessings of that ordinance in harmony with my faithfulness, and can be further prepared on Earth to receive the blessings of a glorious celestial resurrection and exaltation in the world to come

washed[2] - to be cleansed

washing - to intend, as one who truly holds the necessary authority to officiate and the authorization to do so from God's own called, ordained and authorized priesthood leaders on Earth, to administer, without pay, to a baptized, confirmed and otherwise qualified living adult in a dedicated holy temple of God the initiatory ordinance of washing in that revealed manner and mode of symbolic washing recognized by Him as valid, so that they can then receive the powerful blessings of that ordinance in harmony with their faithfulness, and can be further prepared on Earth to receive the blessings of a glorious celestial resurrection and exaltation in the world to come

washing[2] - to intend, as one who truly holds the necessary authority to officiate and the authorization to do so from God's own called, ordained and authorized priesthood leaders on Earth, to administer, without pay, in a dedicated holy temple of God the initiatory ordinance of washing upon righteous living proxy who act in behalf of deceased family members and other deceased persons who are accountable to the laws of God and whose preliminary temple work has been done—so that those deceased persons who are desirous and righteous enough to receive the ordinance work done for them can then receive the powerful blessings of that ordinance in harmony with their faithfulness, and can be further prepared by loving family or other living proxy on Earth to receive the blessings of a glorious celestial resurrection and exaltation in the world to come

washing[3] - to intend to perform a sacred ordinance of washing recognized by God as authorized and binding on Earth and in heaven

washing[4] - to be cleansing

watchful - to be prayerfully alert, attentive, informed and prepared enough to quickly observe and respond as well as I should as God fulfills His prophesies and promises

watchful[2] - to be prone to carefully minimize my own chance or risk of exposure to darkness, vice, corruption, bondage, despair, turmoil and misery

watchful[3] - to be prone to carefully minimize my own chance or risk of exposure to harm or injury

watchful[4] - to be wary

waxing - to intend to advance, increase, grow or progress by improving the enlightenment and virtue of the thoughts I continue to integrate into the thoughts, beliefs, values and characteristics of my heart

waxing[2] - to intend to grow more healthy

weak - to be prone to humbly recognize my utter dependence upon God for all of my energy,

force, power or strength to do and be that which is truly good and of God now and until my death

weaned - to be reconciled to necessary or unavoidable loss

weaning - to intend to reconcile myself to necessary or unavoidable loss

weeding - to intend to remove or root out darkness, vice and corruption from within me

weeding[2] - to intend to remove or root out what is spiritually harmful or noxious

welcoming - to intend to cheerfully and gladly extend to an honorable guest, newcomer or stranger a kindly and warm greeting and gratuitous hospitality upon their arrival

welcoming[2] - to intend to receive a grateful guest, newcomer or stranger with the same kindness, warmth and gratuitous hospitality with which I would like to be received if I were the grateful guest, newcomer or stranger

welfarist - to be godly enough to be made truly chaste, clean, pure and virtuous at heart—and to continue to encourage and help other people by charitable love, kindness, invitation and instruction to be godly enough to be made truly chaste, clean, pure and virtuous at heart

welfarist[2] - to be prone to think, speak and act in virtuous oneness with the dictates of my enlightened conscience

welfarist[3] - to be ascertaining, discerning, enlightened and virtuously integrated enough to become or remain virtuously

Zionistic with one or more other people who are and do likewise welfarist[4] - to be ascertaining, discerning, enlightened and virtuously integrated enough to become or remain virtuously single-minded and single-hearted with one or more other people who are and do likewise
welfarist[5] - to be prone, without expectation of return, to kindly and personally offer what I can afford to the needy and the poor of the world to help provide them with the temporary aid, education, jobs, services, training or other support they cannot provide for themselves—provided they are continuing to demonstrate by their own determined education, training, labors, investments and savings, that they are responsibly striving to become self-reliant net contributors to the virtuously liberating freedom, health, honorable economic prosperity and steady progress of themselves, their families and society
welfarist[6] - to be prone to reasonably use or condone the reasonable use of government taxing and spending authority to offer the needy and the poor of the world the temporary aid, education, jobs, services, training or other support they cannot provide for themselves—provided they are continuing to demonstrate by their own determined education, training, labors, investments and savings, that they are responsibly striving to become self-reliant net contributors to the virtuously liberating freedom, health, honorable economic

prosperity and steady progress of themselves, their families and society
welfarist[7] - to be prone to voluntarily advocate, favor or seek to preserve government which promotes the virtuously liberating freedom, health, honorable economic prosperity and steady progress of its citizens by promoting private ownership of property, self-reliance and service
well - to be good
well[2] - to be healthy
well[3] - to be good-natured
well-accepted - to be received or regarded with much approval or favor from God by my believing and honorably exact obedience to that divinely appointed law upon which receipt of that blessing is predicated
well-adapted - to be prone to adjust well to an honorable and virtuous standard
well-adjusted - to be prone to conform well to an honorable and virtuous standard
well-appreciated - to be prone to personally ascertain and live in harmony with the discernibly enlightening and spiritually verifiable truth that: I am greatly or highly valued in the sight of God
well-aware - to be enlightened or intelligent
well-balanced - to be prone to steadily maintain awareness of and harmonious orientation toward that which is truly good and of God
well-balanced[2] - to be prone to steadily maintain awareness of and harmonious orientation toward that which is true

well-balanced[3] - to be virtuously just

well-behaved - to be prone to think, speak and act in a virtuous manner

well-behaved[2] - to be prone to think, speak and act in a courteous or polite manner

well-beloved - to be generously and sincerely good enough to other people to be greatly loved by them

well-conditioned - to be of virtuous character, behavior and moral disposition

well-conditioned[2] - to be healthy

well-disposed - to be virtuous

well-educated - to be prone to wisely make actual or real the best that lies within me

well-educated[2] - to be much edified and enlightened

well-educated[3] - to be prone to use my learning, knowledge or skill to enhance the quality of my life and the lives of other people

well-educated[4] - to be prone to obtain much learning, knowledge or skill in something

well-established - to be well-grounded

well-favored - to be prone to willingly receive and work to retain many blessings from God by my believing and honorably exact obedience to those divinely appointed laws upon which receipt of those blessings is predicated

well-favored[2] - to be prone to willingly receive and work to retain that which produces, preserves or restores true enlightenment, virtue and integrity within me, my family and society

well-favored[3] - to be prone to willingly receive and work to

retain much benevolent, gracious and kind regard from another person

well-founded - to be well-grounded

well-grounded - to be firmly established, fixed or settled upon a sure foundation of enlightenment, virtue and integrity

well-grounded[2] - to be firmly established, fixed or settled upon a sure foundation of enlightened certainty, reality or truth

well-informed - to be prone to strive for broad and general awareness, discipline, experience, education, information, training or wisdom

well-intentioned - to be prone to think, speak and act in harmony with only good intentions

well-mannered - to be prone to think, speak and act in a polished and polite manner

well-married - to be lawfully and legally wedded to a faithful person of the opposite gender who is filled with true enlightenment, virtue and integrity

well-meaning - to be well-intentioned

well-natured - to be virtuous

well-off - to be exalted

well-off[2] - to be redeemed unto exaltation

well-off[3] - to be redeemed and released from the bondage, burdens and debts of my sins

well-off[4] - to be godly enough to be made truly chaste, clean, pure and virtuous at heart—and to continue to encourage and help other people by charitable love, kindness, invitation and instruction to be godly enough to be made truly chaste, clean, pure and virtuous at heart

well-off[5] - to be enlightened or intelligent

well-off[6] - to be healthy

well-off[7] - to be virtuously affluent, prosperous, rich or wealthy

well-ordered - to be prone to speak or act in harmony with virtuous character, ethics, morality, politics or religion

well-ordered[2] - to be prone to resist anarchy, chaos, confusion and darkness as well as I can and should

well-prepared - to be prepared for exaltation

well-prepared[2] - to be prepared for redemption

well-prepared[3] - to be well enough motivated, qualified and otherwise made ready ahead of time, in advance or beforehand to do only good, come what may

well-prepared[4] - to be well enough motivated, qualified and otherwise made ready ahead of time, in advance or beforehand to vanquish that which produces, preserves or restores darkness, vice and corruption within me, my family and society

well-principled - to be prone to live in harmony with better or higher moral principles

well-read - to be sufficiently informed through reading

well-refined - to be virtuously refined enough to produce, preserve or restore true enlightenment, virtue and integrity within me, my family and society

well-rounded - to be virtuously broad or diverse in ability,

development, interest, knowledge and skill

well-spoken - to be kind in what I say

well-spoken[2] - to be prone to say what should be said as it should be said

well-to-do - to be virtuously affluent, prosperous, rich or wealthy

well-trained - to be experienced, knowledgeable and practiced enough to be well disciplined, educated, proficient and qualified in thinking, speaking and acting in harmony with pure and virtuous thoughts, beliefs, values and characteristics

Western - to be prone to live in harmony with the ways of Western character or culture which produce, preserve or restore true enlightenment, virtue and integrity within me, my family and society

whispering - to intend, when speaking is necessary, to speak very quietly or very softly when virtuous reverence is called for

whispering[2] - to intend to speak very quietly or very softly when good reason requires it

whistle-blowing - to intend to help bring violators of good laws to equal and honorable justice by reporting their known or wisely suspected corrupt, sinful or vicious wrongdoing to patriarchal, parental or other good authority having rightful jurisdiction

whistle-blowing[2] - to intend to faithfully continue to exercise my personal freedom and my right to patriotically wield personal civic authority and political power to defend, protect, preserve and sustain my good local, state and national governments by informing them of known or wisely suspected violators of our good laws

white - to be prone to live in harmony with the ways of character or culture of those with naturally light-colored skin to the extent those ways produce, preserve or restore true enlightenment, virtue and integrity within me, my family and society

whole - to be exalted

whole[2] - to be redeemed unto exaltation

whole[3] - to be redeemed and released from the bondage, burdens and debts of my sins

whole[4] - to be godly enough to be made truly chaste, clean, pure and virtuous at heart—and to continue to encourage and help other people by charitable love, kindness, invitation and instruction to be godly enough to be made truly chaste, clean, pure and virtuous at heart

whole[5] - to be truly intelligent

whole[6] - to be truly healthy

wholehearted - to be integrated-at-heart

wholehearted[2] - to be virtuously sincere

wholehearted[3] - to be prone to refuse to be hypocritical or schizophrenic to any degree

wholehearted[4] - to be prone to refuse to be viciously deceptive or false

wholesome - to be whole

wholesome[2] - to be clean

wholesome[3] - to be healthy

whole-souled - to be prone to continuously and faithfully strive with all of the energy, might, power, strength and will of my soul to be made truly chaste, clean, pure and virtuous at heart and to continue to encourage and help other people by charitable love, kindness, invitation and instruction to be godly enough to be made truly chaste, clean, pure and virtuous at heart

wide-awake - to be sharply alert and acutely observant

willful - to be prone to voluntarily retain in remembrance and practice within my mind and heart that which I have ascertained is the mind and will of God, and to thus allow His mind and will to continue to influence what I think, say and do and who I am at heart

willful[2] - to be prone to demand the freedom or liberty to think, speak and act for myself in a harmless, lawful and legal manner, along with the responsibility to account for what I say and do

willful[3] - to be prone to demand the freedom or liberty to speak or act in a deliberate, intentional, volitional or voluntary manner, along with the responsibility to account for what I say and do

willing - to intend to choose, control, decide or determine in harmony with that which I have ascertained is the mind and will of God

willing[2] - to intend to choose, control, decide or determine in harmony with that which is truly good and of God

winning - to be progressing

winning[2] - to be increasing in true enlightenment, virtue and integrity within me

winning[3] - to intend to persevere in doing my very best to achieve, conquer, prevail, succeed or surpass as a participant in an honorable competition or contest until it has ended or until I cannot contribute or give any more

winnowing - to intend to discriminate that which is truly good and of God from that which is evil or satanic in order to divide or separate myself from that which is evil or satanic

winnowing[2] - to intend to discriminate enlightened certainty, reality or truth from confusion, error and falsehood in order to accurately divide or separate that which is truly good and of God from that which is evil or satanic

wiry - to be enduring or persevering enough to dispel or withstand evil or satanic adversity, affliction, defeat or hardship

wise - to be intelligent, practical, pragmatic and providential

wise[2] - to be prone to improve what I know and the good I do with what I know

wise[3] - to be prone to truly build my life on a sure foundation of righteous desires and good works

wise[4] - to be prone to truly discern and judge in favor of that which is truly good and of God instead of that which is evil or satanic

wise[5] - to be prone to truly discern and judge in favor of that which is enlightened certainty, reality or truth instead of that which is confusion, error or falsehood

wise[6] - to be prone to truly discern and judge between that which is real and that which is imaginary, so as to avoid confusing them with each other

wise[7] - to be prone to discretely use the best available means to correct, rectify or resolve

wise[8] - to be prone to refuse to produce, preserve or restore darkness, vice and corruption within me, my family and society

wise[9] - to be prone to refuse to think, speak or act in an imprudent, indiscrete, senseless or unwise manner

wise[10] - to be prone to refuse to think, speak or act in an excessively or needlessly careless, foolhardy or unsafe manner

wise[11] - to be prone to refuse to squander my time, talents and other valuable resources on disappointing and viciously worthless desires and works

witting - to intend to make actual or real the best that lies within me

witting[2] - to be in possession of increasing true enlightenment, intelligence or wisdom

witty - to be judicious

womanish - to be a girl or woman who is womanly

womanized - to be a girl or woman who is feminized

womanizing - to intend to help a girl or woman be feminized

womanly - to be a girl or woman who is feminine

wonderful - to be amazingly or astonishingly good

wooing - to intend to steadily use truly loving words and actions in order to steadily induce, influence or persuade growth and improvement in the truly virtuous love I enjoy with my lawfully and legally wedded husband or wife

wordcrafting - to intend to create and introduce a new word symbol and to connect to it a clear definition of a certain designated portion of enlightened certainty, reality or truth previously abandoned, forgotten, lost, unexplained or unknown as a part of my language

working - to intend to apply or direct action, effort, exertion, labor or toil to the accomplishment or production of something good

working-class - to be one of those who seek to earn through honest labor or toil the income or wages we and our families need

world-class - to be one of those people of the world who produce, preserve or restore the greatest true enlightenment, virtue, integrity, liberty, hope, peace and joy within ourselves, our families and society

worldly-wise - to be prone to refuse to think, speak and act in harmony with the ways of worldly people

worldly-wise^2 - to be aware of how to effectively avoid the pitfalls and snares laid by worldly people

worriless - to be prone to refuse to be worried

worshiping - to intend to constantly choose to charitably, faithfully, hopefully, lovingly, meekly and reverently gift my whole-souled and unreserved adoration, devotion, honor, obedience, praise, respect, service and will to God so that He can help me and the other people I serve to be exalted

worshiping^2 - to intend to constantly choose to give my whole-souled and unreserved adoration, devotion, honor, obedience, praise, respect, service and will to God in harmony with the dictates of my enlightened conscience

worthful - to be prone to personally ascertain and live in harmony with the discernibly enlightening and spiritually verifiable truth that: I am one of God's children who has divine potential and can receive divine power to do and be only good by my faithfully repentant and honorably exact obedience to those divinely appointed commandments, covenants, laws and ordinances upon which receipt of that power is predicated

worthful^2 - to be godly enough to be made truly chaste, clean, pure and virtuous at heart—and to continue to encourage and help other people by charitable love, kindness, invitation and instruction to be godly enough to be made truly chaste, clean, pure and virtuous at heart

worthful^3 - to be prone to produce, preserve or restore true enlightenment, virtue and integrity within me, my family and society

worthful^4 - to be prone to help remove darkness, vice, corruption, bondage, despair, turmoil and misery from within me, my family and society

worthy - to be exalted

worthy^2 - to be redeemed unto exaltation

worthy^3 - to be redeemed and released from the bondage, burdens and debts of my sins

worthy^4 - to be godly enough to be made truly chaste, clean, pure and

virtuous at heart—and to continue
to encourage and help other people
by charitable love, kindness,
invitation and instruction to be
godly enough to be made truly
chaste, clean, pure and virtuous at
heart
worthy[5] - to be prone to
continuously and faithfully strive
with all of the energy, might,
power, strength and will of my
soul to keep my thoughts, words
and actions truly chaste, clean,
pure and virtuous in the sight of
God
worthy[6] - to be commendable in
merit
wrathful - to be virtuously just in
dutifully administering by rightful
authority that penalizing equal and
honorable justice which is
charitably loving, just, right and
wise in the sight of God, to an
extent or in a manner which is not
prohibited by the good law of the
land
wrestling - to intend to contend,
strive or struggle for self-mastery

X

xenophilic - to be xenophilous
xenophilous - to be very attracted
to learning about foreign
languages, people, places and
things

Y

yeasty - to be effervescently and
virtuously thriving
yellow - to be prone to live in
harmony with the ways of
character or culture of those with
naturally brownish-yellow-colored
or yellowish-colored skin to the
extent those ways produce,
preserve or restore true

enlightenment, virtue and integrity
within me, my family and society
yielding - to intend to actively,
faithfully, humbly and meekly
submit or surrender my mind and
will to believing and honorably
exact obedience to that which I
have ascertained is truly the mind
and will of God
yielding[2] - to intend to produce,
preserve or restore greater true
enlightenment, virtue, integrity,
liberty, hope, peace and joy within
me, my family and society
yielding[3] - to intend to give up,
give in or give way to that which
produces, preserves or restores
greater true enlightenment, virtue,
integrity, liberty, hope, peace and
joy within me, my family and
society
yogic - to be prone to seek virtuous
communion, oneness or unity with
the Supreme Being
youthful - to be prone, as a youth,
to think, speak and act in the
hopeful, peaceful and joyful
manner of godly youth who have
experimented with true
enlightenment, virtue and
integrity, and have used them to
become liberated from darkness,
vice and corruption
youthful[2] - to be prone, as a youth,
to think, speak and act in the
carefree and energetic manner of
healthy and innocent youth
youthful[3] - to be prone, as a youth,
to enjoy true personal betterment,
improvement or progress
youthful[4] - to be prone, as a youth,
to avoid being viciously faddish,
fashionable, stylish or trendy
youthful[5] - to be prone, as a youth,
to do all I can and should to avoid

the suffering of teenage ignorance, immaturity or weakness

Z

zestful - to be prone to enliven someone with enjoyably hearty and vigorous activity

Zionist - to be godly enough to be made truly chaste, clean, pure and virtuous at heart—and to continue to encourage and help other people by charitable love, kindness, invitation and instruction to be godly enough to be made truly chaste, clean, pure and virtuous at heart

Zionist[2] - to be prepared and ready—in harmony with the divinely granted true higher priesthood authority and power of heaven, celestial law, divine commandment, prophetic utterance and ongoing personal enlightenment, inspiration or revelation from God—to live in a holy and ideal society in which all members are filled with enough true enlightenment, virtue and integrity to willfully and collectively become of one pure heart and of one mind in virtuous oneness with God, with my family and with society, to be blessed with prosperity in the land, to enjoy plenty, to have all things common, to be without poor among us, and to dwell together in liberty, hope, peace and joy by our combined faithfully repentant and honorably exact obedience to celestial law

Zionist[3] - to be prepared and ready—in harmony with the divinely granted true higher priesthood authority and power of heaven, celestial law, divine commandment, prophetic

utterance and ongoing personal enlightenment, inspiration or revelation from God—to join with others who are pure-in-heart to build up a holy city or nation of peace unto God, as did the prophet Enoch when he built up the City of Enoch or the City of Holiness, even Zion

Zionist[4] - to be prepared and ready—in harmony with the divinely granted true higher priesthood authority and power of heaven, celestial law, divine commandment, prophetic utterance and ongoing personal enlightenment, inspiration or revelation from God—to willingly cooperate in a holy and ideal society within one of many holy cities or lands of God in which the class of poor is abolished as members collectively and voluntarily consecrate and pool ownership of capital, land and all but essential personal property along with that belonging to other community members, before duly authorized and commonly sustained priesthood leaders allocate enforceable rights of ownership of needed real property, resources and individual productive stewardships among heads of existing and newly formed family households, before each household keeps what they need from what they produce prior to voluntarily donating, along with other family households, any remaining surplus into community property, and to willingly allow those priesthood leaders to continue to distribute community surplus among members in harmony with the needs and reasonable wants of recipients

Zionist[5] - to be one of those who are justly and truly chosen, favored or selected by God—in whatsoever land we dwell—to inherit or receive His greatest earthly blessings by our faithfully repentant and honorably exact obedience to those divinely appointed commandments, covenants, laws and ordinances upon which receipt of those blessings is predicated

Zionist[6] - to be one of those who are justly and truly chosen, favored or selected by God to inherit or receive from Him by divine commandment the divine right to occupy some blessed or promised land in which He will bless us by our faithfully repentant and honorably exact obedience to those divinely appointed commandments, covenants, laws and ordinances upon which receipt of those blessings is predicated

Zionist[7] - to be prone to join with others who are pure-in-heart to build up a holy city or nation of peace

Zionist[8] - to be prone to produce, preserve or restore greater true enlightenment, virtue, integrity, liberty, hope, peace and joy within me, my family and society

Zionist[9] - to be prone to build, improve and strengthen the virtuously liberating freedom, health, honorable economic prosperity and steady progress of all people

zoophilous - to be very attracted to, affectionate toward and curious about animals

Zoroastrian - to be prone to live in harmony with the teachings of Zoroastrianism which produce, preserve or restore true enlightenment, virtue and integrity within me, my family and society

Introduction . . . . 28 pages
Textbook . . . . 100 pages
Dictionary . . . . 322 pages
Note Space . . . . 4 pages
_____
= . . . . 454 pages

End Pages . . . . 2 pages
= . . . . 456 pages

This Book Belongs to:

Note Space - 2

Note Space - 4

www.ingramcontent.com/pod-product-compliance
Lightning Source LLC
Chambersburg PA
CBHW070917150426
42812CB00047B/794